THE CENTURY PHILOSOPHY SERIES
Sterling P. Lamprecht, *Editor*

OUR
PHILOSOPHICAL
TRADITIONS

STERLING P. LAMPRECHT

AMHERST COLLEGE

OUR
PHILOSOPHICAL
TRADITIONS

A Brief History of
Philosophy in Western Civilization

New York
APPLETON-CENTURY-CROFTS, Inc.

PREFACE

HISTORY, as any schoolboy or schoolgirl can tell us, deals with the past. But what the past *is* is by no means clear to the minds of most people. The past is not something which once was and is no more, so that we can properly turn our attention from it and live, without further reference to it, in our own exciting present. Time has a greater continuity than most people realize; and the past, at least in many of its vital phases, provides the institutions and alignments, the ideas and principles, by which we are today surrounded and in the context of which we must work out such degree of salvation as we may achieve. Our political life in America bears the ineffaceable marks of John Locke's hopes and fears; our economic life reflects the optimism of Adam Smith and is shadowed by the towering figure of Karl Marx; our religious life moves in large part along channels established by St. Paul and St. Augustine and St. Thomas; our educational life rests squarely upon that courageous readiness of Plato and Aristotle to explore the world and to appraise men's lives under the guidance of human reason. The strands from the past have been woven into a complicated fabric, and only too often the threads are tangled or torn or knotted.

Nothing which has come down to us from the past has come down in finished form. Nothing, just because it is ancient, can bind us authoritatively or can be set up as a model for us to imitate and to repeat. Yet without understanding of the past we shall never understand where we now are and hence be able to formulate wise programs of how further to proceed. Or, to change the metaphor, without the materials which the past provides, we shall never find the resources which we need today in our struggle to fashion a civilized society and to lead the life of reason.

This book, as its subtitle indicates, is a history of philosophy in the western world. But it is more than that. It is explicitly intended—more directly and self-consciously, perhaps, than other existing histories of philosophy—to help its readers to discover in the past the philosophical traditions which have entered into the molding of western civilization and are dominant in our current world. Sometimes a great tradition develops slowly toward ever greater clarity and adequacy, as empiricism developed from Locke through Berkeley and Hume to Woodbridge and Dewey. Sometimes a tradition receives in the genius of its first eloquent defender a classic form which excels in merit all subsequent attempts to restate it, as humanism found its normative expression in the dialogues of Plato. This book does not minimize the importance of single figures; it seeks, rather, to make apparent the enormous indebtedness under which we stand to the intellectual giants who, one after another, have appeared throughout the centuries. But history is more than a succession of individuals. For the individuals we meet in history have sometimes transmitted and sometimes created traditions which live as vital forces for as many decades as the individuals live years or even minutes.

Sometimes one hears a voice which condemns dependence upon tradition. And there is, of course, a sound element in the attitude of him who wishes to be free and unrestrained. No wise person wants to be a mere echo of bygone days. But the technique of freedom is, not immunity from the influence of traditions, but understanding of the import of traditions. To the extent to which a man scorns traditions, he is exposed to errors and inadequacies which go with isolation and ignorance. To the extent to which a man gains wide understanding of the traditions of his own culture and the rival cultures of his world, he ceases to be in servitude to those traditions and is equipped to use them as tools for analyzing his place in history.

There are many reasons, even many good reasons, for studying the history of philosophy. The world view of each great thinker may be taken apart from context and contemplated as a work of art; it is as much a work of art as a poem or a painting or a symphony, and can be appreciated for its esthetic balance and color. The variety of opinions and beliefs among the famous figures of history may wean the student from provincial narrowness and broaden his intellectual horizons. Out of the clash of antithetical philosophies may emerge a new insight into truth; and such insight is more likely to come through historical studies than through resolute trust in one's own private views. These three, and doubtless other, good reasons may be listed for historical studies of philosophy. Only one bad reason calls for a word of reproach. History ought never to be viewed as a museum of antiquities. The history of philosophy ought never to be studied as a set of amusing errors maintained by men who did not have the advantage of belonging to the supposedly enlightened school of thought to which the would-be historian belongs.

But of all the reasons, and good reasons, for studying the history of philosophy the most important is that indicated by the deliberately chosen title of this book. Study of the history of philosophy brings understanding of intellectual traditions and so orients the student in the current world where those traditions are playing an effective role. Past, present, and future are intricately interrelated. We can deal wisely with our present, only provided that we understand the past which is part of its *actual* structure and anticipate the future which is part of its *potential* significance.

My acknowledgements, if completely recorded, would be very lengthy. My students for more than twenty-five years have helped me, through their questions and protests, to make clearer to myself the meaning of the philosophical ideas and traditions I discuss in this book. I should like to pay some of my indebtedness to them by helping new generations of students to possess these same traditions more humanely. I thank the friends who have read portions of my manuscript or have listened patiently while I have read portions aloud to them. But I wish to express gratitude, specifically and publicly, to three friends who have been major sources of aid to me in writing this book. First of all, I am immeasurably indebted to the late Frederick J. E. Woodbridge, whose teaching of intellectual history and philosophy of history was and still is a model to emulate. I thank my colleague Professor James Alfred Martin for his judicious suggestions on Chapter IV, "The Formative Years of Christianity." And, finally, I owe more than I can easily indicate to Professor Joseph Katz, who has read the entire manuscript (some of it more than once), has given me scores of detailed and salutary criticisms, and has shown a personal interest in my book for which I am profoundly grateful. I, of course, make no one except myself responsible for the summaries of fact and the interpretations of history which this book sets forth. But I am sensitively aware of how much I owe my various students and friends, and I hope my book is evidence that their aid was not given in vain.

S. P. L.

Amherst College

CONTENTS

Part III. MODERN PHILOSOPHY

PART ONE

GREEK PHILOSOPHY

Greek Philosophy

In beginning the history of philosophy with the ancient Greeks we follow a tradition long since established among historians of our western world. Doubtless it is a wise tradition and has ample justification. For in the city-states of ancient Greece a considerable number of remarkable men appeared in the sixth and later centuries b.c. And their reflections about the world and about man's place in that world resulted in the formulation of many ideas which, in one form or another, have influenced much subsequent thinking and still play an active role in our own intellectual life today. We could not omit the ancient Greeks from our history without at once depriving ourselves of some basic elements of our cultural heritage and obscuring our current intellectual situation.

We ought to be sure to understand, however, the full import of the tradition according to which our histories of philosophy usually begin with the ancient Greeks. We cannot properly say that philosophy began with the Greeks or that the Greeks were the first philosophers. There may well have been other men in earlier times and in other lands whose reflections, did we but know them, would seem to us to deserve mention in the first chapter of our histories of philosophy. There is no first moment in time, and there is no absolute beginning in history. But in addition to the accident of limitations in our sources of information about the past, a further factor compels us to begin our writing and studying of history with the Greeks. We cannot, however thorough we may make our histories, repeat the past. We cannot, however zealous we may be in our historical researches, pay equal attention to every phase of the past. We may well cultivate an eager curiosity about other times and places and seek an objective judgment concerning such matters. Yet we inevitably select some aspects of the past, and not others, for our attention; and in this process of selection we tend to notice those aspects which are important for, and relevant to, an understanding of our current interests and needs and problems and purposes. History, even when meticulously accurate in its reports and judgments, is yet itself a philosophical enterprise. That is, it embodies an element of experimental judgment concerning what phases of the past are requisite for explaining and evaluating ourselves and human affairs today. A history of law or of

3

religion might begin with the Romans or the Hebrews. But a history of philosophy—for us, at least, who belong to "western civilization"—normally begins with the Greeks. It is to the Greeks that we owe many of the dominating principles which hold sway among us. We are in part created by the traditions which come down to us from them; and, conversely, our history of that past then fortifies these traditions by picturing them as the sources of our intellectual life. We shall not become narrow by working under these inevitable limitations, provided that we understand the nature of our historical enterprise. Rather, we may gain an understanding of our history which will be at once appreciative and critical.

Greek philosophy may be conveniently divided into three main chapters: philosophy in the Greek colonies, philosophy at Athens, and philosophy in the Graeco-Roman world. The Greek colonies were cities planted on the Aegean coast of Asia Minor, on islands in the Aegean Sea, in Sicily, and in the southern parts of the Italian peninsula. In these colonies philosophy flourished in the sixth and fifth centuries B.C. Many of these colonial cities had a prosperity from sea-borne commerce which released certain men from pressing tasks in the struggle for existence and afforded them a leisure in which the intellectual life might favorably develop. Certain thinkers in these colonies during these centuries put forward creative and fresh ideas that spread widely throughout the Greek world. Philosophy at Athens came later; but when it did come, in the fifth and fourth centuries B.C., it reached one of the most glorious levels to which the human mind has ever risen. Here Socrates lived and talked; here Plato taught and wrote; here Aristotle carried on his work during the most important years of his life; here were centered the intellectual activities of others who, although not always native Athenians, found Athens a congenial and profitable residence. Then with the fall of Athens from power and importance came a troubled period, and Rome finally succeeded to control over the Greek cities and the entire Mediterranean world. Even in this period, which culminated in the political dominance of Rome, it was Greeks who usually furnished the intellectual stimulus and provided the instruction on which further intellectual movements were based. Hence we may justly consider philosophy in the Roman world as a last chapter in the history of Greek philosophy.

I

Philosophy in the Greek Colonies

1. HISTORY AND TRADITION

OUR KNOWLEDGE of philosophy in the Greek colonies differs markedly
from that in any subsequent period of the history we have to consider. For every later period we have the writings, or at least many of
the writings, of the men whose ideas and principles are most important. But for philosophical developments in the Greek colonies
we are circumscribed tightly by tradition. We can list one or two
dozen men, name their respective cities, and put down certain alleged dates for their lives and activities. The alleged dates, however,
are quite unreliable; indeed the evidence for them is sometimes so
contradictory that nothing definite can be concluded with accuracy.
Even the person of Pythagoras has been challenged as legendary
rather than historical, although the Pythagoreans always believed,
probably correctly, in his historicity. Our knowledge of the colonial
period in Greek philosophy comes to us from fragments quoted in
the writings of later philosophers or authors. Plato referred to many
of his predecessors; Aristotle wrote a useful summary of certain
phases of the thought of earlier times; and other authors of still later
generations add further information.[1] None of these men, however,
has given us sufficient and sufficiently reliable material to enable us
to reconstruct the history of philosophy in the Greek colonies. Their
purpose usually was not historical but controversial. They often
quoted the colonial thinkers as foils to their own ways of thinking
and may well have changed the original intent of the colonial
thinkers by quoting them out of context or in a new and misleading
context. Occasionally the passages quoted are long paragraphs, but
more often they are merely brief sentences; and often these sentences are of quite cryptic nature. Yet, whether or not these fragments
reflect adequately the thought of the colonial thinkers, they have

---

[1] For example, Theophrastus, who was friend of Aristotle and his successor as head
of the Lyceum; Chrysippus the Stoic; Sextus Empiricus the Skeptic; and a series of later
pagan and Christian writers.

given rise, in the course of time, to a certain tradition concerning the philosophical ideas which were developed in the Greek colonies in the sixth and fifth centuries B.C. This tradition expresses what the colonial Greeks meant to their successors. Hence it cannot but express what they mean to us. Only as that kind of a tradition can we deal with the colonial philosophers today.

2. THE MILESIAN SCHOOL

THALES, 640–550 B.C., of Miletus. He is listed among "the seven wise men of ancient Greece." Many tales are told of him. He is said to have fallen into a well when he was making observations of the stars one night and to have been rescued by a maidservant. He is reputed to have foretold an eclipse of the sun and to have given the people of his city sage political and military advice. From Aristotle comes the story that he observed one year that there was going to be an abundant crop of olives and that he shrewdly hired all the olive presses in the country and thereby gained much wealth. In telling this story, Aristotle added the amusing remark: "Thus we learn that a philosopher can be rich if he chooses; but normally his heart is set on loftier things." Urstoff = H₂O

ANAXIMANDER, 610–540 B.C., of Miletus. Boundless

ANAXIMENES, fl. 540 B.C., of Miletus. Air

XENOPHANES, 580–480 B.C. He is not always included among the Milesians, but is reputed to have been born at Miletus. He was a kind of itinerant preacher who wandered from city to city, spreading his message as he went. He may possibly have visited Elea or even settled there for a time. In the latter case, he would be a link between the Milesian and the Eleatic schools.

THALES IS famous for the alleged remark that water is the principle of all things. This generalization has sometimes been interpreted to mean that water is the stuff out of which all other things are made. Perhaps, however, it rather meant that water is the indispensable condition by which all important changes in nature can be explained. For Thales is supposed to have pointed out that the seeds of all things and the nutriment to support all things are moist.

Whatever the fragment about water means, the important thing about Thales is that he was obviously trying to turn from the earlier efforts (like those, for example, of the poet Hesiod) to account for the world in terms of the activities of gods or supernatural forces. He stands out conspicuously in tradition for what we call a naturalistic theory of the world. He was seeking to find within nature an observable factor by means of which we may account for the course of nature. His significance is well summed up in the statement that "he is an acknowledged leader of his people, a man to consult in crises, when other nations performed a human sacrifice or took the inarticulate and dangerous advice of a sacred snake." [2]

Anaximander is reputed to have carried on some bold and imaginative speculations. To him is attributed the first complete naturalistic cosmology with which tradition acquaints us. The outlines of his cosmology are imposing. Earth, air, fire, and water are not the ultimate substances which they were supposed to be in much popular Greek thinking. Rather, they are all forms which a more ultimate substance assumes in the course of its manifold changes. This ultimate substance, since from it come many varied things, can best be called the Boundless. Earth, air, fire, and water are respectively the dry, the cold, the hot, and the wet forms which appear out of the Boundless. No one of these forms, however, can ever assume a dominating role in the cosmos. Each element tends to encroach in various ways upon the others; but the mutual encroachments are so adjusted in accord with a principle of balance that all things "pay retribution and reparation to one another for their injustices." [3] No one state of the world is fixed or final. Rather there has been and there always will be a succession of worlds, a succession of innumerable worlds of which our particular world is of course but one. The present world, however, is the only one of those innumerable worlds which we have evidence to describe. The earth, said Anaximander, is shaped like a drum of a column, with water, air, and then fire surrounding it in the order of their weights. The encircling fire, however, has evaporated much of the water; and the mists thus produced have enveloped the fire and have shut it up in great rings or tubes. There are three such rings which encircle the drum of the earth. Hence, in looking up, men do not see very much of the fire that encircles the earth. They see only such bits of the fire as dart through holes or

[2] Gilbert Murray, *The Rise of the Greek Epic* (Oxford, Clarendon Press, 1924), p. 262.

[3] *Hubris,* or an overweening insolence, was one of the traditional vices denounced by many Greek writers and was supposed to lead to destruction of the guilty person. Anaximander's theory seems to make reparation in nature akin to the destruction due to an insolent man. But whether or not Anaximander attributed moral quality to nature is not clear from a reading of the available fragments.

perforations in the rings of mist. The stars are escaping flames from the smallest ring, which is the ring nearest to the earth; the moon is flame escaping from the middle ring; and the sun is a vast circle of flame escaping from the third or largest ring. Eclipses are to be thought of as temporary stoppages in the holes in the rings. And all the elaborate cosmic structure exhibits mathematical proportions: the height of the drum of the earth is one-third its breadth, the ring of the moon is eighteen times, and the ring of the sun twenty-seven times, the height of the drum of the earth.

Anaximander, in addition to formulating this bold cosmology, made suggestions concerning the origin of living things. Life first appeared in the ocean. Then, as the waters were evaporated by the encircling fire, certain lands appeared above the level of the sea, and some animals were tossed upon the land. Although many of these animals probably perished at once, some managed to survive and to produce new species of living things. That man is one of the animals that descended from other species which lived earlier is indicated by the helplessness of the human infant and the long period of infancy.

Anaximenes rejected Anaximander's theory of the Boundless and sought to find an ultimate element among the determinate materials of our present world. For some reason not clear to us, he decided that the ultimate element is air and that all other things come from air through the processes of condensation and rarefaction. When air becomes thick, it becomes wind, then cloud, then water, and finally earth, and even rock. When it becomes thin, it becomes fire. And not simply is air the ultimate material, but it is also the ultimate force that holds the world together. Life depends on breath, which is air. Air distributes all things to their respective places. The earth is a flat disk and the heavens surround it like a hat. The sun and moon and other heavenly bodies are bits of rarefied air which just because of their rarefied condition look like fire. And these heavenly bodies are blown against the heavens and held in position by air.

Xenophanes is not known to have originated any cosmological theory or to have adopted any one of the theories formulated by his predecessors. But he seems to have accepted the naturalistic type of explanation of the earlier Milesians and to have been much concerned to enforce certain consequences of that way of regarding the cosmos. He utilized the naturalistic type of explanation as a weapon with which to attack the religious ideas and beliefs that many Greeks had adopted under the influence of Homer, Hesiod, and other such teachers. He insisted that although we may not know the exact origin or present form of the world, we are entitled to believe that the truth, whatever it be, must surely be in line with the naturalistic, non-theological theories of the Milesians. The common ideas of the gods were immoral and could only lead to a low morality among men. Furthermore, these common ideas were intellectually ridiculous. Men have usually treated the gods as having been born, as having shapes akin to the human, as acting like men. This anthropomorphism in religion, according to Xenophanes, is an absurd error. Ethiopians believe that the gods are snub-nosed and black, and Thracians believe that they are blue-eyed and red-haired. So cattle and horses and lions, if they could paint or talk, would represent the gods in their own respective forms. Actually, no one has ever known, and no one will ever know, the truth about the gods; and if by a strange chance someone spoke the truth about the gods, he would have no credible reason for believing in what he said. Xenophanes is credited with some fragments which read as if he hinted at a monotheistic conception. But these fragments are not in line with the other fragments and are quite obscure. Possibly these obscure fragments, if correctly attributed to Xenophanes, mean only that if there is anything men can properly call divine, that thing is the universe itself. This last conjecture is historically quite uncertain. But it is clear that Xenophanes attacked popular religious beliefs as both immoral and absurd.

3. THE PYTHAGOREAN SCHOOL

PYTHAGORAS, 580–500 B.C. He is a dim figure about whom little is known. What he taught is quite impossible to separate out from what his various followers believed and taught. Tradition is that he was born on the island of Samos, that he migrated for political reasons to Crotona, that he spent most of his life in southern Italy and died there, and that his disciples came back from Italy to Thebes and other cities in Greece, disseminating their ideas and forming a brotherhood which became widespread in the fifth century.

PYTHAGORAS MAY HAVE been earlier in time than Xenophanes. But he is the alleged founder of a school of thought so distinct from that of the Milesians that he is best treated after Xenophanes. And in any case it is with the fifth-century Pythagoreans that tradition mainly acquaints us.

Pythagoreanism is an assemblage of ideas which often seem not wholly consistent. Among these ideas two are central and controlling. One of these ideas is that number is the principle by which to explain everything in the world. The Pythagoreans were fascinated by numbers. They devised the scheme of representing numbers by figures and formed the figures by clusters of dots. They spoke of triangular, oblong, and square numbers (the last kind of which is still a fruitful device in mathematics today). They discovered the theorem that the square on the hypotenuse of a right-angled triangle is equal to the sum of the squares on the other two sides. They knew how to find a square equal in area to twice the area of a given square. They could divide a line into parts related to each other in what is called the golden section. They knew that the side and diagonal of a square are incommensurable.

The Pythagoreans took a step of immense importance when they went on to apply number to an interpretation of the world. Their applications were especially fruitful in the fields of music, medicine, and astronomy. In music they discovered the numerical ratio between a note and its octave, its fifth, and its fourth. Thus they came to realize that noise becomes music when sound assumes form and that number is the principle of form. In medicine they viewed the body as a correlation of certain elements, the hot and the cold, the wet and the dry; and they believed that health was contingent upon establishing the due numerical ratios among these elements. Disease is discord, and health is harmony. Disease is to health as chaos is to form, and, again, number is the principle of form. In astronomy different Pythagoreans held different views. Some seem to have adopted the cosmological picture of Anaximander and to have gone on to identify the distance of the three heavenly rings to the earth with the ratios of the musical fourth, fifth, and octave.[4] Others, probably later on in the fourth century, developed the view that the earth is itself a sphere and revolves around a central fire. They seem not to have identified this central fire with the sun. Rather, they regarded the sun as a sphere which, like the earth, revolved around the central fire. They attempted to determine the numerical ratios in this system of revolving bodies; but the detail of these attempts is today obscure and confused.

---

[4] This notion, interpreted poetically, gave rise in later times to the supposition that the heavenly bodies produce musical harmonies which, however, men are not able normally to hear. This supposition of "the harmony of the spheres" is a misunderstanding of the Pythagorean doctrine. In Greek the word *harmony* meant mathematical ratio. Only when mathematical ratios are applied to the specialized case of vibrating strings or similar matters does harmony become a musical phenomenon.

The Pythagoreans treated other things also in terms of numbers. Marriage, some of them held, corresponds to 3, justice to 4, man to 250, plant to 360. Some critics have endeavored to find some significance in these correlations; others have been inclined to dismiss them as nonsense. Actually, we have no clear indication as to what was meant and so can hardly judge the full purport of the various suggestions. Through all these suggestions, however, runs an idea of characteristically Pythagorean nature, namely, that exact and finite form is needed for merit or excellence. The indefinite, the inexact, the infinite are bad; the definite, the precise, the finite are good. Mathematics thus has ethical significance in its application to things. Everything, including man, comes into its best form when it manifests due proportion in all its parts and all its activities. This idea was to enter into the thought of Plato and much subsequent philosophical reflection.

The other central idea of the Pythagoreans was purity. And it was probably in the search for purity that Pythagoreans became welded together into that type of association which we refer to as a brotherhood. In stressing the search for purity the Pythagoreans were very closely connected with, and were probably directly influenced by, Orphism and certain still older Greek rites and beliefs. Possibly Pythagoras himself, certainly some later Pythagoreans, believed in the transmigration of souls; they taught that escape from the prison house of the body could be effected only by that soul which was wholly pure. Critics of Pythagoreanism from Plato's day to our own have pointed out that the kind of soul which can escape from endless rebirths and have existence altogether independent of a body can hardly be identified with the kind of soul whose health is contingent upon proper bodily harmony. But within the Pythagorean order both ideas of the soul were advanced, possibly at times by the same Pythagoreans. In any case, and whatever the soul be, the soul needs purification. Many techniques for purification were advanced. The soul needs to be kept pure from external contaminations; and to accomplish such purification Pythagoreans adopted and advocated the observance of many taboos which probably can be traced back to quite primitive times but had lingered on as popular superstitions.[5] Furthermore, the soul is supposed to be helped if the body is purged physiologically; and to effect such purgation some Pythagoreans, with their interest in medicine, developed some knowledge of cathartics and

---

[5] For example, Pythagoreans were forbidden to eat beans or the heart of animals, to sit on a quart measure, to leave the mark of a pot in the ashes, to leave the imprint of one's body in the bedclothes, to pick up what has fallen, and so forth.

the value of cathartics for health. But above all, the soul needs to be purified by music and philosophy, so that it may become free of evil passions, worldly desires, and undue absorption in affairs. Pythagoreanism thus came to contain, at least at times, considerable asceticism.

Pythagoreans were wont to express their doctrine of purification by using a dramatic metaphor. Men go to the Olympic games, it was said, for different reasons. The least worthy go to sell goods and make money; the more worthy go to compete and to win a prize; but the noblest go to witness the games and so to obtain understanding. Similarly, in human life, some men are absorbed in commerce for the sake of gain; others struggle for office for the sake of honor; but the noblest engage in contemplation for the sake of wisdom. Thus Pythagoreans, in accord with this teaching, sometimes cultivated in themselves and taught to others a scorn for worldly affairs, for the practical, for the earthly scene. A true lover of wisdom, they held, will separate his soul from the world and prepare himself for a bliss the world does not ordinarily understand.

As time went on, the Pythagorean brotherhood seems to have divided into two groups. The one favored what we might call the scientific application of the idea of number; the other became mystically rapturous over an insight which number was supposed to give them in spiritual matters. The former favored high moral instruction and discipline to purify the soul from sordid purposes; the latter became mystically concerned with a world not present to the senses and correspondingly indifferent to political and civic affairs. It is tempting to speak of the mathematical-moral branch and the magical-mystical branch of the brotherhood. But the record is very confused and the tradition is very elusive; and our only assurance is that Pythagoreanism contained a variety of none too consistent opinions.

4. HERACLITUS

> HERACLITUS, 530–470 B.C., native of Ephesus. He is reputed to have been heir to a high office in the religious life of his city and to have retired in favor of his brother. The reason for his retirement from the office is alleged to have been that he preferred a quiet life of speculation.

HERACLITUS, surnamed the Dark, was scornful in his attitude toward mankind. Most people, he is said to have maintained, are ignorant of even that which they see and hear. "Eyes and ears are bad witnesses for men unless they have souls that understand the language." Indeed, nature is so complex and so subtle that men who trust their observations of nature are like "fools who are absent when present." The senses are faulty and apt to mislead, except when reason is able to penetrate beyond surface appearances.

The most famous saying attributed to Heraclitus is "All things flow." This saying is usually interpreted to be a denial that there are any permanent substances in nature. Flux alone is real. Change alone does not change. And if tradition be reliable, Heraclitus was wont to express his beliefs in striking epigram. No one, he is reported to have said, can step into the same river twice because fresh waters are ever flowing upon him. Indeed, in the words of one of Heraclitus' admiring followers, no one can step into the same river once or can remain the same person as he steps, because both the river and the man who steps change during the event. But change is never lawless or chaotic. However ceaseless it be, it occurs according to an invariable cosmic pattern. The man who judges by sense alone will fail to grasp the law within nature; but the man who has sufficient reason will detect that all that he sees and touches changes in definite and intelligible ways. "The sun will not exceed his measures," said Heraclitus, nor indeed will anything else exceed its. Change is measured change. The structure of change has a rhythm which makes change itself an embodiment of reason.

Tradition also attributes to Heraclitus a number of sayings according to which fire is both the ultimate material out of which other things are made and the animate principle by means of which man is conscious and able to reason. It would be tempting to regard these strange fragments as symbolical utterances; for fire is so restless that it is suggestive of endless flux and so brilliant that it is suggestive of penetrating reason. But the fragments do not sustain such an interpretation and leave us without any clue as to the relation of the doctrine of fire to the other doctrines of Heraclitus.

5. THE ELEATIC SCHOOL

PARMENIDES, 520–440 B.C., of Elea. Author of a long philosophical poem *Concerning Nature,* of which considerable sections are extant. He is reported to have visited Athens in his old age, when Socrates, then a youth, met him.

ZENO, 490–430 B.C., of Elea. Pupil of Parmenides.

PARMENIDES IS traditionally set over against Heraclitus as representative, even as creator or founder, of the antithetical view. As Heraclitus stressed the fact of change, so Parmenides stressed the fixity and permanence of genuine reality. According to Parmenides, the world of many things and incessant flux, the world we seem to have visibly about us and in which we pursue our normal human interests, is illusory and unreal. The chief proof of its unreality is that all the opinions we express about it can be shown to be full of contradiction and cannot be rid of contradiction. And, of course, any opinion which contains contradiction is false. Reality can be properly defined in only one way, namely, as an unchanging, immovable, and indivisible unit. Like many others who have disparaged the reality of visible objects and events, Parmenides is more persuasive in attacking what he regards as error than in establishing his positive thesis. In one fragment attributed to him he stated that what *is* is "like the mass of a well-rounded sphere, equally balanced from the center in every direction." This is an obscure statement. Perhaps Parmenides meant that what *is* is a material, continuous plenum and, hence, that there is no empty space either within the plenum or beyond it.

The type of argument by which Parmenides is reported to have defended his view is what is called dialectical. That is, it seeks to prove an assertion by showing that the denial of the assertion leads to contradiction and so is logically untenable. It never appeals to evidence in the sense of observed facts; for it seeks to establish the contention that all the facts of observation or of sense experience are illusory or untrustworthy. Among his arguments are the following. (1) What *is* is; and nothing else is at all. For suppose that what *is not* is too. This is contradictory. Hence only what *is* is. (2) What *is* is both uncreated and indestructible. For suppose that it is created. If created, it was created either by what is or by what is not. But what is not cannot create; and what *is* is identical with, rather than the cause of, what is. Similarly suppose that what *is* is destructible. Then what is can be destroyed either by what is or by what is not. But again, what is not cannot act; and what is must be if it acts and so is not destroyed. Hence what *is* is neither created nor destroyed. (3) What *is* is unchanging. For suppose it changes. Then it ceases to be what it is and becomes what it is not. But it is unintelligible to suppose that what *is* is not what it is, or that what *is* is what it is not. And what is unintelligible is surely false. Hence what *is* is unchanging. (4) What *is* is indivisible. For suppose it is divided. Then it must be divided either by what is or by what is not. To be divided

All is being.

by what *is not* is to remain undivided. To be divided by what *is* is to be homogeneous, continuous, and so undivided. Hence what *is* is indivisible. And if indivisible, it is, of course, also one or single. Thus the entire case of Parmenides (particularly in its negative side or its denials) is demonstrated by dialectical means.

Parmenides is reported to have written out his views in a long poem. The first part was the "Way of Truth" and gave such arguments as have just been sketched. The second part was the "Way of Opinion" and gave a summary of alternative views, especially Pythagorean views, which Parmenides himself rejected.[6] Thus the two parts of the poem presented a contrast between truth and opinion, knowledge and error, reality and appearance, intellect and sense. And this contrast, whether in Parmenides' fashion or in modified ways, has found repeated expression in subsequent philosophical speculations.

Zeno the Eleatic is traditionally represented as a kind of popularizer of Parmenides' technical theories. The fragments attributed to him advance no idea that is not already found in the fragments from Parmenides; rather they deal with Parmenides' ideas in dramatic and picturesque fashion. Zeno forced home his point by use of paradoxes. It is possible that he was trying to defend the standpoint of Parmenides against the natural tendency of most men to believe in the reality of many objects and of change; or he may have been defending that standpoint against the Pythagorean theories which implicitly asserted pluralism (instead of monism) and change (instead of permanence).

Among the paradoxes of Zeno the most famous are the following. (1) Empty space is inconceivable, or space is not itself real. For by space is meant a continuum which is made up of parts. These parts (or points) must either have magnitude or be without magnitude. If the former, they are not points because they can be further divided; if the latter, they are such that no assemblage of them would ever produce what has magnitude. Thus the conception of space as a reality is absurd. (2) If Achilles, the Fleet-of-foot, and a tortoise, which is slow in movement, should run a race in which the tortoise had a headstart, Achilles could never overtake the tortoise. By the time Achilles came to the point where the tortoise was, the tortoise would be some distance, however small, ahead of that point. This same relation would of course be continued endlessly. Hence Achilles could

---

6 It has been plausibly suggested that Parmenides was himself a Pythagorean in early life and that the second part of his poem thus dealt with opinions he had once held but had come to regard as inadequate.

never overtake the tortoise. (3) An arrow which is shot into the air cannot really move. For it always occupies a space exactly equal to its own length, and whatever occupies a space equal to its own length is at rest in that position. It obviously cannot move when it is where it is, and it obviously cannot move where it is not. Therefore the arrow cannot move at all.

These paradoxes, however playful in form, are highly serious in intent. They were designed to throw discredit upon ordinary ideas of space, of motion, and of the reliability of the evidence of the senses.

6. THE PLURALISTIC SCHOOL

EMPEDOCLES, fl. 444 B.C., native of Akragas, Sicily. He lived much of his life in Thourioi in southern Italy. He impressed his contemporaries as a man of more than normal human powers. According to an unfriendly legend, he wished to make people think him a god and therefore dramatically threw himself into the flaming crater of Etna.

ANAXAGORAS, fl. 440 B.C., of Clazomene in Ionia. He spent some years at Athens and is reputed to have been friend of Pericles. He had to flee from Athens to save his life. Possibly political plotting was the real cause of his flight; but the charge of impiety was made against him on the ground that he taught that the sun was not a god but a hot stone.

DEMOCRITUS, 460–360 B.C., of Abdera. He is reported to have traveled extensively in Egypt and Asia. An imposing list of writings on many subjects indicates that his literary work was extensive; but only fragments of these writings have been preserved.

ACCORDING TO THE traditions about the pluralists, they may be regarded as having sought to mediate between the view of Heraclitus that all things are in flux and the view of Parmenides that reality is one and changeless. At least they attributed constant change to the macroscopic and complex things we see and handle, and they assigned changeless unity to each of the microscopic elements of which they took the macroscopic things to be composed. That is, changing things are made up of unchanging parts; and the changes that occur in things are due to redistribution of the same constant and indivisible ultimate elements. The world is a pluralism, each element of which is indivisibly one.

Empedocles was the earliest of the pluralists, and his views departed less than did those of his successors from traditional notions of popular Greek thought. There are, he held, but four kinds of ultimate particle out of which all things are composed. These four kinds of ultimate particle are earth, air, fire, and water. He called the particles roots, probably choosing that metaphorical term because it is from roots that all else grows. But from these four types of roots, a vast variety of compounds is incessantly arising; for the proportions in which the four roots are combined differ endlessly in the macroscopic things they come to form from time to time. We normally call each compound after the type of root which predominates in its composition. But in the many compounds which we name, for example, earth, there may well be many variations of kind. One name often serves indiscriminately for a large number of quite different macroscopic things.

Empedocles is reputed to have performed an experiment to establish the reality of the particle air. He does not seem to have doubted that men generally would acknowledge the reality of earth and water and fire. But he seems to have supposed that since air is more elusive to the senses than the other three elements, many men might hesitate to regard it as an ultimate element. He therefore sought to give a demonstration of the substantial nature of air. This he did by submerging in water a vessel which contained a certain volume of air and by showing that the water cannot then force its way into the submerged vessel until the air is released.

Empedocles sought to give an explanation of the agencies by which the roots are brought together into compounds and are again separated out. These agencies, he believed, are two: love and hate. The first is the force which brings the roots together into macroscopic things, and the second is the force which dissolves macroscopic things again into their individual elements. He seems to have thought of these forces as external to the elements and as operating upon the elements from without. How anthropomorphic or how metaphorical Empedocles was in his view of love and hate we cannot easily determine from the fragments we have of his writings. When love brings elements together, there result harmony and peace; when hate drives them apart, there ensue strife and discord. Thus order and chaos succeed each other in ever recurring cycles.[7]

Anaxagoras continued the pluralistic point of view but differed from Empedocles in details. Earth, air, fire, and water, according to Anaxagoras, are not the only four types of element, because the qualitative diversity of macroscopic objects is very great. There are, he inferred, many types of ultimate elements or particles. These elements he called "seeds." The seeds are both infinite in number and very small in size. All sorts of qualities are in some or others of these seeds; and a compound has the qualities derived from the kind of seed that predominates in the mixture of which it is composed. Among the seeds is one kind that is purer or more vaporous or more delicate than any of the others. This kind, not entering into compounds in the way in which the others do, is nevertheless the directive power over everything and causes the motions of all things. This element Anaxagoras called mind. It is what animates man; it also imparts order to the entire cosmos. Critics of Anaxagoras, even early critics like Plato, have complained that Anaxagoras did not carry out his theory of mind competently but resorted instead to mechanical accounts of the way in which events are produced.[8] But in defense of Anaxagoras it might be pointed out that he regarded mind as a material substance, so that the difference between explanation in terms of mind and explanation in terms of mechanism probably never occurred to him.

Democritus, surnamed the Laughing Philosopher, carried out the pluralistic position in an incisive and thorough way. He gave it a form which is one of the great contributions of Greece to subsequent thinking and has remained ever since one of the major philosophical points of view. He used the term *atom* to designate the ultimate unit of material substance, thus indicating that it cannot be further cut up. But his view about the atoms was different from that of Empedocles and Anaxagoras about their roots and seeds. In two respects he took positions that proved to mark real advances in thought. In the first place, he taught that the atoms differ from one another in size and shape only, that is, in quantitative respects only. He did not attribute to them any of the qualitative characters which we observe in macroscopic objects. He held that qualitative characters arise in compounds because of the structural manner in which the homoge-

[7] Empedocles, as also Anaxagoras and Democritus after him, speculated on other matters not here mentioned. For example, he advanced theories of the way in which material impact gives rise to sensations in animal bodies.

[8] *Phaedo,* 97–99.

neous atoms happen to come together. Quantity is thus more ultimate than quality in the cosmos or, in other words, quality is a function of quantity. All scientific explanation therefore ought to aim at resolution of qualitative differences into the precisely measurable quantities upon which they depend. In the second place, he resorted to no outside force like love and hate or mind in his explanation of motion, change, growth, and decay. Rather, he held that motion is intrinsic to the atoms and hence that all changes arise from the nature of the atoms themselves. Indeed the changes that arise are the natural and spontaneous result of the atoms that are involved in the course of those changes. Breaking with the Eleatic denial of empty space, Democritus affirmed the reality of the void. The void is not, of course, a substance. But it is a precondition for the motion of the atoms. Indeed, were it not for empty space, the atoms could not successively produce the vast assortments of things which constitute the processes of the cosmos. Democritus thus set forth a position which has been well summarized in the words "mechanism as to motion, atomism as to structure, materialism as to substance." [9] Although reflections on other subjects have come down to us in the traditions about Democritus, it has been his theory of atoms and the void by which he has been most often remembered.[10]

7. THE SCIENTIFIC TRADITION

THE COLONIAL PERIOD of Greek philosophy, in spite of the fragmentary and even legendary manner in which knowledge of it was transmitted to later ages, made a great contribution to the traditions of western culture.

It was in the colonial period that certain ideas were first announced which have proved fruitful through all succeeding centuries. The rise of new animal species from accidental changes in the environment of earlier species, the swinging of the earth like the sun and the planets in space, the succession of worlds no one of which is everlasting, the applicability of unchanging natural laws to restlessly changing things and events, the distinction between appearance and

[9] George Santayana, *Three Philosophical Poets* (Cambridge, Mass., Harvard University Press, 1910), p. 27.

[10] For example, he is reputed to have given a certain refutation of the relativism of Protagoras and to have defended a certain theory of morals. The former has been more or less forgotten because of the historic importance of Plato's refutation of Protagoras. The latter is a phase of the development of hedonism and is discussed below in connection with the Cyrenaic-Epicurean tradition. Cf. Chap. III, sec. 1.

reality, the atomic constitution of matter—these ideas, fostered by imaginations which ran far beyond the available evidence to support them, have echoed across the ages, have stimulated later minds to seek more adequate evidence, and have been built into the texture of the intellectual outlook of the whole of western civilization. And more fruitful still, in all probability, there was the Pythagorean insight that numbers furnish one of the effective techniques whereby the interlocking structures of cosmic events can be made intelligible to the human mind. Whenever scientists have used mathematics to formulate principles for the explanation of nature, as notably in the sixteenth and seventeenth centuries, and again in the twentieth, Pythagoras can be seen to be once more a master of the intellectual life.

The significance of the philosophers of the Greek colonies is the more evident when the historian places their contribution to western culture side by side with the ways of thought which characterized life in the great empires of Asia Minor and Mesopotamia and even, though here less markedly, Egypt. In these empires the intellectual life was practiced almost exclusively by the priestly classes and for the sake of such fortification as theory might bring to vested religious interests. The contrast between the oriental and Greek mentalities is not of course absolute. Greek thinkers borrowed important ideas from non-Greek (particularly Egyptian) sources; and of course certain Greek thinkers, such as the group of Pythagoreans who revived attention to ancient popular taboos, were reactionary rather than in line with any creative advance. Nonetheless, after all qualifications have been granted, the historian may properly conclude that the Greek philosophers of the colonial period stand out, so far as our knowledge of the past goes, among all the thinkers of their own or earlier ages. The really notable Greek philosophers of the sixth and fifth centuries B.C. were not members of a caste which had commitments to ancient cosmogonies. They looked at the world around them freshly; they sought to explain this world by analyzing it in terms of what they found in it. Even when they spoke of things that lay beyond their own experience, they tried out their ideas of such things by reference to facts they could observe. They took steps toward supplementing observation by experiment, setting up conditions for observations which would then have crucial importance for testing ideas. They regarded nothing as too sacrosanct to be investigated; they deemed some things sacred in the sense of precious but nothing at all sacred in the sense of exempt from study and criticism.

The colonial philosophers of Greece may fairly be said to be the source for western culture of the scientific spirit. The tradition they began has waxed and waned periodically in the history of western culture but cannot be traced to any earlier manifestations of import. The word *science* sometimes is bandied about today controversially: the "merely scientific" is contrasted with the humane, the moral, the spiritual, or some other favored means of insisting upon notions which, imported into affairs, lack evidence properly to support them. But the word *science,* understood in the sense in which it describes the spirit of inquiry in the philosophers of the Greek colonies, cannot fairly be put in any such contrast. Science, so understood, is knowledge which comes from disciplined imagination in patient and unbiased examination of things, that is, of the world and man and society. The scientific spirit is one of honest curiosity—of curiosity which has no antecedent commitments to dull the senses in their observations or to warp the mind in its judgments. From the Greek thinkers of the colonial period the heritage comes to western civilization of that scientific spirit. This heritage is culturally even more important than the various special ideas which those thinkers, practicing inquiry in that spirit, succeeded in enunciating.

II

Philosophy at Athens

1. THE GREEK SOPHISTS

PROTAGORAS, 480–410 B.C., of Abdera.

GORGIAS, 483–375 B.C., of Leotini.

HIPPIAS, fl. 420 B.C., of Elis.

PRODICUS, fl. 420 B.C., of Ceos.

THRASYMACHUS, fl. 420 B.C., of Chalcedon.

ISOCRATES, 436–338 B.C., of Athens.

FOR A GENERATION or two before the cosmological speculations in the Greek colonies died out, another philosophical movement arose among the Greeks. This movement had its center at Athens which reached the apogee of its wealth and power during the second half of the fifth century. Its sponsors were not usually native Athenians but came from many cities in the Greek world. They gathered at Athens, however, because they found there conditions favorable to the development of their interests. This period is commonly called the age of Pericles and was pre-eminent for political achievement, literary glory, and a widespread recognition of the dignity of the arts. Athens was indeed so renowned for its cultural atmosphere that men from other Greek cities often sojourned at Athens and participated in Athenian society. Among these men were those whom we call Sophists.

The word *sophist,* as commonly used in tradition and in current speech, is a term of reproach. It has come to connote rhetorical pre-tense, intellectual shallowness, and even moral insincerity. He is often called a sophist who, as the old phrase puts the point, "seeks to make the worse appear the better reason." And there are facts in Greek history which give partial warrant for this usage of the term. Plato spoke of a Sophist as "a paid huntsman of rich and distinguished young men"; and Aristotle characterized a Sophist as "one who seeks to make money out of apparent wisdom." ¹ In the fourth century, when Plato and Aristotle wrote, the Sophistic movement had deteriorated; it had come, at least in part, to deserve such condemnation as they administered. But even in the fifth century, when the Sophistic movement was at its best, the Sophists had the reputation of being arrogant in their claim to be "wise men." They did not hesitate to assert that they were equipped to give instruction in good manners, in the art of social success, in the means of swaying assemblies by eloquent speeches, in the tactics by which a man could climb to power in the state.

If there was some merely pert arrogance in the praise which Sophists sometimes poured out upon themselves, the Sophistic movement also played a serious and important role in Greek philosophical development. It was an effort to provide a needed theoretical foundation for the genuine and growing concern of intellectuals for literary, artistic, and political affairs. It was the philosophical correlate of the glorious social achievements of the Periclean age. Certain Sophists continued the cosmological and naturalistic interests of the colonial philosophers. But the emphases of the Sophistic movement were basically humanistic. Hence, in its impact upon Greek life, the Sophistic movement marks a shift in the objectives of philosophical inquiry—a shift from physical nature to man, from disinterested science to a primary concern for practical human problems, from the more ultimate to the more immediate, from analysis of the world to elaboration of techniques and methods for men's dealing with the world. It was concerned with grammar and rhetoric, with the arts of oratory and poetry, with the merits of different kinds of literary style, with education and politics. It was normally, if not always, skeptical concerning the possibility of reaching any satisfactory solution for problems of cosmological inquiry; but it was confident that even in a world the objective nature of which remained a puzzle, man could yet come into a profitable development of his own powers in the social life of his cities. The Sophists were polite, urbane, cosmopolitan, fond of prosperity, concerned with living well. They seem to have confused two senses of the phrase *living well,* namely, living comfortably or even luxuriously, and living nobly or excellently. Perhaps they sometimes thought that to live comfortably is to live excellently.

The Sophists whose names mean most in subsequent history are those whom Plato pictured in his writings. Isocrates is the only one

¹ Plato, *The Sophist,* 223b. Aristotle, *De Sophisticis Elenchis,* 165a22.

of those listed at the outset of this chapter whose writings have come down to us. He wrote many pretty moralistic essays in which he cultivated a flowery style. The other Sophists are not known by extant works. They appear to us primarily through the rather unsympathetic and surely ironic characterizations which Plato gave. Plato facetiously praised Hippias for having invented a memory system. He portrayed Prodicus as guilty of labored and pedantic zeal in drawing fine distinctions between the meanings of nearly synonymous words. Plato gave more serious attention to Protagoras, Thrasymachus, and Gorgias, but he treated only the first of these at all favorably.

Protagoras is famous in tradition for the maxim "Man is the measure of all things." [2] All that we know about Protagoras can be treated as an amplification of the idea in this maxim. Protagoras seems to have desired to emphasize the necessity of judging all things by the manner in which they appear to human beings and by the role they play in human affairs. He was repelled by what seemed to him the fantastic extravagances of the cosmological and mathematical speculations of the Eleatics and Pythagoreans and others of the colonial philosophers. He was protesting against the dialectical devices by which the Eleatics had been led to reject the evidences of the senses. He was protesting against the atomists' analysis of the everyday objects of common experience and their explanation of these objects in terms of roots or seeds or atoms which no one can possibly observe. He was protesting against the Pythagorean insistence that the side and diagonal of a square cannot be measured by any common unit however small. He was protesting against the attribution of reality to abstractions like the Boundless or points or numbers. Against all such abstruse theories he sought to maintain the standpoint of the unsophisticated man, namely, that only those things are real which men actually see and touch or otherwise experience through the senses. Men lose all sanity, he seems to have meant, when they once venture to distrust their senses.

But Protagoras is important, not just for his reliance upon normal and uncriticized human experience but also for the further tenets to which this reliance led him. For him, as often for defenders of what are alleged to be "common-sense beliefs," the initial pronouncement proved to be difficult to maintain without acknowledging further implications of radical purport. For if that alone is real which men observe through their senses, then reality is bound to be one thing to one man and quite another thing to the next man. Wine is sweet

2 Plato, *Theaetetus*, 152a.

to a man in good health but bitter to a sick man. Water is warm to one and cold to another. Colors and shapes vary as they are observed by several men at one time and by one man at several times. And since dreams are perceived as immediately, and illusions occur as genuinely, as anything else, dreams and illusions are as real as any other things men observe. Protagoras had no way, once he had made man the measure of all things, of appealing beyond private experiences to objective and more-than-private realities. He could find no meaning in the supposition of a world that is independent of all human experience or is common to various human experiences. A man's opinions, Protagoras held, are naturally founded on what appears to him; that is, to perceive is then to know. Therefore, just as what one man observes is real for him and may not be real for another, so what one man believes is true for him and may not be true for another. Thus, in Protagoras' development of his maxim, both reality and knowledge are relative to the individual.

This frank and abandoned relativism of both reality and knowledge could be treated in more than one fashion. All the Sophists, so far as we can tell from the available evidence, accepted the basic relativism. But different Sophists developed this relativism in different ways. Relativism could lead to a rampant individualism, or it could be curbed by an appeal to convention. Gorgias, a Sophist contemporary with Protagoras, seems to have delighted in pressing the former alternative. He is reputed to have uttered a strangely epigrammatic statement: "First, nothing exists; secondly, if anything existed, it could not be known; thirdly, if anything were known, the knowledge could not be communicated." The meaning of this cryptic remark is not certain. But the meaning may be that nothing exists in the way of an object prior to, and independent of, its appearance to some observer; that such an object, if it did exist, could not be known by men who must rely on nothing but their observations; and that knowledge of an independent object, if by chance one man gained such knowledge, could not possibly be transmitted to others who had not had the same observation. Such a position, however, if indeed it be Gorgias' meaning, did not seem wise to the much more conservative Protagoras. Protagoras preferred to teach that for practical purposes a man ought to accept those objects as real and those opinions as true which were accepted by the consensus of his fellows. A man can, on the basis of the relativistic theory, afford to do this, at least in many cases. For he has no ground for insisting on his own private views when he can win success by tactful compromise. How far Protagoras would have had a man go in the direction of submitting to social conventions, we cannot now exactly determine. But he is known at least to have warned men against an exuberant and stubborn insistence on their favorite opinions. A wholesome respect for convention is the only means by which effective adjustment can be secured among the conflicting assertions of separate individuals. Gorgias seems to have been willing to press relativism into defiance of convention. Protagoras seems to have desired to use relativism to bring men into moderate and happy relations to the conventions of their time and their city.

The application of the relativism of the Sophists to matters of morals was the most controversial aspect of the Sophistic movement. All the Sophists, so far as we can tell, rejected the age-old religious sanction for morality. The very existence of the gods is doubtful; and even if there are gods, a man is not bound to submit his will to theirs. Each man is the best judge of what is good for himself. His good is what he wants and what serves his interests. No one is under obligation to sacrifice his own good to any theological, political, or social pressure. Zeus, Protagoras is made to say in one of Plato's dialogues, gave every man "conscience and a sense of honor." [3] The reference to Zeus was for Protagoras a merely rhetorical device. The point of the remark is the notion that conscience and a sense of right are private convictions which arise from a man's inner feelings and are not capable of further training or objective correction. Men feel about good and bad as they feel; and there is no valid ground for argument among men whose feelings do not happen to be in accord.

This relativism in morals, like that in theory of reality and of knowledge, is again capable of being pressed into radical individualism or of being guided into conservative channels. Thrasymachus is famous in tradition for the former alternative. He is represented by Plato as having maintained the thesis that "justice is the interest of the stronger." [4] What passes as justice in any community is but the will of the strongest man who then imposes his preferences and tastes upon the mass of weaklings who submit to him. A man is of course quite entitled to defy the will of his ruler if he is able successfully to do so and to escape punishment for his defiance; but he thereby proves that it is he, and not the ruler, who is really the stronger. Protagoras, however, in morals as in other questions, would not push relativism to this extreme individualism. He advocated a much more

[3] *Protagoras*, 322.
[4] *Republic*, Bk. I, 338c.

cautious procedure. A man who wishes to succeed in life dare not be too bold. For a man is never strong enough to stand alone against his city or his community. He will win more success for himself by working out his purposes within the existing framework of his society. Nothing, to be sure, can be called good by nature; but there are many things that can be said to be good by convention. The wise man is he who knows how to adjust his tastes and desires to the social forces through which alone his own advantage can be gained. He will know when to insist and when to yield. And since conventions vary from time to time and from group to group, morality, of course, will vary too. What is good at Athens may be evil at Sparta, and vice versa. To live well a man must adapt himself to fluctuating conventions. But no absolute moral injunctions have any binding force upon a man who is intelligent enough to win the favor and sway the sentiments of his fellows. And even when a man is intelligent and realizes the wisdom of recognizing the conventions about him, he has no authority to guide him in moral matters except his own desires and his estimate of his chances of getting what he wants.

2. SOCRATES

SOCRATES, 469–399 B.C., was born, lived, and died at Athens. He came of a middle-class family. His father was a sculptor, his mother a midwife. He was trained in his father's profession. But he seems to have neglected this profession and to have been very casual about engaging in any means of supporting himself and his family. He was married and had several children. His wife, Xanthippe, is traditionally represented as a shrew who henpecked him; but, if Plato's *Phaedo* can be trusted, she and he stood in affectionate and tender relations. His chief business in life was reflection on moral problems. This reflection he persistently carried on in public, engaging anyone who would listen to him in discussions. Whether on the street corner or in the gymnasium or the market place, he was frequently surrounded by a group of fond admirers and curious bystanders. He made many bitter enemies by his impertinent questions and ironic comments; and he won many friends by the engaging and noble traits of his character. He left no writings. But the influence of his conversations was widespread and profound, so that he looms up in history as a figure of great philosophical importance. Pictures of

him are given by three of his personal acquaintances—
Plato, Aristophanes, and Xenophon. These pictures do
not agree; and we today have no clear grounds for determining their relative reliability. But the picture which
Plato gave has been the historically accepted one, so that
the Socrates who moves through the pages of Plato's dialogues, whether he be unduly idealized or accurately portrayed, is the Socrates who also lives in literary and philosophical traditions. He was gay, witty, fond of dinner
parties and drinking parties. He was eventually accused
of "being impious and corrupting the youth." He was
found guilty and condemned to death by the Athenian assembly. His trial and death are presented, through Plato's
eyes, in the *Apology, Crito,* and *Phaedo.* His character,
as Plato probably thought of it, is presented through the
mouth of Alcibiades in the closing pages of the *Symposium.*

SOCRATES AND Plato are so intertwined in literature that they are
difficult to separate in historical fact. Socrates is the chief speaker in
all of Plato's dialogues except a few of the latest. How much of what
Plato put into Socrates' mouth was spoken by the historical Socrates,
and how much was added by the literary and philosophical genius
of Plato, cannot be determined today with assurance.[5] A probable
hypothesis on this moot point is that the earlier dialogues of Plato
are chiefly Socratic in their general content but that the later dialogues give Plato's own mature thought. Socrates clearly began the
line of reflection which Plato then carried on. Plato surely was too
acute a thinker to remain all his life within the limits of borrowed
ideas. But no sharp division between the Socratic germ and the
Platonic development can, of course, be drawn.

The best available means of distinguishing between Socrates and
Plato is probably contained in the comments which Aristotle made
on Socrates. Aristotle never knew Socrates: he was not born until
some years after Socrates' death. But he knew Plato for many years
and associated closely with Plato. Therefore it is quite probable that
he learned more from discussions with Plato than we can infer by

[5] Two of the most brilliant recent historians of Greek philosophy, John Burnet and
A. E. Taylor, have maintained that all of Plato's dialogues can be taken historically at
their face value. They base this supposition on the belief that Plato was too scrupulous to
put a remark into a person's mouth unless he had actually heard that person make that
remark. This extreme position is far from convincing to most other scholars. Good
grounds for rejecting it are given by Paul Shorey, *What Plato Said* (Chicago, University
of Chicago Press, 1933), p. 21.

subjective impressions from our reading of the dialogues. And he wrote long after the time when Socrates was a controversial figure in Athenian life, and he seems to have had no reason either to exaggerate or to detract from the importance of Socrates.

If we accept Aristotle's judgment, we have a disinterested guide to an estimate of Socrates' contribution to philosophy.[6] Using this estimate from Aristotle and applying it to Plato's dialogues, we may summarize Socrates' position in the history of philosophy as follows:

Socrates busied himself with ethical matters. He did not concern himself with the world of nature. He rather sought the universal in ethical matters, and he directed attention, for the first time, to definitions.

Socrates was akin to the Sophists in the field of his major interests. He, like the Sophists, turned from cosmological speculations to the analysis of human affairs. But the ground for his neglect of cosmological problems does not seem to have been the same as theirs. The Sophists held a theory of perception which cut the human mind off radically from any possibility of reaching objective evidence about the nature of the physical world. Socrates, if Plato's dialogues be taken as just, was neither so relativistic nor so subjectivistic as that. He was indeed skeptical about many matters. But he was skeptical, not because he held a general theory of knowledge which made complete skepticism alone tenable, but because he realized the difference between unfounded guessing and genuine knowledge. He seems to have so respected the empirical demand for evidence about any matter of fact that he refused to entertain opinions on any matter of fact that lay beyond the reach of his experience. He repeatedly professed, in Plato's accounts of him, to be very ignorant; and this profession, often ironically pressed for rhetorical purposes, was probably fundamentally sincere. He assured the Athenian people at the time of his trial that he had not, like Anaxagoras, affirmed that the sun is a stone and not a god.[7] But in saying this, he gave no indication that he deemed a naturalistic explanation of the sun morally or religiously dangerous. He seems rather to have desired to dissociate himself from those who pressed opinions for the truth of which there was not sufficient evidence. He wished to confine himself to matters with which he could deal directly and in connection with which he could offer supporting reasons. And above all, he wished to emphasize his concern over ethical problems and not to allow others to confuse the settlement of such problems by dragging in irrelevant considerations.

[6] Aristotle, *Metaphysics,* 987b1–4. See also, 1078b17–31.
[7] Plato, *Apology,* 26c-d.

He had no disdain for natural science, but he had an acute and sensitive respect for the difference between opinions speculatively advanced and conclusions carefully sustained.

Socrates was diametrically opposed to the Sophists in moral theory. He would not trust a man's desires until those desires had been certified by standards of objective validity. He would not trust feelings as a guide to what is genuinely good. He was always appealing beyond some particular end a man might choose to a universal criterion by which that particular end might be judged. A universal may be difficult to know. But there are universals, and prolonged discussion may enable us to discern them. Knowledge of universals is preliminary to judgment upon particulars. Socrates would constantly try to direct men to turn from listing various just acts or various pious acts and to define the nature of justice or piety. Plato repeatedly represented him as making the kind of distinction which appears in the following passage: [8]

I did not ask you to name one or many of the pious acts which may be performed, but to set forth the nature of piety by virtue of which all pious acts are pious.

In his most abject professions of his own ignorance, he always (in Plato's portrayals of him) indicated a firm conviction that universals might be brought to light through long, serious, and sustained intellectual search.

Socrates held, on the one hand, that particular things or acts may be observed but cannot be defined and, on the other hand, that universals may be defined but cannot be sensibly observed. He therefore disparaged the senses, and exalted reason, as a means to moral knowledge. A universal may be reached by inductive generalization, however; that is, a universal may be discovered by taking the common element in all the cases in which the universal is present. But this procedure involves a difficulty; for we do not know what the cases are in which a universal is present unless we have knowledge of that universal to guide us in selecting and listing the cases. Hence Socrates seems to have regarded the search for universal criteria as an almost endless quest. He never supposed that he had come to the end of that quest. He thus never became the defender of any settled body of moral instruction. He was, in the words of one metaphor, a "gadfly" sent by the gods to sting the sluggish beast, Athens, into more earnest reflection.[9] He was, in the words of another metaphor, a midwife who

[8] *Euthyphro*, 6d-e.
[9] Plato, *Apology*, 30e.

worked upon young men instead of young women and assisted in the birth of ideas instead of children.[10] Even, however, if men do not come to final determination of the exact nature of the universals they seek, they profit from the search for the universals. They come through the search to a better knowledge of themselves, their capacities, and their limitations. Socrates thought of himself as fulfilling the mission of stimulating men to ethical reflections. Yet even though he took his mission with deadly seriousness, he took himself humorously and lightly. He stands in history, not for any final conclusions, but for a method and a purpose. The quality of his life, as well as a central point of his philosophy, is summed up in a remark which Plato put into his mouth: "An unexamined life is not worth living." [11]

3. PLATO

PLATO, a native Athenian, lived from approximately 427 to 347 B.C. Though he belonged to an aristocratic family whose young men would normally aspire to public life, he never entered into active politics in his native city. In his early manhood he met Socrates and became one of the group who listened to, and participated in, the discussions which Socrates stimulated. He remained throughout his life under the inspiration of Socrates' character, purpose, and method of inquiry. In spite of his refraining from active politics in Athens, he had a genuinely practical interest. He founded a school at Athens which is known as the Academy, the first in time and the first in importance of the "four schools of Athens" which are listed in tradition. Here he reputedly gave lectures and encouraged debates of philosophical problems. He thus sought to bring men to an understanding of the principles by which, as he conceived, their personal lives and the affairs of cities might best be guided. He is reported to have gone to Syracuse in 367 and once or twice later, in the hope of assisting the tyrant of that city to perfect the government. But his honest and idealistic efforts encountered undercurrents of opposition and intrigue which made them unsuccessful. His writings have come down to us in quantity, probably in their entirety. They consist of dialogues in which Socrates is usually the chief speaker. The earlier ones prob-

---

10 Plato, *Theaetetus*, 149–150.
11 *Apology*, 38a.

ably reflect the kind of discussion, penetrating but not coming to any explicit conclusion, for which Socrates was famous. The later ones, particularly the *Republic,* seek to establish the truth of certain principles which, carefully put together, constitute a consistent body of philosophical opinions. His name is attached also to thirteen letters, the authenticity of which has been disputed. The longer and more important of these letters are probably genuine and, if they be so taken, furnish autobiographical material and some philosophical comments of consequence. His influence through both his writings and his teaching in the Academy was widespread in his own day and has continued as a potent force in western civilization for more than two thousand years.

THE PHILOSOPHY of Plato differs, in the form of its presentation, from that of most philosophers. Plato never formulated a systematic treatise on philosophy or, indeed, on any subject. He even made the statement (if, as is probable, the seventh letter is genuine) that he never reduced and would never be willing to attempt to reduce his philosophy to written form. Philosophy, he said, cannot be put into words like other studies but can be kindled in men's minds through close companionship only.[12] But he did compose many dialogues in which philosophical themes are penetratingly and tirelessly explored. These dialogues may be considered, not merely as a reflection of the method and purpose of his teacher Socrates but also as samples of the instruction which he himself carried out more thoroughly in the Academy. They would be, in this interpretation of them, a kind of prospectus of the achievements reached in personal contacts between Plato and his pupils. The earlier or Socratic dialogues, even when not bringing a discussion to a definite conclusion, always disclose some firmly held convictions in the course of the analyses they give. The later or more entirely Platonic dialogues, however, do quite deliberately state precise conclusions. These various convictions and conclusions, brought together in sympathetic fashion, constitute what we may properly call Plato's philosophy.

Plato's dialogues present ideas through the medium of portraits of various persons. They exhibit the handsome, impulsive, unscrupulous, but affectionate Alcibiades, the vain and stupid sectarian Euthyphro, the manly and inquiring youth Theaetetus. They present various types of Sophist, the blustering Thrasymachus, the high-minded

12 Seventh letter, 341c-d.

Protagoras, the pedantic Prodicus. Above all, they give an elaborate description of Socrates; they make clear why and how he irritated some of those whom he prodded with his almost impertinent questions and also why he endeared himself to his many friends and admirers. These portraits may or may not be historically reliable. That of Alcibiades includes no reference to the corruption and overt treason which Thucydides revealed in his sinister picture of the same man. That of Socrates does not resemble the pictures of Socrates given by Xenophon and Aristophanes. All the portraits, however, if historically uncertain, are philosophically powerful; for they are portrayals in concrete form of abstract ideas to which the reader, in his very observation of the persons, is progressively led. The dialogues, exploiting the portraits, are really intellectual dramas in which ideas are set over against one another in ironic but earnest discourse. The *Laches,* for example, discusses courage or manliness; the *Gorgias* deals with the claims of Sophists to teach eloquence; the *Phaedo* examines the significance of death and the fate of the soul; the *Symposium* and the *Phaedrus* consider the nature of love, its lower and higher forms, and the effects of these various forms upon the soul; the *Protagoras* and the *Meno* debate the possibility and means of teaching virtue; the *Timaeus* presents some current theories about the structure of the universe and contains some profound suggestions toward a cosmology; the *Republic* gives a definition of the just or excellent life for a man and for a state and develops a theory of knowledge and a scheme for education.

Plato's dialogues, taken for the philosophy that is in them, may be said to achieve two purposes. On the one hand, they promote consistent thinking. They take an idea, define it, and trace its implications. They are thus forays in logical analysis, revealing what some initial stand entails in the way of necessary consequences. They show that we can, if we choose, examine the import of an idea without seeking to make any commitment as to the truth of the idea. The dialogues which confine themselves to this type of analysis are Plato's earlier ones and were written when the influence of Socrates over him was still authoritative. On the other hand, and more and more in the later dialogues, Plato supplements logical analysis with an effort to determine objective truth on the problems which he was considering. The *Republic,* for example, exhibits both purposes. It first section or "book" (which some critics think may once have been an independent dialogue) is in this sense Socratic, and the great body of the dialogue is more completely Platonic. For, after subjecting various ideas of justice to critical examination of their meaning and implications, Plato went on so to define the term *justice* as to establish a rational norm or standard by means of which he thought an informed mind could truly appraise events and could soundly guide action. Hence, although Plato did not give us any systematic treatise, he did enunciate a philosophical point of view from which, as he believed, all human problems may be systematically studied and genuinely solved. This point of view Plato quite clearly regarded as indispensable for any man who seriously wishes to live well. In pointed criticism of some of his predecessors and many of his contemporaries, he endeavored to show how men may best seek order in the midst of confusion, security in the midst of change, and certainty in the midst of doubt. For, as he plainly insisted, it is only as men gain order, security, and certainty that they may come to live the good life which is their potential glory and their prerogative as rational creatures.

PLATO'S IDEA OF VIRTUE

Plato explored themes in many fields of philosophical interest— ethical, political, logical, epistemological, aesthetic, metaphysical. But his primary concern, or the focal center from which he was then led on into other fields, was ethical. Always, from his earliest to his latest writings, he was directly or indirectly engaged in examining the import of his major question: What is the best life a man may lead?

Fundamental to Plato's treatment of the good life for man is a conception which along with other and often incompatible notions was embedded in Greek moral traditions prior to his time. He had the genius to bring out this conception clearly and to put it in explicit opposition to the other notions. This conception is that the good of anything is to be found in the most mature or the most fully developed form of that thing. Man's good, then, is the perfection of his potential form. Other things, of course, have their respective fulfillments too. But the specifically human form of good is what we human beings are naturally most concerned to know and to achieve. So we give it a special name. This name, which in Plato's Greek is *aretē*, is often translated as "virtue." [13] Virtue, then, in the context of Plato, is not mere innocence or lack of evil; it is rather the achievement

---

[13] Virtue is a particularly happy translation of *aretē* if one keeps in mind the etymology of the English word. Virtue is a word which comes from the Latin *vir* which means "man." Virtue, then, is "man-ness," or "manliness," or the quality which would, if fully realized, make a person the embodiment of the perfection of which a human being is capable.

of positive excellence, the ideal fulfillment of the entire powers of a man in mature accomplishment.

Plato proceeded to bring out the implications of his conception of virtue. Man is not virtuous by original nature; indeed, by original nature man is neither good nor bad. Original nature is related to the achievement of virtue as raw material is related to finished product. On the one hand, no original element of human nature is to be condemned as evil or to be excluded from its legitimate place in the developed life; and on the other hand, no original element of human nature is to be entirely trusted or given free rein or allowed to dominate or suppress other elements. According to Plato's conception, the good life for man is won only through the development of all the latent resources of human nature in a wholesome integration. It comes, not through abstinence, but through positive realization of capacities in unified action. In a word which Plato borrowed from the Pythagoreans, human good or virtue is a kind of harmony. The good man is one who has "set his house in order." Without guidance and wise planning a man is likely to be either a riotous welter of warring impulses or an unbalanced assertion of some one partial impulse. But with guidance and wise planning a man may achieve a rich manifold of adjusted interests within the harmonious structure of an embracing order. The good man is one who has become completely himself.

In formulating this basic conception, Plato rejected other theories which were more or less current in his day. His basic conception is indeed a mean between two other types of theory, and he gave detailed analyses of these two other types and their inadequacies.

On the one hand, certain people thought of the proper life for man as obedience to an authority outside himself. This external authority might be a human authority, like civil law or social convention, or it might be an alleged divine authority, like the will of the gods. But this type of theory, in both its secular and religious forms, implicitly denies the moral autonomy of man. Plato had great respect for social conventions and even more for civil law; he would not lightly run counter to conventions and laws because both of them often embody the instruction of much past human experience. But neither would he take these factors as in themselves necessarily binding. Laws and conventions have to be judged by standards to which they are properly subject and are not themselves to be erected into standards. Plato pictured his beloved Socrates as sometimes boldly defying and sometimes piously accepting the edicts of the laws.[14] Similarly Plato would not accept religious authority as any more final than civil orders or social pressures. He regarded it fitting for a man to participate in the established religious ceremonies of his city. Such participation he seems to have deemed a matter of good taste. But he did not think it ethically sound for a man to take the alleged commands of the gods as unquestionable. He once made Socrates ask whether an act is right because the gods will it or whether the gods will the act because it is right.[15] And the answer he had Socrates sponsor is obvious. Even the will of the gods is subject to judgment by standards of objective moral validity. Divine power (if indeed there be gods and they have power—and on these points Plato made no claims) could not by fiat make right wrong or wrong right. Unless the gods will for man what is genuinely in accord with man's intrinsic moral integrity, their will would not be virtuous and so would not properly receive man's obedience. Religion, like politics and social affairs, is material for ethical criticism, not the source of the standards by which such criticism can be soundly made. Religion and politics and social life all contribute enormously to human fulfillment when and if they are rightly conducted. But they are to be measured by the degree to which they are means to such fulfillment; they cannot properly be turned into ends to which man is to be subjected as to outside authorities.

On the other hand, certain people, reacting against the authoritarian point of view, resorted to a subjectivistic position. Plato was here attacking the Sophists. Such people supposed that a man is morally entitled to do anything he wishes or to satisfy any desire he deeply entertains. In extreme form, this point of view is found in the mouth of Thrasymachus in the *Republic* when he defined justice as the interest of the stronger.[16] In gentler but more insidious form, it is found in the Sophistic teaching that a man's good is what he most wants. But the stronger, whether he appeal to physical prowess or to political control, may or may not know his own best interest and, relatively to those over whom he exercises his strength, may be a tyrant who imposes a deforming mode of life on others. Furthermore, a man's desires may or may not be in accord with the real good of his potential nature. Desires do not always bring to consciousness all the latent capacities of a man's entire nature. Desires, like brute strength, need criticism. A man may need more than or other than he

---

[14] Cf. *Apology*, 31, and *Crito*, 51–54.
[15] *Euthyphro*, 10a.
[16] *Republic*, Bk. I, 338c.

desires. One of the chief problems of ethical criticism is to find ways and means of bringing to explicit and conscious desire what would be in accord with the total fulfillment of a man's capacities. Only when desires have been thoroughly examined by reasoned analysis of those capacities and their most harmonious and complete fulfillment, can they be known to be in accord with the conditions of the good life.

THE PERFECT CITY AND THE GOOD MAN

In carrying out his fundamental conception that the good of anything lies in the most mature or most fully developed form of that thing, Plato was therefore driven to raise and answer many other questions. And through his answers to these further questions he built up a body of moral philosophy. Among those other questions, three are of major importance for an understanding of his position. First, what is the nature of man whose mature development would constitute human virtue? Secondly, what are the qualities of character in which such a being as man would find his fulfillment? Thirdly, by what means can that development most effectively be promoted? The first question calls for anthropological and psychological analysis. The second requires the definition of standards which will serve as criteria of moral appraisal. The third necessitates the formulation of a theory of education. The three questions are interrelated, and the answers to them are interdependent.

In considering the nature of man Plato made use of an analogy, an analogy which becomes itself so absorbing as almost to distract attention from the purpose for which Plato introduced it. A city, Plato said, is a man "writ large against the sky," and, just because it is larger, is easier to observe and to analyze. The social classes within a city, the types of relationship these classes may have to one another, the methods of training men to perform the due functions of their respective social positions, and the virtues proper to the various social classes and to the city as a whole—all these points of the analogy bear significantly upon an understanding of the good life for man. Ethics and politics are intimately interinvolved; neither can be thoroughly discussed apart from the other. And Plato obviously became increasingly interested, as he carried out his analogy in detail, with the political aspects of his theories. Plato is here characteristic of the best phases of Greek thought, according to which an individual man could realize his own personal development only through participation in the organized life of society. Plato was therefore bound to study man in his social context. But he never forgot the individual man who was both the occasion of his first introduction of the political analogy and the final concern of his elaborated political reflections.

A city, Plato started out his analogy by maintaining, differs from a collection of separate individuals in that it is organized according to the principle of the division of labor. Some people raise food for others, some construct houses for others, some make coats or shoes for others, and so on. The number of occupations can be increased almost without limits, as the city grows larger and richer. All those who work at tasks which administer to the needs or to the pleasure or entertainment of others can be thought of as constituting the class of producers. But a city is more than a class of producers; its well-being makes requisite that some men be chosen to protect the city against attack by jealous neighbors and to keep order and to regulate the common life. These chosen men, Plato pointed out, will constitute two further classes. Some will be soldiers to protect the city from internal and external foes. Others will be rulers to determine policies and to plan for civic welfare; they will be concerned both to define the ends which the defense of the soldiers will safeguard and to provide for the conditions which will make the industry of the producers most wholesome for the city as a whole. A city, as Plato pictured it, thus consists of three classes: producers, soldiers, and rulers.

Cities, however, may be of many different degrees of excellence. Only if a city is rightly ordered will it be perfect. But if it is rightly ordered, it will really be perfect, and in it will then be found the virtues for which Plato's discussion was searching: temperance and courage and wisdom and justice. Plato did not in all his dialogues give exactly the same list of virtues. He sometimes, for example, included piety. But the four virtues just mentioned are the ones he stressed; indeed he stressed them so constantly and emphatically that the literary traditions of subsequent centuries have usually referred to them as the cardinal virtues. The English words by which Plato's names for the virtues are customarily translated do not colloquially convey the full and rich meaning Plato put into them. We must therefore take care to note all that Plato intended.

Plato explained the virtues by showing exactly where they would be located in his well-ordered city. Wisdom, of course, resides in the ruling class. It is more than technical knowledge such as the various producers must possess for the competent performance of their several tasks. It is more than knowledge of means whereby separate objectives may be gained. It is rather knowledge of the final and inclusive ends for the realization of which all competent perform-ances and all means at men's disposal may best be utilized. It is knowl-edge of the ends which the integrated life of a city may achieve, of the ideal values which all who share in a city's life may be taught to enjoy, of the full excellence toward which a truly united city may aspire.

Courage is the peculiar virtue of the soldier class. It is not identical with physical prowess. It includes such prowess, but it also includes firmness against indulgence in distracting pleasures and against fear of impending pains. It is loyal performance of the purposes which wise rulers specify as requisite to a city's welfare.

Temperance is a virtue which ought to be found distributed throughout a city. It "is unlike courage and wisdom, each of which resides in a part only"; it "extends to the whole, and produces a harmony of the weaker and the stronger and the middle class, whether these be stronger or weaker in wisdom or power or numbers or wealth." [17] Temperance is a principle of balance, of due expression of every interest. It is good taste in all actions, sensitive appreciation of what is fitting, regard for one's own dignity as a person and for the feelings of others. It is moral harmony of a man within himself and in his diverse civic relations.

Plato's fourth virtue was justice. Yet Plato did not conceive it as one more virtue on a par with the other virtues. He conceived it rather as that culminating excellence to which the other virtues collectively lead. It is the fine quality which accrues to the life of a city when every class and every person exhibits the other virtues and fulfills perfectly all requisite functions relatively to one another and the whole. Without it, the other virtues become difficult and turn into inadequate imitations of their proper forms. It entails the other virtues, and the other virtues collectively eventuate in it. Plato be-lieved that he could distinguish the four virtues in idea, but he thought that it was hard to find them separately in their occurrence. Virtue, he was prone to say, is one. Courage and temperance are im-possible without wisdom; courage without temperance becomes a kind of bold defiance; and temperance without courage becomes effete mediocrity. A city is in principle a unit; and, hence, existing cities must be judged by the degree to which they possess or lack the perfec-

17 Cf. *Republic*, 431–432. In tradition through subsequent centuries, the full meaning of Plato's definitions of the virtues has often been obscured. Wisdom degenerated at times into prudent regard for one's own concerns, and courage into mere physical prowess. Temperance especially suffered; it became a kind of abstinence, a negative with-drawal from the lure of the world or mere moderation in such appetites as desires for food and drink. Justice tended to lapse into a merely legal concept or became identified with honesty in the handling of property.

tion which the conjunction of the several virtues gives them. And this perfection he indicated by the word *dikē* which, perhaps unfortunately, is normally rendered "justice" in English translations of his Greek.

Plato applied his analogy of the city step by step to the individual man. The three social classes represent the three "parts of the soul" or elements in human nature. Parallel to the class of producers is the mass of desires or affections or passions which emerge in man's consciousness. These are often amorphous and troublesome; they tend, unless they are rigorously trained and directed, to lead a man into unbalanced indulgence and chaotic activity. Parallel to the class of soldiers is spirit. This element in human nature is not at all what in other moral traditions is called spirituality. It is the dynamic energy or forcefulness which we refer to in using the phrase "a spirited man." And parallel to the class of rulers is intelligence or reason—the ability of a man to judge, to foresee, to criticize, to know. This element is a distinctively human possession, and in its proper use and fulfillment lies a man's specifically human glory. The complete man is a whole within which the three aspects are distinguishable. And the kind of person a man becomes depends on the way in which the three aspects are developed and related. A man can be compared, Plato said, to a chariot drawn by two steeds, one black (passions) and the other white (spirit), and driven by a charioteer (reason).[18] As the rulers of a city are the only class suited to control and organize the city, so the reason of a man is the only element suited to preside over and to integrate his life. But the rulers exist for the sake of the city, and reason exists for the sake of man. The whole, not merely the noblest class or part, is the entity with which moral criticism is concerned.

The virtues requisite for a good city, Plato maintained, are also requisite for a good man. Wisdom ensues when reason discerns the ends proper to the organized life of the entire man and guides all other elements of a man's nature to unified fulfillment. Courage ensues when spirit loyally submits to reason's direction, spurning to indulge in the lure which some one exciting passion might offer, refusing to cringe before some hardship or pain which the course of nature or the iniquities of society may threaten. Temperance ensues when each one of a man's many desires is expressed to precisely that degree which keeps it from thwarting other interests and enables it to contribute to the richness of the unified whole of life.

[18] *Phaedrus*, 246.

It is a kind of moral poise. And, finally, justice ensues when the complex man so becomes one harmonious person that internal discord gives way to exuberant expression of all latent capacities in integrated action. As in a city, so in a man, possession of the three preliminary virtues culminates in excellence of the ordered whole. The moral worth of a man depends not only on development of parts but also on the way the parts are put together. Only in the entire man, if anywhere, can justice be found.

THEORY OF EDUCATION

As Plato's philosophy arose from a primary ethical concern, so it culminated in a theory of education. For his view of man's nature and of man's fulfillment led him to inquire concerning the means by which the original nature can be transformed into the finished product which would be that fulfillment. And as he found three classes in a city and three elements in human nature, so he specified three means by which a city might train its citizens and a man might attain his due development. Plato's thought on these related subjects, although not stiffly schematic, is thoroughly systematic and may be summed up in the following fashion.

Producers Soldiers Rulers	go to make up a	City.
Passions Spirit Reason	go to make up a	Man.
Temperance Courage Wisdom	go to make up	Justice.
Music Gymnastic Dialectic	go to make up	Education.

In each case Plato distinguished three parts which when duly related make possible the unified whole he was seeking to analyze and to appraise.

Music and gymnastic, in Plato's theory of education, are the staples of elementary training. Plato's discussion of them is not entirely clear on all points. But he probably meant that all the youth of a well-ordered city would be trained in these two elementary subjects. For Plato did not wish to have sex differences determine the status of men and women in society. A city, he said, ought, of course, to give women exemptions from certain tasks in order to promote healthy conditions for the bearing of children. But otherwise, men and women, as he conceived the matter, should share in the fruitful life of producers, the military life of soldiers, and the political life of rulers. All youths, then, ought to receive training in music and gymnastic, as much training, indeed, as they prove fit to receive. The point at which anyone ceases to profit from the training would be the point at which he dropped out of the course of education; and the point at which he dropped out would determine the class in society, even the status in the particular class, to which he would then belong. Only those who completed the course of training in music and gymnastic would proceed to the further training in dialectic, which is requisite for the class of rulers.

The term *music,* in Plato's usage of it, includes very much more than the English term includes today. Music is a name for all the arts over which, in Greek mythology, the Muses preside. Its main branches, so far as Plato's detailed treatment goes, are what today would be called literature and music. Plato would utilize this whole field of study to make men gentle in their manners, moderate in their sensitivities, discriminating in their tastes. He did not for a moment suppose that such studies, as practiced in the world of his day, had these beneficial results. He therefore advocated strict supervision and control of these studies. He would forbid the telling of unseemly stories about the gods and the heroes, about fear of death, about prosperity for the wicked and misery for the just. He would forbid also the playing of such melodies and the use of such harmonies as arouse either softness or wildness in those who listen to them. But he believed that the arts, thus controlled, could profitably be used for moral ends and would cultivate in young people the virtue of temperance.

Plato advocated gymnastic for moral ends too. Men say, and, as he acknowledged, they say correctly, that gymnastic is good for the body as music is good for the soul. But Plato, accepting this trite notion at the outset, proceeded soon to modify it. For vigor of body, health, strength, and grace, although physical assets, have their effects upon the soul too. They make the spirit clean and manly. They lead to sturdiness of fiber, resoluteness of will. Viewed in terms of the city, gymnastic helps to produce good soldiers; viewed in terms of the man, it helps to cultivate the virtue of courage.

Plato seems to have believed that most people would only continue their education to some period of the study of music and gymnastic.

But he held that a few would complete that preliminary training and exhibit a fitness to go further. These few are those intellectual elite who might, through a more advanced training, gain the more subtle and difficult virtue of wisdom. Obviously no city can afford to base its policy, and no man can afford to build his career, on opinions that rest on guesswork or limited experience. Men must have more than casual opinions, they must have genuine knowledge, in order to live well. Thus Plato was driven, in the context of his ethical reflections, to consider problems of knowledge. And his answers to these problems involved so much of a break with conventional theories in the Greek world that they are often treated as the major part of Plato's philosophy. We will understand them best, however, if we recall that they came before Plato's mind in connection with his search for the good life for men to live.

THEORY OF KNOWLEDGE

The distinction between opinion and knowledge in all Plato's dialogues is unqualified and absolute. Opinion and knowledge differ, to be sure, in degree of certainty; but, were this the whole difference between them, the distinction would be merely relative. Opinion at its best is a matter of probability, and knowledge at its least is entirely sure. And back of this difference and accounting for this difference is a distinction between two kinds of object with which opinion and knowledge respectively deal. Plato was here accepting, and probably developing, the position of Socrates. Opinion is judgment concerning some particular act that occurs or some particular thing that exists or some collection of particular acts and particular things. All these particulars, as one may call them, are continually changing, becoming what they were not or ceasing to be what they are; they are ephemeral, contingent, difficult to characterize in any stable fashion. Knowledge, however, is directed toward objects of another sort which Plato called ideas or forms. Forms, in contrast to particulars, are intelligible objects and, as such, are fixed, unchanging, untouched by the passage of time, hence eternal. Because the object of knowledge is form, knowledge can be and is reliable and exact.

The relation between particulars and forms is one upon which Plato never tired of elaborating. We draw diagrams of circles in the sand; the geometrician deals with *the* circle. We tune two strings on our musical instrument to sound an octave; the scientifically trained musician knows that the strings, if equally taut, must have lengths of a *fixed* ratio of 2 to 1. We deem a certain man just; the wise man defines the *nature* of justice. The particulars, Plato was wont to say, imitate the forms; the forms define the ideal of which the particulars are more or less adequate instances. There is but one form of the circle, and there is a myriad of approximately circular diagrams. There is but one form of justice, and there is a myriad of somewhat just men. We cannot, Plato seems to have thought, reach knowledge of forms by generalizing from particulars; for the forms have a perfection which particulars, however close they come to the requirements of the suitable form, probably never fully embody. Seeing a particular or hearing it or otherwise sensing it may be for us the occasion upon which our minds are pricked into an intuition of form. But the form is never one among the particulars we see or hear or sense.

Plato, of course, ran counter to the prejudices of those men who are accustomed to think that only the visible or the solid is real. Against such prejudices he was wont to insist that a form is, of all objects, the most deserving of the predicate "real." [19] A form, he maintained, is an object of whose reality particulars partake without exhausting its eternal perfection. But Plato, in emphasizing the reality of forms, never meant to deny that there are other objects too. He never questioned that the many particulars—things and events in the world about us—exist, come into being, and pass away, and are vitally important for us to deal with as effectively as we can. He wanted men to acknowledge the reality of forms just because there are the particulars which can never be wisely managed except as instances of the forms. Men must discern the forms before they can strive successfully to better themselves or to handle other things in the world about them. Forms are indeed the only real objects, relatively to the problem of defining human excellence or the significance of particular things. Plato did not ever speak of forms as real in any absolute or general sense; he spoke of them as real always in the context of inquiry into the means whereby we may hope to make our dealings with particulars genuinely effective. Men live, as it were, in two worlds, although not all men realize the fact. They live simultaneously in the inferior world of particular things and particular events, where perfection constantly eludes their grasp, and in the superior world of forms, where all objects are perfect, unchanging,

---

[19] The English word *real* is the usual translation of one of Plato's phrases. A more exact translation would be "that which is" or even "that which truly is." But however his Greek is put into English, the phrase will be misleading to modern readers unless they note the context in which the phrase is used.

and serene. The few men of able minds and good purposes will sensitively discern the forms and will rule the affairs of the inferior world
in the light of the vision they gain of the perfect forms. Knowledge
of the forms—and nothing else—will give them a technique of
achievement of a better order in the world of particulars. Relatively
to judging particulars and acting wisely upon them, only forms are
"real." And the priority of forms to particulars in this sort of inquiry
was what Plato meant by the reality of forms.

A certain inadequacy, even, so to speak, a certain confusion, can
be detected in Plato's treatment of the forms. The form *man* is the
nature of many existing particulars; the form *justice* is an ideal of
what might be but perhaps never wholly is. Plato made no clear
distinction (as Aristotle, building upon the foundation Plato laid,
was soon to make) between forms in which particulars participate
and forms in which particulars ought to participate. Men are often
confronted with such corrupt situations that the full demands of
certain ideal forms cannot easily, perhaps cannot possibly, be there
brought to pass. But even in those cases, men must at least discern
the ideal forms in order to use them as measures of the degrees of
imperfection with which they are constrained to grapple. Plato's
failure to distinguish the two types of forms made him, with his deep
ethical concern, speak of the world of particulars as a shadow world.
He spoke of forms as both a logical analysis of the world of affairs
and a moral pronouncement upon that world. Some of the things he
has to say about each of these types of forms do not strictly apply to
the other. That, perhaps, is why there is in his writing a certain note
of sadness; for he realized that neither he nor other men can carry
out the full import of the ideal forms in the confused and corrupt
world in which their bodies move and their actions occur. That is
also why he somewhat too eagerly urges men to love the forms for
the beauty, precision, and symmetry which the forms manifest and
to remain always loyal to the vision which intuition of the forms
brings before their minds.

Plato set forth, in the closing pages of Book VI of the *Republic,*
an outline of the way in which the intellectual life may develop from
the lowest ignorance to the highest knowledge. He described this
development in what is called his "figure of the divided line." The
line, he said, has four sections which represent four stages of intellectual development: conjecture, belief, understanding, and reason.
The first two stages are both on the level of opinion but differ as more
shoddy and more competent opinion. The last two stages are both

on the level of knowledge but differ as more elementary and more advanced knowledge. Conjecture is snap judgment or guesswork, based on prejudice or superficial glance or subjective preference, as, for example, when a man estimates the strength of an enemy by his height. Belief is judgment based on the accumulation of several or many instances of some phenomenon. It varies in competence according to several factors: how well the instances are selected, how wide the range of experience is from which the instances are selected, how aptly the instances are organized in reaching a generalization. Belief is found, for example, when a physician judges that a certain herb is a remedy for a certain ailment. Such a belief may be false or true. But since belief, like conjecture, is based solely on observation of particulars, it does not reach the discernment of any form or principle, does not enable its possessor to deal with novel situations, and so does not afford a reliable basis for guiding action in the complex and variable world of affairs.

Understanding and reason are knowledge and involve discernment of form. Men may wonder how we human beings are able directly to apprehend or have intuition of forms. Plato repeatedly insisted upon the fact that we do have intuitions of forms. But he realized that the fact is indeed hard to explain. So he resorted to mythical explanations of the fact. The myth he most frequently used was borrowed from the Pythagoreans. If they meant it literally, he meant it figuratively. The souls of men, he said, existed elsewhere before they were fated to be plunged into "the prison house of the body" and to live in the world of particulars. In this prenatal state men's souls dwelt above the vault of heaven with the deathless gods and the pure forms. The descent of these souls into bodies and the world of particulars made them forget the forms. But occasionally, and for some men, earthly experience stimulates a soul to recall some form it knew before it was born. Knowledge therefore, as Plato was prone to say, is recollection. In using this manner of speech, Plato was aware that he was telling a myth and, indeed, took pains to warn his readers explicitly that he was doing so. But the myth, like all the many myths to which Plato resorted, has a point which Plato meant seriously. The point is that in knowledge there is an element which no accumulation of particular instances however vast can ever account for. This element is not a particular at all but a form or principle which, once discerned, is a superior means for guiding choice and for handling particulars to which it is relevant. The human mind is more than a witness of the facts given in sense. It has a power to penetrate beyond these facts and to discover forms requisite for the interpretation and appraisal of these facts.

Understanding and reason, the third and fourth sections of the divided line, differ in degree of organization, just as do conjecture and belief on the level of opinion. Understanding is that cognitive development which ensues whenever a form, even a single form, is discerned, as, for example, when a geometrician, confronted visibly with a number of diagrams, thinks of the nature of the perfect circle. Forms, however, unlike particulars, have logical interrelationships with one another. They imply and are in turn implied by other forms. They can be elaborately put together into systems such as the science of geometry.[20] When a man goes beyond intuition of a single form or some few forms toward a systematic body of logically interrelated forms, he is approaching the level of reason, the final section of the divided line and the culminating glory of the intellectual life. Thus reason is organized and systematic understanding. Plato seems to have believed that if anyone ever reached the ideal goal of such organized and systematic reason he would have a body of knowledge which would be the true and entire interpretation of the whole world. Such a man, Plato thought, would become a "spectator of all time and all existence." [21]

Plato's ideal of knowledge has seemed to some of his critics to justify them in speaking of him as a monist. For if one integrated body of knowledge can be an interpretation of the whole world, then the world must in some sense be one system of things. But this line of criticism goes beyond what Plato clearly said. Plato never claimed to have himself gained the high level of reason, nor did he indicate that he believed anyone else had gained it or even was likely ever to gain it. He presented the level of reason as an ideal of knowledge, not as an achievement. It is an ideal of knowledge toward which all our intellectual efforts point as to their crowning perfection. It is a measure of the cognitive worth of such understanding as we do possess and so gives meaning to all our intellectual endeavors. Even those who live on the level of understanding can at least see that a higher level is theoretically possible, a higher level on which our many sciences would become parts of one inclusive science and on which our

20 Euclid lived about 300 B.C., nearly a hundred years later than Plato. But his geometry can be taken as just the kind of intellectual enterprise which Plato wished men to cultivate. Euclid was not the original discoverer of most of the propositions of his *Elements*. But he was the one who had the genius to arrange the various propositions within the structure of one logical system, thus transforming a lot of previously scattered bits of geometrical understanding into a reasoned science of geometry.

21 Cf. *Republic*, 486a.

estimates of even high degrees of probability would give place to entire certainty. The more organized a man's understanding is, the nearer he has approached the ideal of reason or of one rational grasp of truth in a total and final insight.

But we must return to Plato's theory of education in connection with which he developed his theory of knowledge at such great length. He believed, as we have seen, that most men are preoccupied with the particulars that lie visibly about them and seldom raise their minds to the realm of forms. But he sought for an advanced course of education which would give the select few youth of his city an insight into the nature of the intellectual life. This course of education would consist of the study of the mathematical sciences: arithmetic, plane geometry, solid geometry, astronomy, harmonics, and, finally, dialectic.[22] For these sciences deal directly with forms and deal with forms systematically. And dialectic was Plato's word for the most determined intellectual effort to bring together systematically every consideration that is relevant to the understanding of any subject or problem. "According as a man understands or does not understand a subject as a whole," wrote Plato, "he is or is not a dialectician." [23]

Plato sought to indicate how men's intellectual life could best be advanced from the level of understanding to the level of reason. His suggestion on this point is a kind of prophecy; for, as has been pointed out, Plato did not suppose that anyone had really advanced to the level of reason. His suggestion is also quite difficult to interpret; his discussion of it is one of the most obscure passages in his dialogues. The organization of all other forms into an inclusive system of reason, he maintained, can best be effected through use of a highest principle, a principle of principles. Plato asserted that this highest principle is "the form of good." But in developing his point he used extravagant and mystical language. He wrote: [24]

The form of good confers on all other objects the gift of being known and confers on them their true and essential being. Yet so far from being akin to other forms, it transcends them all in dignity and power.

This passage has meant different things to different readers. Christian theologians have been prone to find in it an act of theistic faith, and

---

[22] Astronomy and harmonics, in the sense in which Plato meant them, were branches of mathematics. Astronomy was a matter, not of looking up at the stars as at so many particular objects but of formulating the principles or laws of moving bodies. It was what today we would probably call vector analysis and mechanics. Harmonics was a study of the mathematical ratios and proportions of which musical arts would be particular applications.

[23] *Republic*, Bk. VII, 534b.

[24] Cf. *Republic*, Bk. VI, 507b–509c, especially, 509b.

others have so interpreted it as to read into it some sort of anticipation of their own favored convictions. No interpretation can be advanced with assurance. But we ought at least to remember that the central concern of Plato's philosophy is always ethical; and we may not then go astray if we fit his rapturous language about the form of good into that way of thinking. Possibly his meaning is something like the following. Nothing is properly known and nothing can be given its most significant status relatively to other things until it is viewed in the light of the function which it potentially has and the good which would be its ideal fulfillment. Things are what they are because they serve the ends they do serve and have the values they do have. And knowledge, then, if it is to reveal the ultimate nature of things systematically, must be organized around the idea of function or value or good. Knowledge, that is, must be teleological in its principle of organization. An analysis of things in terms of the values latent in them is the only and indispensable means of putting them into that cognitive context which best discloses their full nature and their interconnections. Other types of explanation are possible but less fruitful. Mechanical explanation, for example, deals with things in terms of multiplicity of parts but ignores what holds these many parts together in a significant unity.[25] But things as they exist are more than their momentary actuality and structure; they are also the seat of values that lie beyond this momentary actuality and are yet their genuine, though ideal, ends. Only a teleological explanation can take account of these values and relate the many things about us to the inclusive ends these many things may be made to serve. By no other intellectual device can men dispel confusion and establish order, control change and promote security, remove doubt and gain certainty.

PLATO'S IDEALISM

Plato, as his critics have often said, was an advocate of aristocracy in government. He distrusted the kind of influence, for example, which skillful rhetoricians and orators might exercise over legislative assemblies. There is ideally a genuine art of ruling a city, but there is actually a spurious art to which ambitious men too facilely resort. Plato had seen the populace of Athens find his beloved Socrates guilty of impiety and condemn him to death. Orators have a knack of play-

25 Cf. *Phaedo*, 97c–99d. In this passage Plato pictured Socrates as rejecting Anaxagoras' attempt to explain a man's acts by listing the anatomical elements involved in the motions of the man's body.

ing upon the prejudices of an assembly even though they entirely lack understanding of the true good of their city and of the means by which this true good may be promoted. In all human affairs the distinction between the spurious art and the genuine art is evident. A cook may flatter the palates of people, but only a trained physician can tell people what is really good for their health. A vendor of jewels and cosmetics may induce men to adorn themselves, but only a trained gymnast can tell them what will really benefit their bodies.[26] Similarly, in politics, a popular speaker may sway crowds of voters by his eloquence, but only the trained statesman can tell them what are the proper ends of political action and the best means toward those ends. Plato aimed, in all the concerns of mankind, to educate people so that they would abandon the spurious arts and cultivate the genuine arts. And the genuine arts are those practices which depend upon a thorough understanding of the theories of which the arts are applications. Understanding begins in the discernment of the forms which define excellence and culminates in a dialectical grasp of many interrelated forms. Only a wise man can be a genuine artist, that is, can be a trained physician, a trained gymnast, a trained statesman. Only the man who has passed through all the stages of sound education and has risen toward the level of reason is fit to rule a city.

But Plato's advocacy of aristocracy in government ought not to be misunderstood. Plato was concerned to formulate a standard of criticism for political or any other human affairs, but he was not drawing up a program for a city to adopt. He emphasized the importance of moral and intellectual integrity and did not find this integrity widespread among men. He did indeed profess to believe that his ideal of a perfect city might by some chance come about in fact. But he was not prophesying such an achievement. One would need a perfect ruler in a perfect city in order to set up a perfect educational system, and one would need a perfect educational system in order to produce a perfect ruler and a perfect city. Plato was aware of the dilemma in the practical situation, and he himself failed to bring about satisfactory reforms in Syracuse. He was far from supposing that the march of events led naturally toward perfection. He did allow that if one perfect ruler and a persuaded city were to exist the vision of perfection might be realized. But he quickly added that it was not the purpose of his inquiry to show how such realization might occur. His purpose was rather an ethical one and had two closely related aspects.

In the first place, the pictures of the perfect city, of the wise ruler,

26 These analogies are developed in the *Gorgias*, 462c–466a.

in western culture. This humanism is not properly to be regarded as an antithesis to the scientific tradition, which had its source in the colonial Greeks. It is, rather, an application to human affairs and aspirations of the same patient kind of unbiased inquiry which the colonial Greeks applied to the cosmos. It is called humanism because over against those theologies which scorn human nature and bring some other-than-human standard to bear upon mankind, it maintains a twofold thesis: (1) that the highest good of man lies in the fulfillment of his natural potentialities, and (2) that the only sound method of promoting that fulfillment is the use of man's natural powers of reason to restrain and guide the passions and the will.

Humanism as a term for the tradition that stems from Plato's moral philosophy is a mean between two extremes which Plato found current around him and explicitly rejected. It has remained a mean between the same two extremes throughout the continuity of its re-expressions in the history of western culture and is, indeed, such a mean today. It is, to be more specific, a mean between subjectivism and authoritarianism. It agrees with each extreme in one respect and differs with each extreme in another respect. It is like subjectivism in that it treats man as having his own proper moral end in a world which permits but does not chiefly pursue that end; and it is unlike subjectivism in that it holds that man has objectively a nature which ought to be analyzed for an understanding of its ideal potentialities and which ought to be respected for its genuine moral purport, no matter what desires may momentarily impel a man or incline him to neglect the rightful claims of his integral being. It is like authoritarianism in that it distrusts the casual impulses or transient passions of any moment of consciousness and seeks to discipline these impulses and passions by an ideal to which the impulses and passions ought to be obedient and even contributory; and it is unlike authoritarianism in that it finds the needed ideal, not in some sanction imposed upon man from without but in the harmonious development of the intrinsic potentialities which analysis shows to be latent within human nature itself. Subjectivism has always tended toward caprice. Authoritarianism has always tended, even when put forth in the name of religion, toward repression and dogmatism. Humanism has been historically a tradition which has served as a corrective of the more extreme positions.

Humanism, like any tradition with so long a history, has been different things in the hands of its various adherents and expositors throughout the centuries. It received partial expression in such diverse systems as the theologically controlled ethics of St. Thomas, the dilettante courtliness of Castiglione, and the Renaissance ideal of the gentleman. But the historian would be just who pointed to Plato's dialogues as the definitive expression of the humanistic tradition and to the other expressions as deviations from that Platonic norm. And the philosophical critic would not be guilty of exaggeration who maintained that Plato's own statement of humanism is the most effective and most adequate presentation of the humanistic ideal with which the entire course of western culture acquaints us.

4. ARISTOTLE

ARISTOTLE, 384–322 B.C., was born at Stagira in Thrace. He was the son of Nicomachus, court physician to the king of Macedon. At the age of sixteen, he entered Plato's Academy, and he continued his studies there until the death of Plato twenty years later. In 343 he became tutor to the youthful Alexander of Macedon. When Alexander entered actively into political affairs three years later, Aristotle returned to Athens and established there his own school, the Lyceum. This was the second of the "four schools of Athens." Aristotle taught in his school for nearly twenty years. In 323, when Alexander died and the Athenians could more openly express their opposition to the encroachments of Macedon, Aristotle became suspect for anti-Athenian sympathies. He fled to Chalcis, where he died the next year. His voluminous writings constitute an amazing achievement, both for the range of their interests and for their intrinsic merit. They include works on physics, astronomy, anatomy, physiology, metaphysics, logic, ethics, politics, rhetoric, theory of art, psychology, and natural history. Some of these writings are lucid and even eloquent. Others, particularly the *Metaphysics,* are at times obscure, seemingly contradictory, possibly corrupt. The difficulty of interpreting the *Metaphysics* is increased by the fact that this treatise, in the form in which it has come down to us, consists of essays from quite different periods of Aristotle's intellectual development. Recent scholarship, notably that of Werner Jaeger, has succeeded in distinguishing three periods, the first of which is quite Platonic, the second transitional, the third maturely Aristotelian. The jumbling of essays from the three periods into what at first glance seems to be one continuous book has made Aristotle seem to stand for many different views to readers of many different schools of thought. The earlier or Platonic essays proved grist to the mill of Christian theologians, particularly in the Middle Ages. The latest essays, entirely naturalistic in tone, are more generally regarded today as the best parts of the treatise.

ARISTOTLE SHARES with Plato the fame of expressing Greek thought at its apogee. Some critics have been prone to draw a sharp contrast between Platonism and Aristotelianism, as if the two philosophies stood in antithesis to each other. The schoolmen of the Middle Ages sometimes made this contrast, and modern writers have occasionally followed this lead. Certainly the systems which have passed in history as Platonism and Aristotelianism have really been opposed systems of thought. But tradition, in reducing the two philosophies to two alternative systems, has accentuated the differences between the two men themselves. Plato and Aristotle held quite similar views on many subjects. Aristotle seems to have been inclined to think of himself as a Platonist. He not infrequently opened a discussion of a question by saying that he would "consider the opinions of the many and of the wise"; and by the "wise" he always meant Plato and members of Plato's school. In his latest period, however, he did depart more and more from the position of Plato, or from what he took to be the position of Plato—and he departed in important ways. But when all the differences between Plato and Aristotle have been fully taken into account, it remains true that Aristotle accepted throughout his life many of Plato's ideas and that he developed and brought to completion one line of thought which is implicit in Plato. Indeed, the philosophy of Aristotle is one of two major forms of thought which arose as historical results of the inspiration and instruction of the teachings of Plato.[29]

Insofar as Plato and Aristotle do differ, historians have sometimes sought to explain the difference by noting that the former was a mathematician and the latter a zoologist. This judgment is suggestive but does not go to the root of the matter. A more exact judgment would be that Plato began with man and went on to view nature as merely the setting of man's search for the ideal, and that Aristotle began with nature and went on to view man as a specialized case, at

[29] The other of these two major forms is the philosophy of Plotinus. Cf. below, Chap. III, sec. 4.

once typical and distinctive, of nature's general ways. The difference between the two men is then one of emphasis and starting point. But much of the tenor of any philosophy depends on the starting point. Because he began with a definition of the ideal, Plato tended to be impatient with the delinquencies and shortcomings of actual men; and because he began with analysis of nature, Aristotle tended to recognize the natural limitations that make the best human efforts fall short of the ideal. Plato is more idealistic in aspiration; Aristotle is more realistic in analysis.

ARISTOTLE'S FUNDAMENTAL POSTULATE

A fundamental conviction is present in all of Aristotle's reflections. This conviction is that reality ultimately consists of many concrete, individual things, such as those we constantly find in the world about us. There are many such things—men and animals and plants, sticks and stones, mountains and rivers and seas, sun and moon and stars, and so on indefinitely. These many concrete things, he held, are real in a primary sense; and then, in a derivative sense, the qualitites of these things are also real, and the relations among them, and any others of their states or aspects. This conviction he opposed to various opinions which he attributed to his predecessors. He opposed it, for example, to the supposition of the atomists who placed reality in minute particles and thought of macroscopic things as derivative from the particles. He opposed it also, for another example, to the supposition (which he attributed to followers of Plato if not to Plato himself) that ideas or forms have superior reality and that concrete things are but inferior copies or imitations of the ideas. This fundamental conviction of Aristotle is what has led some historians to speak of his philosophy as an epitome of "common sense," that is, an elaboration of an attitude generally entertained by most of mankind.

The more detailed exposition of Aristotle's fundamental conviction often entails certain linguistic difficulties against which readers of Aristotle's writings ought to be on their guard. Aristotle spoke of each concrete, individual thing as an *ousia,* a word which Cicero put into Latin as *substantia* and which modern translators into English call substance. But *ousia* and substance are both terms which merely promote confusion unless they are very carefully used. The word *substance* came to mean many things in later European philosophical literature which were not in Aristotle's intent and ought therefore never to be read into his text. And *ousia* can properly be employed, in Aristotle's Greek, of other existential facts than the many concrete, individual things. *Ousia,* literally translated, is *being.* To call a thing a substance is therefore, in the framework of Aristotle's reflections, to do no more than so say that the thing has being or that the thing is.

There is a sense, however, as Aristotle went on to point out, in which *ousia* can be affirmed of much else besides concrete, individual substances. And we cannot, without doing violence to good usage, use the term *substance* as widely as he used *ousia.* For example, red and cold and sweet have *ousia;* that is, they all are. But red and cold and sweet are surely not concrete, individual things, and we should not find it easy to speak of them as substances. It is the flower that is red; it is the water that is cold; it is the wine that is sweet. Red and cold and sweet are qualities, and qualities are real only as qualities of some concrete, individual things. So, for another example, being close together and being far apart have *ousia,* sitting and standing have *ousia,* striking and being struck have *ousia.* And, again, we can hardly wish to call any of these items a substance. Being close together and being far apart are relations that occur between concrete, individual things; sitting and standing are positions which concrete, individual things take; striking is an action, and being struck is a passion, of some concrete, individual thing.[30] Aristotle could say, indeed he did say, that qualities, relations, positions, actions, and passions, just as much as concrete, individual things, have *ousia* or are. But concrete, individual things have *ousia* in a more fundamental way than relations, qualities, and the like. Hence, as Aristotle put the point, we discover *ousia* in a primary sense and *ousia* in a secondary sense. We should be linguistically ill advised if we always translated Aristotle's *ousia* as substance. Our English does not lend itself to such word-for-word rendering of Aristotle's Greek. We shall be more faithful to Aristotle's intent if we say that concrete, individual things are substances or have being in a primary sense, and that qualities, relations, and the like, although not "substances," have being in a secondary sense. And by speaking in this fashion, we shall make clear Aristotle's fundamental conviction that reality consists ultimately of many concrete, individual things and that nothing else is real except insofar as it in some way pertains to these things.

Aristotle summed up the significance of his fundamental convic-

---

30 The word *passion* is here used in a sense far different from its current colloquial sense. But such usage will probably not in this case cause confusion of thought. *Passion* is the word normally employed by translators of the text of Aristotle and so is here retained. As *action* is what one individual, concrete thing does to another, so *passion* is what one concrete, individual thing has done to it by, or suffers from, the act of another.

tion in his discussion of the categories. A category, in Aristotle's use of the term, is a basic concept which the world around us forces us to use in our analysis of it. We cannot view the world in any way we choose; at least we cannot so view it if we seek the truth. The world is prior to our thought about it. Our reflections, from the most casual to the most technical, presuppose the existence of the world, or of some part or parts of the world, as subject-matter for our reflections. And the terms of discourse which we use in our analysis of the world therefore depend upon what the world happens to be. Among the terms of discourse we use about the world, some are more basic than others. The term *man,* for example, is not a category; for we do not need to use such a term in analyzing the stars. Nor is the term *star* a category; for we do not need to use it in analyzing man. But some terms are requisite to any and every analysis of any and every existing subject-matter. Men and stars are both substances, that is, concrete, individual things. And substance is a category; for every investigation we make of the world about us proves to be an investigation, if not about a man or a star, about some such concrete, individual thing or things. So are quality and relation categories. For though qualities are of many sorts—sensible qualities like red or cold, moral qualities like temperate and just, physiological qualities like healthy and strong—some sort of quality or qualities characterizes any substance we can possibly examine. Similarly, though relations are of many sorts—spatial relations like on-top-of and at-the-side-of, biological relations like son-of and cousin-of, political relations like citizen-of or enemy-of,—again, some sort of relation or relations characterizes any substances we can possibly examine. When Aristotle gave a systematic list of the categories which he believed we needed for anything like a thoroughly adequate analysis of the world, he listed ten. These ten are, first and foremost, substance in the primary sense, and then also quality, quantity, relation, spatial determination, temporal determination, action, passion, position, and condition. This list is not without its difficulties, for some of the ten categories seem closely equivalent to others. But the list is significant in its main point, namely, that our thinking about the world is controlled by the nature of the world, and that the nature of the world, in spite of all the varieties in things, exhibits also certain universal traits which can be summed up in a relatively few terms of discourse.

Throughout all of his philosophy in its many branches, Aristotle applied his doctrine of the categories so as effectively to throw light upon the subjects he discussed. For example, he asked whether the soul is a substance; and he gave the reply that it is not a substance but an action. A particular man is a substance, but his soul is what he does. This preliminary consideration so fixes the direction of subsequent investigation of the soul that the entire science of psychology receives suitable organization. Similarly, for another example, he asked whether virtue is an action; and he gave the reply that it is not an action but a condition. A particular instance of justice is an action, but the virtue of justice is a condition—the condition, namely, of having a well-established habit. This consideration of the category under which virtue falls so illumines the nature of the moral life that the entire science of ethics receives appropriate organization. Only after one has determined clearly under what category a certain subject of investigation falls can one go on to formulate profitable questions and to discover illuminating answers concerning that subject. Aristotle's doctrine of the categories thus ties together the various branches of his philosophy and also provides organizing principles for each of the branches in turn.

ARISTOTLE'S PSYCHOLOGY

Aristotle's treatise on psychology is usually called *Concerning the Soul*. The term *soul,* however, is not quite clear in English today, because it suggests religious conceptions which Aristotle did not intend. His term was *psyche* and might better be translated "life." When we examine the many substances which collectively constitute the system of nature, we find a number of different kinds. We find further that we can arrange these kinds in a series or hierarchy. The principle of classification which Aristotle used in making this hierarchy is degree of complexity of organization. With increased complexity of organization there always goes a consequent increase in variety of functions which a substance can manifest. The more complex the organization of material, the more varied and intricate the functions. For example, a lump of earth and a beet may not differ in the ingredients of which they are composed; but they do differ in the organization of those materials. And as a consequence of its organization or structure, the beet exhibits certain characteristic functions which the lump of earth does not exhibit. Among these functions are nutrition, growth, and reproduction. The lump of earth is not alive, but the beet lives. The life of the beet is the course of its characteristic functions. Life, then, is not a substance; it is a way of behaving, an activity, a process, a function which goes with a requisite kind of organization of materials or bodily structure.

Vegetative life, such as a beet exhibits, is the first or simplest level of life. A second level is animal life. This is an activity which ensues when, in addition to the organization requisite for vegetable life, certain further specialized organs or structures appear in the bodies of living things. The functions of animal life are those of vegetative life and the further ones of sensing (for example, seeing, hearing, smelling), desire, and locomotion. There is no sharp line between vegetative and animal life; indeed there are certain living things (like sponges and sea anemones) which seem borderline cases. Yet the level of animal life is clearly an advance upon the vegetative level, an advance in both complexity of organization and range of function.

Finally there is rational life. Thinking, believing, knowing, and all other cognitive activities arise when the bodily structure of an animal becomes sufficiently and appropriately complex. Again, the line between merely animal life and rational life is difficult to draw with precision; but we may safely say that the human animal or man is the only living thing to manifest rationality to any marked degree. Each of the more complex levels presupposes and involves the lower levels; that is, animal life never occurs without the functions of vegetative life, and rational life never occurs without the functions of both vegetative and animal life.

If we generalize the results of these observations and this analysis of types of life, we may say that life (or soul) is the activity of a certain sort of organized body. Life, Aristotle said, is to body as cutting is to the ax or as vision is to the eye. Life cannot be identified with body; and yet life is inseparable from body and from body of a definite and specifiable kind.[31] Or, in other words, life (or soul) is the form of a

---

[31] There are passages in Aristotle's psychology in which he expressed an idea which is difficult to harmonize with the views outlined above. Possibly these passages are due to the earlier Platonic affiliations of Aristotle rather than to his own more mature reflections. But whatever the explanation may be, the fact is that he wrote that reason is the only part of the soul which can possibly be considered as capable of continuing independently of the body. He never directly asserted that reason did exist apart from the body; indeed, the statements are, more than anything else, an assertion of the mortality of vegetative and animal life. Cf. *Concerning the Soul,* 413b24–33; 403a5–18. In subsequent history, however, these remarks were taken out of context and utilized for theological purposes as an endorsement of the doctrine of the immortality of the soul. His idea was, perhaps, that whereas sight has changing things as its objects and so is subject to corruption, reason has eternal truths as its objects and so is not subject to corruption.

living body.[32] As cutting is the form or soul of an ax, and as vision is the form or soul of an eye, so the various levels of life are the respective forms or souls of certain suitably organized types of body.

ARISTOTLE'S ETHICS

The psychology of Aristotle led directly into his ethics, and that in turn led directly into his politics. The functions of a man are many and diverse and need ordering relatively to one another. And since no man is sufficient to himself alone or can perform his due functions in isolation from his fellows, his fulfillment involves organized society or the state. Ethics and politics are for Aristotle two mutually interdependent phases of one line of inquiry. Ethics is an examination of how men may best live; and since men cannot live well apart from organized relations with other men, ethics finds its completion in politics. Man, said Aristotle, is a political animal; he is a political animal, not by chance and accidentally, but by nature and unavoidably. He who is not member of a state is either more or less than a man: he is either a god or a brute. Gods are deemed so self-sufficient that their perfection may come in isolated existence, and brutes have not the potentiality of such social development as have men. But if men are ever to express their nature adequately, to perfect their several capacities and powers, to enter into their specifically human type of excellence or happiness, they must play their requisite roles in social life. It is from society that all men receive their nurture and training, and it is in society that they find their noblest fulfillment.

Aristotle was following Plato in the basic conceptions of his ethical theory; indeed, he followed Plato more closely in ethics than in any other part of his philosophical speculations. We call Aristotle's ethical position *eudaimonism,* because he used the word *eudaimonia* for the moral end men ought to pursue. Ordinarily this word is translated into English as "happiness"; but its meaning is much the same as what Plato meant by the word we translate as "justice." It is the complete well-being of the mature and superbly developed man. It is not equivalent to pleasure, though the words *happiness* and *pleasure* are sometimes used interchangeably in modern English. Pleasures may be good pleasures or bad pleasures; they may be a part of human happiness or of its antithesis. Only the pleasures of a good man are good; those of a bad man are bad. Of course, the good man will have

---

[32] The full import of the term *form* in Aristotle cannot be clear until his metaphysics has been studied, but the term can hardly be omitted here.

abundant pleasure; indeed, that man is not yet wholly good who does virtuous acts reluctantly instead of finding in their performance a zest and delight that perfect his activity and thus crown his development and complete his happiness. But no adequate estimate of the worth of a man is possible through an attempted measure of the amount of pleasure he enjoys. We may praise such pleasures as the good man feels; but we cannot properly deem a man good just because his pleasures are many and intense.

Aristotle modified somewhat Plato's analysis of human nature and, consequently, Plato's list of virtues. He seems to have found Plato's picture of the elements of human nature and the corresponding virtues a bit too schematic. He pointed out that human nature has many irrational elements [33] and also a rational principle, and that the irrational elements are in part beyond the power of reason to control and are in part subject to control by reason. Thus human nature, considered as the raw material for transformation in accord with the good life or happiness, has three parts:

(1) the irrational part which is not subject to rational control;
(2) the irrational part which is subject to rational control;
(3) the rational part.

And corresponding to these three parts there will be three kinds of excellence and, likewise, three ways by which happiness comes, if indeed it comes at all.

Corresponding to the irrational part of human nature which is not subject to control by reason is natural excellence. This is the result of good fortune or luck. It is not properly to be called virtue, because those who lack it cannot be blamed for their unfortunate condition. It is better to be handsome than ugly, well born than ill born, citizen of a free state than slave to another, tall than short, and so forth. But although the former alternative in each of these contrasts is better than the latter, he who is fortunate, however much he may therefore be admired, is not necessarily more virtuous than he who is unfortunate and lacks natural excellence. Aristotle differed markedly from Plato at this point. Plato loved the ugly Socrates. But Aristotle was realistic rather than romantic. He was realistic enough to recognize

---

[33] All the standard translations of Aristotle into English use the term *irrational*, so that use of the term in this text could hardly be avoided wisely. But it needs a word of explanation. The elements of human nature which are called irrational are not illogical or faulty in their reasoning. They simply are not rational elements. They are the nonrational or prerational elements of human nature—the appetites, the passions, the emotions. They are the whole of human nature except for the element of reason.

that there are phases of happiness which, though they are beyond man's power to regulate, are yet involved as minor elements in the complex whole of happiness. Men live in a world that stretches far beyond them and lies in part outside their power to modify; and though they may use reason to control much of their destiny, they are subject to factors more numerous than they can hope ever to learn to master and to regulate. As regards these factors, their happiness then depends on good luck.

Corresponding to the irrational part of human nature which is subject to control by reason is moral virtue or moral excellence. This depends upon the formation of right habits. What Aristotle called moral virtue is equivalent to what Plato called temperance. But Aristotle's treatment of the matter is much more pluralistic. As Aristotle stated his position, men have many impulses and desires, each of which deserves consideration, but none of which ought to be permitted to be dominating. For any and all of these impulses and desires, the excellent state is a mean between deficiency and excess. Moral virtue occurs to that degree to which the mean is realized. Courage, for example, is a mean between cowardice and rashness; liberality is a mean between stinginess and prodigality; friendliness, between brusqueness and obsequiousness; justice, between wanton disregard of others and timid yielding to others; good temper, between indifference and irascibility; sobriety, between narrow asceticism and abusive indulgence; and so on. There are as many forms of moral excellence as there are kinds of impulse or desire. To achieve the mean is not easy and depends upon long training and practice; indeed, it depends upon long enough training and practice to eventuate in the formation of strong habits. A man may hit the mean in some particular instance as the result of blind chance or passing impulse; but a man can exhibit the mean with constancy and dependability only when he has a habit of action that is well formed and deeply ingrained. Just as we learn to play the flute only by playing the flute, so we learn to be courageous only by acting courageously, to be friendly only by acting in a friendly way, and so forth. By consistently acting in virtuous ways, we acquire habits of virtue. Doubtless we need to be guided by others in the years of our immaturity; but we can eventually guide ourselves in the formation and reformation of our habits. The possession of well-established habits is what we mean by character; and character is good or bad according to the nature of the habits. Character is thus the outcome of a long and consistent period of moral training. A man of character is one who is not tempted in various directions every time he is called upon to act; he is rather one who acts directly and reliably in accord with his established habits.

In a noteworthy passage which summarizes much of his ethical theory, Aristotle wrote that an act is genuinely virtuous only if it meets three tests: (1) the act is done with knowledge of what is being done; (2) it is chosen deliberately and for its own sake; and (3) it flows from a well-established habit.[34] All three conditions are important; but the last is the one Aristotle emphasized most. A man can hardly be deemed virtuous, therefore, in the light of one act, however admirable that one act may be. He can be deemed virtuous only in the light of considerable stretches of time, perhaps in the light of the entire course of his life. "One swallow does not make a summer, nor does one day make a happy man." [35] Happiness comes, if it come at all, only through consistent, not sporadic, performance.

Corresponding to the rational part of human nature is the third type of excellence, intellectual virtue. This is gained by teaching and sustained reflection. Intellectual virtue has many forms, according to the subject-matter with which reflection is occupied. It may be prudence in the provision for, and care over, one's domestic affairs. It may be statesmanship in the administration of one's city. It may be speculation concerning the course of nature and the first principles which are manifest in the cosmos as a whole. The larger the subject-matter of which a man has competent understanding, the finer his degree of intellectual virtue. Prudence and even statesmanship are chiefly instrumental, serving ends beyond themselves; but the sheerly speculative life is an end in itself. As in his psychology Aristotle regarded rational life as the specifically human life, so in his ethics he regards speculation as man's greatest glory. Those critics, however, have misunderstood him who have interpreted him as favoring retirement from affairs; for speculation is not profitable when the person speculating is removed from contact with his subject-matter. Speculation is a life, not a retreat from life. It is a life that is free from the needs of quick and hurried application of partial wisdom. It is a life such as we might conceive the gods to lead; and, hence, men become most godlike when they succeed in living speculatively. It is a real and final end, because all else may serve to advance it, but it is carried on for its own sake. As the final end, it may be said to issue in the highest wisdom.

[34] *Ethics*, Bk. II, chap. 4, p. 1105a30–34.
[35] *Ethics*, Bk. I, chap. 7, p. 1098a18–19.

Aristotle's eulogy of the speculative life [36] has much in common with Plato's praise of the highest form of intellectual development or reason in his figure of the divided line. Plato is perhaps more of the reformer, stressing the point that reason is always instrumental toward a better integration of personal and social life. Aristotle is perhaps more of the disinterested inquirer, stressing the point that knowledge, apart from its uses, is in itself a source of the greatest happiness. But both men grant both points, and the difference between them is one of emphasis. Aristotle in subsequent tradition [37] was sometimes interpreted as one who would lure men from affairs into aloof reflection. Actually, however, Aristotle's view of the speculative life was that it was best lived, not in contemplation of fancies or idle possibilities, but in the intelligent interpretation of human activities, of the political life, and of the world as the scene within which the political life occurs.

ARISTOTLE'S POLITICAL THEORY

Aristotle's treatment of the state differs in many ways from that of Plato; for his interest lay, not in picturing an ideal by which to judge the actual, but in determining the best procedure to follow in practice. Although states were probably first formed to secure the bare necessities of life for their members, they afterward come to serve broader and more ideal ends. They arose in order to enable men to live, and they survive and are cherished because they enable men to live well. They serve such ends as the education of their citizens, the stabilization of socially profitable policies in laws, and, at least at their best, provision for some of their citizens to pursue the speculative life. In actual organization, Aristotle would not, like Plato, make the few best men supreme and subject to no authority beyond themselves. Rather, he would try to effect a balance of authority among several groups. He would put the best men in the highest offices; he would leave a right to criticize (in both legislative and judicial matters) to the mass of the people; and, above all, he would have all men, rulers and other citizens alike, subject to established laws. "The laws, when good, should be supreme." [38] The problem of determining which laws are really good remains, of course, a perennial problem; but it is a practical problem and has no

---

[36] The *locus classicus* for eulogy of the speculative life in the literature of western civilization is probably that in Aristotle, *Ethics*, Bk. X, pp. 1176a30–1179a32.

[37] For example, in Petrarch, *Life of Solitude,* in defenses of monastic contemplation, even in the idea of "the ivory tower."

[38] *Politics*, Bk. III, chap. 11. p. 1282b2.

general theoretical solution. In defining a state abstractly, one may safely put all policy into the hands of the wise, as Plato advocated. But in managing an existing state concretely, one has to recognize, Aristotle maintained, a plurality of factors, all of which deserve some scope in action. Laws which have stood the test of time are likely to contain residues of wisdom which the limited experience of even the wisest of men might overlook. Laws play the same role in the state that habits play in the man: that is, they establish social habits and are the safest guide to policy until superseded by better laws enacted by the appointed legislative bodies.

Aristotle thus assigned their respective roles in a state to the few best men, to the mass of people, and to the laws. He warned against reducing a state to too great a unity. "The nature of a state is to be a plurality." [39] The principle of division of powers is the most desirable procedure in practice and the most sound idea in theory. The unity proper to a state ought not to be sought by imposing administrative centralization upon it; it ought to be achieved by fostering common purposes among the various interacting but co-operating elements. If this unity is precarious, so is life everywhere and under all conditions. The purpose of ethical and political theory is not to solve practical human problems and thereby to remove all moral hazard from life. The purpose is rather to exhibit the kind of moral problems and moral hazards which both men and states, as long as they exist at all, will inevitably have to encounter in their daily practice. It is, in other words, to make men aware of the factors with which in all practice they will have to deal.

A minor point in Aristotle's political theory, but one which has attracted considerable attention, is his defense of the institution of slavery. Aristotle did not commend the form of slavery which existed in his own city and his own day. He asserted that many persons who were then held in slavery (perhaps as the result of military conquest) did not deserve to be slaves at all. But he did believe that some people are "natural slaves," namely, those who do not themselves possess sufficient reason to share in the rule of a city and would even profit from following the reason and the commands of others who are then their natural masters. But aside from such men as are natural slaves (and Aristotle did not hazard an estimate of the number there would be of these natural slaves), all other men were in Aristotle's theory properly citizens who were admitted to participation in political life.

[39] *Politics,* Bk. II, chap. 2, p. 1261a18.

ARISTOTLE'S METAPHYSICS

Aristotle wrote on many phases of nature besides psychology; he produced works on physiology and anatomy, astronomy and physics. And he came to realize more and more that there are certain general presuppositions in all these many lines of investigation of nature. There are, he saw, certain highly general truths which all the special sciences use and are justified in using. These presuppositions or general truths, he thought, deserve explicit treatment in a distinct science which, even if formulated after the other sciences, is logically prior to them. This distinct science he developed in the work we call his metaphysics.

The term *metaphysics* does not occur in Aristotle's writings: it did not exist in Aristotle's day. It was coined, after Aristotle's death, as the result of an historical chance which occurred in connection with the transmission and editing of his writings. Andronicus of Rhodes, in the first century B.C., prepared a complete edition of Aristotle's many works; and finding one work which had no title, he chose to put it immediately after the work on physics, with which, indeed, the unnamed work had close affiliations. The unnamed work therefore came to be called "the work *after* the physics," or the *meta*physics. The term *metaphysics* thus had no meaning originally except as an indication of the position the unnamed work had in the first collected edition of Aristotle's writings. But the term has been used much in subsequent centuries and has acquired a variety of meanings. Some of these meanings are quite different from anything Aristotle ever had in mind to try to discuss. We ought, in dealing with Aristotle, to employ the term *metaphysics* for only that exact type of intellectual enterprise which Aristotle carried on in the otherwise unnamed work which Andronicus placed after the work on physics.

Metaphysics is not a first science in the order of its formulation; for its content would hardly occur to anyone who had not already been studying many phases of nature. But it is a first science in the order of its logical position; for it seeks to give the over-all intellectual framework within which all other investigations of phases of nature receive their final sanction. Metaphysics in this sense, as Aristotle pointed out, is quite as scientific as any body of knowledge could be and is, at the same time, completely general. It does not take as its subject matter some selected part of nature or some phase of nature that occurs now and then but not always. Rather, it takes as its subject matter all substances and relations and processes which collectively constitute the natural world, and it then seeks to state the principles which hold good everywhere and universally. In other words, metaphysics is the science of the basic traits of existence *qua* existence, and it leaves to the special sciences the task of stating such additional principles as hold good of some particular existences but not of all.[40]

One of the most famous passages in Aristotle's *Metaphysics* is that in which he gave his "doctrine of the four causes." The English word *cause* is here used in a most unusual sense. It is used as a translation of Aristotle's term *aitia*. *Aitia* was a term used in the Greek law courts to mean a line of attack. Hence, in metaphysics, an *aitia* is a line of attack upon nature or a type of investigation into nature. Had Aristotle's Greek been translated into English before it was translated into any other language, no translator, in all probability, would have chosen to render Aristotle's term *aitia* by the English word *cause*. But Cicero had translated Aristotle's *aitia* into an equivalent Latin legal term, namely, *causa,* and from Cicero's *causa* we have come to employ the English word *cause*. The curious course of these linguistic changes has obscured the meaning of Aristotle's text. We must therefore take care to recover that meaning. Only one, or at most two, of Aristotle's four causes can be said to have anything to do with what the English word *cause* means in colloquial speech. The word *cause,* in discussions of the "doctrine of the four causes," must be taken in the sense of the Greek *aitia;* that is, it must be taken to mean a line of attack upon, or an approach to the investigation of, nature.

Aristotle did not believe, as Plato evidently did in his discussion

---

[40] The conception of metaphysics explained above is that which is expounded in the latest or most mature parts of Aristotle's treatise. But a quite different conception is present in the earlier or more Platonic parts. This earlier conception, superseded in the course of Aristotle's development, nevertheless has had great historical influence and deserves attention therefore by the student of history. According to the earlier conception, metaphysics is a study of the highest kind of being and thus is equivalent to theology. There are, Aristotle said in his earlier period, three kinds of being. The lowest kind is the terrestrial bodies; these move irregularly and in unpredictable directions and, hence, can hardly be the subject-matter of any science. A higher kind of being is the celestial bodies; these move in perfect circles and, hence, can be a proper subject-matter for science and can be described in general formulas. The highest kind of being is pure form without any admixture of matter. This highest kind of being Aristotle called god. The term *god* here meant, as indeed it often meant in Greek literature, nothing of religious value, but an ultimate beyond which lay nothing further. This highest kind of being (because it has no admixture of matter) does not move from place to place but nevertheless is the source of all movements of celestial and terrestrial bodies; that is, it is the prime mover of the universe. When Aristotle changed over from this earlier view of metaphysics to his more mature view, he abandoned the supposition of three levels of being and the idea of god which was involved therein, and he treated all substances alike and regarded them all as capable of receiving the same kind of analysis.

of the epistemological significance of the form of good, that there was one supreme principle from the adoption of which all knowledge of nature could be brought into one complete system. Rather, Aristotle contended, there are four ways of examining nature, each legitimate and none primary to the others. These four ways of examining nature are then the four causes. No matter what it is which one chooses to study, one may properly ask four distinct questions and, provided that one is able to carry his inquiry through successfully, will be able to get four answers. The four questions one may ask of any and every thing which exists are:

(1) What is it made of?
(2) What is it?
(3) What produced it?
(4) What is it good for?

And the answers to these questions, though, of course, they will vary according to the things one is examining, will be in terms respectively of:

(1) Matter, or the material cause;
(2) Form, or the formal cause;
(3) Agency, or the efficient cause;
(4) Purpose, or the final cause.

Every substance is a union of matter and form, resulting from the activity of some agent and lending itself to some end it naturally serves.

The first two of Aristotle's four causes can best be treated together. In saying that every substance is a union of matter and form, Aristotle was explicitly repudiating what he took to be Plato's theory. He was repudiating any separation of forms and particular things into two different orders of reality, with the consequent treatment of forms as prior realities and of particular things as secondary and derivative. If the Platonic dualism were allowed, it would follow, Aristotle held, that what we know most clearly would not exist and what exists could not be clearly known. But, as daily experience teaches us, knowledge of particular substances *is* possible and, furthermore, this knowledge is our first and our most certain knowledge. We know, for example, that Socrates is a man, that a certain visible object is a ship, and so on with countless other particular matters of fact. The form in each case is the nature of the existing substance; it is an inseparable element of every substance's existence. A substance could not be at all and yet have no nature. Every substance, however, is more than its form or nature; for otherwise everything we think of or imagine would at once exist. This something more than form is what Aristotle meant by matter. The matter of every substance is as inseparable an element of its existence as its form. We recognize the matter in a substance whenever we say that there really is a thing of such-and-such a nature, for we are insisting in any such judgment that such-and-such a nature is embodied in an existing thing. Socrates is a man; but so are Plato and Xenophon and many other particular human beings. Form is repeatable in many substances which nevertheless are distinct existences. Form is the principle of individuality; that is, form is what makes a substance the kind of thing it is instead of some other kind of thing. But matter is the principle of particularity; that is, matter is what makes each substance the numerically distinct being it is among perhaps a large number of other beings of the same form. Nothing could be a substance and fail to have both form and matter. Or, to put the point in language which has been used often since Aristotle's day, form is a name for *what* a thing is, and matter is a name for the fact *that* it is.

Aristotle's insistence that every substance is a union of form and matter has important consequences for his history of our human knowledge of substances. On the one hand, the form of a substance is what makes a substance intelligible and hence knowable. When a substance confronts a man and the man knows the substance, the form of the substance is also the idea in the man's mind. The entire substance does not enter the man's mind, but its form does. Then the man can be said to know what the substance is. But when a man has a certain idea in his mind, he cannot thereupon at once conclude that a substance of that form exists, because a substance is not constituted of form alone. If an idea in a man's mind is to be knowledge of substance and not merely unfounded fancy, the idea must be discovered to be a form embodied in matter so as thus to constitute a substance of the type the idea designates. On the other hand, the matter of a substance is what makes it requisite for a man to await evidence before affirming that the substance exists, and evidence is always some indication through the senses that the substance exists. It is through the senses, and through the senses alone, that a man discovers by what particular substances he is confronted. The matter of a substance is what makes it impossible for a man to infer the existence of the substance from an idea of its nature, however clear that idea may be. Or, in language which came later to be used in exposition of Aristotle's position, the matter of a substance is what compels a man to proceed empirically in his efforts to know the substances which comprise the actually existing world.

A further comment on Aristotle's treatment of matter may be useful. A pot is made of clay; a ship is made of wood; an altar is made of stone; and so forth. There is no existing thing which has come to exist from nothing. Clay, wood, and stone, however, are prior substances and so are constituted of matter and form. They are materials which can be utilized to make pots, ships, and altars. They are materials because they are themselves more than form, that is, because they have in them the element of matter. Matter, as Aristotle came to formulate his position, is not some inchoate and formless stuff out of which clay and wood and stone are derived.[41] Matter is rather a name for the way in which any and all existing substances differ from imaginary things. It is because existing substances are matter as well as form that they (and not imaginary things) function as materials which human beings or any other agents may operate upon and transform into new things.

The third of Aristotle's four causes is the efficient cause. The efficient cause is the agent, whether animate or inanimate, which produces change in things. "Everything that comes to be comes to be by the agency of something." [42] The operation of an efficient cause is requisite for any change, whether the change be in the position, the size, the state, or the nature of a substance.

The fourth of Aristotle's four causes is the final cause. The use of the word *final* in English is here again, as in the case of the word *cause,* due to Cicero. Aristotle used the word *telos.* Cicero translated *telos* into his Latin word *finis,* which English scholars merely anglicized into *final.* A *telos* is an objective or an end-toward-which a thing tends, whether the thing reach that end or not. So a final cause is not a temporally last cause but an end in the sense of purpose or value. For example, the final cause of an acorn is an oak tree, as Aristotle said, whether the acorn grow into an oak or be prevented by unfavorable circumstances from reaching its natural end. To exist at all involves (along with the other three principles) teleological purport. To exist at all involves necessarily being good for some specific end or

41 The supposition of an inchoate and formless material prior to the actual or substantial materials we have about us in nature has been upheld by some thinkers. It is found, for example, in the opening lines of Genesis and in what some of the Schoolmen called *materia prima.* It has been attributed by some critics to Aristotle too. And there are some obscure passages in the *Metaphysics,* particularly in its earlier portions, which may seem to warrant this attribution. But the position sketched above is quite clearly Aristotle's main intent and mature view.

42 *Metaphysics,* 1032a13.

ends. These ends may be clearly conceived and consciously sought (in the case of rational beings like men), or they may be entirely latent and unaccompanied by consciousness (in the case of nonliving beings). A drug is good as specific for a certain disease, whether administered deliberately by a watchful physician or taken unsuspectingly and by chance. Indeed, purpose in the sense of intent or design is but a special case of purpose in a more general metaphysical sense. Purpose in the sense of design would not even be possible at all, were not natural utility genuinely a universal trait of substance. A physician could not use a drug to heal a patient unless the drug naturally served that end. Conscious beings could not exploit nature's ends, were nature not itself teleological apart from, and prior to, their conscious intent.

Aristotle's defense of teleology in nature has often been misunderstood. Theologians have turned it into a doctrine of providence, as if things could not naturally have certain utilities unless God created them for those uses or assigned those uses to them. Vitalists have turned it into the doctrine of a resident force within living things which consciously produces bodily organs to accomplish the ends they then come to serve. But Aristotle's intent was nothing of this kind. Final causes, as he conceived them, are evidence of neither antecedent design nor vital impulse. Teleology, in short, is not an indication of the kind of efficient causes that produced the things that are teleologically significant. Final causes, Aristotle insisted, ought not to be turned into a special kind of efficient cause. That way lies superstition. Final causes do not generate; they ensue. However a thing comes into being, that is, however a thing is mechanically conditioned, it yet has some kind of utility. The thing is of course somehow produced, but its utility is not produced. Clay is good for making pots, and wood is good for building houses, no matter what the agencies were which brought the clay and the wood into existence. Clay and wood would not be what actually they are unless they had their respective utilities. So in general, the utility of any substance is an aspect of the substance without which the substance would not actually be just what is is. Purpose is thus as genuine a metaphysical feature of nature as are matter, form, and agency.

In one of the latest and most mature parts of his *Metaphysics*, Aristotle discussed the relation of his doctrine of the four causes to the course of change in nature. Substances are not timeless entities, as are Plato's forms. Rather, they are temporal affairs and require the passage of time in order to exist at all. Change is therefore the normal status of a substance. Even when a substance endures for a time without visible change, it is continuing through time and is changing in its relationships. Socrates is a man; but to be a man is to be a living being, and to be a living being is to develop from earlier to later stages of a typical process. As in his psychology Aristotle said that the soul is the form of a certain kind of body, so in his metaphysics he said that all existing forms are the natures of temporal substances. No substance could be what it is if it did not act or function as it characteristically does. Substances come into being, endure for a period of time, and then pass away. A universal condition of the substantial being of any and every thing is that it change.

Change, moreover, is not irregular and capricious but follows along lines that depend upon the nature of the substances which are changing. An acorn grows, if it grows at all, into an oak tree and never into a hawthorn; a beet seed grows, if it grows at all, into a beet and never into a rosebush. Whether acorn and beet grow at all is a contingent matter, a matter contingent upon the operation upon them of certain kinds of agents. But the way in which they grow is characteristic of their own nature. Aristotle's point, put generally, is that every substance has certain potentialities within the limits of which the development of that substance is bound to lie. A substance is never so inchoate in its intrinsic possibilities that the agents operating upon it may make it into anything they may capriciously wish. The potentialities are always multiple or plural, to be sure. A boy may become a musician, a soldier, a pilot, or a statesman; a stone may become a doorstep or the drum of a column; an acorn may become an oak tree or may rot in the ground or may be devoured by and nourish an animal. But the potentialities of a substance, even though multiple, are always definite and specific. Change is thus the passage from potentiality to actuality. No matter how powerful the agent is that operates upon a substance, the course of the ensuing change lies within the limits of the potentialities of the substance. Actuality is what at any given moment a substance is or does; potentiality is what it is capable of becoming. Potentiality is therefore as real a trait of nature as is actuality.

There is therefore a contrast, Aristotle pointed out, between the actual state of many substances and the more complete reality which, if favorable conditions prevail, these substances may become. The complete reality he called the entelechy. An acorn has its entelechy in the oak tree; the boy has his entelechy in the man; the man has his entelechy in happiness. An entelechy is the fulfillment which each substance by its very nature ideally indicates. The simpler the substance, the more often and more easily its entelechy is actualized; the more complex, the less often. Complexity of organization increases the degree of precariousness for the realization by a substance of its entelechy and exposes a substance to more chances of disorder and of ill fortune. Hence it is harder for a man to be a happy man than for an acorn to become an oak tree. The entelechy, however, even when not actualized, is potential. It is not to be thought of as a secret inner force or a subtle power that operates to bring about its own actualization. All forces, inner and external alike, are actualities, but an unactualized entelechy is a potentiality and depends for the occasion of its actualization on factors other than itself. Therefore the perfect, as Aristotle once put his point, is in a sense a condition of the existence of the imperfect. Things could not be the imperfect things they usually actually are, did they not potentially have the entelechy which serves to measure the very extent of their actual imperfections.

Aristotle proceeded to point out that it is just because change is passage from potentiality to actuality that the course of change in nature is contingent. Some philosophies deny or ignore potentiality and then come to think of change wholly as passage from one actual state to another actual state; and since actuality is always specific and determinate, these philosophies are driven to think of change as proceeding according to an inevitable and necessary pattern. But there is more indetermination in nature than such philosophies take into account. Potentialities, as Aristotle insisted, are always plural. The actualization of any one potentiality often means that others cannot be actualized and hence may even cease to be potentialities altogether. But before an agent so operates as to bring one potentiality of a substance into actuality and thereby to eliminate (permanently or for a time) all other potentialities, all the potentialities are equal in status. Aristotle did not regard contingency as complete indetermination. For, as has already been pointed out, he maintained that potentialities are limited and specific, not general and amorphous. The range of potentialities of a substance sets bounds to the possibilities of change in that substance's development. But within the bounds thus imposed there are many genuine and yet different lines of change which may occur. Contingency in nature is recognized practically in daily life, where choices are made and selected ends pursued; it is understood theoretically as soon as the full significance of potentiality and its pluralistic possibilities is grasped.

ARISTOTLE'S LOGIC

Aristotle's logical treatises, collectively known as the *Organon,* set forth a theory which is closely bound up with his metaphysics. Logic is an analysis of the nature and the criteria of knowledge. But knowledge is concerned to report truly about the world. Logic, then, is bound to reflect in its formal principles the metaphysical structures of the world. As existence pertains to things, so truth (or error) pertains to propositions about things. And the structure and interconnections of propositions will necessarily depend upon, and run parallel to, the structure and interrelations of things. Without reference to some existence, a proposition could be neither true nor false. Aristotle accepted Plato's insistence that knowledge is reached only when form is apprehended. But Aristotle, unlike Plato, went on to say that discernment of form is knowledge only when the form is properly predicated of some substance. A substance is (directly or indirectly) the subject of a proposition; and the form of that substance, or some part of the form, constitutes the predicate of the proposition. The unit of knowledge for Plato was a detached form; but the unit of knowledge for Aristotle was a judgment, expressed in a proposition, in the predicate of which the form appears. To separate the intuition of form from the role of form in an integral judgment is to suppose that we can have knowledge without its being knowledge of anything.

Aristotle discussed the various types of proposition which we use in judging things and the way in which these propositions may be related to one another in a body of systematic knowledge. The nature and connections of propositions will parallel the nature and relations of things. Form is repeatable; hence certain propositions will be universal (for example, "All men are mortal"). Substances vary in many respects; hence certain propositions will be particular (for example, "Some men are temperate"). Each substance is distinct; hence certain propositions will be singular (for example, "Socrates is snub-nosed"). Substances fall into more inclusive and less inclusive classes, so that the terms by which we designate these classes will be *genera* and *species.* And the propositions in which genera and species occur will then be found to have certain relations of necessary implications among them. Everywhere our thinking, if it is to be logical and eventuate in knowledge, must follow the facts and structures of the natural world.

A science or body of related knowledge, Aristotle went on to say, will contain different kinds of propositions. Each science will have some appropriate first principles and certain further subordinate propositions which, if discovered one by one in separate investigations, will receive their logical organization from the first principles. This logical organization, Aristotle thought, will often be expressible in syllogistic form. The syllogism, he thought, was the most perfect form of argument. "A syllogism is discourse in which, certain things being stated, something other than what is stated follows of necessity from their being so." [43] Aristotle carried out his treatment of the syllogism in great detail and with great skill, thus creating what has ever since his time been a major part of what has come to be known as formal logic.

Aristotle did not regard his logic as merely a device for presenting or arranging knowledge in a convincing way. It is, of course, such a device; but it is, he believed, much more. It is, he held, a technique for the discovery of new truth or the gaining of further knowledge. To treat logic as purely formal would be to forget that thinking parallels existence. The first principles of a science, however, cannot themselves be demonstrated. They are truths which anyone familiar with a given subject-matter would, Aristotle supposed, discern as requisite for any discussion of that subject-matter. These truths but make explicit the basic forms which attentive observers will discover to be embedded in the substances with which the particular science deals. "The premises of demonstrated knowledge must be true, primary, immediate, better known than, and prior to, the conclusion, which is further related to them as effect to cause." [44] The premises are indemonstrable, not in the sense that they are question-begging or capricious or even hypothetical, but in the sense that they are evident, and evident without proof, to any competent mind who is familiar with the relevant subject-matter. All demonstration, Aristotle thought, depends on prior knowledge. Hence, if there were not primary, indemonstrable truths to be gained before demonstration begins, demonstration would never get a start, and science would not occur at all. These primary, indemonstrable truths become apparent through direct acquaintance with the substances with which the science that employs them as first principles is concerned. If there were not a world of substances with which we are in contact before our reflections and analyses begin, as well as during and after those reflections and analyses, thinking would not be significant, and propositions would not be capable of being true.

[43] *Prior Analytics*, 24b19.
[44] *Posterior Analytics*, 71b20.

THE NATURALISTIC TRADITION

The influence of Aristotle in the course of western culture has been enormous. Aristotle was often referred to in medieval philosophy as "The Philosopher," and Dante characterized him as "the master of them who know." [45] His influence, however, was chiefly on separate points taken apart from their context in his integral philosophy. It was rarely on the central and controlling ideas which run through all his writings and tie his treatment of many fields together into a consistent whole. And even the special points, when subsequently woven into other philosophies, were often considerably altered from the meaning they had in his own statement of them.

The influence of Aristotle is apparent, for example, in the contention of medieval nominalists that there is nothing in the intellect which was not first in sense and in the contention of modern empiricists that all ideas are copies of antecedent impressions. His influence is also apparent, though in perverted form, in the contention of various materialisms that matter is the one underlying and permanent substance and all else is but a casual by-product of material processes. His influence is again apparent, and more justly represented, in a reinforcement his *Ethics* gave to the humanistic tradition that stems from Plato. St. Thomas Aquinas, for instance, uses Plato and Aristotle as if, in ethical theory, they spoke in kindred terms.

That historian must be bold who goes beyond these and other such single influences and tries to detect, in the intellectual life of western culture, a tradition which preserves a central Aristotelian position. That historian would be negligent, however, who refuses to try.

The tradition which embodies the central Aristotelian position, intermittent in its enunciation but repeatedly rediscovered, is hard to name except by the controversial term *naturalism*. For Aristotle's philosophy in its comprehensive scope and many fields of inquiry is throughout an exposition of the structure and potential values in that course of events which he called *phusis*. The English word *nature* has, of course, many meanings. If one chooses to define nature as a system of physicochemical forces devoid of all purpose and all value, then one must go on to say that Aristotle did not believe in nature and his position is not a naturalism. But if one uses the English word nature to mean what Aristotle meant by *phusis*, then one must say that Aristotle's philosophy is a naturalism. And naturalism in this Aristotelian sense, in which the term is a detailed ex-

---

[45] *Inferno*, canto 4, l. 131.

position of the significance of *phusis*, can perhaps be summed up in the following three theses.

The first thesis is that nature is a vast array of substances which are not fixed entities that merely appear endlessly in new arrangements but raw materials that are continually undergoing many sorts of transformations and are full of potentialities, all of which indeed may not ever have been brought to fruition. The second thesis is that among the potentialities of nature's substances are life and mind and beauty and happiness and all the values which adhere thereto when the raw materials of nature are so transformed, in accord with their intrinsic teleology, as to bring into actuality their ideal fulfillments. And the third thesis is that all the actualities within nature, from the inanimate lump of clay to the cognitively alert and esthetically and morally sensitive man, come into being, endure for a time, and pass away in accord with structural uniformities which prevail in all processes of becoming.

Naturalism in this Aristotelian sense may be said to be the general metaphysical position which best sustains, justifies, and verifies the humanistic ethics. The humanistic theory of man and the naturalistic theory of nature, so to speak, go together logically. Santayana, among other recent critics of Greek philosophy, has seen this point clearly. "In Aristotle the conception of human nature is perfectly sound; everything ideal has a natural basis and everything natural an ideal development." [46] However specifically human and distinctive from the rest of nature man is, his life exhibits, though in a peculiarly human form, the generic traits which run through the whole of nature. The same sort of remark could be made of every other natural occurrence, too. Mankind is not the end toward which *phusis* as a whole aims or tends. But the intelligent and happy man is one of the ends nature has brought to pass, one of the ends which instances some of nature's ideal possibilities, one of the ends which discloses that nature has not merely raw materials but eventuations of beauty and of moral worth.

[46] George Santayana, *Reason in Common Sense* (New York, Scribner, 1905), p. 21.

III

Philosophy in the Graeco-Roman World

1. TEMPER OF THE HELLENISTIC PERIOD

THE PERIOD between Aristotle and St. Augustine, a period of some seven hundred years, was very different in character from that of the apogee of Greek civilization at Athens. Athens had reached its artistic and political splendor under Pericles in the fifth century; and if it reached its intellectual supremacy with Plato and Aristotle, these two men still thought in hopeful terms of such achievements as lay in their immediate past. The Peloponnesian War brought much ruin in its train; it was not so much a victory for Sparta as a defeat for Athens and all Greece. The Greek city-states were gone forever, and with them faded the hopes and ideals which for a time had flourished within them. Alexander the Great had died a year before Aristotle; and although the three great states into which his empire divided preserved their independence for a century, the power of Rome began to march across the Mediterranean world and to subjugate province after province to its imperial sway. Of the Athenians after Aristotle, Mommsen wrote: "They too were powerless, and hardly anything, save the halo of Attic poetry and art, distinguished these unworthy representatives of a glorious past amidst a multitude of petty towns of the same stamp." [1]

Greek influences, however, dominated the culture and thinking of Rome. Greece, defeated militarily and politically, was still the school teacher for Rome. But Greek ideas, in the process of molding the intellectual life of the vast Roman domain, were also greatly modified in their new habitat. Historians need adjectives to characterize the cultural quality of the periods before and after the death of Aristotle. They tend to speak of the former as Hellenic, the latter as Hellenistic. Hellenistic culture has its roots in Hellenic culture

---

[1] *History of Rome* (London, Richard Bentley, 1867), Vol. II, p. 221.

but lacks the same kind of robust vitality. It seems to have cringed a bit from the awful magnitude of practical problems and to have hoped for protection from disaster rather than for the joy of achievement.

Hellenistic culture is marked by what has been called a "failure of nerve." [2] In the Graeco-Roman period there was less originality of ideas, except in the field of jurisprudence, than in the Hellenic period. Erudition took the place of creative thinking. A host of names can be given of men in this period whose philosophical reflections are chiefly an effort to appropriate borrowed ideas, to make an eclectic synthesis, and to compose learned commentaries on their predecessors. All the notable developments of philosophy in Hellenistic times exhibit a basic world-weariness, although the forms in which this world-weariness found expression are numerous and often antithetical to one another. Abandoning confidence of winning control in the world of affairs, the philosophers rather sought quiet shelter from misery or escape to some better realm. They deplored the misfortune of their inevitable human limitations and longed for peace from strife, security from attack, or help from some more-than-natural source.

Hellenistic philosophy is therefore characterized by a preoccupation with moral and, to some extent, religious problems. It shows a decline of interest in the natural world except insofar as that knowledge is a preliminary to protection or escape. It becomes a discussion, sometimes a rather effete discussion, of "the art of living." It thus often came to be crystallized into sets of doctrines which were erected into accepted authorities, even into revelations. About each set of doctrines would gather a kind of brotherhood of men of kindred minds. Each brotherhood would often repeat and transmit its set of doctrines as an established technique for safe living. To depart from strict allegiance to the set of doctrines was frequently regarded as dangerous to the hope of salvation. Philosophy became a profession of this or that "school" or cult. Rival schools spent much time in refutation of one another rather than in disinterested search for truth. To exhibit novel beliefs was then unbecoming, and to be loyal to one's own tradition was a notable virtue.

There are five schools of thought in the Hellenistic period which deserve particular mention. Christianity is one of these, that is, Christianity in its more primitive forms. But discussion of it will

---

[2] This happy phrase, which has indeed become famous, is taken from Gilbert Murray, *Five Stages of Greek Religion* (New York, Columbia University Press, 1925), p. 155.

be saved for another chapter, and only the other four schools of thought will be included in this chapter.

2. THE CYRENAIC-EPICUREAN TRADITION

ARISTIPPUS, 435–360 B.C., of Cyrene.

EPICURUS, 331–270 B.C., chiefly at Athens.

LUCRETIUS, 96–55 B.C., of Rome.

THE CYRENAIC-EPICUREAN tradition is the earliest known defense of the ethical doctrine known as hedonism. Hedonism is the theory that pleasure is the one intrinsic good and that all else, if it be of value at all, is valuable for its use in producing pleasure. The earlier Cyrenaic form of hedonism is quite different in temper from the later Epicurean form. The development in hedonism from the earlier to the later forms is an instructive illustration of the general character of the Graeco-Roman period in philosophy.

Best known of the Cyrenaics is Aristippus. He had been attracted to Athens by the reputation of Socrates, conversed at length with Socrates, and claimed to have derived his leading ideas from Socrates. But he gave a very different interpretation than did Plato to the position of Socrates, for he said that he learned from Socrates that pleasure is the only intrinsic good.[3] Of most things we may well be skeptical, because our experience discloses our own approach to the world rather than the nature of the world itself. But of the worth of pleasure no one can doubt. Happiness, Aristippus asserted, is a sum of pleasures. That man is therefore happiest who has the largest number of the most intense pleasures. The best man then must of course be sensitive to pleasures from many sources, and he must be able to exercise prudence in so directing his actions as to obtain the maximum total of pleasures. He will readily possess bodily pleasures and the pleasures of riches and honor and social recognition, and he will add thereto the further pleasures of friendship and intellectual discourse. No man can be happy, however, who trusts the fleeting impulses of the moment and who fails to realize the natural cause-and-effect connections which human interactions with the natural world are bound to entail. The good man must therefore regulate his actions by esti-

---

[3] A few passages in Plato's dialogues seem to attribute a hedonistic position to Socrates; cf. the closing part of the *Protagoras*. The hedonism of such passages is probably assumed for dialectical purposes.

mates of the total consequences which are likely to ensue from any choice he makes. He must, that is, be prudent. Prudence, as Aristippus conceived it, is very different from Plato's virtue of wisdom; it is not so much a vision of a transcendent value as a mundane calculation of personal profit and loss.

Democritus (whose materialistic and atomistic cosmology was outlined in Chapter I) defended a hedonistic ethics about the same time as Aristippus. But his hedonism was more sober and more disciplined, perhaps because it was not accompanied by so much skepticism. As reason penetrates beyond the appearances of the senses to the ultimate atoms that are prior to all sensation, so, maintained Democritus, reason also penetrates beyond the lure of every passing pleasure to the abiding and, hence, the best pleasures. Democritus condemned the violent pleasures, hence, the bulk of bodily pleasures and pleasures of the senses. He recommended the peaceful or tranquil pleasures which come when men, instead of becoming ensnared by some immediate desire, act calmly and in harmony with the whole course of nature. The good life is not one of agitation but of undisturbed poise such as only those can fully secure who lead the intellectual life.

Epicureanism is hedonism rooted in a conviction of inevitable defeat. Epicurus had a strange and, for the earlier years of his life, an unhappy existence. He was poor, afflicted with constant ill health, and, for a time, a political exile from Samos and a refugee. Then in 310 B.C. a group of his disciples bought him a house and garden in Athens, and he retired to this property for the rest of his life. Here he established a school, called the Garden, the third of the "four schools of Athens." In his Garden he received his friends who accepted his words of wisdom almost as an oracle. Epicurus never recovered from the feeling produced in him by his early misfortunes. He seems to have been convinced that he lived in a hostile world, a world that is indifferent to human good, a world that will torment men unless they build some wall to shut it out from their gardens, a world that will surely destroy all men in the end. Wisdom consists in making the wall around one's garden high and strong, in order to keep the world out as long as possible. Only in the quiet that ensues upon renunciation of the world can men find a certain limited and temporary pleasure.

The development of hedonism from Aristippus through Democritus to Epicurus was thus marked by a steady decline in confidence that man could win more than a brief modicum of happiness. History has been ironically unfair to Epicurus in assigning to him, or to his tradition, the maxim "Eat, drink, and be merry, for tomorrow you die." This adage, taken as an incitement to sensuous living or indulgence, is a gross misinterpretation of Epicurus' position. Epicurus, rather, stressed a need for restraint in order to escape entanglements with the hostile world: he was almost ascetic in his advice to his followers. He cautioned men against bodily pleasures and against participation in worldly affairs. He thought of the good life for man as one that is undisturbed by catastrophe from without and by passions from within. The Epicurean ethic might indeed be expressed diagrammatically as follows:

$$\text{Happiness} = \frac{\text{Achievements}}{\text{Ambitions}}$$

But whereas some moralists would recommend that men make their happiness greater by increasing the value of the numerator of this fraction, Epicureanism recommends that they make it greater by decreasing the value of the denominator. For, in the opinion of Epicurus, it is almost impossible, in the face of a hostile world, to add achievement to achievement. It is necessary, therefore, to relinquish ambition after ambition.[4]

Epicurus differed considerably from Democritus in the grounds on which his quietism rested. Democritus admired the majestic course of nature and despised the petty desires of men. He therefore urged men to acquire some of the superb poise which nature has. Epicurus, however, regarded nature as hostile, alien, and even abusive. He therefore urged men to safeguard themselves against nature's encroachments and to cultivate in themselves a poise which, as he thought, exists nowhere else in nature than perhaps in themselves. Democritus was joyful in his challenge to men to discipline themselves, but Epicurus sounded a note of profound sadness. Epicurus would gladly have taken more pleasure if he had believed he safely could. He was constrained by the misery of the human predicament to take less. But the wise man will never allow this sadness to turn into bitterness. Ill temper against the cosmos would but destroy the very serenity of mind which the wise man must cultivate.

The definitive expression of Epicureanism in world literature is Lucretius' poem *On the Nature of Things*. By the time Lucretius wrote in the first century B.C., the main doctrines of Epicureanism

---

[4] The suggestion for the fraction given above came from William James, who, in his *Principles of Psychology* (New York, Holt, 1890), Vol. I, p. 310, defined self-esteem as success divided by pretensions.

had become established as a fixed tradition of the Epicurean brother-hood. The hedonism of Epicurus was the central commitment of this brotherhood, and the materialistic atomism of Democritus pro-vided the cosmology which seemed to give the hedonism its meta-physical sanction. Lucretius often paid glowing tribute to Epicurus as to a revered master. Lucretius is great, not because his ideas were newly conceived, but because in his poem the Epicurean faith assumes the grandeur and the sweep of an epic.

The world was not made for man, Lucretius emphasized at the outset of his poem, nor indeed is there any purpose or plan in nature. All things occur according to uniform laws of matter or because of unpredictable and blind chance. The only ultimate things that exist are atoms and the void. Atoms are minute particles, of varied shapes and sizes, which drop downward through the void. Happening to swerve slightly from the downward course,[5] they become entangled with one another and thus come to be arranged in the complex bodies we now find to exist and to constitute the things of our present world. All of these complex bodies are transient; indeed, our whole present world is but a passing structure which was doubtless preceded by earlier and will in turn be superseded by later worlds unlike it. Only the atoms are everlasting. They are solid, indivisible, indestructible. All complex bodies are produced by their union and are dissolved again by their separation. Even the soul is made up of atoms. It is made up of atoms of air and breath and heat and a fourth, very fine atom for which we have no name. The soul is thus born by the union of these four kinds of atom and perishes when the union is broken up, though of course the atoms, including the atoms of the unnamed sort, persist forever as all other atoms do.

The world, though it has no purpose, is the scene within which many wonderful things have come to pass. Among these, the most wonderful of all is the race of men. Nature was not made for them; but nature produced them and is to an extent favorable to their temporary growth and to the civilization they slowly build up. The sounds men naturally uttered came gradually, in the course of long generations and slow accretions of understanding, to be systematic speech. The fire which resulted from lightning, destructive in large part, chanced to instruct men in the arts of cookery and of the making of tools. But with the increasing complexity of human ways of life,

---

[5] In introducing the idea of the swerve of the atoms, Lucretius departed from the teaching of Democritus. He thought he needed chance in nature as a basis for free will in man. And unless man were free, man could not exercise choice to stand out against the ruthless course of nature's inhuman ways.

there came two unfortunate developments. One of these was the custom of distributing nature's resources as private property, even of treating gold as a basic form of wealth by which all else might be secured and without which no one could hope long to keep possession of any other goods. Thence arose ambition, greed, war, crime, and countless other ills which agitate and trouble the minds of men. The other of the two unfortunate developments was belief in gods, in survival of the soul after death and its subjection to frightful torments in its future state, in the need of propitiating the gods with gifts, and in all the other errors of religion. Religion is perhaps the worst affliction from which man suffers because it is the chief cause of his fears and consequent terrors.

Lucretius varied in mood as he pictured in his poem the nature of human civilization. At times (particularly in Book V) he seems to have hoped that through reasonable foresight and prudent action men could fashion within the hostile world a comparatively fine structure of social order and personal happiness. All such order would, of course, be temporary, and all such happiness precarious. Yet the order and happiness might be won—and Lucretius almost invited men to seek them through disciplined effort. But at other times and more usually, Lucretius condemned civilization as a dangerous lure against which prudent men would safeguard themselves. Civilization appeared to him usually as a sham, tempting at first glance but corrupting men's moral fiber as they become entangled in its meshes. Men, he seemed to think, would be better off if they withdrew from civilization's enticements and lived quietly in the retirement of their protected garden walls.

Lucretius has often seemed to critics to have had considerable scientific interest in nature, and much of his poem is certainly occupied with giving analyses of physical phenomena. He did delight in suggesting causes to account for the amazing occurrences which succeed one another in the course of nature. But the motive of his speculations about these causes was his desire to prove that no occurrence in nature was the result of miracle or divine intervention. He was not concerned with science for the sake of science, that is, for the sake of adding to the sum total of human knowledge about nature. He was not even concerned to sponsor any particular speculations as surely true. He was interested only to insist that the correct explanation of nature would release men from any taint of religious or supernaturalistic explanation, and that this release, if it were effected, would win men to the moral position he sought to uphold. Lucretius said, for example, that men's possession of fire may have been due to a conflagration set by lightning or to the friction of trees which rubbed against one another in a storm or to the heat of the sun's rays in dry fields. Any of these suggestions might be true, or none of them. But that kind of explanation was requisite in order to show that fire was not a gift from Prometheus or any other god. The possession of fire has moral consequences, to be sure; but its causal antecedents had no moral intent, indeed, no intent at all and no moral quality. Of other things, as of fire, Lucretius similarly said that their genesis is a phase of the unforeseeing course of the motions of the atoms in the void. And only on the foundation of a clear understanding of that point of view can men become so emancipated in mind as to be able to live sanely, modestly, peacefully. The alleged scientific interest of Lucretius was but a means of preparing men to accept such advice as the following: [6]

If a man governs his life by true reasoning, he will gain the great wealth of living frugally with an undisturbed mind; for never can there be a lack of the little he needs. . . . Piety is not a matter of being often seen with veiled head turning toward altars . . . but it is rather a matter of being able to behold all things with a mind at peace.

3. THE CYNIC-STOIC TRADITION

ANTISTHENES, 440–370 B.C., of Athens.

DIOGENES, 412–325 B.C., of Sinope.

ZENO, 340–265 B.C., of Citium.

SENECA, 4 B.C.–A.D. 65, of Rome.

EPICTETUS, A.D. 60–120, of Nicopolis.

MARCUS AURELIUS ANTONINUS, A.D. 121–180, of Rome.

CONCURRENTLY with the formulation of the Cyrenaic position there arose the movement known as Cynicism. And in much the manner in which the former led into the sophisticated and disillusioned brother-hood of the Epicureans, the latter developed into a mature and dis-ciplined school of Stoicism. Epicureanism and Stoicism both reflect the world-weariness of the Graeco-Roman period. Both expressed in their peculiar ways the conviction that men cannot lead the good life by acquiescing in the prevailing customs of society and the popular notions of what constitutes success. In many respects, however,

[6] *On the Nature of Things*, Bk. V, ll. 1116–1117, 1198–1204.

Epicureanism and Stoicism are antithetical in their principles. Whereas Epicureanism sought to teach men how to shield themselves against the harshness of the hostile world, Stoicism summoned men to struggle valiantly against the evils of the world even if in that struggle they chanced themselves to perish. Whereas Epicureanism recommended that men seek a temporary and partial pleasure in some sheltered spot, Stoicism urged that men, without a thought for their personal pleasure or pain, give unstinted service to a purpose in comparison with which their own fortunes were insignificant and in realization of which they might be called on to play but a minor part. "Do thy duty though the heavens fall," the Stoics are reputed to have been prone to say. Unswerving loyalty to duty is the high privilege of men, whatever the cost may be in sacrifice of personal ends.

The Cynics took a position which anticipated and furnished a partial background for Stoicism. Like Cyrenaicism it claimed to derive its ideas from Socrates, although the Socrates to whom it appealed was different from the Socrates of Plato and the Socrates of Aristippus. Antisthenes, its earliest known advocate, accepted and elaborated upon Socrates' idea that no harm can happen to a good man.[7] He interpreted this idea to mean that men ought to be completely free from emotional involvement in what lies beyond the range of their own powers to control, free from fear of catastrophe, free from desire for external goods, free from dependence on the favor or disfavor of others. Conventions are artificial and therefore bad; and natural wants can be satisfied without ties that bind men to others. Man has no social duties: he ought to stand alone and rely only on himself. External fortune, pain and pleasure, office in the state, friendship and reputation among men—these are all morally indifferent. Even knowledge, except insofar as it enables a man to understand himself and to secure his moral separateness from the world, is unimportant. Virtue alone is good; vice alone is evil. Vice arises when a man allows himself to be perverted by compliance with the pseudoconventions of society. Virtue arises when a man, hurling a cry of defiance against all about him, stands firmly in his due place in the world and proves himself entirely self-sufficient.

Diogenes contributed no new ideas to the Cynic tradition and can hardly be considered a philosopher. But he exemplified the Cynic attitude in such a picturesque way that he has become a symbol of Cynicism in practice. One early tradition reports that his father was thrown into prison for defacing the coinage, and another attributes

---

7 See Plato's attribution of this idea to Socrates in *Apology*, 41c-d.

this experience to Diogenes himself.[8] Whatever the truth may be on this matter, Diogenes may be taken as one who sought to deface all the conventions that passed as current coins in the world.[9] He regarded civilization as a network of degrading institutions and unsound pretensions, bolstered by arbitrary standards and superstitions. He would reject existing civilization, not to put some nobler social order in its place (as the great Athenian philosophers had sought to do) but to restore men to the untrammeled integrity of their own individualities. He praised the dog's manner of life because a dog has few wants, no false shame about bodily functions, and no hypocrisies.[10] He took up his abode in what has long been called a tub but was perhaps a large grave jar on the side of the Acropolis in Athens. His character is indicated by a story of his encounter with the great Alexander. Alexander, curious to see the eccentric Diogenes, made a visit to this unusual shelter. Diogenes, however, refused to bow before a mere emperor but dismissed Alexander with a slighting gesture and the remark, "Stand aside out of my sunlight." Unperturbed by pleasure and pain, undismayed by physical or social events, indifferent to civic and human ties, he stood alone against a cosmos he scorned.

Stoicism, unlike Cynicism, was a fully developed philosophy. It met in a peculiarly effective way the emotional and moral needs of the troubled times and quickly became one of the dominant trends of Hellenistic thought. It almost supplanted Platonic influences at times and even became the accepted teaching of the Academy in certain periods. It entered profoundly into the complex texture of moods and ideas which marked the growth of Christianity. It has remained across twenty centuries a potent force in western culture.

Stoicism might be characterized as Cynicism rooted in a religious faith. It retained the Cynic conception of the good man as one who is completely free of emotional entanglement in affairs. But it rejected the Cynic notion that the good man would be free of moral involvement in affairs. For the world about us, the Stoics maintained, is the expression of a central purpose that runs through all things and assigns to every men his due place and his proper duties. The Stoics extolled two prime virtues, one of which may be considered as

8 Diogenes Laertius, *Lives of Eminent Philosophers,* first paragraph of the section on Diogenes the Cynic. This book by Diogenes Laertius, written perhaps about A.D. 200, is full of gossip of dubious historical value.

9 This interpretation of the tradition concerning the defacing of the coinage is offered by Gilbert Murray, *op. cit.,* p. 117.

10 Our word *cynic* (which is derived from the Greek word for dog) is due to this saying from Diogenes.

negative and the other as positive. Their negative virtue was apathy, or passionlessness, or indifference to both the lure of pleasure and the fear of pain. Their positive virtue was loyalty, dispassionate and purely rational loyalty to a cosmic principle or teleological trend which governs the whole course of events. The good man, the Stoics conceived, would be free of personal ambitions and private hopes and yet would be unstinting in fulfillment of the role which the all-embracing purpose of the cosmos allotted to him.

Some symbolic significance may be attached to the social status of the founder and of the three greatest literary expounders of the Stoic school. The reputed founder of Stoicism was a man named Zeno, whom tradition describes as a Semite from the East. Shipwrecked on the coast of Attica, he remained in Athens and there founded the Stoa which was the fourth of the "four schools" of that city. He was thus a man of the Diaspora or that scattering of Semites throughout the cities of the Mediterranean world which ensued upon the ravaging of their homelands. Like many others of the Diaspora, Zeno, an expatriate from his own country, had interests which were cultural but not civic. He was loyal, not to the particular spot where he chanced to live, but to the ideals and faith which he sought to teach. He founded a community, not of walls and boundaries, but of sympathy and purpose. His community cut across all accepted boundaries and sought to unite men of kindred beliefs and moral principles; it was a community in, but not of, the world.

Seneca, Epictetus, and Marcus Aurelius are the three later Stoics whose writings have survived to our day.[11] They occupied very different social positions. The first was a rhetorician and tutor of Nero, the second a slave who was freed by his master, and third an emperor of the Roman Empire. Stoicism is thus seen to be able to bring men from the most varied levels of society into substantial intellectual and moral agreement, so that it cuts across social distinctions among men as across political boundaries. Stoicism throughout its history has been a cosmopolitan force.

The good man, as the Stoic tradition conceived him, was entirely rational. Whereas Plato and Aristotle had pictured the good man as one whose passions and desires are under the control of reason, the Stoics pictured him as one whose passions are rooted out and whose

---

11 A list of names of other Stoics between the time of Zeno and the three mentioned above is given in many histories. There are, for example, Cleanthes (whose "hymn to Zeus" is extant), Chrysippus (the titles of whose writings are listed by Diogenes Laertius), Panaetius (who is reputed to have brought Stoicism to the city of Rome), Boethus of Sidon, and Posidonius.

acts are motivated by wholly rational considerations. Emotions, the Stoics thought, are a moral disease which interferes with the exercise of disinterested judgment concerning right and wrong. The wise man will have no private desires and no emotions. He will be free from fear, from the lure of pleasure, from agitation and worry over the course of events, from every excitement that might pervert the soul and produce errors of judgment concerning moral values. He will be free even from pity for human misery and from sympathy for the unfortunate. Although he will serve his fellow men without stint and will sacrifice himself without hesitation, he will do so not because of personal inclination but because of his judgment of obligation. If he is unable to avoid a consciousness of bodily appetite or physical pain, he will nevertheless scorn these frailties as deviations from perfect well-being. The "sage," as the Stoic wise man is often called, will be passionless and calm.

The Stoic position in ethics was reinforced by a suitable metaphysics. In certain passages in Stoic writings this metaphysics appears in decidedly materialistic form, according to which fire is the ultimate element, the animating force, even the soul of the universe. But this materialistic contention, whether figurative in meaning or a revival of some earlier influence like that of Heraclitus, is much less important than another doctrine. This other doctrine is that the universe is informed by a rational purpose, that the course of nature is teleological, that all events are contained within one unitary and intelligible plan. As the human body contains the human soul, so the material world has, as it were, its soul.

This metaphysics is nowhere worked out with convincing success in the writings of the Stoics. It has been called "a system put together hastily, violently, to meet a desperate emergency." [12] The goals of the cosmic purpose are not clearly specified by the Stoics but remain inchoate and vague. Doubtless the skepticism of the Cynics continued to influence the Stoics at this point. But whatever the cosmic purpose may be, it is assuredly both rational and noble. This purpose realizes values which, if the wise man did but know them, would meet with the approval of his disinterested judgment. The wise man can supposedly understand his proper role in carrying out the cosmic purpose, even if he does not succeed in understanding its entire meaning.

A maxim common in Stoic writings is "Live according to nature." Nature here is not a name for the material world. It is, of course, not a name for human nature, which is largely evil and, indeed, ought to

[12] Edwyn Bevan, *Stoics and Sceptics* (Oxford, Clarendon Press, 1913), p. 32.

be suppressed rather than expressed. It is, rather, a name for the cosmic purpose which runs through all things. It may be called providence; it may even be called god. With it men may feel a mystic sympathy which will sustain them in unyielding resolution to fulfill their duties. Human beings are thus like actors in a cosmic drama: they have their assigned parts to play and hence have no right to invent their own lines or choose their own course of action. Whether their station in life be humble or exalted, they should feel no shame and no pride. Their part in the cosmic drama may be comic or tragic; but nothing matters except that they play their assigned roles well and hold true to their vocation.

All things are fitting for me, O Universe, that are fitting for your purpose. Nothing that is in due time for you is too early or too late for me. Everything that your seasons bring, O Nature, is fruit for me. . . . That which seems to be chance lies within the warp and woof of the course of Providence. That is good for every part of Nature which Nature brings about and which fulfils its course. . . . Do your duty, whether cold or warm, whether weary or rested, whether maligned or praised, whether dying or busy with work.[13]

The more the Stoics talked in terms of providence, the more the rigor of the Cynic defiance of the world was modified by a spirit of humility and prayer. But to the end there is always in Stoicism a hard element. We mortals are told to serve our fellows and to bear and forbear. This service is never to be performed because of any rapture of friendship or spontaneous affection but because of a stern sense of duty. Even our harmony with Nature, the Stoics taught, ought to be one of rational consent rather than emotional congeniality.

4. THE SKEPTICAL TRADITION

PYRRHO, 385–275 B.C., of Elis.

ARCESILAUS, 315–241 B.C., of Pitane.

TIMON, 320–230 B.C., of Athens.

CARNEADES, 213–129 B.C., of Cyrene.

AENESIDEMUS, c. A.D. 100, of Cnossus.

SEXTUS EMPIRICUS, c. A.D. 250, of Alexandria.

CONTEMPORARY with Epicureanism and Stoicism there arose in the Graeco-Roman world a widespread Skeptical movement. And in the

13 Marcus Aurelius, *Meditations*, Bk. IV, par. 23, Bk. II, par. 3, and Bk. VI, par. 2.

case of the men who gladly designated themselves Skeptics, this Skepticism was quite thoroughgoing. Doubts on some specific matters may of course go hand in hand with assured convictions on other points. A philosopher, for example, may believe he knows the constitution of matter and may at the same time doubt the possibility of knowing any objective standard of virtue; or he may believe he can demonstrate the existence of the gods and may doubt the possibility of determining the nature of the physical world. But Skepticism as a school of philosophy is more than honest doubt on some or even on many specific points. It is rather a universal, deliberate, and, one might say, professional doubt concerning the possibility of ever reaching knowledge on any subject whatsoever.

Skepticism was fostered in Hellenistic times by controversies among the "four schools of Athens" and among the adherents of those schools in many cities of the Mediterranean world. The continuity of these schools across the centuries is, to be sure, quite uncertain, even improbable, though there is an ancient legend that the four schools all continued in being until officially closed by imperial order in A.D. 529. The Academy probably had the longest history; for if it went out of existence at times, it was then re-established. But whether the schools were in being or not, the influence they exercised, especially the influence of the Academy, the Garden, and the Stoa, was potent wherever Greek culture penetrated. And philosophic Skepticism was the negative side of this influence. The more rigid the orthodoxies of the schools became, the more outspoken was the criticism of the grounds on which these orthodoxies rested. The profession of Skepticism may sometimes have been a pose which was pressed with humor and was enjoyed as an intellectual game. But Skepticism seems to have been more than such a profession. It was also at times a serious contention among many prominent leaders of philosophical discussion. It served as a tonic against too ready adherence to the orthodoxies. It penetrated the Academy, so that many heads of the Academy are traditionally listed among the Skeptics. It was furthered by a tendency of the post-Aristotelian age to dispraise the intellectual life and to view philosophy as a practical way to salvation.

The Greek Skeptics are known to us only in fragments of their writings, particularly in references to them by their opponents. Pyrrho, the reputed founder of the school, composed no writings, perhaps esteeming silence the becoming attitude for a Skeptic. Yet Aenesidemus, nearly four hundred years later, wrote "eight books" in summary of Pyrrho's alleged teachings. Pyrrho is a peg on which Skeptics generally hang their witty sayings, so that the word *Pyrrhonism* has come to be used almost interchangeably with excessive Skepticism. Certain brief documents have survived which purport to be from Sextus Empiricus. But we find it difficult today to disentangle the various Skeptics and may rest content with a summary of the views which tradition assigns to them as a group.

Greek Skepticism, like Cyrenaicism and Cynicism, had a kind of Socratic basis. The Skeptics took over Socrates' profession of ignorance without preserving the serious moral purpose which was latent in Socrates' expression of that profession. They rather put this profession in the context of Sophistic subjectivism. They followed Plato's conviction that men can have only opinions, and never knowledge, of the world of particular things. But they entirely vitiated the significance of Plato's conviction, for they regarded Plato's affirmation of a world of forms as preposterous and therefore denied the possibility of knowledge altogether. There is, they thought, no reliable criterion of objective truth. All reasoning is covert expression of varying tastes of differing individuals. Deductive inferences are all untrustworthy because they proceed from premises which are assumed and not demonstrated. Inductive inferences are also all untrustworthy because they rest on private experiences which may not indicate the genuine nature of the things that occasion those experiences. Hence, not simply metaphysics and physical science (with their generalizations about nature) but even particular assertions about specific things are unreliable. Such efforts to report objective truth are useless theoretically because they give rise to endless disputes and are useless practically because they merely express individual biases. Even beliefs shared by large groups of people are unfounded dogmas; for such beliefs result from conventions and social pressures, and social conventions are no more trustworthy than private hopes and fears. Law and custom may be good guides for practical purposes but cannot be rationally defended. We must confess, the Skeptics contended, that all men, including the Skeptics themselves, are doomed to remain in unrelieved ignorance. We have no certainty; we have little ground for probability; we deal exclusively in groundless opinion. Wise men, consequently, will acknowledge that suspense of judgment on all matters is a major virtue.

The Skeptics, like the Sophists, made much of the relativity of sense experience. Men's sense organs differ, and no one can boast that his organs are superior. These organs, moreover, present things in accidental relations which constantly fluctuate. No sensation is free from elements of interpretation which minds unsuspectingly add to the elements that come from without. The objects which produce sensations, if indeed there be objects at all, may or may not be like the sensations they produce. These objects may have many qualities which our sense organs do not detect and may not have the qualities which our sense organs lead us to observe. All appeal to experience is therefore capricious and vain.

Some of the Skeptics—and tradition here points particularly to Carneades—delighted in applying their irony to religious beliefs. They did more than list the variety of incompatible beliefs which various cults maintained with equal zeal. They went on to point out that each belief in turn is inconsistent with itself. A god, if there be such, is either incorporeal or corporeal and is either all-powerful or limited in power. If incorporeal, he cannot be detected by men, who must rely on sensation for evidence of any existence. If corporeal, he is exposed, like other bodies, to change and decay and death. If all-powerful, he cannot be virtuous in permitting so much evil and ignorance to abound. If limited in power, he is subject to forces superior to him and hardly deserves to be called divine. All ideas concerning a god are thus untenable. Gods may yet exist, the Skeptics caustically granted; and some Skeptics continued for social reasons to submit to conventional religious exercises and even, as priests, conducted these exercises. But men's ideas about the gods are worthless, as indeed are all ideas which profess to give knowledge of what lies beyond the subjective realm of private fancy.

In comments on moral problems, the Skeptics had nothing original to say. They carried on, but with an even more deliberately destructive intent, the relativism of the Sophists. Carneades, for example, when once in Rome, is reported to have given two speeches on justice on two successive days. In the first speech he elaborately defended the ethical position of Plato; and in the second, he systematically refuted this position. All moral standards, he evidently meant to maintain, are subjective preferences and lack objective validity. The Skeptic will doubtless receive much amusement in watching the zealous efforts of others to force their preferences on one another. But he himself will remain aloof from such efforts and will not even seek to be consistent in the professions and actions in which he from time to time indulges.[14]

---

[14] Edwyn Bevan, *op. cit.*, p. 124, made a telling comment on the attitude of the Skeptics: "It was a wonderful deliverance to realize that you need not mind not knowing."

5. THE NEO-PLATONIC TRADITION

PLOTINUS, 205–270, of Lycopolis, Egypt.

PORPHYRY, 233–305, of Phoenicia.

JAMBLICHUS, died c. 330, of Chalcis, Syria.

PROCLUS, 412–485, of Byzantium.

NEO-PLATONISM IS the name used today for the philosophy which begins with Plotinus. The term, of course, is a modern one. Plotinus would never himself have dreamed of using it or seen any need for its use by others. He supposed that he was reviving the genuine philosophical position of Plato. And he wished to revive this position in order to combat the Stoicism and the Skepticism which had at times crept into the teachings of certain heads of the Academy, as well as other corruptions, as he viewed them, which the ideas of Plato had suffered in the Hellenistic world. But the ideas he borrowed from Plato came to have, in the system into which he built them, a very different meaning from anything which Plato seems ever to have intended. What he thought of as Platonism, we have therefore come to call Neo-Platonism.

The historian must nonetheless assign to the philosophy of Plotinus a unique and significant place. Neo-Platonism ranks, in both intrinsic importance and long-continued influence, as one of the two major forms in which ideas of Plato have been adopted and developed. It was so influential, both in the days of its first formulation and during many subsequent centuries, that it almost entirely eclipsed for hundreds of years the other major (Aristotelian) form of the philosophy of Plato. It has even eclipsed to some extent the philosophy of Plato itself: at least, it has often been regarded as equivalent to Plato's philosophy and has then led many enthusiasts for Plotinus to read it back into the dialogues of the master. Both Aristotle and Plotinus found the genesis and the inspiration of their philosophies in Plato. Both, however, came to maintain independent positions. Aristotle, using many ideas of Plato, formulated a philosophy that is naturalistic and pluralistic. Plotinus, also using many ideas of Plato, formulated a philosophy that is idealistic and monistic. Aristotelianism and Plotinianism are entirely distinct and, on certain points, antithetical. Plotinus did not himself realize how different his views were from Aristotle's because he focused on the earlier or more Platonic portions of Aristotle's writings and interpreted the more mature Aristotle in the light of the early Aristotle. But a careful critic will see Plato, Aristotle, and Plotinus as representing three distinct philosophies. And whether he will regard Aristotle or Plotinus as closer to the major intent of Plato, will depend on his way of reading Plato.

The founder of Neo-Platonism and his more prominent followers all came from eastern Mediterranean provinces of the Roman Empire. They all shared, in varying degrees, the religious yearnings which had produced in those provinces many curious and exotic religious cults. Jamblichus remained chiefly in Syria, and his version of Neo-Platonism is saturated with mystical and even magical ideas from that oriental milieu. Proclus lived many years in Athens where he became head of the Academy, and his writings exhibit, though to a lesser degree, the same eastern quality. Plotinus himself, however, and Porphyry, his intimate companion and biographer, settled in Rome. In Rome, Plotinus founded the school through which he disseminated his interpretation of Platonism; here he read and discussed philosophy with his pupils, using chiefly certain commentaries which had recently been composed on works by Plato and Aristotle. And in Rome, Plotinus composed his essays, which, far superior to the writings of his ancient or his Renaissance followers, remain the definitive statement of Neo-Platonism. Rome, therefore, rather than the more mystical eastern provinces, was the first home of Neo-Platonism. The original and finest form of Neo-Platonism stems directly from the rational and humanistic traditions of the apogee of Greek philosophy. Only later did accretions of oriental magic and superstition mark phases of its development.

Plotinus wrote many philosophical essays. Most of these he submitted to Porphyry during his lifetime, and all of them he entrusted to Porphyry at his death. Porphyry then edited the essays with pious care and devoted allegiance to his friend. Porphyry arranged them in six groups of nine essays each. And to this arrangement we owe the fact that Plotinus' writings go under the title of *Enneads* or "sets of nine."

PLOTINUS' DUALISTIC OPPONENTS

Six hundred years lay between Plato and Plotinus. And during that time Plato's influence, always extensive, had sometimes been strangely felt. Various enthusiasts, only some of whom can properly be called philosophers, had not infrequently taken phrases and figures of speech from Plato's dialogues and had turned them into quite un-

Platonic, even into bizarre notions. These notions usually depended on forcing Plato's imagery about the relation of soul and body into a system of cosmological dualism. This dualism was as inchoate as it was prevalent. But two of its forms deserve attention here, both because they were widely disseminated and because they furnish elucidation of the background of the more reputable philosophy of Plotinus.

Neo-Pythagoreanism may have been, as its name suggests, historically continuous with the Pythagoreanism of the sixth and fifth centuries B.C. But in its Hellenistic developments it was surely controlled by, if it was not derived from, Plato's way of using Pythagorean language. Plato had used this language partly because he thought colorful metaphors and myths pedagogically effective, partly because he wished to extract from the myths certain rational elements which he thought they contained. But the Neo-Pythagoreans interpreted the language literally and transformed it into set doctrines. Central in their thinking was the belief that the body is the prison house of the soul and that personal salvation can be won only by the soul's escape from the control of the body. Hence they found other Hellenistic philosophies (such as Epicureanism, Stoicism, and Skepticism) too austere, too demanding, too resigned. They longed feverishly, not for courage to face earth's miseries directly, but for escape from these miseries to the ecstatic joys of some other realm. They normally believed in transmigration of souls, treating Plato's metaphor that knowledge is recollection as evidence of the truth of that belief. The body, indeed all matter, is evil; the soul, indeed all spirit, is good. Confinement of the soul in the body is punishment for the defilement which the soul suffered from the bodies of its previous incarnations. The course of salvation is therefore a warfare of the soul against the body. Escape from the body may come through ascetic practices and suppression of bodily desires; and in carrying out this supposition, Neo-Pythagoreans revived many primitive taboos. Release from the body may also come through the more-than-natural help of some divine being; and in carrying out this supposition, Neo-Pythagoreans affiliated themselves with various mystery cults of the oriental provinces. These cults often celebrated the triumph of some god or hero over death and his consequent entrance into the supernal bliss of some spiritual heaven. The same triumph and the same bliss the Neo-Pythagoreans hoped to gain for themselves through participation in the god's cult. Neo-Pythagoreanism ought not to be identified, but it was certainly closely associated, with a recrudescence of many primitive taboos, with trust in dreams and omens and charms, with sympathetic magic, even with erotic religious practices.

Gnosticism was a more sophisticated movement than Neo-Pythagoreanism. It had an articulated philosophical theory of the nature of the cosmos and of history. No writings of the Gnostics have survived to our day, except for fragments quoted from them by their bitter opponents. The names of Saturninus, Basilides, and Valentinus have come down to us, all of them Gnostics of the early second century A.D. And at about the time of these three men Gnosticism seems to have been rife in both pagan and Christian circles. *Gnosis* is a Greek word for knowledge, and Gnosticism is therefore, by etymology, a claim to knowledge. But the knowledge which the Gnostics boasted of possessing was not such knowledge as might come through scientific investigation or through any exercise of intelligence. It was, rather, a revelation, a mystically revealed and usually a secret knowledge of the means of salvation. It was a knowledge of the names of gods or spiritual beings to whom those possessed of this knowledge could effectively address their supplications for help.

For the Gnostics believed they needed help. Their world view was such that without divine help they could not win their salvation. The world is the scene of a warfare between the realm of spirit and the realm of matter. These two realms, the Gnostics believed, are antithetical in origin and in destiny. The realm of matter or the visible world, they supposed, is the creation of an evil divinity and is ruled by this evil divinity. It was produced by the evil force which they, using a Platonic term out of context, called the Demiurge; and it continues to exist under the sway of this Demiurge. Men are spirits imprisoned in matter and cannot effect their own escape. Escape comes only to those who, initiated into the proper secrets, have the knowledge to enable them to appeal to the spirits who will then deliver them from matter and the Demiurge.

The spirits to whom the Gnostics believed they could appeal were numerous and differed from Gnostic to Gnostic. The Christian Gnostics, of course, appealed to Christ, whose person they entirely deified, denying that his human form had been anything more than a semblance of genuine humanity. Other Gnostics appealed to the gods or heroes or spirits of all sorts of other oriental cults or to spirits they believed they had themselves discovered. Some appealed even to Platonic forms, evidently entertaining the supposition that these forms were agencies that could and did act.[15] And many seem to have also believed that complete salvation from matter could come only through death, when the human spirit, if purged sufficiently, would be forever freed from matter and would enter into the blessed realm of disembodied spirits.

THE ONE AND EMANATIONS FROM THE ONE

The philosophy of Plotinus is, among other things, a rejection of dualism in all its forms. There are not, Plotinus believed, two disparate realms of being at war with one another. There is but one order of being, a vast order of being, to be sure, containing various levels and different kinds of existences. This entire order depends upon, and owes its being to, a central principle, which Plotinus normally called the One. The One, as we discover when we think rationally, is a logical presupposition of anything else we may happen to consider. But it is more than a logical presupposition: it is also an ontological precondition of all else that is. It alone is all-sufficient. All else is derived from it and manifests the inevitable consequences which ensue from it. A wise man will seek to escape from the limitations of his inferior status and to rise to participation in fuller being; but he will even then recognize that his earlier inferior status and his later higher status alike are necessary expressions of the plenitude of being of the One. And hence he will not regard his escape as a leap from a wholly evil world to an allegedly different realm, for that way lie philosophical fantasy and moral vanity. He will seek, rather, through understanding his earlier limitations as deficiencies of being, to become a more adequate expression of that fullness of being which is the One.

A man, Plotinus said, is not wise if he "does not know how to accept necessary things." [16] And among necessary things are the human body and its limitations. The body is necessary in two senses. On the one hand, the body is the locus which defines the present status of the soul. And if that status be temporary (as a man may well resolve to make it), it is yet the requisite point of departure for all sound efforts to change it for another and nobler status. On the other hand, the body, along with all other finite and partial existences, is an inevitable

---

15 St. Paul was castigating the Gnostics when he referred to the supposition that men need appeal to angels and principalities and powers and height and depth and such "creatures." Cf. Romans 8:38–39.

16 Quoted from the translation of Ennead II, essay 9, by Joseph Katz, *The Philosophy of Plotinus* (New York, Appleton-Century-Crofts, 1950), p. 100.

outcome of the One. And if anyone were foolishly to condemn it as wholly evil, he would be implicitly condemning the One, which is the source of all being and of all good.

Plotinus was, of course, a mystic. But his mysticism was very different from that of the mystery cults, the Neo-Pythagoreans, and the Gnostics. It was not a repudiation of the finite and visible world. It was, rather, a sensitivity to the presence within the finite and visible world of what is infinite and invisible. The One, he insisted, is transcendent. The One is transcendent in beauty, transcendent in goodness, transcendent in fullness of being. The One is therefore far more than the partial indications of its infinity, which we can detect in the midst of the finite. A man may indeed hope ultimately to rise above the finite and visible world into union with the transcendent One. But the One, Plotinus insisted with equal earnestness, is immanent too. The One is as present within the finite as infinity can be. The One accounts for that lesser degree of beauty, that lesser degree of goodness, and that lesser degree of being which characterize the finite and visible world. A man will never achieve union with the transcendent One who lacks appreciation of the immanence of the One in the finite effects which must necessarily ensue from the One.

Plotinus' position perhaps can best be expounded through a metaphor he himself was fond of using. Suppose that there were one, great, all-inclusive source of light. That central light, because of its supernal splendor, would not then contain all light within itself. It would rather radiate light in every direction and in every lesser degree of brightness. All lesser degrees of light would be inevitable consequences of the central light, would owe their occurrence and their relative brightness to the central light, would express the glory of the central light in various degrees of finitude. Darkness would not be another reality opposed to light, but would be the ideal limit, a limit possibly never wholly reached, of the diminution of the ever spreading radiance of the central light. So with the One. The One is in a sense the only being. But the One has such full being that it cannot alone be but brings into being all degrees and forms and types of derived being. The One has such full being that there is, in a phrase used by subsequent writers, a consequent "plenitude of being." Insofar, then, as a finite being is at all, it, too, like the One, is good and beautiful. But it only partially has being, and so it is only partially good and partially beautiful. Nonbeing is not another being opposed to the One. Nonbeing is the ideal limit, again a limit possibly never wholly reached, of the diminution of the being of the One.

Plotinus called nonbeing by the name *matter*. This bit of his terminology has caused much confusion in traditions that flow from Plotinus. For the word *matter,* in most systems of thought (Democritean, Aristotelian, dualistic) had quite different significance. Matter, in Plotinus' usage, does not exist at all; at least it does not exist at all as a real being or by itself. But matter, in Plotinus' usage, is, at the same time, an aspect, and a necessary aspect, of everything that is except the One itself. For all things except the One lack full being or, as Plotinus could then say and did say, all things except the One suffer material limitations or are mixtures of being and nonbeing. Matter is the negative side of finite reality, as being is its positive side. Materiality is but a name for that diminution of being which marks the relative distance of finite beings from their source in the One. No such thing as mere matter has being; for anything, in becoming mere matter, would, so to speak, cease altogether to be.

THE CHIEF HYPOSTASES

If the controlling insight of Plotinus was mystical, the method he employed in its defense was far from mystical. His method was thoroughly rational. Porphyry stated in his biography of Plotinus that during the period he and Plotinus lived together, Plotinus achieved union with the One on four occasions. But Plotinus did not dwell on these or other such experiences in composing his essays. Rather, he argued with all the techniques of logic at his disposal and sought to prove to his readers the necessity of recognizing that all existence is due to the One. The philosophy of Plotinus is therefore of that type in which the ultimate aim and the technical procedure of its implementation are distinct.

The procedure of Plotinus was to argue that we can detect empirically in the world about us evidences of transcendent realities upon which that world depends. These transcendent realities he called hypostases because they stand under or support the finite and visible world. There are many such hypostases; indeed, there must be many, for the fullness of being of the One requires every other possible form of being to come about as its necessary expression. But among these many hypostases three are most important: the level of soul, the level of intelligence, and, finally, the One itself.

The level of soul, Plotinus believed, is evident in the very structure of the finite and visible world, and, indeed, in each and every part of that world. Nature is not a mechanical jumble of brute forces but a teleological system. And a teleological system can be sustained only by souls in whose embrace a multiplicity of parts receives its purposeful interrelationships. The human soul, for example, holds together the many distinct parts of the human body in an organic unity. Similarly, a world soul is implied by the even more completely organic texture of the whole of nature. The human soul accomplishes an organic togetherness of parts on a smaller scale, and the world soul on a larger scale. Wherever organic togetherness is found—and it is found everywhere—soul can be known to be at work. For organic togetherness is effected through a rational contemplation of ends not yet wholly realized in the finite but nonetheless foreseen and implicit. And only soul is capable of rational contemplation. In nature as a whole, just as in that fragment of nature which is man, a "living reason . . . exerts its productivity within the begotten being." [17] Indeed, the human soul could not live the rational life of contemplation and fulfill its specific teleological function, were not nature already the same kind of system of which the human soul is a notable instance. "Everything derives from contemplation and everything is contemplation." [18]

But the level of soul can hardly be the ultimate hypostasis. For what contemplates is made possible only through a superior realm which it contemplates. Thus Plotinus was led to affirm that the level of soul derived from a higher level of being, namely, the level of intelligence. He thought he was here but repeating Plato's point that particulars are imitations of, or participate in, the forms. The level of soul expresses imperfectly and under limitations of finitude and of time the ideal perfection of the level of intelligence. The level of intelligence is superior because deviations from principle do not occur in it, nor does change mar its timeless adequacy of fuller being. Intelligence is merely potential in soul, and what is potential cannot produce, but always presupposes, the reality through which it then comes to pass. The level of intelligence, although it makes possible, even makes necessary, the lower level of souls and bodies, is not dependent in any way upon the contemplations which soul may have of it. It is, hence, subject to none of the imperfections which haunt all creatures on the lower level of time and space.

Even the level of intelligence, however, is not ultimate. For in it the many forms remain distinct or separate from one another, much as finite things are separate. And the supreme principle of being must

[17] Joseph Katz, *op. cit.*, p. 44.
[18] *Ibid.*, p. 50.

be truly and entirely single and simple. Plotinus was thus led to insist that beyond even the level of intelligence lies the One. Unity is indeed implicit in all being. A man, for example, is made up of many parts; but only insofar as these parts are brought into some degree of unity can a man be at all. Being always manifests some kind of oneness, and full or entire being must be completely one. Plotinus did not suppose that he could conclusively demonstrate that the One is and is ultimate being. For all demonstration moves from premise to conclusion in the realm of multiplicity. He merely followed the course of reason as far as reason could carry him, hoping that he then indicated a prior being that lies beyond even reason. The proper outcome of sheer rationality, he believed, comes in the mystic awareness which supersedes and surpasses reason. Reason may point out the very limits of reason; and then mystic vision passes on to the One which transcends all else.

There is nothing, Plotinus frankly admitted, that we can say about the One except that it is. To affirm any predicate of it is at once to introduce duality of subject and predicate. Even the assertions that the One is beautiful and that the One is good, though properly to be made and as near the truth as utterance can reach, are inadequate efforts to express the ineffable. These assertions ought to be taken as ways of praising the One, rather than ways of describing it. We can do no more than acknowledge that the One is and that from the One comes about all else that is. The manner in which all else comes about from the One, Plotinus called emanation. Emanation is not the kind of causality which we find about us in the finite world, where cause produces effect through the exercise of efficacy; for the exercise of efficacy occurs only when some deficiency is present and, hence, some effort for something more is requisite. The One has no deficiency and requires nothing more than itself. Emanation, as Plotinus conceived it, is a production that is due, not to any act of one thing upon another, but to the sheer essence of the superior principle. We can say no more than that because the One wholly is, all lesser beings are too. The level of intelligence is an emanation from the One, and the level of soul and the finite and visible world are emanations from the level of intelligence. Thus reality can be treated as "a downward way of becoming from the One." The One is beyond space and time and distinctions; yet it is the source of all the distinguishable things that come to pass in space and time.

THE UPWARD WAY OF SALVATION

If the metaphysics of Plotinus was expressed in the idea of the downward way of becoming, his ethics was expressed in the compensating idea of the upward way of salvation. Plotinus, like the Epicureans, dispraised the active life of struggle for worldly success, for office, for power. But he did not dispraise it for the same reason. The Epicureans dispraised it because the material world (which is the scene of the active life, indeed, of all action and all change) seemed to them to have more reality than the feeble powers of men can cope with. But he dispraised it because that world seemed to him to lack the full reality for which men potentially yearn. He sought a higher life than the finite and visible world ever grants. He sought a life in which the soul rises through contemplation to the level of intelligence and through mystic union to absorption in the One itself. He seems to have been not altogether consistent in his theory of the salvation to which soul may aspire. For he regarded the upward way of salvation as both a sloughing off of the limitations of finitude which cling to whatever has individuality and a realizing of potentialities which would bring fuller being to those individuals who gain salvation.

In his list of virtues Plotinus followed the language of Plato and some suggestions of Plato's dialogues. But he transformed what he took over from the master. Whereas Plato aimed at such achievement within the world as a knowledge of forms made possible, Plotinus aimed at such a rise in the scale of being as leaves the finite world entirely behind. The virtues of Plotinus are on three levels that correspond fairly closely to the three hypostases of his metaphysics.

On the level of soul as it finds itself in the finite and visible world, Plotinus commends the four major virtues of Plato's *Republic*. These virtues, far from being sufficient, are treated by Plotinus as preparatory to much that is higher. Temperance, he held, is release of the soul from desires for particular ends. Courage is readiness to remain firm against the lure that drags the soul toward particularity. Justice is that treatment of all particulars which ensues when the soul has no desire for personal acquisitions. Wisdom, the highest of the preparatory virtues, is such absorption in contemplation of pure forms as comes with complete indifference to all "imitations" of these forms in the finite and visible world.

Then to these preliminary virtues on the level of soul, Plotinus added three further virtues on the level of intelligence: art, friendship, and logic. Or, to speak more exactly, these three are models of virtue on the level of intelligence which call for imitation on the level of soul. Art, Plotinus taught, is concerned, not with the sensuous charm of some particular materials, but with the idea or form which may be expressed through these materials. Friendship in its ideal occurrence is not attachment of one person to another person but a higher ideal unity in which distinction of persons is lost in aspiration for the good. And logic is an exercise in dialectic which, emancipated from attention to "imitations" in the visible world, is concerned with the timeless interrelationships of pure forms for one another.

Finally, the soul, in Plotinus' upward way of salvation, may achieve union with the One. The state of this union, he frankly asserted, cannot be described in words. But it may be won by the soul who, through the discipline of all the prior virtues, is completely purified from the contaminations of finitude and materiality.

If one rises beyond oneself, an image rising to its model, one has reached the goal of one's journey. When one falls from this vision, one will, by arousing the virtue that is within oneself, and by remembering the perfection that one possesses, regain one's lightness and through virtue rise to Intelligence, and through wisdom to the One. Such is the life of gods and of divine and blessed men, detachment from all things here below, scorn of all earthly pleasures, and flight of the alone to the alone.[19]

Thus the ideal goal of human existence, like its ontological source, is the One. Salvation for Plotinus is an upward flight of the soul— a flight of that which is alone in the sense that it is apart to that which is alone in the sense that it only is.

PLOTINUS' SUCCESSORS

Later Neo-Platonists did not attain philosophic distinction equal to that of the *Enneads* of Plotinus, except perhaps Porphyry. But Porphyry was more of a scholar than a philosopher. In addition to editing Plotinus' essays, he wrote a *Life of Plotinus*. He also wrote fifteen books, *Against the Christians,* which had wide influence in his day but, except for fragments, have been lost. Of his other works in rhetoric, biography, and literary criticism, the most important for subsequent history were his *Introduction* to, and *Commentary* upon, the *Categories* of Aristotle. These treatises, more than any other document, mark the transition from Greek philosophy to the scholastic philosophy of the Middle Ages. For in them Porphyry raised and discussed the problem of whether genera and species are real beings

---

19 Joseph Katz, *op. cit.,* p. 158.

in themselves or are real only as concepts entertained by the minds which think them. He was here dealing with a basic problem which is at stake in the opposition which tradition came to find between Platonism and Aristotelianism. The manner in which Porphyry posed the problem occupied the attention of scholastics for some hundreds of years and became what is called the problem of universals.

Jamblichus wrote commentaries on Plato and Aristotle, and from him or his school came a work *On the Egyptian Mysteries*. In this development of Neo-Platonism there was introduced a maze of superstitions concerning divination, astrology, soothsaying, the interpretation of dreams and trances, demonology. Proclus, too, wrote commentaries on various dialogues of Plato, a treatise *On the Theology of Plato*, treatises on grammar, and *Elements of Theology*. In the last of these he recommended, as means of purification of the soul, prayers at set times of the day, hymns to various deities, theurgical ceremonies, and the like. Neo-Platonism thus declined in quality from the third to the fifth centuries, and, apart from incorporation into the context of Christian thought, has never been re-expressed with the fine distinction which it had in the *Enneads* of Plotinus himself. Neo-Platonism, the historian may fairly judge, was saved from degenerating into a riot of fantasies through the use of it by certain Christian thinkers, particularly St. Augustine. But in the process of its incorporation into the texture of Christian philosophies, it was radically transformed. Plotinus' One, for example, became identified with God. Translators of Plotinus into English, happening to read Plotinus' *Enneads* in the light of Christian Neo-Platonism, have usually erred in using the word *God* where the Greek text of Plotinus gives no warrant for that terminology. Both Jamblichus and Proclus on the one hand and St. Augustine and other Christian Neo-Platonists on the other hand are much further removed from Plato than was Plotinus himself.

6. THE CRY FOR SALVATION

HELLENISTIC philosophies were primarily theories of the way in which men could best live amidst the evils of the world. Their advocates exhibited little interest in natural science and, except for the Neo-Platonists, less in metaphysics, exploiting these subject-matters, when they touched upon them at all, mainly for the purpose of buttressing their already firmly defined ethical doctrines. They manifested almost a scorn for the daring Hellenic hopes that men might, through the very aid philosophy would provide, construct a better order within the natural world. They recurrently emphasized the folly, as they regarded it, of the vain pursuit of these hopes.

Salvation in Hellenistic times, moreover, was a personal or individual objective. The Hellenistic philosophers had no antisocial animus. Even the Epicureans, who, more than other schools of thought, summoned each man to live his own private life prudently, had no brutal intent. None of the Hellenistic thinkers, however, was deliberately and consciously political. The Stoics to be sure included in their number an emperor who lived in the service of the state; but insofar as his action resulted from his theory, he lent himself to this service, not for the sake of the state he served, but for the sake of keeping his own soul untarnished from the world. No Hellenistic philosopher spoke specifically in the interests of the state or the corporate life of mankind. These philosophers were all inattentive to social reform. They were preoccupied in urging each to reform himself.

In spite of the similarities of attitude among Hellenistic philosophers in the respects just noted, many differences can also be detected in their concepts of salvation. For salvation, here as always, is a complicated concept. Salvation is always *from* something rejected, *to* something prized, and *by means of* some trusted device. All the complications of theory in the entire record of philosophies of salvation can be understood as shifting values of the three variables just distinguished.

The following chart presents a summary interpretation of some of the theories of salvation embedded in the Hellenistic philosophies. It includes the chief philosophies discussed in this chapter and also two forms of Christianity which will be discussed in the next chapter. Christianity in its origin and formative years, as students of history need constantly to remember, was a competing cult within the Hellenistic world and had its rival idea of salvation. Informed observers in the Roman Empire did not usually consider it as important or likely long to survive. Modern Christians are prone to interpret its earlier phases in the light of its subsequent history. But at the outset it was thoroughly Hellenistic in temper. St. Paul lived before the three great Roman Stoics and Plotinus and voiced a typically Hellenistic cry for salvation. St. Augustine, though later than all those mentioned in this chapter except Proclus, gathered much of Neo-Platonism within the massive structure of his system and shared the hopes and fears of the troubled age of which his philosophy marks the close.

SALVATION	FROM	TO	BY MEANS OF
Epicureanism	suffering	pleasure	retirement
Stoicism	lure of pleasure	harmony with nature	freedom from passion and the voice of reason
Skepticism	error	freedom from commitment	destructive criticism
Paulinism	sin	justification	grace of God
Neo-Platonism	deficient being	fuller being	contemplation and mystic union
Augustinianism	corruption	favor with God	offices of the Church

PART TWO

PHILOSOPHY IN CHRISTENDOM

Philosophy in Christendom

CHRISTIANITY IS primarily, not a philosophy, but a religion. Its practice, that is, did not arise because its adherents entertained a philosophy which then led logically to the practice. Rather, the practice, in the course of years, generated various philosophies, each of which was an attempt to justify the practice. Philosophical interpretations of Christianity often led to modifications in the practice and thus contributed to the multiplicity of divergent practices which, more and more, Christianity has manifested. But the Christian religion was prior in origin to all the philosophies it has generated and has continued in its history to be related to these philosophies in the same way in which any subject-matter is related to theories about that subject-matter.

Any and all religions, however, whether Christianity or others, require for their full and proper development, as indeed do all human activities, a theoretical interpretation and an attempted justification. For, in the words of the opening sentence of Aristotle's *Metaphysics*, "all men are naturally curious." Seldom do men long remain satisfied with an activity to which they cannot give articulate intellectual expression. Men crave to understand what their activities are, what grounds those activities rest upon, what values those activities have or promote, what degree of reasonableness those activities can have assigned to them. Even though practice is historically the initial fact and theory is subsequent thereto, theory is nonetheless inevitable if men are long to continue a practice and to sustain it as a valued phase of human affairs. The Christian religion gave rise to Christian philosophies because Christian men yearned for theories which would justify their commitments and support their hopes.

Christianity, like any religion which develops beyond its elementary stage and comes to have a history of many hundreds of years, has given rise, not to one single and consistent philosophy, but to many philosophies. This is in part due to the complex implications of religious practice. A highly developed religion requires many sorts of theories in its elucidation—theories perhaps about the gods or God, theories about the world and its relation to the gods or God, theories about man and his origin and his destiny, theories about the religious life and about religious institutions, theories about the supreme values which the religion aims to promote. But the diversity among Christian philosophies is also in part due to the way in which, religiously as well as intellectually, Christianity has been at odds with itself. Many Christians of the first and second centuries, for example, did not fully accept the teachings of St. Paul. They did not accept these teachings, partly because they did not understand them precisely, partly also because they did not practice the kind of religious life of which these teachings were a defense. Revivals of St. Paul's teachings were to come in later centuries, as notably in St. Augustine and in Luther. But these revivals differed in important respects from the original they professed to follow. The Catholic Church, although it canonized St. Augustine, refused, after considerable deliberation, to accept all the details of the ideas which St. Augustine thought he had taken over from St. Paul. And the Protestant bodies of modern times seldom gave assent to the full rigor of Luther's Paulinism. Christianity, it was said at the outset of this chapter, is a religion. A more just historical comment would be that Christianity has been many religions, some of which are closely akin, and others of which are fundamentally antagonistic. And if the religious unity of Christianity be but nominal, the philosophical expressions to which it has given rise are even more pluralistic. Some Catholic historians, following the instruction of a favored dogma, have maintained that within Catholic Christianity and central to its religious integrity, a unity or consistency of development has occurred. Yet even here, institutional continuity has been more manifest than intellectual conformity. Catholics have usually been wont in recent generations to point to the philosophy of St. Thomas Aquinas as the definitive form for Catholic thought. Yet St. Thomas himself made emphatic protests against other Catholic philosophies, such as that of St. Anselm; and some Catholics today would regard the authority of St. Thomas as excessive and would put some other philosophy, perhaps that of Bergson, in its place. And among Protestants, with their appeal to the right of every individual to be his own religious authority and guide, the diversity of philosophies is even more extreme.

No history of "Philosophy in Christendom" can list all the forms of thought to which Christianity has given rise. The aim of the following group of chapters is to select, from among the various Christian philosophies of the centuries before the Renaissance, those which are most important. And the criteria for determining importance are chiefly two: the intrinsic greatness of a system of thought and the degree of influence a system of thought has had upon subsequent thinking. These two criteria, to a considerable extent, prove in practice to coincide.

IV

The Formative Years of Christianity

1. THE RELATION OF JESUS TO CHRISTIANITY

CHRISTIANITY, as its name indicates, is a religion which centers in the person of Christ. The word *Christ,* however, was originally, not a proper name, but a title. It is a Greek word, a word used to translate into Greek the Hebrew word which is customarily put into English as "Messiah." The Messiah was thought of by the Hebrews in various ways. Sometimes the Messiah was an individual person, sometimes the whole Jewish people collectively. Sometimes the Messiah was regarded as the agent of salvation to the Jews alone, sometimes the agent of salvation through the Jews to all mankind. But always the Messiah was the central figure in the process by which salvation comes. And since the earliest followers of Jesus were mostly Jews, they naturally called him the Messiah or the Christ. Later Christians, most of whom had never been Jews, found the Jewish terminology obscure and uncongenial. They made the title into a proper name, thus coming to speak, not of Jesus the Christ, but of Jesus Christ. The role which Christ played according to their ideas of salvation they then came to express by such other terms as *Son of God* or *Lord* or *Savior.* Different meanings, frequently quite vague and impossible to define with precision, were intended by these Christian terms. But in all cases a continuity of meaning between Judaism and Christianity is apparent. Christians continued to mean by their terms, as Jews had meant by the term *Messiah,* that Jesus Christ is the person through whom the kingdom of God, however that kingdom be conceived, is proclaimed and brought to pass.

Jesus of Nazareth, however, was not a Christian but a Jew. He was, to be sure, a Jew of distinctive quality of life and belief. He stood in the great prophetic tradition of Judaism. And that tradition, whatever else it also was, was throughout its history a dynamic effort to reform current Judaism and thus to make Judaism a purer and nobler religion. We have no reliable sources for a detailed knowledge of what Jesus did, of what Jesus said, or of what Jesus believed. The four gospels in the New Testament, and even more surely all other early Christian writings, are propaganda documents; that is, they are documents by which certain authors, not easily identifiable, sought to disseminate their beliefs and to demonstrate the truth of their conviction that Jesus Christ is Lord. The gospels are not narratives of primarily historical intent. They have, indeed, great historical value in informing us concerning the developments of Christianity in the middle and end of the first century A.D. They give some indications concerning earlier times and concerning events in the life of Jesus; but these indications must be employed with caution and even hesitation. One of the indications, an indication which is perhaps the most nearly reliable basis of inference from the gospels to Jesus, is that Jesus had no intention of making a break with his ancestral religion. The gospels indicate that Jesus would have been profoundly shocked by the supposition that his work and teachings would become the occasion for the rejection of Judaism and for the founding of a new religion.

Judaism had been a religion which centered in respect for the Torah, or the Old Testament law, as the disclosure of God's will for men. Christianity, from its earliest days, was a religion which centered in acceptance of Jesus as the Christ. Christians of the first generation after Jesus, therefore, would hardly have spuriously attributed to Jesus such remarks as the following: [1]

Think not that I am come to destroy the law, or the prophets: I am not come to destroy, but to fulfil. For verily I say unto you, Till heaven and earth pass, one jot or one tittle shall in no wise pass from the law, till all be fulfilled.

These words assign to Jesus an attitude which any good Jew would understand. Jesus clearly sought to give his own interpretation of the fundamental significance of the law. And in so doing, he seems to have been a revolutionary force. But he was a revolutionary force within, not against, Judaism. Some early followers of Jesus thought they could combine loyalty to the Old Testament law with acceptance of Jesus as the Christ. But their compromise position was soon banned; it seemed to many Christian leaders to lessen the high significance of the person of Christ and the entire and sufficient adequacy of Jesus' teachings. The advocates of this compromise were condemned as

[1] Matt. 5:17–18.

"Judaizers." Christianity, in all its reputable forms, has respected the Old Testament and the Old Testament law. But Christianity has never been willing to take the attitude of Jews toward this law. Jesus, however, did take this attitude. Thus Jesus, in his intended loyalties and his conscious affiliations, belongs among the Jews rather than among the Christians.

The full story of the origins of Christianity as a religion distinct from Judaism remains obscure even after meticulous and zealous research by scholars. These origins surely lie, however, not in any design of Jesus, but in ideas about Jesus which were advanced and promoted by certain other men in the years immediately after Jesus' death. They probably do not lie in the faith and teaching of any single man. But among those who were creative forces in the fashioning of Christianity, St. Paul seems to have been foremost. He is certainly foremost in the records which have come down to us. We can point to no other figure comparable with him in insisting that faith in Jesus as the Christ meant the beginning of a new gospel which would liberate mankind from the burden of the Jewish law, or Torah. He, then, rather than Jesus, accomplished, for better or for worse, the break with Judaism which brought Christianity into existence. Whereas Jesus sought to refashion Judaism, St. Paul sought to put a new gospel in the place of Judaism. And, measured by their respective intents, Jesus failed and St. Paul succeeded. St. Paul succeeded, however, by using Jesus, thus giving to Jesus a role in subsequent history which made Jesus in his failure a far more influential person than was even St. Paul in his success.

2. ST. PAUL

St. Paul of Tarsus, a Jew and a Roman citizen, lived from about A.D. 10 to perhaps about 60. He received training in the rabbinical traditions of Judaism. He at first regarded the followers of Jesus as dangerous to the religious integrity of his ancestral religion, and devoted much time and strength to a campaign to suppress them and to free the synagogues of their presence and influence. Then, in circumstances which in The Acts of the Apostles are described in terms of a miracle, he was converted to faith in Jesus as the Christ and became as zealous in propagating the new religion as he had formerly been in attacking it. He made a number of missionary journeys among eastern provinces of the Roman Empire, establishing Christian churches or fortifying the faith of already established Christian groups. His extant writings consist of eight or nine letters which he addressed to certain Christian churches, as well as fragments of other letters which are now embedded in letters that are not entirely his. His opposition to orthodox Judaism got him into violent disputes with leading Jews who seized him and took him before Roman authorities. He appealed his case to Caesar and was shipped to Rome for trial. There he disappears from history. According to tradition he died the death of a martyr.

St. Paul was not a technical philosopher. He was a missionary whose ardent labors so exhausted his time that he never had opportunity for a systematic statement and development of his ideas. His writings are what are called "occasional" letters; that is, they are letters written to meet certain immediately pressing crises in various Christian churches and do not give a well-rounded summary of his views. But he stated certain ideas with great power. And these ideas became controlling intellectual principles in many subsequent Christian philosophies. Among these ideas the central ones were those of sin and of grace.

Sin and grace were not ideas with which ancient Judaism had been much concerned; nor were they, in their Pauline form, very closely akin to Neo-Pythagorean or other Greek traditions. They seem to have arisen as interpretations which St. Paul made of his own personal religious experiences. In his early preconversion days, St. Paul had felt oppressed by a burden of inner unworthiness. The Jewish law or Torah, he was quite willing to grant, was a holy law, the law of a holy God. But he had within himself a sense of utter inability to bring his will into harmony with the requirements of this law. And he generalized from his own experience and so imputed the same inability to all men. A man might, if he were sufficiently resolute, make his outward acts conform to the prescriptions of the law, although such conformity was indeed rare. Even then, however, a man would find himself inwardly craving for what the law forbids. And the gnawing consciousness of those cravings would make him realize the moral irreconcilability of his nature to the demands which God, through the law, imposed upon him. Loyal acceptance of the law as holy, far from relieving a man of sin, only accentuated the realization of the power sin had over him. "By the works of the law," he wrote, "shall no flesh be justified." [2] Man, as long as he remains a

2 Gal. 2:16.

fleshly creature, is under the dominion of sin. He cannot effect escape from this dominion by means of good works. For his inner being remains in the control of sin, no matter what overt acts he performs. Nothing in a man's natural powers—neither reason nor native gifts nor education nor the utmost determination of will—can accomplish man's escape from sin's control. Man is therefore doomed to rejection by God and exclusion from God's presence until, and unless, some nonhuman power enters into him and accomplishes for him what he cannot accomplish for himself.

Then came St. Paul's conversion. The conviction of sinfulness seems to have become such an obsession with him that it approached hysteria. The conversion brought him the sense of a new power within him, a power that had come to him from without, a power that transformed his nature, a power that drove out sin and made him over into a "spiritual" man. And here, as before, St. Paul generalized his experience and regarded what had happened to him as the sole and necessary means by which other men, too, might receive salvation. Spirit, he taught, is not a natural human endowment but a divine intrusion into human life. It is not a natural potentiality of man but a gift of God. A transformation of human nature alone can end the control of sin and begin the control of spirit. It alone can bring man into inner peace and serenity; it alone can make man acceptable to God. Outward acts, of course, change too when this transformation has once occurred. The works of the flesh, St. Paul said, are adultery, strife, hatred, envy; the works of the spirit are love, gentleness, temperance, goodness.[3] Good works, however important, are but expressions in overt conduct of an inner change that is even more important. The inner change is "justification"; that is, such a reconciliation of man to God as to bring man into favor with God. As flesh is always sinful, spirit is always righteous. The spirit-possessed man is then no longer under the law. He needs no external guide to the righteous life. He can rely with assurance on the new power within himself; for he is no longer a fleshly creature but a spiritual being. He thus is free at last. He is free from sin, free from the specifications of the law, free from the need of practicing Jewish ceremonies and rites. He is free to a joyous life of confident expectations of blessedness, free to the promptings of spirit, free to enjoyment of justification before God.

The term St. Paul used for the bestowal of spirit upon a man was *grace*. Sin and grace, in his treatment of them, are more than moral

---

[3] Cf. the famous passage in Gal. 5:19–23.

attitudes men may take; they are more than inclinations of will toward evil and good respectively. They are what, if St. Paul had used technical philosophical language, might be called substantial forms, for they give to particular men the natures which these men then have and manifest. Men are born with sinful natures, and many remain sinful throughout their lives, committing overt sins because their natures are sinful. Some men receive grace and thereby become different in their natures and consequently perform righteous acts. Grace is not a human achievement; it is not won by those who receive it because they have earned it. It is a gift from God, a gift which, if conferred according to God's wise purposes, nevertheless seems to men to be given or withheld arbitrarily. It is, every time it comes to a man, a miracle in the sense of a divine activity beyond the powers of human beings to regulate or to direct.

St. Paul's thought has been called dualistic. But it is not dualistic in the same way in which Neo-Pythagoreanism, for example, is dualistic. St. Paul did not regard the cosmos as a warfare of two opposed powers. He believed, rather, as Judaism had maintained for centuries, that the world is God's creation and the scene of God's beneficent providence.[4] He may not have been altogether consistent in asserting, on the one hand, the entire disparity of flesh and spirit and, on the other hand, the universality of God's providence. There are doubtless a number of philosophical problems about the relations of God and the world to which he gave no answers, indeed no attention, in the "occasional" letters we have from him. Other and later Christian thinkers, taking his phrases, were to press his ideas into rigid speculative doctrines to which, however, he might never have been willing to assent.[5] He was kept by his ancestral Judaism from excesses of dualism such as were rife in the more purely Greek thinkers of the Hellenistic age.[6]

[4] He is akin at this point to Philo, a Jewish philosopher who lived at Alexandria in the first half of the first century A.D. Philo was much more affected by the Greek traditions of the Hellenistic world than was St. Paul. He believed that the human soul was a spark of the divine, that it hovers between rising toward God and falling back toward matter, that there are many "powers" or angels who may assist the human soul to rise toward God. But he veered away from such dualism as the Gnostics sponsored. He was kept by his ancestral Judaism from putting his theory of spiritual mediators into the framework of a general cosmological dualism. Whether or not Philo influenced St. Paul is a moot historical problem. He probably did influence some later Christian writers. Yet his theories were so much an expression of widespread trends of thought in the Hellenistic world that the later Christian writers could well have received these influences from the intellectual climate of their age.

[5] Consult on this point Matthew Arnold, *St. Paul and Protestantism,* one of the wisest and most just books ever written on St. Paul.

[6] Such, for example, as the dualism of the Neo-Pythagoreans and of the Gnostics. See above, pp. 97–99.

St. Paul's dualism, if that term be used at all, was not between God and the material world; it was, rather, between two dispensations by which God ruled mankind. The whole world is God's world; matter and spirit are alike God's creation. Of the material world as much as of anything else, St. Paul would have confessed in the words of Scripture that "God saw that it was good." [7] But in dealing with his world, God chose to employ two different means of control and regulation. The "old dispensation" was that of the law; the "new dispensation" was that of the gospel. The purpose of the law was educative; its function was to convict men of sin; its validity was local and temporary. The purpose of the gospel was redemptive; its function was to save men by grace; its validity was universal and everlasting. The law, if it succeeded in bringing men to a consciousness of sin, could do no more than lead them to throw themselves entirely upon the mercy of God. The gospel, transforming men into spiritual beings, brought entire salvation. Salvation, as St. Paul thought of it, was not some future bliss such as the mystery cults purported to offer but a state into which men might enter at any moment of their lives. St. Paul manifestly believed in immortality, but he had no wish to suggest that salvation need await a triumph over death. He did use language akin to that of the mystery cults. Men, he said, must "die with Christ" and be "raised with Christ." But the death and resurrection of which he was speaking were death to the flesh and resurrection in the spirit. And that death and that resurrection could, and did, occur whenever, during earthly existence as truly as in any future state, men received the gift of grace and thereby became transformed in nature.

St. Paul's usual word for the state of grace was "justification." To be saved is to be justified in the eyes of God. And justification, he insisted, is never gained by good works. Indeed, men who deem their good works sufficient to win them favor with God are arrogant; they are still unaware of the corruption of their inner nature and, hence, too proud to be sensitive to the need for grace. Justification comes only through "faith." Faith, however, in St. Paul's usage of the word, is not belief. St. Paul never supposed that a man could offer correct belief in lieu of good works as a means of salvation. Faith was for him an act of the will rather than of the intellect; it was unhesitating trust by a man in the power and guidance of the spirit of God. And such trust is not within a man's power to display unless, and until, that man is stirred by grace to display it. Men of faith will,

---

[7] This is a recurrent phrase in the first chapter of Genesis.

of course, be ardent in good works; they cannot have faith and not exhibit its practical consequences. But the faith that is in them, rather than the works to which faith leads, is what makes them acceptable to God. Justification, then, is by faith, not by works; it is an immediate outcome of the indwelling spirit in a man's life.

St. Paul's treatment of the spirit is in some ways far from clear. He appealed to it constantly, pointed out the consequences of its presence, and warned of the moral ruin of its absence. But he never developed a consistent theory of its nature. He used interchangeably such phrases as the spirit of God, the spirit of Christ, and the spirit. Christians were sometimes troubled, in both his lifetime and later centuries, by the problem of explaining the relations of God and Christ and the spirit to one another. Official leaders of the Church soon came to affirm a doctrine of the trinity in order to settle disputes on this moot point. But this doctrine was more of a restatement of the problem than its solution and led to a series of controversies in which theories were formulated, most of which were quickly banned as heretical. Here, as elsewhere, St. Paul was prevented by the urgency of his missionary labors from working out the full philosophical import of the ideas he proposed.

Nonetheless, St. Paul's influence on intellectual and cultural developments was extensive and permanent. In the first place, St. Paul's claim that Christ is sufficient for salvation made the break with Judaism marked and irretrievable. It meant that Christians relegated the Jewish law to the role of a temporary code of a peculiar people. Christianity could then find support among citizens of the Roman Empire who would never have been willing to accept the particularities of the Jewish law. Christianity could at once begin its own autonomous development. It could freely feel the influences of Greek philosophy and Roman ideas of empire and could embark upon a new synthesis of ideas and cultures. In the second place, St. Paul's claim that Christ is in some way to be identified with Jesus of Nazareth enabled Christians to regard themselves as heirs of whatever seemed best to them in historic Judaism. Christians thus took over the canonical literature of Judaism (which they called the Old Testament), its monotheism, its moral wisdom and sanity, and that prophetic power which Jesus had manifested. Christianity, therefore, though breaking with Judaism and becoming more cosmopolitan than Judaism, nevertheless preserved a cultural continuity with a notable past.

In the third place, St. Paul's claim that Christ is the only and indispensable means of salvation raised a new problem, a problem entirely absent from Greek philosophy, a problem characteristically and intrinsically present in Christianity. This is the problem of the relation of reason and faith. For if, as St. Paul taught, men have within themselves no power to work out their own salvation, human reason must play a subsidiary role and must be subject to guidance and authority from another source. Greek philosophy had typically exalted the life of reason; it had made reason the proper tool for both the investigation of nature and the ordering of human affairs. With this humanism of Plato and Aristotle, however, Paulinism stands in sharp antithesis. St. Paul himself never disparaged reason. He ignored it. He did say that "the foolishness of God is wiser than men," [8] thus indicating that his gospel need not be brought under the scrutiny of human reason. He put foremost in human life a gift of grace which, because it comes from a source independent of man, makes criticism by reason an impertinence and a mark of unregeneracy. Later Christian expounders of their faith sometimes turned St. Paul's silence about reason into an explicit defense of irrationalism. They would not submit faith to check by reason but would rather submit the findings of reason to the authority of faith. And even when opposition to reason did not assume the extreme of deliberate irrationalism, reason was often allowed only a limited jurisdiction over a lesser area of human affairs than that over which faith held sway.

We thus find, in passing from Greek philosophy to Christian thought, a change of intellectual climate.

3. THE CATHOLIC IDEA OF THE CHURCH

JUSTIN MARTYR, c. 100–c. 165, of Syria.

TERTULLIAN, c. 150–c. 220, of north Africa.

ORIGEN, c. 185–254, of Alexandria.

ST. CYPRIAN, c. 200–258, bishop of Carthage.

ST. ATHANASIUS, c. 296–373, bishop of Alexandria.

ST. AMBROSE, c. 340–397, bishop of Milan.

ST. JEROME, c. 345–420, of Rome.

BETWEEN St. Paul and St. Augustine lay almost four centuries of formative years in the making of Christendom. In St. Paul's days the

[8] I Cor. 1:25.

various groups of Christians in the cities of the Roman Empire had no uniformity of discipline and organization, no commonly accepted set of beliefs, no universally recognized standards of moral practice. In St. Augustine's days the Church, to a considerable extent, had become one in official polity, one in creedal formulas, one in ethical ideals. Dissidents there always were and continued to be. But the Church became more and more unified and institutionalized with the passing generations, and its leaders usually took strong measures to suppress disturbing factions. In other words, the informally associated groups of early Christians came to be succeeded by the Catholic Church.

The Catholic Church did not come into being as the result of philosophical reflections. It was a product of a number of factors—primarily religious and moral factors, but also economic and political and social factors. The philosophical factor, in comparison with the others, was negligible.

The period between St. Paul and St. Augustine is commonly called the patristic period, and the writers who in this period expressed their religious and moral ideas of the Christian faith are commonly called the Church fathers. Some of the Church fathers looked on philosophy with suspicion, even at times abjuring it as a heathen conceit. Such men, often lacking philosophical ability and training, tended to view Greek thought as a purely human invention which stood in antithesis to the divinely revealed and divinely inspired faith. Tertullian, for example, explicitly rejected philosophy in all its forms as a foe of the Church. The gospel, he insisted, is from God and so needs no defense from men. He and other enemies of philosophy indeed had, from their point of view, grounds for their enmity. For not infrequently there were speculative minds among the Christians who took over ideas from Greek thought, elaborated these pagan suggestions in systematic form, and reached conclusions which proved to be at variance with one or another of the religious beliefs current in Christian circles. Councils of bishops, and even at times single bishops, condemned such speculative minds as heretical and excluded them from the Christian brotherhood. Such condemnations made the very enterprise of philosophy itself seem suspect. A widespread fear of heresy haunted Christian circles and made many Christians view philosophy as destructive of vital Christian faith.

An attitude of hostility to all philosophy, however, could hardly remain a permanent or characteristic Christian position. For, as Christianity spread and became increasingly powerful, certain Christians were bound to wish to defend themselves against their educated opponents, even to seek to convert these opponents. They were bound to wish, moreover, to formulate for their own sakes a view of God and man and the world which would enable them to justify their religious faith as a rational venture. Men of philosophical ability began to appear among the Christians, for example, Justin Martyr, Origen, St. Athanasius, St. Ambrose, St. Jerome; and some of these men held high office and exercised wide influence in the Church. In their philosophical reflections they utilized concepts and principles which they borrowed from the diffused Greek thought, particularly Platonic and Neo-Platonic thought, which had been disseminated across the Mediterranean world. They utilized these ideas because indeed there was no other body of philosophic thought to which resort was possible. But the great majority of Christians, it may be said, tolerated philosophic reflections only when the reflections proved clearly to fortify the faith. And even when they granted such toleration, they regarded the faith as resting on grounds prior to, and more reliable than, any considerations which philosophical speculations could subsequently adduce.

The philosophical significance of the patristic period, however, does not lie primarily in the philosophies it now and then produced. It lies rather in the import of the outstanding achievement of the period, an achievement which philosophic minds did little to promote. This outstanding achievement was the molding of the Church into a Catholic body. Any great institution, even if it does not have its genesis in any philosophic concern, is bound to embody and to disclose an idea which has correspondingly great philosophic import. So with the Catholic Church, once it came into being. The Catholic Church required, for its defense and its stability, the formulation of a new philosophical principle. The *de facto* catholicity of the Church made requisite the formulation of a new idea which, germinating gradually in minds but dimly aware of its meaning, was to regulate philosophical speculations for a thousand years and—what is even more important—was to be itself a major premise within the philosophical systems it entailed. Christians did not make the Church catholic because they first entertained the idea of catholicity. Rather, they discovered that in dealing with religious and moral problems the Church had become catholic, and then, they sought to define that idea which would best explain and justify the nature of the Church they already had.

One of the most pressing of the practical problems of the Christians of the second, third, and fourth centuries was the quest for unity— unity in belief, unity in moral practice, unity in organization. For how could the Christians stand effectively against the powers of the pagan world; how, even more, could they hope to convert these pagan powers to their own Christian faith, unless they worked with harmonious ranks and consistent aims? And how could they achieve harmony and consistency unless somewhere they discovered a dominant voice which they could recognize as entitled to speak for them all and to speak with authority? This quest for unity entailed a long struggle among contending forces until some one of those forces proved to have a *de facto* claim to exercise final control over all the other forces. The kind of unity which was practically most important was unity of organization. For once unity of organization was firmly established, means would be at hand to require unity in other respects. A dominant authority could then regulate belief and practice; it could at least enforce conformity in the more public professions of faith (such as the officially approved creeds) and in the more outward matters of human conduct. And in the case of the Church, as often elsewhere in human affairs, the very existence of a *de facto* claim over a period of years would give opportunity for the framing of a *de jure* justification of this claim. With the *de facto* power, the Catholic Church would have come fully into being. With the *de jure* justification, its catholicity would receive philosophical recognition and gain increased favor among the educated classes of society.

The course of the historic struggle for unity of organization was not uniform in the various parts of the Roman Empire over which Christians had spread. But a certain logic of development is evident among the facts. The struggle was in part a sheer struggle for power among contenders for leadership. But it was also in part a serious intellectual contest to find a criterion by which the truth of religious ideas and the validity of ethical ideas could be certified. Early Christians who had come from Judaism naturally differed on many points with other early Christians who had come directly from the pagan world. Furthermore, among both Jewish and pagan Christians, diversities of belief and moral practice were rife. If the diversities were to be controlled and were to be superseded by an officially approved religious and moral position, some norm had to be found, some criterion of judgment upon the diversities had to be formulated. And this effort to formulate a criterion, even if confused by the passions of contending claimants for power, was a genuinely philosophical enterprise.

THE QUEST FOR A STANDARD

In our present retrospect upon the developments of Christianity in the first few centuries, the position of St. Paul stands out as the first decisive theory concerning the proper way to determine truth. St. Paul had claimed to find within himself the witness of the spirit, and he had regarded this witness as coming from God and, hence, as being infallible. But the appeal to an inner witness was an appeal to something wholly subjective. It enabled different men to justify different opinions and different practices. It failed to furnish a clear test of the relative soundness of the different opinions or the relative correctness of the different practices. The Pauline type of appeal was therefore quite chaotic in practice and generated strife and contention among the early Christians. St. Paul had explicitly rejected the supposition that any objective test was requisite for the authority of the inner voice of the spirit.

The Jews require a sign, and the Greeks seek after wisdom. But we preach Christ crucified.[9]

Yet others, too, claimed to preach Christ crucified. And when these others differed in point of view with him, he had no other recourse than to vilify them. He did this with a rigor which left no doubt about the assurance with which he preached his gospel.

There be some that trouble you, and would pervert the gospel of Christ. But though we, or an angel from heaven, preach any other gospel unto you than that which we have preached unto you, let him be accursed.[10]

Two potent influences operated among the early Christians against the subjectivism and the dogmatism of the Pauline position. One of these was the great tradition of Judaism, in the history of which effort after effort was made to state the principles of righteousness in the light of human experience, human sufferings, and human achievements. The other was the great tradition of Greek philosophy, according to which, even in the diffused form in which it had spread over the Mediterranean world, all alleged inspiration was made to submit to rational criticism and to adduce evidence in its support. St. Paul's position, therefore, although continuing to influence subsequent developments, proved inadequate for the needs of the Christian com-

9 I Cor. 1:22–23.
10 Gal. 1:7–8.

munities. The other two traditions at this point contributed effectively to the fashioning of the Christian position.

A second effort to establish a criterion for the faith was an appeal to the words of Jesus. Oral traditions concerning Jesus' words were abundant, and written records of certain of his teachings had been made within a very few years after his death. Both the oral traditions and the written records later contributed to the four gospels in the form in which we have them today. St. Paul knew and used these traditions and probably the earliest of these written records. Nothing was more natural than that the early Christians, especially in the midst of strife concerning the voice of the inner spirit, should turn to the words of Jesus as an authority or criterion.

Both oral traditions and written records, however, proved ambiguous in their purport because they were far from being uniform in the positions to which they testified. Appeal to the words of Jesus settled an old issue but at the same time raised a new controversy concerning the relative reliability of different versions of Jesus' teachings. In their endeavors to determine which documents were most trustworthy, Christian leaders used three tests: the alleged apostolicity of the authors of the writings, the conformity of the writings to current Christian practices, and authentication of the writings by one or more of the powerful churches. Certain approved documents thus came to be recognized as constituting the canon of the New Testament, or the body of early Christian writings which were officially proclaimed to have been divinely inspired. Many more writings were excluded than included in this canon. The tests were hardly defensible; but the result came to command general consent. The authority of the canon seemed temporarily to provide a criterion for genuine revelation.

But any such body of literature as the canon of the New Testament is capable of diverse and antagonistic interpretations. The search for a sure criterion could hardly rest in an appeal to any such written material.[11] A fourth solution of the quest for a criterion was to appeal to the bishop in each community for an official interpretation of the New Testament, for an official interpretation, indeed, of all

---

11 In the Protestant Reformation in the sixteenth century some of the early Christian ideas concerning the criterion of truth were revived. Luther began with a Pauline appeal to the witness of the spirit within him. But the exigencies of his political struggle with the papacy led him soon to muddy his own position by appealing to the text of Scripture. Calvin followed this second position more clearly than did Luther. Later forms of Protestantism, relying firmly on the principle that each believer had the right to formulate truth for himself, brought both Luther's and Calvin's positions into disrepute, at least among large numbers of Protestants.

oral and written traditions. For the bishop was often, perhaps usually, the best-informed and, normally, the most powerful man in each community. His voice carried weight; and in the confused days of early Christianity, the weight of office was difficult to distinguish from the criterion of truth.

Then came a fifth and, in its bearing on the present discussion, the final position concerning the reliable criterion of religious and moral truth. Bishop often disagreed with bishop across the Christian world. Appeal to a single bishop could never solve a problem for the scattered Christian communities. Consequently, more and more, appeal was made to councils of bishops which met from time to time to settle strife and to allocate power. And the logical end of this appeal was, of course, to recognize the authority of ecumenical councils. An ecumenical council is, by derivation from the Greek, a council of "the inhabited world." It is, in fact, a council in which the entire body of Christians, wherever situated, representatively share.[12] Such a council, and only such a council, could unequivocally pronounce on contested points, because there was in practice no further corporate body to which appeal could be taken. Hence, in the formulation of the conciliar theory of the Church, the long quest for a criterion of judgment on religious and moral problems reached a *de facto* solution. And this *de facto* solution was what led to the careful formulation of one of the important ideas of history, namely, the Catholic idea of the Church.

THE NOVATIAN HERESY

The formulation of the Catholic idea of the Church occurred during, and was proffered as a solution for, two crises in the affairs of the Church in northern Africa. Both crises arose as the result of persecutions of the Christians by the Roman civil authorities. In A.D. 250, at the order of the emperor Decius, all residents of the provinces were required to make sacrifices to the imperial gods and to

---

12 Historically, the formation of Catholicism culminated in the claim that an ecumenical council is the ultimate authority in Christendom. The Roman Catholic Church has qualified this position by making the voice of the bishop of Rome, that is, the pope, supreme above all councils. The centrality of the city of Rome in Christendom, the imperial traditions of Rome, and the economic and military prestige of Rome favored the rise of the Roman pontiff to actual supremacy. This rise had begun by the third century or earlier. And the actual supremacy was given a dogmatic basis by the proclamation in the nineteenth century of the doctrine of papal infallibility, according to which the pope is infallible when he speaks *ex cathedra* on matters of faith and morals. But from the point of view of the entire Catholic world, the Roman Catholic Church is but one of the many Catholic churches, and the dogma of papal infallibility is an erroneous departure from the basic Catholic position.

the emperor himself as a god. The Roman government was normally tolerant of the many religions which were practiced in one or another part of the empire; and, to the Roman mind, Decius' order constituted no infringement of the principle of toleration. Everyone was permitted to have such other gods as he wished; but, for the purpose of promoting civic loyalty, he was required to hail the emperor also as an object of religious regard. From the Christian point of view, however, obedience to Decius' order would have been disloyalty to the Christian faith. When the order was enforced in the city of Carthage, a persecution ensued. Some Christians saved themselves by flight; some met martyrs' deaths; and still others yielded to the exigencies of the moment and performed the required sacrifices to the emperor. The last group were referred to as "the lapsed." And the lapsed caused quite an administrative and also quite a doctrinal difficulty for the Church. For when the persecution died out in the following year and many of the lapsed sought readmission to the Church, the Church was bitterly divided on the question of their readmission. A local Christian leader, Novatian, denied readmission to the lapsed on the grounds that the Church was the body of the elect, that is, of the Christians who showed true faith and led righteous lives. But the newly installed bishop of Rome, Cornelius, counseled the readmission of the lapsed; and, late in 251, a council under Cornelius' sway excommunicated Novatian. Novatian had a strong Christian tradition behind him; his theory of the nature of the Church had been held by some Christians in every preceding generation of Christendom. But when he led a minority movement of the *katharoi*, or "the pure," in resistance to Cornelius, he became a heretic, and his theory, under the name of Novatianism, became a heresy.

St. Cyprian, more effectively than any other Christian leader, formulated the principle which justified the position of Cornelius and became the official idea of the Church. The Church is not the community of those who are already saved; rather, it is the "ark of salvation" into which all men are invited in order that through its offices some may then receive salvation. Schism, consequently, is the greatest sin; for separation from the Church means separation from the only known and reliable means of salvation. And the bishops of the Church, as the successors of the Apostles, are the sole dispensers in this world of Christian truth and of divine grace. The idea of the Church thus involved, as one of its corollaries, the idea of Apostolic Succession. Without the bishops there is no Church; and without the Church there is no salvation. "He who has not the Church for his mother has not God for his father." Doubtless there was moral earnestness on Novatian's side; but on St. Cyprian's side there were stern necessity and farsighted statesmanship. The Church, in the implications of St. Cyprian's position, was real apart from the individuals who might at one time or another enter into it. It was not brought into being by the individuals who chanced to assemble within it.[13] Rather, it was prior, temporally prior and logically prior, to all such individuals and had a reality in and of itself.

THE DONATIST HERESY

The second of the crises mentioned above brought the Catholic idea of the Church to its final form. Again there was an imperial order for worship of the emperor—this time in the reign of Diocletian in A.D. 301. Again there was a persecution at Carthage. Again there were some who "lapsed." Again the persecution died out, and the lapsed wished to return. But this time the issue was more acute, and the precedent of the former crisis did not enable its easy settlement. For this time the lapsed included some priests who now sought to be permitted to resume their priestly offices. Was the reinvestiture of the lapsed clergy to be sanctioned? A strict party denied reinvestiture on the ground that a priest of imperfect character could not administer valid sacraments. Another party favored reinvestiture on the ground that the validity of the sacraments could not safely be made contingent upon the character of the priests who administered them. In 313 the case was tried at Rome. Donatus, a newly chosen leader of the strict party, was condemned. He led certain Christians in a schism which lasted more than a hundred years; but his position became a heresy which is named Donatism. The rival party won and became the orthodox party for all subsequent history.

THE HOLY CATHOLIC CHURCH

Through the defeat of Novatianism and Donatism, an idea of the Church was developed which was the intellectual counterpart and proffered justification of that administrative unity of the Church that had already come to pass. This idea had far-reaching meta-

[13] This theory of the Church which St. Cyprian rejected is one which was sponsored in later centuries by some bodies of Protestants. These Protestant groups, influenced by the nominalistic traditions of medieval philosophy, normally put all reality in separate and distinct individuals and regarded the institution of the Church as having a reality borrowed or derivative from such individuals as momentarily came together to compose it. Thus the Catholic and Protestant positions are often fundamentally opposed on the idea of the Church.

physical and epistemological implications which succeeding centuries would investigate. According to this Catholic idea of the Church, the Church is real in and of itself and does not owe its reality to the various human individuals who chance at any one time to become its members or to the various congregations of individuals who happen to gather in various places. It is, moreover, holy in and of itself. That is, the nature of the Church is not determined by the events which occur during the history of its visible manifestations. Its offices are holy, no matter what the character of the men who at one time or another occupy those offices. The validity of its sacraments depends upon the holiness of the Church, not upon the degree of holiness of one or another of the officiating priests who administer the sacraments. The Church, independently of the fluctuating exigencies of time and circumstance, is the sure repository of divine power, divine holiness, divine grace, and, hence, the divinely established means of salvation. The Church, in words which came to be added to some of the earlier creeds, is "the holy Catholic Church."

The position of St. Paul had already raised the problem of the relation of reason and faith. His position had relegated human reason to lesser concerns, to mundane affairs, to the discovery of ways and means to pursue ends which faith made evident to whoever had the spirit within him. Faith rested upon a prior assurance which needed no empirical verification. For if the spirit was present within a man and the spirit was of God, the findings of the spirit were beyond all doubts. This position of St. Paul was now modified, although the breach between reason and faith was continued. The spirit, according to the Catholic doctrine, spoke primarily through the Church. The Church has never rejected the claim that an individual man might be the recipient of revelations through the spirit. The authority of St. Paul himself, as well as the genius of certain other mystics throughout the centuries, was too strong to permit repudiation. But the Church has been suspicious of mystics and of their claims to direct promptings by the spirit. The Church has transferred the normal operations of the spirit to the Church. It has been content when the vitality of mystic experience has reinforced the official doctrines and practices of the corporate body of the Church. But it has been fearful of the implicit individualism of the mystic way of life, and it has banned all mysticism which veered toward a tendency to exempt mystics from the authority of ecclesiastical discipline.

The Catholic idea of the Church meant, among other things, that the intellectual life and all philosophical speculations were subject to control by the Church. The intellectual life was not enjoined, but it became subordinate to the dogmatic position of the established faith. The faith contained many problems, it was acknowledged, which the human intellect might well investigate; but the investigations of the problems of the faith could not properly end in rejection of that faith. As a scientist may investigate rocks or comets or plant life, so a theologian may investigate dogmas. But as the scientist is never entitled to reject the reality of the subject matter of his investigations, so the theologian is never entitled to reject the dogmas he is seeking to elucidate.

A further historical bearing of the Catholic idea of the Church upon philosophy is important. Acceptance of the Catholic idea of the Church meant more than the supremacy of dogma over all legitimate speculations. It also meant, though at first glance this fact may seem paradoxical, the rise of a new kind of rationalism. For the dogmas of the faith, certified by the Church, were capable of becoming the premises of sheerly deductive reasoning. Whenever men suppose that they have a body of indubitably certain propositions, they can then proceed to reach conclusions therefrom by syllogistic and other such rationalistic inferences. They will, for such reasoning, need no empirical evidence and no factual confirmation of their conclusions. And just this philosophical situation resulted from acceptance of the Catholic idea of the Church. To the extent that the Catholic idea of the Church prevailed, philosophy became, not wholly but in large part, a searching out of the logical conclusions which could be derived from the premises furnished by revealed dogmas.

4. ST. AUGUSTINE

St. Augustine, 354–430, was born in Tagaste, a small town southwest of Carthage in North Africa. His father was a Roman official and, throughout most of his life, a pagan; his mother Monica was a devout Christian. He was sent to Carthage to study and manifested striking literary ability. When near the end of his life he wrote his *Confessions,* he pictured his youth as wayward and worldly; but, like most converts, he probably painted his preconversion days too darkly. He taught rhetoric in Carthage, Rome, and Milan. In Milan he came under the influence of St. Ambrose. He had been inclined to accept the materialistic ontology of the Manichees and the Skeptical epistemology of the academic schools. But in his early twenties he underwent what are frequently called two conversions, though the latter grew out of and supplemented the former. The former, primarily intellectual, was due to his reading of Platonic literature, mostly of the Neo-Platonic type; it led him to a firm belief in the reality of ideas and immaterial substances. The latter, moral and practical, was due to an accumulation of Christian influences and his reading of the New Testament; it led him to devote himself to spreading and defending the Christian faith. Both conversions had important intellectual and philosophical consequences. The second he dramatically described in a famous passage in Book VIII of his *Confessions*. He was consecrated priest about 391 and became bishop of Hippo near Carthage five years later. Then for thirty-five years he worked zealously in the affairs of his diocese and turned out an amazing number of writings, many of which were in confutation of what he considered heresies. He died in Hippo during the siege of that city by the Vandals.

IN THE PHILOSOPHICAL position of St. Augustine western thought reached one of its great culminations. On the one hand, it brought together, in effective if unstable synthesis, several of the earlier philosophical traditions which had previously seemed opposed strands of thought. On the other hand, it announced powerfully certain theses which played a conspicuous role in the reflections of medieval and modern thinkers for more than a thousand years.

St. Augustine did not, of course, think of himself as playing the role of synthesizer of traditions; he sought rather to express systematically and comprehensively what he believed to be the truth which various earlier strands of thought had helped him to reach. The disparate nature of these earlier strands is more apparent to careful readers today than seemingly it ever was to him. In his first writings, such as his *Soliloquies,* he adhered faithfully to the Neo-Platonism of Plotinus; he there spoke of God (as Plotinus spoke of the One) as the truth, the goodness, the wisdom "in whom and by whom and through whom" all things are true and good and wise that are true and good and wise. God, said St. Augustine, is either identical with eternal truth, or, if there be anything more excellent than this truth, is that more excellent thing.[14] God, in this way of thinking, is the

14 "If there is something still more excellent, that rather is God; if however there is nothing, then truth itself is God." *De Libero Arbitrio,* Bk. II, chap. 39. Quoted from

timeless ground of all being and is treated in terms of formal and final causes of the world. Then, in his later writings, composed during the stress of administering the affairs of his parish, St. Augustine modified this almost sheer Neo-Platonism in the direction of ideas taken over from the Judaic-Christian theism of the Old and New Testaments, especially from St. Paul. He now spoke of God as the active and transforming power of the indwelling spirit. God is still, in a sense, the ground of all else and is conceived as beyond time; but he is now being treated in terms of efficient cause, even if a transcendent efficient cause. Thus the earlier Neo-Platonism, never abandoned, became greatly altered in import. St. Augustine's basic philosophical and theological doctrines—of God and man, of sin and grace and salvation—resulted from his efforts to hold at one and the same time the two disparate positions. Much of the subtlety of his thought lies in the intellectual techniques by which he endeavored to harmonize the two traditions upon which he relied.

THEORY OF KNOWLEDGE

However much St. Augustine was influenced by earlier traditions, he also had originality and creative genius. He has been called "the master of the inner life." Gifted in forensic debate and in administrative affairs, he was acutely proficient in observation and analysis of the workings of the mind and the will. Every man, he contended, can have intuitive knowledge of his own existence as an immaterial or spiritual being. A man may err in many ways. But even in erring, in doubting as truly as in knowing, he can be absolutely certain of himself as existing. Knowledge of the self is not dependent upon sense experience or anything else: it is immediate and indubitable. St. Augustine expressed this position in a famous epigram: *Si fallor sum,* "Even if I err, I am."

St. Augustine had escaped from the impasse of academic Skepticism when, and only when, he succeeded in formulating his own theory of knowledge. And what he found personally useful he regarded as philosophically requisite. Any systematic outline of his philosophy therefore begins best with his theory of knowledge. The Skeptics had usually maintained, on the one hand, that ideas are but mental notions which are private to those who entertain them, and, on the other hand, that sensations are but subjective effects which no one is justified in taking to be disclosures of external objects. St. Augustine

Richard McKeon, *Selections from Medieval Philosophers* (New York, Scribner, 1929), Vol. I, p. 56.

formulated his theory of knowledge in answer to these Skeptical positions.

Against the former of these Skeptical positions St. Augustine asserted, in typically Neo-Platonic fashion, that ideas are real entities which have being prior to, and independently of, their discovery by our minds. The ideas are indeed immediately grasped in our intuitions of them but are yet themselves unaffected by our intuitions of them, as indeed they are unaffected by our failure to have intuitions of them. They are not inferences; they are not reached through the senses or through anything other than themselves; they are not mental facts, though our intuitions of them and inferences from them are mental acts. They are not in time or space and, hence, unlike material bodies, are immutable. They confront our minds directly in intuition whenever our minds receive an "illumination" which, as St. Augustine was later able to add, comes from God.[15] When a man's mind receives illumination, he observes ideas and thus gains knowledge of eternal and immutable truths. These eternal truths, like the ideas, are objective; they are not fashioned by the mind but are revealed to the mind and hence have authority over the mind. The mind may change in its intuitions of now this and now that idea; but no idea changes, and, therefore, the truth concerning ideas is unchanging. To knowledge of eternal and immutable truths St. Augustine gave the name wisdom.

Against the latter of the Skeptical positions St. Augustine asserted that sensation is not an effect which bodily changes produce in the mind but a mental act in which the mind freely chooses to observe certain changes in the body. The human body, like all bodies, is, of course, in constantly changing relations with other bodies and passively receives many impressions from its contacts with those other bodies. But the mind is wholly different in nature from the body. The mind is a simple and immaterial substance; the body is a complex and material substance. The mind uses the body; it is not a product of the body. Nor is sensation an influence from the body. Sensation is the mind's observation of some of the changes which occur in the body. The mind does not observe all the changes which occur in the body; it observes only such bodily changes as are relevant to its own purposes. When we see or hear or have any sensation, we witness some change that is going on in our bodies and, hence, ac-

---

15 As Frederick Copleston, S.J., points out: "divine illumination takes the place in Augustine's thought of reminiscence in the Platonic philosophy," *A History of Philosophy* (London, Burns, 1950), Vol. II, p. 64.

quire some information about those changes. Sensation is indeed a path to knowledge; it is a purposeful act, revealing both the mind's intent and something of the bodily situation to which the mind's act is related. Even in its simplest form, therefore, sensation already contains intellectual and volitional elements. It is implicitly judgment concerning the animal body and such other bodies as are in contact with the animal body. This kind of knowledge, fruitful in enabling men to deal with material affairs, is, in St. Augustine's view, less admirable than knowledge of eternal and immutable truths, because its objects, being but bodies in the world of change, are less admirable than ideas. But it is genuinely knowledge, inasmuch as in it the ideas are involved. For the ideas, though in themselves entities beyond the world of the senses, are also the natures of the bodily things we observe through the senses. That is why the world of bodies is knowable through sensation. To this second and lowlier kind of knowledge St. Augustine gave the name *science*.

St. Augustine's theory of knowledge fitted neatly into the Catholic position. St. Augustine accepted what had become the orthodox position, namely, the primacy of faith to reason. But he never countenanced a blind and unreasoning faith. It is necessary, he maintained, to believe in order to know; for only if we first believe, will we gain that contact with, and illumination from, the divine which eventuates in knowledge of spiritual matters. But also, and just as truly, it is necessary to understand in order to believe with peaceful assurance. We cannot, indeed, have a full Christian faith without understanding. Men may often reach, through their own unaided human efforts, the kind of knowledge called science. But although St. Augustine thus made place for science and scientific investigation of temporal and mundane things, he was not himself concerned to devote his energies to accumulation of such knowledge. The higher kind of knowledge called wisdom, he held, requires divine illumination. And this knowledge, both a consequence and a fulfillment of faith, is what brings men an understanding of spiritual realities and of God.

GOD AND THE WORLD

St. Augustine believed, as he himself asserted, that his doctrine of God, the sound Christian doctrine of God, had historic connections with the philosophical tradition which went back to Plato. His Plato, of course, was the Plato of Plotinus, and the doctrine of God which he found in Plato was Plotinus' doctrine of the One. In stating this

Platonic doctrine, he was able to make the doctrine sound like a trinitarian formula. He wrote: [16]

In God are to be found the power which brings things into existence, the rationality which makes things intelligible, and the purpose which gives moral order to life. For if man has been so created that through what is noblest in himself he reaches out to that which is absolutely the noblest of all things—that is, to the one true, supremely good God, without whom no nature comes into being, no doctrine enlightens the mind, and no con-duct proves advantageous—let him be sought in whom all things are made secure for us, let him be discerned in whom all things become clear to us, let him be esteemed in whom all things become justified for us.

This passage repeatedly emphasizes the threefold relationship of God to the world and to man: metaphysical, epistemological, and ethical relationships. Thus there came to be established, through the use St. Augustine made of the Platonic tradition, the conviction that Plato was in harmony with Christian dogmas.[17]

As St. Augustine met the responsibilities of administering his diocese, he came to differ more and more from Plotinus' position. At the outset of his literary career, his idea of God, like Plotinus' idea of the One, was that God is the sole source of being and of good. In prayers to God, he used typically Neo-Platonic language at times.

O God, founder of the universe, grant me first of all that I may ask of thee what is fitting . . . God, through whom all things come to be which have no being through themselves . . . God, from whom all good things flow continually to us, by whom all evil things are driven from us. God, above whom is nothing, outside whom is nothing, without whom is noth-ing.[18]

Yet, in spite of his debt to Neo-Platonism, St. Augustine was not content to regard the world and man as emanations from God. The emanation theory tended, whenever it was introduced into Christian theology (as often later by the Scholastics), to turn into pantheism. St. Augustine regarded God and the world as different in kind of being, not merely in degrees of being. And what led him to qualify the Neo-Platonic tradition was the Judaic-Christian tradition and

16 *The City of God,* Bk. VIII, chap. 4. In introducing this chapter, St. Augustine re-ferred to Plato as properly to be preferred to all the other philosophers of "the gentiles," and extended his praise to those Platonists (that is, Neo-Platonists) who were most skilled in interpreting Plato.

17 The passage is, in language, reminiscent of Plato's discussion of the form of good in *Republic,* 509b. See what was said about this passage above, p. 48. But since Plato came to St. Augustine through Plotinus or other Neo-Platonists, St. Augustine's Pla-tonism was of the mystical and theological sort.

18 *Soliloquies,* Sec. I, pars. 2–4.

his own personal experience. According to the former, God created the heavens and the earth. In the latter, St. Augustine was vividly aware of will in himself and over against himself; he had, in moments of both rebellious and responsive will, a sense of encountering God's will. And it is because the doctrine of creation deals with God in terms of will that St. Augustine espoused it. Creation is technically different from emanation; it views the world as resulting from the efficacious power of God rather than ensuing from the formal nature of God's being. Thus the idea of creation does not involve any suggestion of pantheism. Although St. Augustine followed the Neo-Platonic tradition that God is beyond time and, in that sense, transcendent, he followed the Judaic-Christian tradition in thinking of God's relation to the world in terms of power. God is still immanent in the world, to be sure, for St. Augustine as for Plotinus; but he is immanent in power, not in substance. Where for Plotinus the One is fullness of being, for St. Augustine, God is almighty will. Where for Plotinus the world, insofar as it is at all, partakes of the being of the One, for St. Augustine the world, in its occurrence and its history, manifests the power of almighty will. Plotinus' theory of a spiritual world thus became in St. Augustine a theory of spiritual power.

Never before St. Augustine had the Platonic tradition treated the timeless and eternal ground of the world in terms of power and will. The new position had grave difficulties; but St. Augustine sought to resolve these difficulties by formulating a new theory of the relation of time to consciousness. A mere human being, he pointed out, holds together in the unity of his finite consciousness a certain range of time: he remembers the past, he enjoys the present, and he expects the future—and he encompasses past, present, and future (a certain limited amount, to be sure, of past, present, and future) in a synthetic act of consciousness. What man does on a small scale in his finite consciousness, God does on an infinitely vast scale in his all-embracing consciousness. God, that is, contains the entire course of time in one eternal, immutable, and ineffable vision. Men, of course, cannot share this divine vision, but they can at least understand it as a limit which is partially, if feebly, prefigured in their own capacity for synthesis. Nothing is either past or future for God. God, existing beyond time, grasps the entire course of time in one comprehensive act— an act which, in its several aspects, is creative power, complete knowledge, and fulfilled purpose.[19]

St. Augustine was required by his theory of time to restate two

[19] For St. Augustine's theory of time, see *Confessions*, Bk. XI, and much of *De Trinitate*.

ancient Christian doctrines, creation and providence. Creation is not properly to be regarded as an event which took place at any one time, much less at a time long ago. Rather, it is a name for the relation between the timeless cause of the world and the whole course of events in time. God created time in creating the world of changing things, for time is the measure of change. God can be said to have been before the world. But that expression, however natural to us creatures who live in time, is not to be taken in a chronological sense. It is to be taken in a logical sense; that is, God as the eternal ground of the world is logically prior to the temporal world as the consequence of God's power. God is no more closely related to any one event in time than to all other events. His providence, therefore, is not a purpose gradually worked out, bit by bit, as time rolls on. His providence is found rather in there being the kind of world which the whole course of time synthetically presents when grasped in its totality. From the human point of view particular providence may be said to occur in this or that event taken separately. But such instances of *particular* providence have their full significance in the way in which those events occur in the sweep of all events, which collectively indicate the nature of God's *general* providence. Of God's providence St. Augustine wrote as follows.[20]

> For he does not will, now this, now that. But in one all-embracing and consistent act he wills all the things which he wills. He does not will bit by bit, again and again, now these things and now those. He does not will later on what before he did not will, and he does not refrain from willing what he formerly willed. For a will of that sort is a changing one, and no changing thing is eternal. But our God is eternal.

St. Augustine maintained that the providence of God is compatible with freedom of choice on the part of such rational creatures as men. The doctrine of the providence of God requires that God be acknowledged to have foreknowledge. But God's foreknowledge is not knowledge at an earlier time of an event which will then happen at a later time. Such foreknowledge would indeed make men victims of external control and would deprive human choices of much of their moral significance. St. Augustine condemned such a notion of divine foreknowledge as the breeder of beliefs in divination, astrology, soothsaying, and other such superstitions; he deemed these beliefs and practices evil. God's foreknowledge must be understood in the light of God's eternal vision of all time in one simultaneity. God's foreknowledge and men's freedom are related as the eternal is related

[20] *Confessions*, Bk. XII, chap. 15.

to the temporal. What for men is successive, so that one thing is earlier and another thing later, is for God all contained together in one timeless synthesis. Men are genuinely free because they are so created by God as to be responsible agents. Men are genuinely free both when they turn to God and obey his commandments and when they turn from God and fall into sin. But, just as divine foreknowledge is compatible with human freedom, so is the occurrence of moral evil compatible with the righteousness of God's all-controlling will. For God had to will a world in which men could freely choose evil if he was to will a world in which choice would be morally significant. A world which permits and therefore contains evil, St. Augustine believed, is a better world than a world would be in which all human behavior was constrained by external necessity and from which genuine choice was therefore absent.

St. Augustine's view of man involved, of course, an analysis of the nature of evil or sin. And here difficulties emerge with which St. Augustine labored in many controversial tracts, but never with entire success. Evil, as he often dealt with it, is a Neo-Platonic concept; it is deficiency or corruption of being. As we see darkness only by not seeing, and as we hear silence only by not hearing, so we are evil only by not being. This negative concept of evil, however attractive for its consistency with the Neo-Platonic tradition, did not wholly satisfy St. Augustine. Sin, as he usually dealt with it, is a Judaic-Christian concept, less metaphysical and more psychological and moral than the concept of evil. Sin, that is, is a more positive concept; it is at least a concept of a very positive factor in human experience. It is the moral degradation of character which ensues from pride, conceit, self-reliance over against dependence upon God. In Neo-Platonic fashion St. Augustine said that "all natures, then, inasmuch as they are . . . are certainly good." [21] Yet, as he also held, moral degradation is other than deficiency of being; it is guilt.

Such reconciliation as St. Augustine effected between the two concepts of evil and sin he effected by formulating the idea of original sin. This idea can indeed be traced back through Christian thought to St. Paul himself. But it was never expressed, before St. Augustine, in the vigorous and explicit manner in which St. Augustine expressed it. It was his most deliberate recognition of the logical gap between the Neo-Platonic doctrine of evil and the Judaic-Christian doctrine of sin. It was his most deliberate attempt to bridge that gap. But St. Augustine never succeeded in working out his compromise position so as to free his idea from obscurity and ambiguity. The idea of

[21] *City of God,* Bk. XII, sec. 5; see also, sec. 7.

original sin, at least in the form in which he used Neo-Platonic language to express it, involved in its statement a confusion between the host of individual men and the Platonic idea of man. For example, he wrote: [22]

God created man upright. He is the author of all natures [that is, the author of human nature and of all other natures, too] insofar as they are, but certainly not of the blemishes in them. But man, having become deliberately depraved and justly condemned, begat depraved and condemned children.

St. Augustine, of course, was referring to Adam when in this passage he said "man." But he had to mean man in the sense of human nature in order to account for the ensuing corruption of all men who, as descendants of Adam, are embodiments of human nature. In the particular man Adam, corruption was sin; in the form of man, corruption was deficiency of being. The former, however, supposedly produced the latter. Then from the corruption of the form of man all subsequent men come to be instances of this corrupt form. But, even apart from subsequent sins to which this corruption of nature may lead them, the corruption is accounted to them as sin or guilt. Men, even before committing any overt sinful acts, are already guilty in the eyes of God; and men, in the acts which are entailed by the deficient nature with which they are endowed, are also held responsible for their sinfulness and can never hope for salvation unless their original nature is altered by the gift of grace. Men cannot even deserve the gift of grace until they have first received it (in some part, at least), and profited enough therefrom to begin to deserve further grace. That God does save some men through his grace and does not save others St. Augustine believed to be a fact of experience. But, as he clearly acknowledged, it is a hard fact to accept and to reconcile with the goodness of God. He sought to resolve the difficulties of his position by maintaining that the salvation of the righteous is evidence of the mercy of God and the damnation of the wicked is evidence of the justice of God. When pressed, he then confessed that though we call God just, divine justice is not what justice is for men or what justice for men ought to be. He insisted, nonetheless, that both the mercy and the justice of God's relations to the saved and the damned show forth the glory and majesty of God.

St. Augustine's treatment of the intricate questions of human freedom and sin and grace became the occasion of long and acrid controversies in his own day and for centuries to come. His most con-

[22] *The City of God*, Bk. XIII, sec. 14.

spicuous opponent in his own day was Pelagius.[23] Pelagius cut through the difficulties by denying original sin and by making human choices independent of God's will. This position satisfied an ethical interest by emphasizing the moral status of man and by removing a seeming taint of willful arbitrariness from the character of God. But it violated a religious interest by implicitly denying that God's will lies behind all the events of history. St. Augustine wrote many anti-Pelagian tracts, and successive councils of the Church during the next two centuries condemned Pelagianism as heresy. But here, as often in the history of Church doctrinal development, the negative pronouncement in condemnation of an alleged heresy was not equivalent to a positive definition in affirmation of an alleged truth.

St. Augustine's theory of grace contains the same difficulty as his theory of sin. Here again St. Augustine labored to synthesize the two traditions on which he depended. In Neo-Platonic fashion he thought of grace as that fullness of being which overcomes the deficiency of original sin. Since being is good and all things are therefore good insofar as they are, increased fullness of being makes the men who receive it more and more acceptable to God. But, in accord with teachings of Judaism and of Jesus, he also thought of grace as forgiveness which God gladly bestows on those who freely repent of their sins. In the former tradition grace is a condition of holiness; in the latter, a reward for holiness. With both of these alternate positions St. Augustine now and again agreed, making grace both antecedent and consequent to holiness. He tended more and more, as with the years he found it practically important to insist upon the authority of the Church, to allay the theoretical impasse by emphasizing the role of the sacraments in the religious life. It is in the sacraments, for most men and for practical purposes, that divine grace comes to men. In the mystic worship of God in the sacramental offices of the Church men are at once fortified in their righteous resolves and restored to divine favor. Mystic communion with God is at the same time a metaphysical transformation and a moral regeneration. St. Augustine never forgot his claim that we must believe in order that we may know; but he never supposed that understanding of God's infinite mysteries is complete. Thus philosophical analysis is not the whole duty and privilege of man, and, by its very difficulties, it often leads to the act of prayer. For example: [24]

23 A British monk who served at one time as a papal legate. He died about 420.

24 *Confessions*, Bk. X, chap. 6. The ease with which St. Augustine turned from analysis to prayer is what would partially justify Santayana's statement, or rather his telling overstatement, that St. Augustine's philosophy was hardly born out of rhetoric before it was smothered in authority.

I love thee, O Lord, not with a doubting but a convinced mind . . . But what is it I love when I love thee? Neither beauty of the body, nor the glory of a moment, nor the splendor of light, which is indeed pleasing to these our eyes, nor the sweet melodies of all sorts of songs, nor the fragrance of flowers and ointments and spices, nor manna and honey, nor limbs enticing to carnal embraces. I do not love these things when I love my God. And yet I love a kind of light, a kind of tone, a kind of fragrance, a kind of nutriment, and a kind of embrace when I love my God—the light, tone, fragrance, nutriment, and embrace of my inner man, where that which no space can contain shines in my soul, where that which time cannot carry away resounds, where that which breath cannot scatter yields fragrance, where that which voracious eating does not lessen has relish, and where that which satiety does not destroy remains firm. This is what I love when I love my God.

PHILOSOPHY OF HISTORY

One of the most remarkable books St. Augustine wrote, and perhaps the most influential, is *The City of God*. In this book St. Augustine presented, along with many curious and interesting digressions, his theodicy, that is, his vindication of the Christian interpretation of history, or his justification of the ways of God in dealing with human misery and sin.

The City of God was a timely book. The emperor Constantine had legalized Christianity in 313 in his Edict of Milan, thereby putting Christianity on equal footing with the many pagan cults throughout the empire. But troubled times followed in the fourth century. The empire weakened, and the power of Rome declined; barbarian invasions occurred, and the empire split into eastern and western parts. The Church was rent by heresies like Donatism, Arianism, and Pelagianism, and by acute political rivalries. About 360 the emperor Julian tried to revivify paganism, and for two decades or more hostility to Christianity was in fashion. In 388 the Roman senate debated whether to make the worship of Jupiter or Christ the official religion of Rome. Then in 393 the emperor Theodosius I prohibited the practices of paganism. Two years later the Visigoths crossed the Danube and spread ruin across vast areas of the imperial provinces. The poet Prudentius wrote tracts in which he contended that only because of Christ and his servants had God spared the city of Rome from destruction by the barbarians. But in 410 the Goths sacked Rome. And many persons in Rome and elsewhere in the empire were prone to join in the cry "Rome has perished in its Christian days." A more able and realistic defense of Christianity than that of Prudentius was obviously called for. St. Augustine sought to give this defense in the twenty-two books of *The City of God*, which he wrote between 413 and 426. His theodicy has survived the Vandals' sack of his own city of Hippo and the decline and fall of the Roman Empire and has become one of the most widely accepted philosophies of history through all subsequent centuries of western civilization.

History, according to St. Augustine, is the continual warfare of two opposed forces—the earthly city and the heavenly city. Countless illustrations can be given of this warfare—Cain and Abel, the Flood and Noah, the people and the prophets, Herod and Jesus, the world and the Church Invisible. The former in each of these illustrations is marked by cruelty, pride, extortion, and debauchery; the latter, by faith, hope, and charity. The warfare began with the beginning of time and will continue until the Last Judgment. "These two cities are entangled in this age and will be intermingled with each other until separated at the Last Judgment." [25]

The earthly city is often manifested in the state because the state often is characterized by greed and sordid ambition. And the heavenly city is best witnessed in the Church because the Church is the abode of many noble men. But St. Augustine never meant to identify the state with the earthly city or the Church with the heavenly city. He was not giving a theory of the relation of church and state; he had no occasion for dealing with a problem which only became prominent in the centuries after his time. The state, he believed, can be, and at times may possibly be, a noble institution. It is, indeed, a necessary institution for human welfare, necessary because of original sin and the evil acts of wicked men. It is, in St. Augustine's sympathetic analysis of Cicero's conception of *res publica,* an association of persons with a community of interests and under the rule of law. Were the state synonymous with the earthly city, no Christian could properly hold civic office or assume the role of citizen. St. Augustine never meant to undermine men's sense of civic responsibility and their willingness to serve the state. He meant rather to insist that only when the community of interests is a community of noble interests and the rule of law is a rule of just law will life in the state become compatible with loyalty to the heavenly city. He himself appealed to the power of the state to assist in suppressing the Donatists. The material things of this world are not evil if rightly used; and government is not subservient to the earthly city if justly conducted. Though the existence of the state is made necessary by the evil in the world, the conduct of the state need not be evil. St.

[25] *City of God,* Bk. I, sec. 35.

Augustine quite obviously lacked that keen sense of the dignity of the political life which Plato and Aristotle had; he did not exhort men to devote their lives to seeking opportunities to hold political office. But he respected the kind of state and government which functioned in accord with Christian principles. His constant condemnation of the states and governments of history and of his own day was due to his empirical observation that they did not customarily so function. And he did regard the Church as a nobler institution than the state, because only through the admonitions of the Church could members and rulers of the state learn Christian principles.

Similarly, the heavenly city is not identical with the visible Church. St. Augustine could not have maintained that position without espousing the very Donatist theory of the Church against which he wrote many of his tracts. The Church, for him as for St. Cyprian, is the ark of salvation, not the body of the elect. There is indeed a body of the elect, and that body may be said to constitute the Church Invisible. No man knows who is and who is not in the Church Invisible; only God in his omniscience knows that. The Church as it exists in this world contains righteous and unrighteous. Without the Church there is no accessible means of salvation; through the Church salvation becomes possible; but within the Church are many to whom salvation will never come. Imperfect as the Church is in the mass of its adherents, it nonetheless, because of its divine origin and its holy status, is the nearest of all visible institutions to the heavenly city. And in all issues between state and Church, St. Augustine's sympathies and teachings were quite naturally on the side of the Church. But until the Last Judgment, the warfare between earthly and heavenly cities will continue to be waged within the portals of the Church as genuinely as, if less disastrously than, in the more corrupt confusion of the rest of the visible world.

PLATO, PLOTINUS, AND ST. AUGUSTINE

Plato, Plotinus, and St. Augustine are the three greatest figures in the ancient world in the history of what, for want of a better term, we may call the Platonic tradition. By the fourth and fifth centuries, however, the genuine teachings of Plato had been overlaid with Neo-Platonic language and Neo-Platonic conceptions. The genius of St. Augustine consisted in combining that philosophically sophisticated Neo-Platonic tradition and the much more simple, almost naïve theism of the Judaic-Christian tradition (two traditions to which the learned Christianity of scholars and the popular Christianity of the masses respectively have tended to return). He combined them with great skill, if not with entire success. And each of these two traditions served to benefit the other with which St. Augustine associated it. The Judaic-Christian tradition, with its firm monotheism and its reliance on the words of Jesus, saved Neo-Platonism from the absurdities of theurgy, soothsaying, and superstition into which, in the later writers of the school, it was more and more drifting. The Neo-Platonic tradition, with its rationality and its emphasis on the glory of the intellectual life, saved Christianity from the crudities of anti-intellectualism, unreasoning dogmatism, and brutal authoritarianism into which, in some of its untutored leaders, Christianity was tending to be snared. In effecting something of a synthesis of these two great traditions, St. Augustine was enormously aided by the conception of the Church as the repository of the world's wisdom, a conception which, however much transformed by St. Cyprian, was a legacy left to subsequent centuries by the Roman idea of empire.

Plato, Plotinus, and St. Augustine, although three interdependent figures in the history of the Platonic tradition, represent three quite different forms of that tradition. Briefly and perhaps therefore somewhat inadequately expressed, the different forms are these. Plato is the *locus classicus* in history for a vision of the spiritual values which define the ideal fulfillment of man's natural resources and powers. Plotinus is the *locus classicus* in history for the argument that in spite of the seeming multiplicity of finite existences everything has its respective status in one all-inclusive and spiritual world. St. Augustine is the *locus classicus* in history for the faith that above and beyond all the changes in the lives of men and nations lie the wisdom and the goodness of one spiritual power. Spiritual values, a spiritual world, and spiritual power are not themes which exclude or necessarily contradict one another; but they are distinguishable themes. Neither are vision, argument, and faith incompatible enterprises; but they give distinguishable qualities to those whose work is primarily one rather than the others.

V

The Early Middle Ages

1. THE NATURE OF SCHOLASTICISM

PSEUDO-DIONYSIUS, a name now used for an unidentified Christian author whose works appeared about 500. These works purported to be written by Dionysius the Areopagite, whom St. Paul converted to Christianity in Athens (cf. Acts 17:34). The works bear such titles as *Mystical Theology, Divine Names, Celestial Hierarchy*. They present a form of Neo-Platonism and were probably written in Syria under the influence of Proclus.

ANICIUS MANLIUS SEVERINUS BOETHIUS, 480–524, was a Roman of distinguished rank in affairs of state and a scholar of wide learning. He was imprisoned and finally executed by the Gothic king Theodoric. The book he wrote while in prison, *The Consolations of Philosophy,* has served almost as a book of devotion in medieval and modern times. Of more philosophical importance were his translation of Aristotle's logical works and his commentary on Porphyry's *Introduction* to Aristotle's logic. Whether one deems him Christian or pagan will depend on whether or not one deems genuine three treatises on *The Trinity.*

ALCUIN, c. 730–804, studied in the school in York. At the request of Charles the Great, he became head of the Palatine School, 782–796. (This school, moved to Paris later by Charles the Bald, was one of the schools which united to become the University of Paris in 1215.) He spent his last years as abbot of the monastery of St. Martin in Tours.

PETER LOMBARD, c. 1100–1160, an Italian who became bishop of Paris. He is best known for his *Four Books of Sentences,* composed about the middle of the twelfth century.

THE FOUR CENTURIES from the death of St. Augustine to the reign of Charles the Great were less productive in philosophy than any other period of equal length in the history of western civilization. Two men stand out in the first quarter of the sixth century, Pseudo-Dionysius and Boethius; they represent respectively the Platonic and Aristotelian traditions and are important primarily because they were channels through which these traditions were transmitted to the Middle Ages. Otherwise, however, the centuries were philosophically sterile; they were indeed, as they are commonly called, the Dark Ages. Barbarian hordes which had begun in the fourth century to make inroads into the Roman Empire continued to sweep in devastating numbers across the provinces and into Italy itself. The authority of Rome in military and political matters declined; and with that decline went a decay of learning and the arts. The Graeco-Roman epoch of western civilization was ending.

When western civilization began once more to flourish its scene was no longer the Mediterranean world but the lands to the west and the north. As Rome in conquering Greece proceeded then to go to school to the Greeks, so now the barbarians in sacking and breaking up the Roman Empire had in like manner to go to school to those who, in scattered abbeys or monastic orders, preserved memories of Graeco-Roman culture. The barbarian peoples had the vitality and energy which, once trained by long discipline, would yield momentous results. But no mere revival of Graeco-Roman culture occurred. The barbarian peoples were Christianized, at least nominally Christianized, before they achieved literary and philosophical competence. Hence, even if the ideas and techniques of their culture came from their heritage of classical culture, the subject-matter to the interpretation of which these ideas and techniques were applied was the content of the Christian faith. Thus a quite new epoch began for western civilization.

The Dark Ages gave way gradually to the period which has come to be called the Middle Ages. The transition to the Middle Ages was long and toilsome; its progress was sporadic. The stages of its advance are marked, as if by milestones, by the founding of schools. An initial step was taken when, in 787, Charles the Great enacted an ordinance for the establishment and endowment of schools in connection with the monastic institutions of his domains. Teachers for these schools, oddly enough, often came from lands which lay at the boundaries of the western world. Certain missionary expeditions had been sent out by Christian leaders in earlier centuries into the most distant provinces of the Roman Empire. These missionary enterprises had led to the founding of abbeys in which, because they were remote from the swaths cut across the empire by the barbarian invasions, some knowledge of ancient culture and some degree of learning had been preserved from generation to generation. Then in the eighth and ninth centuries the direction of missionary effort was reversed, so that "after many days" the more central areas began to receive intellectual succor from the very edges of the known world. The idealistic zeal behind the founding of the schools, if not a strictly factual account of the movement, is indicated in the following passage from *The Acts of Charles the Great,* a late ninth-century chronicle by a Frankish monk.[1]

When the illustrious Charles had begun to reign alone in the western parts of the world and the study of letters was everywhere well-nigh forgotten, in such sort that the worship of the true God declined, it chanced that two Scots from Ireland lighted with the British merchants on the coast of Gaul, men learned without compare as well in secular as in sacred writings; who, since they shewed nothing for sale, kept crying to the crowd that gathered to buy, If any man is desirous of wisdom, let him come to us and receive it; for we have it to sell. . . . At length their cry being long continued was brought by certain that wondered at them or deemed them mad, to the ears of Charles the King, always a lover and most desirous of wisdom: who, when he had called them with all haste into his presence, enquired if, as he understood by report, they had wisdom verily with them. Yes, they said, we have it and are ready to impart to any that rightly seek it in the name of the Lord. When therefore he had enquired what they would have in return for it, they answered, Only proper places and noble souls, and such things as we cannot travel without, food and wherewith to clothe ourselves. Hearing this he was filled with great joy, and first for a short space entertained them both in his household; afterwards when he was constrained to warlike enterprises, he enjoined the one, by name Clement, to abide in Gaul; to whom he entrusted boys of the most noble, middle, and lowest ranks, in goodly number, and ordained that victual should be provided them according as they had need, with fitting houses to dwell in. The other he despatched into Italy and appointed him the monastery of Saint Austin beside the Ticinian city, that there such as were willing to learn might gather together unto him.

This narrative, if unreliable in detail, probably gives quite faithfully the purposes of the founders of, and teachers in, the schools. Charles the Great did bring Alcuin from York to his court, and Alcuin then founded a school at Tours from which other teachers later went out to found schools elsewhere. The various schools flourished or declined and disappeared according to the competence and reputation of some one or more teachers. There came to be

---

[1] Quoted from R. L. Poole, *Illustrations of the History of Medieval Thought* (London, Williams and Norgate, 1884), pp. 16–17.

schools in York and Canterbury; in Paris, Cluny, Reims, and Chartres; in Munich and Salzburg; in Rome, Naples, Padua, Bologna, and Florence. During the twelfth and thirteenth centuries some of these schools developed into universities, at which division into separate faculties (such as law, medicine, and theology) was followed and degrees were awarded to students who completed prescribed courses of study.

The curriculum of the schools of the early Middle Ages (that is, of the ninth to twelfth centuries) normally conformed, wherever resources permitted, to a standard which was widely recognized. It consisted of two main parts. The trivium comprised the three elementary and propaedeutic subjects: grammar, rhetoric, and logic. The quadrivium comprised the four more advanced subjects: arithmetic, geometry, physics, and music.[2] And philosophy, which came more and more to be referred to as "the queen of the sciences," was conceived both as the presiding spirit of rationality and as a synthesis in which other branches of knowledge culminated. When the several subjects were represented pictorially in frescoes or low relief on walls or portals of churches and abbeys, philosophy was sometimes portrayed as a fair damsel with her head in the clouds and with a ladder in her hands by which aspirants for knowledge could mount aloft toward the skies. Philosophy thus came to be closely associated with theology, for, of course, theology also was concerned with heavenly things.

The term *Scholasticism* has come to be used, and aptly used, for the philosophical reflections of thinkers in the Middle Ages. This term needs to be rescued from the obloquy into which in modern times it has often been plunged. Philosophers of the sixteenth and seventeenth centuries, confident that they were making a momentous break with what they regarded as the unscientific and unprofitable philosophies of the Middle Ages, led their followers to regard Scholasticism as a synonym for logic-chopping, verbal futilities, and obscurantism. This quite historically unjustified attitude toward medieval philosophy, due to Francis Bacon more than anyone else but also to such men as Descartes and Locke, lasted, at least in Protestant circles, until well into the nineteenth century and even, to some extent, into the twentieth century. But the term *Scholasticism,* when properly used,

[2] *Physics* and *music* are here used in the Greek sense of the terms, so that physics means "natural sciences" and music means "liberal arts." In another sense music is one of the seven liberal arts.

is a name for the philosophical reflections of all the men who lived and worked in the schools of the Middle Ages. Scholasticism is not one single body of philosophical doctrines or one uniform line of philosophical development. It is a number of philosophies, as modern philosophy, too, is a number of philosophies, which had in common their connection with the schools or the centers of learning during the approximately six centuries (from the ninth through the fourteenth) which constitute the Middle Ages. In this considerable number of philosophies are many and often conflicting philosophical positions, different premises, different methods, different conclusions. The Middle Ages produced a rich diversity of philosophical opinions, even though all speculations of the schools were carried on under the auspices of the Church and were committed, in their broad outlines, to agreement with the dogmas of the Christian faith.

Through all the diverse philosophies of the Middle Ages, however, there are constantly manifest a deep respect for authority and a consequent readiness to refer, usually with deference, to the opinions of the great Greeks, the Greek and Latin fathers of the Church, and passages of Scripture. This respect seemed to many critics in early modern times to be a mark of intellectual servility or blind subservience. Actually, it was nothing of the kind in the case of all the most distinguished writers of the Middle Ages. It was rather an indication of two mental traits which prevailed widely in the school.

Medieval respect for authority, in the first place, sprang from a firm conviction that philosophy was an effort to understand and to interpret a subject matter which was not produced by philosophy but was presented to philosophy. St. Augustine had already made the claim that faith, although requiring the illumination of reason, was requisite to give to reason materials upon which to operate. This claim was frequently repeated by his successors. St. Anselm, for instance, was but reaffirming St. Augustine's position when he wrote: [3]

I do not seek to understand in order that I may believe, but I believe in order that I may understand. For this also I believe, namely, that I should not understand unless I believed.

No thinker, in other words, was accounted fit to grasp the fundamentals of a subject matter which lay beyond his experience. Just as no one would understand political rights and duties who had not been a citizen, so no one would understand what religion involves who had not led the religious life. And the Scriptures and the fathers of the

[3] *Proslogium*, chap. 1.

Church are guides in leading a wholesome and well-rounded religious life. Only through respect for authority, then, could one gain that familiarity with religion which it would be the business of philosophy to examine rationally.

Respect for authority, in the second place, was deemed a mark of intellectual competence. It meant distrust for an untutored mind. For, as the schoolmen realized, authority, when rightly used, is not constraining but liberating to intelligence. Only he is entitled to speak on a given subject who has first disciplined his judgment by acquainting himself sufficiently with what has already been said and thought on that subject. He who could quote no authority was evidenced by that very fact to be ignorant of the history of the problem under discussion. He who quoted authority, especially if he quoted ample authority and authorities on several different sides of a problem, thereby gave some indication of a readiness to proceed with the formulation of his own opinion.[4] It is indeed a striking and significant fact that Scholastic philosophers referred to authority as frequently on matters where established dogmas were not involved as on matters where dogmas had been proclaimed and rigidly defined. As Latin was the universal and international language of learning, so respect for authority was recognition of the need that learning be well grounded. It was to promote learning that Peter Lombard composed his *Sentences* (about the middle of the twelfth century), a collection of opinions by many earlier writers on many subjects, and, similarly, that St. Thomas Aquinas, Duns Scotus, William of Ockham, and others wrote commentaries on the *Sentences*. It was for the same reason that Abelard wrote his *Yes and No* (about the same date or possibly a few years earlier), another collection in which opinions on one side of each question were set over against opinions on the other side, so that the various known ways of answering the questions might all be reviewed on their merits. St. Thomas Aquinas composed his great *Summa Theologica* in accord with a method which discloses the exact significance of the medieval respect for authority. He began his consideration of every topic by asking a question; he then listed a group of authorities who answered the question in one way and another group of authorities who answered the question in an opposed way; and only then, after he had utilized the authorities as a kind of preliminary exploration of the question, did he proceed to argue vigorously for his own position and to give refutations of the au-

---

[4] This point has been well made by Richard McKeon, *Selections from Medieval Philosophers* (New York, Scribner, 1929), Vol. I, p. xv.

thorities with whom he differed.[5] The Scholastic references to authority are an indication of intellectual sophistication rather than of credulity or naïveté.

The provenance of medieval philosophy in the schools is reflected in the form of the writings in which medieval philosophy was cast. Medieval philosophy, more than the philosophy of any other period of western civilization, was presented in dialogues and commentaries. Back of these writings lay the day-by-day teaching in the schools. This teaching was often accomplished by conversation. And, where lecturing occurred, it was often presented point by point, like a debate, as Schoolman answered Schoolman or challenged response to a given thesis. The teaching, moreover, was usually concerned with the explication of some text, of which a school was proud to possess a copy. Books there were of course none, and manuscripts were costly and scarce. Scholars would go from school to school, when conditions permitted, in order to see and hear some writing of antiquity which they had not previously had the means to examine. And just because opportunity for consultation of a text was rare, comment on the text and written summaries of its contents and significance were part of the normal procedure in the dissemination of knowledge. In the dialogues of medieval philosophy one can today see a reflection of students gathered at the feet of a master; in the commentaries one can see a reflection of the treasured manuscript about which master and students alike were gathered.

2. THE PROBLEM OF UNIVERSALS

THE PROBLEM OF universals, as it has come to be called, was more prominent in discussions of the early Middle Ages than at any other period in the history of western civilization. It is, to be sure, a problem which may properly concern any thinker at any time. It arises naturally in the analysis of human experience. We human beings perceive many particular things and quickly begin to make statements about them. We say, for instance, that this thing is a tree and that thing is a rock. We refer to particular things by means of general

[5] At no point do medieval and modern philosophers stand in more marked contrast than in their respect for authority. Modern philosophers often sought to set aside all previous philosophies as so many failures and to make what they themselves supposed to be entirely fresh beginnings. The spirit of modern philosophy, in contrast to medieval philosophy, is clearly found in the phrase which Kant chose as title for one of his works—*Prolegomena to Every Future Metaphysics.*

terms. We treat particulars as instances of a species or a genus. In doing so, however, we often ignore the features which make each particular thing unique or at least distinguishable from others of the same kind and consider only those features in which a particular thing resembles many other particulars of the same kind. We may then turn our thoughts away from the particular things altogether, may treat what the general term means as another and quite different kind of object, and may try to define it. What the general term means is not, when thus considered, a particular object at all; it is a universal. It is certainly not a physical object, though it may be an intelligible object. Every genus and every species, indeed the meaning of every general term by which particular things are described and analyzed, is a universal. The problem of universals is an inquiry as to what status universals have, whether they exist in nature or only in men's minds, and how they are related to particular things. This problem at once involves other problems concerning the nature of being, the validity of thought, and the way in which thought is related to things.

The problem of universals was forced upon thinkers of the early Middle Ages by the manner in which the traditions of Greek philosophy came down to them through the Neo-Platonists and St. Augustine. A century after St. Augustine, Boethius raised the problem in the form in which philosophers continued to discuss it from the ninth to the twelfth century. In his *Commentary on the Introduction of Porphyry,* that is, in his commentary on Porphyry's introduction to the logic of Aristotle, Boethius quoted some historically influential passages from Porphyry.[6]

Since it is necessary, Chrysaor, to know what genus is, and what difference is, and species, and property, and accident, as well for that doctrine of categories which is in Aristotle as for the imposition of definitions and in general for those things which are in division and demonstration, I shall try briefly, in this useful contemplation of such things, to approach as if in an introductory manner those things which have been said by the ancients. . . . I shall refuse to say concerning genus and species whether they subsist or whether they are placed in the naked understandings alone or whether subsisting they are corporeal or incorporeal, and whether they are separated from sensibles or placed in sensibles and in accord with them.

What Porphyry said he would refuse to discuss, Boethius proceeded to discuss thoroughly. The questions which Porphyry raised and Boethius discussed were exactly the questions which philosophers of

[6] Quoted from the translation of Boethius by Richard McKeon, *Selections from Medieval Philosophers* (New York, Scribner, 1929), Vol. I, pp. 81, 91.

the early Middle Ages argued among themselves for several centuries. Much of the heritage of ancient philosophy came down to the Middle Ages in the context of these considerations about the problem of universals.

Plato's quest for standards of moral judgment had led him to insist on the reality of forms or ideas; and in the Platonic tradition, especially as this tradition developed in the hands of the Neo-Platonists, these forms came to be regarded as more real than the particular things subsumed under them and as both logically and ontologically prior to the particular things. Aristotle's inquiry into the generic traits of existence had led him to affirm that form and matter are two distinguishable but ontologically inseparable aspects of particular things; and in the Aristotelian tradition, the forms, never acknowledged to exist as independent realities, came to be regarded either as the objective natures of particular things or as ideas which minds, in coming to have knowledge, abstract from particular things and entertain as mental tools of discourse. Neither Plato nor Aristotle directly attacked the problem of universals; but they advocated views which seemed to have irreconcilable implications on that problem. Thus, in tradition, Plato and Aristotle became the reputed founders of the two chief but opposed schools of thought concerning universals. Platonism became the position that universals are real *per se* or in themselves or "absolutely." Aristotelianism became the position that universals are not real *per se* or in themselves and that they are, in an English phrase employed for translating medieval Latin, "absolutely nothing." [7] The former position is called realism or (to distinguish this usage of the term *realism* from its meaning in other literary and philosophical contexts) medieval realism or logical realism. The latter position is called nominalism.

The two terms *realism* and *nominalism* need to be used cautiously. For both schools of thought received quite varied expressions in the Middle Ages, sometimes rather extreme, sometimes more moderate; and moderate realism and moderate nominalism are not as different as some of the differences within each school. The philosophers called realists divided among themselves on such issues, for example, as the relation of universals to particulars, but they always maintained that universals subsist in themselves. [8] The philosophers called nominalists were opponents of realism. They were sometimes

---

[7] See, for example, Richard McKeon's translation of Boethius, *op. cit.*, Vol. I, p. 93.

[8] The term *subsistence* was used and is still often used to signify the kind of reality universals have in contradistinction to the kind of reality particulars have.

accused by realists of reducing a universal to a mere *name* or a puff of breath (*flatus vocis*); they of course gained their designation as *nomin*alists from this accusation. The accusation, however, was made in the heat of controversy and was a gross distortion of the facts. Nominalists did not deny that universal concepts had some objective basis in the nature of things. What they did deny was that universals exist absolutely. Nominalism, therefore, properly means little more than a rejection of the realistic position.

The prominence of the problem of universals in the early Middle Ages and the bitterness with which philosophers debated the problem were due to the fact that any solution of the problem bore acutely on various articles of the Christian faith. St. Augustine had himself been converted to Christianity through his prior conversion to Neo-Platonism and its insistence upon the reality of the spiritual world. Other Christians have reached their faith or defended it on quite other grounds; and some Christians have deemed a philosophical defense of Christianity unprofitable. But to many of the sophisticated minds of the early Middle Ages, the authority of St. Augustine was greater than that of any other philosopher, and the Augustinian use of the Neo-Platonic philosophy therefore seemed, not simply a permissible procedure, but the only sufficient basis for a reasoned and conclusive faith. St. Augustine had so ably stated certain Christian doctrines by means of Neo-Platonic conceptions that the doctrines seemed to many men of subsequent centuries to stand or fall with that philosophy. Three illustrations may be given of this point.

A fundamental doctrine is, of course, the existence of God. God, St. Augustine had said, is either identical with eternal truth or even more excellent. But eternal truth is found, not in dealing with particular things in the realm of change, but in intuition of unchanging forms or universals. And the more excellent thing, if there be such (and St. Augustine had come to put God, as Plotinus had put the One, above the eternal forms), is surely unchanging and eternal too. One could hardly be consistent, it seemed, in both denying the reality of eternal forms and asserting the existence of an eternal God. To question the absolute being of universals was therefore to undermine the accepted ground for a philosophical defense of the Christian faith. To question the absolute being of universals was dangerously close to atheism; it was to equate reality with the visible and temporal world of becoming, even, possibly, to reduce God to an idea which has only subjective status in men's minds. The heathen had often pictured their gods as particular beings who moved around in the visible world like glorified human beings. Doubtless many simple Christians naïvely entertained similar conceptions of God. But this anthropomorphic manner of thinking seemed superstitious to many philosophically trained minds. A Christian faith for scholarly and sophisticated thinkers therefore seemed to be bound up with an affirmation of the reality of universals and, once the timeless being of universals was assured, with a further affirmation of God as the unitary being on which the multiplicity of universals depends.

Another fundamental doctrine of Christianity, at least of Christianity in its Catholic and medieval forms, is that of the Church. Here again St. Augustine, particularly in his anti-Donatist tracts, had utilized a technique borrowed from his Neo-Platonism. The Church, according to the decisions which settled the Novatian and Donatist heresies, is real apart from all its many manifestations in particular assemblies of men; it is real in such a way as to be above all contingencies in the world of change; it is pure in itself and a source of purity which even the impurity of lax priests cannot sully. Such a Church, it seemed, must be eternal, not temporal. It must then be like a universal. The phrase *Church Universal* may have originated in other contexts. But however it originated, it can be used to indicate the kind of reality the Church must be affirmed to have if the Catholic theory of the Church is to be sustained. To question the reality of universals, therefore, was to undermine the basic authority of medieval Christendom. To question the reality of universals was to make the Church Universal a fiction, even to reduce it to the arbitrary power of whatever individual official was momentarily strong enough to prevail.[9]

A third doctrine which illustrates the importance for the Middle Ages of the problem of universals is that of original sin. St. Paul had said that "as in Adam all die, even so in Christ shall all be made alive." [10] St. Augustine expressed the idea of original sin by restating the Pauline doctrine in Neo-Platonic terms. In Adam's sin man became guilty. This manner of thinking, as was suggested above,[11] may not be entirely consistent. But it at least requires a realistic position on the problem of universals. Men are sinful, according to the Augustinian statement of this doctrine, even before they perform an overt sinful act, because man is sinful. Man, then, must be conceived as real prior to, and apart from, particular men. To question

[9] It was the implicit nominalism of the sixteenth-century Protestants which, philosophically considered, led to the break-up of the medieval unity of Christendom.
[10] II Cor. 15:22.
[11] See above, pp. 139–140.

the reality of universals was to imperil that theory of human nature upon which depended the chief claim for the indispensability of the sacramental offices of the Church to human salvation.

The Schoolmen of the early Middle Ages debated the problem of universals on its merits and as a philosophical exercise. But constantly in the background of the debate was the rumble of ecclesiastical authority, and occasionally into the debate intruded harsh ecclesiastical discipline. The officials of the Church normally favored the realistic solution of the problem, as consideration of the three given illustrations would lead one to expect. The situation, however, was far from simple. Realism of an extreme kind seemed to lead to pantheism; for if all that is emanates from the One and partakes of the being of the One, the Christian distinction between God and his creatures appeared to be endangered. Nominalism might make difficult the philosophical statement of certain doctrines; but nominalists normally professed orthodox beliefs and submitted to Church authority, even when they rejected the realistic manner of arguing for and interpreting the orthodox doctrines. Realists and nominalists were both prone to use dialectic devices to convict one another of heretical tendencies. But the analysis of the problem of universals was usually disinterested and often competent, even though the doctrinal bearings of the proffered solutions occasionally raised storms of bitter passion and even unfair personal abuse.

Medieval preoccupation with the problem of universals had far-reaching consequences beyond strictly philosophical considerations. Affirmation of the absolute reality of universals had, as one of its social correlates, insistence upon the fixed and unalterable status of all human beings in the social classes to which by birth they belonged. It is no mere historical coincidence that the growth of nominalism at the end of the Middle Ages occurred at the same time as the breaking down of the established class distinctions of the feudal system. Even in the fine arts a correlate of medieval realism may be observed. Portrayals of such Christian themes as the crucifixion evidence the influence of a realistic attitude. Artists sometimes presented the crucifixion partly in accord with the gospel stories but partly also with such figures as St. Augustine, St. Jerome, and St. Ambrose gathered about the foot of the central cross. These portrayals do not indicate, when understood, any anachronistic intrusions. They are partly portrayals of an historic event but partly also portrayals of a dogma. A dogma, according to one way of considering it, is a definition of that universal of which an important historic event is the notable disclosure. Artists who created such portrayals were doing more than showing that the whole of mankind should worship at the foot of the cross. They were using the techniques of the plastic arts to present, as best they could, a timeless universal.

3. FROM ERIGENA TO ABELARD

JOHN THE SCOT, c. 810–877, usually called Erigena (possibly because he came from Ireland). Spent his mature life on the continent, largely at the court of Charles the Bald. Translated the writings of Pseudo-Dionysius into Latin. Wrote commentaries on some writings of Pseudo-Dionysius and on Boethius' *The Consolations of Philosophy*. His major speculative work was *The Division of Nature,* in five books, written in dialogue form.

ST. ANSELM, 1033–1109, was born in Aosta, Italy, studied in France, entered the Benedictine Order, became prior and then abbot of the monastery in Bec, France, and, in 1093, was made archbishop of Canterbury. Among his writings are *Discourse (Proslogium), Soliloquy (Monologium)*, and *Why God Became Man*.

PETER ABELARD, 1079–1142, was born near Nantes, France, studied in several schools in France, established his own school first elsewhere and then at Paris, retired, after the well-known love affair with Heloise, to the abbey of St. Denis, taught in his own school in Le Paraclet between 1121 and 1125, became abbot of a Brittany monastery for four years, taught again in Paris for a dozen years, was condemned for heresy in 1141, after which he lived in retirement in Cluny. Author of *Yes and No (Sic et Non)*, an ethical treatise *Know Thyself (Scito te ipsum)*, several theological treatises, and *Glosses on Porphyry*.

AMONG THE Schoolmen of the early Middle Ages, Erigena, St. Anselm, and Abelard are here selected for discussion, partly because they are probably the most notable and partly because they represent the chief types of positions taken on the problem of universals. Erigena was an heretical realist of the Neo-Platonic tradition; nineteen propositions from his writings were condemned at an ecclesiastical synod in 855. St. Anselm was a realist of a more moderate sort; he received the blessing of the Church. Abelard was a nominalist; he incurred the hostility of St. Bernard of Clairvaux and even of the pope. But this hostility was due to the provocative manner in which he flaunted his opinions rather than to his so-called nominalism.

Erigena, following the lead of Pseudo-Dionysius, developed a philosophy which emphasized and deliberately exploited a strain of skepticism which was latent in Plotinus and the Neo-Platonists. God, he maintained, is the One from which all things come. But though men may know assuredly the existence of God, they cannot possibly know the nature of God. Even God himself could not know his own nature. The inability of men and God to reach knowledge of the divine nature is not due to feebleness of intellect (though the human intellect is indeed feeble); it is due, rather, to the very nature of God which transcends all predicates. In seeking knowledge, men proceed by either affirmation or negation (Erigena took this point over directly from Pseudo-Dionysius). All affirmations concerning God, however, are inadequate. Such affirmations disclose attitudes which men may take toward God but do not disclose God's nature. Men say, for example, that God is personal. But to be personal is to be an individual or one thing among many, and God transcends individuality. Men also say that God is good and wise. But God transcends these predicates too. Men indeed do better when they turn from vain attempts at affirmation and resort to negation. They might say that God is not personal or good or wise, and in these negations they would, to speak strictly, be correct. They would not properly mean by these negations that God is something other than a person or that he is evil or limited in understanding. They would properly mean that God's nature is above all distinctions such as are found among the particular things of the visible world. Even the trinitarian formula, which men ought to accept on the authority of the Church, is a figurative expression, indicating, not what God really is, but what God appears to be in relationship to the world of creatures. God is in no species and in no genus. God is superessential.

From God all reality proceeds. It proceeds by division, in the language of Erigena; that is, it proceeds by coming to be characterized by what one predicate rather than another predicate specifies, or, in other words, by limitation of full being or by individuality and finitude. Every level of reality in this downward way of becoming is capable of knowing the levels lower than itself. God alone knows all the levels that proceed from God. Indeed, all those levels may be said to come into being because God knows them; for in knowing them God possesses their forms or ideas, and they "subsist more truly in their ideas than in themselves." [12] All that proceeds from God is therefore in God substantially; to be at all is to be known as God knows. In the particularity which finite things incur in their procession from God, these things become contaminated by all sorts of accidents which arise and pass away. But particularity, and therefore, of course, evil, are nonbeing or defect. Only in their essence are all things, since they are then divine ideas, eternal and wholly real.

Human knowledge, of course, is quite limited. Men have both sense and reason. But of levels of reality above them, men have only negative knowledge. They may know *that* the higher levels are but not *what* they are. Of levels of reality below them, they may have positive knowledge; for the ideas of these lower things are inherent in men in the same way in which the ideas of all things are in God. This knowledge of lower things, however, is only of those things as they appear in their finitude. Sense presents things to men in their multiplicity instead of in their fundamental unity in God. And even reason, though it grasps the ideas of things, views things in their occurrence as appearances in the world of becoming, in their separateness, in their relatedness. Human knowledge, in addition to being fragmentary, is also inevitably inadequate, for human reason cannot by its own powers view things as the perfect essences they are in God.

Salvation, for Erigena, is absorption into the unfathomable being of God. As the One, by descending into the lower levels of reality, becomes many without ceasing to be One, so the lower levels of reality, by returning to their divine source, become one without ceasing to be many. Salvation, thus conceived, is in part a rational process just because being and knowledge are one. But its rationality exceeds merely human rationality because, in the upward way of salvation, the inadequate ideas which men entertain of things in their particularity give place to the adequate ideas which are the essences of things as they subsist in God. Salvation therefore is also in part and eventually a mystic achievement. It culminates in a spiritual apprehension wherein men's particularity disappears in God's fullness of being as "stars at the rising of the sun."

Erigena, though he regarded himself as a faithful Christian, incurred the displeasure of Church authorities. He was accused of being a pantheist, though the truth or falsity of that charge depends on an arbitrary definition of the term. The basic reason for the displeasure he incurred was probably that in spite of his skepticism and

[12] *The Division of Nature*, Bk. IV, chap. 8. Quoted from McKeon, *op. cit.*, Vol. I, p. 127.

along with his mysticism he was, in principle, an uncompromising rationalist. He maintained, to be sure, that sound reason and true authority cannot conflict, but he did not put faith before reason. He viewed authority as an enunciation of that truth which reason had already reached in the person of earlier thinkers. Men used authority, he confessed, because they are not themselves infallible. But neither were the earlier thinkers infallible. Scripture may perhaps be called infallible; but the meaning of Scripture has to be determined by fallible men. Scripture is largely allegorical, and allegory calls for ample interpretation. Moreover, Erigena used pagan philosophers more abundantly than he used Scripture, defending his use of them by saying that as the Israelites despoiled the Egyptians, so Christians may turn the pagan writers to their uses. In the end, it was his own judgment alone which he trusted in philosophical matters.

ST. ANSELM

St. Anselm, more than two hundred years later than Erigena, represents another type of medieval realism, a type more orthodox in its bearing on Christian doctrines. His philosophical affiliations are quite Augustinian. Like St. Augustine, he maintained that faith is prior to reason and so provides a subject-matter which men may then seek to understand through reason. Like St. Augustine, he held that God exists beyond time and brought space and time into existence with the rest of creation. Like St. Augustine, and at this point even more than St. Augustine, he practiced philosophy as a kind of prayer, as a manner of devoting his talents to the praise of God. Whereas most men praise God by candles or songs or good works, St. Anselm, with devoted piety, sought to praise God by logic and dialectic. The title of his most famous work, the *Proslogium,* is usually translated into English as *Discourse;* but the work is a special kind of discourse, and the title might be better translated *Prayer.*

For a faith in God already firm and settled, St. Anselm sought such demonstrations as were appropriate to one who, in accord with a chief tenet of the Platonic tradition, affirmed the absolute reality of universals. Among the demonstrations he proffered two are most notable for their influence. Neither of these two was wholly original with him: each was embedded in the writings of St. Augustine. But both received from St. Anselm what may fairly be called their definitive statement.

The argument of St. Anselm's *Soliloquy* repeats the argument of St. Augustine's *Soliloquies.* There are, he reasoned, innumerable goods, experienced by the bodily senses or discerned by the mind. Some, like a swift horse, are good for their utility; others, like a beautiful work of art, are good because of their intrinsic character. But all goods, utilitarian and intrinsic, must be good through that one and same being through which all goods exist; and this one good, the greatest good, must be good, not through something other than itself, but through itself alone. This supreme good cannot properly be said to possess goodness, for in that case it would be good through another. It must then *be* goodness, that is, God.

The same argument, of course, can be stated in terms of being instead of goodness. And St. Anselm, having given his argument in the one form, proceeded at once to give it in the other. There are many beings. Every being must be through something or through nothing. But no being exists through nothing. Nor can the many beings be through an ultimate plurality of independent causes, for the many independent causes, if they have being (as causes indeed must), would participate alike in being and so depend on one more ultimate cause, which is being itself. There is therefore some being which supremely is and which "supports and exceeds, encompasses and penetrates all other things." [13] This being, of course, is God. St. Anselm evidently felt a religious rapture at the way in which by dialectic he was able to support his faith. He wrote: [14]

God is in every place and at every time, because he is absent from none. And he is in no place and at no time, because he cannot be put in space and time at all. He does not receive into his nature distinctions of places and times. He is neither here nor there, nor anywhere; nor now nor then, nor at any time. He is not in this fleeting present which we now experience, nor has he been in the past nor will he be in the future; for to be in any of those ways is a property of only such things as are limited and mutable.

The other and even more influential of his two arguments for the existence of God St. Anselm gave in his *Discourse*. This argument has come to be called the ontological argument for the existence of God because it claims that the idea of God implies the existence of God. St. Anselm began this argument dramatically by quoting the first verse of the fourteenth Psalm: "The fool hath said in his heart, There is no God." But, as St. Anselm proceeded to maintain, the fool only proves by his utterance that he is a fool, for what he says is self-contradictory. In denying the existence of God, the fool acknowledges that he has in his understanding the idea of God. And the idea of

[13] *Soliloquy*, chap. 14.
[14] *Soliloquy*, chap. 22.

God is the idea of that than which nothing greater can be conceived. But that than which nothing greater can be conceived cannot exist in the understanding alone; for what exists also in reality is greater than that which exists in the understanding alone. Therefore that than which nothing greater can be conceived must exist both in the understanding and in reality, or, God exists.

St. Anselm's ontological argument for the existence of God has often been attacked both in his own day and since. In his own day it was attacked by Gaunilon, a monk of Marmoutier, in a brief essay, *In Behalf of the Fool*. Gaunilon contended that the concept of a being than which nothing greater can be conceived must, of course, be conceived as existing in reality. But what men conceive to exist in reality does not always so exist in reality; rather, men are often mistaken concerning what exists and what does not exist. Although the man who denies the existence of God may be a fool, we cannot dispose of his denial by merely pointing out that he has a concept in his mind of what he is denying. And Gaunilon merrily went on to illustrate his position by an analogy. We may have in our minds the idea of an island more excellent than all other countries inhabited by mankind. But from the idea of this island nothing follows at all concerning the real existence of such an island. Indeed, not the person who doubted the real existence of the island but the person who supposed the existence of the island to be implied by the idea of the island would be the bigger fool.

St. Anselm replied to Gaunilon, claiming that Gaunilon had misunderstood his position. The kind of reasoning he had used in dealing with the idea of that than which nothing greater can be conceived does not, he contended, hold good in connection with any other idea. And he facetiously went on to promise Gaunilon that if Gaunilon could sustain the analogy between the idea of God and the idea of a perfect island, he would "give him his lost island, not to be lost again." [15] The merits of the controversy between Gaunilon and St. Anselm are difficult to determine precisely, and the historian in dealing with the controversy is in danger of foisting more sharply defined opinions upon the two men than the men explicitly expressed for themselves. But a likely interpretation of the controversy is that Gaunilon, like many other critics of St. Anselm (particularly modern critics like Kant) missed St. Anselm's intent. Gaunilon and St. Anselm seem to have been using the term *idea* in different senses. Gaunilon used the term to mean a mental state or concept, and he

---

[15] See St. Anselm, *Apologetic in Reply to Gaunilon*, chap. 3.

was arguing that one cannot proceed by logical devices from a mental state to a nonmental existence. St. Anselm was using the term to mean a form or Platonic idea which, if it happen to be in the understanding, is also real in itself. Ideas in this latter sense of the term, which is taken for granted among medieval realists, are objects concerning which eternal and immutable truths hold good. St. Anselm was passing not from the mental to the nonmental but from essence to existence. He was affirming that the realms of being which in medieval terminology may be called subsistence and existence meet in the one being God. In all other cases essences are one kind of object and existences are another kind of object. That than which nothing greater can be conceived must be omnipotent, for power is better than impotence. It must be compassionate, for compassion is better than indifference. It must also exist, for existence is better than nonexistence. To deny the existence of that than which nothing greater can be conceived would then be equivalent to affirming that what one was thinking about was not really what one was thinking about. God thus viewed is not essence rather than existence nor existence rather than essence but both. St. Anselm's theory of the bearing of logic on ontology may not be sound, but it was not fairly met in the criticism of Gaunilon.

If the interpretation here given of St. Anselm be correct, St. Anselm marks a shift, even a decline, in the influence of the Neo-Platonic tradition. St. Anselm's argument for God in his *Soliloquies* is quite Neo-Platonic, for particular existences are there treated as derived from that higher order of being which is the realm of forms. But his ontological argument in the *Discourse,* although making the crucial exception that in God essence and existence coincide, otherwise treats essences and existences, as Plato treated forms and particulars, as two distinct orders of being. He thus began a reorientation in the discussion of the problem of universals which prepared the way for nominalists like Abelard and moderate realists like St. Thomas Aquinas.

ABELARD

Abelard is the outstanding figure among the Schoolmen of the twelfth century. His mature life fell in the generation after the death of St. Anselm, a generation which probably exceeded any other generation of the scholastic period for acrimony of debate, personal rivalry of teacher with teacher, and violence of controversy. Abelard said of St. Anselm that he was like a tree with many leaves but no fruit or a fireplace with much smoke and no light. Certain Schoolmen whose writings have not come down to us and whose views are consequently preserved only in the refutations pressed against them by their opponents—these Schoolmen appear in tradition as extremists in the discussions of the problem of universals and as foils for those who attacked them. Roscelin (c. 1050–1120), a teacher successively in several schools in France, appears as the arch nominalist. He is reputed to have said that genera and species are only words and that propositions about them reflect, not the nature of things, but the arbitrary rules of grammar. William of Champeaux (1070–1120), a teacher in the cathedral school in Paris and a pupil of Roscelin, appears as the archrealist. He is reputed to have said at the outset that universals are the only real things and that individuals of the same species all have the same substance and differ from one another only accidentally. Then, under the criticism which Abelard made of this doctrine, William supposedly altered his position extensively. He seems to have come to hold that only individuals exist, but that these very individuals are species or genus when considered in those respects in which they are alike. The detail of these controversies is not clear, because the writings of Roscelin and William are not extant. The fury of the controversies, however, is quite apparent. And Abelard (who studied under both Roscelin and William) seems to have delighted in the opportunities the controversies gave for repartee and forensic triumph.

Abelard believed that the position he took was similar to that of Aristotle, but he obtained his Aristotelianism chiefly through the commentaries on Aristotle by Porphyry and Boethius. He contended that the problem of universals was not an ontological problem at all, for all existences are individual things. The problem of universals is wholly a logical one, for it first arises in connection with our discourse about individual things. Only words can be universals. The realists erred, he argued, who made universals the substance or even the essence of things; they were thereby led astray into ignoring the many differences among things or into treating these differences as merely external to their real being or adventitious and accidental. Individuals are real in the full and entire richness of their concrete existence. If we could handle and refer to every individual separately in its integral and specific actuality, we should not need universal terms at all. We resort to universal terms because practical exigencies require us to make propositions in which we apply one predicate to many individuals at once. But in applying one predicate to many individuals at once, we are, of course, forced to overlook the full being of these individuals, to focus attention on only some respect or respects in which the individuals are alike, and, hence, to lose much of the full reality with which we started. The bread we see and eat is always some particular loaf. But we do not usually need to single out any special one of the many loaves which may exist. We need, rather, anything called bread. The term *bread* is a universal; it is a general word for the many individual loaves which, however particular in their occurrence, are yet alike in their value as food. The universality of the term *bread* consists in the fact that the term is equally applicable to a multitude of loaves numerically distinct. None of the loaves is merely bread; each loaf has its distinguishable traits (color, weight, size, position in space, and so forth), and hence a richness of nature that exceeds what the universal term designates. In dealing with universals, therefore, we are not carrying on an exploration of existence but are making an analysis of our human way of discoursing indefinitely about many individuals at the same time. A universal, even if faithful to the many individuals called by the same name, is thus inadequate to the entire actuality of any one of these individuals. A universal, consequently, far from being more real than the individuals grouped together by it, is marked by a certain decrease in reality. A universal is not a way of existing or of subsisting; it is a way in which minds sometimes refer to chosen aspects of one or more individuals. In so referring to individuals, minds may often refer truly, but they never thereby refer to the complete individuality of anything that exists.

In defending his contention that only words can be universals, Abelard was led to attend to the psychology of human thinking. Thinking, he contended, is a substitute for perception, a substitute that is in one respect less adequate and in another respect more useful than perception. It is less adequate ontologically, for it does not, as does perception, depend on the bodily senses and put integral individuals before us. It is more useful logically, for, since it requires no bodily organs, it enables us to deal with the absent as well as the present and informs us about connections among things which perception could never elucidate. Thinking proceeds by the use of images of things, that is, by the construction through the imagination of mental representations of existing individuals. These images may be quite faithful to some individual, as, for example, when we recall some intimately known friend. They may, however, be quite vague and even obscure, as, for example, when we think of man or animal or substance in general. All images come from, and reflect some aspect of, a prior perception. But they are always selective, including, at best, some features of one or more individuals and excluding all else. And often they are confused. They are confused because they are not derived from one single individual thing but from many individual things which are only more or less alike.

Knowledge is more than imagination, however, even if it is dependent on imagination. Knowledge arises when the word attached to an image is referred to some object. And knowledge may be either concrete or abstract. The sharper an image, the more likely it is that the mind will refer the corresponding word to one single individual object and the more concrete knowledge will be. The more confused an image, the more likely it is that the mind will refer the corresponding word simultaneously to many individual objects and the more abstract knowledge will be. Confused images are concepts. The words attached to sharp images, like the words attached to individual objects, are singular terms. The words attached to confused images or concepts are universals. It is not the images, any more than it is the individual objects, that are universal; all images, as much as all existent things, are individual. Only words can be universal, and these words indicate, not the images as so many mental occurrences, but the reference which the mind makes of the images to their alleged objects. Truth and falsity arise in the acts of reference which the mind makes of its images to things.

A universal, then, for Abelard, is a partial understanding of many things. It is neither a thing that has absolute reality, nor a subjective mental state (like the confused images he called concepts), but a way words function in intellectual processes. It has reference to existent things, and the truth or falsity of this reference depends on what these existent things objectively are. But it occurs only in the context of reflection.

Abelard's answer to the problem of universals would deprive the Church of that support for its doctrines which realistic theories seemed to afford. St. Bernard rebuked Abelard as one who preferred Plato to Moses and who, in trying to make Plato a Christian, only succeeded in making himself a pagan. But this rebuke was doubly mistaken and discloses St. Bernard's lack of understanding. Abelard was far from Plato. His curious identification of concepts with confused imagery was in complete antithesis to Plato's serene conviction that forms were the clearest possible objects of knowledge. And he was far from being a pagan, though he clearly was unconventional, perhaps heretical, in his Christianity. He did assent to the authority of the Church, affirming that one must believe the doctrines of the Church whether or not one understands them. He went so far as to assert, against the Augustinian tradition, that many doctrines are not such that they can be understood. Faith, for him, ought not to seek understanding. Rather, faith depends on authority, and understanding is confined to such matters as come within the range of sense experience. No student of history can be surprised that the leaders of the Church feared the influence of Abelard. For if faith lies beyond the realm of reason, then faith is in a sense irrational, and what is irrational is dangerously near to the absurd.

VI

The Thomistic Synthesis

1. THE RECOVERY OF ARISTOTLE

AL-FARABI, died c. 950, Arabic scholar of the school in Baghdad.

AVICENNA, 980–1037, Arabic scholar of the school in Baghdad.

ALGAZEL, 1058–1111, Arabic scholar of the school in Baghdad.

AVICEBRON, died c. 1070, Jewish scholar of the school in Cordova, Spain.

MAIMONIDES, 1135–1204, Jewish scholar of the school in Cordova, Spain.

AVERROËS, 1126–1198, was born in Cordova, served as court physician to Moorish caliph, was banished, and crossed to Morocco.

ROBERT GROSSETESTE, C. 1175–1253, taught at Oxford and was given title of Chancellor. Later he was bishop of Lincoln. He wrote on natural science, dealing with problems of sound, light, comets, colors, the rainbow, heat, and motion. He translated some works of Aristotle from Greek into Latin.

VINCENT OF BEAUVAIS, C. 1190–c. 1264, a French monk. He wrote *Speculum Maius* about 1250, an encyclopedic work which had as one of its sections a compendium of information on natural history.

WILLIAM OF MOERBEKE, died c. 1286, translated works of Aristotle from Greek into Latin, while residing at the court of Urban IV.

ST. ALBERT THE GREAT, 1206–1280, was born in Swabia. He became a Dominican monk in 1223, studied in Padua, then in Paris, where he took his doctorate. He taught in Paris and Cologne and wrote works on natural science, such as *De Vegetalibus* and *De Animalibus;* paraphrases of Aristotle's works; a commentary on the *Sentences* of Peter Lombard; and certain logical tracts which dealt with the problem of universals.

St. Bonaventura, 1221–1274, was born in Tuscany. He taught in Paris and entered the Franciscan Order, of which he became minister general in 1257. He was created cardinal in 1273 and is sometimes called the Seraphic Doctor.

Roger Bacon, c. 1212–1292, studied at Oxford under Grosseteste and became a Franciscan monk. He taught mostly at Oxford but briefly in Paris and was primarily interested, like his teacher, in natural science. He became a center of considerable controversy. Some of his opinions in astronomical matters were condemned as "novelties" in 1278, after which he apparently was some time confined in prison for heresy. He wrote *Opus Maius, Opus Minor, Opus Tertium,* and compendiums of philosophy and theology. He is sometimes called Doctor Mirabilis.

THE THIRTEENTH CENTURY witnessed a considerable change in the development of Scholasticism. This change was due in large part to the recovery of the text of Aristotle and a gradually augmented and corrected understanding of its meaning. Some of Aristotle's logical ideas—his treatment of the categories and of the syllogism—had come through Porphyry and Boethius to the early Middle Ages. But from the sixth to the twelfth centuries most of the rest of Aristotle's philosophy was misjudged and even unknown. Such interpretations of it as circulated among the schoolmen of those centuries were Neo-Platonic in purport and were based on the early and more Platonic and more theological portions of the text of Aristotle's works. A compilation of three of Plotinus' *Enneads* had been put forth in the ninth century under the title *The Theology of Aristotle.* The scientific works of Aristotle and the more naturalistic sections of the *Metaphysics* were almost unknown in the Christian circles of western Europe until manuscripts were discovered and eventually translated into Latin in the late twelfth and the thirteenth centuries.

The history of the fortunes of Aristotle's writings is a romantic story. Tradition reports that the writings were left in Aristotle's will to Theophrastus who succeeded Aristotle as head of the Lyceum. They may possibly have been passed along to Theophrastus' successors. They were certainly available in the first century B.C. when Andronicus of Rhodes arranged them in what is called his edition; and some of them were still available when Alexander of Aphrodisias in the second century A.D. and Boethius in the sixth composed their commentaries. Even when not studied, they were highly respected in antiquity. They were once hidden, according to Strabo, in a cellar in northwest Asia Minor, in order to save them from the ravages of war; but they are reported to have suffered physical damage in that refuge and to have become badly jumbled and soiled. They are said to have been carried through the streets of Rome in the triumphal procession of Sulla, as if they, like the seven-branched candlestick from the temple at Jerusalem, gave added luster to the splendor of a conquering general. But once the authority of the Neo-Platonic version of the Greek philosophers prevailed, the texts of Aristotle disappeared from the ken of scholars and thinkers of western Europe.

During the centuries when the text of Aristotle was almost unknown in Christendom, it was preserved and treasured elsewhere. It was translated into Syriac in the fifth and sixth centuries and, later on, into Arabic and Hebrew. A reputable Aristotelianism flourished wherever Mohammedan or Saracenic culture spread, first with the Arabs in the east and, then, as Islam swept across North Africa, with the Moors in Spain. A succession of Aristotelian philosophers brought fame to a school in Baghdad: al-Farabi, Avicenna, and Algazel. These men taught a Neo-Platonic, mystical Aristotelianism, turned, in the case of Algazel, into a defense of Jewish theism. Another succession of Aristotelian philosophers brought equal fame to a school in Cordova, Spain. Here Aristotle became the philosopher of Jewish scholars who enjoyed under the Moors an intellectual freedom not often granted to Jews within Christendom. Among the Jewish Aristotelians were Avicebron and Maimonides. A mystical Aristotelianism also got into parts of the Jewish Cabala and was carried in that form into all the countries of western Europe.

The greatest Aristotelian philosopher in western Europe before the thirteenth century—greatest probably in his intellectual genius and greatest certainly in his influence upon Christendom—was the Saracenic scholar Averroës. He was at one time court physician to the Moorish ruler at Cordova and, though banished from Cordova and forced to retire to North Africa, disseminated interest in medicine, law, and philosophy wherever Saracenic civilization continued. His influence was carried by the conquering Normans to Sicily and the schools in Salerno and Naples. In opposition to Christian beliefs in miracle, prophecy, providence, and the efficacy of prayer, he taught a thoroughly naturalistic philosophy. In opposition to the Christian belief in creation, he taught the indestructibility of matter and hence the endless existence of the material world. In opposition to the Christian beliefs in spiritual substances and in future rewards and punishments, he taught the dependence of the soul on the body and, hence, the mortality of the soul.) He made theology entirely subordinate to philosopohy, seeking to preserve his standing among orthodox Mohammedans by explaining that the seeming contradictions between his philosophy and their theology were due to use of allegory by theology and of scientific literalness by philosophy. Whatever fate he incurred with those who professed an orthodox Mohammedan faith, he became in the eyes of Christians one of the most feared archheretics of history. Christian painters, for example, sometimes portrayed him, along with Judas Iscariot and Arius, prostrate under the feet of the saints.[1] Nonetheless, he had not a few zealous disciples among western intellectuals who remained within the Church.

At the end of the twelfth century Aristotle was widely associated in Christendom with the hated Jews, the hated Moors, and the hated heretics. He was a symbol of a rationalism which ignored the Augustinian ideal of intuitive wisdom and the claims of a faith that goes in advance of or beyond reason. In 1210 the use of Aristotle's writings was proscribed at the University of Paris, and similar proscriptions were repeatedly pronounced through much of the thirteenth century. Nonetheless, attention to the works of Aristotle continually increased. Portions of them appeared in Latin translations, sometimes from the Arabic (as in Spain and Sicily), sometimes directly from the Greek of newly acquired manuscripts. Certain Schoolmen who were more interested in natural science than in metaphysics, like Roger Bacon at Oxford, found themselves permitted to examine freely the scientific writings of Aristotle. By 1260 Aristotle's metaphysics, psychology, ethics, and politics had been put freshly into Latin from Greek originals by Robert Grosseteste and William of Moerbeke. Successive popes and other ecclesiastical authorities had to yield gradually to the enormous concern of many scholars to become acquainted with Aristotle and to relate Aristotelian ideas to other ways of thinking. Those who favored Aristotelian ideas promoted a change in the official attitude toward Aristotle by drawing a distinction between Aristotle himself and the Averroist interpretation of Aristotle. The earlier proscription was viewed, by the middle of the thirteenth century, as a temporary measure designed to remain in force only until proper translations of Aristotle could be made and legitimate interpretations put in place of the Saracenic. In 1215 the

[1] Dante, to be sure, put Avicenna and Averroës, as he put Plato, Aristotle, and his beloved Virgil, in limbo rather than in the sixth circle of hell with the Epicureans. But Dante wrote a generation after the death of St. Thomas Aquinas when, among intellectuals at least, the contribution of all who had made Aristotle available to philosophers could be more safely recognized.

Organon was explicitly exempted from proscription, and other works, one by one, then came into general use. In 1263 the pope ordered a new translation of all the works of Aristotle, and in the fourteenth century every candidate for a master of arts degree at Paris was required to exhibit a knowledge of the entire philosophy of Aristotle. The Aristotelian Schoolmen who appeared heretical were condemned as Averroists rather than as Aristotelians. And Aristotle, if not actually Christianized, was deemed helpful in the discussion of certain philosophical problems.

In the history of the process by which Aristotle was adapted to the use of Christian philosophers the most notable figures were St. Albert the Great and his pupil St. Thomas Aquinas. St. Albert designed a grandiose project of rewriting the works of Aristotle, of incorporating therein his own additions when Aristotle seemed to him deficient or incomplete, and of thus achieving a finished and systematic statement of philosophical truth. He was willing to use existing Latin translations of Aristotle insofar as they were adequate. But since these translations were often so poor as to be quite unintelligible, he proceeded to examine many manuscripts and to make new translations, weaving therein his own expositions of what in his judgment Aristotle had intended to say or ought to have said. This grandiose project St. Albert carried through with considerable success; he thereby offered to the thirteenth century a version of Aristotle which, if not altogether reliable historically, made Aristotle not merely tolerable but almost essential to the philosophical defense of Christianity.

The recovery of Aristotle did not by any means end Platonic influences in medieval philosophy. It did, however, end some suppositions which had been prevalent in the early Middle Ages. It ended the uncritical belief that Platonism and Aristotelianism were two alternative positions between which philosophers were forced to choose. The greatest of the Schoolmen, St. Thomas Aquinas, is as conspicuously Platonic at some times as he is Aristotelian at others.[2] It ended also the vogue of the extreme realism which treated universals as absolutely real in themselves and particular things as emanations therefrom. It meant a kind of return from Plotinus' to Aristotle's conception of matter. That is, it meant that individuality came once more to be conceived, not as deficiency or corruption of the fuller being which something else possesses, but as concreteness or substan-

[2] Not simply was St. Thomas conspicuously Platonic, but he referred to Pseudo-Dionysius as an authority more often than to any other philosophical authority except Aristotle himself.

tiality which marks the genuineness of finite existences. The recovery of Aristotle thus meant that interest in, and study of, the physical world received a fresh metaphysical sanction. To many men of the thirteenth century "Aristotle came as a revelation; he taught men that visible nature is something more than a theological cryptogram and richly repays study on her own account." [3] Interest in the physical world had never been wholly lacking in western Europe, even if many thinkers from St. Augustine to the thirteenth century were preoccupied with eternal truths and the fate of the soul. But in the early Middle Ages compendiums of natural lore made little distinction between facts observed and fanciful stories reported by ancient authors and travelers. And as late as Vincent of Beauvais, whose *Speculum* appeared about the middle of the thirteenth century, this earlier medieval attitude continued. St. Albert the Great, however, whose mind was stirred by the recovery of Aristotle, collected specimens of plants, birds, fish, insects, animals, and minerals, and he indicated the kind of concern he took in nature by his remark: "Experiment alone is trustworthy in such matters" (*Experimentum solum certificat in talibus*).[4]

With the revival of Aristotelian influences there continued respect for the authority of Platonism—a Platonism somewhat closer to the position of Plato himself than that which had been disseminated through Pseudo-Dionysius and the extreme realists. One might fairly say that in the thirteenth century Aristotle became a chief guide in the investigation of the natural world and Plato remained a guide in efforts to understand the further problems raised by the Christian faith. St. Bonaventura (1221–1274), minister general of the Franciscan Order and cardinal of the Church, said expressly that Aristotle was sound in his analysis of natural objects but was weak in metaphysics. The Franciscans of the thirteenth century were less favorable to Aristotle than the Dominicans; they conceded as much as they could to the new enthusiasm for Aristotle but held firmly to the Augustinian doctrine of illumination. St. Bonaventura summed the matter up by saying that Aristotle excelled in science, Plato in wisdom, St. Augustine in both. Dominicans, however, generally followed the lead of St. Thomas Aquinas in accepting Aristotle more fully; but St. Thomas' Aristotle was one who had grown up in Plato's school and taught a metaphysics which culminated in a theology. The sheerly

[3] A. E. Taylor, "Ancient and Medieval Philosophy," in *European Civilization*, ed. E. Eyre (New York, Oxford University Press, 1935–1939), Vol. III, p. 820.

[4] Quoted from Etienne Gilson, *Histoire de la philosophie medievale* (Paris, Payot, 1922), Vol. II, p. 12.

naturalistic Aristotle was deemed by almost all thirteenth-century Schoolmen within Christendom to be a fabrication of the heretical Saracens.

The recovery of Aristotle facilitated a new solution to the problem of universals. This solution, formulated by St. Albert and accepted by St. Thomas, has come to be called moderate realism. It is a realism because it affirms that what in the mind is universal exists also in things as their form; and it is moderate because it denies that universals or forms exist absolutely. Particular things, as Aristotle taught, are unions of matter and form. Matter is the principle of individuation; form is the principle of intelligibility. Were forms not in matter, individual things could not be. Were matter not formed, knowledge could not occur. The same form which in any individual thing is that thing's actuality or quiddity (or whatness) is also, in any mind which knows that individual thing, an idea of the thing or the thing's essence. Unless the identical form were at the same time a thing's nature objectively and a mind's idea subjectively, the thing would not be intelligible and the mind would not be cognitive. Furthermore, when a mind once possesses a form as its idea, that mind may cease to be preoccupied with the individual thing which has the form as its nature and may consider the form as the possible nature of many individuals. Thus considered and only when thus considered, the form may properly be called a universal, though indeed that form may actually be the nature of only one individual. A universal, in St. Albert's way of expressing the point, is "an essence apt to give being to many, even though it may never give being." [5] A universal, therefore, if one uses language strictly, is only in the intellect; for apart from the intellect, form is always individuated in matter.

In the order of existence things are prior to universals. For a subject-matter is always prior to knowledge about that subject-matter; that is, things are what they are whether known or not, and only when the mind comes to know them, do their forms (denuded of their matter) enter the mind and become ideas of them. But in the order of knowledge universals may in a sense be called prior to things. For universals are wholly and exhaustively intelligible; indeed, they are the only entirely intelligible objects, lacking as they do the principle of matter resident in all individual things which resists apprehension by the mind in ideas. Only in the order of God's creative

---

[5] *Short Natural Treatises on the Intellect and the Intelligible,* Treatise II, chap. 2. Quoted from the translation by Richard McKeon, *Selections from Medieval Philosophers* (New York, Scribner, 1929), Vol. I, p. 359.

mind do universals come before the things of which these universals then later become the actuality or quiddity. Only in God are the intelligibles which express his creative purposes prior to both the existential order and the order of human knowledge.

This moderate realism of St. Albert and St. Thomas has frequently been summed up in histories of Scholasticism in an apt formula: that universals, although never existing absolutely, do exist *ante rem, in re,* and *post rem.* In this brief Latin phrase moderate realism is neatly defined. Universals are *before things* as the rational plans of God's foresight and creative power; they are *in things* as the things' natures; and they are *after things* as the ideas or the knowledge which finite rational creatures may come to have concerning things.

2. ST. THOMAS AQUINAS

ST. THOMAS AQUINAS, 1225–1274, born near Naples, was younger son of a count of Aquino. He studied at the Benedictine monastery of Monte Cassino (where an uncle of his was abbot) and in Naples and became a Dominican monk in spite of opposition from his family. He also studied at Paris and Cologne under St. Albert. He was so quiet and preoccupied by his studies that he was dubbed the Dumb Ox by his fellow students. He taught in Paris and at the courts of three successive popes, set up a curriculum for schools of the Dominican Order, and wrote prolifically. Among his important works are *Being and Essence;* commentaries on Aristotle's physics, astronomy, psychology, metaphysics, ethics, and politics; a commentary on Peter Lombard's *Sentences;* several treatises against the Averroists, of which the most famous is *Summa contra Gentiles;* and the stupendous *Summa Theologica,* which in translation into English under the auspices of the English Dominicans fills twenty-nine volumes. He is referred to in tradition as the Angelic Doctor.

THE SYSTEM OF theology and philosophy which St. Thomas Aquinas produced has been called, in the tributes paid to it by some of its admirers, the supreme synthesis. It is certainly one of the notable culminations of medieval Scholasticism and may fairly be said to stand beside St. Augustine's system as a momentous expression of a Catholic theory of God and man and the world. And, like St. Augustine's system, it was indeed a synthesis, though its elements were not quite the same as those which furnished materials for St. Augustine's thought. St. Thomas wrote during the controversial days of the Aristotelian revival; he preferred the Aristotelian to the Neo-Platonic analysis of the visible world and of the nature and development of human knowledge. But in adding much which he learned from Aristotle to his synthesis, he exhibited a keenly critical mind. His system was not a mechanical hodgepodge of ideas from diverse sources. It was the product of his own original genius and incorporated elements from his predecessors and contemporaries only when these elements, judged on their merits and put in their due places relatively to the overarching grasp he had of the whole of his system, contributed to the advance of his integrated understanding of truth. St. Thomas was an innovator. Viewed in his intellectual environment in the thirteenth century, he was a bold innovator. The vogue into which his system eventually came and, above all, the sanction which in recent times the papacy has given for the study of his system in Catholic colleges and seminaries across the world ought not to blind the historian to the daring originality of a mind which could see how Platonism, Augustinianism, Aristotelianism, and even at times Averroism, could be utilized to expound a total point of view which, in his judgment, was faithful at once to all the experienced facts of everyday life and to all the orthodox dogmas of Catholic Christianity. Had St. Thomas' mind not been both original and bold, he could not have borrowed effectively from sources widely suspect in his century; nor could he have achieved what has proved to be one of the most durable syntheses in the traditions of western culture.

RELATION OF THEOLOGY AND PHILOSOPHY

St. Thomas made a fundamental distinction between theology and philosophy. Theology begins with dogmas that are given in revelation; philosophy begins with experienced subject-matters that are given in observation. Both theologian and philosopher will use reason and will develop their respective bodies of knowledge rationally and in accord with the principles of logic. Theology and philosophy may even on occasion enunciate the same propositions, as, for example, that God exists. They may well be found in the same treatises; indeed, St. Thomas himself included large quantities of philosophy in his *Summa Theologica* and considerable theology in his *Summa contra Gentiles* in which he was controverting the philosophical position of the Averroists. Such combinations of theology and philosophy he deemed desirable. One function of reason is to arrange and correlate all our knowledge into one system—a task which in principle is possible because truth is one consistent whole. But even when theology and philosophy meet and concur in affirming the same propositions, the two kinds of knowledge remain distinct, and neither one can ever become the other. For theology and philosophy reach these propositions by different means. Theology proceeds through deduction from revealed premises, and philosophy through inference from observed facts. Theology and philosophy do, to an extent which is highly significant, deal with different problems. Theology deals, for example, with the triune nature of God about which philosophy can say nothing; and philosophy may deal with problems of heat or sound about which theology chances to disclose nothing. Any knowledge reached by philosophy might, of course, be given by theology; and, indeed, some such has been given, though also much has not been so given. But the fundamental difference between theology and philosophy lies in the procedures by which the two branches of knowledge are respectively pursued. Theology is authoritarian, using reason to explore the full meaning and implications of dogmas revealed to faith, and philosophy is empirical, using reason to draw such conclusions as it can from the facts of human experience. Philosophy is natural knowledge.

In some of his shorter treatises St. Thomas treated his themes philosophically and without any theological setting. In each *Summa*, however, he developed his philosophy in a structure determined by the pattern of his theology, beginning with God and proceeding from God to God's creatures. This method of presentation, St. Thomas held, is philosophically sound, even if not philosophically requisite. Philosophy, pursued apart from theology, may properly begin either with God or with the visible world. It must begin, if it is to be systematic and clear, with that which is prior. But, as St. Thomas said in agreement with Aristotle, there are two distinct kinds of priority. That which is prior in the order of being is not the same as that which is prior in the order of the growth of human knowledge. God is prior in the former sense, and the visible world in the latter. St. Thomas, more interested as he was in the nature of being than in an account of the gradual development of human knowledge, preferred the former method of exposition. But he granted that the latter method may be helpful to many inquiring minds.

The latter method is the one which is adopted in the discussion of this chapter. It is adopted because it enables the student of the history of ideas to discern from the outset the difference between

Augustinianism and Thomism. This difference is chiefly due to two factors: first, St. Thomas' espousal of the moderate realism which he had learned from his teacher St. Albert, and second, his incorporation into the synthesis already made by St. Augustine of a great deal of Aristotelian naturalism.

St. Thomas rejected St. Augustine's distinction between science and wisdom. Against that Augustinian position he sponsored the theory of knowledge according to which "nothing is in the mind which was not first in sense" (*nihil est in intellectu quod prius non fuerit in sensu*).[6] The mind of man, he insisted, does not immediately and directly apprehend the eternal forms. The mind of man in its actuality is void of ideas until it gains ideas through acquaintance with the forms of natural substances in the natural world.[7] Human understanding, St. Thomas said, is to truth as the eye of a bat is to the sun. Men indeed, St. Thomas argued, can reach some knowledge of God and of immaterial substances. For once the mind of man has encountered the forms of substances in the natural world, the mind is able, through its own powers and without divine illumination, to contemplate these forms and to know truths concerning them. But the knowledge of God which men reach through philosophy cannot be obtained apart from the plodding and mundane method of science.[8] Knowledge of other than the visible world is philosophically possible only insofar as the visible world is discovered to stand in relationships to something beyond itself. The knowledge of higher things which we gain through philosophy constitutes what St. Thomas considered

[6] This phrase is sometimes quoted in histories of medieval philosophy as the typical thesis of nominalism. It is indeed applicable to much of the antirealistic tradition. Boethius quoted it in his exposition of Aristotle's logic (in his commentary on Porphyry's *Introduction to the Categories*), and Abelard repeated it in his *Glosses* on Porphyry. But it also expresses the position of St. Albert and St. Thomas: it sums up the so-called moderate realism according to which forms resident in material things may become ideas in men's knowing minds.

[7] St. Thomas' denial that the human mind apprehends the eternal forms without prior sensible experience of substances in which these forms are materialized was condemned in 1277 by the bishop of Paris. Ecclesiastical authorities feared St. Thomas' break with Augustinianism. Their fear is evident from the fact that along with his condemnation of St. Thomas' denial of the Augustinian position, the bishop of Paris also condemned over two hundred other points taken chiefly from the Averroists.

[8] This contention, more in accord with Aristotelian naturalism than with Augustinianism, marks a great historic change in the course of European philosophical speculation. It can be taken to indicate the beginning of modernity in philosophy. Franciscan criticisms of Thomism, which began shortly after St. Thomas' death, reacted strongly against his theory of knowledge because of the way in which that theory led on into naturalistic ontology. But modern thought generally operated on the same supposition as St. Thomas, holding that the method of science is the only method available for natural knowledge. Modern thought also generally rejected St. Thomas' reliance on revelation for theological truth, thus making the method of science the only means of knowledge. However much St. Thomas would have deplored many modern developments, his theory of knowledge prepared the way for them.

natural theology. But natural theology, in his view of it, is a branch, not of theology (which in contradistinction to natural theology may be called revealed theology), but of philosophy and rests upon natural knowledge. We do not reach knowledge of God or, indeed, of any substantial reality by a consideration of forms as such. As a genus is not more real than a species subsumed under it, so a form of any degree of abstraction is not more real than the substance of which it is the form. A form is the whatness of a thing. When a form is abstracted from the thing which has that form, the form is an idea, and an idea is the way in which a thing exists in the intellect or the way in which a thing is known. We do not obtain knowledge of reality by arranging abstract forms in some sort of logical hierarchy, though we may and, as St. Thomas believed, do discover a hierarchy of beings. We must therefore, for all branches of natural knowledge —for knowledge of higher realities as well as of lesser realities—begin with an analysis of nature or the visible world. Only after we have reached considerable knowledge by this humble procedure which alone is appropriate for man, can we then go on to reorder the knowledge thus gained according to a hierarchy we discover in being itself.

THE VISIBLE WORLD

Through his espousal of moderate realism and his consequent rejection of St. Augustine's distinction between science and wisdom, St. Thomas was able to introduce much Aristotelian naturalism into his synthesis.

In the order of the growth of our natural knowledge, we begin, St. Thomas held, with the visible world. And when we observe and reflect upon this visible world, we discover many truths about it. Among the truths which St. Thomas expounded about the visible world are the following. (1) The visible world is the realm of composite substances. The substances are composite because, as St. Thomas said in agreement with Aristotle, they are all unions of matter and form. (2) Composite substances are all subject to generation and corruption. (3) While continuing in existence, these substances change in many respects—in size, quality, location, posture, activity, and so forth. Through all such changes, however, they remain the same substances. Thus we discover the difference between substance and accidents.[9] (4) Composite substances are much more potentially than they are actually. They are tendencies toward what they are capable

---

[9] St. Thomas was here re-expressing Aristotle's doctrine in the *Categories*, namely, that of the ten categories one refers to being in a primary sense, and the other nine refer to being in a secondary sense.

of becoming but are not yet and may or may not ever become. They point to fulfillments they may or may not realize. Hence we cannot properly identify the entire being of any composite substance with what at any one time, or even perhaps at all the times of its continued existence, it actually is. (5) Composite substances are contingent. They are contingent in two respects. On the one hand, they are dependent for their generation, for the changes in their successive accidents, and for their corruption, upon other composite substances which are external to them and play upon them from without. On the other hand, they are dependent, in the whole order of their unstable and precarious existence, upon some necessary being which determines the natural order and is not itself exposed to contingency at all. For that which is contingent involves that which is necessary, as that which is below involves that which is above. (6) The realm of composite substances manifests a graduated scale of being, a diversity of kinds within an ordered hierarchy—from inorganic substances, through plants, and animals, to men; and this hierarchy in the realm of composite substances is part of a larger hierarchy which leads on through the various levels of angels to necessary being or God. This hierarchy of being, as we come to understand when once we have demonstrated the existence of God, is known to result from the beneficence of God's creative power.[10]

Hence in natural things species are seen to have been ordered in ascending steps. Compound things are more perfect than the elements; plants, than mineral bodies; animals, than plants; and men, than other animals. Moreover, in certain cases within these main groups, one species is found to be more perfect than the others. Therefore, just as divine wisdom, in order to promote the perfection of the whole, is the cause of differentiation among things, so also it is the cause of the inequality among things. For the whole would not be perfect, if only one degree of goodness were found among things.

(7) The visible world, St. Thomas believed, is teleological throughout. Not simply is every grade of goodness realized in the world, but many types of end are served. Three of these types of end are easily apparent. Every part of the world exists for the sake of its own proper act, as the eye for vision. Every less honorable part exists for the sake of the more honorable, as the senses for the intellect or the stomach for the man. And each and every creature exists for the sake of the whole, and the whole for the sake of showing forth the glory of God.

As we examine this scale of hierarchical being from the lower to the higher stages, we discover, St. Thomas maintained, a difference

[10] *Summa Theologica*, Pt. I, qu. 47, art. 2.

in the way in which form is related to matter. On the lower levels form is so completely embedded in matter that the substances thus constituted manifest no activities apart from the matter in which the form resides. That is, the activities of the lower substances are all material activities. Such are the activities of plants (nutrition, growth, and reproduction) and the further activities of animals (sensation, locomotion, and appetite). On the higher level of the angels, there is no matter at all. Man lies midway between the animals and the angels. Man manifests all the activities of the lower forms of life but also the specifically human activities of thinking and judging. The souls of plants and animals, since their activities depend wholly on bodily organs, are, like their bodies, corruptible and, hence, mortal. And to the degree to which the human soul resembles the lower types of soul, the same conclusion must be drawn. But the mind or intellectual soul is capable of activities which are not bodily and, hence, is free of corruption, has being apart from the body, and is immortal. The intellectual soul has a status which other parts of the human soul do not have. Insofar as the human soul is capable of functioning by itself and apart from the body, it is self-subsistent.

St. Thomas believed he was following the psychology of Aristotle closely. He regarded the human soul as more closely united to the body than did St. Augustine. He reviewed the theories of the ancients and pronounced in favor of Aristotle. The early Greeks, he said, erred in regarding the soul as a corporeal entity. Plato and the Platonists (among whom he included St. Augustine) separated the soul too much from the body. St. Thomas expressly rejected the theory (which he attributed to the Platonists) that the soul is in the body as a sailor is in his ship. Aristotle, he contended, took a sound position between the early Greeks and the Platonists, for Aristotle treated the soul as the form of the organic body. The human embryo, St. Thomas taught, has a vegetative soul from the first moment of its genesis and is able of its own powers to develop into an animal soul. But only so far do the powers of the natural organism go. A miracle then occurs when God infuses into the developing embryo an immaterial and rational soul. But God so infuses the rational soul as to make the entire human soul one unitary form. And as long as a man lives, he is a material being whose form is individuated by his body, as all other composite substances are individuated by matter.[11] But because the intellectual

---

[11] St. Thomas regarded his position as an enlargement of Aristotle's suggestion that the rational soul may exist without the body. Cf. the discussion of Aristotle above, p. 60, n. 31.

soul is not wholly dependent on the matter which individualizes it during the present life, it survives the body. In such survival, however, it requires some body as its natural and eventual manner of existing. The doctrine of the immortality of the soul thus demanded, for St. Thomas as for the Christian tradition generally, a doctrine of the resurrection of the body. St. Thomas' theory of the human soul in its entirety is an unstable conjunction of Aristotelian naturalism and Christian dualism.

St. Thomas believed that there are problems about the visible world which cannot be solved by philosophy, that is, by human reason on the basis of evidences in nature. One such problem, for example, is whether the visible world has always been and will always be or is limited in its duration in time. We know, St. Thomas insisted, that the visible world has existed for but a finite time and that it and time came into existence together. But that knowledge is not part of our natural knowledge. That knowledge comes from faith or revelation. So far as human reason can discover from analysis of the world, both solutions to the problem are tenable, and neither solution can be demonstrated. St. Thomas argued against the Averroist claim to have proved the endless existence of the material world. But he argued against it, not to put an alternative proof in its place, but to show that reason is here dealing with a problem beyond its natural powers. In his own words: [12]

The proposition that the world has not always existed is known by faith alone: it cannot be proved demonstratively . . . For the will of God cannot be investigated by reason, except in regard to those points which it is absolutely necessary for God to will. But what God wills concerning his creatures is not among the absolutely necessary points . . . Hence the proposition that the world had a beginning rests on faith and cannot be demonstrated nor proved. And it is profitable to consider this matter, lest perchance someone, presuming to put forward a demonstration of what is strictly a matter of faith, should entangle himself in specious arguments. And were this to happen, it would give an occasion of ridicule to unbelievers, who would then think that we accept the articles of faith on invalid grounds.

ANGELOLOGY

Composite substances are not the only type of substances. There are also, St. Thomas maintained, simple substances. Simple substances are higher in the hierarchy of being than composite substances, for they

[12] *Summa Theologica*, Pt. I, qu. 46, art. 2.

owe nothing to matter but are immaterial and naturally immortal. Simple substances are the various types of angels—angels, archangels, principalities, powers, cherubim, seraphim, and so forth. They exist in exceeding great numbers, far beyond the number of material or composite substances. St. Thomas worked out his angelology in great detail and with great skill. No two angels, he held, are of the same species, for where things of the same species occur, they require matter for their individuation. "In these substances more than one individual of the same species are not found, but however many individuals there are, just so many are the species." [13] Angels are in a place, not as material substances are, but only insofar as they exercise power upon any place. They can move from place to place, but their motion is not continuous, for they pass from one place to another without passing through the intervening places. Angelology, however, is a branch of knowledge which quickly leads beyond philosophy. Angels are above the range of our human intellects; we can know them, not as they are in themselves, but only indirectly as they affect us. St. Thomas developed his angelology, not from the Aristotelian principles which he used in his analysis of the world of composite substances, but from Neo-Platonic principles, particularly from the Neo-Platonic principle that God's plenitude of being requires that every possible kind of being should actually be. The more St. Thomas turned to consideration of what lies beyond the material world, the more his Aristotelianism was qualified by, and put within the framework of, the Platonic tradition.

PROOFS FOR THE EXISTENCE OF GOD

St. Thomas' theory of the gradation of being culminates in his discussion of God. This discussion contains both Aristotelian and Platonic elements. The Aristotelian influence is apparent in St. Thomas' firmly maintained insistence that the existence of God is not self-evident but requires demonstration and that the demonstration must proceed from such effects of the existence of God as are manifest to us in the world about us. The proposition that God does not exist is indeed false, but it is not self-contradictory. The Platonic or Neo-Platonic influence is apparent in St. Thomas' claim that we human and finite beings cannot know the essence of those levels of the hierarchy of being which are above us. Our natural knowl-

---

[13] *Concerning Essence and Existence*, trans. George G. Leckie (New York, Appleton-Century-Crofts, 1937), p. 23.

edge can go only as far as it is led by sensible things. The blessed, to be sure, have another degree of knowledge: through the infusion of faith they see the essence of God—and at this point St. Thomas appealed to St. Augustine and even used the term *illumination*. But in this mortal life no one can see the essence of God; and even the blessed who receive the light of grace and so are enabled to see the essence of God do yet not fully comprehend God.

St. Thomas gave five proofs for the existence of God. The first three are forms of what has come to be called the cosmological argument. They are so called, because they offer as evidence certain experienced traits of the cosmos or world. They depend upon, or at least they follow, the theological parts of Aristotle's *Metaphysics*. The fourth is a more Platonic argument: it is akin to the argument of St. Anselm in his *Soliloquies*. The fifth is what has come to be called the teleological argument. It is so called because it proceeds on the basis of evidence of design in the world. It is historically the most ancient argument for God in the traditions of Judaism and Christianity and goes back at least to the Psalms. But nowhere did St. Thomas resort to the ontological argument of St. Anselm's *Discourse*. In fact, he explicitly rejected that argument, thus again displaying his boldness as an innovator in his day. Some few Schoolmen of the thirteenth century (of whom St. Albert was one) expressed no critical judgment concerning the ontological argument. Most of the Schoolmen of the first half of that century, however, even if they handled it cautiously, were Augustinian enough to give versions of St. Anselm's ontological argument; they deemed it impossible to deny the existence of God without becoming involved in contradiction. St. Thomas was the first to give philosophical grounds for rejecting it.[14] He had to reject it consistently with his theory that we human beings, though we may know that there are beings higher than ourselves in the hierarchy of existence, cannot know their essence.

The basic form of St. Thomas' cosmological argument for the existence of God is the third of the five arguments in his *Summa Theologica*. The argument is compact. All things in nature are possible to be and not to be, since they are generated and corrupted. But not all beings could be merely possible. For what is merely possible requires for its being something other than itself. Were every possible thing caused by another merely possible thing, all existence would be contingent. But what is contingent requires for its oc-

[14] Once St. Thomas had made his position clear, most Schoolmen rejected the ontological argument, almost as a matter of course.

currence something that is necessary. Therefore there must be something the existence of which is necessary. "This all men speak of as God."

The two other forms of St. Thomas' cosmological argument for the existence of God are, one of them from motion, the other from efficient cause. Motion occurs. But what is moved is moved by another than itself. Motion is passage from potentiality to actuality. What moves another must be actual. And, ultimately, the source of motion must be sheer actuality without potentiality, for otherwise it would require another to act on it and would not be the source of motion. There must therefore be a first mover, moved by no other. And "this all men speak of as God." Similarly, efficient causes occur. But unless, in addition to the host of intermediate causes in the series of causes, there be a first cause, there would be no efficient causes at all. Hence, there must be a first cause. And "this all men speak of as God."

The fourth argument begins with the fact that there are many gradations of goodness in things. Some things are less good, some are more good. But things are less or more good only as they resemble less or more something which has the maximum of goodness. There must therefore be something which is the cause of goodness in all other things. And "this all men speak of as God."

The fifth argument begins with the fact of purpose in the world. Even unthinking natural bodies act for ends and achieve their ends, not fortuitously, but designedly. These things must therefore be directed by some being with intelligence, "as the arrow is directed by the archer." And "this all men speak of as God."

God, as St. Thomas conceived him and argued for his existence in the five proofs, is related to the world which is his creation as the timeless ground to the temporal order. God is first cause, not first chronologically, as if he had existed and acted a long time ago, but first ontologically. That is, God is not the first member of a long series of causes; he is not a member of a series at all. He is outside the series as the ground upon which the whole series depends. So he is unmoved mover, and all else moves as by another; but as unmoved mover, he is equally the source of every motion, of present or future motions as truly as of past motions. Since God is timeless, he has in his being no taint of the merely potential, but, alone among all beings, is sheer actuality. Where all else is contingent, he alone is necessary. And his goodness and purpose are evident in his works. But when one has said of God all that St. Thomas said, one has not said anything significantly positive about the essence of God. Rather, one has spoken about God in terms of God's relation to the world. As the arguments for the existence of God begin with analysis of the world, so the enlightenment to which the proofs lead men's minds is found in a better understanding of the privileges and duties of men in the world. What these privileges and duties are St. Thomas further explained in his treatment of providence and freedom, of evil, of law and miracle, of human virtue, and of the gift of grace.

RELATION OF GOD TO THE WORLD

Since God is first cause of the world and intelligent first cause, the world is the manifestation of God's providence. That the world is at all is expressed in the doctrine of creation; what the world is is expressed in the doctrine of providence. St. Thomas, like St. Augustine, regarded God as timeless in his being, so that God, in his creation and his providence, is related to each and every thing and event as immediately and closely as to all others. But he emphasized, more than could St. Augustine with his Neo-Platonic principles, the causal integrity of finite substances. Providence, he explained, has two aspects: it is the ordering of affairs to an end and the execution of this order. In the former aspect of providence God's purpose is immediate and controlling. In the latter aspect it is realized, in most cases, by subordinate or secondary agents. St. Thomas insisted that in the temporal order finite substances are genuine agents. God is always first cause, because he creates time with the world. But the things he creates are second causes. Second causes are, in St. Thomas' vocabulary for his theory of providence, not merely apparent or illusory causes, but causes which operate with true efficiency within the framework of God's world. St. Thomas spoke frequently of "the dignity of second causes." God created a world in which finite agents would operate with finite degrees of power. There are, as St. Thomas thought we can all directly observe, three kinds of finite agents in the natural world. Some things act without foresight, indeed, without consciousness, as a stone moves downward. Some things act with conscious appetite but without capacity of understanding the import of their instinctive impulses, as a wolf seizes its prey. Men, however, act —at least, they can and sometimes do act—from judgment, that is, from a decision which follows reflection and understanding both of ends sought and of means toward those ends. All three kinds of acts are occasions of natural contingency, because God's providence brought about that kind of a world. But only in the third type of

act is natural contingency turned, through the rational nature of the
agent, into free choice. The stone and the wolf are true agents; but
their acts follow the single course of events which their natures lead
them to perform in the situations in which they exist. Men also are
true agents; but their acts, guided by consideration of the varied
potentialities of the situations about them, are deliberate choices
among these potentialities. Only rational agents can be free agents.
Freedom is a consequence of the concurrence of two factors: natural
contingency and rationality.

Some individual actions [of individual agents] are contingent. And hence,
in these cases, the decision of reason can move in alternate ways and is
not determined to any one single outcome. Therefore, from this very
fact, namely, that man is rational, it is to this extent necessary that he
also have free choice.[15]

Were God a temporal being and only chronologically prior to men's
acts, either God's providence would annul the possibility of human
freedom or human freedom would be an exception to divine providence. But because God is prior to time and the creator of time,
God's providence and human freedom are theoretically consistent
and actually concurrent.

St. Thomas' answer to the problem of evil follows from his doctrine
of providence. The world, as orthodox Christianity has always maintained, is an expression of God's beneficence; yet it contains, as
orthodox Christianity has also always maintained, much evil, both
natural evil and moral evil. In accord with these orthodoxies, St.
Thomas at the same time affirmed that God so created the world that
evil occurs, and he denied that God can properly be spoken of as the
source of evil. There is no defect in God; nor is there defect in his
world. God's very goodness is what makes requisite that both what
is unable to fail in goodness and what is able to fail in goodness occur
in the finite world of creatures. A creation which contained no things
able to fail in goodness would not express adequately the infinite
creativity of God's beneficence. But when there are things able to
fail in goodness and those things are genuine agents, some of them
will fail in goodness and so evils will occur. God's providence orders
a world in which agents will cause evil, and God forsees the occasions
of evil; but though he permits such evil, he does not directly will
it as an entity in itself.

Evils are sometimes classified under two heads, natural and moral.
St. Thomas, however, explained both types in the same manner.

15 *Summa Theologica*, Pt. I, qu. 83, art. 1.

Natural evils such as ravages of physical nature, suffering, and mortality, are an inevitable consequence of finitude of being. Some good things could not be at all unless these evils occurred too. Hence, the evils bear testimony to the amplitude of God's creative beneficence, just as "the introduction of moments of silence makes a chant pleasing." Without them many things could not be which add to the beauty and excellence of the visible world. Moral evils are but a special case of the same finitude of creatures. "There is no such thing as human virtue unless man acts freely." [16] Freedom in rational creatures is a supreme instance of the goodness of God's creation, but it could not occur without the real possibility, and, hence, the occasional actuality, of choice of evil rather than of good by the free finite agents.

St. Thomas developed a theory of miracle in connection with his explanation of the nature of God's providence in order to combat the entirely naturalistic Aristotelianism of the Averroists. The providence of God, he maintained, has established a world in which we find regularity and uniformity in the operation of natural causes and the occurrence of natural effects. But this providence also leaves room for the occasional occurrence of effects without the operation of the proximate causes which normally produce these effects. God, St. Thomas urged, never acts outside the plan which expresses in the temporal order the course of his providence. But he sometimes acts outside that part of his plan which is expressed in the agency he has allotted to his creatures. A miracle can then be defined as an act of God which is outside the usual order assigned to things. Miracles are not due to afterthoughts on God's part, because God is neither before nor after but timeless; nor are they corrections in the general course of his providence. They ensue in God's providence as every particular type of things ensues, namely, because God's creative power requires every possible type of existence to be contained within the structure of the created world. Miracles are a special case of providence; they are related to the regularities of nature as particular providence to general providence.

VIRTUE AND GRACE

St. Thomas' moral philosophy is a synthesis of the humanistic tradition which stems from Plato and Aristotle and of the Christian tradition which stems from St. Paul. It consists accordingly of two

---

[16] For a careful discussion of the problem of evil, see *Summa contra Gentiles,* Bk. III, chap. 71. The phrases quoted above are from chaps. 71, 73.

parts. In the first part St. Thomas dealt with happiness as the fulfillment of the highest potentialities of human nature under the direction of reason; in the second part he dealt with blessedness as that vision of God which goes beyond the natural capacities of men but is possessed by the saints. In exposition of this moral philosophy he gave two lists of virtues: on the one hand, the four natural or cardinal virtues of Plato, temperance, courage, justice, and wisdom; and on the other hand, the three theological or supernatural virtues of St. Paul, faith, hope, and love.

Natural virtues, St. Thomas said, may be classified as moral and intellectual. He here followed Aristotle closely. Moral virtue differs from intellectual virtue, he said, as appetite differs from reason. Speculative insight is the most excellent occupation of mankind. Reason, directed toward that insight (what indeed Aristotle called *theoria*), finds its natural perfection in wisdom, the noblest of the four cardinal virtues. Reason, however, is also needed to guide the passions toward the other three cardinal virtues. In this latter role it leads to prudence and is an element in the achievement of the moral virtues. When a man achieves the four cardinal virtues, he has won natural happiness and has gained his natural good.

St. Thomas' moral philosophy is not as Aristotelian as it at first sounds, partly, of course, because he regarded natural happiness as but a lower stage of full human excellence, partly because he put his Aristotelianism in the context of the Christian tradition of original sin. Men may be capable of understanding the nature of happiness and the conditions of its achievement through the exercise of their natural reason. That fact is indeed made evident from the books of Aristotle and Averroës who both made their analyses without appeal to, or regard for, any more-than-natural basis for morality. But men are not now capable, through their creaturely and sheerly human powers, of achieving the happiness they thus understand. They are burdened by the weight of original sin and cannot proceed far toward even natural happiness without assistance from the grace of God. The so-called "human nature" which would find its perfection in happiness is that integral human nature which Adam had in the state of innocency before the fall. It is not the corrupt human nature which all men have had since the fall. Corrupt human nature must be regenerated through grace before it can become even the theoretical basis for the practice of the cardinal virtues to any satisfactory degree. Only a redeemed man has the kind of nature which would find its fulfillment in happiness.

Furthermore, even in the philosophical statement of the nature of human happiness, St. Thomas was prone to qualify his Aristotelian naturalism by constant references to the dependence of all things upon God. It is true, he granted, that natural happiness is a fulfillment of the capacities of human nature, once human nature is in a state of innocency. That philosopher would then be in error who sought to reduce morality to obedience to any arbitrary fiat, human or divine. But God, as St. Thomas conceived God, is incapable of any arbitrary fiat; God is wholly rational and his will is in accord with his intelligence. Nonetheless, though human nature is what it is and consequently has the natural fulfillment it has, this human nature, like the natures of all creatures, is an expression of divine creativity and providence. God could not have created man as he did create him and then have made natural happiness to be other than what the wise philosopher, through his analysis of human nature, finds the fulfillment of human nature naturally to be. That is, God cannot be conceived as unreasonable. Yet, since the world is God's world, moral philosophy is, in St. Thomas' view, more than a humanistic enterprise; it is also grounded in the will of God.

Man is more than a natural being; he is also an immortal soul. Achievement of all the natural virtues will therefore not lead to man's ultimate end, which is blessedness. Blessedness is not within the range of man's own powers, even when man has been restored to the state of innocency before the fall. It requires the three theological or supernatural virtues and depends upon the unmerited gift to man of divine grace. The object toward which these virtues is directed, as well as the cause which alone can produce them, is God. As God is the most excellent of all objects, so the theological virtues are the noblest state to which man can conceivably be brought. Faith is that intellectual insight which, going beyond natural wisdom, reaches truths not ascertainable by human reason. Hope is that direction of the will toward acts of piety and devotion which may seem foolishness to the natural man but are wisdom to God. And love is the eager joyfulness of union with what faith discerns and hope envisages as of ultimate value. These virtues come, if they come at all, only through infusion; they depend for their inception and their increase on the gift of grace. In their case there is not, as there is with the cardinal virtues, any mean between defect and excess; rather, with them there cannot be excess. Man may be granted some degree of the theological virtues in this present human life, though here they occur precariously and may be possessed only to be lost again. They are securely and adequately enjoyed only by the saints in paradise.

St. Thomas' moral philosophy thus begins with the potentialities of human nature and ends with the vision of God. St. Thomas accepted the humanistic principles of Plato and Aristotle. But he regarded the Greek theory of natural happiness, even as outlined by the two men whom he deemed the greatest of the non-Christian philosophers, as but propaedeutic to a Christian understanding of blessedness. He put the Greek humanistic principles in the context of the Pauline cry for divine aid to carry man beyond the merely natural. The burden of St. Thomas' long discussions of ethical theory is that the soul needs grace throughout its entire progress toward the good. Some knowledge of the good and some slight amount of moral achievement are possible without grace. But grace is needed to heal the natural man of his corruption, to restore human nature to that integrity which it had before the fall, and to raise even that restored human nature toward the divine source, which is also the final end of all things.

POLITICAL THEORY

St. Thomas' political theory, like that of Aristotle, grows out of his ethics. In his subordination of the state to the Church he followed the theory of St. Augustine; but in his respect for the state as a natural and ethically worthy institution he took over some elements from Greek thought. Men, he believed, are incapable of much happiness in isolation from their fellows. They need intimate associations with one another, and these intimate associations need the stability and order which only political institutions can afford. The state is morally requisite for three purposes. First, it regularizes human relations and puts them in their proper hierarchical arrangement. Secondly, it enforces obedience upon the more refractory members of the human family and punishes infringements of social peace and order. And thirdly, its provides the ways and means by which all men may be educated in natural virtues and the Church be given due opportunity to furnish education in theological virtues. The state then can be considered to be in accord with God's will for mankind. However much St. Augustine distinguished the state from the earthly city, the influence of Augustinianism was to associate the state with corruption and evil. St. Thomas' political theory rescued the state from this kind of sinister association. Far from being intrinsically evil, the state, St.

Thomas made clear, is an expression of reason and has legitimate and ideal ends.

St. Thomas' political theory centers in the conception of law. Law is of several sorts: human law, natural law, divine law. But generically, law is a principle of reason for the promotion of the common welfare, promulgated by whoever has responsibility for the protection of that common welfare. God has such responsibility, and the divine law is the supreme law. Human reason has such responsibility on a lesser scale and over a smaller area, and natural law (which is the rules of right reason) is the objective standard of morality. The ruler of a state has such responsibility, too, even if to a still smaller degree, and so human law deserves respect and obedience. Civil statutes, however, are properly law only when they conform to the generic definition of law. That is, they deserve respect and obedience only insofar as they implement natural law and follow the instruction of divine law. St. Thomas' political theory thus recognizes the right, even the duty, of men to refuse submission to bad law and to revolt against a wicked ruler. But St. Thomas was far from inciting men to rebellion. He believed that occasions for rebellion would seldom arise; he insisted that individual citizens be patient in venturing to make judgments at variance with those of the established authorities; and he even advised men humbly to accept a wicked ruler as God's punishment upon them for their sins. In the actual vicissitudes of life, men would be wise, instead of hastening into open strife with the state, to repent, to pray, and to throw themselves on God's mercy. St. Thomas' incisive logic in thinking through the implications of his generic definition of law was thus tempered by his respect for the established order.

As natural virtue is but propaedeutic to theological virtue, so the state is by its very nature subordinate to the Church. The state is concerned with the natural man and natural happiness; the Church is concerned with the whole man and his blessedness. Men are dependent to some degree upon the state for their temporal happiness, but they are completely dependent upon the Church for their salvation. The best life, St. Thomas concluded, is the religious life in which all else that men prize is valued for its contribution to more adequate possession of a vision of God.

THE THOMISTIC TRADITION

Thomism and Augustinianism, which may be summarily if inexactly characterized respectively as Aristotelian and Platonic Christianity, remain the two outstanding achievements of philosophy in Christendom. Sharing many convictions which through their joint authority have become the orthodoxy of Catholic faith in the western world, they nevertheless stand in other respects in marked contrast. The contrast between them is consequent upon their different theories of knowledge more than upon anything else. St. Augustine distinguished wisdom from science, elevating the insight of the former above the plodding hesitations of the latter. From his influence on this point have come all the subsequent theologies and philosophical idealisms which, after granting the right of scientists to carry on investigations of the natural world, have virtually despised the results of scientific inquiry as indifferent to men's more lofty concerns and have formulated the guiding ideas of faith in complete or nearly complete independence of the methods and conclusions of the sciences. St. Thomas rejected this dichotomy in the intellectual life. He insisted that faith has its role to play as well as reason, so that theology is not dependent upon, though it may well be significantly aided by, philosophy. But he as firmly maintained that knowledge has its human origins in men's sensory contacts with the visible world, and that no scientific or philosophical certainties can be reached apart from observations of the course of natural events. From his influence on this point come all the subsequent theologies and reasoned cosmologies which, acknowledging revelation and exulting in a faith founded on authority, nevertheless recognize that natural theology and natural religion must submit to the same tests and adduce the same kind of evidence as do the physical and social sciences.

The historian, however, ought to add that the difference between the Augustinian and Thomistic traditions is more marked than that between the personal attitudes of St. Augustine and St. Thomas. For, on the one hand, St. Augustine as truly as St. Thomas recognized a legitimate place in human affairs for curiosity about the visible world and for the pursuit of scientific understanding of that world. And on the other hand, St. Thomas did not himself, any more than St. Augustine, wish to devote time and thought to scientific matters. St. Thomas did not share the concern which his teacher St. Albert evinced for observation of, and experiment with, natural substances and processes. St. Thomas made an amazing synthesis, perhaps the supreme synthesis, of certain philosophical traditions. But his writings did not reflect, as did, for example, the writings of the Aristotle on whom he deeply depended, all the human interests which, as he himself granted, men may properly cherish. In his own century the claims of natural science were beginning to be voiced, as in St. Albert and in Roger Bacon, and these claims were pressed in the immediately ensuing centuries with increased vigor. New philosophies were bound to arise to express the significance of the scientific interests and pursuits. And the very fact that St. Thomas had praised Aristotle as "the philosopher" and had fought for respectful appreciation of the soundness of many Aristotelian principles—this very fact is probably the historical reason why Aristotle soon fell into disrepute with scientific workers and scientifically inclined philosophers. St. Thomas' lack of personal interest in science made him willing merely to cite scientific opinions of Aristotle as satisfactory. And since some of these opinions, though incidental to the fundamental philosophical principles of Aristotle, were based on inadequate evidence and often were mistaken, St. Thomas led scientifically inclined thinkers to regard Aristotle as an obstacle to scientific advance. So it came about that the philosophies of science which appeared after St. Thomas had an Aristotelian as well as a Thomistic animus.

Thomism has remained and is today one of the great traditions of western culture. Although St. Augustine rather than St. Thomas was the ancient authority to which Protestant thinkers, both in the early days of the Protestant Reformation and again in our own time, have most frequently appealed, St. Thomas has more and more become the officially sanctioned authority of Catholic theology and of Catholic scholarship generally. Under St. Thomas' influence the Catholic Church has contended that reasoned arguments and reasoned demonstrations are of value to theology. It has been unwilling to view theology as entirely a matter of revelation, and it has been suspicious of appeals to intuition or nonreasoned ventures of faith. It has condemned as a dangerous heresy the so-called fideism according to which men's natural powers of reason are unable to reach a knowledge which contributes to the support of orthodox faith.

Catholic historians sometimes call Thomism the supreme synthesis. St. Augustine had already synthesized, as was said above, ideas from Plato and from the Jewish-Christian theistic tradition, especially from St. Paul. St. Thomas brought Aristotelian ideas into his synthesis, boldly using even such Aristotelian writers as were enemies of Christianity. He thus modified the Augustinian synthesis notably; he modified it in the direction of naturalism in its theory of the visible world and in the direction of empiricism in its theory of human knowledge. Thomism is the last great synthesis of its kind. It is the last great synthesis which took pains to weigh the merits of the philosophies of the ancient world and to build together such elements of those philosophies as were deemed true and so had their proper place in a comprehensive system of thought. It is thus a culmination and a termination of a long period of intellectual history.

VII

The Late Middle Ages

Duns Scotus, c. 1266–1308, possibly English, more probably Scotch. Entered the Franciscan Order. Studied and taught at Oxford, then Paris. In 1307 he was sent to Cologne, where he died. Many treatises were attributed to him. Some of these are almost surely spurious, though from what may be called the Scotist School. Among the genuine writings are two commentaries on *The Sentences,* certain other logical treatises, *Questions on the Metaphysics, Quodlibeta,* and *De Primo Principio.* He has been called the Subtle Doctor.

William of Ockham, c. 1280–1349, was born in Surrey, England. He entered the Franciscan Order and studied and taught at Oxford. His writings include a commentary on *The Sentences,* commentaries on Aristotle, *Quodlibeta,* and certain logical treatises. He became a protagonist of the Emperor Louis IV against the pope (during the early days of the papal residence at Avignon). His political writings in defense of the supremacy of the secular power in political affairs influenced Marsiglio of Padua (1270–1343), author of *Defensor Pacis.*

1. THE DECLINE OF SCHOLASTICISM

THE PERIOD FROM the death of St. Thomas Aquinas to the fifteenth century is one which exhibits a reaction against the Thomistic confidence in reason as a means of establishing a systematic body of truth about the natural and supernatural worlds. The two most notable Scholastics of the period were Duns Scotus and William of Ockham. Their philosophies were consciously opposed to that of St. Thomas. They espoused a position which is generally called voluntarism in contrast with St. Thomas' intellectualism. They were, to a considerable extent, critics of the mainstream of Scholasticism throughout the entire Middle Ages. For in spite of vigorous protests on the part of certain nominalists, the chief Scholastics of the ninth to thirteenth centuries regarded reason as an ally of revelation in the quest for truth. So much so is this true that confidence in the powers of reason is a leading characteristic of Scholasticism in the days of its finest achievements. And by contrast, and in this specific sense, then, the late Middle Ages mark a decline in the vigor and the hopes of Scholasticism.

Whether Scholasticism after St. Thomas suffered a decline in a more general sense is a moot point at the present time. The great authority which St. Thomas has exercised has led historians to neglect, until recently, the philosophies of Duns Scotus and William of Ockham. Confusion in regard to Duns has been promoted by ascribing to him certain writings which almost surely are not his and by reading back into him the not altogether consistent views of some of his followers. Scholars are now at work upon the documents which have come down to us from the late Middle Ages and will probably soon throw light upon the authorship, dates, and significance of these writings. Until these writings are sorted out, competently edited, and made more available, we are bound to view Duns Scotus and William of Ockham in the half-adequate manner current in recent decades, that is, to treat them primarily as foils for St. Thomas.

The philosophy of Duns Scotus is particularly difficult to determine and to assess. Oxford, where Duns and William were trained, has often been regarded as a center of an Augustinian revival, and affiliations of the thought of the two men with the Augustinian tradition have been pointed out. But Duns at least, and possibly William also, seems in some important respects to be more Aristotelian than St. Thomas himself. The place of Duns and William in the development of philosophical thought cannot therefore be understood clearly until many detailed points of scholarship have first been settled. Duns has often been called a "destroyer of systems" and has been deemed a witty and caustic critic who aimed to bring his predecessors' ideas into ridicule. And, in turn, he has himself been made the butt of others' hasty jibes.[1] For example, he has been twitted for concerning himself with the question of how many angels can dance on the point of a needle. But in raising this seemingly pert question, he was really dealing with the serious problem (treated before him by St. Thomas) of how immaterial substances like angels may manifest themselves

---

[1] The English word *dunce* was derived from his name. But the point of this etymology is not evident until one realizes that dunce originally meant a caviling sophist rather than a stupid person.

under the spatial limitations to which all material substances are subject. Even when viewed in the half-adequate fashion recently current, Duns Scotus and William of Ockham stand out as able thinkers; and further study may show them to be philosophers of great stature.

2. DUNS SCOTUS

DUNS SCOTUS is notable in the history of ideas for his advocacy of voluntarism over against what he regarded as the excessive intellectualism of St. Thomas. He held that God is infinite and almighty will, and fearlessly faced the implications of this position. God does not will what he does will because he is in any way restrained by his reason. That is, God does not will what he does will because he has first judged what he wills to be good. Rather, he wills freely, and then he sees that what he wills is good. God's creation is not guided by an antecedent plan formulated through his own eternal ideas. Indeed, there are not, Duns maintained over against St. Thomas, any ideas *ante rem* in the mind of God. God's will is absolute in the sense that his will is determined, not merely by nothing outside him, but by nothing within him. The created world, consequently, is an expression, not of eternal reason, but of almighty power.

Duns agreed with a number of St. Thomas' principles. But he modified, in the light of his voluntaristic position, the significance of these principles.

Duns agreed with St. Thomas, for example, in making a distinction between theology and philosophy. But he limited, much more rigorously than had St. Thomas, the area of natural theology. He accepted the argument for the existence of God from the contingency of the world. But he rejected the argument from motion. The latter argument, he pointed out, begins by proclaiming the principle that whatever moves owes its motion to something outside itself, but then passes to the idea of a cause which moves but owes its motion to nothing outside itself. There may be an unmoved mover, but the existence of an unmoved mover cannot be demonstrated from a premise contradictory to the conclusion drawn. Furthermore, Duns continued, an unmoved mover, if there be such, might very well not be identical with what men call God.

In similar fashion Duns criticized St. Thomas' arguments for the immortality of the soul. One of St. Thomas' arguments, Duns noted, rests on the assumption that every natural human desire (such as man's desire to survive death) is somehow fulfilled in a universe which manifests divine benevolence. But the lower animals, Duns said in comment, as truly as man, have the desire to survive death, and a denial of immortality to the lower animals is not taken to be a challenge of divine benevolence. Another of St. Thomas' arguments for immortality, Duns went on to insist, utilizes the assumption that a function like reason (which may indeed be performed without any specific organ on which it depends) is not subject to dissolution with the body. But Duns put forward the suggestion that what does not depend on any specific organ may yet depend on the manner in which the many bodily organs are arranged in their mutual interrelationships.

To seek to establish theological doctrines by philosophical means, Duns asserted, is often to confuse proof with a plausibility which is relative to the hopes and fears of particular men. We are much less able than St. Thomas supposed to prove by reason the doctrines of the faith. Theology is properly a matter of revelation, and knowledge through reason is knowledge of the natural world. Reason is unable to prove the existence or to ascertain the nature of that which is prior to reason. Reason in God himself is recognition and understanding of whatever his free and unconstrained will brings into being. Reason in man is basically acceptance of God's creation, once man has encountered, or insofar as he has encountered, this creation and has discerned its nature. Once existence is given, human reason may know it, may rationally conclude what it involves, may rationally discover what is desirable for man to pursue or to avoid. But since reason does not determine God's will, reason cannot possibly be used to investigate the ground of the created world.

Duns agreed with St. Thomas, for another example, in affirming the principle that man in his present state gains all his natural knowledge from direct observation of the substances in the world about him. But, unlike St. Thomas, he regarded man's cognitive life as subject to the same limitations to which man's powers of observation are subject. Man cannot, by his natural reason, reach knowledge of objects which lie beyond those he has come in contact with by means of his senses. Man cannot justifiably treat these objects as effects and then presume to make inferences therefrom concerning some supposedly higher level of being. Duns accepted St. Thomas' own principle that man must encounter forms *in re* in order to have ideas *post rem.* He interpreted this principle, as St. Thomas did not, to limit philosophy to analysis of the visible world.

In both God and man, Duns maintained, the will is primary and the intellect subordinate. God's will provides the being which his intellect then knows. And while man's reason begins with assent to what God's will has created and hence consists in conformity to God's will, his will is not bound to follow the instruction of his reason. Man may be guided, if he so chooses, by his knowledge; but he may not choose to be so guided. Even when his will is guided by knowledge, his will is not so determined. For he can always turn from what knowledge discloses as good and will otherwise. Man's will is a free power which in every resolution could have chosen something different from what it actually does choose. Freedom therefore is not rationality in action; nor does man's salvation depend on his understanding. Man's salvation depends rather upon an act of will which harmonizes his will with that divine will which is prior to even the divine reason and therefore surely beyond the powers of merely human reason to investigate.

3. WILLIAM OF OCKHAM

WILLIAM OF OCKHAM brought together the voluntarism of Duns Scotus and a thoroughgoing nominalism, thus pressing the anti-Thomistic criticisms of Duns to yet more radical conclusions.

The most common allusion in general literature to the philosophy of William of Ockham is to what has come to be called Ockham's razor.[2] This maxim called his razor, however, is so fundamental in William's thinking that it may well serve as introduction to any sketch of his ideas. The Latin words William used are *Entia non multiplicanda sunt praeter necessitatem*. That is, in free translation, "no one ought in making an explanation to assume more than the minimum necessary." One ought not to postulate undiscernible entities as a purported ground for the occurrence of what is evident and may well be sufficient in itself. One ought not to entertain unverifiable hypotheses as satisfactory ways of accounting for experienced facts. Rather, one ought, in choosing between different possible theories, to prefer the simpler or less elaborate. William developed the principle of his razor in different contexts and, hence, in different forms. He applied the principle, among other problems, to the problem of

---

[2] The metaphor of the razor is due to the idea that the maxim shaves thought and removes all undesirable growths from it.

the relations of theology and philosophy and to the century-old problem of the nature and status of universals.

All theology, William held, is revealed theology. Man can formulate all sorts of possible theological hypotheses, but he cannot establish by reason the truth of any of these speculative possibilities. The various proffered arguments for the existence of God, William claimed, are none of them satisfactory as demonstrations. They are at best *credibilia,* that is, propositions believed, not propositions proved. They may indeed be persuasive to those who already believe, but they all rest on assumptions which are not critically examined. Even the argument from contingency (which Duns Scotus retained) is dubious. We observe the world, but we do not know whether it depends on one necessary being or whether, if it does rest on one necessary being, that being is God or whether, if that being is God, God has the attributes affirmed of him in Christian faith. William was a devout Catholic and orthodox in his acceptance of the dogmas of the Church. But he maintained that theology is, from the point of view of human reason, quite arbitrary, and that reason is, from the point of view of theology, utterly irrelevant. Since, as he held in common with Duns, God's will is not grounded in reason, God's will cannot be demonstrated; it can only be disclosed. We know by revelation that God loves all men; but so far as reason could ascertain, God might be indifferent or hostile. We know by revelation that God instituted the Church as his channel of grace for men; but so far as reason could ascertain, God might have established some other scheme of salvation or none at all. We know by revelation that God was incarnate in the man Jesus; but so far as reason could ascertain, God might have become incarnate in an ass or a stone or not incarnate at all.

As with theological doctrines, so with moral principles. Voluntarism led William to fiat morality. Moral principles are not rational but arbitrary. God has ordained, for example, that theft and adultery are wicked. But he could by his will make those acts good, though he has not done so. What is right and what is wrong are consequent to the unconstrained will of God.

William upheld a rather extreme form of nominalism. Everything which exists is a unique individual. Genera and species are not in things as their natures. As Duns had denied that universals are *ante rem* in the mind of God, so William went on to deny that they are *in re.* Universals are only *post rem* as ideas in the mind. Moreover, universals are vague ideas. They are mental representations which serve as signs of groups of things but are so blurred that they serve loosely as signs for any one of a number of things but for no one of the things exactly. A precise and wholly clear idea is the sign of a single object. The more universal an idea is, the more objects it indicates, but also the more vaguely it indicates those objects. A general proposition, therefore, is a rough summary of partial information about a number of single facts; and insofar as our knowledge of these single facts depends on the general proposition, our knowledge is inadequate to the many single facts. Just as there is no knowledge of existing things without direct experience of them, so there is no entirely adequate knowledge of them apart from sense experience. There is a disparity between the unique individuals in the world about us and the inadequate universals we entertain in our minds.

William drove home his point by making a distinction between two sorts of propositions: those about concrete things and those about relations among our universal ideas. And there is a consequent distinction between two sorts of science. On the one hand, propositions about concrete things rest upon direct experience of individuals insofar as we note both *that* the individuals are and also *what* they are. Such are the propositions that Socrates is white and that man is an animal. We know such propositions insofar as they state what we have already been aware of in observation of the existing individuals with which the propositions are concerned.[3] The natural sciences (physics, botany, mineralogy, and so forth) are comprised of such propositions and aim to give as much truth as possible about the existing world. On the other hand, propositions about our universal ideas do not refer to things directly observed and are not concerned with truth. Such are the propositions that black is not white and that baldness is lack of hair. We know such propositions by examining the necessary relations among ideas and without reference to existing things. Logic is the science which enables us to deal with these propositions, and logic, therefore, is concerned not with truth but with validity. The logician *qua* logician does not care whether or not his propositions correspond to existing objects. He is explicating the relations among ideas rather than exploring relations among objects, and he has no assurance, and he desires no assurance, that the relations among ideas are in accord with the relations among objects.

The radical nature of William's reaction against Thomism was

---

[3] William used the phrase *notitia intuitiva* for direct observation of concrete individuals. The word *intuitive* in English, however, has connotations which make it difficult to use in translation of this phrase. *Notitia intuitiva* is a prelogical awareness which includes both sensation and intellectual discernment of what it is that is present in sensation.

a consequence of his joint affirmation of voluntarism and nominalism. He was driven to deny that logic can be utilized to determine that a certain thing exists, what that certain thing is, and how that certain thing is related to other things. Logic is not a tool for obtaining knowledge of any matters of fact.

4. THE END OF THE MIDDLE AGES

THE LAST CENTURY or century and a half of the Middle Ages contributed little of note to the history of philosophy. Quarrels between Thomists and Scotists, embittered by rivalries between Franciscans and Dominicans, did hardly more than provide opportunity for making exaggerated restatements of points already more carefully made. In these quarrels one may see zeal for partisan advantage rather than disinterested search for truth. For example, some Scotists pressed the distinction between theology and philosophy to a bizarre extreme. They went so far in their opposition to intellectualism as to maintain that what is true in theology may be false in philosophy and vice versa. A Christian, one of them said, is a person who accepts on the basis of authority what his reason finds absurd. Emphasis on the arbitrariness of the divine will led at times to skepticism. There may really be no natural substances, it was suggested. For if God's power is absolute, he may cause us to have perceptions of what are seemingly substances, even though none such exists. Thus there is no ground upon which reason may proceed to investigate the natural world, because, indeed, there is no evidence that a natural world exists at all.

Scholasticism, through its lack of great minds to guide it along sound lines, came to a dreary end.[4] The distinction which William of Ockham made between natural science and logic, in a fashion unforeseen by him, hastened this disastrous outcome. For Scholastic philosophers were inclined to leave the natural sciences to specialists and in secular hands and to occupy themselves with logical matters. But if logic be unconcerned with questions about concrete things, it turns out to have no significant subject-matter. Scholasticism in its latest phase thus seemed to degenerate into dialectical futilities and into what modern philosophers regarded as unprofitable logic-chop-

---

[4] Scholastic philosophy has been revived in the nineteenth and twentieth centuries. Its revival was due largely to a desire to combat the secularism toward which modern philosophy progressively tended. Recent scholasticism has been predominantly Thomistic, though not exclusively so. Its revival aimed to recover a rational basis for theological dogmas and a rational theory of the relation of God and man or God and the world.

ping. And so the very term *Scholastic,* like the term *Sophistic* in the fourth century B.C., became a term of reproach. The rich content of earlier Scholasticism was forgotten, and Scholasticism was identified with verbal trickery. The fate overtook Scholasticism which is prone to occur whenever preoccupation with methodology supplants the investigation of concrete affairs.

Contemporary with the decline of Scholasticism went a conspicuous revival of mysticism. Mysticism, of course, is not an exclusively medieval development. It runs through the many centuries of western culture and flowered repeatedly and in many contexts. It was a phase of many of the great systems of thought of earlier and later times. We encounter it in St. Thomas, Pseudo-Dionysius, St. Augustine, and emphatically in Plotinus; we encounter it, according to some critics, even in such parts of Plato as the ladder of love in *The Symposium* and the ecstatic treatment of the form of good in *The Republic.* We encounter it again in many of the Protestant leaders, like Luther himself, in the Cambridge Platonists of the seventeenth century, and in many poets of modern literature. But in the fourteenth century mysticism flourished as a compensation for the growing barrenness of philosophy. The historian may say that in the fourteenth century mysticism became, not a phase of philosophical systems, but a self-sufficient system of philosophy. Feeling, in the sense of an alleged immediate consciousness of the presence of God, was made an autonomous ground for religious faith, and reason and its labored arguments were sometimes looked upon as distractions and worse than useless diversions.[5] The philosophical consequences of such mysticism were skepticism concerning the role of reason, voluntarism, individualism, and attention to the inner life of man rather than to the natural world.

Medieval philosophy or Scholasticism was a richly diversified group of theories and systems. There was no more one medieval philosophy than there was one Hellenistic philosophy. There were many medieval philosophies, presenting different, often antithetical, views. Medieval philosophies can be characterized collectively for their primary concern with the existence of God and the relation of God to the world, also, though less consistently, for their respect for the integrity of human reason as a tool of investigation. When that tool was no longer deemed capable of investigating the problems of primary concern, medieval philosophy declined and ended.

[5] Prominent mystics of the fourteenth century include John Eckhart (c. 1260–1327), John Tauler (c. 1300–1361), Henry Suso (1295–1365), and John Ruysbroeck (1293–1381). Two anonymous mystical writings also deserve mention: *Imitatio Christi* (c. 1400) and the much later *Theologia Germanica* (c. 1516).

PART THREE

MODERN PHILOSOPHY

VIII

The Transition to Modern Philosophy

1. A BREAK WITH THE PAST

MODERN PHILOSOPHY involved a marked break in the continuity of ideas in the history of western culture. The great systems of philosophic thought which were formulated in the seventeenth, eighteenth, and nineteenth centuries (the period of time which the term *modern* here indicates) were concerned with new problems and followed new methods of inquiry. The break between modern philosophy and all the philosophical speculations of earlier times was not accidental; it was a result of a deliberate desire and intent on the part of the early modern philosophers. At no other moment in the long history of western culture did so extensive a break occur. Plato commented upon and made rejoinders to the Pythagoreans and Sophists; Aristotle often opened his discussions of a subject by reviewing the opinions of his predecessors. Hellenistic thinkers utilized ideas borrowed from Hellenic philosophers. The Dark Ages, to be sure, were a long interruption in the productivity of western philosophy; but when philosophical activity began again in the ninth century and continued through the Middle Ages, the Schoolmen were proud to cite views of the ancients, the Bible, the Church fathers, and such writers as Boethius and Pseudo-Dionysius. Modern philosophy began not so much after an interruption as after a break. So much so is this true that 1600 (or some such date) marks a more complete break in the continuity of western philosophy than any other date which could be mentioned.

The extent of the break can be illustrated by reference to the words of Francis Bacon and René Descartes, the first great philosophic figures of modern times and the oft-styled founders of modern philosophy. The views of these two men were sharply opposed on many points. But they were nonetheless alike in their distrust of tradition and authority and in their confident reliance on their own personal resources to reach truth. Bacon used vituperative language in referring to the leading philosophers of his own day and all previous times. He called them defilers of truth and falsifiers of things. He did speak somewhat kindly of Democritus (for his honest materialism and his denial of final causes in nature) and scarcely less so of Plato (for his inductive method of investigation). But he denounced Aristotle for substituting words for thoughts and spoke of Aristotle's logic as largely verbiage. He damned Scholasticism as a degenerate version of Aristotelianism; he accused the Schoolmen of supposing that whenever they made a verbal distinction they were discovering real differences among things. Similarly with Descartes. Descartes wrote that "no single thing is to be found in philosophy which is not subject to dispute and, in consequence, is not dubious." He therefore resolved, in regard to all the opinions he had been taught, that he "could not do better than endeavor once for all to sweep them completely away, so that they might later be replaced, either by others which were better, or by the same, when they had been submitted to the scrutiny of reason." [1] Bacon and Descartes both believed that dependence on tradition was a baleful catastrophe and reliance on authority was abject cowardice. A serious seeker after truth, they held, ought surely to make a fresh start, to begin anew, to build his own foundations, to free himself from the incubus of errors which had led men of previous ages astray.

This deliberate rejection of dependence on the past led Bacon and Descartes to formulate new methods whereby truth, they supposed, could be more surely won. Bacon wrote his *Novum Organum,* or new tool, for reflective procedure. His choice of his title was a deliberate rebuke to Aristotle, whose logical writings had collectively long been called the *Organon*. Descartes' first published work was his *Discourse on the Method of Rightly Conducting the Reason and Seeking the Truth in the Sciences*. The two proffered methodologies are strikingly different and on some points opposed; but the aim of the two authors is the same. Their common aim was to teach a method which anyone can then follow so as to be certain of avoiding old blunders and of reaching reliable knowledge. Descartes opened his *Discourse* with the striking sentence: "Good sense is of all things in the world the most equally distributed among men." [2] That is, all

---

[1] *Discourse on Method*, Pts. I and II.

[2] Some critics have alleged that Descartes was being highly ironic in this sentence. But these critics fail to realize the intensity with which Descartes sponsored his method as a tool whereby anyone could proceed with assurance.

men have a native capacity for reaching truth, and, moreover, they will succeed in reaching truth if only they are given a cue as to the proper manner in which to utilize their capacity. Equipped with clear understanding of the right method, men can supposedly look forward to further and further extension of knowledge of the world about them and can thus progress to greater and greater achievements in the ordering of human affairs. Bacon taught that by knowledge of nature's ways men could establish a kingdom over nature. And Descartes proclaimed that by use of his method men would become "masters and possessors of nature." Descartes appended to his *Discourse* three essays (on optics, meteorology, and analytical geometry) as samples of the way in which his method can lead to profitable results, and he appealed to intellectuals everywhere to join him in further research. Neither Bacon nor Descartes saw any natural limits to the increase of human knowledge of the world around us. Neither of them saw any insurmountable obstacles to improving the comforts of life and the happy ordering of human affairs. Adoption of a new and proper method, each of them believed, is the key to a glorious future.

Not all subsequent philosophers in modern times shared the serene confidence of Bacon and Descartes in the sufficiency of making a fresh start with a new method. Some of them, struggling with the problem of relating the opposed Baconian and Cartesian methods, found that a definition of a truly satisfactory method was itself the most baffling of problems. Some of them found that any definition they gave of a supposedly sound method put unforeseen obstacles in the way of using that method to reach assured conclusions about other matters. And so some of them were reluctantly driven to skepticism instead of optimistic reliance on their own powers. But from the hopeful announcement of the Baconian method of induction at the outset of the seventeenth century to the defiant proclamation of the Marxian method of dialectics in the nineteenth century, a resolute confidence in the power of a new method keeps on emerging in various contexts. And whether confidence in methodology be preserved or skepticism prevail, modern philosophy throughout the three centuries of its history is characterized by the Baconian-Cartesian distrust of the past and a desire to make a fresh start.[3] To make a fresh start, modern philosophers generally supposed, is to make a better start. To begin

---

[3] Spinoza, it ought to be added, had more knowledge of, and more respect for, tradition than any other of the great modern philosophers. He is, however, the least typical philosopher of modern times.

anew, they not infrequently supposed, is a necessary precondition of progress.

One significant consequence of the break which modern philosophers made with traditions of the past is that they became preoccupied with epistemological problems. Modern philosophy is predominantly and persistently epistemological. Modern thinkers, of course, were concerned with metaphysical, ethical, political, even theological problems, too. But in most cases they began with theory of knowledge, inquiring into how knowledge may best be obtained and what its nature and limits are. And when they went on to other considerations, their views were usually determined, if not wholly, at least in large part, by the implications of their prior answers to the epistemological problems. Their theories of the world often resulted not so much from discoveries which came from direct investigations of various things in the world as from implications which they were compelled to draw from their own epistemological premises and conclusions. Many scientists during modern times were indeed engaged in direct investigations of the structure of the world and of some of the particular things in that world. Bacon and Descartes conceived of themselves as participating in those investigations, even as organizing and taking the initiative in them. But after the middle of the seventeenth century modern philosophers were more and more drawn, by their very preoccupation with problems of methodology, into speculations concerning the origin, nature, and limits of knowledge. They sometimes intended their speculations to be appraisals of the methods scientists were using. But they sometimes found that their speculations led them to doubts as to the reliability of the conclusions the scientists reached. The medieval distinction between philosophy and theology thus was succeeded by a distinction between philosophy and science. More conspicuously than ever before in western culture, the relation between philosophy and science became itself a controversial philosophical problem. That such a problem became central for philosophy is an outcome of the modern temper.

2. THE BACKGROUND OF MODERN PHILOSOPHY

MODERN PHILOSOPHY, though it involved a break with traditions from ancient and medieval philosophy, was conditioned in important respects by new social and intellectual forces of the sixteenth and seventeenth centuries. Those two centuries were a time of vast changes in many phases of western culture. Geographical explorations opened up new areas of the earth to the knowledge of western Europe. Trade expanded beyond the old feudal boundaries, and evidences of a new capitalistic economy appeared. National states gradually supplanted the older feudal ties. A growing middle class slowly arose and pressed for a share in political power. But the most important of the new influences for the course of modern philosophy were the Renaissance, the Protestant Reformation, and momentous developments in astronomy and other physical sciences. These many changes were inter-related in complex fashion.

THE RENAISSANCE

The Renaissance was initially a literary movement. The rebirth, which the word indicates, was a revival of interest in more of the ancient authors than the Schoolmen had found useful to their purposes. Many of these ancient authors were innocently or even aggressively secular in their views. The Renaissance began at least as early as Petrarch (1304–1374), who, although only slightly later than Dante, exhibited different attitudes on many points. Petrarch and other so-called Humanists felt a growing hostility to the Scholastic manner of treating ancient literature; they disliked the way in which the Schoolmen treated that literature primarily as a source for opinions on the problems they themselves were considering. The Humanists exulted in the classics for their intrinsic beauty and their worldly wisdom. Their appeal to the classics was virtually a quest for new attitudes to the dignity of the individual (in his freedom from ecclesiastical control), to the world of nature (in its own integrity and apart from its dependence on supernature), and to personal experience (in contrast to submission to tradition). Man, the Humanists learned from the classics, was a rational being, autonomous in many fields of human concern, privileged to pursue his chosen ends without constant supervision by authority. The spirit of the Renaissance was enormously furthered by the invention of printing presses and the consequent accelerated distribution of books. Pico della Mirandola (1462–1493) wrote *Oration on the Dignity of Man,* in which he said: "The beneficent God has given to man to have whatever he (man) chooses and to be whatever he (man) wills." Castiglione (1478–1529) wrote *Book of the Courtier,* in which he pictured the excellent man in a manner reminiscent of Plato, adding thereto a praise of the courtly activities common at the palaces of Italian princes. As the Renaissance spread from Italy to northern countries, it often became more religious in its affiliations (as in Erasmus of Rotterdam, 1466–1536) and more impassioned for economic and political reform (as in St. Thomas More of England, 1478–1535). It reached its apogee, perhaps, in the essays of Montaigne (1533–1592), whose Catholicism was outward and nominal and whose vast learning in the classics enabled him to become a wise commentator on the customs, foibles, and ideals of his own day. The influence of the Renaissance was to increase respect for the individual, to break down subservience to authority, to make men ready to question established customs, and to foster reliance on the critical powers of human reason.

THE REFORMATION

The Protestant Reformation in the sixteenth century was in some ways akin to the Renaissance in its influence and in one important respect antithetical thereto.

Leaders of the Reformation promoted both the individualism of the Renaissance and the concern of the Renaissance for the present world and social affairs. Luther (1483–1546) wrote at the outset of his *Christian Liberty:* "The Christian man is most free lord of all and subject to none; he is most dutiful servant of all and subject to everyone." He fought for the right, and the duty, of each individual man to settle fundamental matters of religious faith in the light of his own conscience; and Protestants have repeatedly emphasized this contention in the doctrine of the universal priesthood of all believers. This individualism was even more thorough than that of most of the Renaissance Humanists; for although the Renaissance Humanists usually remained faithful sons of the Catholic Church in matters of religion, Protestant reformers insisted, in principle, on entire freedom for the individual in both the formulation of dogma and the acceptance of ecclesiastical control. Exigencies of political strife between Protestant groups and the Catholic Church, and soon among differing Protestant groups, led some Protestants to seek to enforce conformity in faith and discipline upon members of their own groups. But the genius of Protestantism was thoroughly individualistic, and more and more, as Protestantism developed and quick new orthodoxies were proclaimed by successive Protestant leaders, the influence of Protestantism was so individualistic as to be divisive and chaotic.

Protestantism was also akin to the Renaissance in emphasizing the importance of activity in the social affairs of the present world. Luther firmly maintained the doctrine of justification by faith (not by works). But he maintained that doctrine, as had St. Paul, with the further insistence that true faith is quickly and surely expressed in deeds of generosity and service to one's fellow men. Protestants affirmed God and immortality as seriously as Catholics. But they have seldom glorified the contemplative life or retirement from this world for purposes of monastic discipline. Rather, they so held their faith in God that it proved to be a driving force toward full participation in human affairs. Calvin (1509–1564), to be sure, was less concerned than Luther with social service; he was more occupied with the negative duty of keeping oneself unspotted from the world. Therefore, wherever Protestantism has been consciously Calvinistic, Protestants have thought of morality largely in terms of abstinence from evil acts and from indulgence of bodily passions. But the weight of the Protestant ethic has been upon the religious significance of the present life. Protestants have characteristically sought to find that significance in the joyousness of human living, the preciousness of human relations, the bearing of religious faith upon the reorganization of economic and political practices, and the right of a Christian man to possess abundantly the natural goods of God's world.

Protestantism was unlike the Renaissance in one respect. The great figures of the Renaissance are often called Humanists just because, in accord with the Platonic and Aristotelian ethic, they trusted reason as the best guide to the good life for man. But Protestant leaders, through the early generations of Protestantism at least, and in some cases to our own day, have disparaged a trust in reason as a form of human presumption (even, at times, as evidence of original sin). Man lives sinfully, they held, until faith is implanted in him through divine grace. And faith is a conversion of the will. The conversion is both by God and to God. Luther had been an Augustinian monk before he broke with Rome, and he may well have been influenced, if not by Duns Scotus and William of Ockham, at least by the voluntarism which spread abroad from their teachings. But his emphasis on will apart from reason is an exaggerated form of the Augustinian position. For Luther and for many Protestant leaders after him, faith is a commitment which, from the point of view of reason, may be arbitrary; and reason is a snare which, from the point of view of faith, is not merely irrelevant but even arrogant.

It was the individualism of Protestantism and its attention to the social and natural worlds which, harmonizing with the similar teachings of the Renaissance, influenced the course of modern philosophy. Other features of Protestantism left modern philosophers indifferent or even made them hostile. Protestantism exhibited quite a trend toward fideism, that is, toward a faith which not only had no grounds in reason but defiantly scorned the support of so worldly, so secular, so feeble a faculty as reason. The Protestant Reformation, for all its importance, was not an intellectual movement, and Protestantism has never produced a theologian of the rank of St. Augustine or St. Thomas or others of the great Schoolmen. Protestant theologians have been dogmatic theologians rather than philosophical theologians. Calvin is perhaps the nearest claimant to front rank among Protestant theologians; but although he was exemplary in his definitions of doctrines and in the logic with which he carried out the implications of his premises, he would not be numbered among men of genuine philosophic concern. Philosophers who are also Protestants have indeed been numerous in modern times; and many of them, both before and since Kant, have argued for God, freedom, and immortality. But their philosophic interests have arisen in other contexts than theology. Locke is typical of them when he protested against the rival contentions of the quarreling Protestant sects as so much "enthusiasm," that is, so much unprofitable assertion of unproved opinions on emotional grounds. And increasingly, as the eighteenth and nineteenth centuries succeeded the seventeenth, modern philosophers have tended, sometimes toward skepticism, more often toward secularism. The Thomistic distinction between theology and philosophy has become, in Protestant hands, an almost complete separation between theology and philosophy. Modern philosophers have reduced to a minimum the number of theological tenets they saw the slightest philosophical justification for accepting or have rejected theological tenets altogether.

THE DEVELOPMENT OF MODERN SCIENCE

Even more decisive than the Renaissance and the Reformation in influence upon the genesis and development of modern philosophy was the series of epoch-making achievements of astronomers and physical scientists in the sixteenth and early seventeenth centuries. Both the conclusions of the scientists and their method of procedure, particularly the latter, made a strong impact upon modern philosophical speculations and raised new problems which now received the attention formerly given to the traditional issues of the ancient and medieval worlds.

The revolution in scientific views gained its first great victory with the publication in 1543 of Copernicus' *De Revolutionibus Orbium Coelestium.* Some scientists of the ancient world had believed that the earth swings in space and even that it moves around the sun. But these beliefs had been submerged for centuries because of the authority of Ptolemy's geocentric views. Copernicus (1473–1543) not merely defended the theory that the earth is one of the planets and moves, like the others, around the sun, but he also marshaled the reasons in favor of this heliocentric theory. A preface to Copernicus' book by one of his politic and cautious friends argued that Copernicus offered his theory, not as the truth about the physical universe, but as a convenient hypothesis which promoted ease of calculation in astronomical matters. Passages in Copernicus' own text can be cited to corroborate the friend's argument. But Copernicus quite probably himself believed that his theory was more revolutionary than the preface indicated, and such was certainly the historical purport of his book. For he made the important contentions that motion is relative to the position of the observer, that no point in space is privileged or central, and that the only meaning of truth in selection of an arbitrary point of reference is the resulting simplicity of a theory and the ease of calculation which ensues from a theory. Copernicus' presentation of the heliocentric theory was faulty in certain respects, largely because he favored the circle as the most perfect geometric figure and hence affirmed that the orbits of the planets about the sun are circular. But the heliocentric theory, even in faulty form, made evident that the physical universe is enormously vaster in extent than opinion through the Middle Ages had ordinarily supposed. It demoted the earth, the scene of human life, from the center to the periphery, so to speak, of the cosmos. It deprived man of his proud position as the chief denizen of the main body to which then all other bodies in the heavens were ornaments or appendages and turned him into a being who clings to the surface of a minor planet of only one of the suns, and a comparatively small sun at that, of the stellar universe.

Kepler (1571–1630) solved some of the difficulties with which Copernicus' formulas were encumbered and made more evident than before the significance of Copernicus' method. He worked in turn with various mathematical possibilities and compared the outcome of these mathematical calculations with the actually observed positions of the planets in their relation to the earth.[4] He finally found that he must abandon two suppositions which were retained in the thought of Copernicus: (1) that the orbits of the planets about the sun are

---

[4] He worked for years as assistant to the Danish astronomer Tycho Brahe, in whose observatory had been collected the most extensive and most accurate data available up to that time in the history of western culture.

circular, and (2) that the rate of motion of the planets in their orbits is constant. He discovered that with different suppositions on these two points he could maintain "the simplicity and ordered regularity of nature" and could fit together the outcome of mathematical calculation and the observations of the astronomers. He reduced his conclusions to what are called his first two laws: that the planets move about the sun in elliptical orbits, with the sun at one of the foci of the ellipses, and that the planets sweep out equal areas of the ellipses in equal times. He thus became convinced that the structures of the physical universe could be summed up in harmonious mathematical formulas which were applicable universally and uniformly to the whole course of nature. He continued to hunt for mathematically expressible relations in the physical world. One such he stated in his third law, namely, that the squares of the periodic times of the planets in their orbits about the sun are proportional to the cubes of the major axes of the ellipses of those orbits.

Galileo (1564–1642) carried the scientific revolution into the fields of mechanics and formulated the laws of motion. The story is famous of the manner in which he discovered the law of the pendulum. He watched the swaying of a chandelier in the cathedral at Pisa, counted the time for each of the motions against the beatings of his own pulse, and thus uncovered a hidden rhythm among the welter of sense experiences visible on the surface of events to any casual observer. So in the examination of other kinds of motion he found mathematical uniformities in what to the untrained senses might seem a chaos. He set forth formulas concerning the parabolic path of all falling bodies or projectiles and concerning the uniformity of acceleration with which all bodies fall. He made himself a telescope and, with it, discovered the mountainous character of the surface of the moon, four of the satellites of the planet Jupiter, and the phases of the planet Venus. He was so forceful in proclaiming the revolutionary nature of the work of Copernicus, Kepler, and himself that he stirred up opposition in ecclesiastical and academic circles. Copernicus' book was placed on the Index of the Church until it received some "correction," and works by Kepler and Galileo were placed on the Index and remained there for two centuries.

The scientific revolution from the middle of the sixteenth century to the middle of the seventeenth involved a rejection of certain ideas which had been current for centuries, particularly in the Neo-Platonic tradition and in the medieval version of Aristotle. It gradually undermined, for example, the notions of a hierarchy of being, of a distinction of kind between celestial and terrestrial motions, and of the kindred distinction between the perfection and regularity of the heavens on the one hand and the imperfection and irregularity of earthly changes on the other. The entire physical universe, according to the new science, was subject to one set of uniform laws of nature which could be stated with precision in mathematical terms.

But for the history of modern philosophy, the most profound influence of the scientific revolution was in raising two old problems in a new form and in stimulating philosophers to seek answers which would justify the procedures the scientists were already successfully using. These two problems are the relation of reason and sense in the acquisition of knowledge and the relation of human experience and the realities of nature.

The relation of reason and sense had long been debated in philosophy. One common theory on this problem, a theory which had been expressed repeatedly from the early Greeks to the great Scholastics, was that reason, although it carried the mind beyond the facts observed through the senses, had to respect and conform to those facts. St. Thomas, for example, insisted that theory must always "save the appearances." And he recognized that alternate theories might seem at times to be equally consistent with the observed facts, in which case neither of the alternate theories could be asserted as proved. St. Albert stated that "a principle that does not agree with experimental knowledge acquired by the senses is no principle but quite the opposite." [5] However far reason might go, it began with the real substances first presented before the senses. Copernicus was not far from this traditional position; but Kepler and Galileo, particularly the latter, were moving toward suspicion of sense experience as inadequate and subjective and, hence, were inclined to trust reason and its mathematical clarities as sufficient in and by themselves for obtaining knowledge. Kepler and Galileo were too busy with their scientific work to speculate in detached manner upon epistemological problems. But they both, and Galileo more notably, commented on their own procedures in such a way as to compel sophisticated philosophical minds like Descartes to make explicit the epistemological tendency in their procedures. Galileo, for example, wrote: "Against appearances in which all men agree, we make headway with reason,

[5] Quoted from Lynn Thorndike, "Natural Science in the Middle Ages," *Popular Science Monthly*, Vol. 87 (1915).

either to confirm the reality of that experience, or to discover its falsity." [6] Here there is no empirical confidence in sense experience as giving evidence necessary to test out the adequacy of the hypotheses of reason. Rather, there is rationalistic confidence in the power of the intellect to formulate mathematical assurances which will account for the curiously inadequate appearances of things in sense experience. Sensation has come to be regarded as not merely superficial but even somewhat deceptive—deceptive, at least, until accounted for and explained in terms of the principles which reason alone can detect clearly. Descartes laid bare the import of Galileo's position when he wrote: [7]

Bodies are not genuinely perceived by the senses or by the faculty of the imagination, but by the intellect only . . . they are not known from their being seen or touched, but only from their being understood.

But if it took a man with philosophic flair like Descartes to see all that Galileo's method involved, the demotion of sensory experience and the exaltation of reason were already present in Galileo's work.

The other problem of the relation of human experience and the realities of nature was tied up with the problem of the relation of reason and sense. Galileo stated that he would not accept a theory which violated what sense experience presented to an observer. And to an extent he was therefore still accepting the principle that theory must "save the appearances." But the word *appearance* is equivocal. As applied to Galileo's position it does not mean what it meant in the older view. In the older view appearances are the direct presence of substances before an observer; in Galileo's view they are effects which substances produce in an observer's mind and hence are mental states. In the former case they are objective realities in the realm of nature; in the latter case they are subjective entities which have to be validated by reason before they can be taken as cues to the existence and nature of external substances. In Galileo's theory appearances are not themselves substances but images which may or may not adequately represent the substances which produced them. Hence, for Galileo, sense experience, in and by itself, is untrustworthy and even misleading, and reason is requisite to determine the degree of cognitive value we may properly assign to it.

Thus there arose the contrast between appearance and reality which was to haunt modern philosophy for the next three hundred years.

---

6 Quoted from J. H. Randall, *Making of the Modern Mind,* rev. ed. (Boston, Houghton Mifflin, 1940), p. 221.

7 *Meditations,* Pt. II, closing paragraph.

Galileo held that all the mathematically formulable qualities and relations of things are objective. The figure and size of things, the number of things, the position and motion of things are inseparable from things, though such matters cannot be competently judged from our human ways of perceiving those things through the senses but must be established by principles discerned by reason. Whatever cannot be formulated in mathematical terms, Galileo regarded rather as subjective and resident in human minds. A feather, he said, may produce a tickling in a man when it is drawn in a certain way across his skin. The tickling, however, is not in the feather but in the man. Similarly, colors and tones, sensations of hot and cold, odors and tastes are not in the substances about us but in us. The objective world is regular, immutable, mathematical; men's subjective experience through the senses is fluctuating, relative in part to the condition of men's bodily organs, and somewhat chaotic. Experience, at least sense experience, arises in men because nature is what it is. But this experience is not a disclosure of what nature is; nor is experience really part of the events which comprise the course of nature.

The scientific revolution began in Copernicus to change the traditional view of man's place in nature from centrality to that of a casual and even insignificant spectator. It developed in Galileo so as to change the traditional view of the value of the senses in gaining knowledge of things. Reality and appearance, nature and experience, reason and sense, instead of being correlative aspects of unitary occurrences, became antitheses which presented logical dichotomies with which modern philosophers struggled for many years.

IX

A Century of Philosophy on the Continent

1. DESCARTES

RENÉ DESCARTES, 1596–1650, was born of a noble French family, educated at a Jesuit college at La Flèche (near Tours), and, after his father's death, possessed a sufficient income to make him financially independent. He was bored by social life in Paris and decided at the age of 21 to seek solitude for scientific and philosophical reflections. He found some solitude by enlisting in peacetime in the Dutch army for two years and then in the Bavarian army for another two years. Later, he served three years in a French army which besieged the Huguenots in La Rochelle. In 1629 he went to Holland, the country where at that time there was more intellectual freedom than anywhere else in western Europe, and made his residence there for twenty years. During these years he kept in touch with the learned world chiefly through Père Mersenne, a French monk whose cell in Paris was a center for European intellectuals. In 1649 he was persuaded to go to the court of Christina of Sweden, where, exposed to unaccustomed cold, he fell ill and died. His writings deal with the many scientific questions of his time, such as optics, meteorology, the formation of the solar system, eclipses, and tides. He formulated the basic principles of analytical geometry. He completed a book *De Mundo* by 1633, but he withheld it from publication and even destroyed sections of it, partly because he timidly wished to avoid such ecclesiastical censure as Galileo incurred, partly perhaps because he wished to lead Catholic authorities gradually to a more favorable attitude toward the new science and sought to avoid shocking them. In spite of his prudence, Protestant theologians raised objections to him in Holland, and the Catholic Church put his works on the Index in 1663. His most important philosophical works are *Discourse on Method* (1637), *Meditations on First Philosophy* (1642), and *Principles of Philosophy* (1644). An earlier work, *Rules for the Direction of the Mind,* may have been written by 1626, but was never published until 1701. The *Discourse* was written and first published in French, probably because Descartes wished to address as wide an audience as possible. The other three philosophical works, intended primarily for scholars, were first written and published in Latin.

WHEN IN HIS early manhood Descartes looked out on the world of learning, he decided that the writings of philosophers were comparatively futile and the discoveries of recent scientists, particularly Galileo, were exciting and illuminating. He set himself the task of formulating a new philosophy which, freed from burdensome philosophical traditions, would justify the accomplishments already made by the new science, would prepare the way for further scientific progress, and would arrange all actual and future scientific knowledge in the context of a well-rounded system about God and man and the universe.

In both the *Discourse* and the *Meditations* Descartes cast his reflections in the form of an intellectual biography. This biography, dramatic and a bit histrionic, is characteristic of the modern spirit in its emphasis upon the author's own individual development (for the two works use the first personal pronoun throughout) and in its optimistic confidence that a new age of human enlightenment and human happiness is dawning. Descartes heightened the popular appeal of his biographical sketches by picturing himself as plunged initially into almost hopeless doubts that assail him on every side and then as rescued from all his doubts by a series of absolutely certain insights which together form the principles of the new and irrefutable philosophy.

THE METHOD OF DOUBT

Descartes' initial doubts were primarily two. Both of them arose from his study of the method of Galileo. He admired Galileo's work and wished to justify it. But he, the philosopher, saw in the method two epistemological problems which Galileo, the scientist, had not noticed or at least had not discussed. He expressed his doubts in extreme form in order to make his eventual resolution of them more triumphant and attractive.

One of the doubts was concerning the value of sense experience as a basis for opinions about the world around us. The senses have the defect of being sometimes illusory, and they have the much more serious defect of being entirely subjective. That is, the sense experiences we have are nothing but ideas in our own minds and contain no indication of whether or not they resemble the things outside of us which supposedly produced them within us. Indeed, they contain no indication even that there *are* things outside of us. They are "modes of consciousness" or "modes of thought." We have such modes of consciousness or such ideas in our dreams when supposedly no things exist such as we seem to perceive. Possibly, then, all the sense experiences of our so-called waking life are likewise in us without external things to produce them. They may arise in us, so far as our ideas reveal to us, through our own unsuspected generating powers or through the direct agency of God or through the malicious machinations of a demon who delights in leading us astray. So far as sense experiences instruct us, there may be no material world at all and no God and no demon. Although we indubitably do have the modes of consciousness or ideas and do normally believe them to come to us through our bodily sense organs from material things outside of us, we may really have no bodies, no sense organs, and no contacts with material things.

The second of Descartes' initial doubts was concerning the power of our minds to transcend the subjectivity of sense experience and to reach knowledge of the world outside ourselves. Descartes came only gradually to appreciate the gravity of this issue. In two of his early works he sponsored the method of Galileo without indicating any suspicions of the epistemological problems inherent in it. In *Rules for the Direction of the Mind* he confidently exclaimed that mathematics "is a more powerful instrument for knowledge than any other which has been devised by man and is indeed the source of all others." [1] And in *De Mundo* he exultingly cried out: [2]

Whoever examines carefully the rules I have laid down and the truths thereby reached, will be able to proceed to demonstrations *a priori* of everything that occurs in the world.

No more ardent support of Galileo could be given. And Descartes never withdrew this support. But he did realize that Galileo's tech-

[1] Rule 4. For Descartes' full discussion of the point, see *The Philosophical Works of Descartes*, ed. E. S. Haldane and G. R. T. Ross (Cambridge, Cambridge University Press, 1911), Vol. I, pp. 10–13.

[2] See *Oeuvres de Descartes*, ed. Charles Adam and Paul Tannery (Paris, Cerf, 1897–1913), Vol. XI, p. 47.

nique presented an epistemological problem which Galileo had him-self done nothing to solve. We need some guarantee, he became aware, that the real objects outside of the mind and independent of it are yet in accord with the mathematical principles which are clear and simple to the mind. In the *Discourse on Method* he wrote: [3]

In examining some of the simplest demonstrations of the geometers, I noted that the great certitude universally accorded to these demonstrations is based solely on the fact that they are conceived with clarity. . . . But I noted also that there was nothing at all in the demonstrations to assure me that objects such as those being discussed really existed.

The power and resources of the natural world may be very vast; and the principles of mathematics, however lucid, are general and simple. What assurance can we then have that our lucid principles enable us to lay bare the intricacies of the world outside of us?

STEPS TOWARD CERTAINTY

Descartes' solution of the epistemological problems raised by these doubts consists of three steps, each of which, if taken in its proper order, seemed to him so indubitable as to remove every vestige of speculative uncertainty. These three steps Descartes presented as three stages in the development of his intellectual biography.

The first stage is the bedrock of certainty upon which all else in Descartes' subsequent system of philosophy rests. It is the assurance he comes to have of his self-existence. In the midst of the most thorough and extreme doubts he can possibly raise, he becomes aware that he must himself exist in order even to doubt. What he believes he sees may be illusion, but he must himself exist in order to suffer illusion. What he infers by logical and mathematical principles may contain some unnoticed error, but he must himself exist in order to err. Descartes' own words, in the French of the *Discourse*, are *Je pense, donc je suis,* and in the Latin of the *Meditations,* are *Cogito ergo sum.* And he felt intuitively certain of the nature as well as of the existence of this self. [4]

I admit nothing which is not necessarily true when I say that I am precisely and only a thinking thing, that is, a mind or spirit, an understanding, or a reason—terms the significance of which were until now unknown to me. I am, indeed, a real thing and really exist. But what thing? I answer: a thinking thing.

This thinking thing (*res cogitans*) stands apart from body and from physical nature; it does not require any place or position in space.

[3] Pt. IV, par. 5.
[4] *Meditations,* Pt. II.

From the fact that he intuitively knows his own existence while he continues to doubt everything else, it follows, Descartes thought, that his self is a substance [5] the entire essence of which is to think. The knowledge he has of his own self is intuitive; that is, the knowledge is due to immediate inspection. His own self is indeed the only existent thing of which he can possibly have intuitive knowledge; it is not simply the *first* existent thing he can know with certainty but the *only* existent thing he can know directly. Whatever else of existence he may subsequently come to know, he has to come to know by demonstration from this initial intuitive knowledge.[6] The knowledge he has of himself, Descartes maintained, is the indispensable foundation upon which, and upon which alone, the entire structure of knowledge of other existences can be built securely.

The second stage in Descartes' solution of his epistemological problem is demonstration of the existence of God. After he comes to know his own existence intuitively he is still in doubt about all other existence, for he has only his own ideas immediately present to inspection and may be the victim of the malicious demon. He needs some guarantee of his right to use his reason about other existences. This guarantee he believed he found, and he believed he found it in God.

In his chief argument for the existence of God [7] Descartes made use of a classification he proposed of all his ideas into three kinds. Some of his ideas he called adventitious, because they appear to be produced in him by things outside of him; for example, the sound he hears or the heat he feels. Others of his ideas he called factitious, because he forms or invents them himself; for example, the ideas of a siren and a chimera. Still others of his ideas he called innate. Descartes' philosophy depends to no small extent upon his claim that some ideas are innate, and yet his definition of what the word *innate* means is not wholly clear. The innate ideas are not ideas

---

[5] Descartes later defined this technical word in the *Principles of Philosophy*, Pt. I, principle 81, as "an existent thing which requires nothing but itself in order to exist."

[6] Descartes admitted only two kinds or degrees of knowledge—intuition and demonstration. Intuition is basic. It is, in the language of the *Rules for the Direction of the Mind*, rule 3: "not the fluctuating testimony of the senses or the unreliable construction of the imagination, but the indubitable conception which a pure and attentive mind gives us so directly and distinctly that we are freed from all doubts concerning that which we know." Demonstration is a supplementary form of knowledge. It is inference which follows necessarily from intuitive knowledge. There is intuitive knowledge of certain principles of logic and mathematics as well as of the existence of the self. But there is no intuitive knowledge of *existence* except of the self.

[7] He also made use of the ontological argument in a form closely akin to that of St. Anselm.

always present in his mind, much less are they ideas he had in his mind at birth; in that sense of the word *innate* he has no innate ideas. They are rather ideas "imprinted on his mind by nature." [8] Perhaps the most nearly satisfactory explanation he ever gave of innate ideas is in some notes he composed near the end of his life and did not intend for publication. He there said: [9]

When I observed that there are thoughts in me which proceed neither from external objects nor from the determinations of the will but solely from my capacity to think, I called these thoughts innate ideas, thereby distinguishing them both from those which come from without and from those which are fashioned by myself.

We all can formulate some innate ideas through our purely intellectual powers, he contended, whether or not we are ever skillful and attentive enough to bring them explicitly before us in clear consciousness. Among the innate ideas he found in himself he listed his idea of himself; his ideas of what are called a thing and a truth and a thought; his ideas of certain mathematical axioms, like the principle that things equal to the same thing are equal to each other; and his ideas of certain philosophical axioms, like the causal principle that an efficient cause, though it may have more perfection than the effect it produces, cannot have less perfection than that effect. And such also, Descartes believed, is his idea of God.

The motivation behind Descartes' insistence upon innate ideas was his desire to maintain the integrity of the intellectual life. If all our ideas came, as do our adventitious and factitious ideas, from the mechanisms of physical stimuli and bodily organs, then, he feared, our beliefs would be built up in us in mechanical fashion. We would believe what mechanical forces compelled us to believe, and we might believe false ideas as easily and as earnestly as true ideas. We would have no objective criterion of truth, no standard of genuine knowledge. If some of our ideas are capable of leading us to discern the difference between truth and error, then, in his opinion, these ideas must arise in our minds apart from the mechanisms of the material world. They must, in short, arise from our pure or uncontaminated intellectual powers. Descartes was above all else, a champion of the ability of the intellect to ascertain truth. He wished to preserve the authority of the intellect over against the pressure of the passions

---

[8] See his *Reply to Objections III to the Meditations.*

[9] *Notes Directed Against a Certain Program Published in Belgium in 1647.* See the note written against art. 12 of this program. These *Notes* may be found in an English translation in *The Philosophical Works of Descartes,* ed. E. S. Haldane and G. R. T. Ross (Cambridge, Cambridge University Press, 1911), Vol. I, pp. 431–450.

and the strength of the impact of physical forces upon the bodily senses. Even in dealing with physics, we ought not to allow our minds to be swayed by adventitious ideas or sense experiences; we ought to pronounce upon our sensory data in the light of principles which are innate. For once we conceive innate ideas clearly and distinctly, we have, Descartes firmly held, the one sure means to truth. And what is the case in physics is surely, too, the case in matters of fundamental philosophical concern. Innate ideas, once they are in our minds, enable us to escape from the physical and social forces which naturally incline most men's minds to most of their beliefs. They bring to our minds "a natural light" which is "pure intellection" and so is utterly different from a mechanical impetus. They issue in rational judgments which are not physiologically conditioned inclinations but clear discernments of necessary truths.

His innate idea of God, Descartes said, is an idea of "a substance infinite, eternal, immutable, independent, omniscient, omnipotent, and by which I myself and all other existences (if indeed there be any such) were created." [10] This idea, he contended, contains much which could not have come from himself, much indeed which could not have come from any finite being. He is therefore at once compelled to conclude that he is not alone in the world, but that another being exists which has caused this idea in him. And the being which caused this idea in him must have at least as much perfection as the idea which is its effect. Ideas of other finite substances, like inanimate things or other men or animals, he might form by himself because he is himself a finite substance and is animate. But the idea of God could come only from a being who had the perfection which the idea contains. This being, of course, is God. And therefore God surely exists. In Descartes' words: "I should not have the idea of an infinite substance (since I am myself finite) unless the idea had been given me by a substance which is genuinely infinite."

The third and last stage in Descartes' solution of his epistemological problem is the validation of the right and the power of his mind to reach knowledge of the bodies which collectively constitute the natural world. This right and this power he had originally questioned. He believed that he recovered this right and this power through his demonstration of the existence of God. The world, he believed, is God's world, and his mind is God's gift. His mind, therefore, is fitted to discover truths about the world, provided that his mind is properly used. And his mind is properly used, he maintained, once it is de-

10 *Meditations*, Pt. III.

tached from his senses and from all inclinations of his nonintellectual nature. God, the perfect being, cannot be guilty of fraud or deception (which are imperfections). Hence, as Descartes felt warranted in concluding, he can trust all the capacities which God has given him whenever he uses those capacities in fitting fashion. He does, he confessed, sometimes fall into error. But errors arise from the abuse of his faculties. Errors never arise from the undisturbed activity of the intellect but from impetuosity or even arrogance of the will. The will has a wider range than the intellect and tends to press forward to judgments beyond the limits within which the intellect is able competently and confidently to determine truth. But, as Descartes triumphantly concluded, he will never err if he refrains from making judgments on anything he does not clearly and distinctly perceive. A God-given intellect is, within its proper domain, an infallible instrumentality for reaching truth and providing indubitable knowledge.

Thus Descartes' epistemological problem received its solution. Descartes began in sheer subjectivity with consciousness of self; he utilized his doctrine of innate ideas to reach a demonstration of the existence of God; and he ended with a militant proclamation of his right to an unfettered use of his pure intellect in the pursuit of knowledge of all other things.

MATERIAL SUBSTANCE

An urgent question for Descartes, because of his zeal for the natural sciences, was the essence and the existence of material things. This question he made his first concern, once his epistemological problem was solved to his satisfaction. And in typically Cartesian fashion, he sought to determine the *essence* of material things before going on to demonstrate their *existence*.[11] On account of his views of the subjectivity of sense experiences, he supposed himself to have no material things given to his mind for inspection and analysis. He thus had to begin his discussion of material things by considering their essence —to clarify the ideas he held of them—and only then to pass from clear and distinct ideas in his own mind to corresponding existences outside of his mind. He described his own procedure thus: [12]

Before considering whether such objects as I conceive exist outside of me, I must examine the ideas of them, insofar as these are in my mind, in

11 Critics have not often noted the significance of the order of topics discussed in *Meditations,* Pts. V and VI. As the titles of these two meditations show, Descartes dealt in the former with the *essence* of material things and in the latter with their *existence*.

12 At the outset of *Meditations,* Pt. V.

order to determine which of the ideas are distinct and which are confused.

There are two kinds of ideas, Descartes pointed out, which he has concerning material things. On the one hand, he has various sense experiences—colors, sounds, odors, tastes, pains, and the like. On the other hand, he has the idea of extension in three dimensions, or quantity, with all the particular specifications thereof, such as figure, size, number, and motion. The former ideas are confused and obscure; the latter, clear and distinct. The former seem to come to him through some interrelation or mixture of his mind with a body; the latter are conceptions of the pure intellect. And in accord with the epistemological principle he had already established, Descartes affirmed that he ought to trust the mind alone, and not the mind and body in conjunction, as a means of knowing the truth about existences.

When I considered all the most clear and distinct ideas of material things which I find in my understanding (which are figure, size, and motion) and the principles of geometry and mechanics by which these three things can be diversified by one another, I reached the judgment that all the knowledge men can have of the natural world must necessarily arise from this source alone. For all the other notions we have of things through the senses are confused and obscure, and so not only can not afford us knowledge of what is outside of us but may even serve to impede us in reaching this knowledge.[13]

Material things, if they exist at all, may not be like what we perceive in sense experiences, but they must be like what we clearly and distinctly conceive in geometry and mechanics. The essence of bodies or material things is clearly and distinctly perceived in geometry and mechanics to be extension. Every material thing, therefore, if there be such at all, is an extended substance (*res extensa*). The material world is an extended world. Of it, all the theorems of geometry and mechanics must hold good. About it, if its existence can be shown, we have abundant knowledge; for its essence is extension.

Descartes' proof of the existence of material things is a consequence of his realization that he has in his mind a clear and distinct idea of their essence. God, he has demonstrated, exists and is no deceiver. Hence, Descartes believed that he can trust his ineradicable inclination to believe that his ideas of bodies are conveyed to him by material things. But he can trust this inclination only if he safeguards it against hasty abuse. He may, indeed he must, conclude that all his ideas of

[13] *Principles of Philosophy*, Pt. IV, principle 203. This passage was not in the original Latin edition of 1644. It first appeared in the French translation of 1647, a translation made by Descartes' friend Picot but revised and expanded by Descartes himself.

bodies are conveyed into his mind by something very different from his own mind. But when he says loosely that he perceives colors and other such confused sensations in bodies, he can properly mean nothing more than that he perceives something of the real nature of which he is ignorant. This something he may take as the cause of his sensations, but he may not take that something to be like the sensations. When, however, he says that reflection on his sensations gives him clear and distinct ideas of length, breadth, and depth, then he may properly affirm that he knows the existence of bodies with exactly those properties.[14] Thus he has demonstrated, in a manner appropriate to his epistemological position, the existence of the material world.

Descartes was enabled, on the basis of this epistemology, to adopt the discoveries which such scientists as Galileo had made and to proceed himself to further discoveries of the structure and processes of things in the natural world.

RATIONALISM AND DUALISM

Descartes has often been classified by historians as a rationalist and a dualist. And correctly so. He is a rationalist in epistemology and a dualist in ontology. But there are many types of both rationalism and dualism in the history of ideas, and care must be exercised to specify the exact character of Cartesian rationalism and Cartesian dualism.

Rationalism, in general, is the principle that human reason is the final authority in all matters of opinion and conduct. Cartesian rationalism is concerned only with matters of opinion (for Descartes was willing to leave conduct to be guided by the laws of the state and the instruction of the Church). But in matters of opinion Cartesian rationalism is an extreme position. It is the epistemological theory that the intellect, freed from the confusions of sense experience, can by its own powers formulate ideas and determine the truth of these ideas.

Descartes, the historian ought not to forget, himself performed many experiments. When in 1630 Mersenne inquired of him how to make useful experiments, he commended the writings of Francis Bacon.[15] He illustrated his position by suggesting that after one has observed that all the shells on European seashores have spirals which turn in the same direction, one ought to examine shells from below the equator and see whether the spirals of those shells turn in the

---

14 *Principles of Philosophy*, Pt. I, principle 70; Pt. II, principle 1.
15 See below, Chap. X, sec. 1, for a discussion of Bacon's views.

same fashion. But he at once added to this illustration that no experiment is profitable unless it is guided by general knowledge which the experimenter already has. And Descartes' point in making this last remark is not hard to detect. He regarded the experiment, not as laying some portion of the world open before one's eyes, but as producing in the experimenter's mind some sense experiences upon the occasion of which the pure intellect could discern a structure that could be described in terms of necessary principles.

It may well be that Descartes was not altogether consistent in his expressions of his rationalism. In one letter to his friend Mersenne he wrote: "To seek geometrical demonstrations in matters of physics is to seek the impossible." [16] And in another letter to Mersenne a few weeks later he wrote: "I accept no principles in physics which are not also accepted in mathematics." [17] If the historian is to effect a reconciliation of these statements, it would perhaps be this: that the principles of physics and mathematics are so general and the events in nature so multifarious that subjective sense experiences are requisite to guide the intellect in choosing appropriate principles for each given event.[18] But in any case, Cartesian rationalism is the theory that the senses put confused ideas between the mind and the world and that the intellect, aloof from this confusion, is itself capable of determining necessary principles and of reaching truth *a priori*.

Dualism, in general, is the belief that reality consists of two distinct and irreducible kinds of being. One dualism will differ from another according to what the two kinds of being are which are regarded as distinct and irreducible. Platonic dualism, if that term is used, is the belief that all realities are either forms or particulars. Cartesian dualism is the belief that all realities are either souls or bodies, that is, spiritual substances or material substances. Soul cannot be reduced to body or to a function of body or to a dependency upon body. And body cannot be reduced to soul or to the ideas of soul or to a product of soul. Only because he took this position firmly could Descartes call both soul and body substances, that is, existing things, each of which is what it is without reference to any other thing. Soul is thinking and unextended substance; body is unthinking and extended substance. Man is a certain union of soul and body and therefore belongs to both realms of being. As a soul he is a spiritual being, and as a body he is a material being. But although man is a

16 This letter is dated May 17, 1638. See *Oeuvres de Descartes,* Vol. II, p. 142.
17 This letter is dated July 27, 1638. See *ibid.,* Vol. II, p. 268.
18 Just this position is expressed in *Discourse on Method,* Pt. VI, par. 3.

union of soul and body, the two substances in him ought never to be confused.[19]

MAN AND NATURE, OR MIND AND BODY

Descartes viewed the natural world as a mechanical system of physical forces. This view followed from his firm conviction that the principles of mathematics and physics applied to it with unbroken regularity. In holding this view Descartes displayed great boldness, for his century was a time of widespread credulity. King Louis XIII consulted his court astrologer for guidance in the siege of the Huguenots at La Rochelle. Even the scientist Pascal (1623–1662) reported miraculous cures by the application of a sacred thorn to sore eyes and he wrote to inform Mersenne that a certain man had died at just the time predicted by an astrologer. But Descartes swept nature free of intrusions which would upset the uniform operation of the laws of physics. He went so far as to deny that these laws could be interfered with by even God and the angels. His demonstration of the existence of God and his recognition of the soul as a spiritual substance seemed to him to be sufficient to satisfy the needs of religion. He wished to leave the natural world, as an entirely material system, to the investigations of the scientists. To allow spiritual agencies to interfere with nature, he believed, was to slander the spiritual as well as to upset the natural; it was to turn the spiritual into an erratic and perverted disturbance of the world. He insisted with equal zeal upon the two sides of his dualistic system: he made the doctrines of God and the soul independent of any considerations the scientists might raise, and he made the doctrine of the mechanical character of the natural world free of any intrusions which theologians might seek to allege.

The point at which Descartes most nearly came into difficulty with his theory of the mechanism of nature was in discussing the position of man in nature. With animals other than man he had no difficulty at all, for he advocated the thesis that animals are automata, have no consciousness, and are complex but wholly material machines. (He broke here entirely with the Aristotelian tradition concerning the three levels of soul—vegetative, animal, and rational.) As the circulation of the blood (which he had learned about from Harvey [1578–1657] and had himself discussed in Part V of his *Discourse*) is a mechanical process of pumps and conduits, so all animal behavior,

[19] All that is said in this paragraph about dualism is subject to such qualification as may be needed in the light of Descartes' avowal that God created both souls and bodies.

like the behavior of winds and floods, is mechanical. Descartes thus absorbed what we should call biology wholly into physics and denied it any independent principles. The human body, too, he put without reservation into the mechanism of the natural world. But man is soul as well as body, and so the position of man in nature is a point which required special consideration from Descartes.

Descartes met this problem by his theory of interaction of soul and body. The human soul and the human body have a point of contact, namely, at the pineal gland, a small organ at the base of the brain. Physical stimuli which play upon the human body and are transmitted through the nervous system to the pineal gland cause sensations to arise in the soul. And, conversely, acts of will and deliberate choices so rearrange the motions in the pineal gland, that influences from the soul, beginning in the pineal gland, are transmitted through the rest of the human body and thence into the external world. Body thus affects soul, and soul affects body. Descartes did not attribute to the soul the power to increase or decrease the *amount* of motion in the physical world; he gave it the power merely to alter the *direction* of some of this motion. And since the theory of the conservation of motion had not been so stated in Descartes' lifetime as to apply to direction of motion as well as to quantity, his theory of interaction seemed to him adequate to the known facts. Moreover, two basic interests, Descartes believed, are safeguarded by the theory of interaction. On the one hand, the significance of human volition for religion and morals is preserved intact because the will is made genuinely efficacious. On the other hand, the mechanism of the natural world is left undisturbed, so that scientific investigations will never be thwarted.

THE INFLUENCE OF DESCARTES

Descartes' influence on the seventeenth century during his lifetime and after his death was profound. The scientifically enlightened intellectuals of that period generally prided themselves on being Cartesians. Descartes' championing of the revolution in science, rather than his formulating epistemological and metaphysical doctrines, was the primary cause of his reputation. And yet the epistemological and metaphysical doctrines had many notable effects upon subsequent developments in philosophy. His problems, at least, were discussed and rediscussed, even if his answers to those problems were not always favored. He had some loyal disciples, to be sure. But he was an intellectual stimulus to thinkers who would not be considered, either by themselves or by an historian of ideas, as Cartesian in their professions. Some of his special doctrines, often out of the context of the entire body of his thought, set up radiating lines of influence. They were sometimes adopted in part, but were more often so criticized, so restated, so torn asunder, that the resulting philosophical positions would often have been repudiated by Descartes as egregious errors.

One line of influence from Descartes was to bring the problem of the relation of mind and body into the center of discussion. The theory of interaction had its weak points and was, moreover, bound up with Descartes' dualism. Later thinkers found it difficult to conceive how a physical stimulus could possibly produce a sensation or how an act of will could possibly change the direction of a moving body. Spinoza criticized Descartes on just this point; he not merely rejected interactionism but even denied that mind and body are substances at all.[20] A less radical break with Descartes came in the theory of Geulincx (1625–1699), a Dutch disciple of Descartes and leader for a time of the group who liked to think of themselves as the Cartesian school. Geulincx retained the dualism of Descartes. But he came after physicists had restated the law of conservation to specify that the total quantity of motion in nature in a given direction is constant. So he was forced to reject Descartes' notion of the way in which volition proved efficacious. Body and mind, he held, are so disparate that neither can cause an effect on the other. They appear to interact, to be sure, but they cannot really do so. Two clocks, he suggested, might be so synchronized that one would point to the hour and the other would strike the right number of chimes; hence, perfect co-ordination between the two clocks might occur without either one causing any effect on the other. So with mind and body. God controls all mental and bodily events so that mind and body behave as if each affected the other even though neither produces a change in the other directly. A sensation arises in the soul on the *occasion* of a certain nervous change in the body, and a motion of nerves and muscles occurs in the body on the *occasion* of a certain volition in the soul. Thus the name *occasionalism* was given to Geulincx' theory. According to occasionalism, even more thoroughly than according to Descartes' interaction theory, the material world is freed from the intrusion of spiritual forces, and yet all glory is given to God for the ingenuity of his wonderful foresight and his powers of minute correlation. But a difficulty emerged in occasionalism, too. For the

[20] See the next section of this chapter for discussion of Spinoza's views.

soul now seemed, in its independent changes, to follow exactly the kind of pattern exemplified by the mechanical order of the material world. Hence, Geulincx' occasionalist theory seemed to tend toward the outcome that soul, as much as the body, would have to be treated in mechanistic terms.

Some fifty years later La Mettrie (1709–1751) departed still further from the position of Descartes. His position is indicated by the title of his book *The Man-Machine.* La Mettrie was Cartesian in accepting the position that animal bodies are automata; but he was un-Cartesian in extending this same position to include human bodies. Not simply sensation, but all aspects of consciousness, emotional, intellectual, even volitional, are, he maintained, products of physical stimuli and bodily processes. Men may, for some inexplicable reason, have consciousness accompanying certain of the nervous changes in their bodies, but they behave at all times and in all respects as they would behave if there were no consciousness. They are physical machines which have consciousness as a by-product. There is no substantial soul. There is no spiritual substance, human or divine.

In spite of the difficulties of the interactionist theory, Descartes' dualism proved, in its historical influence, to be one of the recurrent metaphysical positions of modern times. The dualism was philosophically unstable. La Mettrie turned it into a materialism in which matter and motion are the only effective realities. Leibnitz turned it into an idealism in which consciousness alone is real and matter is but appearance.[21] But dualism survived these un-Cartesian versions of Descartes' views. Dualism has been a congenial position to many people in modern times because it assures them of a spiritual world for religious faith and, at the same time, gives them respectable standing as friends of the natural sciences. Scientists particularly have frequently veered toward Cartesianism because they can then grant the propriety of religious faith and the dignity of man as a spiritual being and still have the whole realm of the natural world for scientific investigation without fear of running up against any intrusion in the regularities of natural processes.

Another line of Descartes' influence on modern philosophy is visible in the order in which modern thinkers were often wont to discuss their problems. Seldom did later philosophers make proof of the existence of God a necessary preliminary to proof of the existence of a material world. St. Thomas had held that the first object of natural

21 See sec. 3 of this chapter for discussion of Leibnitz' views.

knowledge is the world around us and sought to rise from analysis of this world to knowledge of God. Philosophy for him is the handmaid of theology. Descartes reversed this sequence. For at the inception of his epistemological inquiries he has no world; he has only himself and his own states. He can, he insisted, never come to know another existing thing with the intuitive certainty with which he knows himself. And he therefore approaches knowledge of the world by indirection. He has first to prove the existence of God if he then is ever to determine valid means of reaching knowledge of the world. Theology is for him, one might almost say, the handmaid of philosophy, at least of natural philosophy. But Descartes' stand on this point never produced conviction among most later philosophers. The world generally seemed to them, as to Wordsworth, only too much with us.

But Descartes did lead many subsequent thinkers to make self-knowledge the basic article of epistemological assurance. Indeed, the most profound influence of Descartes on modern philosophy was in inducing these thinkers to suppose that they must begin their epistemological analyses with their own selves, with their private states of consciousness, with their subjective ideas. Even St. Augustine had not been as subjectivistic as was Descartes. His *Si fallor sum* was an anticipation of Descartes' *Cogito ergo sum*. But St. Augustine never reduced the content of the mind wholly to mental states. He considered that certain ideas are real beings, like Plato's forms, and that sensations are the mind's observation of some events in the body. Descartes is the first major philosopher in western culture to regard all the ideas of the mind, sensory ideas and intellectual ideas alike, as "modes of thought" which are in their occurrence wholly within the mind. Descartes thus made the individual mind with all its ideas a realm separate from the rest of existence, so that a man's experience does not, in its appearance to him, contain anything other than his own privacy. Modern thinkers did not generally agree with Descartes as to the way in which a man may transcend the calamity of his privacy and reach knowledge of God and the world. But they often did espouse a totally subjectivistic position as the only proper starting place for epistemological speculations. This subjectivism proved to enable Descartes to find his bedrock of certainty; it proved to engulf many later thinkers in a morass of skepticism. In the history of science Descartes is notable primarily as a bold discoverer of mathematical truths about the world. But in the history of epistemology and metaphysics he is notable primarily as founder of that school of thought which maintains that the only data of experience, or the most assured data, are private states of consciousness which then cut the mind off from direct contact with things other than itself.

2. SPINOZA

BARUCH (or BENEDICTUS) DE SPINOZA, 1632–1677, a Dutch Jew. His family had fled from Portugal to escape the Inquisition. His father became a prosperous merchant in Amsterdam and a prominent member of the synagogue. He himself became known, when he was about twenty, as an heretic. He was offered, for his father's sake, an annuity on condition that he remain silent on theology. This bribe he rejected. His father died in 1653, and he was excommunicated from the synagogue in 1656 with violent maledictions. He went to law to establish his rights against his sister as one of his father's heirs; but after winning the case, he voluntarily relinquished most of his patrimony in the sister's favor. He proceeded to support himself by grinding lenses, an occupation requiring great skill and keeping him in touch with the new science which was then concerned with problems of optics. In 1660 he retired to a small village Rijnsburg (near Leyden) where he lived for many years, but eventually he moved to The Hague. He declined on one occasion a professorship of philosophy at Heidelberg, fearing that institutional ties might impair his intellectual freedom. He accepted a small annuity from the son of a close friend, though he insisted upon taking a smaller sum than the son offered. His life was secluded, quiet, and unremittingly devoted to philosophical reflections. He died of tuberculosis of the lungs. Only two of his works were published during his lifetime: *Principles of Descartes' Philosophy* (1663) and *Theological-Political Tractate* (1670). The latter was a pioneer work in scientific criticism of the Bible and also defended theories of an entirely secular state and principles of intellectual and religious toleration. Others of his writings appeared posthumously in 1677, among which were his greatest work, *Ethics Demonstrated in the Manner of Geometry,* and an unfinished *Political Treatise* (which expressed views similar to those of Hobbes). A century later there was published *Treatise on the Improvement of the Understanding,* which had been written before the *Ethics*. Still later appeared *A Short Treatise on God, Man, and His Well-Being* (1862). For a century after his time Spinoza was neglected and misunderstood. Locke, for example, spoke of him as "that justly reprobated atheist." He has been enthusiastically eulogized by many thinkers from the time of Lessing and Goethe to our own day. He was given the name Baruch as a Jewish child; but after he was excommunicated from the synagogue, he translated his Hebrew name into Latin and called himself Benedictus.

SPINOZA, LIKE PLATO and others of the ancients, conceived of philosophy primarily as a serious and prolonged search for the best life a man can live. In the opening sentence of what is probably his earliest writing he said: [22]

After experience had taught me that all the things which ordinarily happen in social life are vain and futile—when I saw that all the things I feared had neither good nor evil in them except insofar as the mind was agitated by them—I at last resolved to inquire whether there might be something which is truly good and able to impart its goodness to me, and by which alone (after all other things had been rejected) the mind might be affected, whether indeed there might be something through the discovery and acquisition of which I might come eternally to possess continual and supreme happiness.

Fame, riches, and sensuous pleasures are the goals most men seek; but these are all ephemeral, and their loss, if indeed they be momentarily possessed, only plunges men into abject misery. Happiness or unhappiness, he decided, depends upon this one consideration alone, namely, the quality of the object to which a man is tied by his love. Love of what is perishable is, in the kind of a world we live in, the occasion of ceaseless perturbation of mind. Love of what is "eternal and infinite" brings to the mind uninterrupted and intense joy. "Wherefore," he concluded, that which is eternal and infinite "ought to be greatly desired and sought for with all our strength."

This conception of the prime purpose of philosophy led Spinoza to give the name *Ethics* to his great systematic work. And quite properly so. But an ethics which was designed to disclose an eternal and infinite object for human love and then to instruct men in the means of so disciplining themselves as to turn with whole-hearted and single-minded devotion to that object—an ethics of this sort was bound to be an ethics in the grand manner. And such, indeed,

[22] *Treatise on the Improvement of the Understanding.*

Spinoza's *Ethics* is. It contains a system of metaphysics, because pursuit of the eternal and infinite requires thorough examination of the nature and structure of reality. It contains an elaborate psychology, because human nature cannot be disciplined until it is competently understood. It contains a theory of knowledge, because every resource of the intellect must be engaged in gaining the desired end. Spinoza's *Ethics,* more than any other work in modern philosophy, ranges systematically over wide areas of philosophical concern [23] and organizes its reflections thoroughly and compactly. Ethics without metaphysics, epistemology, and psychology would be, in Spinoza's judgment, abortive, whimsical, and fruitless. Man can determine his noblest destiny in the world, only provided that he understands the world, his own weaknesses and potential strength, and the techniques of moral adjustment of his own being to the forces among which he is constrained to live.

The best way to comprehend Spinoza's thought, since he gave that thought a carefully prepared plan of development, is to proceed page by page through the *Ethics.* Aside from his writings in political philosophy, the other works of Spinoza are ancillary to the main work.

DEMONSTRATION IN THE GEOMETRICAL MANNER

When a reader first opens Spinoza's *Ethics,* he is likely to be appalled by the method of exposition Spinoza adopted. The full title of the work is *Ethics Demonstrated in the Manner of Geometry,* and the form of discussion is exactly what the title indicates. The *Ethics* is divided into five parts. Each part begins with axioms and definitions; and the propositions which follow are proved in turn by reference back to the axioms, definitions, and earlier propositions. The thought of Spinoza is thus presented as a deductively organized system.

Critics of Spinoza have often misunderstood the purport of his method of presenting his system of philosophy. They have charged him, quite unjustifiably, with the fallacy of begging the question by dogmatic assertion of indemonstrable axioms and arbitrary definitions. Three considerations can be made in refutation of this charge. In the first place, Spinoza's method is one of exposition, not of discovery. Spinoza's discussion of levels of knowledge shows clearly that he did not suppose he knew the axioms and definitions first and then reached the successive propositions later on. He was not, like Descartes, sketching a purported order of discovery. Rather, he worked

23 Only Hume's *Treatise of Human Nature* approaches Spinoza's *Ethics* for its comprehensive philosophical sweep, and it lacks the tight organization of the *Ethics.*

out his entire philosophy before he began to write; and finding that philosophy to be complex and difficult, he chose for purposes of exposition a method which had proved to be a model of clarity in mathematics.

In the second place, the definitions and axioms given in the *Ethics* may not have been the only ones or the first ones with which Spinoza experimented in his efforts to effect a compact organization of his ideas. Evidence on this point is lacking, because Spinoza wrote in retirement and left no account of his personal progress on his book. But the supposition is likely that he tried out several organizational principles and found them unsatisfactory before he at last formulated the principles he finally adopted.

And in the third place, the axioms and definitions, taken in themselves and apart from the entire work in which they stand, are often obscure, even unintelligible. They first receive explicit meaning in their development in the particular propositions they are said to imply. The particular propositions may often be established as true by observation. These particular propositions are the proof of the organizational utility of the axioms and definitions. Or perhaps more accurately, the truth of the organized body of ideas is really the proof of the separate axioms, definitions, and propositions. Were the axioms and definitions not clarified by the successive propositions, they would not be known to be true, either by Spinoza himself or by his most enthusiastic adherents. In Spinoza's theory of knowledge, the abstract is not known first and the concrete known by deduction therefrom. Rather, a welter of confused ideas comes first, more adequate ideas may be gradually reached to correct the initial confusion, and finally (if indeed knowledge ever reaches its ideal goal) a comprehensive intellectual grasp of some large area of existence puts these adequate ideas into an ordered and rational system. A man ought therefore to hesitate to write philosophy until he has arrived at an advanced stage of knowledge; but when he has so arrived, he may properly present his finished system rather than his earlier meanderings with confused ideas. In the light of this theory of knowledge, one cannot fairly accuse Spinoza of failing to distinguish his starting point and his achieved goal. In one of his letters Spinoza claimed that he had the true philosophy but confessed that he might not have the best philosophy.[24] This distinction between the true and the best philosophy can mean only one thing; namely, that Spinoza was convinced that the content of his philosophy was true but was also willing to

24 *Letter* LXXVI.

concede that the axioms and definitions chosen for its presentation might not be the best possible.

For these three reasons Spinoza can be surely acquitted of the charge of begging the question. Instead of committing that stupid blunder, he was rather seeking, by the geometrical manner of exposition, to promote clarity of mind and ease of understanding.

SUBSTANCE OR NATURE OR GOD

Part I of the *Ethics* is entitled "Concerning God." But the God of Spinoza is so different from traditional ideas of God that the term misleads unwary readers. The appendix to Part I specifically argues against these traditional notions. God, Spinoza said, is not creator of the world. For a creator is necessarily distinguishable from his creation: a creator would have some attributes, and the created world would have others. God, conceived as creator, would be limited by the creation over against him, or, in other words, would not be infinite. And a God that is not infinite would be a contradiction in terms. Moreover, if the world were regarded as needing a cause beyond itself, so, by the same principle, would the cause of the world in turn need to be accounted for by its cause. And still further, there are, Spinoza thought, no final causes in nature, no evidences of design which require the notion of a designing agent behind nature. Spinoza thus rejected the idea of God commonly affirmed in the Judaic-Christian tradition. He spoke later on [25] of "God or nature," thus proclaiming that the two terms, in the context of his thought, referred to one and the same vast and admirable system of existential being. And Part I of the *Ethics* gives the argument which, he thought, not merely permits but requires this identification of God with nature.

Part I contains the metaphysical background of the rest of the *Ethics*. It begins with a statement of certain highly formal definitions and then develops in subsequent propositions the full meaning which Spinoza intended the definitions to convey. Three of these definitions are of major importance for an outline of Spinoza's thought. They are: [26]

By substance I mean that which is in itself and is conceived through itself, that is, that of which the conception does not require a conception of anything else upon which it depends.
By attribute I mean that which the intellect perceives to constitute the essence of substance.

[25] *Ethics*, Pt. IV, preface.
[26] Definitions 3, 4, and 5.

By mode I understand the modifications of substance, or that which is in something else through which it is conceived.

These definitions, far from clear in their initial abstract statement, become clear in their development in the argument for which they serve as organizing principles.

The definition of substance is equivalent in meaning to Descartes' definition of substance as that which requires nothing but itself in order to exist.[27] But Descartes' own definition, Spinoza proceeded to make evident, was logically incompatible with the applications Descartes made of it. Bodies (Descartes' extended substances) and human minds (Descartes' thinking substances) are created things, and they are affected in various ways by one another. Bodies and human minds, then, ought not to be called substances. They exist, to be sure; but they depend in their occurrence and their history upon many conditions. They are, therefore, modes, not substances. They are modes of substance; but the substance of which they are modes is the self-sufficient and all-encompassing system within which they have their finite existence. There can be only one substance, Spinoza pointed out. There cannot be in the universe two (or more) substances with the same attribute; for two things with the same attribute would impose limitations upon one another, would have to be understood in the light of those limitations, and so would be modes. There likewise cannot be in the universe two (or more) substances with different attributes; for two things with different attributes would involve negations of one another's natures, would be finite in the richness of their essences, and so again would be modes. Substance necessarily exists because it cannot be produced by anything other than itself. It is necessarily one because it cannot be limited by anything other than itself. It is necessarily (and, of course, for the same reason) possessed of an infinite number of attributes, each of which expresses its eternal and infinite essence. Whatsoever there is which exists must be either the one substance or modes of the one substance. Indeed, without reference to the one substance, nothing can either be or be conceived.

The first fifteen propositions of Part I of the *Ethics* give the argument summed up in the preceding paragraph. But in Spinoza, even more than in most other philosophers, the average reader does not readily ascertain the philosopher's position from the technical statement of it. Spinoza was expressing, in language reminiscent of Scholastic and Cartesian writings, a position which in our own day is

[27] See above, p. 226, n. 5.

called naturalistic. He believed that there is a vast system of nature (the one substance) within which an endless variety of many things (modes) comes to exist. This system of nature contains everything that ever occurs (it is infinite), has no beginning and no end (it is eternal), and has a productive power that is manifest in the rich display of particular things that have already appeared or may yet appear in accord with the laws of its being (it has an infinite number of attributes, each of which expresses its infinite and eternal essence). From the resources of the system of nature there "follows an infinite number of things in infinite ways." [28] And all this infinite number of things occurs inevitably according to natural regularities and uniformities in the causal sequences and mutual interdependencies of the natural structures among the finite particular things.[29]

There is a sense, Spinoza proceeded to make clear, in which nature is ever the same, and there is another sense in which nature is always changing. He fixed these two senses by the use of two terms: *natura naturans* and *natura naturata*.[30] *Natura naturans,* on the one hand, is nature as active or creative. That is, it is the fructifying energy which brings all things to pass, but which brings them to pass according to uniform, constant, and permanently established principles. Though itself dynamic in its efficacy, it always operates in an eternally unchanging manner. For example, water always freezes at a set temperature (when other conditions are the same); certain drugs are always poisonous to living things; and men are always mortal. *Natura naturata,* on the other hand, is nature as passive or existent at any one moment. That is, it is a condition of affairs which has been produced and temporarily prevails. But what nature actually is at any one instant, nature almost surely never was before and never will be again. That is, water is not always freezing, drugs are not always poisoning animals, and men have not always existed and therefore have not always been dying. The order of nature is one and the same at all times and places; but the particular state of the cosmos is changing from moment to moment. Any one of the endless number of particular states of the cosmos Spinoza called "the face of the universe" at the moment of its occurrence. But the face of the universe is subject to a ceaseless variety of expressions. The world is a closed mechanical system within which such fixities prevail as that indicated by the law of the conservation of motion and energy. But it is also a flux of

[28] *Ethics*, Pt. I, proposition 16.

[29] At this point, that is, in denying contingency in nature and in affirming strict necessity, Spinoza's naturalism differs from the naturalism of Aristotle.

[30] *Ethics*, Pt. I, proposition 29, note.

changing circumstances which come and go in accord with the fixed principles for the generation and corruption of all things. On the one hand, there is never any change in the laws of *natura naturans;* on the other hand, there are incessant alterations in *natura naturata*—alterations in the successive modes, in their diversities of position, quality, and arrangement, and in the processes of their becoming other than they were.

The thirty-six propositions of Part I of the *Ethics* reveal why Spinoza tended to use interchangeably the three terms nature, substance, and God. Nature is the basic term. It is what we find wherever we look. It is nature because everything within it occurs according to its own principles and without guidance from without. It is substance because it, and it alone, is what the definition of substance specifies. And it is God because it (rather than the personal deities of the positive religions, pagan, Jewish, and Christian) has the properties which orthodox believers list as pertaining to God. For it is infinite, eternal, the ultimate source of all being, and the one necessary being. Moreover, in Spinoza's judgment, it is perfect. Its perfection, however, is not a moral matter; it is a consequence of its unbroken order and its inexhaustible power. Spinoza held that the more power a thing has, the more perfect it is, and he maintained that nature or God has power without limit. Moreover, as the closing part of the *Ethics* explains, love of God is the only technique whereby men can achieve their supreme excellence or blessedness.

Two final words of warning may be added concerning Spinoza's use of the term *God,* for he did not mean by God a personal being such as most readers of his text probably mean. His God is not the God of the Judaic-Christian tradition. The Judaic-Christian concept of God, Spinoza insisted, is confused and inconsistent. If the concept were made clear and consistent, it would become the concept of a vast impersonal system of nature.

One of the warnings is that for Spinoza "neither intellect nor will appertains to the nature of God." [31] There is, to be sure, a sense in which Spinoza also asserted that "thought is an attribute of God, or God is a thinking thing." [32] This last proposition will soon receive comment. But it is not, when rightly interpreted, a contradiction of the denial to God of intellect and will and all typically human traits. Man, Spinoza could well have said, is no more made in the image of God than is a rock or a tree. All finite modes exemplify possibilities

[31] *Ethics,* Pt. I, proposition 17, note.
[32] *Ethics,* Pt. II, proposition 1.

present in "God or nature"; but none of the distinguishing characteristics of any of these finite modes can properly be predicated of God.
Spinoza's God is not personal; it does not act for ends, nor does it
know or carry on intellectual activities. It has no more concern for
man than for any other mode. It does not hear prayers because it
does not hear at all. Men are foolish if they supplicate it; men are
wise if they admire it for its indifference to their passionate cries.

The other warning is that Spinoza's theory of God is not pantheism, although critics abound who have said just that. Spinoza was
not a romantic like the poet Wordsworth who reveled in the beauties
of nature and then rhapsodized about nature as divine. Spinoza did
not apply the name *God* to any momentary state of the cosmos or
"face of the universe," or even to any collection or series of those
states. Each state of the cosmos is a mode, a mode of the highest level,
an infinite mode, but still a mode and not a substance. Each such
state consists of all the finite modes existent at a given moment, as
each of them in turn is a complex of smaller modes, and so on (unless one finally comes to elements that are further indivisible). God
is a term to be applied, not to *natura naturata,* but to *natura naturans.*
God is not the sum total of a lot of beets and carrots, men and animals,
rivers and mountains, planets and comets and stars. The eternal is
not made up of even a vast number of the transitory. God is the fixed
and established system of nature which gives rise in turn to each of
the successive states of nature. God, so to speak, is not so much the
world as the order of the world. The world as it is at any moment
exists in accord with the order of the world but does not exhaust
the fertility or infinity, nor does it possess the eternal unchangeability,
of that order. The order of the world, or the system of nature, is
alone that which may be called either substance or God.

THE ATTRIBUTES OF SUBSTANCE

Part II of the *Ethics* has the title "Concerning the Nature and
Origin of the Mind." In this part Spinoza gave his theory of the relation of mind and body and also his theory of knowledge. In both
of these theories he was explicitly criticizing and differing with the
theories of Descartes.

Spinoza rejected Descartes' doctrine of interaction of mind and
body. That doctrine he regarded as both false and ridiculous in its
implications. One of its implications, for instance, is that it requires
some seat for the soul in the body. But the supposition that the soul
has its seat in the pineal gland or any other organ of the body is so

preposterous, Spinoza said, that "I could hardly have believed the notion to have proceeded from so illustrious a man [as Descartes], if it had been less ingenious." [33] It is preposterous because it both places the mind's activities in nature and alleges that the principles of the mind in its interference with nature are contrary to nature's own principles. Descartes erred, Spinoza maintained, in treating the place of mind in nature as "a kingdom within a kingdom." [34] That is, Descartes viewed mind as purposeful and nature as void of final causes and yet pictured mind as interfering with nature's mechanisms. Man, Spinoza said in rejoinder to Descartes, is quite unable to interfere with the majestic course of nature or to exhibit traits incompatible with nature's laws. To suppose that man interferes with nature is to impute to nature a flaw. Both man's body with its intricate mechanism and man's mind with its many passions, ideas, and acts of will have their natural causes, through which, and through which alone, they can be respectively understood. When we competently trace the causes or effects of any bodily event, we always cite some other bodily event; and when we competently trace the causes or effects of any mental event, we always cite some other mental event. Never, in sound explanation of either body or mind, do we cite the other kind of event. We all speak colloquially in loose fashion, referring to a bodily stimulus as cause of a sensation or to a mental decision as cause of a muscular contraction. But we are jumbling our words when we speak in such fashions, passing back and forth, as it were, from one language to another and violating the rules of each language.

Spinoza's discussion of "the nature and origin of the mind" is the most difficult section of the *Ethics* to understand. Possibly Spinoza was not himself wholly clear as to some details of his own position. He has certainly been interpreted diversely by his critics. He is clear in his objection to Cartesian dualism and interactionism, and in his treatment of body and mind as two distinct ways in which the same identical human activities can be dealt with. But he extended his theory of mind and body beyond human activities and applied it thoroughly to the rest of nature. When he did this, he used the terms *mind* and *thought* in senses they do not ordinarily have.

Man has indeed the two aspects, body and mind. But so, on a lower level, Spinoza maintained, has everything else. Spinoza did not mean that the lower animals are rational or that plants have sensations or that rocks and rivers have consciousness. He is not defending a posi-

---

[33] *Ethics*, Pt. V, preface.
[34] *Ethics*, Pt. III, preface.

tion like primitive animism. Rather, he is arguing that everything in nature has two aspects. And he found it convenient to employ Cartesian language and so to call these two aspects thought and extension. Indeed these two aspects are universally present throughout nature; they are attributes of substance. Or, as the two first propositions of Part II express the point:

> Thought is an attribute of God, or God is a thinking thing.
> Extension is an attribute of God, or God is an extended thing.

The problem of the relation of mind and body in man is therefore only a special case of the relation of the two attributes of substance.

And the relation of the two attributes of substance is one of identity. "Thinking substance and extended substance," Spinoza proclaimed, "is one and the same substance comprehended now under this and now under that attribute." [35] Substance has an infinite number of attributes, of all of which Spinoza said the same thing which he said about thought and extension. In principle, substance may be adequately described, analyzed, and known under any one of its attributes. But we human beings know only two of the infinite number of attributes, and therefore, for us, the problem of the relations among the many attributes boils down to the problem of the relation of thought and extension. And that relation, as has been said, is one of identity. "The order and connection of ideas is the same as the order and connection of things." [36] Every existing mode can be correctly viewed as either idea or body. There are not two things, extension and thought, which mysteriously run along parallel to each other.[37] There is, rather, but one identical thing, though that one identical thing can be adequately conceived under either of the attributes.

In the case of man, and only in his case, the idea of his highly organized body is a mind. In the case of other modes, the body is less highly organized and the idea of the body is not a mind at all. Bodies only become living bodies, and ideas only become minds, when special structural developments occur in nature. Every mode of substance,

---

35 *Ethics*, Pt. II, proposition 7, note.
36 *Ethics*, Pt. II, proposition 7.
37 Unfortunately many critics of Spinoza have misinterpreted him on this point. They have made him into a psycho-physical parallelist. Then they have gone further and made him into an animist who believed that brooks and storms and other natural phenomena have souls as well as bodies. Finally, they have, in some cases, been led to distort his view of God, as if he had thought of God as apart from nature and maintaining by his supernatural power the one-one correspondence between extension and thought. This line of speculation is quite different from what Spinoza said in the *Ethics*.

nonetheless, whether highly organized or quite simple in structure, has the two attributes and can be conceived as either body or mind. So simple a mode, for example, as a line in a plane is an extended thing; it is also an idea which may be expressed in the equation of the line. Any change in the line involves a change in the equation, and any change in the equation involves a change in the line. The line and the equation are not two modes; they are but one identical mode, conceived either under the mode of extension or under the mode of thought. The circle drawn in the sand and the equation $x^2 + y^2 = 1$ are one identical thing. Similarly a certain material event of plunging rock and the idea of avalanche is one thing, and another material event of the spreading out of waters and the idea of flood are one thing.[38] The ideas in these modes are not processes of reflection, but they are ideas nonetheless. Nature must be conceived, Spinoza held, both in its one substance and in its many modes, under the two attributes of thought and extension. Each particular existing idea and the extended body of which it is the idea are one identical and inseparable mode of substance. The one substance or system of nature is both rolled out in space and displayed in ideas. The many extended bodies form one order of continuous extension, and the many ideas comprise one interrelated and integrated system of ideas. But the extension and the truth of things are not two but one.

THREE LEVELS OF KNOWLEDGE

Spinoza's theory of levels of human knowledge differs markedly from Descartes', though expressed in Cartesian language. Since Descartes conceived of the human mind as a spiritual substance, he began with man's distinctively spiritual acts of intuition. Since Spinoza conceived of the human mind as a mode within nature, he began with the confusions which ensue from man's first entanglements in the texture of natural events.

There are, Spinoza maintained, three levels of human knowledge. We human beings all begin on the lowest level, the level of opinion. Some of our opinions are based on hearsay, others on our own sensations. In either case they are unreliable. Hearsay is often unfounded rumor. Sensation results from interaction of human organism with external bodies and gives but very confused ideas of the nature of these external bodies. The body receives many stimuli, and the mind correspondingly has many sensations. But the stimuli are chaotic and

---

[38] Considerable similarity may be seen between Spinoza's position on this point and Aristotle's doctrine that every particular thing is a union of matter and form.

intermittent, and the sensations are incoherent and unsystematic. No idea in our minds is entirely false, inasmuch as every idea and every sensation is the mental equivalent of some aspect of the extended bodies in the world about the human body or of the human body itself.[39] But opinions based on sensation are inadequate because they do not reflect the full nature of the situations in which the human body finds itself. For example, when we look at the sun, we may judge it to be a relatively small disc "about two hundred feet distant from us." [40] We may later learn much more about the physical world, in which case we shall understand why the sun so appears and is bound, in accord with natural laws, so to appear to us. But in the first quite limited contact of our bodies with other bodies about us, the sensations which are the ideas of this limited contact are also a very limited participation of our minds in the system of ideas which is the fuller truth about those bodies. Inadequate and hence confused ideas necessarily arise in our minds, because our bodies are finite, have only a few sensory organs, and are affected by only a few of the stimuli which theoretically might affect them in the physical interrelations of bodies in the vast world of physical forces. Sensations, insofar as they positively occur, are not illusory or deceptive (as Descartes supposed). But they are superficial, they lack comprehensiveness, they are not a measure of the vast range and complex structure of nature.

A higher level of knowledge is reached when we have adequate ideas of things. We come to have some adequate ideas because all things, both all finite modes and the one inclusive substance, have certain common features or traits. What is equally in every part and in the whole of nature cannot be conceived except adequately and is reflected in "common notions," which all men clearly and distinctly perceive.[41] Examples of such common notions are our ideas of extension, motion, rest, solidity, size, figure, cause, surface, line, and, in short, all the fundamental ideas of mathematics and mechanics. Moreover, from these common notions, which are our initial adequate ideas, we can derive further adequate ideas by necessary deduction. Consequently, the means lie at hand, in accord with Spinoza's theory, for the progressive expansion of science and of human knowledge about the natural world.

The third and highest level of knowledge Spinoza called intuition.

---

[39] Spinoza never disparaged sense experience in the wholesale fashion of Descartes.
[40] *Ethics,* Pt. II, proposition 35, note.
[41] *Ethics,* Pt. II, proposition 38 and corollary.

The term is Cartesian, but the meaning Spinoza attached to it is far different from what Descartes meant. Intuition, in Spinoza's usage of the term, is comprehensive knowledge of a complete system of things. Even adequate ideas are only relatively adequate. The common notions, just because they are ideas of what all things have in common, do not give us the full nature or essence of any single one of those many things. Adequate ideas, true as far as they go, find logical fulfillment in an organized understanding in which the abstract clarity of the adequate ideas will be supplemented by a more concrete grasp of the detailed nature of things in their complex interrelationships. In principle, as Spinoza recognized, his conception of intuition presents so ambitious an ideal that its genuine achievement would not be possible for man. But at least it presents a significant ideal by which the various degrees of actual human cognitive achievement can be measured. And if possession of adequate ideas is the base for scientific exploration of the world, aspiration for intuitive knowledge is preliminary to that integrated vision of truth which is the quest of philosophy.[42]

Spinoza worked out his theory of knowledge without resorting to any epistemological legerdemain. His position is implicitly a rebuke to the appeal Descartes made to God as a guarantee for the validity of human reason. Descartes, he held, argued in a vicious circle: Descartes used reason and the innate ideas of the self in order to prove the existence of God and then appealed to the beneficence of God to justify the use of reason and the truth of innate ideas. Against that specious procedure Spinoza boldly proclaimed that "truth is its own standard." Or, in other words:

Whoever has a true idea knows at the same time that he has a true idea and cannot possibly doubt of the truth of what he knows.[43]

There is no way to know, Spinoza was virtually saying, except to discern that an idea is true. Descartes' claim at the end of his epistemological adventures is sound; for when we have a clear and distinct idea, we do know. But we do not need, and Descartes did not need, to appeal to a divine sanction as guarantee of truth. No one needs a divine sanction to authorize him in accepting his discernments of truth as being what genuinely they are.

42 In spite of his use of the Cartesian term, Spinoza was presenting a theory of knowledge much more akin to Plato's than Descartes'. Spinoza's conception of intuitive knowledge is almost the same as Plato's conception of reason in the figure of the divided line.
43 *Ethics*, Pt. II, proposition 43 and note.

PSYCHOLOGY OF THE MORAL LIFE

Part III of the *Ethics,* along with some propositions in Part IV, gives Spinoza's psychology, especially such psychological views as are most relevant to the working out of his ethical position.

The title of Part III is difficult to translate into simple English, because there is no easy equivalent for the Latin word *affectus* which Spinoza employed. An *affectus,* Spinoza said in the third definition of Part III, is any way in which a human being is affected by the forces which impinge upon him in his interactions with other modes in the world around him. It involves certain modifications of the human body and also certain modifications of the human mind (in accord with Spinoza's doctrine of the equivalence of bodily event and mental event). The title of Part III might be translated "Concerning the Origin and Nature of the Ways in which a Human Being Is Affected by Other Things." The discussion of this problem is cast in terms of a fundamental distinction which Spinoza defined in an explanatory footnote to definition 3. When an *affectus* so increases a man's powers that it can be understood in terms of the man's own nature, then the *affectus* is an action.[44] And when it so diminishes those powers that it can be understood only in terms of the external forces which produced it, it is a passion. Or, in other language which Spinoza also used, an action occurs in a man when he is adequate cause of what he does, and a passion occurs in him when he is only an inadequate or partial cause of what he does. In the former case, a man is expressing his own nature and powers; in the latter case, he is the creature, at least in part, of forces that play upon him from the external world.

The good life for man to live, as Spinoza conceived it, is one in which a man is active or becomes the adequate cause of his conduct. But this kind of life is difficult to lead. For every man has many inadequate ideas; some men have more, and some have fewer, but all men have some. The nearest approach a man can make to living the good life is by gaining as many adequate ideas as possible, and thus by becoming, as far as possible, the controlling agent of his affairs instead of being a victim of agencies in the world around him. No finite mode of nature, not even a man, can be entire master of

[44] This way of using the term *action* is unusual in English. For a man often behaves much more agitatedly and violently in the case of passion than in the case of action. Care must be taken to keep Spinoza's exact sense of the word *action* in mind through the subsequent psychological and ethical propositions.

his career. The tragedy of human existence, as Spinoza saw it, is acknowledged sadly in the proposition: [45]

It cannot happen that man should not be a part of nature and that he should suffer no changes except those which can be understood exclusively through his own nature or of which he is himself the adequate cause.

But we may discern clearly the kind of life which would be the good life for man, even if we cannot expect any man ever wholly to achieve it. Virtue, Spinoza said, is power.[46] But power is not brute strength, muscular or military; it is not unrestrained expression of passionate impulse. Power, rather, is action in accord with the essence of man or with the laws of human nature. What he meant in saying this becomes evident as he develops the propositions of Parts IV and V of the *Ethics*.

Spinoza often wrote of human achievements and failures in terms of *laetitia* and *tristitia*. These Latin words are frequently translated into English, but very clumsily translated, as "pleasure" and "pain." Spinoza was far from being a hedonist. He was not at all ascetic in his tastes, and he rejoiced to see his fellow men in their merry festivities and in their profitable possession of material goods. But he was, as much as Plato and Aristotle, a critic of the notion that pleasure can be used as a criterion of a man's or an action's moral worth. He never used the word *laetitia* indiscriminately for any and every pleasure. When he wished to refer to sensual pleasures, he spoke of the titillation of the senses. *Laetitia* is the joy or elevation of happiness which marks a man's growth in the mature realization of his powers; it is the satisfaction which accompanies the mind's passage to a greater degree of virtue or perfection. And *tristitia* is the reverse experience; it is the sense of futility and meanness which goes with a setback in a man's moral development or with a lessening of his mature powers. Spinoza maintained the position that a man lives best when he realizes within the texture of natural events the full excellence of which he is capable. *Laetitia* is the awareness of moral growth, and *tristitia* is the awareness of failure and degradation.[47]

Spinoza also wrote a good deal in terms of self-preservation. But he wrote two centuries before Darwin. And he had no intent to suggest that a man either naturally does seek, or ethically ought to seek,

[45] *Ethics*, Pt. IV, proposition 4.
[46] *Ethics*, Pt. IV, definition 8.
[47] See *Ethics*, Pt. III, proposition 11 and note, propositions 19–26; Pt. IV, proposition 41.

to triumph in a bitter struggle for existence with his fellows. When he wrote that every individual man, indeed every finite mode in nature, "seeks the preservation of its own being," [48] he was urging men zealously to pursue the enhancement of their status in nature. That is, every man, insofar as he gains adequate ideas and becomes the adequate cause of what he does, expresses his own mature powers and vital human energies, rather than allows himself to be driven helter-skelter by distracting stimuli from the rest of nature.

So far from regarding the good life for man as a ruthless competition against his fellows, Spinoza maintained quite the opposite position. A man finds many things in the world which aid him better to realize his own powers, but none of these things is so effective an aid as co-operation with other men. Two men of kindred purposes are twice as powerful as either one alone—and similarly with still larger groups. The theoretical human ideal, indeed, is that all men should be so adjusted to one another that their minds and their bodies should form, as it were, one mind and one body and that they should collectively seek their common welfare.[49] In an eloquent passage Spinoza wrote: [50]

There is nothing men are less able to do than to live a solitary life, so that many writers have defined man as the social animal. . . . Hence let satirists laugh as they please at human affairs, let theologians scorn them, let the despondent praise the life of crude retirement from society, let them heap contempt upon men and admiration upon brutes. When, however, all is said and done, men find that they are dependent upon mutual support in order to provide the things they need and to escape the dangers which everywhere impend.

To approach this theoretical ideal, however, men would have to be undeviatingly rational. They would have to outgrow their normal passions and to enlarge the active area of their living. Insofar as men are afflicted by passions they strive jealously against one another, disfigure their own lives by hate and others' lives by malicious attack, and tear society into warring factions. Insofar only as they live under the guidance of reason do they promote harmony in their communities, serve the good of their neighbors, and find for themselves the joy of personal realization.

Spinoza added to Part III of the *Ethics* a catalogue of the actions and passions which are conspicuous in human behavior. The essence of man, he asserted in the opening article of this catalogue, is desire

48 *Ethics,* Pt. III, proposition 6.
49 *Ethics,* Pt. IV, proposition 18, note.
50 *Ethics,* Pt. IV, proposition 35, note.

(or yearning or movement toward something not yet possessed). Every desire, then, issues in either *laetitia* or *tristitia*, as is requisite for Spinoza's theory. For when desire leads to moral growth, it is "action" and brings happiness; and when desire leads to moral loss, it is "passion" and brings unhappiness. The definitions in the catalogue (of which there are in all 48) go mostly in pairs—for example, love and hate, confidence and despair, timidity and daring. Insofar as they are not paired, the number of passions exceeds the number of actions—for example, ambition, gluttony, inebriety, avarice, and lust are all opposed to humanity or moderation. In spite of his vision of the theoretical possibility of the accord of men in an ordered society, Spinoza was keenly aware of the sordid as well as the noble phases of human affairs. Neither indulgent nor censorious in theory or practice, he viewed human nature and its problems with disinterested justice.

HUMAN BONDAGE AND HUMAN FREEDOM

Parts IV and V of the *Ethics* indicate in their titles the culminating theme to which the argument of the entire book leads. These titles express eloquently an opposition, and this opposition is developed in a threefold manner. The titles are "Concerning Human Bondage, or the Force of the Impact of Nature upon Man," and "Concerning the Power of the Intellect, or Human Freedom." In these phrases Spinoza contrasted bondage and freedom, nature's impact and man's intellect, force which coerces and power which controls.

Good and bad, like terms of moral judgment generally, do not apply to things when things are considered in themselves and apart from their effects upon men. And they do not apply to nature as a whole. Spinoza called nature admirable, because the system of things, in its vast extent and its marvelous complexity, stirred him by its self-sufficient majesty. He called it perfect, because the course of events is precise, undeviating, and firm. Nature is neither malignant nor indulgent. We human beings have no need to combat its course and no power to alter its laws. An understanding of nature was, for Descartes, a condition of mastery over it; this understanding was, for Spinoza, a prelude to a sheerly intellectual delight in its grandeur. Many men through the ages have sacrificed and prayed to their gods because they hoped to receive favors and concessions in return. Spinoza enjoyed the contemplation of the all-encompassing substance he called God just because God, as Spinoza conceived him, was incapable of partiality or passing whims. This ultimate system of nature which

Spinoza called God could not be perverted from its fixed ways. God is not so much to be utilized as to be respected, to be admired, even to be loved.

But man, produced though he is within the system of nature, is a moral being, capable of lapsing into base servitude to the brute forces about him and capable also of rising in dignity to a finer realization of his own rational powers. Having honestly acknowledged that substance is not a moral entity, Spinoza hastened to insist that many of the modes of substance are good and many others are bad. For many modes further the growth of human powers, and many others retard or thwart that growth. Music, Spinoza said as an example of his point of view, may be good for the melancholy, bad for the bereaved, and neither good nor bad for the deaf. What nourishes a man is good and may be called food, and what upsets a man is bad and may be called poison. Moral predicates may be, indeed must be, applied to many things in nature because of the role of these things in promoting or retarding men's efforts to develop their own specifically human powers. Within an amoral nature man is inevitably a moral being.

In spite of differences between Spinoza's metaphysics and Aristotle's, Spinoza's ethics resembles the humanistic position which Plato formulated and Aristotle systematized. But he emphasized more fully than the earlier advocates of the humanistic position that reason cannot solely by itself act in control over the passions. Man, he believed, can never escape from those interruptions of his life which result from his involvement in the mechanism of nature. An *affectus,* he wrote, cannot be controlled or destroyed except by a contrary and stronger *affectus.*[51] And the pressing problem of practical morality is therefore the means of gaining more of those impacts from nature which will benefit man's quest for the good life.

Spinoza's answer to his problem is in a proposition which is phrased in very formal language.[52]

The mind can bring it to pass that all modifications of the body or images of things are referred to the idea of God.

Human reason or the intellect, of course, is central in the procedure which Spinoza here advocated. For the idea of God is not a modification of the mind which arises in us from a passing stimulus or a casual collection of passing stimuli. The idea of God is an idea of the vast system of interlocking forces which is only superficially re-

[51] *Ethics,* Pt. IV, proposition 7.
[52] *Ethics,* Pt. V, proposition 14.

flected in our sensations and passions. But we human beings find our sensations and our passions qualitatively transformed when all passing stimuli are understood in the light of the entire system of things. A man, for example, will not feel resentment against his bodily pains when he understands that just such pains are inevitable for a finite mode in the natural world. He will not feel anger against another man who insults him when he understands that the insulting behavior is the conduct certain men naturally display in certain situations. He will not fear death when he understands that mortality is the natural status of a finite mode of nature. In summary, a man who understands that all events occur necessarily according to natural laws will be differently affected by those events than will be a man who supposes the events to be disasters deliberately and maliciously aimed at him. Not simply will he be affected differently but also he will be affected more intensely. And this stronger *affectus* will replace the weaker *affectus* he would feel if he did not refer all his experiences to the idea of God or the system of nature as an established order.[53] Fragmentary experiences, not put into their causal order by an understanding mind, are perturbations that disfigure a man's life. But "any passion which nature produces in us ceases to be a passion as soon as we form a clear and distinct idea of it." [54] It then becomes an action. The imprint of nature upon human bodies and human minds continues to occur. But to the man of discerning intellect all imprints of nature are actions rather than passions. They are not perturbations; rather they are enlightening experiences of a mind at peace with the world.

The power of the intellect, Spinoza believed, reaches its maximum when it cultivates in men an "intellectual love of God." No one can hate God; for the idea of God is the most adequate of all ideas, and hate is a passion. In the intellectual love of God a man finds release from pettiness, meanness, agitation of temper, envy, and bodily lusts. In the intellectual love of God a man finds poise of mind, serenity, control of bodily impulses, sympathy with his fellows, and peace with the universe. The intellectual love of God is the key to action, power, virtue, freedom—four aspects of, or names for, the quality of the good life.

BLESSEDNESS

A break in Part V of the *Ethics* occurs between propositions 20 and 21. At the close of the discussion of proposition 20 Spinoza said:

53 *Ethics*, Pt. IV, proposition 11.
54 *Ethics*, Pt. V, proposition 3. See also, proposition 6.

I have in the preceding propositions completed all the things which look toward this present life. . . . It is therefore time to turn to those other things which pertain to the duration of the mind without relation to the body.

The language of Spinoza here conceals rather than reveals his meaning. A mind in his system has no temporal existence, now or in the past or in the future, without a corresponding body. Spinoza is turning from consideration of the temporal to consideration of the eternal. But the eternal is not the immortal; it is not endless continuance through time. The eternal, Spinoza explained, is any existence conceived, not as a mode which occurs here and not there or now and not then, but as an idea in the system of ideas which is the truth about the world.[55] Substance, regarded exclusively under the attribute of thought (without any reference to the attribute of extension), is a system of true ideas. In that system of ideas is the truth about every finite mode. In that system, therefore, is the truth about each and every man, dead, living, and yet to be born. When a man conceives of himself in terms of that idea which is his essence in the infinite system of ideas, he knows the full and final truth about himself. And, of course, the same holds good when he conceives of any other existence in that way. To conceive a thing in this manner is to view that thing *sub specie aeternitatis,* to use Spinoza's famous phrase, that is, in the light of eternity. To conceive a thing in the light of eternity is (in the technical terms of Spinoza's theory of knowledge) to view it intuitively.[56] It is the highest form of human knowledge, as Spinoza said in Part II of the *Ethics.* It is also, as he now came to say, the noblest form of human life. It is man's blessedness.

   Spinoza's doctrine of blessedness is the paean with which the *Ethics* comes to its triumphant close. It is not the same doctrine as that which Spinoza elaborated in his long analysis of virtue, power, *laetitia,* realization of excellence. But without it the rest of the *Ethics* would seem a bit abortive, or at least baffling. For man can never achieve, amid the ceaseless play of external forces upon him, his full measure of moral dignity. Man can never win entire freedom. Man can expect, in his temporal existence, only some limited measure of moral success, only some relatively fortunate degree of happiness. The doctrine of blessedness offers man something different from *laetitia*—something different though not something inconsistent. Blessedness is possible even where full virtue is not. Man can understand the circumstances of his degree of *laetitia* and his inevitable taint of *tristitia;* he can understand, and, through understanding, may become blessed. Blessedness is no substitute for virtue; it is no compensation for moral failure. Rather, it ensues upon the radically just judgment which a finite creature may pronounce upon himself when he regards his finitude in the presence of the infinite. Blessedness is not subject to assaults from the mechanism of external forces, because it is a vision of the eternal. "There is nothing in nature," wrote Spinoza, "which is contrary to the intellectual love of God or is able to destroy it." [57] There is consequently nothing in nature which prevents men from reaching blessedness. They may reach it in the midst of ecclesiastical persecution, political tyranny, economic misery, bodily suffering, and all other inadequacies of finitude. They *may* reach it, Spinoza held. He did not suppose they *would* reach it often. As he said in the oft-quoted final sentence of the *Ethics,* "all things excellent are as difficult as they are rare."

3. LEIBNITZ

GOTTFRIED WILHELM LEIBNITZ, 1646–1716, a German mathematician, lawyer, and philosopher. The son of a professor of moral philosophy, he was reared in academic circles and took a bachelor's and a master's degrees at the University of Leipzig and a doctor's degree at the University of Altdorf. He served the Elector of Mainz and the Duke of Brunswick, traveled extensively, and later became librarian at Hanover. He developed plans for reuniting the Protestant churches, and even for reuniting the Catholic and Protestant churches, and also formulated the principles of the infinitesimal calculus. He became a member of the Royal Society at London, and furthered the establishment of learned societies in the Germanies. He spent a month visiting with Spinoza, to whom he owed a philosophical debt he was reluctant to acknowledge. He wrote a large number of essays on jurisprudence, motion, logic and the methodology of science, metaphysics, epistemology, ethics, and theology. Leibnitz corresponded with many learned men, and thirty thousand of his letters are in the archives of the library at Hanover. His *Theodicy* (1710) is the only book he published in his lifetime. His *New Essays on the Human Understanding,* a

[57] *Ethics,* Pt. V, proposition 37.

criticism of Locke's *Essay*, was ready for publication in
1704; but when Locke died, Leibnitz withheld the manuscript, which was not published until 1765. Among the
best known of his many essays are *Discourse on Metaphysics* (1686), *New System of Nature* (1695), *Monadology* (1714), and *Principles of Nature and Grace, based on
Reason* (1714).

LEIBNITZ SPENT SOME of his years in diplomacy, in the service of
German princes. The diplomatic spirit evident in the philosophical
writings of his later years reflect this early training. Leibnitz attempted
to resolve by logic the controversies which had arisen in European
philosophical circles as a result of the widespread influence of ideas
of Descartes and of problems generated in various Cartesian schools
of thought. In philosophical concerns, as in practical affairs, he sought
for compromises among conflicting views. Compromises, however, are
seldom completely satisfactory to any of the interested parties. Leibnitz' philosophical compromises are no exception to the general rule.
Even a devoted admirer of Leibnitz who can call him "one of the
supreme intellects of all time" says of one of Leibnitz' theories that
it "would never have seemed credible but for the previous history
of Cartesianism." [58] To many readers the theories of Leibnitz (except
some of his mathematical and logical discoveries) do not seem credible
at all. Yet his influence has been considerable. His readers are likely
to be impressed by his imagination and his ingenuity. And his metaphysical theories, if not "credible," have clearly shown the possibility
of one kind of answer to problems which are still "persistent problems" or stock classroom problems some two hundred years after his
death.

Leibnitz had a fundamental theological concern. He wished to
maintain a doctrine of God which would be more acceptable to
the religious traditions of western Europe than was Spinoza's. He
revived the ontological argument of St. Anselm and the cosmological
argument of St. Thomas. He sought to restore to favor the much older
teleological argument or argument from evidences of design in nature
(protesting strongly against the tendency of the science of Galileo
and the philosophy of Descartes to banish final causes from nature).
And he added a new argument for the existence of God from his
own theory of pre-established harmony. But his theistic convictions

[58] Bertrand Russell, *A History of Western Philosophy* (New York, Simon and Schuster,
1945), pp. 581, 588.

required for their support a restatement of various other philosophical issues. These issues Leibnitz discussed in the course of his many essays.

METAPHYSICAL IDEALISM

One of the issues on which Leibnitz expressed original views was the problem of the relation of body and mind. He agreed with Geulincx and Spinoza that interaction of body and mind is inconceivable. An idea cannot move a body, and a body cannot produce an idea. One ought surely to deny the impossible. There is therefore, as Leibnitz firmly maintained, no interaction.

Leibnitz' denial of interaction had two striking consequences which he endeavored to work out in accord with the logic of his system. One of these consequences is what is called his metaphysical idealism, namely, his contention that only spiritual substances exist. He argued for this position by a criticism of the belief of both Descartes and Spinoza that extension can be the essence of a substance. He held that indivisibility is a necessary property of all substances. Only that which is indivisible is substantial. Extension is always divisible and therefore cannot be the real nature of a substance. What a substance really and essentially is we know through our immediate awareness of our own selves. A substance is an independent center of spiritual activity. Not all substances, Leibnitz recognized, are of the sort that can properly be called minds. Many of them are much simpler and of a lower degree of development. They are all, however, more akin to minds than to the material things Descartes talked about. For their real essence is to be found, not in extension, but in their power of resistance to external influences. Substances are like points. Physicists treat of forces at a point; and metaphysicians, Leibnitz argued, ought to treat of substances in a similar way. A substance is an unextended or immaterial entity which maintains its own integrity of separate existence against the assaults, indeed, against the approaches, of all other substances.

The universe thus comes to be viewed as a large number of spiritual substances or souls, arranged in a hierarchy. The chief soul is God. And arranged below God in serial order, there are rational minds, animal centers of consciousness with sensations and appetites, vegetative souls, and, finally, the souls which have very obscure perceptions and give no visible evidence to ordinary observers of their inner spiritual nature. All these souls may be called entelechies because they contain in themselves a latent perfection. The simplest souls are, as it were, in a state of stupor such as we human beings experience in swoons. We ourselves are aware of the manner in which we come back to lively consciousness when we recover from swoons; we know that the recovery is a gradual process and that it comes from a prior state of faint and practically undiscerned consciousness. Such faint consciousness is the continual condition of the simplest souls. But there is nothing dead in the universe. Rather, the universe is spiritual throughout. It may be called "the city of God." God is related to the many other souls as a prince to his subjects or a father to his children.

Leibnitz endeavored to make his theory of obscure consciousness plausible by an ingenious device. When we stand upon the seashore we hear the moaning of the waters but would never notice the sound of the motion of one single drop of water. But as the sea is an assemblage of a vast number of drops of water, so the moaning sound we hear is an assemblage of a vast number of obscure perceptions. There would not be the loud sound, were there not the many faint sounds. The kind of obscure consciousness we do not notice is just the kind of consciousness possessed by the lowest level of substances.

Souls appear to one another, Leibnitz had to acknowledge, as so many bodies. Body, however, is not reality or the essence of things. It is, rather, appearance or the representative manner in which a spiritual substance is symbolized in another's consciousness. Souls act as if there were no bodies, for their successive states occur in them without causal action from bodies. Similarly, bodies act as if there were no souls, for all appearances of souls to one another are exclusively in the representative form of extension. Leibnitz' position on this point shows indebtedness to Spinoza's doctrine that the one identical substance can be fully understood in terms of either of the attributes, thought or extension. But it differs from Spinoza's position in that for Leibnitz soul is the only reality and body is symbolic appearance. Leibnitz thus exploited the subjectivism of Descartes, according to which the only things of which a soul is directly aware are its own states of consciousness. The allegedly material world is but the manner in which a spiritual world is represented in consciousness. Mechanics and physics, therefore, are investigations of the order, sequences, and interrelations of the states of perceptual experience in the unfolding life of souls.

MONADOLOGY

The other startling consequence which Leibnitz was led to draw from his denial of interaction is his monadology. Every soul, he maintained, develops through the principles of its own intrinsic being and without interference or causal influence from anything external to it. Leibnitz utilized for his own purposes Descartes' definition of substance, as Spinoza had done before him. But their purposes were different, and so their applications of Descartes' definition were different too. Descartes' definition was that a substance is that which requires nothing but itself in order to exist. Spinoza, seeing that finite things interact, then logically concluded that finite things are not substances and that only the vast system of nature is a substance. Leibnitz, holding that finite souls are substances, then logically concluded that each of them is completely independent of the others and causes no effects in the others. Each soul he therefore called a monad, that is, a substance which exists in and through itself alone. Every monad mirrors the entire universe. And every monad has in its own being ideas, explicit or obscure, of everything that exists or happens in the universe. When one person speaks and another person hears, the speaking does not cause the hearing. Rather each person lives according to the laws of his own being, though the experiences of the two persons are so harmoniously adjusted that men commonly suppose interaction occurs. Similarly with all the events in the lives of human beings and all other monads. There is no external influence which ever does come or ever could theoretically come into contact with any soul. Every experience of every monad arises in the life of that monad "through an entire spontaneity relatively to itself, and yet with an entire conformity relatively to other things." [59] Leibnitz picturesquely expressed his point by saying that monads are "windowless."

PRE-ESTABLISHED HARMONY

Leibnitz' monadology required for its support an explanation of the means by which countless monads, entirely without interaction, so unfold in mutual adjustment as to seem to interact. This explanation Leibnitz gave in his doctrine of pre-established harmony. God is all-powerful and produced the many finite souls in such a fashion that through all time harmony prevails among the countless lines of independent spiritual development. In his correspondence in defense of his *Discourse on Metaphysics*,[60] Leibnitz compared the universe to a large number of orchestras or choirs. Suppose, he wrote, that several orchestras or choirs are so placed that they neither hear nor see one another. Suppose further that each orchestra or choir follows

[59] *New System of Nature*, sec. 14. See also, *Discourse on Metaphysics*, sec. 28.
[60] In a letter to Arnauld dated April 30, 1687.

its own notes, notes which are assigned it by a master conductor. The whole volume of music would then be one harmonious symphony, though the vast symphony would appear to each orchestra or choir in terms of its own performance only. The order of the universe, Leibnitz concluded, is that kind of cosmic music.

THEODICY

Leibnitz utilized his doctrine of pre-established harmony in an apology for the ways of God in dealing with the world. The world, he maintained, is the best of all possible worlds. It may not be the best of all imaginable worlds, for anyone can imagine a world exactly like the actual world except that some one purported evil, or some few evils, or even all evils were omitted from it. But to imagine such a world is not to show it to be possible. One might say, if one recurred to the metaphor of the many independent choirs, that dissonance, although harsh and unpleasant in its separation from an integral composition, is nevertheless a contributing factor to the beauty and merit of the whole. So what appears to the partial view of finite minds to be evil may be requisite to the excellence of the total universe. In God's mind no evil would be apparent.

This theodicy fitted into some of the currents of religious thought of the eighteenth century and became the staple theme of the so-called philosophical optimism of modern times. Bolingbroke took up the idea and passed it on to Alexander Pope, who utilized it in his *Essay on Man:* [61]

> All Nature is but Art, unknown to thee;
> All chance, direction which thou canst not see;
> All discord, harmony not understood;
> All partial evil, universal good.

But the doctrine that "whatever is, is right" met strong opposition from less traditional minds. Voltaire, for example, caricatured Leibnitz in the Doctor Pangloss of *Candide*.

HUMAN AND DIVINE KNOWLEDGE

Leibnitz formulated some principles which have been important in the history of logic. Two of them, famous in themselves, are also significant for their connection with Leibnitz' metaphysics. These two principles are the law of contradiction and the law of sufficient reason. They are not altogether original with Leibnitz. The former,

[61] Epistle I, ll. 289–292.

indeed, goes back at least to Aristotle. But in their context in Leibnitz' thought they receive a modified and specific meaning.

The law of contradiction states that any contradictory proposition
is false and that any proposition which contradicts a false proposition
is true. By the use of the law of contradiction we are enabled to discover truths of reason. These truths are necessary truths. They can
be known *a priori*, Leibnitz held, because they are really all analytic
propositions. (Analytic propositions are those in which the subject
term already contains, explicitly or implicitly, the predicate term.)

The law of sufficient reason states that no thing exists or no statement is true unless there is a sufficient reason why the thing exists
or the statement is true. By the use of the law of sufficient reason we
are enabled to discover truths of fact. Often, indeed, we human beings
may not know the reasons for the existences we find about us. Our
knowledge of truths of fact is therefore bound to be *a posteriori,* that
is, it is bound to depend on experience. Truths of fact are, for human
beings, contingent truths.

The point at which Leibnitz' discussion of truths of reason and
truths of fact is most original is in his claim that the distinction holds
only for finite minds like those of men. For God, the infinite mind, all
truths are truths of reason and are known *a priori*. In the mind of
God, the subject term of every true proposition already contains the
predicate term. Only because of our lesser acuteness must we human
beings await experience to disclose to us what God would know in
advance of experience. For example, we have to turn to experience to
learn that a particular man dies at a certain moment; but the idea
of that particular man contains, in the mind of God from all eternity,
the idea of his death at the certain moment. In other words, all truth,
ideally considered, is logically necessary, though men, unable to follow
the import of ideas as God knows them, must pursue a halting method
in their investigations of the world and must await the instruction of
experience. The implication of this position seems to be that the
more a man knows about the world the less he needs to await experience. Leibnitz' ideal of knowledge is completely rationalistic, even if
he granted that men need more than their reasons to gain knowledge
of truths of fact.

X

English Philosophy in the Seventeenth Century

1. FRANCIS BACON

FRANCIS BACON, 1561–1626, was the son of an English knight in government service and a nephew of Lord Burghley of the Cecil family. Admitted to the bar and granted public office through the grudging aid of the Cecils, he rose slowly under Queen Elizabeth and rapidly under James I, finally becoming lord chancellor in 1618. He was knighted in 1603 and was created Baron Verulam in 1618 and Viscount St. Albans in 1621. In 1621 he was brought to trial on the charge of accepting bribes from suitors in his court. He confessed and was sentenced to pay a large fine and serve a long imprisonment. The fine was remitted, and the imprisonment lasted only a few days. But he was permanently excluded from public office. Commenting on his trial and sentence, he said (in what was probably a fair and objective opinion): "I was the justest judge that was in England these fifty years; but it was the justest censure in Parliament these two hundred." He was one of the great essayists in English literature; he published a volume of essays in 1597 and enlarged editions in 1618 and 1625. His leading philosophical works are *The Advancement of Learning* (1605) and *Novum Organum* (1620). He incorporated these works in a projected compendium of science and philosophy which he called the *Great Instauration* and wrote fragmentary parts of other sections of the compendium. An unfinished fantasy of philosophical significance, *The New Atlantis*, was first published at the end of *Sylva Sylvarum* in 1627.

BACON WAS A CHILD of the Renaissance, with its brilliance and its limitations.[1] A generation earlier than Descartes, he shared some of

[1] See above, Chap. VIII, sec. 1, for a preliminary discussion of Bacon's role in the Renaissance.

Descartes' enthusiasms, but he represents, in the detail of his philosophical thought, a quite different type of position.

Bacon was the herald of the empirical tradition in modern philosophy. Empiricism was not his word; nor would he have countenanced its use as descriptive of his intellectual stand. For an empiric, in the language of his time, was a dabbler, almost a quack, rather than a learned man; he was one who might proceed by some homely rule of thumb but did not understand the principles which might justify (if they did not condemn) his procedure. But in the nineteenth century and our own times, the term *empiricism* acquired a new meaning. It designates a theory of knowledge opposed to the kind of rationalism advocated by Descartes. It is the epistemological position according to which human knowledge arises gradually in the course of experience through observation and experiment. And experience, as empiricists usually conceive it, is initially and primarily sense experience. Empiricists are generally suspicious of first principles, of innate ideas, of the constructions of reason. They are generally friendly to the contention that we best know what things are by looking at them, by handling them, by trusting to our perceptions of them. They are prone to regard the ideas of reason as fictions of the imagination unless and until those ideas chance to receive confirmation in the observation of facts. And in this recently acquired sense of the term, we may justly call Bacon the herald of empiricism.

Bacon was the prophet rather than the founder of the empirical tradition. For he did not succeed in developing the position adequately and was seemingly unaware of some of its theoretical implications and of certain difficulties it was later shown to involve. He had no time for system-making. He was announcing a gospel for the times. He tried to lure scholars out of their studies into the open air of the natural world. He urged thinkers to turn from preoccupation with their deductive systems of ideas to a fresh examination of the many facts within the range of observation.

Bacon regarded knowledge not so much as an end as a means. He did not so much praise the joys of the intellectual life as emphasize the practical fruits of knowledge. In his first book, *The Advancement of Learning,* he set out to explain his attitude.[2]

Moral philosophy . . . decideth the question touching the preferment of the contemplative or active life, and decideth it against Aristotle. For all the reasons which he bringeth for the contemplative are private, and

[2] Bacon took a different stand in *Novum Organum,* Bk. I, aphorism 129. But the passage quoted above is more characteristic of him.

respecting the pleasure and dignity of a man's self. . . . But men must know, that in this theatre of man's life it is reserved only for God and the angels to be lookers on.

The subtitle of his *Novum Organum* is "Aphorisms Concerning the Interpretation of Nature and the Kingdom of Man." Bacon dismissed theological problems, regarding them as irrelevant to the task of philosophy. He professed to have religious beliefs, but he excluded all such beliefs from the field of philosophy. We have, he once said, no knowledge of God, but only wonder and worship. Philosophy is concerned with the visible world and human life.

Bacon had a keen realization of the need for co-operative effort by large numbers of scientific workers if men were ever to pursue and apply knowledge effectively. He drew up plans for an ambitious work of many volumes, for which his own writings would be parts, indeed the architectonic parts, but for which other trained scientific workers would supply further parts. This massive joint work he proposed to call *The Great Instauration,* and he wrote prefaces and introductions to various projected sections of it. In the opening preface he said: "I have taken all knowledge to be my province." But he did not mean to work alone. He wanted others to join him in making observations, in recording observed facts, in arranging facts in tables which would, he hoped, indicate their significance and value. He made a review, in *The Advancement of Learning,* of the existing state of the various sciences in order to expose deficiencies and gaps in current knowledge and to direct future efforts to the most needed supplementary inquiries. Actually he did not succeed, he did not know how to succeed, in enlisting other workers in a co-operative enterprise of research and experiment. Yet he had the vision of a society organized about an institution which would bring scientists together in joint efforts to expand the frontiers of human knowledge and to apply that knowledge to the improvement of human affairs.

Bacon's philosophical fantasy *The New Atlantis* pictures an English ship blown into uncharted seas by a great storm and finding haven in the harbor of an island previously unknown to the mariners. On this island the English sailors find a magnificently ordered society with countless devices to add to the happiness of the inhabitants. The civilization on the island centers in a great institution of experimental research called Solomon's House. When the sailors inquire concerning the nature of this institution, they receive the eloquent reply: "The end of our foundation is the knowledge of causes and secret motions of things; and the enlarging of the bounds of human empire, to the effecting of all things possible."

This typically Baconian utterance is both impassioned and sober. It is impassioned because it envisages vast progress in scientific knowledge and consequent improvement in the ways of human living. It is sober because it limits men's achievements to what is naturally possible; it does not rapturously extend those achievements to all things desired or to all things imaginable. Men cannot hope, Bacon recognized, to do all things. They can hope, however, to do much if they but learn to submit to nature's ways. By submitting to nature's ways, men may gain greater powers of control within nature and enrich their own destinies.

Bacon may be said to have eulogized, perhaps more eloquently than any other figure in history, the glory of the natural sciences, their fruitfulness in human affairs, and the dignity of their pursuit.

HIS NEGATIVE MESSAGE: THE IDOLS OF THE MIND

Bacon's discussion of the empirical method for the advancement of human knowledge consists of two chief parts: the negative part, in which he pointed out dangers which frequently lead men astray, and the positive part, in which he outlined proper procedures for scientists to follow.

Bacon is at his best in the negative part. He thundered magnificently against the arrogance of too confident rationalism and the folly of premature conclusions. He expressed his views in a series of metaphors which have become part of the legacy of English literature. For example, he wrote: [3]

Though it be true that I am principally in pursuit of works and the active department of the sciences, yet I wait for harvest-time, and do not attempt to mow the moss or to reap the green corn. For I well know that axioms once rightly discovered will carry whole troops of works along with them, and produce them, not here and there one, but in clusters. And that unseasonable and puerile hurry to snatch by way of earnest at the first works which come within reach, I utterly condemn and reject, as an Atalanta's apple that hinders the race.

The same point Bacon made again when he contrasted what he called anticipations of nature and interpretations of nature. He wrote: [4]

[3] In an introductory passage called "Plan of the Work" for *The Great Instauration.*
[4] *Novum Organum,* Bk. I, aphorism 1.

Man, being the servant and interpreter of nature, can do and understand so much only as he has observed in fact or in thought of the course of nature; beyond this he neither knows anything nor can do anything.

He never explained what he meant in telling men to observe nature "in thought." He seems to have wanted nature to talk to men and men to listen to nature. What specifically that means he did not make clear. It is obvious that he urged men to avoid such haste that they would pervert the facts and merely voice their own prejudices. That is why he denounced anticipations of nature. But he never sufficiently amplified his phrase about interpretations of nature. He seems to have been advising men to keep their minds passive if they wished to observe facts objectively. He seems to have supposed that a large number of facts, recorded in tables and so stored up "in thought," would somehow themselves generate an interpretation of nature.

The most famous of all Bacon's metaphors are those in which he discussed "the idols of the mind." [5] An idol is any tendency of the mind which, unless restrained, will involve a person in error. Bacon distinguished and defined four such idols and gave them picturesque names.

The idol of the tribe comprises all those dangerous impulses to error which are characteristic of the whole tribe of mankind. The human understanding, Bacon said, is always liable to being easily led astray by the affections and the will. From their love of simplicity, men naturally believe that the planets move in circles. From analogy with their own quest of ends, they believe that nature, too, pursues final causes. From the intensity of their own hopes and fears, they believe that their prayers will be heard and answered.

The idol of the cave refers to the specific tendencies to error which are more or less peculiar to each individual person. Every human being, Bacon explained, has a cave of his own. And when a man retires into his own cave, the light of nature may enter but is likely to be discolored in some particular fashion. About this idol one cannot generalize, as Bacon pointed out. Men belong to factions, read different books, and have varied tastes. Each man ought to study himself and discount his own subjective inclinations.

The idol of the market place is a name for the manner in which men are deceived by words. For men go to the market place not merely to buy and sell but to converse and gossip. Men are prone to believe there is a reality corresponding to every word. So men

5 *Novum Organum*, Bk. I, aphorisms 41–44.

have at times worshiped Fortune as a deity, have built up idle speculations about prime matter or unmoved mover, and have engaged in numberless empty controversies.

The idol of the theater consists of those loyalties to historical traditions which only too often warp men's judgments and make them partisan. Bacon may well have seen Shakespeare's kings and nobles walk the stage and have had them in mind when he coined this figure of speech. "The received systems," wrote Bacon, "are but so many stage-plays, representing worlds of their own creation after an unreal and scenic fashion." The worst examples of this idol are to be found in the effect of religious superstitions and theology upon men's judgments. Other examples occur in the similar effects of all philosophic sects.

HIS POSITIVE MESSAGE: THE METHOD OF INDUCTION

The positive part of Bacon's discussion of empirical method is his doctrine of induction. Our reliable conclusions come, not through the syllogism or deductive inference from cherished ideas, but through instruction from large and well-ordered assemblages of observed facts. We cannot sweep a floor clean with a broom which lacks a band to hold its rushes in proper position. So we cannot survey nature competently with a fund of information which lacks a principle of sound organization. The secret of scientific method, Bacon maintained, resides in a technique of so arranging observed facts that truths about nature will become apparent. Induction, Bacon held, is that technique.

Bacon illustrated the inductive method by a long discussion of the nature of heat. We need first a table of presence, that is, a list of instances of the occurrence of heat, such as the sun's rays, meteors, thunderbolts, and flame. We need next a table of absence, or a list of instances, as like as possible to those in the first table, in which, however, heat is not found. Bacon here listed such instances as the moon, northern lights, and the scales of fish which shine the dark. And, finally, we need a table of degrees or instances in which varying amounts of heat are found in changing conditions—intermittent fevers, differing temperatures of different parts of the same animal bodies, or different degrees of heat from ignited coal and wood. From these three tables of instances, Bacon concluded, or he wrote as if from them he concluded, that heat is a species of motion, expanding from center toward circumference, moving upward and rapidly.

Bacon's long discussion of heat does not produce conviction in most readers. Most readers suspect that he borrowed his conclusions from more competent scientists and failed to find suitable instances to support those conclusions. The idea behind Bacon's three tables, nonetheless, was a germ which in future times was developed into canons of induction and was made a central tenet of empirical methodology or theories of empirical procedures.

After completing what he had to say about the three tables, Bacon took pains to insist that instances of a phenomenon differ greatly in evidential value. Some aid the mind to draw clear conclusions; others do not. We ought, then, he urged, to take care to collect "prerogative instances." And he gave a long list of the respects in which instances may be prerogative. There are, for example, "bordering instances," such as a flying fish (between fish and bird) or a bat (between bird and animal) or an ape (between animal and man), all of which might throw light on the proper classification of forms of life. There are "migratory instances," such as the white color of pulverized glass or of the foam on tossing waters, which might help one to determine the nature of color. Or there are "instances of the door," such as observations made with telescope or microscope, which admit an observer into the secrets of nature more quickly than do ordinary observations. The ingenuity of Bacon and his felicity in coining happy phrases are more evident in this discussion than is his scientific competence.

HIS LIMITATIONS AND HIS INFLUENCE

If Bacon was the herald of empiricism, he was yet not a competent expositor of the empirical method or of the issues, epistemological and metaphysical, which acceptance of the method implicitly raises.

Bacon, strangely enough, did not have adequate understanding of the methods which were being used by scientists of even his own day. He spoke slightingly of Copernicus as "one who cares not what fictions he introduces into nature, provided his calculations answer." [6] He was probably unacquainted with the writings of Kepler. He praised Galileo for perfecting the telescope; but he had none of Descartes' acuteness in ferreting out theoretical difficulties in Galileo's procedures. One great weakness in Bacon was that he lacked realization of the role of mathematics in scientific thinking. He thought of natural science in terms of qualitative descriptions of things rather than in terms of quantitative measurement. He had no glimpse of that basic

---

[6] Quoted from J. M. Robertson, *The Philosophical Works of Francis Bacon* (London, Routledge, 1905), p. 685.

principle of modern physics according to which qualities can be correlated with, or can best be expressed by means of, quantity and number. He had the fault of taking some things uncritically for granted, which many acute thinkers of the early seventeenth century found reason to question. With all his brilliance of mind, his wit, and his imaginative vision, he had but a limited understanding of the role of science in the life of the mind.

Furthermore, Bacon was almost naïve in supposing that one gains knowledge of things by looking at them and in expecting laws of nature to emerge somehow from collections of facts and their arrangement in tables. He could, indeed, describe the empirical method colorfully. For example, he wrote: [7]

Those who have handled science have been either men of experiment or men of dogmas. The men of experiment are like the ant; they only collect and use. The reasoners resemble spiders, who make cobwebs out of their own substance. But the bee takes a middle course; it gathers its material from the flowers of the garden and the field, but transforms and digests it by a power of its own. Not unlike this is the true business of philosophy; for it neither relies solely or chiefly on the powers of the mind, nor does it take the matter which it gathers from natural history and mechanical experiments and lay it up in the memory whole as it finds it. Rather it lays it up in the understanding altered and digested.

The passage is beautifully phrased, and its point is sound. But in most cases Bacon proceeded himself much more like the ant than the bee. And the reason he did so is probably his unconquerable fear of the prejudices of the human mind. He disliked finespun distinctions. He deplored the readiness of men to observe only those facts which accord with their own antecedent theories. He granted, in the passage just quoted, that a scientist may lay his observations up in his understanding "altered and digested." But he is quick to thunder against any alteration by the mind as if it were distortion and against any digestion as if it were annihilation. He lacked understanding of the role of hypotheses in scientific investigation; he seemed to regard an hypothesis as a dangerous commitment to a corrupting bias.

The historian may well find a premonition in Bacon of the subsequent development of empiricism in modern times. Bacon's empiricism is more negative than positive, in outcome if not in intent. That is, it is much more successful as a warning against errors than as an elucidation of a positive technique. Likewise, from the time of

---

[7] *Novum Organum,* Bk. I, aphorism 95.

Bacon through the eighteenth century and well into the nineteenth century, the empirical school of thought has been more concerned to attack credulity, unwarranted "enthusiasm," and premature beliefs than it has been to proclaim any positive doctrines about the world. The role of classic empiricism in history has been to act as a catharsis of the mind rather than to draw up an outline map of nature. Scientists have received little guidance from philosophers of the empirical school. But those philosophers, hearty in their approval of the sciences, have been fruitful in demolishing obstacles in the way of popular acceptance of the views the scientists have suggested.

2. HOBBES

THOMAS HOBBES, 1588–1679, was born near Malmesbury in Wiltshire, England. His mother gave birth to him prematurely at the time of the approach of the Spanish Armada to the English coast. He wrote, late in life, that "she brought forth twins—myself and fear." At the age of twenty he became attached to the Cavendish family (among whose members were dukes of Devonshire and marquises of Newcastle). He served successive generations of this family as tutor to young sons and as trusted advisor and friend, and he remained retainer to the family, except for one interruption of three years, until his death more than seventy years later. He spent many hours with Francis Bacon during the last five years of the latter's life, taking dictation and translating Bacon's *Essays* into Latin. He fled from England in 1640 (shortly after the flight of his patron the duke of Devonshire) and spent the next eleven years in France. He became known to Père Mersenne, and wrote at Mersenne's invitation one of the sets of "objections" to Descartes' *Meditations*. He and Descartes are reported to have met once when they were both Mersenne's guests. He served for a time as tutor in mathematics to the young English prince who later became Charles II. In 1651, again following the example of his patron, he made his peace with Cromwell and returned to England. But like his patron he welcomed the accession of Charles II in 1660, after which time he was occasionally in attendance at the king's court. His first published work was a translation of Thucydides (1629), and among his last works were translations of the *Odyssey* and *Iliad* (1676).

He engaged in a running controversy with two distinguished mathematicians, Seth Ward and John Wallis, publishing nearly a dozen tracts against them, in which, among other things, he claimed to have squared the circle and cubed the sphere. In another controversy he defended against Bishop Bramhall his theory of liberty and necessity of the will. His philosophical writings are numerous, though they repeat one another to some extent, even at times using the same phrases. The chief of these writings are *De Cive* (privately printed at Paris in 1642, brought out in three distinct editions in 1647 by the Elzivir press, put into English by Hobbes himself in 1651); *Human Nature* (1650); *De Corpore Politico* (1650); *Leviathan, or the Matter, Form, and Power of a Commonwealth Ecclesiastical and Civil* (1651); *Of Liberty and Necessity* (1654); *De Corpore* (1655); *De Homine* (1658); and *Behemoth: The History of the Civil Wars in England* (1679, 1682). Against attacks on his person as well as his ideas he published two defenses: *Mr. Hobbes Considered in his Loyalty, Religion, Reputation, and Manners* (1662) and *Thomae Hobbes Malmesburiensis Vita Carmine Expressa* (1679).

THOMAS HOBBES IS THE complete secularist. He lived through troubled times of religious strife and civil war, and he blamed much of the destructive turmoil of the social order upon overly zealous espousal of sectarian religion. He believed most theological doctrines to be vain indulgences of human fancy as well as incipient threats to the security of the state. He proposed to end the nuisance they caused by subjecting religion to strict regulation by the government. He affirmed, to be sure, the existence of God, on the ground that we are driven to recognize some first cause for the world. And he once hazarded the statement that "God who is always one and the same was the person represented by Moses, the person represented by his Son incarnate, and the person represented by the apostles." In hazarding this utterly heretical version of the doctrine of the Trinity, he supposed it in conformity with the then existing legal establishment of the English Church. He would have been quite willing to make some different statement if the laws of the realm had so demanded. And in this strange attitude he was not being capricious; he was rather carrying out faithfully his own serious philosophical theory. For he was firmly convinced that the only available means of ending dangerous bickering over religious dogmas and practices is to subject religion in all its phases to the sovereign authority of government. And what he did to religion he would have been willing, if need arose, to do also to education, science, philosophy, and letters. Need might not arise; and he hoped it would not. He was himself a searcher for truth; he liked, for himself and for others, the privilege to investigate truth freely and to publish the truth thus discovered. But he judged social chaos the greatest peril to education, science, and the arts— a far greater peril to them, indeed, than control of them by government would be. Therefore, as a precondition to civilization and its treasured aspects of culture, social order must be preserved at all costs. We should be even worse off in anarchy and war than in a sovereign state in which the ruling power subjected the arts and sciences to deleterious forms of control. Citizens of a state, in many cases, may deem submission to authority highly undesirable; but they can hardly deem it, if they are wise, so undesirable as to prefer resistance and consequent violence. Hence, Hobbes believed that conformity to an established government is a prerequisite to social peace and order, and peace and order, in turn, a prerequisite to every other personal and social good. Hobbes concluded that all human interests ought to be subordinate to the secular power of a sovereign state.

THE STATE OF NATURE

Two themes are interwoven in the position of Hobbes just summarily sketched. One is the striking difference between the confusions of social disorder and the security of civil government. The other is the social necessity for strong, even for absolute, sovereignty in the civil government. Hobbes's political writings expound these two themes in their interconnections and their implications. The two themes, as it happens, are picturesquely portrayed in frontispieces to two of his published works. The former theme is portrayed in the frontispiece of *De Cive*,[8] the latter in that of *Leviathan*. Each of these two frontispieces will be described below as part of the exposition of Hobbes's themes.

The frontispiece of *De Cive* shows two personages, named respectively *Libertas* and *Imperium*. The Latin names can best be translated Anarchy and Sovereignty. Anarchy, on the one hand, is a forlorn and haggard female, nearly naked, carrying a broken bow. Behind her is a landscape where a rude stockade can precariously protect

---

[8] Only, to be sure, in the privately printed edition of 1642 and in the first of the three Elzivir editions of 1647. In the second Elzivir edition of 1647 and all subsequent editions and translations of *De Cive*, a strangely altered frontispiece appears which unfortunately fails to indicate the thought of Hobbes.

a few miserable inhabitants. Outside the stockade thieves assault a man, and a woman seeks to escape from the violent embraces of another man. Amid scenes of robbery and rape men have no inclination to plant and cultivate crops, so that the country is bare and unfruitful. Sovereignty, on the other hand, is a strong and handsome young woman, crowned, and bearing sword and scales as symbols of power and justice. Behind her is a prosperous landscape with a fair city on a distant hill. Before the city, merchants travel in security, mothers suckle their young by the banks of a stream, and farmers reap their plentiful crops. In a panel above the two figures of Anarchy and Sovereignty is a representation, in the traditional manner of medieval art, of Christ and the Last Judgment. This bit of iconographical symbolism expresses Hobbes's conviction that just as popular thought dwells on the unbridgeable gulf between the saints in heaven and the damned in hell, so he had found an equally unbridgeable gulf between the citizens of a strong and wise sovereign power and the helpless savages of a wild and barbarous turmoil.

The theme which expresses the difference between Anarchy and Sovereignty Hobbes formulated freshly from his observations of men and their ways. It was not a deduction from some antecedent theory, though Hobbes eventually tried to build it into a place in an embracing philosophical schematism. But in expressing his theme in language, he made use of certain terms which had been common in political thought from ancient times, often in senses Hobbes himself did not intend to retain. Three such terms are *state of nature, right of nature,* and *law of nature.*

The state of nature, in Hobbes's usage, is anarchy. It is anarchy wherever found, whether in the past or the present or the future. It is not some original condition of mankind. It is not an historical period from which men have escaped by framing governments. Rather, it is a constant factor in human life. It is sometimes so covered up that it is overlooked and forgotten; it is sometimes so prominent that it dominates society. It is always evil, and men are not rational if they allow it to prevail. It is the base way in which men live whenever they are deprived of two beneficent forces. One of these beneficent forces is the authority of government, which regulates affairs according to firm laws. The other of these beneficent forces is human reason, which may at all times discern the sound principles for human conduct but may at some times be impotent to implement its decisions. The state of nature is what would be left when civil institutions are weak and human reason fails to receive due respect. And reason is sure to fail to receive respect when civil institutions are weak. For men dare not amid scenes of violence do what reason might lead them to do in more favorable circumstances. They dare not keep their promises when they fear they are themselves about to be cheated. They dare not share their modest means generously with others when they fear others are intending to snatch all they have and perhaps to assault and kill them as well. When the laws are silent, Hobbes maintained, reason is silent too. And in place of law and reason, passions of fear and hate and greed and lust operate without restraint in human lives. Such is the state of nature.

The state of nature is, in Hobbes's words, a state of war. And he characterized the state of war with glowing rhetoric because he hoped thereby to help to make men avoid it. One of his most famous paragraphs is this: [9]

Whatsoever therefore is consequent to a time of war, where every man is enemy to every man; the same is consequent to the time, wherein men live without other security, than what their own strength, and their own invention shall furnish them withal. In such condition, there is no place for industry; because the fruit thereof is uncertain: and consequently no culture of the earth; no navigation, nor use of the commodities that may be imported by sea; no commodious building; no instruments of moving and removing, such things as require much force; no knowledge of the face of the earth; no account of time; no arts; no letters; no society; and which is worst of all, continual fear, and danger of violent death; and the life of man, solitary, poor, nasty, brutish, and short.

No orthodox Christian theologian with doctrines of original sin and total depravity ever pictured the condition of the damned more forcefully than Hobbes pictured the state of nature. No orthodox Christian theologian ever sought to save man from his unredeemed state more earnestly than Hobbes sought to rescue man from the state of nature.

THE RIGHT OF NATURE

The right of nature, Hobbes wrote, "is the liberty each man hath, to use his own power, as he will himself, for the preservation of his own nature." [10] It is not a moral principle; and Hobbes defined it with ruthless thoroughness, not to incite men to its exercise, but to induce men to remove the ground for its deplorable occurrence. When no government or only a weak and ineffective government exists, and when, consequently, reason too is deprived of the means of directing

[9] *Leviathan*, chap. 13.
[10] *Leviathan*, chap. 14, opening sentence.

affairs to desirable human ends, men have no resource at their disposal except the unrestrained assertion of all their brute strength and all their selfish wiles. In the absence of a neutral and lawful judge over social relationships, a man cannot do other than be a law unto himself and fight with passionate vigor for life and food and bodily satisfaction. In the state of nature, therefore, every man is enemy to every man. "In the state of nature, to have all, and do all, is lawful for all." [11] In the state of nature there is no measure of right except profit; and there is no measure of profit except the desires of him who acts. "Nature hath given to every one a right to all."

THE LAWS OF NATURE

The law of nature is "the dictate of right reason, conversant about those things which are either to be done or omitted for the constant preservation of life and members, as much as in us lies." [12] In this statement Hobbes was much more in harmony with traditional conceptions than on many other points. The law of nature is the law of reason; it is the divine law; it is the standard of morality. It is not law in the sense that it describes natural uniformities. Quite the reverse. It describes principles utterly at variance with the behavior men exhibit in the state of nature. It sets up norms of ethical judgment. It specifies ways by which men can escape from the state of nature and can enter into a civilized state (which, for Hobbes, is always a civil state). It can be elaborated in a series of maxims of almost indefinite extent, some of which are general and universally applicable to human life, and others of which are detailed and carry the voice of reason into any and every possible phase of human affairs.

The first and fundamental law of nature proclaims that men should seek peace by every means at their disposal. This law, Hobbes immediately went on to explain, contains implicitly the provision that men relinquish all their natural rights in favor of a power competent to regulate society in peace. Peace without sovereign power is a vain hope. Peace is a product of a power so strong that even human passions cannot override it. The first law of nature therefore demands that men should cease to act as independent individuals and should regard themselves bound, as it were, by a covenant with their fellows under the authority of a ruler whose word is law.

Other laws of nature require men to perform their contracts, to

[11] *De Cive,* chap. 1, sec. 10.
[12] *De Cive,* chap. 2, sec. 1.

manifest gratitude for services received, to render themselves useful
to others, to show mercy to the penitent, to disdain vengeance, to
be humble and just, to refrain from gluttony and drunkenness—in
short, to exhibit the virtues which, as Hobbes put it, are delivered by
God in Holy Writ. These laws are unchangeable. They may be
summed up in the rule that men ought not to do to others what they
would not have others do to them.

The laws of nature, however, in Hobbes's judgment, cannot, in most
cases, be safely observed in the state of nature and, hence, are not
binding in that state. Some few are always binding: such, for example,
as the law against gluttony and drunkenness. For these few are wholly
within a single man's province of control over himself and do not depend on other people's co-operation. But most of the laws of nature,
Hobbes maintained, are dependent upon the assent of two or more
men. These laws are always binding *in foro interno,* that is, in a man's
conscience. They ought, even when not practiced, to be regarded with
reverence. They ought, even when deliberately set aside, to be deemed
the desirable principles of procedure. But they are not binding *in
foro externo,* that is, in overt behavior, until and unless men find
themselves in situations which give some guarantee of reciprocal observance of the laws on the part of their fellows. Reason is able, even
in the state of nature and in the midst of war, to perceive the moral
desirability of peace and honesty and mutual kindness. But reason
itself cannot make conditions prevail in which reasonable men can
reasonably perform reasonable acts. The laws of nature do not require
a man to expose his innocence to the brutal aggressions of others. As
soon as a sovereign power is in being through which social order is
established, the laws of nature are binding *in foro externo* as well as
in foro interno. But in the absence of such a sovereign power, or to
the degree that an existing government lacks control, the laws of nature, although remaining admirable ideals for a possible future, are
actually without sanction and hence have no jurisdiction over men's
conduct.

SOVEREIGNTY

The second of the two interwoven themes which together constitute
the dominant tenets of Hobbes's political philosophy is the need for
vesting government with absolute sovereignty.

This theme is portrayed in the frontispiece of *Leviathan.* In the
upper half of the frontispiece is shown the large figure of a man,
crowned and bearing symbols of his power. He seems at first glance

to be clad in chain mail; but he is rather built up, as careful scrutiny reveals, of the heads and shoulders of a vast multitude of little men. The meaning of the graphic device is clear: it is that sovereign power is built up through surrender to a ruler of the thousands of natural rights of thousands of little men. Men become citizens when they vest their natural rights in a sovereign. The symbols of power which the sovereign or "leviathan" [13] carries in his hands are a sword and a crozier. The indication Hobbes intended is that the sovereign has entire control over both civil and religious affairs, or that religion is essentially one of the areas over which secular power properly has entire jurisdiction. And below the sword [14] and the crozier are further symbols, arranged in significantly contrasted pairs, which emphasize the two areas over which the power of the sovereign extends. These symbols are the castle and the church, the king's crown and the bishop's mitre, the cannon and the bolts of excommunication, the panoply of warfare and the instruments of dialectic, and the tourney and the heresy trial. Hobbes wished the sovereign to have absolute power everywhere in human affairs; but his emphasis, because of the social confusions caused by religious differences, was on sovereign control over religious doctrine and ecclesiastical institutions. Half of the *Leviathan* is devoted to castigation of the temporal claims of the Catholic Church and of the political arrogance of Protestant divines.

A state of civil society or a commonwealth may arise, Hobbes pointed out, in several ways—rarely by compact, but more often either by foreign conquest or by the triumph of a strong man or a strong faction within a society. Hobbes would have men judge governments, however, not by the ways in which they come to power, but by the social consequences of their exercise of power. He was not concerned to defend any principle of legitimacy. A *de facto* government might prove more desirable in its outcome, he insisted, than a *de jure* government; and once a *de facto* government prevails, it ought to be cherished for its fruits. Hobbes, of course, offended the many partisans who argued in his day for the "right" of some monarch to

---

[13] Hobbes took this word over from the 41st chapter of the Book of Job. At the top of the frontispiece are the Latin words of verse 24 as this chapter is printed in the Vulgate: *Non est potestat super terram quae comparetur ei* ("There is no power on earth which can be compared with him"). This verse is verse 33 of the King James translation of the Old Testament into English and there reads somewhat differently.

[14] The sword, of course, symbolizes the sheer might of sovereignty, though it may well mean more than this. For in medieval iconography the sword often stands for justice, and Hobbes's frontispieces follow medieval conventions on many points. In that case, the sword stands for the justice which prevails when the sovereign fully controls both church and state.

succeed to the throne or for the "right" of the people to choose the kind of government under which they wished to live. Any government, he held, once that government is firmly established, ought to be treasured for its value in ending the state of nature and in arbitrarily enforcing its chosen type of social order. Every government, since it is conducted by fallible men, will doubtless deviate at times from wise and morally just administration of affairs. But perfection in human affairs he thought unattainable. Hence the subjects of a sovereign power may not properly seek to restrain the government or to disobey it or to punish the ruler or even so to criticize the government as to impair its authority. Divided authority, he contended, is a contradiction in terms; for where there is division of authority, men slip back into a state of war among lesser powers until there again be some greater or sovereign authority to regulate the relations of the lesser powers. By the very nature of sovereign power, that power must be absolute in all respects. Hobbes knew only too well from his own experience that some governments are better and others are worse. He talked at length about the duties of rulers to their subjects. He announced emphatically that rulers are morally obligated to observe the laws of nature which are the principles of morality. But a fundamental claim he made throughout his writings is that a faulty government is better than the state of nature and that, consequently, citizens of a state are not morally justified in overthrowing even a bad government. No one, in short, is judge over a sovereign except God. Men therefore ought to submit to whatever sovereign power exists over them and to leave judgment upon the foibles or the iniquities of rulers to the Last Judgment.

Hobbes classified governments in the three traditional types which were distinguished in Aristotle's *Politics:* monarchy, oligarchy, and democracy. He himself preferred monarchy, or the supreme rule of one man. He preferred monarchy, among other reasons, because the selfish desires which divide a sovereign's interests from public interests are more quickly and more inexpensively satisfied where sovereignty is vested in one single man than where it is shared among many men or all men collectively. But this point, though it aroused anger against Hobbes in his own day and dislike for him in many recent readers of his books, is a minor point and not intrinsic to Hobbes's general theory.

The duties of a sovereign to a commonwealth over which he presides are numerous, according to Hobbes. A wise sovereign may well leave certain areas of human affairs to the free decisions of his people, or at least to some of his more intelligent and favored subjects. But no general rule can be laid down on such points, because the vital needs of a commonwealth may vary from time to time. The sovereign may not be expected to leave any human activity unregulated when in his opinion regulation is requisite to the security or the welfare of the commonwealth. Legislative and judicial functions are subordinate to the sovereign's will, as are economic and industrial procedures, educational practices, and religious institutions. The sovereign may determine what property is, how property is to be used, what civic obligations his subjects are to fulfill. He may take counsel where he deems fit and refuse to hear advice when he is so inclined. He may impose punishments and grant rewards according to laws he has defined or according to decisions he makes for special occasions. "To the care of the sovereign," Hobbes said," belongeth the making of good laws." [15] But the sovereign, without restriction from the people he rules, is sole judge of what laws are good. Hobbes regarded sovereigns as obligated to respect all the laws of nature. But, as he said in exposition of the nature of this obligation: [16]

Theft, murder, adultery, and all injuries, are forbid by the laws of nature; but what is to be called theft, what murder, what adultery, what injury in a citizen, this is not to be determined by the natural, but by the civil law.

What specifically and in detail the laws of nature require of citizens of a commonwealth, Hobbes put without reserve in the power of the sovereign. The duties of a sovereign, therefore, can be summed up in the statement that he must give concrete meanings to the otherwise quite abstract laws of nature.

THE PHILOSOPHY OF BODY

Hobbes had the ambition to arrange his philosophical reflections in the form of a comprehensive system. This system, he thought, can be achieved by adopting the concept of body as an organizing principle. The system would then have three parts, which he clearly indicated in titles of three of his writings: *De Corpore, De Corpore Humano,* and *De Corpore Politico.* Nature, man, and the state are, respectively, the three considerations of the three parts of Hobbes's materialistic system. All substances, he came to believe, are material substances. Man is a special kind of body, and the state is an ordered arrangement of bodies of this kind. To understand the nature of

15 *Leviathan,* chap. 30.
16 *De Cive,* chap. 6, sec. 16.

body and the laws of motion, Hobbes concluded, is the whole business of philosophy.

Hobbes did not work out the detail of his materialistic profession with much success. He accepted Galileo's laws of motion as the basic principles of metaphysics or philosophy of nature. He extended the idea of mechanism to the processes of human life and social affairs. When he wrote his "Objections" to Descartes' *Meditations,* he rejected the maxim "I think, therefore I am." He maintained against the Cartesians that our observation of thinking proves only that thinking occurs. There is no self other than the organic body. Sensations and other mental states he viewed, sometimes as the effects of bodily motions, sometimes as identical with those bodily motions. And he never straightened out his ambiguity on this point. He probably did not even notice the ambiguity, because his concern in the matter was polemical rather than constructive. He wanted to oppose the supposition of a spiritual reality exempt from the mechanical laws of matter and motion. And provided that this was done, he hardly cared how it was done. He contributed, nonetheless, to the development of a materialistic psychology. He defined ideas as "decaying sense," [17] that is, as after-images of earlier sensations. He seemed to suppose that he thereby reduced reasoning to mechanical processes, for reasoning and all reflective processes he called "trains of imaginations." [18] He never managed to carry out this materialistic supposition in his description of such activities of reason as are involved, for instance, in his own formulation of the laws of nature; and he never gave any detail to back up his confident proclamation that problems of political life can all be solved in terms of the laws of motion. But he was militant in his materialism. He obviously believed that materialism would prove to be a bulwark to his secular political theories. Did we but know enough, he held, we could deduce psychology from mechanics and politics from psychology.

HOBBES AND HOBBISM

The traditions in which the philosophies of even the greatest thinkers are handed down from century to century are seldom, if ever, wholly faithful to the original intent of those thinkers. Platonism was so colored by Neo-Platonism as to turn Plato's quest for standards of moral judgment into a technique of escape from the scene of political action. Augustinianism was so utilized in the strife of

[17] *Leviathan,* chap. 2.
[18] *Leviathan,* chap. 3.

pope with emperor as to turn St. Augustine's contrast between the heavenly and earthly cities into a contrast between church and state. Epicureanism has been false to its founder Epicurus whenever it has been represented as an invitation to hasty indulgence in sensual gratifications.

Never, however, in the entire history of ideas, has a tradition been less fair to its reputed sponsor than has Hobbism been to the thought of Hobbes. Over fifty attacks were made upon Hobbes before the end of the seventeenth century, and only two defenses appeared in print. Hobbes aroused the fury of all ecclesiastics, Catholic and Protestant, because of the secularism of his political theory, and of all legitimists in politics, Stuart and democratic, because of his argument in favor of any strong *de facto* government. He was also denounced for his materialism, for his atheism (which he never professed), for his profanity (which is certainly not present in his writings), and for his wickedness of character (which is directly contrary to the testimony of friends and patrons who knew him best). Misrepresentations of the philosophy as well as the person of Hobbes were common in Hobbes's lifetime and not uncommon in subsequent times. Students of the history of ideas may well distinguish Hobbism from the philosophy of Hobbes and may justly recognize that the former, unfortunately, has been more influential in tradition than the latter. Hobbism, of course, has its roots in the text of Hobbes's writings but was constructed by wresting phrases from those writings and giving the phrases a meaning Hobbes did not intend.

Hobbism is a caricature of the ideas of Hobbes. It is a way of thinking about man and the state which may be summed up in the following articles. (1) Man is thoroughly evil in nature, without conscience and without the possibility of genuine inner regeneration. He feigns at times to have worthy motives, but those pretenses only add to his evil. He professes to know certain right principles for conduct (the laws of nature) but ignores and defies them. He has no social sympathies but is brutal and ruthless to all about him. (2) Civil society is but a thin veneer of hypocrisy. Both ruler and subjects remain evil men. The ruler gratifies his own passions under a cloak of serving the common good. The subjects obey the ruler insofar as fear of punishment leads them to conform to statute laws but secretly defy him insofar as they dare to disregard these laws. (3) The very notion of virtue and good is a sham. There is no objectively valid distinction between right and wrong, but only artificial injunctions which rest on the superior power of the ruler. Whatever the might of a ruler ordains is *ipso facto* called right, and whatever that might forbids is called wrong. But there is no genuine measure for the worth of actions except success in gratifying the passing whims of passion.

Hobbes, accused of being a Hobbist, was called "the monster of Malmesbury." He presented his picture of the state of nature as a portrayal of what man without the restraints of social life and the guidance of reason would become. He was accused of exulting in what he held up as a terrible warning. He was accused of exulting in the free exercise of animal passions and of encouraging others to the same evil course. The attribution of Hobbism to Hobbes is one of the ironies of intellectual history.

3. NEWTON

SIR ISAAC NEWTON, 1642–1727, was born near Grantham. He was surprisingly studious, even as a boy, neglecting his farm chores in order to slip off and work at mathematical problems. He was sent to Trinity College, Cambridge, in 1661, became a fellow of his college in 1667, and professor of mathematics in 1669. He spent over thirty years at Cambridge. He represented his university in Parliament in 1688–1689, when the establishment of the House of Orange occurred. The new government appointed him Warden of the Mint in 1696 and Master of the Mint in 1699; and these appointments enabled him to live in London. He was knighted in 1705, was elected president of the Royal Society every year from 1703 until his death, and became an associate of the French Academy of Sciences in 1699. He knew Boyle, Locke, Henry More, and other thinkers of his time. He was difficult in his personal relations and had quarrels with Leibnitz, Hooke (who anticipated some of his scientific ideas), and Locke. He formulated many of his leading ideas when in his early years at Cambridge but committed them to writing only under pressure of controversy or at the solicitation of friends. His two greatest works were *Philosophiae Naturalis Principia Mathematica* (1686) and *Opticks: Or, a Treatise of the Reflections, Refractions, Inflections, and Colours of Light* (1704). He called philosophy "an impertinently litigious lady," and he professed to have less interest in his scientific work than in theology and Biblical chronology. He attacked the Roman Catholic Church with vigor, and he rejected the doctrine of the Trinity. He accepted the Bible unquestioningly as inerrant authority. His influence worked in favor of the deistic movement.

NEWTON, MORE THAN Bacon before him and Locke after him, formulated ideas which came to be regarded in many circles as the proper framework for a scientific attitude toward the world. These ideas held sway, especially in England, for about two hundred years. Their acceptance meant the decline of the method and some of the principles of the Cartesian philosophy. Newton had influence along two lines: he enunciated rules for scientific procedure, and he defended conclusions which, though he did not really mean them to be such, were viewed as the outlines of a cosmological system.

Newton's method combined respect for experimental observations with recognition of the role of mathematical deduction. The natural world, Newton believed, was thoroughly rational in the sense that the truth about nature would necessarily follow from the right fundamental principles. But no one, he insisted, can begin with these fundamental principles, because the principles can be reached only by induction from "phenomena," that is, from observed facts. Descartes' appeal to the inerrancy of "clear and distinct ideas" is an unjustified resort to unprofitable fictions and personal fancies. An oft-quoted maxim of Newton (repeatedly expressed in his books and letters in one or another phrasing) is "I do not spin hypotheses." By this maxim he did not mean that he refused to make tentative suppositions to be then tested by further experimental investigation. He meant that he refused to entertain alleged principles which had not been reached inductively from ample observations. He proclaimed that from mathematical principles which he had established in Books I and II of his *Principia,* he then proceeded in Book III to deduce the forces of gravity in the planetary system and the motions of such other bodies as comets, the moon, and the tides of the sea.[19] And he went on to say that he wished to reach knowledge of all other natural phenomena by the same kind of reasoning, that is, by further deductions from the principles of mechanics. But the principles of mechanics, indeed all fundamental principles, play an intermediary role in scientific thinking. Nature is such, he held, that it may be entirely disclosed in the framework of a deductive philosophy. But the principles of this deductive philosophy are hard to discover. The principles he used were gen-

---

[19] See Newton's preface to the first edition of the *Principia* in H. S. Thayer, ed., *Newton's Philosophy of Nature* (New York, Hafner, 1953), p. 10.

eralizations from phenomena and required verification by their application to further phenomena. Moreover, our knowledge about the world is so limited that we can never be certain that we have discovered the principles of a final and all-inclusive deductive system. Hypotheses or general principles, he wrote, may properly be used to explain things only insofar as the explanation arises from observations and also eventuates in experimental observations which substantiate the explanation.[20] Science proceeds from fact to fact through the mediation of principles of explanation.

The nature of bodies is known to us only by experiments. But we may conclude that the qualities which belong to all bodies within the range of our observations belong to all bodies whatsoever. Among the qualities universally present in bodies are extension, hardness, impenetrability, mobility, and inertia. These qualities are not subject to increase or decrease of degree; hence, they are immutable. All bodies, moreover, manifest a principle of mutual gravitation.[21] The universal and constant presence of such qualities in bodies is due, Newton held, to the fixed nature of the ultimate particles of which all bodies are composed.

Newton made popular in modern times, with more authority than any other thinker, an atomic theory of matter. He opposed Descartes' identification of body with extension because he could not view the world as a *plenum*. We observe that bodies of the same size vary in density, and this fact requires us to conclude that the ultimate particles of which they are composed are packed together, sometimes more compactly, sometimes more loosely, with varying amounts of empty space among the particles. Vacuum (such as the pores in bodies) must be granted. And the motion of the ultimate particles, unimpeded by any obstacle until the particles collide with one another, seems to occur in unresisting, hence empty, space. The particles may well have different shapes and sizes because they serve many different ends. All the qualities of the ultimate particles are immutable, and the universally present qualities of all bodies are a consequence of this fact.

Newton seems to have regarded time and space as even more ultimate than the particles of bodies, as if they existed first and bodies

20 Thayer, *op. cit.*, pp. 5–6.
21 Newton's formula for gravitation (that bodies attract one another in proportion to the product of their masses and inversely in proportion to the square of the distance between them) was not, of course, a matter of observation. It was a mathematical principle based on observation and confirmed by further observation. It "saved the appearances"; it brought its use of mathematics to the test of experience.

were then put into them. He used the expressions "absolute time" and "absolute space." Absolute time flows equably "of itself and from its own nature," [22] whether or not there is anywhere in nature an equably moving body which would enable us to measure absolute time exactly. Absolute space, too, may be impossible for us to measure; for we, the measurers, are ourselves on a moving earth when we endeavor to make our measurements. Our human measurements of time and space are relative to arbitrarily adopted centers from which we make our observations. But in all our experiments, whether with a pendulum clock or with eclipses of the satellites of the planet Jupiter, we deduce the reality of "true and mathematical" time and space as the absolutes to which we seek to have our measurements approximate. Relative time and relative space are precise enough for most of our practical purposes; but in "philosophical disquisitions" we ought to realize the difference between our sensible estimates and "things themselves." [23] All bodies are movable, and the relative place of a certain body (for example, the place on a ship where a sailor lies asleep) moves with that body. But movable bodies and movable places presuppose immovable space, even though our measurements of the latter are manifestly inexact.

Newton's theory of ultimate particles and absolute space is closely akin to Democritus' and Lucretius' theory of "atoms and the void." But Newton, unlike the ancient atomists, did not regard an analysis of nature as a sufficient account of the cosmos. He put physics in a theological setting. He believed that physical nature is the handiwork of God. God created the ultimate particles, gave them their shapes and sizes to fulfill his purposes, and distributed them through space at the proper time.[24] Newton appears to have relished natural philosophy primarily because it seemed to him to make evident the dependence of all things upon God's power. He called God an infinite, eternal, and perfect being who created and governs all things. God has no body, yet exists somehow always and everywhere. We know God through his power and attributes, but we do not know, nor are human beings capable of understanding, God's substance or his intrinsic nature. We may properly say that God sees all things and knows all things and acts upon all things. But the manner in which God sees and knows and acts is not a human manner of seeing, knowing, and acting, and, indeed, cannot be grasped by the human mind.

[22] Thayer, *op. cit.,* p. 17.

[23] Thayer, *op. cit.,* p. 20.

[24] He supposed that the date of creation could be fairly accurately determined from scriptural statements and that it was only a few thousand years before Christ.

We are not able to penetrate the mystery of the divine being, but we need to confess that God is Lord over us and the world.

In reconciling divine creativity with natural mechanism Newton came to picture the world as a vast machine, originally set going by omnipotent and omniscient power and now functioning smoothly without further divine interference. Newton's philosophy of nature as a scheme of things organized in stable fashion and deducible from fundamental principles required him to regard God's work as finished. Nature was produced by God, but, once produced, nature operated, and continues to operate, uniformly according to unbroken laws and through the forces resident within it.

Newton's chief influence on philosophy was in propagating the theory of the world machine. To Newton himself his theology was more important than his physics. But here, as often elsewhere in the history of ideas, a man's influence does not lie along the lines of his intent. To many who came after Newton and depended upon the physical teachings of Newton these physical teachings were quite capable of standing alone and needed no theological support at all. Newton thus promoted, though he did not intend it, a naturalism and even a materialism. The world is a machine, no matter how it first came into being, or even if it never came into being because it always existed; and its operations are according to unbroken necessity, no matter whether its laws were imposed on it or are intrinsic to its own material nature. When Newton's theology came to be forgotten, except as a quaint superstition of an eminent scientist, his physics and the theory of the world machine continued to control the thinking of thousands of men.

4. LOCKE

JOHN LOCKE, 1632–1704, was born in Wrington, near Bristol, England, and died in Oates, twenty miles north of London. His father was captain of horse in the Parliamentary army in the 1640's. Locke was sent to Westminster School and Christ Church College, Oxford. He regarded his training in scholastic philosophy as a waste of time. But discovering Descartes' works for himself, he read them avidly, and he showed considerable influence from Descartes in his own later writings. He was a fellow of Christ Church College for more than twenty years. He was elected a fellow of the Royal Society in 1668, assisted Robert Boyle in investigations of the nature of the atmosphere, was a friend of Newton in his later years, took the degree of doctor of medicine, and occasionally used his medical knowledge in treatment of friends in emergencies. In 1666 he met Lord Ashley, who was created the first Earl of Shaftesbury, became attached to the Shaftesbury family as tutor of the earl's grandson and as political advisor, and probably had some part in the earl's conspiracies against the succession of the king's brother (who became James II in 1685). After his patron's death in 1682 he went into voluntary exile, lived in Holland and France, and became acquainted with certain continental intellectuals. He was friend of William and Mary, returned to England upon their accession, accepted a minor government position which took little time and supplied him with income, and lived quietly in Oates until his death. His first two works, serving as tracts for the time, were of tremendous social and philosophical influence in England, on the continent, and in America: *Letter Concerning Toleration* (1689) and *Two Treatises of Government* (1690). His greatest philosophical work was his *Essay Concerning Human Understanding,* begun as early as 1671 and published in four editions in his lifetime (1690, 1694, 1695, 1700). Among other writings he produced are *Some Thoughts Concerning Education* (1695) and *The Reasonableness of Christianity* (1695). He engaged in several controversies, writing three defenses of his views on toleration, two of his views on religion, and three of the *Essay* (in replies to attacks by the bishop of Worcester); and he composed other writings on economic, religious, and scientific subjects. A chapter which he was intending to add to the *Essay* was published posthumously as a separate work under the title *On the Conduct of the Understanding* (1706).

JOHN LOCKE LIVED through most of the social turmoil of seventeenth-century England through which Hobbes had lived, but he was born more than a generation later and lived on, as Hobbes did not, to the Glorious Revolution of 1688–1689, when the House of Orange succeeded the Stuarts on the English throne. His philosophy expressed, in a great variety of forms, that confidence in the wisdom of peaceful compromise and tolerant adjustment of which his life and his personal loyalties were embodiments.

Locke was unwilling to trust sovereignty or absolute power to any one person or any one group. He welcomed the monarchs William and Mary to the throne just because their accession was conditioned by their acceptance of the Declaration of Rights, according to which certain important matters were legally placed beyond the power of the monarchs. He exulted in the fact that so far as he could detect, no person and no group in England had the kind of jurisdiction over other persons and groups which Hobbes considered essential to the establishment of peace. He thought that peace was much more likely to be gained if no one had sovereign power and no one even knew who, if matters came to a showdown, had greater power than others had. The Declaration of Rights bestowed upon Parliament some rights which the Stuart kings had claimed for themselves and supposedly left to all citizens some "inalienable rights" which no government could invade. Locke hoped, indeed, he expected, that all the factions in England—the monarchs, the Parliament, the increasingly powerful middle class of rich merchants, the universities, the ecclesiastical organizations, even the common people—would settle down, in some practical working compromise, to a wise and mutually acceptable adjustment of their conflicting claims. If this happy issue occurred to end the long strife of the seventeenth century, no one would need, in either theory or practice, to find out where ultimate power really resided. No indication of the temper of Locke's philosophy is more telling than the fact that he could write a long treatise on government without once mentioning the word *sovereignty* or even referring to the idea for which that word stands. His treatise was a plea for such moderation that no one would need to know who, if anyone, was actually sovereign in Hobbes's sense of that term.

THE NEED FOR TOLERATION

Fittingly to Locke's character and convictions, his first published work was *A Letter of Toleration*. The central problem of this letter, opportunely for England in 1689, was the relation of church and state. Locke approached the problem by proclaiming in his note "To the Reader" at the outset of his *Letter*: "Absolute liberty, just and true liberty, equal and impartial liberty, is the thing that we stand in need of." Where Hobbes had tried to settle strife by erecting a supreme power over conflicting interests, Locke tried to effect the same end by persuading contending parties to be more moderate and thus to escape the dire need of adopting Hobbes's menacing remedy. A state or commonwealth, he maintained, is a society of men constituted to preserve and advance their civil interests, by which interests he meant life, liberty, and property. A state has nothing to do with preparing its members for a future life and hence may ignore religious organizations and credal differences altogether. A church is quite a different kind of organization. It is a free and voluntary society, into which men may or may not enter according to their choice. It exists for the purpose of conducting the worship of God in that manner which its members consider pleasing to God and requisite to their own salvation. The state, therefore, ought to leave all churches unregulated, provided only that the churches do not incite their members to immorality or owe allegiance to a foreign prince.[25] It ought to leave all citizens unmolested in their acceptance or nonacceptance of membership in a church, provided only that atheists not be tolerated.[26] Churches and individuals, in receiving from the state the privileges of freedom of worship, will then owe a reciprocal obligation to the state. They will owe the obligation of making no claims to control the doctrinal commitments and the ritual practices of those who are not members of their own religious persuasion. Locke was himself a member of the Church of England, believing that in its comprehensiveness, it might bring all men of moderate views cooperatively together in loyal pursuit of basic English ideals. But he abhorred acts of conformity; he deemed such acts illicit aggression on the part of the state and dangerous incitements to resistance on the part of the nonconformist groups.

Locke espoused mutual toleration of religious differences for a further reason. He was sensitively aware of the distinction between knowledge and opinion. He was no doctrinaire skeptic. He believed he could demonstrate the existence of God.[27] He believed, too, in the immortality of the soul, though he did not suppose this latter belief capable of demonstration. But the doctrinal peculiarities of sectarian Christianity he deemed unprofitably speculative, vainly contentious, and completely without evidence for their support. He would not interfere by political means with others' beliefs, even when these beliefs seemed to him fantastic and incredible. But he did wish, for the sake of intellectual honesty as well as for the sake of social peace, to bring people to understand the difference between conclusions based on evidence and dogmas embraced on emotional

25 Englishmen of 1689 had acute fears lest the Catholic Church instigate Catholic princes to undertake the subjugation of England. The Spanish Armada had approached the English coast only a hundred years before. Locke shared a widespread feeling that the Catholic Church was an enemy of civil liberty and national independence.

26 Locke supposed that atheists, just because they lack faith in God, have no moral principles. See *Essay Concerning Human Understanding*, Bk. II, chap. 28, sec. 8.

27 His demonstration (*Essay*, Bk. IV, chap. 10) is a loose restatement of Descartes' cosmological proof. It is one of his most "rationalistic" passages. See below, pp. 308–309.

grounds. He deplored what he called enthusiasm.[28] An unerring mark of the love of truth for truth's sake, he wrote, is "the not entertaining any proposition with greater assurance than the proofs it is built upon will warrant." Many men make claims to revelation, he pointed out; but no man is entitled to embrace any alleged revelation unless and until he has reason to judge it genuine. Appeals to an inner light or to an "illumination without search" he castigated as "conceits of a warmed or overweening brain." Against the acrimonious strife of rival enthusiasms he sanely proclaimed that "reason must be our last judge and guide in everything." [29]

LOCKE'S RELATION TO DEISM

Locke's insistence that evidence is needed to substantiate religious beliefs as much as scientific beliefs leads historians to regard him as belonging in the deistic camp. Deism is a vague word; it refers to a trend in theological thinking of the seventeenth and eighteenth centuries, according to which the essential articles of Christian faith are those only which can be established as part of natural religion. Deism is, so to speak, a minimum Christianity. The men called deists were wont to reject claims of revelation, appeals to Scripture as authoritative, assertions concerning the purported occurrence of miracles, and speculations about the person of Christ and about divine grace. They repudiated the need for a priesthood, and some of them even regarded priests as imposters and charlatans.

Locke was actually none too friendly to the deists who agitated religious controversies during his lifetime. He considered them as arrogant in their negative convictions as the orthodox were in their positive convictions. He explicitly attacked the position of Lord Herbert of Cherbury (1581–1648) because Lord Herbert set forth his five positive doctrines as innate ideas.[30] Locke devoted the entire first book of his *Essay* to an argument that there are no innate ideas in the human mind. In some sections of this book he probably was intending to express a rejoinder to Descartes' doctrine of innate ideas (though, if this be the case, he was not at all successful in meeting Descartes' point). But in most sections he was directing his attack against the spurious methods of religious partisans who too quickly argued that what they firmly believed was infallibly true. The doctrine of innate ideas, in Locke's telling phrase, "eased the lazy from

---

[28] He added a chapter on enthusiasm to his *Essay* in its 4th edition in 1700. See *Essay*, Bk. IV, chap. 19.

[29] See *Essay*, Bk. IV, chap. 19, secs. 1, 7, 14.

[30] *Essay*, Bk. I, chap. 2, secs. 15 ff.

the pains of search," [31] but really dodged the most important intellectual need of man—the need for evidence to accredit opinions and so to turn these opinions, once evidence was forthcoming, into genuine knowledge.

Although Locke objected to Lord Herbert's method of proof and was suspicious of deists generally for their tendency to scoff at the sincere, if overcredulous, beliefs of others, he shared the deistic inclination to reduce Christian faith to a few simple essentials. The fewer articles a man is required to affirm, Locke held, the more likely he is to espouse Christianity. Doubtless there are many further truths which, did we but know them, we would wish to proclaim. But what we know is all we have a right to affirm and, also, all we can reasonably ask others to join us in affirming. Christianity, by being made simple, can be made persuasive. And so Locke, in his influential work *The Reasonableness of Christianity,* pared Christian faith down to three "fundamentals": that one supreme and invisible God, creator of all things, is to be acknowledged and worshiped; that Jesus is the Messiah; and that men should repent of their sins and obey the laws set forth by God through Jesus. The first of these three fundamentals Christianity shares with Judaism. The other two are "the indispensable conditions of the new covenant."

In his discussion of the two specifically Christian articles Locke was quite vague. He never explained just what it means to say that Jesus is Messiah, and he never listed the laws set forth by God through Jesus. He was not trying to be precise; he was seeking to inculcate a generous attitude of good will among men. He himself enjoyed reading and meditating on the words of the Bible; and in his old age he occupied himself with writing a long (and tedious) paraphrase of the letters of St. Paul. He doubtless hoped that others would use the guidance of the Christian Scriptures. But he feared to go further than to promote a general atmosphere of pious moralism, lest he become guilty of infringing his own principles of toleration.

The influence of Locke upon the development of deism after his time was considerable. It was hardly what he would have wished, however, because his neglect or even rejection of many traditional Christian doctrines received more attention than his acceptance of the two vaguely expressed Christian fundamentals. Two young admirers of the older Locke exploited the negative side of his teaching. John Toland (1670–1722), in *Christianity Not Mysterious,* asserted that whatever in historic Christianity is obscure or incomprehensible

[31] *Essay,* Bk. I, chap. 3, sec. 25.

is a spurious accretion to the simple gospel. Matthew Tindal (1653–1733), in *Christianity As Old As Creation,* argued that the only true parts of historic Christianity are the doctrines which Christianity shares with all the other religions of mankind. Both of these men maintained that faith ought never to go beyond reason. And Locke's former pupil, the Anthony Ashley Cooper (1671–1713) who became the third Earl of Shaftesbury, in his rambling *Characteristics of Men, Manners, Opinions, and Times,* contended that morality is entirely independent of religion and needs no support from theistic faith (though he added that doubtless God stands behind the harmonies of the natural and social world). Locke's philosophy promoted these later books. These books, critics may fairly say, are more consistent with Locke's theory of knowledge than Locke was himself in his vague theological generalities. Thus Locke's treatment of religion, apt as it was to the decade of its composition, proved to be a chapter in the history of the spread of deism.

CIVIL GOVERNMENT

Locke wrote his *Treatises of Government,* as he himself says in the preface, "to establish the throne of our good King William." But in doing that he took occasion also to frame a political philosophy which, without dealing directly with the theories of Hobbes, accomplished two things which he thought Hobbes failed to do. In the first place, he so divided political power among the branches of government and the people that ultimate issues would not arise and require anyone to determine the factual seat of sovereignty. In the second place, he so made moral principles prior to political power that all persons and all institutions would be subject to moral judgment.

Locke held that men had existed in a state of nature before they entered into civil society, and he pointed to the American Indians as an instance of a prepolitical society. All men in the state of nature are endowed with certain rights, among which the chief are rights to life, liberty, and property. These rights are inalienable and are possessed by all men equally. In the state of nature men have

perfect freedom to order their actions and dispose of their possessions and persons as they think fit, within the bounds of the law of nature, without asking leave, or depending upon the will of any other man.[32]

The law of nature is the instruction of reason which requires every man to respect the equal rights of every other man and so to pro-

---

[32] *Treatise of Civil Government,* sec. 4.

mote peace in the social order. Men are naturally social beings, so that society is prior to civil institutions or the state. The state of nature would indeed be, if men were only sufficiently reasonable, a condition of concord and happiness.

Unfortunately, the state of nature is not idyllic. It degenerates into the state of war because some men, if not all, are tempted to be rapacious and to invade the rights of others. And so the decent majority of mankind, compelled to take measures to preserve their rights against assault, band together in a compact for mutual protection. This compact necessitates that the men who enter into it surrender some of their rights to the officials chosen to implement the compact in subsequent action. They do not surrender all their rights; they do not surrender any more rights than necessary to vest the officials with power sufficient to fulfill their functions. Locke wrote as if convinced that the state of nature, if it were not violated by the malicious few, would be more desirable than the state of civil society. For to possess all one's natural rights is better than to preserve some rights through the surrender of other rights. But the state of nature is unstable; it oscillates between the state of war and the state of civil society. And the state of civil society is so superior to the state of war that all sophisticated or experienced societies have entered into compacts to live under the protection of political power. The state of nature, abstractly considered, may be the best condition for men; but the state of political society, practically considered, is the best condition which men can devise for the joint possession of considerable freedom and sufficient security. The state of civil society is a kind of insurance policy against the state of war.

No government is legitimate, Locke sternly insisted, unless founded through mutual consent of its subjects. No government has moral claims to obedience if established by conquest or by brute force of the strong over the weak. And, indeed, as Locke proceeded to declare, if a government, even one legitimately set up, exceeds its designated functions and invades the personal rights its citizens have retained within their individual jurisdiction, it is at once at war with its own subjects and may rightfully be overthrown. Locke was not a radical anxious to experiment with frequent changes in governments. He acknowledged that a limited right of revolution is vested in citizens of a state, not merely because he was seeking to substantiate the Glorious Revolution of 1688–1689 in England but also because recognition of that right, he thought, would sober rulers, would restrain rulers within legal limits, and so would tend to decrease the number of occasions when the right of revolution would need to be exercised. He was placing the officials of government, as he had already placed the mass of citizens, under the moral authority of the law of nature. "Wherever law ends, tyranny begins." [33] And tyranny invites, and properly deserves, defiance.

A state of civil society or a commonwealth exists when, and only when, three conditions are met. There must be a known and settled body of statute laws and, hence, a legally constituted lawmaker. There must be a known and impartial judge before whom disputes may be brought and by whom disputes may be resolved in accord with the statute laws. And there must be a known executive powerful enough to enforce the laws and to support the judge's decisions. These three branches of government are collateral, co-operative, but free of one another's control. By the division of political power among them, Locke expected, governments may be tamed and rendered useful, rather than dangerous, to the preservation of comparative freedom for individual citizens.

Locke's *Letter Concerning Toleration* and *Treatise of Civil Government,* more than any other documents which could be named, are the *locus classicus* for a tradition, frequently called "liberalism," which has characterized modern political life. This type of liberalism has normally manifested a combination of qualities which Locke himself exhibited. It has been genially skeptical about the range of human knowledge; content with vague, unformulated, and attenuated articles of religious faith; tolerant over wide areas of affairs where assurance is difficult and variety may add to the spice of life; insistent upon individual rights and yet sensitive to social duties; anxious to muddle through political problems without allowing issues to be sharply drawn; willing to make threats of resistance but reluctant to execute these threats; and above all, hopeful that evil is not very evil and good is likely soon to abound. The spirit of Locke lives in this form of liberalism.

HISTORY OF THE WRITING OF THE *ESSAY*

Locke's *chef-d'oeuvre* is his *Essay Concerning Human Understanding.* This long and rambling work was begun in 1671, was written at various times during the next twenty years, was first published in 1690, was revised for later editions, and was undergoing a further revision when Locke died in 1704. Locke worked upon the *Essay* at scattered intervals over a period of more than thirty years. He

---

[33] *Treatise of Civil Government,* sec. 202.

was animated at the outset by the irenic purposes he of course entertained throughout his life in social, religious, and political affairs. But he soon turned to the more general problems of human knowledge as it is sought in all the fields of scientific investigation. He was early influenced by the work of English scientists like Boyle, who, in accord with the Baconian tradition, stressed the importance of accumulations of factual data; and he tried later to take some account of those conceptions of sense experience and scientific method which he encountered in Galileo and Descartes and the rationalistic continental traditions. His *Essay* reflects the stages in his intellectual development and the gradual changes of his opinion on moot points. Some of the terms he used most freely—such as *experience, ideas,* and even *knowledge*—become equivocal and elusive in meaning. And he felt driven at times toward conclusions he certainly had not foreseen in the earlier years of his writing, did not really wish to adopt, and only acknowledged with reluctance. His philosophical odyssey is instructive, not because he came eventually to one clearly announced point of view (for he never did this), but because he faced all his successive difficulties with unflinching honesty and intellectual candor.

Locke gave the following account of the way in which he began and continued the writing of his *Essay:* [34]

Were it fit to trouble thee with the history of this *Essay,* I should tell thee, that five or six friends meeting at my chamber, and discoursing on a subject very remote from this, found themselves quickly at a stand, by the difficulties that rose on every side. After we had awhile puzzled ourselves, without coming any nearer a resolution of those doubts which perplexed us, it came into my thoughts that we took a wrong course; and that before we set ourselves upon inquiries of that nature, it was necessary to examine our own abilities, and see what objects our understandings were, or were not, fitted to deal with. This I proposed to the company, who all readily assented; and thereupon it was agreed that this should be our first inquiry. Some hasty and undigested thoughts, on a subject I had never before considered, which I set down against our next meeting, gave the first entrance into this discourse; which having been begun by chance, was continued by intreaty; written by incoherent parcels; and after long intervals of neglect, resumed again, as my humour or occasions permitted; and at last, in a retirement where an attendance on my health gave me leisure, it was brought into that order thou now seest it.

The "subject very remote from" a generalized theory of knowledge was the principles of morality and revealed religion.[35] The proposal

[34] In "The Epistle to the Reader" which he put at the beginning of the *Essay.*
[35] Locke did not himself disclose this fact. We learn it from James Tyrrell (1642–1718),

"to examine our own abilities" led Locke to a principle he firmly embraced and never relinquished, namely, that we can gain knowledge of things only insofar as we have experience of them. Revealed religion, he believed, was concerned with things which lie beyond experience. We may hazard opinions on such matters, but we ought to realize that these opinions are precarious and do not constitute knowledge. We can easily know the things we observe and handle in our daily experience, and we can extend our homely knowledge by scientific research if we will but set ourselves systematically to make observations scrupulously (as he himself did, for example, in aiding Robert Boyle to investigate meteorological phenomena). Physical scientists, Locke noted, are constantly increasing human knowledge; but theologians are engaging in unprofitable disputes about the origin of the world and the Last Judgment, about the fall of man and divine grace, about angels and heaven and hell and a host of other things we are not in a position to examine directly. We ought, therefore, Locke contended, to distinguish sharply between knowledge and opinion. Knowledge of the things that exist may not go as far as experience goes (because we do not always attend carefully to all the contents of experience), but it certainly never goes further.

LOCKE'S EARLIER THEORY OF KNOWLEDGE

Locke's earliest theory of human knowledge is a simple and untechnical realism defended by a thoroughly empirical method of procedure. In a preliminary version or draft for the *Essay* [36] he wrote that the measure of truth is "the real existing of the thing thus and thus, and the discoveries we make thereof by our senses." We probably do not ascertain through our senses the "settled and distinct complete nature of things." But we do observe things directly, even if partially. "Finding things without us, and examining them by those faculties nature has bestowed on us suited to such objects, the best we can, we frame ideas of them and then give them names."

In the four published editions of the finished *Essay* Locke continued, not consistently but occasionally, to express this same point of view. Even a child, he wrote, knows what an apple is and what fire

a friend of Locke who was present at the meeting in Locke's chamber. Tyrrell made a notation to this effect in the margin of his copy of Locke's *Essay* (now preserved in the British Museum).

[36] Several drafts for the *Essay* which Locke did not intend to publish were fortunately preserved among Locke's papers and have recently been made available in printed form. The draft here used was published in 1931 by Benjamin Rand under the title, *An Essay Concerning the Understanding, Knowledge, Opinion, and Assent.* The three quotations given above are from pp. 300 and 154 of this draft.

is, and so quickly assents to the proposition that "an apple is not fire." [37] And natural philosophers, with wider experience than a child and with that experience properly systematized, know that "two bodies cannot be in the same place" as surely as we all know that "white is not black" and that "a square is not a circle." [38] No one indeed, child or scientist, knows about the great ocean of being that surrounds the little island of our experience. For if we take the ideas we gain from experience and try to use them in speculations concerning things unexperienced, we may form opinions that please us and may possibly become precious to us, but we are not entitled to indulge our fancies and to regard these opinions as knowledge. Our reliable knowledge is reached through observing things directly.

This simple and untechnical position of the drafts and of some passages in the finished *Essay* was soon overlaid with complex and technical theories. But it was qualified with reluctance, was never wholly abandoned, and determined to some extent the manner in which Locke stated the later theories. It occurs, for example, in a chapter Locke entitled "The Idea of Solidity." In this chapter Locke said: [39]

The idea of solidity we receive by our touch: and it arises from the resistance which we find in body to the entrance of any other body into the place it possesses, till it has left it. . . . If any one asks me, what this solidity is, I send him to his senses to inform him. Let him put a flint or a football between his hands, and then endeavor to join them, and he will know.

This passage is one of the many illustrations Locke gave of his principle that all our ideas come from experience. Experience, in this and kindred passages, is a matter of touching and seeing and otherwise sensing natural objects, like stones and balls, in the world around us. It is direct contact with, and awareness of, things. And, as Locke went on to point out, we have experience of our own mental actions, too; we know what perceiving and thinking and willing are because we observe the "actions of the mind" [40] as directly as we observe objects around us. That is, experience is of both external and internal things and events. Moreover, the ideas we get from experience are the understandings or judgments we are enabled to make. Ideas are inadequate or false when we guess in faulty fashion about things we glimpse carelessly or do not directly observe. Ideas are knowledge,

[37] *Essay*, Bk. I, chap. 1, sec. 23.
[38] *Essay*, Bk. I, chap. 1, sec. 18.
[39] *Essay*, Bk. II, chap. 4, secs. 1 and 6.
[40] *Essay*, Bk. II, chap. 6.

however, when they are adequate and true, as, for example, our idea of solidity is. To gain the idea of solidity from experience is to know what solidity is.

In the cognitive situation, as Locke was here treating it, three factors are distinguished: the object, the mind, and the mind's way of thinking about the object. The mind's way of thinking about the object is the idea, and the idea is knowledge when it is true and is discerned to be true of the object. In many contacts of the mind with objects, experience is so clear and reliable that even a child, as Locke insisted, may know what objects are like. And scientists can and do gain further knowledge insofar as they plan, by travels across the world or by instruments such as the telescope and microscope, to get similarly clear and reliable experiences of further objects that do not easily come into the daily experience of ordinary people. Scientists may gain knowledge, for example, of the causes of certain diseases, of the distances between bodies in the solar system, or of the marriage customs of remote barbarian tribes. In gaining this further knowledge they are but carrying on under special conditions the same kind of cognitive activity which we all use in coming to our "idea of solidity."

LOCKE'S LATER CONCEPTION OF EXPERIENCE AND OF IDEAS

In the finished *Essay* Locke presented a technical and quite different epistemology from the simple position he took at the outset of his inquiries into the human understanding. He changed from the earlier to the later views under the influence of theories he took over from Galileo and Descartes and the trend of thought which stemmed from modern science. Fundamental for Locke, as he informed himself about this important trend of thought, was the contention that sense experience is an untrustworthy basis for knowledge of the world. Locke never abandoned his early assurance that we have nothing better to appeal to than experience, but he came to assent to the notion that experience consists of subjective effects produced in the human mind by stimuli from external objects. External objects, then, are not directly present in experience but are represented there by sensations which may or may not resemble the objects. Ideas cease to be a way of knowing natural objects and become a material upon which the mind must operate in the hope of getting beyond this material to conclusions concerning the external causes which produce it.

Two passages out of many similar statements in the *Essay* may serve as illustrations of the position Locke came to take.[41]

---

[41] *Essay*, Bk. IV, chap. 21, sec. 4; chap. 1, sec. 1.

Since the things the mind contemplates are none of them, besides itself, present to the understanding, it is necessary that something else, as a sign or representation of the thing it considers, should be present to it: and these are ideas.

. . . the mind, in all its thoughts and reasonings, hath no other immediate object but its own ideas, which it alone does or can contemplate.

Locke now distinguished four instead of three factors in the cognitive situation. There are still the external objects, though they no longer appear directly within experience. There is the mind, though it no longer is directly aware of external objects. And there is knowledge, though knowledge is now sharply differentiated from having ideas. But there is now a fourth factor—the ideas in the mind, which stand between the mind and the external objects. They are, indeed, the only objects given in experience, because experience is no longer an exploration of the world but a series of effects the world generates within the mind. Ideas are not the objects which in most of our inquiries we are aiming to know. They are said to represent external objects. But they do not disclose the nature of those external objects. They are, rather, a kind of curtain which hangs between the mind and the world. They are indispensable for knowledge; our knowledge never extends further than our ideas, if, indeed, it goes that far. But they do not represent objects in the sense in which a portrait may faithfully portray a man. They represent objects in the sense in which signs suggest meanings which to many observers of the signs may be arbitrary, dubious, and even highly obscure. Thus, although indicating the presence of objects to the mind, they hide rather than reveal those objects and leave the mind with conjectures rather than with knowledge about the nature of the things that produce them.

PRIMARY AND SECONDARY QUALITIES

Locke endeavored in one chapter [42] and a few scattered passages of his *Essay* to solve the problem of knowing external objects in a manner suggested by contemporary scientists, especially probably by his friend Newton. Had not Newton and Galileo before him discovered that the real qualities of bodies are those amenable to mathematical treatment? And had not Newton, by determining the nature of the ultimate particles, explained many of the qualities of all the bodies composed of these particles?

Locke therefore considered Galileo's distinction between primary and secondary qualities and put it to use in his epistemological quandary. Ideas, he said, are whatsoever the mind perceives in itself,

[42] *Essay*, Bk. II, chap. 8.

and qualities are powers in objects to produce the ideas. The ideas produced by primary qualities "are resemblances of them [that is, of the qualities], and their patterns do really exist in the bodies themselves." [43] But the ideas produced by secondary qualities are "no more the likeness of something existing without us, than the names that stand for them are the likeness of our ideas." [44] Our ideas of primary qualities, Locke said, are solidity, extension, figure, motion or rest, and number. Ideas of secondary qualities are heat and cold, light and darkness, white and black, sweet and sour, and all the other ideas which are commonly but loosely referred to as "sensible qualities." Secondary qualities, Locke further conjectured, are "modes of the primary," that is, they are powers in the objects which are functions of the bulk, figure, texture, and motion of the minute corpuscles of which the objects are composed.

"This little excursion into natural philosophy," as Locke called it,[45] did not really satisfy him. He came to develop a theory of mathematics very different from that of Galileo and Newton. He held that mathematics was a science which, so far as experience indicates, examines, not the structure of the external world, but the relations among certain complex ideas arbitrarily fashioned by the mind.[46] Moreover, the seen shapes of objects, the experienced motions and sizes of things, can hardly be believed to be the same as the objectively real shapes and motions and sizes of things in nature. Although Newton for physical reasons distinguished relative motion from absolute motion, Locke for epistemological reasons distinguished ideas from things. Locke therefore did not press the suggestions he got from Galileo and Newton as he continued to develop his theory of knowledge. Rather, he became increasingly skeptical concerning the adequacy of all ideas for inferences about the nature of things in the world which produce our subjective experiences in us.

SIMPLE AND COMPLEX IDEAS

The epistemological position of Locke, as he came to develop it in the finished *Essay,* consists of two main parts: a theory of ideas and a theory of knowledge. The theory of ideas is given most completely in Book II of the *Essay.*

The human mind, Locke maintained, is initially like an "empty

[43] *Essay,* Bk. II, chap. 8, sec. 15.
[44] *Essay,* Bk. II, chap. 8, sec. 7.
[45] *Essay,* Bk. II, chap. 8, sec. 22.
[46] Locke called this particular kind of complex ideas "modes." The various kinds of complex ideas are discussed below.

cabinet," "white paper, void of all characters," or "a closet wholly shut from light." [47] It has certain powers of its own. But it has no ideas and, of course, no knowledge innately. It can no more reason until it receives from experience materials upon which to exercise its rational powers than can a carpenter with a fine equipment of tools build a house until he receives materials upon which to use his tools. "The materials of reason and knowledge" are the ideas which come from experience. Some of these ideas are ideas of sensation because they come from the stimuli which external objects imprint on our bodily senses. Others are ideas of reflection [48] because they come from the mind's perception of its own operations. All ideas received through either sensation or reflection come to the mind singly; that is, each idea is "simple." The illustrations Locke gave of simple ideas, however, are varied and not altogether consistent. He listed, in one place or another, white and black, sweet and sour, hot and cold, and other ideas from the senses; solidity, space, motion, and figure; ideas of perceiving, thinking, willing, and other activities of the mind; pleasure and pain, power, existence, and unity. Locke did not bother to systematize his many illustrations of simple ideas, for he was primarily concerned only with the major contention, namely, that all ideas whatsoever come to the mind, not through its own powers, but from the ways in which experience produce them in it.

In addition to the many simple ideas the mind has also, Locke proceeded to explain, a great many complex ideas. The mind fashions complex ideas out of its simple ideas. It does this in various ways— by combining, contrasting, and abstracting the simple ideas. Locke did not give an exhaustive list of our complex ideas; he realized that no one could give an exhaustive list. But he reviewed many complex ideas, especially those which he feared others might regard as exceptions to his general theory of the origin of all ideas from experience. So he wrote chapters on such ideas as duration, extension, infinity, God, substance, causality, moral relations, liberty and necessity, matter and spirit.

Complex ideas, Locke wrote, may be classified in three types: modes, ideas of substance, and ideas of relation. The classification is loose, and the discussion of each type is in certain respects loose also.

[47] *Essay*, Bk. I, chap. 1, sec. 15; Bk. II, chap. 1, sec. 2 and chap. 11, sec. 17.

[48] The word *reflection* has often caused trouble for Locke's readers. It here means what other writers have called introspection or the mind's inspection of itself. Locke complicated things for his readers by using the word elsewhere in another sense, that is, for processes of deliberation or reflective inquiry. But he was here thinking of reflection in the sense in which images are reflected in a mirror. In reflection in this sense, he held, the mind is as passive as it is in sensation.

Modes are complex ideas "which, however compounded, contain not in them the supposition of subsisting by themselves, but are considered as dependencies on or affections of substances." [49] Samples of modes are triangle, gratitude, murder, foot and mile, day and hour. anger, envy, liberty.

Ideas of relation arise, Locke wrote, because the mind is not confined to consideration of an idea by itself but may look beyond it to see how it stands in respect to other ideas. The number of ways in which one idea may stand in respect to other ideas is legion, so that our ideas of relation are many and varied. The ideas of relation Locke took occasion to discuss are cause and effect, identity and diversity, relations of space and time, relation of degree of quality, biological relations, and the relations of human acts to the standards of moral judgment.

Ideas of substances gave Locke considerable trouble. We all find that in our experience certain simple ideas go constantly together in groups. We then tend to think of each of these groups of ideas as derived from one thing and as held together by some support or substratum. What this support or substratum is, however, we do not know and cannot know. Our idea of any particular substance, therefore, is an idea of something-we-know-not-what which holds together a given group of ideas. Our idea of gold, for example, is of something which produces in us, in constant connection, the ideas of yellow, considerable weight, melting without being consumed in fire, solubility in *aqua regia,* and so forth. Our idea of spirit, for another example, is of something which thinks, reasons, fears, and carries on other activities which supposedly, but by no means assuredly, are not performed by material things. Material and spiritual substances are distinguishable only by the different kinds of ideas they produce in us. Neither is discerned in its objective being (so that the possibility that matter and spirit are really two different kinds of substance is a consideration which the honest Locke, though he disliked the notion, had to acknowledge as not beyond doubt). And if we generalize our ideas of the many particular substances we encounter and try to form the idea of substance in general, we can say that the idea of substance in general is an idea of an unknown substratum which has powers to produce in us a group of associated simple ideas.

Locke was criticized in his own day, as well as often since his time, for inventing "a new way of knowledge by ideas." [50] He resented the

---

[49] *Essay,* Bk. II, chap. 12, sec. 4.

[50] This phrase was first used by Edward Stillingfleet, bishop of Worcester, with whom Locke engaged in a long controversy.

criticism. But he did much to deserve it. At the outset of his inquiry into the human understanding he thought of ideas as ways of thinking about things, even, at times, as ways of knowing things. Then ideas became the only immediate objects of the mind in thinking, and their very presence in the mind prevents the mind from discerning the things the ideas represent.

Locke's earlier view may be called direct or natural realism; this later view, representative realism. The theory of representative realism required Locke to continue his inquiry in an effort to determine how much knowledge the human understanding may or may not obtain through the "new way of knowledge by ideas."

THE DEGREES AND EXTENT OF KNOWLEDGE

"Knowledge," Locke wrote in a famous sentence, "then seems to me to be nothing but the perception of the connexion and agreement, or disagreement and repugnancy, of any of our ideas." [51] Where there is this perception, there is knowledge; where it is not, there may be opinion or guesswork but not knowledge.

The agreements or disagreements of our ideas, Locke continued, may be reduced to these four sorts.[52]

(1) Identity, or diversity
(2) Relation
(3) Coexistence, or necessary connexion
(4) Real existence

This classification is not well done. The language is both vague and loose, and the meaning of some terms is far from clear.

One major difficulty with the classification is the meaning to be assigned to "real existence." Insofar as Locke adhered to the position (discussed above) that ideas are the only objects we have given to us for reason and knowledge, he could properly proceed to say that we perceive agreements and disagreements of some ideas with other ideas, but he could not properly say that we perceive agreements or disagreements of ideas with existences other than ideas. This conclusion, however, was utterly distasteful to him. He wanted knowledge of things—of things in the natural world, such as material bodies, as well as of the human mind and of God. He realized that he was faced with a grave problem. He continued, for example, to say that ideas are all the materials we have for reason and knowledge, but he also insisted that we may to some extent reach knowledge of real

[51] *Essay*, Bk. IV, chap. 1, sec. 2.
[52] *Essay*, Bk. IV, chap. 1, sec. 3.

existences (other than ideas) which lie outside the mind. To meet this problem he introduced an adjective into some of his later statements. He came to speak of ideas as the only *immediate* objects of the mind. There are, he hoped, other objects of thought and of knowledge, even if those other objects are not immediate objects. These other objects, he still hoped, can somehow be known by means of the immediate objects or ideas. One kind of knowledge, then, would be perception, not of the relation of idea with idea, but of the relation of idea with external object. And so Locke ventured to list "real existence" among the sorts of knowledge which he sought, insofar as he was able, to identify and to justify.

Locke's epistemological difficulty on this point is obvious. But he added to the difficulty by the manner in which he discussed what he called the degrees of knowledge. For he carried on this latter discussion in thoroughly rationalistic terms which he took over directly from his admired Descartes.

The highest degree of knowledge, he wrote, is intuition. This is irresistible; it is so certain that it needs no proof to him who has it. But when Locke put this theory of intuition in the context of his contention that knowledge goes only as far as experience, he could not make use of it in Cartesian fashion. He could not use reason to leap beyond ideas in the mind to things outside of the mind. He was driven, rather, to recognize that the most certain degree of knowledge is usually possible in only trivial matters. We all know that white is not black, that every idea is identical with itself and different from all others, and so forth. Only one piece of knowledge of real existence, Locke confessed, can be gained through intuition. This is the knowledge each man has of his own existence. Locke here gratefully followed the lead of Descartes' *Cogito ergo sum*.[53] We also know intuitively, Locke held, certain principles, like the mathematical axiom that things equal to the same thing are equal to each other. But because ideas stand between the mind and the external world, intuition does not afford us knowledge of that world.

The next degree of knowledge is demonstration, which Locke again conceived in Cartesian fashion. Demonstration is proof by a series of steps, each of which steps is intuitively evident. We have the perfect instance of a successful use of demonstration in mathematics, and Locke expressed the hope that we might reach an equally valid demonstration of the principles of morality. But demonstration is not much more fruitful in investigation of the real world than is

[53] *Essay*, Bk. IV, chap. 9.

intuition. Locke thought he could demonstrate the existence of God and proffered such a demonstration in a chapter which follows closely Descartes' cosmological proof.[54] But aside from this one important exception (which critics have usually regarded as inconsistent with Locke's claim that knowledge can go no further than experience), Locke concluded that demonstration does not, any more than intuition, afford us knowledge of real existence. Neither intuition nor demonstration, as he acknowledged, yields knowledge of the vast extent of nature.

Locke thus reached a crisis in his epistemological speculations. On the one hand, he espoused a rationalistic ideal of knowledge he found in Descartes. He expressed the assurance that we human beings might realize this ideal if only we could get a basis from which to proceed. He wrote, for example: [55]

I doubt not but if we could discover the figure, size, texture, and motion of the minute constituent parts of any two bodies, we should know without trial several of their operations one upon another, as we do now the properties of a square or a triangle.

He wanted physics to be a demonstrative science like mathematics. He wanted to reach conclusions in physics *without trial*. But on the other hand, he insisted that we are forced to proceed empirically. We do not have the basis for demonstration. We do not know the nature of the constituent parts of bodies. We can work only with the ideas which stand between the mind and physical things. The rationalistic ideal, lovely as it is to contemplate, cannot be realized in our human cognitive predicament. Locke, in loyalty to his determination to distinguish sharply between knowledge and opinion, had to state: [56]

These two, viz. intuition and demonstration, are the degrees of our knowledge; whatever comes short of one of these, with what assurance soever embraced, is but faith or opinion, but not knowledge, at least in all general truths.

But he also, in loyalty to his doctrine of experience, put a qualifying clause at the end of the statement. We can have knowledge of general truths by no means except intuition and demonstration.[57] But we may yet have knowledge, or what is as good as knowledge, of particular truths by a further means, namely, by appeal to our senses. And so,

---

[54] *Essay*, Bk. IV, chap. 10.

[55] *Essay*, Bk. IV, chap. 3, sec. 25.

[56] *Essay*, Bk. IV, chap. 2, sec. 14.

[57] This conviction led Locke to write (*Essay*, Bk. IV, chap. 12, sec. 10): "Natural philosophy is not capable of being made a science." For by science he here meant knowledge, which, in addition to being verified and systematized, is generalized.

to the first two degrees of knowledge, intuition and demonstration, Locke finally added a third degree, namely, sensitive knowledge.

NOMINAL AND REAL ESSENCE

The remaining points in Locke's epistemological theories are consequences of his efforts to justify his introduction of sensitive knowledge to supplement the limitations of intuition and demonstration. "The mind knows not things immediately," he insisted, "but only by the intervention of the ideas it has of them." [58] But ideas surely come to us from without and must give some indication of the external objects which produce them in us. Complex ideas are probably quite often fanciful because they are fabricated by the mind. But simple ideas, if not exact similitudes of the qualities of things, are as useful to us in practical affairs as if they were similitudes. Simple ideas are what God thought appropriate for us to have.

Simple ideas are not fictions of our fancies, but the natural and regular productions of things without us, really operating upon us; and so carry with them all the conformity which is intended; or which our state requires.[59]

And so we are justified, if we realize what we are doing and refrain from dogmatism, in calling simple ideas "real" and "adequate" and even "true." [60] They answer to the powers in things. They are "correspondent" to those powers. They do not "become liable to any imputation of falsehood, if the mind (as in most men I believe it does) judges these ideas to be in the things themselves." Only a crazy person, Locke thought, would act in disregard of the instruction his senses give him about the external world. A wise man will act as if his simple ideas were real objects, or at least real qualities of real objects. Simple ideas from both sensation and reflection, for all practical purposes, give us real knowledge.

In theory, however, if not in practice, Locke warned, men ought to recognize that sensitive knowledge is, so to speak, symbolical and not pictorial. In other words, sensitive knowledge enables us to handle things in terms of their nominal essences only and never in terms of their real essence. Locke defined essence as "the very being of anything, whereby it is what it is." The real essence of anything would then be "the real internal, but generally (in substances) unknown constitution of things, whereon their discoverable qualities depend."

[58] *Essay*, Bk. IV, chap. 4, sec. 3.
[59] *Essay*, Bk. IV, chap. 4, sec. 4.
[60] *Essay*, Bk. II, chaps. 30–32, especially chap. 32, sec. 14.

The nominal essence, however, is the complex idea or an associated group of simple ideas which serve us to make distinctions among things and to arrange them in sorts or kinds.[61] The nominal essence of anything, therefore, is a human construction rather than a natural discovery. We put together ideas which occur together frequently in our experience and think of this collection of ideas as an object. But whether or not the powers which produce these ideas in us are the chief part of the real essence of the object we can never know. Real essences cannot be standard for our thoughts, because our thoughts do not easily pass beyond our own ideas.

Locke wrote an introduction for his *Essay*. It is almost certain that he wrote it after the rest of the *Essay* had taken form and the skeptical implications of its argument were clear to its author. The introduction can be characterized as Locke's endeavor to reconcile himself, and then his readers, to the skeptical doctrines with which the *Essay* ends. Locke did not summon men to a cognitive venture by which they would become "masters and possessors of nature" (Descartes); he did not exult in the discovery that "knowledge is power" (Bacon), though to a degree he could here assent; he had no hope that through the highest kind of knowledge a man could gain a vision of the vast structure of the universe (Spinoza). He did not reach a soul-stirring conclusion as did those other seventeenth-century philosophers. He was moderate and humble. He submitted dutifully to the minor role in nature which God in his wisdom had assigned to man. "Our business here," he wrote, "is not to know all things, but those which concern our conduct." We do know enough to provide reasonably for "the conveniences of life and information of virtue," that is, to discover "the comfortable provision for this life, and the way that leads to a better." We are able, in other words, to solve our economic and political problems and to save our souls. We know *how* to do our human tasks, though we do not know *what* the real constitution of the world is. We are in this world like a sailor in his ship.

It is of great use to the sailor, to know the length of his line, though he cannot with it fathom all the depths of the ocean. It is well he knows, that it is long enough to reach the bottom, at such places as are necessary to direct his voyage, and caution him against running upon shoals that may ruin him.

Other philosophers have begun with confused and confusing problems and have sometimes worked through the problems to what they considered triumphant solutions. Locke did almost the reverse. He began

[61] *Essay*, Bk. III, chap. 3, secs. 15–18.

with a simple confidence in simple human powers, by which men might both plan life sanely and gain increasing knowledge of the world. He retained much of this confidence in the human powers to plan life sanely, provided only that they would be reasonable in recognizing the limits of knowledge. But he lost almost all of his initial confidence in the possibility of gaining real knowledge. In place of knowledge about the world, he presented his readers with knowledge of the narrow limits of human knowledge.

THE EMPIRICAL TRADITION IN PHILOSOPHY

Few if any critics have considered Locke a great thinker, but all recognize that his influence has been both wide and deep. Locke can be said to have presented empiricism in its classic form, as Descartes presented rationalism in its. Even more than Francis Bacon, Locke made empiricism into a warning against unfounded beliefs much more than into an aggressive program of investigation of the world. And the school of empiricism since his time (until, perhaps, quite recently) has manifested the same negative spirit. Most important of all for the traditions which have stemmed from his *Essay,* he tied empiricism up with subjectivism and with agnosticism. For he built his appeal to experience into a structure according to which all the data of the mind in thinking are ideas private within men's minds, and according to which, consequently, men must forever remain agnostic about the real nature of the external world. His epistemology did not arise out of contemporary science, though it shows occasional influences from that science. Rather, it arose out of social problems, even if it was generalized to apply to all problems. Locke therefore marks a point in history at which the investigations of scientists and the reflections of philosophers begin to move in independent directions. He put an unbridgeable gap between ideas and things which scientists did not so much overcome as ignore. But he did bequeath to all future empiricists in philosophy a prime concern with the problem of the relation of experience and nature. He granted that men may, through reasonable attention to experience, cultivate arts to improve human life. But he confessed, with reluctance and disappointment, even with frustration, that men are barred by this very experience from formulating sciences which disclose the real nature of the world.

XI

British Philosophy in the Eighteenth Century

PHILOSOPHY IN THE eighteenth century is in part a critical reply to certain outstanding features of the dominant seventeenth-century philosophies. Particularly is this true of British philosophy in the eighteenth century, though, as will be noted in a later chapter, it is also true of the philosophy of Kant.

Descartes on the continent and Locke in England, different as their views were in other respects, agreed in regarding the content of sense experience as an inadequate basis for knowledge of the real world. Descartes then defended the power of the mind to reach clear and distinct ideas, by means of which reason could surmount the limitations of sense; and Locke sought to reconcile himself to the agnostic implications of those same limitations. But in Descartes and Locke alike, sense experience was a succession of ideas which could not be taken to indicate the real nature of the external bodies which produce those ideas in human minds. In Descartes and Locke alike, there appeared a contrast between experience (which may be called subjective because it inheres in private minds) and nature (which may be called objective because it exists apart from private minds).[1]

The enormous authority of Newton continued to be accepted by most natural scientists during the eighteenth and early nineteenth centuries.[2] But the separation of experience and nature was a fundamental problem for many philosophers—so fundamental that it, rather than the results of the natural sciences, received their first attention. The theory of the separation of experience and nature was attacked by Berkeley at the outset of the eighteenth century, by Hume during the middle of that century, and by most of the greater philoso-

[1] Descartes' and Locke's philosophies are both what Alfred North Whitehead called "theories of the bifurcation of nature." See *The Concept of Nature* (New York, Cambridge University Press, 1920), chap. 2.

[2] Until 1859, one might say, when Darwin's *Origin of Species* appeared and began to modify many scientific views, even outside the field of biology.

phers from that time on. The scientists, the historian may explain in the scientists' defense, were too busy with physical and chemical problems to engage in speculative epistemological problems and, hence, did not worry about the relation of experience and nature. Philosophers, however, the historian may go on to say, are born to worry about just such technical and far-reaching problems. They certainly did worry about the relation of experience and nature through the whole eighteenth century. And an interesting historical point is that the philosophers, as by-products of their epistemological reflections, found occasion to dissent on many points from the dominant Newtonian assurances of the scientists. The theory of the world machine was discredited among philosophers long before it was superseded by new theories among the scientists.

1. BERKELEY

GEORGE BERKELEY, 1685–1753, born in the county of Kilkenny in southern Ireland, was partly English by descent. He entered Trinity College, Dublin, in 1700, and spent twenty years there as student, master, and fellow. He took orders in the Church of England in 1709, became dean of Londonderry (in northern Ireland) in 1724, and bishop of Cloyne (in southern Ireland) in 1734. He conceived a grandiose project of converting the American Indians to Christianity and proposed to begin his missionary work among those Indians by founding a university in Bermuda. Finally he received what he considered a promise of financial support for his project from the British government and, accompanied by his bride, set sail in 1728 for Rhode Island. Berkeley bought land, built a house, but waited in vain for the government subsidy he had expected. In 1731 he left America, bestowing his real estate and many of his books upon what was then the College of New Haven and is now Yale University. He lived in London until 1734, then spent eighteen years in devoted service at Cloyne, and retired to Oxford where he died a few months after his arrival. Throughout the years 1705 to 1753 he concerned himself much with writing. His philosophical works fall into two main groups. The earlier group, generally considered the more important, include *An Essay Towards a New Theory of Vision* (1709), *A Treatise Concerning the Principles of Human*

Knowledge (1710, 1734), and *Three Dialogues Between Hylas and Philonous* (1713). The later group includes *Alciphron, or the Minute Philosopher* (1732), which consists of seven dialogues directed against such freethinkers as Bernard Mandeville and the third earl of Shaftesbury (Locke's pupil), and *Siris: A Chain of Philosophical Reflexions and Inquiries Concerning the Virtues of Tar-Water and Divers Other Subjects* (1744), in which Berkeley combined a defense of a Neo-Platonic position with lengthy encomiums on tar water as a cure for most bodily ills. In the tradition which has been called Berkeleyanism only the earlier works have been noticed, and only these earlier works will be referred to in the discussion below.

BERKELEY, WITH SENSITIVE self-appraisal rare among men, summed up his philosophy effectively in a few words.[3]

I do not pretend to be a setter-up of new notions. My endeavors tend only to unite, and place in a clearer light, that truth which was before shared between the vulgar and the philosophers:—the former being of opinion, that *those things they immediately perceive are the real things;* and the latter, that *the things immediately perceived are ideas, which exist only in the mind.* Which two notions put together, do, in effect, constitute the substance of what I advance.

The exposition of these two propositions, together with that of a third proposition which follows from their joint affirmation, will provide an outline of the philosophical position with which Berkeley's name has been commonly associated.

BERKELEY'S REALISM

Berkeley's first proposition is that the things men immediately perceive are real things. This proposition, Berkeley said, is the truth well known to "the vulgar." That is, it is a truth men know whether or not they are trained in speculative reflections or have pondered upon the technical writings of philosophers. Men have no need of learned treatises to demonstrate (much less to question skeptically) the reality of the things they immediately perceive. Berkeley waxed eloquent on this point. He listed, by way of illustration of his contention, the verdant woods and groves, the rivers and clear springs, the deep ocean and high mountain, an old gloomy forest and rocks and deserts, the glorious luminaries that adorn the arch of heaven, and the host of stars which, undetected by the naked eye, become visible

---

[3] The remark put into the mouth of Philonous on the last page of the third dialogue between Hylas and Philonous.

with the use of a telescope. "All the vast bodies that compose this mighty frame" of the world are evident to all who observe them.[4] They are not conjectures reached through argument; they are assured realities which men observe and so cannot reasonably doubt. Scientists may indeed investigate these real objects in the endeavor to discover further facts about them than those at first observed. They may investigate the motions of the planets, the paths of comets, the distances from the earth of those remote stars "far sunk in the abyss of space." Above all, scientists may seek to formulate the laws which set forth the relations and orders in which these real things occur. But neither science nor philosophy is needed to establish the reality of the things observed; and neither scientists nor philosophers ought to forget that the reality of the things observed is presupposed at the outset of, during the course of, and at the conclusion of, their investigations of these realities. "The choir of heaven and furniture of the earth, in a word all those bodies which compose the mighty frame of the world"[5] are as evident to the vulgar as to the learned. They are evident because they are immediately and directly perceived.

The full import of Berkeley's realistic position[6] is apparent when one considers its relation to certain seventeenth-century philosophies against which Berkeley was voicing protest. Berkeley is famous today, especially among those who know little concerning his philosophy, because he is supposed to have denied the existence of matter. And he did deny the existence of matter. But he did not deny the existence of the many bodies which the vulgar, and, of course, the learned, too, immediately perceive. The matter he denied was the material substance of the philosophers. He denied the *res extensa* of Descartes and the something-I-know-not-what of Locke. He denied the existence of alleged substances which are by definition inaccessible to human experience and are also void of all the colors and odors and other sensible qualities we immediately perceive the bodies around us to have. He was unwilling to entertain the theory, the fantastic theory as he viewed it, that the bodies we do directly perceive need to be ex-

---

[4] From a long speech by Philonous near the beginning of the second dialogue between Hylas and Philonous; see A. C. Fraser, ed., *The Works of George Berkeley* (Oxford, Clarendon Press, 1901), Vol. I, pp. 422–423.

[5] *Principles of Human Knowledge*, sec. 6.

[6] Berkeley is normally referred to in textbooks as an idealist. And in a sense yet to be discussed, he was an idealist. But he was a realist too. He was a realist in the sense that he believed in the reality of all perceived bodies. See the able historical analysis of Berkeley by F. J. E. Woodbridge, "Berkeley's Realism" in *Studies in the History of Ideas* (New York, Columbia University Press, 1918), Vol. I, pp. 188–215.

plained in terms of inaccessible substances we cannot perceive. His keenly empirical mind led him, in opposition to both Descartes and Locke, to trust the evidence of the senses for reliable information, though not exhaustive information, concerning the real objects of the natural world. He rejected Descartes' appeal to intuitions in which the mind supposedly operates apart from the senses. He rejected Locke's distinction between "real essences," which cannot be known, and "nominal essences," which cannot properly be taken to yield knowledge of what things really are.

Berkeley's voice was the first to be effectively raised against the disparagement of sense experience which characterizes much seventeenth-century philosophy and appears, in different ways, in Galileo, Descartes, Newton, and Locke. He regarded himself as the champion of the vulgar against that undue disparagement of sense experience. He refused to follow the philosophical convention which defined reality in terms of what Locke called "minute particles" and which then derogatively demoted colors, odors, and tastes to the status of private illusions. In an early entry in his *Commonplace Book* [7] he wrote (without, perhaps, entire accuracy in his phrasing of the point): "I differ from Cartesians in that I make extension, colour, &c. to exist really in bodies independent of our mind." His point is that extension cannot be regarded as real in any sense in which color is not also real. The bodies we perceive to be extended are colored, and the bodies we perceive to be colored are extended. No one is entitled to pick out one quality, to call it primary, then to call other qualities secondary, and to deny the same objective reality to the latter which is affirmed of the former. One and the same world is both extended and colored, and that world is the world we perceive through our senses. Whatever we perceive bodies to be, those bodies really are. They may, of course, be more than what we perceive them to be, but they cannot be less. The trend of much seventeenth-century philosophy, Berkeley pointed out, was to separate reality (that is, what things are) and experience (that is, what things are observed to be). But such a separation of reality and experience makes reality horribly barren and experience tragically futile. Berkeley denounced such an illicit separation severely: [8]

[7] The jottings in his *Commonplace Book* were made in the years 1705 to 1708 and are sometimes unguarded statements of the positions he expressed more carefully in his published works. The passage here quoted can be found in Fraser, *op. cit.*, Vol. I, p. 50.

[8] Quoted from Philonous' long speech near the beginning of the second dialogue between Hylas and Philonous. See Fraser, *op. cit.*, Vol. I, pp. 423–424.

Is not the whole system [of the world] immense, beautiful, glorious beyond expression and beyond thought! What treatment, then, do those philosophers deserve, who would deprive these noble and delightful scenes of all *reality?* How should those principles be entertained that lead us to think all the visible beauty of the creation a false imaginary glare?

CRITIQUE OF ABSTRACT IDEAS

In his *Principles of Human Knowledge* Berkeley sought to prepare his readers for his denial of material substance by writing an introduction in which he denied the existence of abstract ideas. We can indeed fashion all sorts of ideas by dividing and compounding the ideas we originally get through the senses. We "can consider the hand, the eye, the nose, each by itself abstracted or separated from the rest of the body." We can frame an idea of an animal with "the upper parts of a man joined to the body of a horse." [9] But all our ideas are still particular and concrete. We may speak of our idea of a man in general and suppose we then have an abstract idea. But what we speak of as an idea of a man in general is a particular idea which *"with regard to its signification"* [10] represents all particular men whatsoever. It is the representative function of ideas which makes ideas general, and words then become general when they stand for ideas-in-their-representative-function. Particular ideas derive their generality from the manner in which they denote indifferently a number of particular things.

Berkeley's denial of abstract ideas has led historians to classify him as a nominalist. This classification may well be just. But his critics have often charged him, and with evident justice, of confusing ideas with images; and these critics have sometimes gone on to insist that he reintroduced, in his recognition of the representative function of ideas, what many advocates of abstract ideas have been interested to maintain. What Berkeley was most concerned to proclaim is that the general idea of man stands for a host of men rather than for some further entity which is neither *a* man nor many particular men, and hence, similarly, that the general idea of body stands for a host of particular bodies rather than for some further entity which is neither *a* body nor many particular bodies. That is, he was concerned to proclaim that matter *qua* matter does not exist. He argued that because we have the general word *matter* we are not entitled to suppose the existence of a general entity *matter*. The word *matter* is either sheer nonsense or a word without meaning insofar as it is taken to

[9] *Principles of Human Knowledge,* Introduction, sec. 10.
[10] *Principles of Human Knowledge,* Introduction, sec. 12.

indicate something other than the concrete bodies we see and touch. In saying such things he was thundering against the seventeenth-century doctrines of material substances, real essences, external realities, and something-I-know-not-what. His empiricism was effectively carried through, whether or not his nominalism was expressed in thoroughly satisfactory form.

BERKELEY'S IDEALISM

Berkeley's second proposition is that the things immediately perceived are ideas which exist only in the mind. Although in his first proposition he was hostile critic of the seventeenth-century tradition, he was, in this second proposition, faithful disciple of that same tradition. The first section of his *Principles of Human Knowledge* reads very much like the opening section of Book II of Locke's *Essay*.

It is evident to any one who takes a survey of the *objects of human knowledge,* that they are either *ideas* actually imprinted on the senses; or, such as are perceived by attending to the passions and operations of the mind; or lastly, *ideas* formed by help of memory and imagination—either compounding, dividing, or barely representing those originally perceived in the aforesaid ways.

Berkeley did not follow Locke in maintaining that the original ideas of the mind are simple in the sense of coming singly. The original ideas, he held, often come in steady and seemingly established collections. They "are observed to accompany each other," and are then "marked by one name" and are "reputed one thing." "A stone, a tree, a book, and the like sensible things" are the kind of objects with which, from the outset of our experience, we are confronted.[11]

Nonetheless, as Berkeley maintained in accord with Locke, the things we immediately observe are ideas. And since they are ideas, they cannot have any being apart from the mind. Their very nature is to be ideas. Their *esse* is *percipi*.[12]

The table I write on I say exists; that is, I see and feel it. . . . There was an odour, that is, it was smelt; there was a sound, that is, it was heard; a colour or figure, and it was perceived by sight or touch.

All the bodies which compose the mighty frame of the world are ideas and so have no existence outside of the minds which perceive them. To entertain the idle supposition that things other than ideas exist is either to talk thoughtlessly or to utter nonsense. It is to talk thought-

---

11 *Principles of Human Knowledge*, sec. 1.
12 This famous epigram and the quotation which follows are both from the *Principles of Human Knowledge*, sec. 3.

lessly if, in alleging something other than an idea, one does not notice that he is but mentioning something which is surely in his mind and is therefore his idea. It is to utter nonsense if one professes to believe in something of which he has no idea at all. Berkeley asked his readers whether they could think of anything without having an idea of it, whether they could think of anything without viewing it as like the things of which they have or have had ideas, and whether they could think of anything at all which by nature is unthinkable. To these questions, these rhetorical questions perhaps, he took it that the only possible answer is no. He then felt justified in concluding that it is "perfectly unintelligible" and involves "all the absurdity of abstraction" to attempt to distinguish the being of things from their being perceived.[13]

Berkeley quickly added that, in addition to the many ideas, there are also many minds, and that minds cannot be reduced to, or included among, the ideas they perceive. His own words are as follows: [14]

Besides all that endless variety of ideas or objects of knowledge, there is likewise Something which knows or perceives them; and exercises divers operations, as willing, imagining, remembering, about them. This perceiving, active being is what I call *mind, spirit, soul,* or *myself.* By which words I do not denote any one of my ideas, but a thing entirely distinct from them, wherein they exist, or, which is the same thing, whereby they are perceived.

Reality or existence thus is of two kinds, spirits and ideas, and these two kinds are "entirely distinct and heterogeneous." [15] Spirits, Berkeley held, are active and causally productive, and ideas are passive and inert. Spirits are indivisible and incorruptible substances, and ideas are fleeting and perishable objects. Spirits exist in and of themselves, and ideas are dependent beings which do not subsist by themselves but exist only in minds or spirits.

The language in which Berkeley expressed his position is loose, at least in the first edition of his *Principles.* He repeatedly made the following three statements: that the objects of human knowledge are all ideas, that "there can be no *idea* formed of a soul or spirit," and that each of us has "an immediate knowledge" of himself as "a thinking, active principle that perceives, knows, wills, and operates about ideas." [16] Berkeley seems to have come to realize the linguistic con-

13 *Principles of Human Knowledge,* sec. 6.
14 *Principles of Human Knowledge,* sec. 2.
15 *Principles of Human Knowledge,* sec. 89.
16 These three statements recur throughout the *Principles* and *Dialogues.* The phrase

fusion of which he was guilty. And so he introduced, in the second edition of the *Principles* (1734), the word *notion* which he had already used sparingly in the *Dialogues*. We have a notion of spirit, he came to say, though no idea of spirit. That is, we know what we mean when we speak of spirit or mind or soul, though we cannot present it to ourselves as an idea without falling into the erroneous superstition of confusing spirit with a thin, filmy body or vapor. In this emended expression of his position Berkeley wrote that we have ideas of bodies and notions of souls or minds or spirits. But his clear intent throughout all his writings was to insist that everything which exists is either a mind or an idea in some mind. Minds and their ideas are real, and nothing else is real.

Berkeley's doctrine that reality consists entirely of minds and the ideas in minds is what has come to be called his idealism. Berkeleyan idealism, however, is quite different from the idealisms which stem from Plato and Plotinus. In the older forms of idealism ideas have reality apart from minds and are sharply distinguished from particular things, which then are but "shadows" of ideas. In Berkeleyan idealism ideas subsist in minds, have no being apart from minds, and are, either in their separate occurrence or in the collections of them we commonly perceive, identical with particular things. Both types of idealism are metaphysical in purport. But Berkeleyan idealism makes ideas mental entities—which they never were for either Plato or Plotinus.

BERKELEY'S THEISM

Berkeley's first and second propositions entail a third proposition, in which, indeed, he earnestly desired his philosophy to culminate. This third proposition is that the mind of God sustains in existence the many ideas which constitute the mighty frame of the world. Berkeley regarded his philosophy as a refutation of "the grounds of scepticism, atheism, and irreligion" and a proof of "the immediate providence of a deity in opposition to sceptics and atheists." [17] He felt confident that his philosophy furnished a new and irrefutable proof of the theistic foundations of Christianity.

The argument of Berkeley is an exposition of the logical consequence of his joint affirmation of his realistic proposition that the

quoted in the second statement above is from *The Principles of Human Knowledge,* sec. 27. That quoted in the third statement above is from the third dialogue between Hylas and Philonous and can be found in Fraser, *op. cit.,* Vol. I, p. 450.

[17] These phrases are parts of the subtitles of his *Principles of Human Knowledge* and *Three Dialogues Between Hylas and Philonous.*

things we immediately perceive are real things and of his idealistic proposition that the things we immediately perceive are ideas which exist only in the mind. The real things—the bodies which are the choir of heaven and furniture of earth—surely exist when we do not perceive them as well as when we do perceive them. No one would be so capricious and arrogant, Berkeley supposed, as to maintain that bodies in the natural world exist only insofar as he himself, or even all human beings, had ideas of them, that is, observed them. We all, he granted, have some ideas which subsist in our own imaginations only. But we also have many other ideas, such as our sensations, which are not private to us. The ideas which subsist in our own imaginations only are fancies. Those which the senses disclose to us are bodies which may, and often do, exist before and after we perceive them as well as while we perceive them. The "houses, rivers, mountains, trees, stones" which we observe, and our own bodies, too, do not come into existence when we sense them and go out of existence when we do not sense them. The vast world of nature continues in existence when finite minds do not entertain it as their ideas. But—and here we come to Berkeley's point—if this vast world of nature which we human beings may or may not perceive is indeed a system of ideas (and it is just that), there must be some mind other than a human mind which observes it at all times. That is, there must be some infinite mind whose perceptions are the natural world. This infinite mind is God and the world is his system of ideas. The objectivity of the world is guaranteed philosophically by the omnipresent and omniscient mind of God. Insofar as we finite minds entertain ideas which are not parts of God's system of ideas, we are indulging in fancy or falling into error. But insofar as we observe real bodies and pursue the sciences soundly, we are sharing to some degree in the ideas of the divine mind.

True piety in religion, Berkeley argued, will provide "a method for rendering the sciences more easy, useful, and compendious." [18] The agnostic outcome of Locke's *Essay* is destructive of both sound science and sound religion. On the one hand, it denies to men direct access to God's world, so that the theories of the physical sciences cannot be verified and can only be embraced as a kind of human enthusiasm or pretense. And on the other hand, it has to turn from its empirical profession when it comes to discussion of the existence of God and to employ the rationalistic arguments of Descartes, which, in addition to being unconvincing, banish God from the area of

[18] This phrase is from the subtitle of *Three Dialogues Between Hylas and Philonous.*

daily human experience. Sound science and sound religion, Berkeley insisted, are correlative enterprises. Whoever accepts the two basic propositions in which Berkeley summed up his philosophical position will at one and the same time gain two much to be desired goals: he will have direct access to real bodies, which he can study in their interrelations and sequences, and he will have direct access, since these bodies are ideas in the mind of God, to the thoughts of God and the order of the divine mind. God, Berkeley maintained, "is known as certainly and immediately as any other mind or spirit whatsoever, distinct from ourselves." [19] Each man, indeed, can, if he is attentive to the instruction of his own experience, know God more easily than any other of the spirits in the world around him. For each of us knows other human spirits, as he knows animals, by inference from the form and behavior of their bodies. But each of us can know, if he will, something of the mind of God every time he observes *any* bodies, human or animal or other, because all bodies are collections and arrangements of ideas which owe their reality to their presence in God's mind.

Not simply are all natural bodies collections of God's ideas, but the laws of nature are established procedures of the workings of God's mind. [20] "Food nourishes, sleep refreshes, and fire warms us"; and though men are often lulled by nature's regularities into inattention to the divine volition which sustains these regularities, these normal sequences in nature and all other such sequences are evident instances of the "consistent uniform working of God's power." [21] Berkeley believed, as was pointed out above, that ideas are all passive and inert, and that only spirits are active and causally productive. Causality therefore is always volition. The causal sequences in nature are only occasionally instances of human volitions. The great number of these causal sequences, and indeed all those sequences which exhibit vast cosmic force and power, are divine volitions. The scientific discoveries of laws of nature, in Berkeley's view, are also discoveries of the established procedures of God's mind. The wise philosopher who discovers that food nourishes or sleep refreshes will not properly say that the food *causes* the nourishment or the sleep *causes* the refreshment. He will, rather, regard food as a *sign* of the nourishment which will ensue

---

[19] *Principles of Human Knowledge*, sec. 147.

[20] Miracles, Berkeley believed, are sequences in the divine ideas which are not in accord with these established procedures. Miracles are as possible as are events which exhibit the regular operation of laws of nature. But because God's beneficence inclines him to stimulate men to prudent provision for their own affairs, God normally acts according to the established procedures.

[21] *Principles of Human Knowledge*, secs. 31–32.

and sleep as a *sign* of the refreshment. The genuinely causal efficacy he will, in these and all other such cases of natural sequence, attribute to the volition of God. And when Berkeley considered that it may sound ridiculous to say that a spirit (rather than food) nourishes and a spirit (rather than sleep) refreshes, he replied that "in such things we ought to think with the learned, and speak with the vulgar." [22] "In truth, there is no other agent or efficient cause than *spirit*." [23] God's spirit is what controlled nature before men came into existence and now controls it in the far reaches beyond men's range of vision— just as it is God's perceiving mind which sustained bodies in being before men came into being and began their observations and which now sustains those bodies in being that exist beyond the range and sensitivity of men's powers of observation.

BERKELEY'S INFLUENCE

Berkeley's realism (which is primarily an epistemological doctrine), his idealism (which is primarily a metaphysical doctrine), and his theism (which is the keystone of his philosophy and holds the two other doctrines in place) are the main themes which appear in the pages of his early and his more famous writings. Unfortunately for Berkeley's reputation, however, it has been his idealism apart from his realism that has usually attracted attention from his critics. These critics have thus frequently failed to do justice to his philosophy. The famous Dr. Samuel Johnson, for instance (who was born in the year of the publication of Berkeley's first book), was that kind of a critic. He supposed that anyone could refute Berkeley by kicking a stone. For whoever kicks a stone, Johnson facetiously said, will know that a stone is more than a mere idea. Berkeley anticipated that this kind of objection might be raised to his philosophy. He wrote: [24]

It will be objected that by the foregoing principles all that is real and substantial in nature is banished out of the world, and instead thereof a chimerical scheme of *ideas* takes place. All things that exist exist only in the mind; that is, they are purely notional. What therefore becomes of the sun, moon, and stars?

Berkeley had a quick answer to this kind of objection. Everything we see or feel is as real when known to be an idea as when not so understood. There is a *rerum natura* after, as before, men realize that nature is God's ideas.

[22] *Principles of Human Knowledge*, sec. 51.
[23] *Principles of Human Knowledge*, sec. 102.
[24] *Principles of Human Knowledge*, sec. 34.

A more just appraisal of Berkeley's philosophy would not isolate his idealism from his realism. It would recognize, rather, that Berkeley was concerned primarily with two things. He wished, on the one hand, to attack boldly the separation which earlier philosophers had made between experience and nature. And he wished, on the other hand, to refute finally the Newtonian and Galilean conception that nature is void of the alluring sense qualities of our ordinary experience. Furthermore, and as a consequence of these two major themes, he wished to overcome the atheism which, even if Newton and Locke piously rejected it, other thinkers seemed to deem an outcome of both philosophical and scientific trends. These complicated considerations Berkeley resolved by laying the foundations of a new type of empiricism—an empiricism which does not begin with a separation of experience and nature, which therefore finds within nature all the sense qualities of experience, and which flowers in knowledge of both God and the world instead of ending in denials of the former and doubts concerning the latter.

2. HUME

DAVID HUME, 1711–1776, was born and also died in Edinburgh. He belonged to a Scotch family of moderate means and simple living. His father died when he was quite young, but his mother provided carefully for his education. He gained more from books and libraries than from schools and classrooms. Early in his life, he "fairly got the disease of the learned," as he later wrote in his *Autobiography;* and from then until his death he was animated by a keen desire for literary reputation and always applied himself diligently, no matter what other occupation he also had, to one or another form of writing. "When I was about 18 years of age," he wrote in a letter in 1734, "there seemed to be opened up to me a new scene of thought, which transported me beyond measure, and made me, with an ardor natural to young men, throw up every other pleasure or business to apply entirely to it." He therefore used his meager resources to live quietly in France for three years and to put his thoughts into writing. This writing was his first work, *A Treatise of Human Nature,* of which two volumes were published in London in January, 1739, and a third in 1740. He was disappointed in the reception of this work. Only 1000 copies of the *Trea-*

tise were printed, and a second edition did not appear in his lifetime. He wrote in his *Autobiography* that the *Treatise* "fell dead born from the press, without reaching such distinction as even to excite a murmur from the zealots." Yet a review of the first two volumes (which appeared in a Scotch journal, *The History of the Works of the Learned,* in November, 1739), referred to them as displaying "incontestable marks of a great capacity, of a soaring genius, but young and not yet thoroughly practiced." During the next few years he supported himself by acting as companion and keeper to a mentally deranged marquis and as secretary to a general who served at British embassies in Vienna and Turin. But he continued writing. He published numerous essays on economic and political subjects, and he utilized the material of the three volumes of the *Treatise* in three more readable books—*An Enquiry Concerning the Human Understanding* (1748), *Dissertation on the Passions* (1757), and *An Enquiry Concerning the Principles of Morals* (1751). Then in 1754 and later years were published successive volumes of his *History of England,* which won him a wide reputation and a financial reward which he never gained from his philosophical works. He became, as he himself reported in 1767, "very opulent," with "a revenue of £1000 a year." He went in 1763 to France in the suite of the British ambassador and was gratified by the attention he received from the *philosophes.* But he chose, once he was prosperous, to live in Edinburgh, where he entertained and was entertained in style, kept his carriage, and enjoyed high living. He declined offers of chairs of philosophy at Edinburgh and Glasgow, though he had sought such appointments earlier. He was widely respected and loved for his good humor, modesty, freedom from rancor, and generosity. He was consulted by the youthful Gibbon, whom he encouraged to devote his life to the writing of history. He spent much time from about 1750 until his death in writing and rewriting his *Dialogues Concerning Natural Religion.* He did not choose to publish the *Dialogues* during his lifetime but arranged for their publication according to instructions in his will. He named his friend Adam Smith as the one who had the first right to publish the *Dialogues,* provided that Smith published them within three years. Smith failed to act, probably out of fear of the social consequences of Hume's unorthodox views on religion. A nephew of Hume then fell heir to the *Dialogues,* and he published them promptly in 1779.

HUME HAD A KEEN and restless mind. He was always exploring the meaning and implications of ideas he gained from his reading and his own thinking. He was well versed in the writings of the major philosophers of the seventeenth and early eighteenth centuries and examined sensitively the adequacies and inadequacies of the ideas he there encountered. He formulated tentative positions, developed these positions with searching thoroughness, and expressed doubts concerning them as often as he came to definite conclusions. Even such conclusions as he ventured to suggest he set forth with caution, exposing difficulties in them rather than insisting upon their certain truth. He was a keen critic and an honest inquirer. But he frequently indulged in irony, and, occasionally, when he was arriving at a conclusion which he realized to be likely to offend accepted doctrines of current religious belief, he seemed to pass, near the end of his argument, to the very position against which his argument was clearly directed.[25] In spite of his reluctance (more apparent than real) to face unpopular or "dangerous" conclusions, he maintained certain opinions which were original with him and novel for the times he lived in.

The many opinions which Hume expressed in his successive works do not collectively form a consistent system. To say this, however, is not to charge Hume with holding inconsistent opinions at any one time, though even this charge can be substantiated on minor matters in his earlier writings. It is rather to indicate that Hume, with his restless and searching mind, went gradually but steadily through a course of development as he busied himself with philosophical reflections over a period of many years. On some matters—such as his political and ethical theories—he did hold much the same position throughout his literary life. But on other matters—such as the nature of experience, the relation of experience to nature, and other epistemological issues which had been centers of controversy for a hundred years—he changed his views markedly as he composed his successive works. He discussed the latter matters in the first book of *A Treatise of Human Nature,*[26] *An Enquiry Concerning the Human Understanding,* and

---

[25] For example, at the end of his essays on miracles and on providence (secs. 10 and 11 of *An Enquiry Concerning the Human Understanding*) and in the closing pages of *Dialogues Concerning Natural Religion.*

[26] The *Treatise,* especially its first book, has been called the greatest philosophical work ever produced in the English language. It may well deserve this praise. But the

Dialogues Concerning Natural Religion. The dates of publication of these works are respectively 1739, 1748, and 1779. The dates at which Hume was working on these books stretch from 1734 (when he went to France to compose his thoughts on philosophy) to his death in 1776. During the period of more than forty years between 1734 and 1776 Hume worked his way through subtle, technical, controversial issues in which he was at first entangled, and knew he was entangled, shifting bit by bit from doubts he could not resolve to reasoned opinions he was at last willing to hazard. In the light of this history of Hume's composition of his philosophical works, it is not surprising if the trend of his development from the earliest to the latest proves more important, both historically and philosophically, than the contents of any one of the books alone.

HUME'S EARLIER POSITION

The trend of Hume's development was from subjectivism to realism.[27] That is, he began with a conception of sense experience which was common to Descartes and Locke and was widely held in the seventeenth century, and he ended with a theory quite contrary thereto. The earlier theory dominates the whole of Book I of the *Treatise* and reappears in some brief sections of *An Enquiry Concerning the Human Understanding*.[28] The later theory (anticipated in only a few

historian ought not to praise it for the wrong reason. The historian errs who calls it great on the supposition that Hume here expounded more fully than elsewhere the views he continued to maintain in later years and repeated in watered-down form in the *Enquiry* and blandly ignored in the *Dialogues*. The *Treatise* is great, in spite of the fact that Hume later rejected some of its contentions, because Hume here reviewed with astounding acumen and instructive persistence many involved epistemological subtleties through which he had to make his way before he could ever come to positions more satisfactory to himself. Hume was too harsh in his later years in his judgment on his *Treatise*. For in an "Advertisement" which he wrote near the end of his life and which he requested his publishers to include in all copies of his writings that were still offered for sale, he dismissed the *Treatise* as a juvenile work. Yet he was a sound judge when he added in this Advertisement that in his later works (and he was surely referring now to the *Enquiry*) he corrected "negligences" in the reasoning as well as in the style of the *Treatise*. The *Treatise* is great, partly because it contains the most devastating criticisms ever penned of modern philosophy before Hume, and partly because it made possible the later Hume who profited from his own *Treatise* more, indeed, than have those of his subsequent critics who have taken it to be the full statement of his definitive philosophical position.

27 The term *subjectivism*, as used in this history, means the theory that the things immediately present to a man's mind have, and can have, no existence apart from his mind. It usually entails the further theory that the nature of things immediately present to a man's mind is a function of the manner in which his mind perceives or knows them. The term *realism*, as used above for a position contrary to subjectivism, means the theory that the things immediately present to a man's mind (or at least many of them) exist apart from his mind, so that his perception of them is accidental to their existence.

28 Particularly *An Enquiry Concerning the Human Understanding*, secs. 2 and 3, which repeat without deviation *Treatise*, Bk. I, secs. 1 and 4.

chance phrases of the *Treatise*) is presented in a hesitating manner in *An Enquiry Concerning the Human Understanding* [29] and is then taken unquestioningly for granted throughout the *Dialogues*.

Hume opened his *Treatise* with a sentence similar to the opening sentences of Book II of Locke's *Essay* and of Berkeley's *Principles*. "All the perceptions of the human mind," he wrote, "resolve themselves into two distinct kinds, which I shall call impressions and ideas." The language is in part new; the term *impression* is one of Hume's contributions to terminology. What Locke and Berkeley lumped together indiscriminately as ideas, Hume separated into two distinct kinds: impressions and ideas. He gave several grounds for his distinction, though he made none of them wholly clear. (1) An impression, he wrote, is normally a more lively or vivid perception, though he granted that such is not always the case; and an idea is normally a less lively or vivid perception, though it may sometimes, as in certain cases of memory and of belief, become so vivid as to appear like an impression. Degree of vividness is only an approximate, not a sure, criterion for the distinction between impression and idea. (2) An impression is "original" or prior to any idea which copies it; and an idea is a copy of an antecedent impression to which it must always be referred for its meaning and adequacy. (3) An impression is given to the mind, is not strictly within the control of him who perceives it, and so is in some sense more reliable; and an idea may be quite fanciful and can be trusted only insofar as one can discover the impression it copies. Both impressions and ideas, Hume added, are sometimes simple and sometimes complex. A complex impression (such, for example, as a man's impression of the city of Paris) is a group of impressions which are perceived at the same time. A complex idea, however, is seldom faithful to its prior impressions. Even a man's idea of the city of Paris is hardly likely to represent faithfully the complex impression he has had and is perhaps trying to remember; and his idea of the New Jerusalem is a free invention of the imagination which he fashions without regard to the order he perceived among prior impressions.[30] Impressions thus have an authority which ideas do not have, though Hume did not make clear the basis or the nature of this authority.

Hume's failure to make clear the nature of the authority which impressions have was due to the influence which, in the early days

---

[29] Particularly secs. 4, 5, and 12.

[30] David Hume, *A Treatise of Human Nature,* ed. L. A. Selby-Bigge (New York, Oxford University Press, 1941), p. 3—hereafter cited as *Treatise*, S.B.

of his philosophical speculations, the Cartesian-Lockian conception of sense experience had upon his thinking. "All impressions," he wrote, "are internal and perishing existences, and appear as such." [31] Ordinary people, that is, all the "vulgar" who are not prone to, or trained in, technical philosophy, take impressions to be objects apart from the mind and to exist even when the mind does not perceive them. But this naïve position, Hume contended, is untenable. "The doctrine of the independent existence of our sensible perceptions is contrary to the plainest experience." [32] We all tend to believe in "external existences." We seem to see several impressions exterior to our bodies; the furniture of our rooms is beyond our bodies, the walls of our rooms are beyond the furniture, and the fields or buildings seen through a window are beyond our rooms. But "properly speaking, 'tis not our body we perceive, when we regard our limbs and members, but certain impressions which enter by the senses." [33] So it is with what we call our furniture, our rooms, and the scenes beyond our rooms. These matters, too, are impressions which enter by the senses. We err in attributing either externality or continued existence to our perceptions. " 'Tis impossible for us so much as to conceive or form an idea of any thing specifically different from ideas and impressions," because "nothing is ever really present with the mind but its perceptions or impressions and ideas." [34]

Though Hume retained in his early thinking the subjectivistic theory of impressions and ideas, he never followed Descartes and Locke in affirming a world of "real" objects beyond the impressions. The dualism between perceptions in the mind and realities beyond the mind he called a "false philosophy." If the vulgar are mistaken in regarding impressions as external and continued existences, the philosophers who postulate another order of existences apart from impressions are even further from the truth. Impressions are the final data of experience, and we cannot properly go from them to something more ultimate.

As to those impressions which arise from the senses, their ultimate cause is, in my opinion, perfectly inexplicable by human reason, and 'twill always be impossible to decide with certainty, whether they arise immediately from the object, or are produc'd by the creative power of the mind, or are deriv'd from the author of our being.[35]

31 *Treatise*, S.B., p. 194.
32 *Treatise*, S.B., p. 210.
33 *Treatise*, S.B., p. 191.
34 *Treatise*, S.B., p. 67.
35 *Treatise*, S.B., p. 84. In this passage Hume gave forceful expression to his utter skepticism concerning both the Lockian theory, which treated ideas as effects of stimuli

We start with impressions, he maintained, and we end with impressions. We can never justifiably affirm anything but impressions and the ideas which copy them.

Since all men naturally have a firm belief in bodies, that is, in objects which are distinct from, and independent of, our perception of them, Hume felt called upon, in the light of his contention that all impressions are internal and perishing existences, to account for the prevalence of this realistic belief. The belief cannot depend, he insisted, upon either the senses or reason. It arises in us because of the way in which the imagination works. We do not attribute independent existence to all our impressions but only to some of them. We do not attribute it to our pains, our fears, our loves, our hates, or any of those impressions which in Hume's terminology are passions or sentiments or secondary impressions.[36] But we do attribute it to the impressions of our senses, or at least to many of these. The impressions of the senses often have a constancy which leads us to treat a series of closely resembling impressions as appearances or reappearances of the same identical impression. And even where constancy is lacking, the impressions of the senses often have a coherence or regularity of changes in their succession which leads us to treat them as stages in the development of a single thing. The mind "slips along" among the series of separate impressions and related ideas with such a "smooth and easy" passage, that it "confounds the succession with identity." [37] Thus "what any common man means by a hat, or shoe, or stone," [38] is actually a series of perishing impressions, which, however, "produces a propension to unite these broken appearances by the fiction of a continu'd existence." [39] Neither the senses nor reason can support the supposition of a continued (and hence independent) existence. Although "the imagination is seduc'd into such an opinion," the fiction "is really false." [40]

Hume thus concluded that the basic belief of men in continued and independent objects is both inevitable (because the imagination naturally works to produce the belief) and unwarranted (because criticism shows a total lack of evidence for the truth of the belief). He granted that he himself shared the belief of the vulgar; for his criti-

from an external world, and the Berkeleyan theory, which tried to secure objectivity for some ideas by regarding them as ideas in the mind of God.

[36] For explanation of the distinction between sensations and passions, both of which Hume regarded as equally original impressions, see *Treatise*, S.B., pp. 7–8, 175–176.

[37] *Treatise*, S.B., p. 204.

[38] *Treatise*, S.B., p. 202.

[39] *Treatise*, S.B., p. 205.

[40] *Treatise*, S.B., p. 209.

cism could not indeed arrest the natural operation of his own imagination. But he felt bewildered by his conclusion. He was philosophically distressed to confess that his "refin'd and metaphysical" reflections compelled him to deem a natural and inevitable belief an unwarranted and even a false fiction. He brought Book I of his *Treatise* to a close by confessing that philosophical reflections had reduced him to a state of "melancholy and delirium" and by pointing out that such reflections were entirely divorced from the normal business of human life. He wrote: [41]

I am confounded with all these questions, and begin to fancy myself in the most deplorable condition imaginable, inviron'd with the deepest darkness, and utterly depriv'd of the use of every member and faculty.

Most fortunately it happens, that since reason is incapable of dispelling these clouds, nature herself suffices to that purpose . . . I dine, I play a game of back-gammon, I converse, and am merry with my friends; and when after three or four hours' amusement, I wou'd return to these speculations, they appear so cold, and strain'd and ridiculous, that I cannot find in my heart to enter into them any farther.

Here then I find myself absolutely and necessarily determin'd to live, and talk, and act like other people in the common affairs of life. But notwithstanding that my natural propensity, and the course of my animal spirits and passions reduce me to this indolent belief in the general maxims of the world, I still feel such remains of my former disposition, that I am ready to throw all my books and papers into the fire, and resolve never more to renounce the pleasures of life for the sake of reasoning and philosophy.

HUME'S CRITIQUE OF SKEPTICAL PHILOSOPHIES

Hume's disillusionment over the outcome of Book I of the *Treatise* did not turn him for long from further philosophical reflections.[42] But it did lead him to reconsider the reasoning he had presented in the *Treatise* and to reject much of that reasoning. *An Enquiry Concerning the Human Understanding* was in part a briefer summary of material in the *Treatise* and in part a critical rejection of positions set forth in the *Treatise*, together with a tentative formulation of a

---

[41] *Treatise*, S.B., p. 269.

[42] Critics have sometimes represented Hume's turn from philosophy to history as due to disgust with philosophy; and they have interpreted the omission of some of the most skeptical parts of the *Treatise* from *An Enquiry Concerning the Human Understanding* as indicative of a desire to spare his readers such intricate and difficult material. Both these charges of the critics seem to be mistaken. Hume never abandoned philosophy, though he was glad to use historical writing to gain a larger audience than he could gain through philosophical writing. And the sections of the *Treatise* which have no parallel passages in the *Enquiry* (for example, discussion of continued and independent existences) were omitted from the *Enquiry* because Hume no longer accepted the premises or the outcome of these sections.

new position. The last section of the *Enquiry* is directed against his own earlier work as much as against other philosophies he there mentioned.

The last section of *An Enquiry Concerning the Human Understanding* gives Hume's considered views upon several types of skepticism. It bears the title "Of the Academical or Sceptical Philosophy." Skepticism, he meant, is the philosophy which held sway in the academies or universities of the time—and this was mainly Cartesian or Lockian. He intended, not to uphold these skepticisms, but to expose them. He wished to lay bare the assumptions they made and the considerations which led him to deem them untenable. And in so doing, he revised some of his earlier opinions and departed from much of the doubt which he had expressed in his own *Treatise* about the nature and significance of sense experience.

Antecedent skepticism is that "universal doubt" which was "inculcated by Des Cartes" and made a preliminary to all philosophical inquiry.[43] The doubt Hume was referring to is the methodological doubt with which Descartes opened both his *Discourse* and his *Meditations*. It is a doubt, Hume pointed out, not merely concerning conclusions drawn but even concerning the possibility of having any subject-matter to investigate. One may legitimately have doubts as to what one's subject-matter is; indeed, one may set out to make investigations of a subject-matter just because, before investigations, one is doubtful as to what it is. But if one once entertains a defiant doubt as to whether he has any subject-matter to investigate, one will never recover from his doubts. Initial skepticism, when used in the extreme or "excessive" form of the Cartesian method, is destructive of all efforts, scientific or philosophical, to reach knowledge of the world or any matter of fact in the world. Once universal doubt is entertained as an approach to inquiry, reason is unable to afford any escape.

When Hume said reason is unable to afford any escape from such universal doubt, he was using the term *reason*, it ought to be noted, in a very strict sense. He was using it to mean a faculty of *a priori* reasoning,[44] which, in the absence of evidence from experience, is never-

---

[43] *An Enquiry Concerning the Human Understanding, and An Enquiry Concerning the Principles of Morals*, ed. L. A. Selby-Bigge (Oxford, Clarendon Press, 1894), p. 148. In citing this book hereafter, the two works by Hume will be distinguished by using the notation *Enquiry HU* and *Enquiry PM*.

[44] See David Hume, *Dialogues Concerning Natural Religion*, ed. Norman Kemp Smith (Oxford, Clarendon Press, 1935), p. 198—hereafter cited as *Dialogues*, N.K.S. In this passage, which he wrote shortly before his death, Hume was directing attention to the fact that he had been accustomed to employ the word *reason* in a special sense. In this sense,

theless supposed to be able to reach knowledge of self-evident truths through intuition. Hume was not denying that reflections, supported by evidence which a man gains from some other source than reason itself, may issue in accredited conclusions. He meant, rather, that reflections, following a dogmatic or even a skeptical rejection of the evidential value of all sense experience, can never reach knowledge of matters of fact. Reason apart from the evidence of the senses may succeed, to be sure, in reaching certainty in the abstract sciences or in what Hume usually called inquiry into the "relations of ideas." That is, reason discerns such formal truths as "the square of the hypotenuse is equal to the squares of the other two sides," or "where there is no property, there can be no injustice." [45] These truths do not concern anything existent in nature and are mostly elaborations of the meaning of arbitrarily defined terms. "Propositions of this kind are discoverable by the mere operation of thought, without dependence on what is anywhere existent in the universe." [46] But no one can properly pass, as he supposed Descartes sought to do, from inquiries about relations of ideas to inquiries about "real existence and matter of fact." [47] Descartes' antecedent skepticism, if, indeed, it were more than a pose and were seriously entertained by any thinker, was therefore abortive and afforded no possible escape to knowledge of the world or God or even the self.

Antecedent skepticism, if sufficiently moderate or "mitigated," may indeed be a wholesome corrective to dogmatism. It then becomes an intellectual humility which is indispensable to careful examination of evidence. It weans the mind from prejudices. It limits the human understanding to reflections concerning the real order of, and the genuine connections among, the matters of fact, of which some are already observed and more may be observed. Such reflection arises in a context which sheer reason does not produce and cannot annul and which reflection ought to respect as its requisite setting and the scene of its procedure and the material for its verification. The contrary of every matter of fact is, from the point of view of abstract reason, as possible as what is "conformable to reality"; for the contrary of any matter of fact does not involve a self-contradiction and appears as distinctly and easily to the mind as do genuine matters of fact.[48] Reason-

to judge of any matter by reason and to judge of it in the light of experience are exclusive alternatives.

[45] *Enquiry HU*, p. 163; see also, p. 25.
[46] *Enquiry HU*, p. 25.
[47] *Enquiry HU*, p. 27.
[48] *Enquiry HU*, p. 25; see *Dialogues*, N.K.S., pp. 232-233.

ing is profitable, therefore, only when it proceeds with the handling of materials which the reasoner has accepted, prior to reasoning, on the basis of observation and experiment.

Consequent skepticism is that which progressively undermines our judgments when once "our very senses are brought into dispute." [49] Hume did not single Locke out in condemning consequent skepticism, though he surely had Locke in mind as well as others who deemed the immediate objects of the mind to be its own perceptions. He singled no one out specifically, in all probability, because he was now virtually attacking the repeated contention of his own *Treatise* that all the perceptions of the mind are "internal and perishing existences." Hume did not find it easy to depart from the position he had taken in the *Treatise*. He granted that "the profounder and more philosophical sceptics will always triumph, when they endeavor to introduce an universal doubt into all subjects of human knowledge and enquiry." [50] But to these profound skeptics he opposed men's "natural instinct or prepossession, to repose faith in their senses." We all have this faith except when engulfed in the dialectic of an epistemological system; and he clearly preferred this faith, even if he could not theoretically justify it, to consequent skepticism. He frankly said: [51]

Without any reasoning, or even almost before the use of reason, we always suppose an external universe, which depends not on our perception, but would exist, though we and every sensible creature were absent or annihilated.

Without ever finding any way of explicitly refuting the consequent skepticism of Locke and of his own *Treatise,* Hume proceeded to condemn it as excessive. He would indeed retain a consequent skepticism, provided it was sufficiently "mitigated." This mitigated consequent skepticism, he thought, would promote intellectual humility at the termination of inquiry as mitigated antecedent skepticism did at the outset of inquiry. Hume never ceased to point out that "the senses alone are not implicitly to be depended on." [52] But he came more and more to hold that the senses, prior to reasoning, give us some direct acquaintance with real objects in the natural world and that those senses, guided by reasoning, assist us in correcting their deficiencies and in thus making them "the proper *criteria* of truth and falsehood."

The purport of Hume's discussion of skepticism in *An Enquiry Concerning the Human Understanding,* then, is as follows. No one

[49] *Enquiry HU,* p. 150.
[50] *Enquiry HU,* p. 153.
[51] *Enquiry HU,* p. 151.
[52] *Enquiry HU,* p. 151.

can prove that what he sees or hears or is aware of through the senses is really exactly as he sees or hears or senses it. No one, likewise, can prove that it is not. Speculations on the point are profitless. Moderate or mitigated skepticism amounts to caution in accepting the first glance or a narrow experience as sufficient, and it amounts to readiness to explore the world by further observations under the guidance of reasoning. Even the final glance or the accumulated instruction of careful observation may be insufficient to eliminate all error of judgment about matters of fact. But there is, humanly speaking, no substitute for sense experience in reaching acceptable conclusions. Hume always insisted that the information we gain of the world through the senses is partial and fragmentary. But he abandoned the subjectivism of the Cartesian-Lockian tradition. He favored a cautious acceptance of the trust the vulgar put in their senses. He favored that kind of trust because practically it was productive of reasonable results, even if theoretically it was difficult to defend against the disintegrating criticism of the excessive consequent skeptics.

The last and most mature presentation of Hume's opinions on the reliability of sense experience (as, too, on many other points) is given in his *Dialogues Concerning Natural Religion*. "To philosophise" on the role of the senses and of reason, he wrote, "is nothing essentially different from reasoning on common life." [53] Every man is aware that "external objects press in upon him" just as "passions solicit him." [54] And no one can afford, in the exigencies of living and acting, to linger long in the skepticism of the schools. Our ideas carry us no further than our experience has gone; but of objects familiar to us we may safely make judgments. We have all observed "a thousand and a thousand times" that "a stone will fall, that fire will burn, that the earth has solidity." [55] We really perceive matter, that is, many material objects; and we gain nothing (in theological or any other kind of philosophical reasoning) in resolving "the universe of objects into a similar universe of ideas." [56] We have not sufficient "*data* to establish any system of cosmogony," because "our experience, so imperfect in itself, and so limited both in extent and duration, can afford us no probable conjecture concerning the whole of things." [57] But such ideas as we do have "are copied from real objects," [58] and so enable us to know some things in the natural world around us.

[53] *Dialogues*, N.K.S., p. 166.
[54] *Dialogues*, N.K.S., p. 163.
[55] *Dialogues*, N.K.S., p. 178.
[56] *Dialogues*, N.K.S., pp. 200–201.
[57] *Dialogues*, N.K.S., p. 219.
[58] *Dialogues*, N.K.S., p. 229.

Hume has often been called a skeptic; he has been named the archskeptic of modern times, as Pyrrho was of ancient times. This reputation is undeserved. Actually, Hume, though diffident about almost all conclusions in the *Treatise,* came in his later works to be the hostile critic of skepticism. Skeptical arguments, he wrote, are those which "admit of no answer, and produce no conviction." [59] This definition is highly ironical, though it does reflect Hume's own irresolution in the face of the Lockian theory of the subjectivity of sense experience. No theory, he proceeded to say, can be more skeptical than skepticism itself.[60] Even if one finds himself baffled by efforts to refute excessive skepticism, one is hardly likely to be convinced by such skepticism. One's life is going on in a world which conditions it on every hand, and one cannot fail to act as if, and to come to the belief that, one detects many aspects of this world in his daily experience.

HUME'S RELATION TO LOCKE AND BERKELEY

In Hume the eighteenth-century opposition to seventeenth-century subjectivism reached fulfillment. In spite of the hesitant character of his expression of it, Hume made this opposition more marked than had even Berkeley. Hume did not announce it clearly in his own words, but his analysis of skepticism indicates it sufficiently. The historical relation of Locke, Berkeley, and Hume may be set forth by pointing out their acceptance or rejection of the two principles in which Berkeley had summed up his position. Locke had enunciated the basic principle that the things we immediately perceive are ideas which exist only in the mind. Berkeley had retained this principle but had avoided the subjectivistic implication of Locke's principle by adding thereto his own original principle, namely, that the things we immediately perceive are also real objects in the world about us. Hume, in spite of early hesitations, came more and more to be willing to affirm the latter principle without retaining the former. He did not, so far as the evidence goes, gain this principle from his reading of Berkeley.[61] But he did come progressively, as his philosophical reflections continued, to sponsor just that position. We are aware through our senses, he held, of some of the matters of fact or objects which,

---

59 *Enquiry HU,* p. 155n. Hume gave this comment in connection with his rejection of Berkeley's theory that real objects are ideas in the mind of God. But it has a much wider applicability.

60 *Enquiry HU,* p. 158.

61 Hume confessed some indebtedness to Berkeley. He praised Berkeley's treatment of abstract ideas (as set forth in the introduction of Berkeley's *Principles*). But he was estranged from Berkeley by Berkeley's idealism and did not, so far as his comments show, appreciate the realistic purport of Berkeley's thought.

together with some others we may infer and many others we do not at all know, constitute the real order of the natural world. In Book I of Hume's *Treatise,* as in Locke's *Essay,* experience was a series of subjective perceptions; but in Hume's *Enquiry Concerning the Human Understanding* and *Dialogues* experience was rather a method of dealing with objects the nature of which was not known in advance and could be discovered only by observing and handling them. Empiricism,[62] the historian may then say, ceased in Hume's mature writings to be a theory according to which men must begin with their own mental states and may then try to reach other objects that lie beyond the range of inspection and direct experience; it became, instead, a method of investigation of all sorts of objects, human passions and ideas, to be sure, but also material objects and physical and social events. Hume's empiricism in his mature works makes no commitment as to the kind of object with which the mind may happen to start or with which the mind may choose to end. It is an invitation to investigate the things with which men are concerned in daily life, with an open-mindedness as to the connections of these simple things with other things or as to the nature of the other things which lie beyond the range of present observations. Hume remarked in the *Dialogues* that we have not enough data for any cosmogony, and he went on to indicate that we have not enough data for any cosmology or any sweeping generalizations about the whole of reality. But we have, he insisted, direct evidence of many real things which we possess before we begin to reflect upon them and which we may come through reflection to possess more satisfactorily than before.

HUME'S LATER POSITION

Although Hume's analysis of skepticism marks his break with many of the doubts he expressed in the *Treatise,* his new position is more constructively set forth in sections 4 and 5 of the *Enquiry Concerning the Human Understanding.* Hume here raised a question concerning "the nature of that evidence which assures us of any real existence and matter of fact." [63] There are, he maintained, three kinds of evidence: the present testimony of the senses, the records of the memory, and reasoning founded on the relation of cause and effect. None of the three is infallible; all are useful. The first is the most reliable but

---

[62] *Empiricism* is not Hume's term, but it is a term normally applied to all those philosophies which regard experience as the source of whatever knowledge men secure. Many different kinds of empiricism occur in history, however, because many different views have been taken of the nature of experience.

[63] *Enquiry HU,* p. 26.

also the most scanty. The last is the most abundant but also the most likely to lead us astray. Each serves as a check upon the other two; and the three give tolerably good guidance when used together.

Hume did not discuss the first two kinds of evidence at any length. But he did put them first. He put the present testimony of the senses first of all. He now seldom followed his former practice of using the terms *impression* and *perception* for that which we see and touch and are directly aware of through our senses. He spoke rather of objects, occasionally even of "natural objects," of real existence, or of matter of fact. It is real objects in the natural world which we are aware of through our senses. He did not discuss the reliability of sense experience at length, because he took for granted that sense experience, scanty as it at any one time is, acquaints us with some real objects. He was no longer considering the problem of whether we, beginning with what he, like some other philosophers, had been calling perceptions, can infer the real objects in which the vulgar believe. He was rather considering the problem of how we, beginning with the few objects we directly perceive and reliably remember, come to believe in many other objects and so in a vast world beyond the range of sense and memory. His problem, that is, is to account for the way in which reasoning serves as a third kind of evidence for real existence and matters of fact.

This problem confronted him because he had long contended, and he still firmly held, that reason, as a separate faculty unassisted by experience, can never draw any inference concerning matters of fact. Reason, in this strict sense, can never, from the most precise examination of one matter of fact (such as milk or bread, the motion of a billiard ball or a stone), determine either the causes which lie behind it or the effects which follow from it. "Every effect is a distinct event from its cause"; and reason, by itself alone, can never discover "that crystal is the effect of heat, and ice of cold." [64]

Hume employed some unusual language to express his point, language which many of his readers have misunderstood. He said that events in nature are never connected. But he did not say that events in nature are not related, related causally as well as by resemblance, contiguity, regularity of succession, and so forth. A connection, in Hume's customary vocabulary, is a special kind of relation; it is a rational or intelligible bond such as would enable the human understanding to make a deductive or *a priori* inference from one to another of the things connected. Connections, Hume believed, are

[64] *Enquiry HU*, pp. 30, 32.

found among ideas and only among ideas. That is, ideas are sometimes so "connected" or so stand in logical relations to one another
that we may reason about them apart from experience of the senses.
But connections, Hume earnestly insisted, are nowhere found in the
natural world around us. Things sometimes occur together in a uniformity of sequence, so that we may then speak of them as being
conjoined. These conjunctions, however, are always arbitrary to the
unassisted reason. We may call one thing cause and another thing
conjoined with it effect; but the conjunction, though a constant relation so far as our experience of it goes, is not a connection which
reason can show to be necessary. In the case of every natural conjunction, "there are always many other effects, which, to reason, must seem
fully as consistent and natural" as the effect which actually occurs.[65]
The denial of connections in nature is another way in which Hume
expressed his claim that reason by itself is unable to determine matters of fact.

Reasoning founded on the relation of cause and effect, therefore,
is not a matter of argument or ratiocination, at least in its inception
and in its simpler forms. It is an outcome of the impact of experience
upon the mind. And this impact is not planned with sophisticated
deliberateness (because it is found in peasants and children and even
animals, as well as in educated men); it is, rather, a natural result
which experience has upon all minds. It is even doubtful, as Hume
went on to confess, whether it ought to be called "reasoning" at all.
For it is the work, not of understanding or reason, but of association
of ideas or imagination. By imagination, Hume meant in such passages, not mere idle fancy, but such associations of ideas as experience
establishes in careful observers.

The first time, or perhaps even the first few times, that one object
(*A*) is followed by another object (*B*), the mind observes no relation
between the two objects except that of contiguity. If experience becomes more ample and *A* is followed repeatedly and regularly by
B, the mind comes to associate the idea of *B* with the next appearance
of *A* (and this association may be so well established as to occur even
before the object *B* does actually follow that case of *A*). Nothing further is observed in a long series of instances of the *A-B* sequence than
in the first instance. Nothing further is observed; but an association
has been established meanwhile in the mind of the observer. Regularity in experience produces habits or customs in the mind. The

---

[65] *Enquiry HU*, p. 30.

passage of the mind from another occurrence of *A* to the idea of *B* is the inference that *A* is the cause of *B*. And this inference, psychologically requisite, is not rationally guided. It is not such that reason can defend it or refute it. The ampler the experience is of the *A-B* sequence, the livelier will the idea of *B* probably become. And when the idea of *B* is sufficiently lively, the idea of *B* constitutes belief in *B;* that is, the inference from *A* to *B* leads us to believe that *B* will surely occur. For belief, Hume held, "is nothing but a more vivid, lively, forcible, firm, steady conception of an object, than what the imagination alone is ever able to attain." [66]

"Custom, then," wrote Hume, "is the great guide of human life." [67] Understanding does not first produce custom. Rather, custom, operating under the laws of the association of ideas, produces the possibility of wider understanding of nature than could come from the present testimony of the senses and the records of memory. But, nonetheless, understanding may well revise custom, may submit old customs to further experimental testing, and so may make custom a more and more adequate guide to genuine causal relations. The first customs of a man's mind may be due to chance sequences in a limited experience. They may lead to superstitions rather than to the discovery of nature's laws. Even in the more skeptical *Treatise* Hume formulated rules to guide understanding in the revision of customary beliefs.[68] And he then drew the lesson that by his rules we may learn to "carefully separate whatever is superfluous, and enquire by new experiments, if every particular circumstance of the first experiment was essential to it." And in *An Enquiry Concerning the Human Understanding* he pointed out that other psychological conditions beside regularity of natural sequence may also build up beliefs in the mind that are much more likely to reflect some private passion or some respect for cherished authority than to accord with the facts of natural relations.[69] Hence, through the workings of the imagination, we people our world with many existences beyond those which we ascertain from the present testimony of the senses and the records of the memory. No human imagination can be said to work inerrantly in reflecting the real causal relations in nature. But the normal human imagi-

66 *Enquiry HU*, p. 49.
67 *Enquiry HU*, p. 44.
68 *Treatise*, S.B., pp. 173–175.
69 Hume's famous essay "Of Miracles" enforces this point with vigor. He listed the personal and social conditions which induce belief in miracles among many men, and he concluded that in his own opinion "no testimony for any kind of miracle has ever amounted to a probability, much less to a proof." See *Enquiry HU*, p. 127.

nation so works as to set up "a kind of pre-established harmony between the course of nature and the succession of our ideas." [70] And thus our inquiries into matters of fact may extend very far into nature, and our beliefs may closely reflect nature's genuine ways.

THE IDEA OF NECESSITY OR POWER

After having concluded that we ascertain many matters of fact by reasonings founded on the relation of cause and effect, Hume was led to investigate "the idea of necessary connexion." "There are no ideas, which occur in metaphysics," he recognized, "more obscure and uncertain than those of *power, force, energy* or *necessary connexion.*" [71] We have the idea of power or necessity.[72] But we never find in the experiences we have of the world through our senses, Hume was firmly convinced, any instance of necessity.

In reality, there is no part of nature, that does ever, by its sensible qualities, discover any power or energy, or give us ground to imagine, that it could produce any thing, or be followed by any other object, which we could denominate its effect.[73]

Nor do we find any instance of necessity in the operations of our wills (as Berkeley had held). We are aware of our own volitions, and we observe that in many cases suitable motions of our muscles follow the volitions.

But the means, by which this is effected; the energy, by which the will performs so extraordinary an operation; of this we are so far from being immediately conscious, that it must for ever escape our most diligent enquiry.[74]

Neither in the sequences of nature around us nor in our own volitions, therefore, do we observe power or necessity. We must look elsewhere for the impression from which the idea of power or necessity arises.

When Hume sought the origin of the idea of necessity, it ought to be noted, he was not referring to logical necessity, that is, to such strict implication between one idea and another idea that our thinking

---

[70] *Enquiry*, S.B., p. 54.

[71] *Enquiry HU*, pp. 61–62.

[72] One of the strange ironies of history is that Hume, who in both his *Treatise* and his first *Enquiry* devoted long and closely reasoned sections to tracing our idea of necessity back to the impression from which it arises, is alleged by many of his critics to have denied that we have any such idea at all (see below, n. 75). One wonders sometimes whether the critics have read Hume's discussion carefully. Actually, Hume seems to have taken considerable satisfaction in discovering the impression of necessity, of which our idea of necessity is a copy.

[73] *Enquiry HU*, p. 63.

[74] *Enquiry HU*, p. 65.

(our affirmations and our denials) must properly submit to the rational connections by which we are confronted. Such logical necessity occurs only in "relations of ideas," and there affords the ground which enables us to exercise our reason *a priori* and without empirical checks. He was referring, rather, to that compelling productiveness which makes an antecedent factor in a natural sequence a genuine cause and a consequent factor a genuine effect. It is, of course, necessity in this latter sense only which Hume used as a synonym for "power," "force," or "energy." [75]

We do find in the workings of the imagination, Hume believed, what we do not find in either nature or volition. When uniform experience has built up habits in the mind, we gain a new impression which was not in the imagination before this uniform experience. He emphasized this point with reiteration.[76]

When many uniform instances appear, and the same object is always followed by the same event; we then begin to entertain the notion of cause and connexion. We then *feel* a new sentiment or impression, to wit, a customary connexion in the thought or imagination between one object and its usual attendant; and this sentiment is the original of that idea we seek for.

Hume thus did discover instances of necessity or power. The imagination operates with necessity or power, and we detect that necessity and derive thence our subsequent idea of necessity.

The impression of necessity, however, Hume steadfastly held, is to be found only in the workings of the imagination. It is a sentiment (like pain or love or hate), not a sensation or an observed fact in the world around us. And this conclusion of his effort to explain the idea of necessity made Hume doubtful as to the extent to which we can use the idea of necessity (once we have obtained it) in the interpretation of natural sequences. In the skeptical Book I of the *Treatise* he seems to have supposed that the idea of necessity (like the idea of continued and independent objects) was a fiction which we had no warrant for applying to the realm of sense experience. But elsewhere, as in the discussion of the passions in Book II of the *Treatise* and generally throughout *An Enquiry Concerning the Human Understanding,* he took a different position.[77]

[75] In recent or twentieth-century philosophy the term *necessity* is seldom used except in the sense of logical necessity. This change in vocabulary is perhaps the reason why critics have often missed the point Hume was making. Some recent writers, however, do speak of natural necessity as well as of logical necessity. And in so doing, they are continuing the linguistic practice of Hume.

[76] *Enquiry HU,* p. 78. See also, *Enquiry HU,* p. 75; *Treatise,* S.B., pp. 155, 165, 171.

[77] *Treatise,* S.B., pp. 399–400.

'Tis universally acknowledg'd, that the operations of external bodies are necessary, and that in the communications of their motion, in their attraction, and mutual cohesion, there are not the least traces of indifference or liberty. Every object is determin'd by an absolute fate to a certain degree and direction of its motion, and can no more depart from that precise line, in which it moves, than it can convert itself into an angel, or spirit, or any superior substance. The actions, therefore, of matter are to be regarded as instances of necessary actions; and whatever is in this respect on the same footing with matter, must be acknowledg'd to be necessary.

Once we get the idea of blue, for instance, we may apply it to objects not yet seen (inferring perhaps that certain flowers next summer will be blue)—and we may apply it correctly. So once we get the idea of power or necessity, we may apply it to many sequences in nature, even if we do not observe it except in our imaginations. And, again, we may apply it correctly. But, as Hume insisted with his typical restraint, we must apply it with some caution. We are likely to be misled by our hopes and fears if we proceed dogmatically. We are likely to mistake casual sequences for causal sequences unless we study our experiences meticulously and follow the most exact rules for the weighing of evidence.

CRITIQUE OF THEOLOGY

Hume's *Dialogues Concerning Natural Religion,* his most mature work, is an application to theological questions of the theories of cause and effect which he had developed in his *Treatise* and *Enquiry Concerning the Human Understanding.* The *Dialogues* purport to be a sustained argument among three disputants. Demea is a mystic who distrusts reason as a means to theistic faith, who stresses the point that the nature of God is beyond human understanding, and who nevertheless uses the "sublime argument *a priori*" or ontological argument for the existence of "a necessarily existent Being." Cleanthes is an advocate of what had long been called natural religion; he holds that there is a reliable analogy between the works of human art and the course of nature, and so he uses the cosmological and teleological arguments for demonstration of the existence of God on what he takes to be empirical grounds. Philo mischievously plays off his two antagonists against each other, using points which Hume maintained in his other writings. With Demea, Philo asserts that reason cannot determine matters of fact. With Cleanthes, Philo agrees that evidence is requisite for sound beliefs in matters of fact. Philo, in his criticism of Demea and Cleanthes and in his presentation of his own views, is spokesman for Hume; that is, he defends views which Hume elsewhere stated or which one would be likely to infer from what Hume elsewhere stated. Demea becomes annoyed with Philo's irony and with Cleanthes' reliance upon reasoning, and so he departs from the scene of the argument before the termination of the *Dialogues.*

The *Dialogues,* taken as a piece of philosophical exposition, are chiefly devoted to consideration of the reliability or unreliability of the proffered analogy between human art and the course of nature. They grant that in the case of human art purposefulness is a consequence of design, and they then inquire whether in the case of nature purposefulness can be assumed to be evidence of design. Cleanthes defends the analogy. Philo attacks it. Philo attacks it primarily for the three following considerations. (1) "Order, arrangement, or the adjustment of final causes is not, of itself, any proof of design." [78] For it may well be, so far as we can reasonably tell, that order is intrinsic to matter instead of being imposed upon matter by a mind. (2) Reason (and, hence, intelligent purpose) is found here and there in nature, but not widely, not generally. "With what propriety can we assign it for the original cause of all things?" [79] (3) We can, with tentative inference, assign causal relations to objects which "have always been observed to be conjoined together." But we have no experience at all of the making of a world; much less have we repeated and uniform instances of such a process.[80] We may, in other words, use a causal inference for events within nature, but we have no warrant for extending this kind of inference to the world taken collectively as one object. "Every event, before experience, is equally difficult and incomprehensible; and every event, after experience, is equally easy and intelligible. . . . We have no *data* to establish any system of cosmology." [81]

Philo might have rested his case with these considerations. But Hume was not satisfied with even so much and proceeded to have Philo press still further points. Philo proceeds to show that the argument from analogy, even if allowed, would not lead to the conclusion Cleanthes seeks to draw from it. (1) The argument from analogy would demonstrate, at best, a cause of limited power—of just enough power to produce the actual world. (2) It would also, at best, demonstrate a cause which was incoherent in its undertakings and indifferent to the moral consequences thereof. For the world is full of confusion and evil. (3) It would, still further, do nothing to establish one single

[78] *Dialogues,* N.K.S., p. 180.
[79] *Dialogues,* N.K.S., p. 183.
[80] *Dialogues,* N.K.S., p. 185.
[81] *Dialogues,* N.K.S., pp. 225, 219.

ultimate cause but would be far more compatible with a polytheistic, than a monotheistic, hypothesis about the world. (4) It would, finally, be quite in harmony with ancient superstitions, such as that the gods, like men, have human figures, generate their kind, and are changeable in purpose, even capricious.

Hume realized that to reject Cleanthes' philosophical theology was not to prove Cleanthes' theistic belief false. He was as averse to dogmatic atheism as to arrogant assertion of faith. He did so undermine natural theology, however, that few Protestant theologians since his time have sponsored that kind of theology.[82] And if Protestant theologians have now and then used the term *natural religion,* they are more likely to have meant a faith that is natural or congenial to man than a conclusion which one can reasonably reach from alleged evidences for God in the natural world.

ETHICAL THEORY

In his theory of morals Hume belonged to what is called the moral sense school. The third earl of Shaftesbury (1671–1731), Francis Hutcheson (1694–1746), and Bishop Joseph Butler (1692–1752) had reacted against the rationalistic ethics they found in one form or another in Descartes, Spinoza, and Locke; and Adam Smith (1723–1790) later gave brilliant expression to much the same position as Hume's in his *Theory of the Moral Sentiments* (1759). Hume's treatment of ethics in Book III of his *Treatise* and in *An Enquiry Concerning the Principles of Morals* is perhaps the definitive work of the moral sense school.

Just as Hume deemed reason incapable of determining any matter of fact, so he deemed it incapable of determining any of the ultimate ends of human conduct. His ethical position was vigorously antirationalistic. Reason may show us the means to certain ends; it may enable us to learn, for example, that exercise is good for health and that health is good for the successful pursuit of one's calling. Reason discovers this kind of utility and so in that way helps us to act well. But reason cannot begin effectively to operate until it receives, from some source other than itself, instructions as to what is genuinely good in itself. There are no "eternal and immutable moral principles" which reason can furnish.

The foundation of any general theory of morality, as of all moral practice, is our moral sentiments. Our affective nature here holds

---

[82] Hume has had little influence upon Roman Catholic theology, which customarily is based on the philosophical theology of St. Thomas Aquinas.

priority over our rational nature. "Reason is, and ought only to be the slave of the passions, and can never pretend to any other office than to serve and obey them." [83] Not all the passions, not even all the sentiments (Hume's word for the calm but persistent passions), are guides to right conduct. The moral sentiments are among the passions, however; they are as original and as unresolvable into anything other than themselves as pain or fear or love. They are the work, not of reason, but of the heart.[84] They are a "universal principle of the human frame," in which "all mankind have an accord and sympathy." [85] For "the humanity of one man is the humanity of every one, and the same object touches this passion in all human creatures." [86] Moral judgments are the consequence of "the blind, but sure testimony of taste and sentiment." [87]

The objects which elicit moral sentiments in us, Hume held, were not actions but motives. We approve whatever is benevolent, that is, all motives which are "sociable, good-natured, humane, merciful, grateful, friendly, generous, beneficent, or their equivalent." [88] And we condemn the opposite of such motives as vicious or odious or depraved. What is neither benevolent nor malevolent, we count morally indifferent.[89]

Hume defined virtue as "whatever mental action or quality gives to a spectator the pleasing sentiment of approbation." [90] But he was far from being a hedonist. Indeed, he was opposed to asceticism and undue austerity; he was joyous by disposition and by conviction. But the pleasing sentiment of approbation, he firmly held, is a very special case of pleasure, the only pleasure indeed which has basic moral significance. Good wine and good music please us, and so does the convenience of a home. But the pleasures from such things are not the objects of moral approbation. If, however, a man sought to give good wine or good music or a good home to one of his fellows, that man's motive would at once be approved. The only final object of the moral sentiments is public benevolence or a feeling for the happiness of mankind.

83 *Treatise,* S.B., p. 415.
84 *Enquiry PM,* p. 290.
85 *Enquiry PM,* p. 272.
86 *Enquiry PM,* p. 273.
87 *Enquiry PM,* p. 267.
88 *Enquiry PM,* p. 176.
89 Hume discussed justice at length. But he deemed it an artificial virtue, that is, a virtue which through long experience and association of ideas men have learned to regard as an indispensable means to the practice of benevolence. Hence, he did not include "just" motives among the types which naturally arouse our moral sentiments.
90 *Enquiry PM,* p. 289. Cf. *Treatise,* S.B., p. 475.

Hume was intentionally opposing the selfish view of human nature which he attributed to Hobbes. Every person may love himself more than he loves any other one person. Nonetheless, every person has affections for others too. Men certainly do not always act for their own self-interest. Egoism is a poor pyschology. Sympathy for others and a consequent desire to serve others are as ultimate traits of mankind as any that can be mentioned. Sympathy, to be sure, does not bind a man with equal concern to all his fellows. It is stronger toward those who are close or contiguous to us than it is toward others remote in time or space or acquaintance. But it often does prevail among men. It manifests itself in benevolence, which, then, is the only ultimate object of the moral sentiments.

THE NATURALISTIC TRADITION

Hume's philosophical influence has been prodigious during the last two hundred years. Yet he has been interpreted very differently by his various critics and historians. He has been called advocate of "the ideal theory," skeptic (without qualification), phenomenalist, positivist, associationist, realist, naturalist. The history of Hume's influence would be a history of much modern philosophy since his time. Perhaps the most just of the characterizations just listed is naturalist.[91] Though utterly different in approach, in vocabulary, and in temper from Aristotle, Hume may nevertheless be said to represent in modern times the naturalistic tradition which Aristotle represents in ancient times. Yet if that be said, a further word ought to be added. With Aristotle it is his conclusions which lead us to call him naturalist, but with Hume it is his method. He was suspicious of cosmological generalizations like the Newtonian world-machine theory as well as of theological efforts to account for the origin of the world. He was above all an open-minded inquirer into the world he found around him, uncommitted with any finality to even his own tentative conclusions, ready to reconsider and to revise, more inclined to add bit by bit to the store of human understanding than to spin broad generalizations about the fundamental principles of the cosmos. His critical powers showed one way in which Locke's affiliation of empiricism with subjectivism and agnosticism may be replaced by an empiricism that tends to naturalism.

[91] This characterization has been made in our own day by such able critics as George E. Moore and Norman Kemp Smith.

3. REID

THOMAS REID, 1710–1796, was born in Strachan, Scotland, and died in Glasgow. He graduated at the age of sixteen from the University of Aberdeen and then acted as librarian there for ten years. He entered the Presbyterian ministry and served as pastor until in 1752 he went to King's College, Aberdeen, as professor of philosophy. At Aberdeen he organized a philosophical club at which the chief topic of discussion was Hume's philosophy. In 1764 he became professor of moral philosophy at the University of Glasgow. In 1781 he retired from teaching and devoted his remaining years to arranging and publishing his philosophical lectures. Among his works are *An Inquiry into the Human Mind on the Principles of Common Sense* (1764), *Essays on the Intellectual Powers of Man* (1785), and *Essays on the Active Powers of Man* (1788).

THE PRESBYTERIAN CLERGY of Scotland were not long in coming to the defense of their religious doctrines against the disintegrating effect, as they viewed it, of the philosophy of Hume. Hume's *Treatise* appeared to many of its readers a piece of blatant skepticism, and his essays on miracles and providence (in *An Enquiry Concerning the Human Understanding*) were often deemed not merely heretical but even atheistic. Even before his *Dialogues* came out in 1779 Hume was attacked in sermons and books as an enemy of the Christian faith. The reverend James Oswald published *An Appeal to Common Sense in Behalf of Religion* in 1766. The poet James Beattie (1735–1803) published *An Essay on the Nature and Immutability of Truth in Opposition to Sophistry and Scepticism* in 1770.[92] These books have not proved to be important, but they were acclaimed at the time they appeared. The famous Dr. Samuel Johnson eulogized Beattie, King George III conferred a pension on him, and Kant depended on his *Essay* for some of the information he had about Hume.

Thomas Reid developed a position which made the Scotch protest against Hume philosophically respectable. He is the most eminent

---

[92] The most important fact about Beattie, some people might say today, is that his portrait was painted by Sir Joshua Reynolds. The portrait hangs at Marischal College, Aberdeen. In the portrait Beattie conspicuously holds his book on Truth, a symbolic figure of Truth carries the scales of justice, and three figures representing sophistry, skepticism, and infidelity are thrust aside into darkness. Sir Joshua is reported to have indicated that two of the last three figures could be identified with Hume and Voltaire.

figure in what has come to be called the school of Scotch realism or the common sense school. He protested, as had Oswald and Beattie, against the skeptical outcome of Hume's reflections. But he granted that that outcome was a logical consequence of an initial hypothesis with which Hume began—an hypothesis which he named "the ideal theory." [93] This hypothesis is "that nothing is perceived but what is in the mind which perceives it: that we do not really perceive things that are external, but only certain images and pictures of them imprinted upon the mind, which are called impressions and ideas." [94] Once this hypothesis is accepted, Reid insisted, there is no escape from doubts concerning the reality of permanent objects, the material world, the soul, and God. Reid proposed therefore a new analysis of the nature and course of human experience, an analysis which would be more thorough and more empirical than that which "the ideal theory" had given.

The term *idea*, Reid contended, was used ambiguously by Locke, and, similarly, the two terms *impression* and *idea* were used ambiguously by Hume. In one sense the term *idea* means a process the mind performs, such as thinking, conceiving, apprehending, perceiving, seeing, hearing. In another sense the term *idea* means the objects with which we deal in our thinking or our perceiving. Ideas in the former sense are certainly psychical events; they occur in the mind and only in the mind. Ideas in the latter sense, however, may be anything at all. One is not entitled to call them psychical. One is not entitled to apply to them the character one has properly given to ideas in the former sense. One ought not to be misled by ambiguity of language into affirming that because seeing is "in the mind" the objects seen are also "in the mind." "Ideas," Reid said in commenting sarcastically on the history of philosophy from Descartes to Hume, "seem to have something in their nature unfriendly to other existences." [95] He therefore resolved to abandon the use of the traditional term *idea* and to speak in terms of *sensations* and *perceptions*.

Sensation and perception, Reid went on to explain, are not equivalent situations. In sensation two distinguishable factors are present, namely, the mind and the feeling or operation of the mind. We have sensations often in connection with three of the senses of the body

---

[93] Reid pointed out that Descartes and Locke had held this hypothesis before Hume took it over. Reid also supposed that Berkeley had sponsored the same hypothesis, thus failing to appreciate the realistic element in Berkeley's position. He recognized no difference between Hume's earlier and later positions.

[94] Thomas Reid, *Inquiry into the Human Mind*, dedicatory epistle.

[95] *Inquiry into the Human Mind*, chap. 2, sec. 6.

—smelling, tasting, and hearing. In the case of these three senses we are not normally or easily aware of the object through which the operation is produced in the mind. We may learn to associate a certain smell with a rose or a certain sound with a galloping horse. But the rose and the horse are inferred; they are not given immediately in the sensation. In perception, however, three (rather than two) distinguishable factors are present, namely, the mind, the feeling or operation of the mind, and the object of that operation. We have perception normally in connection with the other two senses of the body—seeing and touching. Perception is all that sensation is and more. Insofar as it is more, it is the direct and indubitable presence of the object through which the operation of the mind is induced. The object is here more than inference; it is datum. We may not be able to explain why three of the bodily organs yield sensations only and the other two yield perceptions. But we ought not to allow our inability to explain that point blind us to the facts of experience. We see and touch material things. "I do perceive matter objectively," said Reid.[96] We thus know, and know beyond question, that we are living in a world external to our minds and in no way dependent on our minds for its existence. And insofar as we perceive certain things in this external world, we know, and know beyond question, some of the things which are occurring in this external world.

Reid's distinction between sensation and perception enabled him to revive in a new form the traditional separation of primary and secondary qualities. Primary qualities are those qualities of external objects of which our perceptions give us a "direct and distinct" awareness. Things may indeed have other qualities than those perceived, but they surely have those perceived. Smoothness and roughness, figure, motion, extension, and position are qualities which Reid lists as primary. These qualities are not sensations in the mind; they are real properties or qualities of bodies of which we have direct awareness and, hence, certain knowledge. Secondary qualities, too, are in the things we perceive, but of them we have no direct awareness. They are the qualities in bodies which produce in us the sensations we experience. Sounds, tastes, smells, colors, heat, and cold are not qualities of bodies at all; they are sensations. But bodies have qualities by which to cause these sensations in us; and these qualities, obscure and inferred rather than clear and given, may well be called secondary.

Reid warned his readers against two errors which our inattention to all the complex facts of daily experience may lead us to make. On

[96] *Essays on the Intellectual Powers of Man*, chap. 2, sec. 6.

the one hand, we may thoughtlessly attribute our sensations to the bodies which produce them, thus overlooking the subjectivity of these sensations and their relativity to our constitutions. On the other hand, we may unjustifiably follow the lead of the epistemological tradition from Descartes to Hume and regard our perceptions as merely complex arrangements of sensations, thus coming to doubt the realities of which experience gives us indubitable assurance. Perception is not merely a sensation to which an inference has come in the course of experience to be associated. It is not the hazardous product of conjecture which we have gradually learned to make. It is as original a type of experience as is sensation. It differs from sensation in that it discloses, as sensation does not, the objects which cause our sensations and so enables us to know at least some of the external conditions within the context of which our experience occurs. "Perception . . . hath always an object distinct from the act by which it is perceived; an object which may exist whether it be perceived or not." [97] There is no more reason to doubt the findings of our perceptions than to doubt the experienced qualities of our sensations.[98]

In addition to his philosophy of perception Reid developed a theory of belief. Belief, he vigorously maintained against the view he attributed to Hume, cannot be resolved into the vividness of ideas. Not all beliefs, it is only too apparent to everyone, are true. But some are true; and among those which are true, some few are indubitably true. These indubitable beliefs Reid called the principles of common sense, first principles, or principles involved in our very nature. They are not innate, for they are not in the mind prior to experience. But neither are they inferences we make from our sensations and perceptions, for they are as original elements in our experiences as are any sensations and perceptions. They are original intuitions of necessary and universal truths, and we discern them by an internal common sense as directly as we perceive the primary qualities of bodies by the senses of touch and sight.

Such original and natural judgments are, therefore, a part of that furniture which Nature hath given to the human understanding. . . . They serve to direct us in the common affairs of life, where our reasoning faculty would leave us in the dark. They are a part of our constitution; and all the discoveries of our reason are grounded upon them. They make up what is

---

[97] *Inquiry into the Human Mind,* chap. 6, sec. 20.

[98] Reid remarked that Cartesians were right over against Peripatetics in refusing to take sensations as giving us knowledge of an external world, and that Peripatetics were right over against Cartesians in trusting the data of our perceptions.

called *the common sense of mankind;* and what is manifestly contrary to any of those first principles, is what we call *absurd*.[99]

Common sense, Reid held, is more fundamental than philosophy. Any philosophy which questions the principles of common sense or even offers to give demonstrations of these principles is "a kind of metaphysical lunacy." Sound philosophy incorporates common sense as its foundation and groundwork, using its principles as axioms known from immediate contact with reality and serviceable as a means of proving many subsequent reasoned conclusions. The power of the mind to judge according to common sense is as natural as the power of swallowing food. Even the vulgar have this power, though they may be wholly innocent of philosophy.

Among the principles of common sense which Reid listed are the following: that the qualities we perceive in sight and touch must have a subject, which we may call body, and that the mental operations of which we are conscious must have a subject, which we may call mind; that whatever begins to exist must have a cause which produced it; that design in the cause may properly be inferred from signs of it in the effect; that we human beings have some degree of power over the determinations of our wills; that our natural faculties are not fallacious; that in the course of nature like causes produce like effects.

Reid was aware that an appeal to common sense might become an excuse for dogmatic insistence upon one's prejudices. His intent was so to formulate the position as to safeguard it from fanatical indulgence. But critics were numerous who enjoyed the chance to accuse Reid of merely stubborn assertion of personal preferences. His most competent follower even altogether abandoned use of the term *common sense.* Dugald Stewart (1753–1828), professor of moral philosophy at the University of Edinburgh and one of the great teachers in the history of Britain,[100] feared that Reid's resort to common sense was akin to settling intellectual problems by counting votes. He chose rather to speak of the laws of reason, without the use of which no argument would satisfy the scrutiny of thoughtful men. But his piety toward Reid led him to make his criticisms so cautiously as to blur the real points of difference between him and his master.

---

[99] *Inquiry into the Human Mind,* chap. 7, sec. 4.

[100] His principal work is *Elements of the Philosophy of the Human Mind,* the three volumes of which appeared respectively in 1792, 1814, and 1827.

XII

The Eighteenth Century in France

PIERRE BAYLE, 1647–1706.
Dictionnaire historique et critique, 1697.

BARON DE LA BRÈDE ET DE MONTESQUIEU, 1689–1755.
De l'esprit des lois, 1749.

VOLTAIRE, 1694–1778.
Lettres sur les Anglais, 1732.
Les éléments de la philosophie de Newton, 1738.
Dictionnaire philosophique, 1764.

JULIEN OFFREY DE LA METTRIE, 1709–1757.
L'homme machine, 1748.

ETIENNE BONNOT DE CONDILLAC, 1715–1780.
Traité des sensations, 1754.

DENIS DIDEROT, 1713–1784, editor of the *Encyclopédie* from 1751 to 1766.

JEAN LE ROND D'ALEMBERT, 1717–1783.
Discours préliminaire (of Diderot's *Encyclopédie*), 1751.

CLAUDE ADRIEN HELVÉTIUS, 1715–1771.
De l'esprit, 1758.

BARON D'HOLBACH, 1723–1789, a German *Freiherr* who settled in Paris.
Le système de la nature, 1770.

JEAN JACQUES ROUSSEAU, 1712–1778.
Discours sur les sciences et les arts, 1750.
Discours sur l'origine et les fondements de l'inégalité parmi les hommes, 1753.
Le contrat social, 1762.
Émile, 1762 (especially *Profession de foi du vicaire Savoyard* in Book IV).

THE EIGHTEENTH CENTURY in France is usually called the period of the French Enlightenment. Kant defined the term *enlightenment* as man's release from subservience to other's opinions and readiness to exercise one's own independent reason. But there is no uniformity of thought among the many French writers of the eighteenth century. Some exalted reason; others reduced thinking to a mechanistic series of sensations and images; and Rousseau elevated feelings above reason as the actual and the legitimate basis for human opinions. Even when reason was praised, it was praised in different senses of the term. On the one hand, it was treated as a faculty by which men discovered intelligible principles of the physical and social worlds and regulated desire and will by knowledge of these principles. On the other hand, it was a play of wit, often ironical, at the expense of religious and political institutions and beliefs. Its jibes often had quite ample point because of the corruption in religious and political life. But it was directed at destruction of old customs rather than at construction of new ideas and new ways. Bayle's *Dictionnaire,* just before the century began, set the fashion for much that followed. With its crumbs of historical learning, it gleefully pointed out the abundant errors of the past, though it failed to establish any serious constructive views. Diderot, d'Alembert, Voltaire, and other writers for the great *Encyclopédie* after the middle of the century often seemed less radical than they were because they hid their genuine opinions in minor articles. They had to dodge, as best they could, the censorship of a suspicious officialdom. D'Alembert wrote to Voltaire that in spite of seeming orthodoxy of views in major articles time would enable readers to distinguish what the contributers to the *Encyclopédie* really thought from what they outwardly professed.

THE FRENCH ENLIGHTENMENT

Among the opinions expressed in the French Enlightenment five trends may be mentioned here. Most of them are extensions, often in exaggerated form, of ideas developed in the seventeenth century.

(1) There was a revolt against convention as arbitrary, and there was a consequent appeal to reason. This appeal to reason came in part from Descartes' rationalism; but it depended much more on two English thinkers, Newton and Locke. French writers, notably Voltaire, regarded English thought as a model of enlightenment. Newton, they held, had shown that men can use reason to discover laws of physical nature which explain all events that occur; and Locke, that men can similarly use reason to ascertain laws for the regulation of all social affairs. This appeal to reason was primarily due to a desire to assert the rights of a thinking individual against arbitrary authority. It was not based on a carefully developed epistemology. It was a

technique for social reform. As Newton gave us a new (and supposedly final) physics, so we may make a new and final social system. We do not need revealed religion; indeed, we must reject it. We may believe, however, that God has given us intelligence enough to ascertain laws for society as well as for physical nature. Montesquieu adopted many of Locke's political principles, such as division of powers, individual rights, and popular welfare as the proper goal of government. He recognized, as Locke does not seem to have done, that since climatic and psychological conditions differ from country to country political institutions may therefore properly differ too. But in all countries the laws that should prevail, he held, may be determined by reason's analysis of the pertinent facts.

(2) There was a widespread trend toward sensationalism. Descartes had taught that the brutes are unfeeling automata; Locke had raised the question (though he decided it in the negative) whether organized matter thinks. Voltaire thought that Descartes' distinction between brutes and men was unsound. Either fleas and grubs, he said, have immortal souls as well as do men, or men, like fleas and grubs, are thinking matter. La Mettrie maintained that the difference between men and other living things is only one of degree of complexity of organization.[1] Condillac then took the Lockian theory that the first simple ideas are separate sensations and developed the thesis that all other so-called mental facts are mechanically determined complexes of these simple ideas and of the pains and pleasures which these ideas elicit. He framed the fiction of an animated statue, endowing it with first one sense and then others; and he concluded that the statue, after sufficient organizational complexity, would become the equivalent of a man. Diderot, somewhat in line with Lucretius, supposed that there had always been living and conscious elements in nature (as well as sheerly physical elements). These elements, he held, had gradually come together in such fashion as to become the souls of animals and men. Helvétius embraced the idea of progressive passage from simple elements to complex forms and applied it to the development of moral codes. Men are all susceptible to pleasures and pains, seeking the one and avoiding the latter. What we call moral codes are the convictions which experience has led men to believe in their pursuit of pleasures. Hence, he added with a burst of optimistic confidence, we can, through intelligently guided education, train men to follow the codes we wish them to follow. We have only to subject their behavior to suitable rewards and punishments, and we can

[1] Cf. above, p. 236.

fashion them into creatures of high moral purpose. Helvétius thus built up a program of moral enthusiasm on what was basically a moral nihilism.

(3) The sensationalistic and associationistic theories of the French Enlightenment tended to favor materialistic and even atheistic views of the world. Voltaire, more Newtonian than others, remained hesitantly but complacently deistic. He inclined to suppose that atheists would have no moral sanctions, and that a society of atheists would therefore be impossible. Moreover, God, he thought in agreement with Newton, is needed as first cause of the world, though God may well be limited in power. Diderot espoused atheism zealously; he deemed that any religious theory flies in the face of the fact of evil and leads to intellectual absurdities. And the sensationalism of Condillac made materialism plausible. The German baron d'Holbach, however, expressed materialism and atheism in an extreme form. Newton, he boldly stated, is absurd when he passes from physics to theology. Teleology is a confused notion. *Esprit* or soul is a meaningless term with no empirical evidence. Consciousness consists of motions in the brain. As the providential God of Christianity is full of contradictions, so the God of deism is a useless fantasy. The real alternatives for philosophy are superstition and materialism.

(4) Back of all the trends we have considered in the French Enlightenment was a yearning for social justice. It was a revolutionary yearning in Bourbon France, and it survived into the period of the Revolution as the other trends did not. D'Alembert struck the keynote of the century when he said in the *Discours préliminaire* of the *Encyclopédie* that his century aspired to alter all the prevailing laws and customs and so to bring about a regime of social justice. The French Enlightenment was a period of condemnation of existing institutions and of unlimited optimism in the hopes entertained for the future.

ROUSSEAU

(5) Rousseau's romanticism is the most notable philosophical contribution of the French Enlightenment, as well as the most original. Rousseau entertained a sentimental love for all mankind, even though in his personal relations he was vain, irritable, and quarrelsome. He abhorred materialism for its coldness and atheism for its indifference to personality. But, like most of the thinkers of his century, he was hostile to the established order. He had no trust in reason for the achievement of a better world; reason, he held, was too set, too fixed,

hence too prone to the defense of whatever prevailed. What men call civilization he deemed to be a series of moral and intellectual blunders which inevitably led to slavery for most men. Only through trust in the native promptings of the heart could men be guided to better things.

His first reputation rested on an essay which won a prize in a competition held by the Academy of Dijon. This essay is his *Discours sur les sciences et les arts*. Possibly his desire to attract attention in the competition led him to state his position in exaggerated form. But once his early ideas brought him success, he adhered to them all his life. The arts and sciences, he maintained, are all born of human vices: astronomy of superstition, oratory of ambition and flattery, geometry of avarice, physics of idle curiosity, moral philosophy of pride. Thus civilization is bound to be reeking of many evils. And there is no cure except through a return to the innocence and simplicity which prevailed in the earliest times. Until men were led astray by the wiles of reason, their native feelings prompted them to love one another and the gods, to live together peacefully in rustic haunts, and to enjoy the beauties of nature.

Having won fame through his prize essay, Rousseau hesitated openly to discard, or even to revise, his hyperboles concerning society. But in his next essay *Discours sur l'origine et les fondements de l'inégalité parmi les hommes* (also written for a Dijon competition but not successful in winning a prize) he introduced significant qualifications into his thesis. History, he now explained, is the passage, not from idyllic innocence to corrupt civilization, but from untutored barbarism to sophisticated evil. The state of nature, then, is not a concept which describes an historical epoch. It is, rather, a picture of a good society. Human nature is originally neither good nor bad; it is the raw material out of which circumstances chance to produce a few good men and many evil men. Civilization has even brought some benefits; but it has also stirred men to strive for power and so has introduced existing unjust inequalities.

In the early essays Rousseau suggested no cure for the evils he deplored. A program of improvement he laid down in his longer work *Le contrat social*. He began this book with the cry: "Man is born free, but everywhere he is in chains." History, he now added, is the passage from social atomism to social involvement. And the problem we face is how to secure, not a return to barbarism, but a regulation of government in the interest of the people. Physical force ought to give place to moral conduct. This great end is contingent upon recognition of the sovereignty of the people. We all, in entering society, voluntarily put ourselves under the direction, not of arbitrary authority, but of the general will. Apart from society men can act only from the slavery of impulse; but in society they aspire to come under the liberty of law. In society, when it is a just society, a man acquires new interests (often unsuspected in advance), personal development, a realization of his true self, and a sense of corporate membership in a larger whole. (Rousseau was announcing here the ideal of "fraternity" which became one of the three slogans of the French Revolution, though a slogan not often understood.)

The concept of the general will has been a troublesome one and, indeed, is not always clear in Rousseau himself. It is not the same as the will of the majority expressed in popular vote, though the two may at times coincide. What makes a majority decision into an expression of the general will is not the number of voters constituting the majority but the recognition by those voters of a common interest for the entire social group. The general will stands to a passionate majority decision as does moral conduct to rash impulse in the individual. A majority decision may oscillate between two policies, as contending passions wax and wane; but the general will is constant, unalterable, and pure. Rousseau nonetheless preferred to have a government by popular referendum than a government in the control of king or hereditary aristocracy.

Rousseau, unlike Hobbes, distinguished sovereignty from unfettered power. A government acts against sovereignty whenever it acts against the general will. Indeed, a government never comes to possess sovereignty until it is in the hands of the people and the people are animated by concern for the common good.

Rousseau held views on religion akin to those of Voltaire and other French deists. He was not troubled, as was Voltaire, by the earthquake at Lisbon in 1755. He saw no need of trying to reconcile that natural catastrophe with God's providence. He rather blamed the catastrophe directly on the folly of the men who herded themselves into tall houses in congested quarters instead of scattering themselves across the countryside. But Rousseau did believe the power of God limited, so as to acquit God of responsibility for much that went on in nature. Where he differed from the deists generally was in his desire to trust feeling, rather than reason, in religious faith. In his *Profession de foi du vicaire Savoyard* he supposedly expressed his own attitude. The vicar does, as a matter of fact, find occasion to echo various scraps of argument which Descartes and Newton and Locke had used for the existence of God. But he does not rely on these scraps; he only uses them in defending to others the position he has himself taken on the promptings of his heart. Rousseau felt forlorn in a world which made no kindred response to him. He did not want to feel alone when he looked out on the beauties of the romantic landscape. In both religion and morals he recoiled from those who tried to deduce conclusions from what he called "the principles of a high philosophy." He had much more trust in his own sentiments and tastes than in abstract reasoning.

Rousseau, more than any one else in history, represents romanticism in philosophy. He did not long idealize primitive life, though he often drifted into paragraphs which read like such idealizations. But he did appeal to feelings against rational judgments. And because he distrusted reason, he never was able even to suggest a criterion by which trustworthy feelings could be distinguished from vain, illusory, or malicious feelings.[2]

[2] If one wants an illustration from American literature of the kind of person Rousseau's philosophy would sanction, he may find it in Mark Twain's Huckleberry Finn rather than in James Fenimore Cooper's noble redskin.

XIII

German Philosophy in Kant and His Successors

1. KANT

IMMANUEL KANT, 1724–1804, was born in Königsberg, East Prussia, in or near which he lived quietly all his life. His parents were poor and pious and reared him in the tradition of Pietism, an undogmatic form of Christianity which emphasized inner purity and moral earnestness. He attended the University of Königsberg. After a few years of tutoring in a private family, he began teaching in the university and, in 1770, became professor of logic and metaphysics. He studied physics as well as philosophy, and his early writings were *Theory of the Heavens* (1755) and *Theory of Winds* (1756). For twenty-five years after these two works appeared he published only occasional papers. He was thoughtfully formulating his own original philosophy. Then in one decade he published five great works: *Critique of Pure Reason* (1781, 1787), *Prolegomena to Every Future Metaphysic* (1783), *Fundamental Principles of the Metaphysic of Ethics* (1785), *Critique of Practical Reason* (1788), and *Critique of Judgment* (1790). In 1794 appeared his *Religion Within the Bounds of Reason Alone*. His powers gradually failed, and his closing years were saddened by loss of eyesight and of memory. A brilliant, if poetically whimsical, characterization of him was written by Heinrich Heine (quoted in translation in Royce's *Spirit of Modern Philosophy*).

KANT WAS IMPRESSED with the fact (or what he took to be a fact) that we actually do have in our sciences much knowledge which we cannot possibly account for on the basis of the theories about knowledge advanced by philosophers of the seventeenth and eighteenth centuries. A sound theory of knowledge, he insisted, ought to recognize the nature of the knowledge we gain in the sciences. Philosophers ought not to set that knowledge aside and try to spin something better out of their personal speculations (as he deemed Descartes and the Cartesians generally to have done). Nor ought they to turn from an examination into the *nature* of our knowledge to a psychological hypothesis concerning the *origin* of knowledge, particularly if that hypothesis would then make it logically impossible for us to reach the knowledge we really do possess (as he deemed Locke and empiricists generally to have done). We may not know when or where or how knowledge began. But we *can* show what the nature is of the knowledge the sciences give us. Kant therefore resolved to begin with the existing body of human knowledge and to formulate a theory of knowledge which will disclose what kinds of knowledge we actually do possess. Thereby we shall obtain a sound epistemology and may also throw light upon the possibility of metaphysics.

When we examine the knowledge we possess, we discover, Kant maintained, that it contains judgments of various kinds. Some of our judgments are analytical, and some are synthetic. And among our synthetic judgments, some are *a posteriori*, and others are *a priori*.

Analytical judgments are those in which the predicate term either repeats the subject term or divides the subject term into elements, in order to make clear some one of the various elements which was already obscurely intended by it. "Body is extended," for example, is an analytical judgment. Even if one is not fully aware of the import of the term *body*, he can reach the judgment by analyzing the term logically and without going beyond the one concept *body*. Similarly, the judgment "Every effect has a cause" is analytical, because having a *cause* is exactly what the term *effect* means. Analytical judgments do not extend our knowledge. But they do render our concepts more intelligible to us, and they put our concepts into a better order than they perhaps otherwise would have.

Synthetic judgments are those in which the predicate term adds something that was not either explicitly or implicitly contained in the subject term. "Body has weight" is a synthetic judgment; for only by looking back to our experiences of body can we connect gravity with what the term *body* itself means. Synthetic judgments, when true, amplify our knowledge. The enlargement of scientific knowledge is due to our becoming able to make synthetic judgments.

Most of our synthetic judgments are based upon experience. That water is heavier than oil, that a certain flower is blue, that a certain farmer owns a field of oats, and, indeed, most judgments about the physical and social worlds—these are all learned by observing the facts and submitting to the instruction which experience, and only experience, can give. But some synthetic judgments—and these are very important because they are fundamental in all the sciences—are *a priori*. They report not merely that an *A* is *B* but that *A* must be *B*. They are necessary. Such, for example, are the judgments that every event has a cause, that the amount of matter in the physical world is constant, that in all motions in the physical world action and reaction are equal, that a straight line is the shortest distance between two points, and many other mathematical judgments.[1] There may be empirical elements in some of these propositions, for it is through experience that we know there are events and matter and motion. But no experience and no accumulation of experiences could enable us to know that these synthetic judgments are and must be true. The judgments are apodictic; that is, they inform us concerning what necessarily *must* be. And they are known to hold good, not merely of such particular instances of cause and matter and motion as we have already examined but of all other instances which ever will or conceivably could be experienced.

Kant, having reviewed much modern philosophy before his time, realized that no one had yet seen the significance of *a priori* synthetic judgments for a theory of knowledge. He therefore took as the first of his basic problems the question, "How are synthetic judgments *a priori* possible?" Cartesians, he thought, never noticed the difference between two kinds of necessity—the logical necessity of analytical judgments and the necessity of *a priori* synthetic judgments. Empiricists were prone to deny the fact of *a priori* synthetic knowledge altogether. Neither of the two earlier schools of thought therefore was able to develop an adequate theory of knowledge. Against both rationalism and empiricism he proffered his new theory of knowledge, giving to it the name *critical*. Criticism, in Kant's sense of the term, is more than intellectual alertness and subtlety; it is a theory of knowledge which lays bare the conditions which enable us to have synthetic knowledge *a priori*.

KANT'S VIEW OF EXPERIENCE

Illustrations of synthetic judgments *a priori*, as Kant maintained them, will be given later. But before becoming involved in detailed discussion of these illustrations, we need to review abstractly Kant's

---

[1] Kant held that all mathematical judgments, or almost all, are synthetical, even, for example, that $7 + 5 = 12$. In order to appreciate Kant's position, the student must put himself into the intellectual atmosphere of the eighteenth century and must not raise objections founded on subsequent developments of mathematical thought of which Kant could not have been aware. That is, the student must here think of mathematical judgments as synthetic.

conception of the nature of human experience. For his acceptance of the belief that we do make some synthetic judgments *a priori* led him to formulate, over against the British empiricists, an entirely new conception of what experience is. He granted that all our knowledge begins *with* experience, but he denied that it all arises *from* experience. We can say that all knowledge begins *with* experience, because we do not have *a priori* knowledge first and then come to have experience of particular matters of fact later on. All knowledge is gained during experience. We have much experience before we come to realize, if indeed we ever realize at all, that some of the knowledge we have is *a priori*. The *a priori* is not chronologically first. It is, nonetheless, what the mere occurrence of experience to us could not give us.

Kant was thus led to a different conception of experience than any of his predecessors had held. Experience, as he viewed it, differed in two important respects from the description of it in the British empiricists. In the first place, experience is not initially of simple elements which the mind then has to arrange in some manner. It is rather, in its first occurrence, a highly complex network of things and events from among which we may select any number of special things for attention. In the second place, experience is not a material given to a passive mind. Rather, it is a world in the first appearance of which the perceiving and knowing mind is actively at work. Things cannot come into experience at all except insofar as they conform to requirements which the mind imposes upon them. Both in perceiving through the senses and in knowing through concepts, mind imparts to experience certain necessary conditions which mind then finds as the universal structural framework which prevails throughout experience. Experience is the joint product of material elements which come to the mind and formal elements which mind contributes. Insofar as the material elements in experience are concerned, we have to wait for the occurrence of experience in order to gain knowledge; that is, our judgments are bound to be empirical. But insofar as the formal elements in experience are concerned, we are dealing with universal conditions for the occurrence of any and every experience; that is, our judgments, even when synthetic, are apodictic and *a priori*. Mind is not dully reproductive of a world which is completely itself apart from mind. Rather, mind is in part constitutive of the world it perceives and knows. The world we perceive and know will always conform to the *a priori* demands of mind, because nothing could appear within experience which did not so conform.

Kant used the term *transcendental* for the *a priori* conditions mind imposes on things for their occurrence within experience. The transcendental has nothing to do with what, if anything, lies beyond experience.[2] Many people may never notice that there are transcendental elements in experience. Indeed, not even the sophisticated rationalists and empiricists before Kant had noticed their presence. But these elements are nonetheless present. And it is their presence which enables us to have necessary knowledge and to make the synthetic judgments *a priori* which are indispensable tools of scientific procedure.

THE COPERNICAN REVOLUTION IN PHILOSOPHY

Kant called his critical theory of knowledge the Copernican revolution in philosophy. His figurative language was apt. Copernicus, he pointed out, radically changed the astronomical views of men. Before him, most men had supposed that the sun moved around the earth; and he reversed the matter and regarded the earth as moving around the sun. Kant claimed that he was effecting a similar revolution in philosophy. Before him, from Aristotle to his own day, men had regarded mind as moving around objects in order thereby to come to know them. And he made objects move, as it were, around the central fact of mind and made them conform to conditions which mind lays down for the entrance of the objects into experience. Mind is the one factor, the only factor, which is always present in experience. And it is legislative for all objects which appear to the senses and are known in judgments. If our judgments had to conform to the nature objects have in themselves, we should always have to wait for objects to inform us about their nature, and we then could not ever have any *a priori* knowledge about space and time and matter and motion. But we do actually have a considerable amount of *a priori* knowledge. Therefore, to the extent to which *a priori* knowledge is possible, objects must conform to the transcendental requirements of mind. They must conform to these transcendental requirements, both in the process of their being perceived in the senses and then in their being known through judgments. Kant was led by this theory of transcendental conditions for the occurrence of objects to say that experience is not so much material for knowledge as itself a mode of knowledge. In all experience mind has already been at work, making objects

---

[2] What lies beyond experience he called transcendent. Unfortunately the two terms *transcendental* and *transcendent* confuse the unwary reader. But the meanings of the two terms are entirely distinct.

conform to its demands for intelligibility throughout experience.

It is not always easy for us to distinguish what in experience is due to the nature of the object and what is due to the conditions imposed by mind. But to aid us in making the distinction, we have two criteria: necessity and universality. And these two criteria are interdependent. Whatever satisfies one also satisfies the other. Objects could not be such as of themselves to give either necessity or universality to our knowledge of them. Not all objects are in any one person's experience; nor is any one object always present. But mind is always present in all experience. Mind, therefore, must be regarded as the source of those aspects of experience which are necessary and universal.

Whatever in experience is necessary is also universal. Whatever in experience is universal is necessary. All else is contingent, empirical, and adventitious. The universal and necessary elements of experience are therefore due to the conditions mind imposes upon objects. The adventitious elements of experience are due to the nature objects themselves have. Thus we can, through sufficient attention to the analysis of experience, determine what elements in experience are transcendental and what elements are empirical.

STRUCTURE OF THE "CRITIQUE OF PURE REASON"

All that has been said to this point about Kant's philosophy is an exposition of the contents of the prefaces and introductions Kant wrote to the two editions of his *Critique of Pure Reason*. The remainder of his long book is a detailed implementation of his point of view and a discussion of the consequences of the Copernican revolution in philosophy.

Kant divided his book into three main parts.[3] For Kant regarded our human faculties, in their cognitive relations to the world, to be three. These three are sensibility (*Sinnlichkeit*), understanding (*Verstand*), and reason (*Vernunft*). Kant took up each of these faculties in turn. In the *Transcendental Aesthetic* he discussed the forms of sensibility which mind imposes upon and consequently finds disclosed in all sensory or perceptual experience. In the *Transcendental Analytic* he discussed the categories of understanding which mind requires all experience to satisfy. And in the *Transcendental Dialectic* he discussed the ideas of reason, in the use of which the mind is

---

[3] Some critics prefer to say that it consists of two main parts: the *Transcendental Aesthetic* and the *Transcendental Logic*. These critics are quite faithful to the text of Kant. Yet the *Transcendental Logic* is, in turn, divided into the *Transcendental Analytic* and the *Transcendental Dialectic*. And in expounding the *Critique* it is easier to regard the book as divided into three parts as stated above.

tempted to pass beyond experience and to know "things-in-them-selves." "Things-in-themselves" are not subject, however, to tran-scendental conditions for their occurrence.[4] The first two of the parts of the *Critique* deal with aspects of scientific knowledge. The third part is the negative or destructive part of Kant's *Critique*. It is destruc-tive, because the ideas of reason, in Kant's judgment, however fruitful they may be in disciplining human thinking, never eventuate in pro-ducing knowledge.

Each of the three main parts of the *Critique* requires attention in turn.

FORMS OF SENSIBILITY: SPACE AND TIME

In the *Transcendental Aesthetic* Kant dealt with the forms of sensibility. These are two in number: space and time. Kant did not mean to imply that our perceptual life is something apart from, and complete without, our conceptual life and our reflections. Indeed, he took care to explain that the isolation of sensibility is an abstraction made for the purpose of promoting clarity of exposition. If, however, we artificially separate from our consciousness of a body all that the understanding thinks about it and all that is given to mind by the object, we are left with the pure forms of sensibility. These two forms, space and time, Kant wished to prove, are imposed upon experience by the perceiving mind. For this contention he offered four arguments. The arguments in regard to space and those in regard to time are identical. Those in regard to space will be summarized here.

(1) Space is not an empirical conception which has been derived from our sensations of color, hardness, and so on. For we should never refer these sensations to something outside of us unless prior to, and independently of, these sensations we had a consciousness of space. (2) We can think away any object we wish to disregard. We can think away all objects. We can regard space as empty. But we cannot think space away. Space, therefore, is an *a priori* form of perceptual experi-ence. (3) Space is one. We perceive different parts of space. We could never get the one inclusive space additively from the perceived parts. Therefore, the one all-embracing space is prior to the perceived parts. (4) Space is presented in our consciousness as an infinite whole, within which are contained in their proper relations all the perceived parts.

---

4 Kant had one of the most formidable and technical vocabularies in the history of philosophy. Forms of sensibility, categories of understanding, ideas of reason, "things-in-themselves," and other terms which he coined for his own purposes are indispensable for an exposition of his thought. They must be learned by the student who wishes to grasp the essentials of Kant's philosophy.

Experience, however, cannot give to mind anything infinite. Mind must therefore give the form of infinite space to experience.

These arguments for space and the similar ones for time Kant regarded as satisfactory proof that space and time are necessary forms contributed by mind to the occurrence of experience. We cannot properly affirm that things-in-themselves are in space and time. But within experience space and time are universally present. Kant expressed his point by saying that space and time are empirically real and transcendentally ideal. They are empirically real because they are really found to occur everywhere in experience. They are transcendentally ideal because, from the point of view of their origin, they are mind-derived. Their ideality is the fact of their being contributed to experience by mind. And this ideality is transcendental because the contribution of mind to experience is not an outcome which each particular mind deliberately chooses in the course of its experience, but a condition which all minds, by virtue of being minds, necessarily impose upon every phase of their perceptual lives. Space, Kant added, is a form for all external experience; and time is a form for all experience external and internal, that is, for all experience of things and for the inner course of our own feelings and reflections.

Kant concluded his *Transcendental Aesthetic* by pointing out the consequences of his position for the work of the sciences. The chief consequence is that geometry (which is an elaboration of the form of pure spatial perception) can be known to hold good of the entire world with which physics and the other natural sciences are concerned. Mathematical calculations, therefore, can be trusted, in advance of experience, as giving a true measurement of the structure of the experienced world. We do not need to appeal, like Descartes, to a theological legerdemain to support mathematical interpretations of the world; nor need we ever despair, as did Locke, of our ability to know the framework of things. Scientists had long been using mathematics as a tool, as notably Galileo and Newton. Kant supposed that he had now for the first time found a theory of knowledge which would underwrite natural science with a reasoned rationale.

DEDUCTION OF THE CATEGORIES

In the *Transcendental Analytic* Kant sought to defend the necessity of the basic concepts by means of which we think about the spatial-temporal world we perceive. These basic concepts he called categories of understanding. They are categories because they are logically prior to all the concepts we empirically reach through generalization from experience. They belong to understanding, because understanding is Kant's term for mind insofar as mind reaches knowledge of the world we experience.

There are in all, Kant supposed, twelve categories, and he derived his list of them from an examination of the types of judgment he thought he could distinguish. The part of the *Analytic* in which Kant developed his list is wooden and unprofitable for most students. But three of the categories are of great importance for Kant's philosophy, however they were reached. These three are the categories of substance, causality, and reciprocity.

The transcendental ideality of the categories is connected by Kant with the transcendental ideality of space and time. We human beings, he held, do not first have perceptual material devoid of meaning and then, by reflection upon this material, add meanings to it. Our perceptual and conceptual lives are intertwined; they are aspects of one integrated life. As a famous phrase of his goes, "percepts without concepts would be blind, and concepts without percepts would be empty." Our perceptual experience, as it first goes on, is already saturated with meanings; and our conceptual interpretations, if divorced from what we see and touch and hear, would be vain imaginings of nothing. The views which Kant developed of space and time in the *Aesthetic* required him to go on to lay bare the *a priori* conceptions which mind requires experience to satisfy and which mind, therefore, will always find experience to exemplify.

The category of substance is closely connected by Kant with the form of space. It is the principle that through all changes in nature runs a permanent element which neither increases nor decreases in quantity. Change would not be change without permanence; it would be the ending of one thing and the beginning of another rather than genuine change. If what we experience is in space, it can only be thought of in terms of the presence to mind of substance.

The category of causality is similarly connected by Kant with the form of time. If the order of events in time is to be intelligible, the order must be, not casual, but necessary, like the succession of moments. And the principle of causality is a recognition of the necessity through which successive moments of time are bound together.

The category of reciprocity is connected by Kant with the centrality of mind in the constitution of experience. Space and time, though two forms, and all the categories, though many, are transcendentally derived from one and the same source. Whatever then is empirically present in the spatial-temporal network of significant things and events is necessarily an interinvolved whole. And so mind can surely pass by some device (which device will depend upon the empirical character of particular experiences) from any one part of experience to any and all other parts. However rich and complex experience may become, it must necessarily be penetrated throughout with meaningful interrelationships. The unity of mind guarantees the wholeness of experience. The category of reciprocity is fundamental to all that we perceive and know. Experience is bound, in Kant's technical language, to exhibit the transcendental unity of self-consciousness or the transcendental unity of apperception.

Kant used the phrase "deduction of the categories" for his proof that experience will always satisfy the categorical demands of mind. He gave, not just one, but many statements of this deduction.[5] Some statements of the deduction he called empirical, because they rest upon observation of the presence of the categories in all we experience. Other statements he called transcendental, because they rest upon the unity of mind and, hence, of the demands which mind imposes upon whatever comes before it. One of the clearest and yet briefest statements may be summarized as follows.[6]

Space and time are *a priori* forms of all perception, inner as well as outer. These forms and all the sensuous material experienced in them, however, are determined to an *a priori* unity. For without this *a priori* unity, nothing could be present to mind and so no experience could occur. This unity is what specifies that experience shall exhibit all the conditions of intelligibility. In other words, this unity requires that whatever appears to mind shall conform to the categories of understanding. Hence the categories may be said to be conditions of the possibility of experience, and therefore the categories hold good *a priori* of all objects of experience.

THINGS-IN-THEMSELVES

The world we experience, Kant said, is the world which the sciences observe, analyze, and describe. Kant was as firm on this point as Berkeley was and as Hume finally became. He therefore belongs to the eighteenth-century reaction against the seventeenth-century theory of the subjectivity of sense experience. And yet, over against experience, he put things-in-themselves.

---

[5] Kant probably wrote out these successive statements at different times and then copied them, one after another, into the manuscript of his book. When he had them printed, he gave almost no indication of where one deduction ends and another begins. The text of his book, particularly of the first edition, is therefore bewildering to a reader who does not realize that Kant is repeating himself over and over again, in the hope of making his difficult point clear.

[6] The words here used are a paraphrase of the text of the second edition of the *Critique*, pp. 160–161.

Kant never defined clearly his conception of the relation of experience to what he called "things-in-themselves." He seems never to have reached a clear conception on this point. He spoke of what we experience as phenomena or appearances. Only of phenomena, he insisted, can we have *a priori* synthetic knowledge, because of nothing except phenomena is the activity of the mind constitutive. Things-in-themselves, he concluded, we do not know through the sciences; nor can we have any experience of them. In one place he said that although space and time are the only forms of sensibility, we must grant that sensibility may not be the only kind of awareness which mind (other than ours) might have of things. Much of his language therefore suggests a return to a Lockian dualism between external objects that are not experienced and appearances that are experienced. And some of the speculations of his *Metaphysic of Ethics* and *Critique of Practical Reason* seem to proceed in terms of this kind of dualism.

But Kant did not want to sponsor Lockian dualism. He had another term for things-in-themselves which he used increasingly in the second edition of his *Critique*. This is the term *noumena*. Etymologically, this term ought to mean objects-as-viewed-by-reason. But reason, he firmly contended, never reaches knowledge of any objects except experienced objects. And certainly the burden of his argument in the *Critique* is that phenomena are the way in which things are necessarily viewed by mind. When he used the term *mind,* he was not contrasting merely human mentality with some other-than-human and superior kind of mentality. He used the term *mind* for the unity of all perceiving and knowing consciousness in which men indeed share but which men do not necessarily pre-empt among themselves alone. Noumena, in contrast with phenomena, would then be things-in-themselves considered in some other way than as mind can conceive them. But this curious position Kant did not explicitly state or defend.

There remained, therefore, as one outcome of Kant's *Critique,* a difficult problem to which Kant gave no clear answer. And it was this problem which some of his successors sought, in one way or another, to resolve. But in resolving this problem and advancing their own views about it, they usually came to conclusions which Kant had already taken occasion to anticipate and repudiate.

THE KANTIAN DIALECTIC

The last long section of Kant's *Critique* is the *Transcendental Dialectic*. A dialectic is as much an activity of reason as is an analytic. But a dialectic, in Kant's sense of the term, is an activity of reason

in which reason refuses to work within the limits of understanding.[7]
And a transcendental dialectic is one in which this refusal is due to
efforts to use the forms of sensibility and the categories of understanding to determine the nature of objects of which mind is in no
way constitutive. Dialectic, Kant pointed out, may have disciplinary
value for the mind, but it never issues, he insisted, in knowledge
or valid doctrines about the objects it considers.

The usual ideas of dialectical thought are the absolute self, the
totality of the world, and the supreme being. Consideration of these
ideas has given rise respectively to rational psychology, rational cosmology, and rational theology. None of the objects of these dialectical
ideas is empirically evident, and none of them is subject to the constitutive work of mind. All branches of dialectical thought therefore
end in a kind of intellectual frustration.

Rational psychology seeks to explain the nature of the soul. It
normally affirms that the soul is a substance, that it is simple, that
it is one, and that it is distinct from its bodily vehicle. These affirmations, however, are paralogisms. A paralogism is an inference invalid
in form, apart from any consideration of its content. The transcendent reference of the affirmations is what makes the affirmations
paralogisms.

Rational cosmology seeks to explain the totality of the world. It
always leads to pairs of contradictory propositions, thesis and antithesis, between which no rational choice can be made. The only proof
for the thesis is the reduction of the antithesis to absurdity, and vice
versa. Each pair of these contradictory propositions is an antinomy.
One antinomy has for thesis the proposition that the world had a beginning in time and is enclosed with spatial limits, and for antithesis,
that the world had no beginning in time and has no spatial limits.
The other antinomies are the thesis of atomism and the antithesis
of infinite divisibility, the thesis of complete determinism and the
antithesis of free causality, the thesis of the existence of an absolutely
necessary being and the antithesis of the denial of such a being. Instead of trying to solve these speculative issues, Kant deemed them
unsolvable. But he did not regard them as having no instruction for
men who grasp the reason why they are unsolvable. The first antinomy, for example, brings to our attention once more that time and
space are universally present in experience and bids us recognize that
with experience our knowledge ends. Similarly with the other antinomies.

[7] The student ought to distinguish carefully Kant's meaning for the term *dialectic*
from Plato's. See above, p. 48.

Rational theology seeks to prove the existence of a supreme being or God. Kant, having reviewed the history of rational theology, listed three major types of proffered proof for God: the ontological, the cosmological, and the teleological arguments (the last of which he called the physico-theological). On the latter two his comments are much like those of Hume's *Dialogues,* though he added the further comment that these arguments, at a certain stage in their development, fall back on the ontological argument to prove that the first cause or the controlling purpose is really perfect and supreme. His analysis of the ontological argument is more original. He pointed out that this argument contains a confusion between a necessary judgment and a necessary being. Men who entertain the idea of a supreme and perfect being must necessarily think of that being as existing; for otherwise they would be toying with fancy instead of considering being. But a necessary judgment, even about a supreme being or an *ens realissimum,* does not entail the necessary existence of that about which one is judging. Existence, indeed, is not really a predicate at all. It is not part of the nature of a thing. A hundred imaginary dollars contain as many cents as a hundred real dollars. The idea of a perfect being implies certain specific meanings which may be analytically deduced therefrom. But since existence is not an attribute, it cannot be deduced from any idea whatsoever. No idea implies the necessary or even the actual existence of the object the idea is about.

Kant's criticism of rational theology has been the most influential part of his *Dialectic.* Its great influence, however, was due to its connections with doctrines presented in his later works.

THE CATEGORICAL IMPERATIVE

The outcome of the *Critique of Pure Reason* was favorable to scientific interests; it certified the right, as it were, of scientists to continue the type of investigations which had been fruitful in such leading thinkers as Galileo and Newton. But it seemed, at least at first glance, quite unfavorable to moral and religious interests. It maintained that so far as experience goes, men are caught in a causal nexus which excludes free choice and therefore moral responsibility, and that knowledge of God is quite impossible. But Kant did not mean his *Critique* to be an attack upon morality and religion. Though he meant it to be a rejection of traditional presuppositions on which many people tried to base their moral and religious ideas, he wished to go on to establish new grounds for morality and religion which would be superior to the old presuppositions. And he made his position clearer in the second edition of his *Critique of Pure Reason* by openly proclaiming that he had denied knowledge of God, freedom, and immortality in order to make room for faith.[8]

Before fully setting forth the faith he believed justifiable, he raised a basic question in his *Fundamental Principles of the Metaphysic of Ethics*. What conditions, he inquired, are requisite to make conduct genuinely moral? Until we know the answer to this question we cannot profitably discuss whether or not men are capable of that kind of conduct.

Moral conduct, Kant insisted, is action performed out of respect for duty, and duty is obligation to act from reverence for moral law. The only thing which is good without qualification is a good will. The things men ordinarily praise as good are not good without qualification. Intelligence is good, and such personal qualities as courage are good, and wealth and health are good. But these many things are morally good only if the will which directs men in handling them is good. Otherwise, these many things, any or all of them, might be pernicious. A good will is the indispensable prerequisite of the moral worth of all else. And the good will is a will which is directed, not to the achievement of intelligence or courage or wealth, but to the use of intelligence and courage and wealth in accord with duty, that is, in accord with sheer reverence for moral law.

A will to act from duty, Kant pointed out, is a will which follows the dictates, not of desire or inclination, but of pure reason. When a mother cares for her child for no reason except that she loves the child, she is not exhibiting ethical conduct. Her act may be exactly the act to which respect for duty would lead. But unless her act is motivated by recognition of duty, her will is not yet an ethical will and her conduct lacks moral worth. No act gains moral value from the objective it pursues, much less from its practical success in reaching its objective. Two acts, one of which gains its objective and the other of which utterly fails to do so, are of the same moral worth if they stem from the same motive. Both of them are moral conduct if they stem from respect for duty; and both are without moral significance if they stem from desire or inclination or yearning for happiness.

The moral law, respect for which makes action morally worthy, must therefore be both rational and purely formal. This rational and formal law can be no other than the principle that a man must act in such a way that he can at the same time will the maxim of his action to be a universal law for all men.

<hr>

[8] Preface to the second edition, p. xxx.

Kant's austere position is easier to understand when taken in connection with one of his illustrations. Lying, he points out, is wrong. For lying is intent to deceive. And if all men were animated by an intent to deceive, speech would cease to be a channel of communication among men, and, hence, lying would become impossible. The maxim that one may lie, therefore, cannot be made a universal law for all men and so is an evil maxim.

Kant gave the name categorical imperative to his formal moral law. There may be many hypothetical imperatives. If one wants health, he must take such-and-such measures; if one wants friends, he must act in such-and-such a manner; and so forth. But there is only one categorical imperative.

The one categorical imperative, Kant proceeded to say, can be expressed in either of two forms. The initial form is that already given: always so act that you can consider the maxim of your action a universal law for all men. The other form of the imperative results from recognition of the fact that all rational agents are capable of discerning and obeying the categorical imperative. And every agent who obeys the categorical imperative has intrinsic worth. Every such agent is an end in himself. Things are never ultimate ends; things are only relatively valuable and may be used as means. A rational agent, however, is not a thing but a person. And because of his possible intrinsic value, no person may be used merely as a means. We thus reach the conception of a society of persons of good will. Such a society would constitute a kingdom of ends. Morality can be said to consist in action which promotes the coming into being of a kingdom of ends. The categorical imperative, therefore, may be restated in the form: always so act as to use all persons, never merely as means but also as ends.

Thus it was that Kant gave his answer to the basic question concerning the conditions requisite to make conduct genuinely moral. His answer to this question leaves unsettled the further question whether men, involved as they are in the thoroughgoing determinism of the world of experience, are or are not capable of moral conduct. For no one can act in accordance with the moral imperative unless he is free to follow the dictates of reason. Only free men can be men of good will. If men are determined by causal forces which play upon them from without, or if they are determined by their natural affections, desires, and inclinations, then, indeed, they cannot obey the demands of the categorical imperative. Rationality is a condition of the possibility of moral conduct; but freedom is a condition of the actuality of moral conduct. Either then men are free or there is no such thing as morality among men. And freedom is an illusion from the point of view to which we are limited in our knowledge of the world of experience. Kant was thus led to consider whether he had any grounds for a faith which transcends the limits of knowledge.

POSTULATES OF FAITH

Kant's *Critique of Practical Reason* is a consideration of principles which may properly guide men in practice, even if these principles have no pertinence to the world men perceive and know. There is no possibility of knowledge that any such principles are true, for knowledge is limited to what goes on in the phenomenal world. But neither is there any possibility of knowledge that all such principles are false, for knowledge does not extend to the noumenal world. And Kant, with his Pietistic background and intense moral earnestness, came to regard it as legitimate to entertain, on the basis of faith, whatever principles are indispensable to sustain men's deep-seated and ineradicable sense of the finality of moral values. These principles can never become articles of knowledge. They are, nonetheless, postulates of the moral life. And since morality is obedience to a rational law, they may be called postulates of practical reason.

The supreme principle of morality, Kant held, is the principle of the autonomy of the will, that is, the ability of the will to set aside all the pressures of the world we experience and to follow a rational law it imposes freely on itself.[9] This principle can be sustained by only one assumption, namely, that things-in-themselves are not related to phenomena in the same way in which phenomena are related to one another. That is, we may assume that the noumenal self is not constituted as is the phenomenal self of the world of experience. This assumption has no cognitive warrant, but neither can anything we know discredit it. It is an article of faith which we must make unless we abandon altogether the supposition that men are moral beings. Thus, the supreme principle of morality leads to the first postulate of practical reason, the postulate that men, considered as noumenal beings, are free.

One can hardly venture upon this faith, Kant held, without then following through to its final implications. The condition of the highest good is the entire harmony of a man's will with the moral law. But such entire harmony is not possible for any one living in

[9] Kant referred to autonomy of will in his *Metaphysic of Ethics* but developed the idea more fully in his *Critique of Practical Reason.*

the world of sense. Such harmony is holiness and requires an infinite progress toward perfection. We must therefore, unless we violate our yearning for the fulfillment of the demands of the moral law, postulate immortality of the soul. We must have faith that somehow and by some means moral agents like men may achieve the goal of their moral development.

Even holiness is not enough to satisfy the moral sense of mankind. Holiness would indeed be the supreme good but not the complete good. Men have an ineradicable sense that virtue ought to be followed by proportionate happiness. Men dare not aim at happiness, for to do that would be to violate the principle of reverence for duty as the one intrinsic good. Nonetheless, the virtuous man ought to receive happiness in order that the supreme good may reach fulfillment in the complete good. And so we are led to postulate the existence of God as the power requisite to bring about, eventually and in accord with his design, the union of virtue and happiness.

Thus, for Kant, the principle of autonomy of the will is found to require for its full justification the three postulates of freedom, immortality, and God. These postulates are not theoretical doctrines; they are, rather, practical commitments which give meaning and dignity to the aspirations of morality. They are not knowledge; they are, rather, faith. But they are a faith which has its roots in reason's discovery of the authority of the categorical imperative.

KANT'S INFLUENCE

Kant's position has seldom been accepted in its entirety. But his influence penetrated, in one respect or another, the philosophies of those who came after him. During the last generation his influence has waned considerably, largely because what he called the Copernican revolution in philosophy has come to seem to many thinkers an unsound theory of the relation of mind to nature.

Seldom did his admirers, even when calling themselves Kantians (as Germans are often prone to do), follow his scheme of thought in any integral manner. Rather, they have selected some one element they liked out of the complex of his thought and have neglected or even denied some other elements. Many of them have made mind so central in the determination of not only experience but also being that they have built up systems of metaphysical idealism quite contrary to Kant's own intent. Some of them have developed what Kant meant by mind into a theory of absolute mind in whose engulfing comprehensiveness have been lost all traces of that respect which

Kant had for the autonomy of the individual. One of Kant's British admirers even sought to interpret Kant himself as at heart an idealist.[10]

Kant's influence upon theology has been as profound as his influence on philosophy—and more lasting. Catholic theologians, remembering St. Thomas, have restated with care the natural theology Kant rejected. Protestant theologians, however, remembering Luther's doctrine of justification by faith, have been prone to seize upon Kant's position as a new way of defending their faith. Some of them were led by their reading of Kant to suppose that science and religion were two utterly disparate concerns and that no matter what the findings of scientists were the theologian was entitled to his articles of faith. The faith they cherished seemed to them to come from a transcendent source and to need no natural sanction.

2. FICHTE

JOHANN GOTTLIEB FICHTE, 1762–1814, was born in Saxony. He was a precocious child, and a prosperous neighbor enabled him to receive education. He studied theology and philosophy. He supported himself for some years by tutoring in private families. In 1792 he published *Critique of All Revelation*. By mistake of the printers his name was omitted from the title page, and reviewers hailed the work as Kant's. Kant promptly explained that the work was by Fichte and praised it. Fichte thus became famous instantly throughout the Germanies. In 1794 he was appointed professor of philosophy at the University of Jena; but a charge of atheism later aroused the Saxon government to demand his expulsion. He wrote various philosophical works, of which *The Vocation of Man* in 1800 is the best known. In 1807 he was aroused by the Napoleonic invasions to publish *Addresses to the German Nation,* and he at once became a center about whom patriotic enthusiasts rallied. He helped to found the University of Berlin and acted as its rector from 1810 to 1812. He resigned his academic post in order to lecture all over the Germanies on behalf of the forces which sought to expel Napoleon and the French from the Germanies. In 1814 his wife contracted fever while caring for wounded German soldiers

10 See Edward Caird, *The Critical Philosophy of Immanuel Kant* (Glasgow, Maclehose, 1889).

in the Berlin hospitals, and in caring for her, Fichte caught the fever and died.

FICHTE WAS IN HIS early life a reluctant believer in a deterministic philosophy. Then in 1790 he read Kant's works, and he enthusiastically adopted the doctrine of faith (in Kant's *Critique of Practical Reason*) as a way of escape from determinism. All philosophies, he came to assert, are commitments of the will and are grounded upon men's moral resolutions.

In *The Vocation of Man* he pictured three different philosophical positions from among which men must choose, not on the basis of evidence or argument, but on the basis of moral faith. All three of these positions can be presented in a consistent fashion by their adherents. And to the adherents of each point of view, experience will then come to seem to substantiate it. Choice of a philosophy is therefore an expression of personal character. He who bows down to forces which play upon him from without will find himself utterly entangled in the mechanism of the world. He who directs attention wholly upon the sensory data of perceptual experience will find both the world around him and his own personality dissolved into figments of the imagination. But he who resolves to be free and to act for the sake of values he cherishes will find that he becomes master of his own fortunes and the world becomes plastic to his moral ends. The three books of *The Vocation of Man* deal in turn with the three philosophies; and Fichte's own commitment is clearly indicated by the eloquent rhetoric with which two of the philosophies are made repellent and the third is made glorious. In his statement of the three positions Fichte used the first person singular of the pronoun, thus treating each of them as an adventure of the spirit which is to be rejected or accepted because of its moral effects on the integrity of the self.

In Book I of *The Vocation of Man* Fichte presented the case for mechanism. If I regard the phenomena of the world, I note regularities of unvarying experience. I find that everything is determined by its antecedents and is an inevitable item in an interconnected whole. I am driven to conclude that I myself am part of this whole and am subject to rigid necessity in body, thoughts, and acts. I am what I am because of the way in which I occurred and now exist in the inclusive system of nature. And I shall be what I shall later become because of the forces which mold me. Even the sentiment of freedom occurs within me by necessity. Hence I am driven to conclude that it is not I who act but it is nature that acts in me. I feel horror at this theoretical outcome because I long to be an I who am genuinely free. But I find no escape so long as I accept the premises of the theory.

In Book II Fichte presented the case for perceptualism. In all perception, if I attend to it carefully, I find I perceive nothing but my own conscious states. I perceive no objects outside of me, no substances, no permanent world. I do not perceive anything I may properly call myself but only the vain succession of perishing sensations and ideas. All notions of enduring things and of an abiding self are figments of the imagination. I may fancy, from some spirit which seems to speak to me, that I have in myself something further than what I regard in the states which flit like illusions, one after another, through my consciousness. But as long as I attend to what is before me, I flounder helplessly in a morass of subjectivity. I find no escape from complete futility as long as I accept the premises of the perceptualist theory.

In Book III Fichte presented the case for the voluntarism he himself came to sponsor. I find in myself something more fundamental than intellect (which leads to determinism) and than sense (which leads to perceptualism). I find impulse to act.[11] I find that my trust in intellect is itself the result of my will's resolution to order my world intelligibly and that my trust in sense is itself the result of my will's resolution to respect the data of experience. Back of both intellect and sense is will. Back of both knowledge and perception is resolution to act. And my will is essentially a moral will. Conscience is the root of all experience and of all reality. I will an ordered world in order to have about me the needed instrumentalities of virile action. I can even say that what I "know" to exist is my own act objectifying itself in order that I may then proceed with power. My ego requires a non-ego as its counterpart in all dynamic action. I make the conditions of my own spiritual developments into materials which I can then use in battling my own way to triumphant achievement. The cosmos, with all its rigor and inflexible causal nexus, is but the challenge I throw out from myself in order to make the progress of my moral life invigorating, noble, and worthy of the moral purpose to which I dedicate myself.

Reality, Fichte concluded, is the material of our duty. It has its

[11] This characteristically German attitude goes back at least to Luther's doctrine of justification by faith and comes down at least to both the theistic and the atheistic existentialisms of our own day. Its definitive expression is probably that in Part I of Goethe's *Faust* (1808). Faust, meditating in his study, casts his eyes upon the verse from Scripture, "Im Anfang war das Wort." He rejects this for "Im Anfang war der Sinn" and then for "Im Anfang war die Kraft." But he finally rests in the conviction, "Im Anfang war die Tat."

origin in the categorical imperative. To drift with impulse is too easy. Conscience demands a hard struggle. But for Fichte in contrast with Kant, the categorical imperative is not a demand for universality of law but a demand for personal growth. So live, the imperative commands, as to grow into ever greater spiritual freedom. Make a world of unbroken law in order to operate upon it under conditions that develop all the resources of the self and so increase personal power. The world has, so to speak, no reality in itself; it is the scene (one might almost call it the scenery) of the free man's vocation.

Fichte retained the second form of Kant's categorical imperative more faithfully than the first. A man, if he is to triumph over the world he opposes to himself, needs close union with other men. These other men, unlike the world of things, are spiritual beings and real in themselves. Only among his fellows can a man be his full self. Separate selfhood is too limited to enable a single man to respond to the non-ego with sufficient power. The free man gains his moral stature only by losing his finitude in the corporate unity of all spiritual persons. Fichte, using an ancient term from the Apostles' Creed, called this corporate unity the communion of saints. The unity, in his view, is neither a matter of mystic sentiment nor wholly a matter of the future life. It is effected by action rather than feeling, and it ought to begin now. It is notably found in the organized life of the state, though the state is after all but a foretaste of the more harmonious and more far-ranging life which lies ahead of mankind.

Fichte may properly be called a voluntaristic idealist. He viewed reality in terms of personality, and he viewed personality in terms of will. He may also be called a romantic moralist to whom the good life is the free and triumphant expression of personal power. He represents a strand which has run through much of German culture, a strand made up of two intertwined threads. These threads are (1) admiration for a strong and technically efficient state and (2) a lyric sense of freedom through active loyalty to this state. His own life provided some of the ferment requisite to arouse successful resistance to the Napoleonic might. And his philosophical theory gave more than momentary sanction to the quest for unrestrained expression of a powerful personal will.

3. HEGEL

GEORG WILHELM FRIEDRICH HEGEL, 1770–1831, was born in Stuttgart. He studied at the University of Tübingen and received his Ph.D. degree there in 1790. He served as tutor in private families, first at Bern and then at Frankfort. His interest in religion led him to study the origins of Christianity, and he wrote a life of Jesus in which he repudiated miracles and orthodox Christology. He professed at first a romantic and mystical interpretation of nature which he derived from Schelling, and, through Schelling, he obtained a teaching position at the University of Jena. He and Schelling jointly founded and edited a *Critical Journal of Philosophy* in 1802–1803. He broke with Schelling's views when Schelling left Jena in 1803, and he gradually developed his own philosophy during the next decade. When he left Jena, he taught at the universities of Nuremberg, Heidelberg, and, finally, Berlin. He came to be regarded as leader of the philosophical world, and he confidently accepted the admiration of his large classes of students and the general public. He died of cholera in the epidemic which broke out in Berlin in 1831. His major writings include *Phenomenology of Spirit* (1807); *Science of Logic* (Vols. I and II in 1812, Vol. III in 1816); *Encyclopedia of Philosophical Sciences* (1817), which gave a synopsis of his system in three parts called *Shorter Logic, Philosophy of Nature,* and *Philosophy of Mind;* and *Philosophy of Right* (1821). From lecture notes he left at his death there were later published other works—*Aesthetics, Philosophy of Religion, Philosophy of History,* and *History of Philosophy.*

HEGEL'S PHILOSOPHY is a form of Kantianism. But Hegel, like most successors of Kant, did not retain the many facets of Kant's unstable position. He eagerly accepted some of Kant's contentions and entirely repudiated others. He thus transformed Kant's critical philosophy into what is called the system of absolute idealism.

Hegel was deeply impressed with Kant's insistence on the rational character of experience. Experience is not, as Locke and Hume seemed to him to have made it, a material which first comes to our consciousness void of rational structure; and reason is not, as Descartes deemed it, an abstract faculty which resides in an individual and proceeds by intuitions apart from experience. Reason and experience are not two but one. Reason is the objective structure of experience. And we human individuals are ourselves most truly rational when we cease to follow the whims of our private psychological trends and allow our thoughts to be molded by the manner in which experience occurs.

Hegel was repelled by Kant's supposition of things-in-themselves. Even Kant, he contended, made reason too adventitious when he taught that it applies to only the phenomenal world and has no constitutive role upon all reality. Reality, of course, is independent of individual minds but cannot intelligibly be regarded as independent of mind altogether. Things-in-themselves, if beyond the range of reason, are nothing at all. Appearances may indeed be contrasted with reality. But the reality with which appearances may be contrasted is not a noumenal world that lies back of experience and entirely apart from thought. It is, rather, the fulfilled experience which our incomplete human experience, fragmentary and therefore still somewhat lacking in rationality, indicates to be the objective order of a more-than-human mind. Appearances are related to reality as is the partial to the whole. Experience is not merely, or even primarily, a human event. It is a vast cosmic process, stretching both spatially and temporally beyond our finite share in it. In any portion of cosmic experience which we have or artificially abstract from the whole, we find confusions, contradictions, obscurities. The wider our finite experience becomes or the more fully concrete we make our vista of the cosmos, the more rationality we discover experience to have. We are thus led to realize that the whole of experience is completely rational. The inadequacies of experience, or what seem to us to be its inadequacies, are all overcome in the progressive movement of the cosmos through time.

ABSOLUTE IDEALISM

Hegel thus came to maintain, in words which have become a famous philosophical epigram, that the real is the rational and the rational is the real. He did not mean to apply this maxim to each moment of human experience separated out from the continuum of history. We find that our seemingly legitimate expectations are often thwarted by the course of events, and so we are confronted in our own lives with a mixture of rationality and irrationality. But Hegel attributed entire rationality to absolute experience, that is, to the full concreteness of the entire temporal cosmos. Hegel, as his critics have often said, introduced into philosophy, or at least emphasized in his own philosophy, that growing sense of history which marked the literature of the nineteenth century in all its phases. But history, as Hegel treated it, is more than an understanding of the past. It is an understanding of the temporal structure of experience in its wholeness, past, present, and future. When we take any so-called single experience, arresting it, as it were, in its onward movement, it is merely phenomenal. But we ought not to attribute to absolute experience the deficiencies of our fragmentary bit of experience. All discord, all lack of meaning, all futility will disappear, not for human minds, but for the absolute mind. In absolute experience everything which occurs has its indispensable place and is thoroughly intelligible.

Hegel, therefore, spoke of degrees of reality and of degrees of knowledge. An illusion really occurs in our experience, but an illusion is appearance and has but a low degree of reality. Similarly, our belief in an illusion is justified from our finite point of view but yields only a low degree of knowledge. Philosophers from Aristotle to his own times had erred, Hegel held, in supposing that reality is already complete and that our purported knowledge of it can ever be adequate and final. Neither reality nor knowledge is ever finished. Reality is endless process, and wholly adequate knowledge of it is possible only to the absolute mind. The world we find about us at any moment of our lives is real insofar as it is given to us as the scene of our operations and the material for our sciences. But that world is an abstraction from the course of world history. And our sciences, precious as they are, are stages of intellectual development, reflecting the degree of mental alertness in the individual scientists and the degree of cultural advance in the community. The only entirely real world is the whole cosmos, and the only entirely adequate knowledge is complete knowledge of that cosmos.[12]

The cosmos, in Hegel's view, is therefore absolute mind. Mind in human beings is a subjective process, but mind in the cosmos is an inclusive historical process whereby the cosmos unfolds gradually toward complete fulfillment of itself. Absolute mind Hegel was willing to call God. This view does not conform at all closely to the dogmas of historic Judaism or Christianity. Hegel's God is neither a first cause nor a final goal. It is not a being set over against the world. He used for it the term *Geist,* which is usually translated "spirit" but might be translated "culture." The absolute is a line of cultural development which is implicated in every thing and every event. It is a vast historical process in which the cosmos passes to

---

[12] Tennyson presented the Hegelian point of view in his poem "Flower in the Crannied Wall" (1869):

> "Flower in the crannied wall
> I pluck you out of the crannies,
> I hold you here, root and all, in my hand,
> Little flower—but *if* I could understand
> What you are, root and all, and all in all,
> I should know what God and man is."

ever increased intelligibility. Not simply is history the process by which we human beings come to consciousness of God or the embracing culture of the world; history is also the process by which God or *Geist* comes to ever fuller consciousness of its own development and its far-reaching implications for its growing future.

THE HEGELIAN DIALECTIC

Hegel realized that his theories of reality and of knowledge required a new logic. He devoted years to the formulation of this logic. He explicitly rejected Aristotelian logic. For Aristotelian logic proceeded on the assumption that there are permanent substances and fixed types to which all substances recurrently conform. Aristotelian logic teaches that propositions are either true or false and that, when true, they are finally true. Hegel wanted a logic which would disclose the pattern of developing things and changing events. We occasionally speak, and Hegel thought we then speak significantly, of the logic of events. The formal logic of the schools is not the source of this logic; it is, rather, an abstraction from this logic. Formal logic deals with fixed terms and inert entities which have been arbitrarily fashioned out of the dynamic processes of the world, but it does not reflect the nature of these dynamic processes. The logic Hegel expounded recognizes the rhythmic movement of thought in the progressive unfolding of absolute mind. This new logic ought to set the pattern for our thinking because it is already, and apart from our finite minds, the pattern of the absolute experience we are ever seeking to know. If we wish to define logic as the science of the laws of thought, well and good. But in that case we ought not to think of the laws of thought as anything specifically human. They are laws of the development of absolute thought or universal culture. The thought of which logic gives the laws is first of all the dynamic development of the evolving world and is only subsequently and consequently the thought of wise men at their best moments of insight. The laws of thought are normative principles of human thinking only because they are first of all actual structures of the temporal course of the cosmos.

History, Hegel maintained, is a rhythmic movement which exhibits three stages. These stages he called thesis, antithesis, and synthesis. They are stages found in the developing life of the world in its military, its economic, its political, its social, and its intellectual phases, and these phases are, of course, radically interwoven with one another in their factual occurrence. In the first stage understanding sums up the significance of the cosmic situation in some dogma. This dogma gives definite statement to some partial truth about the situation. In the second stage criticism points out the limitations of the alleged dogma and cultivates wholesome skepticism concerning the partial truth. In the last stage reason unites the partial understanding and the negative criticism in a more adequate grasp of a larger segment of reality. The partial truths of thesis and antithesis are both preserved in the synthesis and are incorporated into a more integrated view. And this triadic rhythm, Hegel believed, continues endlessly. There is no termination to the process. Every effective synthesis becomes the thesis of a new critical examination which raises new grounds for suspicion of its adequacy and leads on to a more sufficient understanding of a still greater portion of experience.

The rhythmic movement of thought (both in cosmic history and in human reflections) is what Hegel called the dialectic of history.[13] World history, as he expressed the point, is a dialectical process. In the more cosmological portions of his discussion of the dialectical process (in contrast with the portions which deal with human history), Hegel's writing is austere and forbidding to most readers (except a few technical philosophical followers). One basic triad in his *Encyclopedia of the Philosophical Sciences* is being-nothing-becoming. Pure being is the beginning; it is unperceived, unfelt, unimagined, void of determinate form. As such, it is an abstraction and, therefore, nothing at all. Being and nothing are both utterly different and also wholly the same. From the synthesis of these two comes becoming or change. Another triad is quality-quantity-measure. Quality cannot alone be; it is, necessarily, so much of some kind of thing and, hence, subject to quantification. And from the synthesis of quality and quantity there ensues definite amount or measure. Hegel arranged these and other triads in a schematism which enabled him to pass, he supposed, from thought in its entire indeterminateness to the richly intricate and developed thought which is the course of the world as we find it about us in its full concreteness. The point of his use of this schematism is perhaps his insistence that the world is not a vast number of ultimate particles (like Lucretius' atoms) which arrange themselves in a succession of different combinations and orders, but a perpetual growth from comparative emptiness to ever increasing meaningfulness.

Hegel made a much more intelligible and much more influential

---

[13] Hegel's use of the term *dialectic* is quite different from both Plato's and Kant's uses of the same term. Cf. above, pp. 48 and 372 respectively.

use of his dialectical formula when he applied it to the course of human history. He had a vast erudition in this latter field, and he found effective illustrations of his logic in political and social European history from the ancient world to his own day. The idealism of Plato, he stated, was a thesis which generated the materialism of Democritus as its antithesis; and these two opposed views then found their synthesis or reconciliation in the realism of Aristotle. The hedonism of the Epicureans brought about a protest which found expression in the Stoic indifference to pleasure; and these two doctrines, both of which were partially true and partially false, were critically superseded by the more balanced ethic of Christianity. Bourbon pretension to inherited rights for the privileged classes led directly to revolutionary claims by the Jacobins in behalf of equal rights for all men; and these two half-truths were then wrought into the saner theory and practice of legally sanctioned rights for citizens within national states. Hegel showed great adroitness in using his triadic method to expound the clashes in human history and the statesmanlike creation, out of the material of these clashes, of new types of social order.

PHILOSOPHY OF HISTORY

In the introduction to his posthumously published *Philosophy of History* Hegel presented an interpretation of the significance he found in the sweep of human history from the ancient empires of Egypt and Mesopotamia to the western states of his own day. He found four main stages in this story of human development. In the ancient empires despotism prevailed, and such morality as existed was imposed externally on the mass of the people. Such despotism is the childhood of the human race. Then in the Greek world came individualism and the release of all men for autonomous expression of their own personal tastes and ideas. Such rampant freedom is the adolescence of mankind. Still later there arose the balanced regime of the Roman state which adjusted the claims of authority and liberty by giving individuals a discipline of rising to power through service to the institutions of empire. Here is the manhood of the human race. Finally, after the chaos of long centuries, appeared what Hegel did not hesitate to call the fulfillment of this whole process of historical development, namely, the German state, in which life, he ventured to say, is joyous, rational, and complete. Here, then, the maturity of mankind is reached.

ETHICS

Some of the consequences of Hegel's absolute idealism can be seen in his ethical theories.

The individual, Hegel believed, is an abstraction from society, and glorification of natural rights (whether in Locke or the Jacobins) is a moral impertinence. Society is not a mere conglomeration of men. It is a spiritual reality, through immersion in which men may come to consciousness of selfhood. Doubtless the society which conditions a man is not perfect, because it is but a stage in the development of absolute mind. It is, however, the only society a man has. It is the *Geist* of his time and place, the preserver and cultivator, at least for him, of science, art, religion, philosophy, and all phases of culture. To recoil from one's society because it is not perfect is to reject the indispensable ground of one's limited perfection. A man's duty, therefore, is not to live as if he were already in some future society which he fancies may yet supersede the present, but to appropriate as fully as he can the meanings this actual society has for his life. The institutions of a society, such as family and political organization, are stabilizations of that society's meanings. These institutions, even though imperfect, are a sounder criterion of morality than subjective opinions of persons who rebel against established ways. We human beings pass to better things only insofar as we associate ourselves intimately with the dialectical development the absolute mind is taking in our own day. To be moral is to live in accord with the *Geist* of one's own society.

Hegel's ethical theories had as one of their results the strengthening of conservatism and the glorifying of the state. His critics have often accused him of unduly subjecting individual persons to the domination of government authority. And for practical purposes these critics may well be correct. But in theory Hegel had no intention of identifying state and government. Government is an organ of the state, and a very essential organ, but only one of many organs. The state is a political entity, to be sure; but Hegel used the adjective *political* in its Greek sense, referring thereby to all aspects of social living in a compactly organized group. The state is the embracing reality within which are contained all the customs and opportunities and institutions which enable a society to practice the arts, to cultivate the sciences, and to educate the minds of its individual members. It is the carrier of the cultural spirit of a society.

HEGEL'S INFLUENCE

Hegel's influence was strong during the remainder of the nineteenth century and even the early twentieth. The school of absolute idealism held its own in the Germanies and dominated academic philosophy in England and the United States until the revolt of the pragmatists and new realists. Hegelianism, its friendly critics have asserted, has been a grandiose protest against one-sidedness. But a grandiose protest against one-sidedness turns easily into an apology for the *status quo;* for it can make, and Hegelians often did make, every evil as well as every good seem a requisite detail in the sweep of the cosmic process. Just as Augustinianism led in some hands to an identification of the city of God with the existing Church, so Hegelianism led to an identification of the ideal with the actual. Hegelians may properly believe that every actual evil will be transcended in the onward movement of the absolute mind; but they must also confess that every evil, as truly as every good, is a necessary manifestation of the dialectical passage to new disclosures of the thought of the absolute. And any finite agent who tries with reforming zeal to hurry the absolute along in its course is as irrelevant in practice as he is ridiculous in theory. For the absolute does all things in its own way and at its own time.[14]

MARX'S REJOINDER TO HEGEL

The most influential student of Hegel's writings was Karl Marx (1818–1883), a German who, exiled twice from France and once from Belgium, spent most of his mature life in England, working on behalf of the first Communist International and writing his chief work *Capital*[15] in the library of the British Museum. Marx began as Hegel's pupil and eventually became Hegel's hostile critic. He was not interested to develop a general metaphysical position or a cosmology. He devoted himself to defining and defending what he called the materialistic interpretation of history. His philosophical relation

---

[14] Francis Herbert Bradley (1846–1924), the greatest of English Hegelians, wrote an essay entitled *My Station and Its Duties* (published in *Ethical Studies,* 1876). In this essay occur the passages (pp. 173, 174, 180): "History is the working out of the true human nature through various incomplete stages towards completion . . . The morality of every stage is justified for that stage; and the demand for a code of right in itself, apart from any stage, is seen to be the asking for an impossibility . . . If you would be as good as your world, you would be better than most likely you are, and to wish to be better than the world is to be already on the threshold of immorality."

[15] Marx published the first volume of *Capital* in 1867. The other two volumes, completed from his elaborate but unfinished manuscript by his friends, appeared after his death.

to Hegel may be summed up by saying that he rejected both idealism and absolutism but retained the dialectical method.

Marx's use of the term *materialism* for his own position has caused him to be frequently misunderstood. He did not sponsor the supposition that unthinking matter determines the course of social changes. He did not hold that mind is a futile by-product of matter. He was, rather, objecting to Hegel's theory that reality can be defined in terms of mind. He would neither make mind supreme over matter nor make matter supreme over mind. Thought, pure thought, if indeed there can be any such thing, is impotent to produce anything and to effect any change in the world. Thinking men, however, can do many things when they associate themselves together in groups and work upon the materials which are naturally and socially available to them. Many changes doubtless occur in nature apart altogether from human participation. But the changes in which Marx was most interested, the changes which most matter to human welfare, he believed, are changes which men effect through their practical arts and the devices they are intelligent enough to invent. Men make history, and thinking men make history differently from unthinking men. Men may indeed become, Marx recognized, increasingly competent to control their material environment and may in that way gain more and more power to direct the course of future history. But the world is not the unfolding of thought. It is a material world within which thought makes no difference until thought is embodied in material structures and processes.

Marx thundered against Hegel's absolutism. He considered absolutism a bulwark of social reaction (such as indeed ensued in Europe upon the suppression of the revolutionary movements of 1830 and 1848). Hegel, he insisted, bathed social reaction in a mystic and romantic glow and encouraged the privileged classes of society to resist needed reforms. Poverty and human misery cannot properly be sanctioned by saying that they are stages in the unfolding of the absolute mind.

But Marx retained Hegel's dialectical method. His materialism is a dialectical materialism. That is, he viewed history as the unceasing clash of opposed forces, each of which, however entrenched it may be in the institutions of an established society, generates the discontent which may eventually be the condition of its violent overthrow. Individuals, operating each of them alone, have little power to promote change. But classes may find tools of action whereby sweeping changes may come about. Dialectical materialism is a theory of thesis-antithesis-synthesis in which economic groups struggle for power against one another and so determine the course which events take in their time. Marx believed economic motivation to be the major, almost the all-embracing, force in society, deeming art and education and philosophy, even scientific problems and discoveries, to be instruments for furthering the fundamental drive for economic advantage. His own very considerable research into history was centered around the immediate and practical problem of promoting the transition from the prevailing capitalistic system of industrial production to a socialistic system; hence, he did not take time to state his position in general philosophical terms. But the transition from capitalism to socialism he professed to regard as but one of the succeeding instances of the dialectical movement of history.

Marx had little interest in such democratic devices for social change as universal suffrage, the general consent, and representative government. And the course of his influence since his death has made this aspect of his thought particularly conspicuous. If a class waited for general consent as granted through majority vote, that class would never accomplish its purposes. Where history is made by clashes between classes, universal suffrage is bound to reflect either the interest of the class already in power or the lethargy of large masses of people. A resolute minority can accomplish more by direct action than by frittering away its energies in trying to win converts among a herd of voters. The chief bond that ties together the members of a resolute minority will always be a community of economic interest. Only where there is this community of economic interest first of all will the members of a group come to be tied together also by intellectual principles and other social forces. Some individuals may show, indeed have shown, that they will act contrary to their personal interests because they choose to identify themselves with what they consider to be the welfare of their fellows. But the dominant force in history and the chief instrumentality for social change are both economic. Marx's willingness to tolerate the invasion of civic rights for many individual persons was due to his conviction that some individuals are bound to suffer as a by-product of needed social reforms. He, like Hegel, was more concerned with the state as a whole than with the fortunes of individuals within the state.

4. SCHOPENHAUER

ARTHUR SCHOPENHAUER, 1788–1860, was born in Danzig. His
father was a wealthy banker who admired Voltaire and
English ideals of liberty, deemed German culture inferior, and hated Prussia so bitterly that when the Prussians
annexed Danzig in 1793, he moved with his family to
Hamburg. His mother was a minor writer of novels of
the romantic school. He had two years of schooling in Paris
and two more in England. He became proficient in Greek
and Latin and studied classical culture enthusiastically.
He worked for a time in a commercial house in Hamburg
but determined to devote himself, as soon as possible, to
a life of scholarship. When he reached the age of twenty-
one shortly after his father's death, he came into enough
money by his father's will to enable him to be independent. He then entered the University of Göttingen as a student in 1809. He and his mother disliked each other and
had few contacts after his father's death. In 1813 he published his doctoral dissertation *The Four-fold Root of
Sufficient Reason.* He had come to admire Kant's writings,
but he scorned the lectures he heard Fichte deliver at
Berlin. In 1818 his chief work appeared, *The World As
Will and Idea,* but it attracted little attention. In 1819
he was given an opportunity to deliver some lectures at
the University of Berlin. Jealous of Hegel's prestige, he
scheduled his lectures at the same hours at which Hegel
lectured. He thus had few auditors, and he became very
embittered. In 1831 he fled from the cholera epidemic in
Berlin and settled for the rest of his life in Frankfort-on-
the-Main. He seemed surly, even rude, to people about
him and had few friends. He indulged in affairs with a
number of women, was always ashamed of his sensuality,
and came to denounce women as a source of many human
ills. The social disillusionment in the Germanies upon
the suppression of the liberal movements of 1848 made the
tone of his essays more in accord with popular taste at that
time, and he came in his last years to enjoy some of the
reputation he had longed to receive.

SCHOPENHAUER GOT from the writings of Kant a suggestion which
Kant indeed had not intended, and he developed this suggestion

into a complete theory, not merely of the nature of man but of the nature of the entire world. This suggestion came to him when he considered the relation between the *Critique of Pure Reason,* with its discussion of the phenomenal world, and Kant's later writings, with their treatment of the noumenal self as will. Schopenhauer thus came to view the world as both idea and will, though he did not in either respect follow Kant's doctrines faithfully.

VOLUNTARISTIC IDEALISM

The data of experience, Schopenhauer held, in agreement with Kant, are phenomena. But these phenomena, he supposed, in divergence from Kant, are subjective ideas in the private minds of individual human beings. The whole world and everything in it, he maintained, can be viewed in terms of the ideas produced in men's minds by the real things which lie beyond sense experience. But the world thus viewed is a world of appearances only; it is not real apart from men's experience of it. Physics and the other natural sciences may well be called the sciences of appearances. These sciences have a kind of pictorial truth and are certainly of great utility in practice; but they deal with the world in a strictly superficial manner and yield no understanding of what the reality of either ourselves or the rest of the world is. From the sciences therefore no conclusion can be drawn concerning things-in-themselves, that is, concerning either our own beings or the real forces which produce ideas in us. What reality is in itself we can know only if we are enabled somehow to penetrate beyond the realm of the phenomena with which scientists deal.

A philosopher, Schopenhauer believed, can get beyond the superficial realm of scientific knowledge through a study of himself, because in himself he directly encounters one noumenal object. Each of us has his own being available to immediate inspection and may properly take himself as a key to the ultimate nature of all other things too. Each of us finds that in himself he is will, not a moral will primarily, as Kant piously supposed, but an endless striving for what he is not and has not. Then, with an assurance which he nowhere justified, Schopenhauer went on to infer that all the other many things in the world are of the same nature fundamentally as each of us finds himself to be. We find about us the ceaseless drive with which waters rush to the ocean, the dogged persistence with which the needle of a compass points to the north, the urgency with which iron filings seek the magnet, the insistence with which saline deposits assume crystalline shape, the pull of the earth upon our bodies, and the force with which all bodies attract or repel one another. Everywhere about us, once we have come to understand our own nature, we seem to be in the presence of countless wills. Our eyes are the phenomenal form of the will to see, our stomachs of the will to satisfy hunger, our bowels and intestines of the will to digest, our brains of the will to know, our grasping hands and hastening feet of the will to execute their many tasks and purposes. Within ourselves and everywhere around us in the world we witness the ever present impulse of what generically we may call will. All that which appears phenomenally or externally as idea is in itself, as each of us discerns his own true being to be, the restless drive of will.

Will is more fundamental, Schopenhauer insisted, than is intelligence. Some wills are indeed, at least on some occasions, intelligent wills. But intelligence is not universal in the world as will is. Will is often, in the natural world around us, blind striving; it has no foresight of the end it is seeking. Even those wills which can consciously sense their ends cannot adroitly fashion means to reach those ends but drive helplessly as impulse chances to lead. And when, as in man, the will is somewhat aided by intelligence, it is not necessarily a nobler will. For, as Schopenhauer pointed out, intelligence does not guarantee moral conduct; it may invent sordid means to advance the interests of the will. A man has to be intelligent as well as unscrupulous in order to practice subtle deception and make the worse appear the better reason.

The world, then, as Schopenhauer thought of it, is both idea and will. He did not mean that it is will in part and idea in part. Rather, he meant that the world can be wholly interpreted in either of two ways. It is idea to the scientist, who operates with appearances, and it is will to the philosopher, who penetrates to things-in-themselves. Schopenhauer was a voluntaristic idealist. He was idealist in that he interpreted all reality in terms of what in man becomes personality or mind. He was voluntaristic in that he made will primary in all things, including man.

PESSIMISM

To his system of voluntaristic idealism Schopenhauer added the doctrine of pessimism. Neither voluntarism nor idealism implies pessimism logically. Pessimism is one of the many ways in which a protagonist of voluntaristic idealism may choose to develop his system. It is the way, seemingly, in which Schopenhauer's own unhappy life led him to expand his philosophy.

To will, Schopenhauer proceeded to say, is to want what one does not have. It is to lack and, hence, to suffer. When the will reaches fulfillment in possession of its desired goal (as it sometimes does), it dies out and is no longer. It reaches fulfillment, Schopenhauer gloomily estimated, only one time in ten, or even less often. Pleasure, he said, is a negative state; it is but the glow which occasionally accompanies the dying out of gratified will. Pain, by contrast, is a more normal state and is positive and cruel; it is the persistence of longing of the thwarted will. Desire gnaws with wearisome intensity at the root of most consciousness; but satisfaction is "short and scantily measured out." [16] And, ironically enough, satisfaction occurs, if it occurs at all, only to make room for new desires which press forward with their unsatisfied claims.

Schopenhauer drained world literature, so far as he with his wide reading knew it, for examples of the predominance of pain over pleasure in human experience. He insisted that Tantalus (and other figures in Greek mythology) can be taken as fairly conceived symbols of the position of mankind in the economy of the cosmos. Dante's Hell, he said in echo of a common criticism of the *Divine Comedy,* uses materials tellingly gathered out of our everyday world, and so is convincing to most readers; but Dante's Heaven is unrealistic, effete, out of touch with the normal experience of mankind. Suffering is not merely the rule; it is the very essence of will. Life is naturally unhappy, both in its irrational volitional basis and in its empirical occurrence.

TWO WAYS OF DELIVERANCE

Schopenhauer devoted many pages of his *World As Will and Idea* to considering the ways that man may use to gain deliverance from the normal unhappiness of life.

He did not countenance suicide. For the end of this mortal life, he said, is the end of only the phenomenal body and does not bring about the end of the real self with its everlasting will to live. Suicide, therefore, is a superficial and foolish act.

Genuine deliverance from unhappiness requires more profound methods. Two such methods he believed he could offer.

The first of these two methods of deliverance Schopenhauer derived from his long and thorough study of the philosophy and culture of the ancient Greeks, particularly of Plato. Ideas, he main-

---

[16] *The World As Will and Idea,* English transl. R. B. Haldane and J. Kemp (London, Truebner, 1883–1886), Vol. I, p. 253.

tained, are of two entirely distinct kinds. There are first the ideas which are the content of sense experience and the phenomenal objects of daily concern. There are secondly the eternal ideas, which are not subject to the course of becoming and its attendant miseries. To the extent to which men give themselves over to the contemplation of the eternal ideas, they are plucked, as it were, out of the struggles of the restless will and are elevated into a serene world where no change intrudes and, hence, escape from pain is achieved.

The technique by which men may give themselves over to contemplation of eternal ideas, Schopenhauer taught, is the pursuit of the fine arts. Art at its best does not present a particular work of art (statue, painting, poem) for its own sake.[17] Art presents that particular work of art in order to direct attention beyond it to the eternal idea of which it is a transient expression. In successful art the particular object is representative rather than presentative; it is representative of what is not a particular at all. When a man is lost in contemplation of the eternal idea which a work of art brings before his attention, he finds that the course of time stops for him, that his will ceases to struggle, and that agitation gives place to untroubled calm. If we compare the normal course of life to the raging of a mighty storm, then esthetic enjoyment is like a silent sunbeam which, in piercing the storm, is not in the least diverted by the bluster about its path. In art, therefore, the will ceases to rage, loses itself in the timeless, and comes temporarily to rest.

But art, as Schopenhauer in spite of his eloquent rhetoric in its praise did not fail to recognize, cannot be a final solution of life's miseries. Art is a temporary deliverance. The esthetic experience cannot be long maintained. Men need something more.

The second of his proffered methods of deliverance Schopenhauer derived from his sympathy with the philosophies of India, particularly with Buddhism. It is the practice of a morality which begins in a man's sense of kinship with his suffering fellows and culminates in saintliness. When a man realizes that all men are but as himself in their restless wills and their consequent sufferings, he rises above the particularity of his own striving and gains a sense of universal compassion for mankind. He no longer feels fear or envy or anger. He no longer is driven by his own little desires. He sloughs off his miserable particularity. He becomes indifferent to the illusions of

[17] Schopenhauer recognized that some objects offered by artists, such as a portrayal of a nude, may arouse desire for the particular instead of raising men above that desire. He therefore deemed an object of this kind a work of pseudo or perverted art.

the phenomenal world which once troubled him. He is able to look out smilingly upon the hectic course of the world. He is able to deny his own will. He has put on saintliness, for saintliness is life based on denial of the will to live.

5. NIETZSCHE

FRIEDRICH WILHELM NIETZSCHE, 1844–1900, was born at Röcken, near Leipzig. He was reared in a home where his widowed mother and several other female relatives sought to impress their religious piety on him, and he revolted with violence against all forms of religion. At the University of Leipzig he studied classical philology and literature. His philological papers were quickly recognized as brilliant; and at the age of twenty-four he was awarded the chair of classical philology at the University of Basel. In accepting this chair he had perforce to consent to become a Swiss citizen. But he enthusiastically offered his services to the German forces when the Franco-Prussian War broke out, and he was disappointed that his participation in the war was limited to ambulance work. In 1879 he was forced by ill health to resign his professorship. He wandered from resort to resort endeavoring to regain his strength. In 1889 he suffered what has sometimes been referred to as an apoplectic stroke and never recovered his sanity except for brief intervals. The chief of his many writings are *The Birth of Tragedy* (1872), *Human, All Too Human* (1876–80), *This Joyful Wisdom* (1882), *Thus Spake Zarathustra* (1883–84), *Beyond Good and Evil* (1886), *Genealogy of Morals* (1887), *The Will to Power* (1901), and *Antichrist* (1901).

NIETZSCHE WAS A prophet rather than a systematic philosopher. He cared little for metaphysics and theory of knowledge and devoted all his great literary powers to what Germans call *Lebensphilosophie*. He scoffed at Kant as a moral fanatic. He knew the works of Darwin and T. H. Huxley, but he deemed them inferior because, in his interpretation of them, they placed too much value on mere biological survival. The critic who tries to ascertain Nietzsche's view of the world from his writings (a task which is not particularly profitable) can glean only a few vague propositions. Nietzsche thought that the world has no intrinsic order, no controlling purpose, no moral government. He considered it a mistake to apply to the world generally any such predicates as good or bad, beautiful or ugly, machine or organism. The world is a lot of different things interacting in a lot of different ways. Nietzsche boasted that he was too broad-minded to espouse a system.

Even in the field of *Lebensphilosophie* Nietzsche was far from systematic. He could write eloquent paragraphs and sustained essays. But in some of his works he presented series of detached aphorisms. Each aphorism is an ejaculation. The aphorisms are sometimes packed with wisdom, usually trenchant and meaty, and occasionally deliberately provocative. Nietzsche was prone to make overstatements of his ideas, partly to annoy the pious reader, partly to arouse independent reflections in the thoughtful reader. Anyone who dislikes Nietzsche can easily convict him of glaring contradictions by depending on the exact letter of the texts and making no effort to infer his probable intent. Nonetheless, Nietzsche was passionately sincere. He never indulged in wit for the sake of being clever (as Voltaire seems to have done). He had the earnestness of generations of his ancestors who were pastors, even though he aimed at results wholly antithetical to theirs. He wanted to destroy the prevailing morality of the Judaic-Christian tradition and to incite men, or some few men, to new and higher accomplishments. He knew he must risk offending the masses of men (whom he despised for their dismal conventionality anyway) if he was ever to arouse an occasional discerning mind to abandon conformity and to strike out for original works of beauty and excellence. Hence he thundered against accepted standards. He lavished praise on genius, even when genius won its way at the cost of turmoil and pain. And he penned stirring battle cries rather than calm analyses of his ideas.

Nietzsche owed much to Schopenhauer, but even more to the Greeks. And he corrected what seemed to him the errors of Schopenhauer by what he gained from the Greeks. He agreed with Schopenhauer that man is fundamentally will (refusing, however, to follow Schopenhauer in attributing will to all nature) and that man may escape from the crudity and confusion of the world by creating beautiful forms in the arts. The will he called the Dionysian element in human experience, and the contemplation of form he called the Apollonian. But he broke with Schopenhauer's belief that man needs to escape from the impulses of will. He repudiated Schopenhauer's advice to deny the will to live. He knew that the will to live meant that men will suffer. But he did not shun pain. He welcomed pain as a sign that one is living in a virile manner. He wanted a life in which the will to live becomes a will to power. He wanted a life in which the Dionysian ecstasy and Apollonian poise are combined. Only timid people, he held, will cringe before pain and become pessimistic. The brave will defy pain, will endure torments of pain in order to achieve an outstanding end, and will exult in their powers to create through suffering. The proper combination of Dionysian and Apollonian elements in life makes for nobility. This combination, he contended, is the very essence of such tragedy as is found in great literature and in great lives. When the mood of Apollonian poise is carried too far, life becomes overintellectual (as, he believed was the case with philosophers after Socrates who never equalled in power the earlier Greek thinkers). When the intoxication of Dionysian revelry is allowed too free rein, life becomes drunken and degenerate. In men like Homer and Aeschylus and Sophocles, he maintained, the balance of Apollonian and Dionysian elements is just and assures creativity in both the fine arts and the art of life.

Nietzsche had no message, and wished to have no message, for the conventional herd of mankind. He knew that the many weaken at the prospect of pain and that all fine accomplishments cost severe pain. He knew that the many accept moral teachings from their social environment and that any rise above the drab level of society comes only when a strong will, directed by its own moral autonomy, pushes aside the inertia of custom. He knew that the many feel frustrated by a sense of their own guilt, and he sought men who, instead of stewing in bad conscience over their past inadequacies, strike anew for action that will lead to genuine excellence. He knew that the many commend behavior that is obedient, dutiful, moderate, considerate, unselfish, and he scorned those adjectives as "contemptible words." He referred to the many as slaves, slaves to priests, slaves to conventions, slaves to routine. He wanted men ready for knightly endeavor, eager for battle, willing even to "trample" on the many when such trampling was the price requisite to achieve a meed of glory. The truly excellent person is a superman. He will not be brutal; he will be just. But justice is not found in treating inferior persons as the equals of superior persons. Justice is found in treating inferiors as means, provided that they are made means, not to idle revenge or spiteful domination over others, but to the production of great art or the liberation of great ideas.

The excellent man, to use the title of one of Nietzsche's books, is "beyond good and evil." This phrase may mislead the unwary reader. Nietzsche did not mean that the excellent man is beyond distinctions between the really good and the really bad or base. Evil, as he used the word, is whatever men's morbid consciences lead them to fear. Nietzsche reproached men for following such maxims as "Blessed are the meek" and "Blessed are the poor in spirit" and "Blessed are the peace-makers." Men praise meekness and poverty of spirit and fear of struggle because they have taken their own measure and found themselves weak. They then try to foist on others the maxims which, if generally observed, would protect them in their weakness. Evil things are what men fear because they have not the courage to act with power. And the excellent man is, of course, beyond the point where he need respect the fears of weaklings. The excellent man will avoid whatever is bad; he will avoid laziness, complacency, the lure of sensuous pleasure, commercial gain as an end in itself, cheap display for the sake of reputation, and all manner of pretense. He will face risks with exhilaration; he will live adventurously; he will not always hesitate in order first to count the cost. The distinction between good and bad is a real one based on the discovery of the difference between superiority and inferiority. The distinction between good and evil is a spurious one, invented by the weak, partly to excuse, partly to protect, their own flagrant weakness.

Nothing is more morally hideous, Nietzsche believed, than renunciation for the sake of renunciation. Asceticism as ordinarily practiced is foolish and base. Rigorous self-discipline may indeed be a *sine qua non* of achievement, and ascetic practices may be the only path by which the artist or the philosopher is able to rise to the heights he seeks. One may properly give up something for the sake of something better. But one may never properly give up something if renunciation is the goal sought. And so, in some of his strong aphorisms, Nietzsche condemned chastity. He condemned chastity, not because he admired the sensualist, but because he abhorred the man who lacked desire. Strong desires are not a guarantee of excellence, but they are one indispensable prerequisite. Not merely in matters of sex but in all areas of human life, to refrain in order thereby better to achieve is fine, but to refrain in order to practice renunciation for itself is base.

Nietzsche proclaimed that his position involved a transvaluation of all values. And to a large extent he was right. His ideal was perhaps the closest thing in modern philosophy to a revival of the Greek aristocratic ideal.[18] He did not at all agree with the universalistic import of Kant's categorical imperative. All men, he taught, have not a right to the same acts or even to the same judgments. The excellent man may well find it wise to treat his inferiors in a manner in which they would be foolish to treat one another, and he may guide this treatment by considered judgments of his own higher merits. To suppose that only that is right for one which is also right for all is a blunder. Only an ethical sentimentalist could recommend a universalistic principle as a guide for conduct in this world of wide diversities of moral worth.

Nietzsche has been reproved by his critics for certain limitations in his statements. With all his emphasis on the crying need for excellence, he gave no criterion by which men might distinguish what is really excellent from what is proffered as such and really is not. But perhaps this is not a fair line of criticism. No philosopher can answer all the questions which his critics may later want to ask of him. And Nietzsche as a prophet cried for excellence, even if as a systematic philosopher he did not define a formal criterion by which to determine its various degrees of worth. Nietzsche's critics have also sometimes decried the way in which, in his later works, Nietzsche resorted with increasing violence to overstatements of his points which seem ruthless and even brutal. These violent overstatements, however, may be indications of his increasing ill health. But whether one agree or not with such points of unfavorable criticism, one ought not to fail to make one point of favorable criticism. No writer in world literature has ever laid bare as effectively as Nietzsche the moral inadequacy of mediocrity.

[18] Some critics have pointed out a similarity between Nietzsche's superman and Aristotle's high-minded man. Nietzsche did not call attention to the point, perhaps because he counted Aristotle as one of the too intellectual post-Socratic thinkers.

XIV

The Nineteenth Century in England and France

THE NINETEENTH CENTURY in England and France was philosophically quite different from the two hundred years before it. The period produced no great speculative thinkers of the first rank—no thinkers, that is, who rivaled Descartes and Berkeley in formulating systematic world views, or Locke and Hume in probing epistemological questions. It was not a time when men were seeking to become "spectators of all time and all existence." It was, rather, a time when men feared lest speculation be unprofitable, and turned instead to careful examination of limited fields of inquiry.

The more prominent English and French philosophers showed surprisingly little familiarity with the course of German philosophical developments. Coleridge and Carlyle, to be sure, reflected the influence of Kant; but the technicalities of Kantianism were hardly appropriate material for belles-lettres to exploit. Sir William Hamilton (1788–1856), a Scotchman who edited Reid's writings, tried to combine certain ideas he took over from Kant with those he retained from Reid. He maintained a position which he summed up in the phrase "to think is to condition." He held with Reid that in our perceptual experience we are in contact with objects which are real apart from our observations of them, and he held with Kant that we subject these objects to conditions which make our experience of them relative to our ways of observing and conceiving. He therefore taught that metaphysics (that is, knowledge of the objective nature of reality or the unconditioned) is impossible and spoke of human knowledge as affording us only "a science of the conditioned." English thinkers of the period were even less touched by the course of German thought. Insofar as they came in contact with it, they dismissed it as unprofitable. James Mill spoke of "poor Kant," and Herbert Spencer regarded the reading of Kant as a waste of time.[1]

[1] Spencer, in his *Autobiography* (New York, D. Appleton and Company, 1904), Vol. I,

Philosophers of the nineteenth century in England and France were prone to leave to the scientists the task of informing them about the nature of the world. Scientists were indeed doing distinguished work in many fields and accumulating much important information. Philosophers respected this work and accepted with humility the instruction the scientists gave them. Whately introduced a discussion of induction and fresh illustrations from the scientists into his *Elements of Logic* in 1826, and Whewell wrote his *History of the Inductive Sciences* in 1827. These works commended scientific method both as a discipline of mind whereby erratic personal biases may be overcome and as a technique of social progress whereby something of the Baconian ambition for promoting social well-being may be realized. Philosophers generally followed the lead of Whately and Whewell. They seem often to have felt toward scientists as amateurs toward professionals. They either confined themselves to analysis of scientific *method* or (if they dealt at all with the *content* of scientific conclusions) viewed philosophy as a systematic summary of scientific knowledge.

The English and French thinkers of the period were mostly preoccupied with immediate and practical problems of current social life. The Industrial Revolution had begun and was continuing. Philosophers joined with others to describe the misery of many factory workers, the complacence of many factory owners, and the injustice of the prevailing system of distribution of profits from industry. Bentham the philosopher, as much as Charles Dickens the novelist, worked to reform cruelties in the penal code and shocking conditions in the prisons. The philosophic minds of the time were convinced that practical reforms could not be gained except under the guidance of sound theories about human motivations and political techniques and ultimate standards of moral judgment. So they busied themselves with psychology and logic, ethics and politics. They sought so to express fundamental principles in these specific fields as to direct attention to the possibility of desirable changes in the organization of society. They rejected the formulas of the French Revolution on the ground that these were both abstract and rationalistic; but they likewise deplored the post-Napoleonic trend toward reaction and dogmatic insistence upon ancient privileges and prejudices. They

p. 289, gave an account of his one contact with Kant's writings. In 1844, when he was twenty-four years old, he chanced on a copy of the *Critique of Pure Reason*. "This I commenced to read," he wrote, "but did not go far. The doctrine that Time and Space are 'nothing but' subjective forms . . . I rejected at once and absolutely; and, having done so, went no further."

wanted a change—they wanted many extensive changes—in the customary ways of life; but they were convinced that in order to obtain these changes wisely and securely they must first have a sound philosophy for their own guidance and an improved educational procedure for winning converts. Philosophy and action, they believed, ought to go hand in hand. A group of left-wing Whigs organized informally as "Philosophical Radicals" and founded the *Westminster Review* in 1824 and the *London Review* in 1835 as organs for disseminating their views. They did not indulge in sheer propaganda for partisan purposes. They emphasized, rather, the general principles of which the desired reforms would be specific applications, confidently trusting that applications would quickly ensue upon understanding of the principles. They were philosophers as well as men of action. But their concern for reform left them little time for the formulation of synoptic and inclusive visions of the world such as occurred in philosophy during the two previous centuries.

1. THE EARLY UTILITARIANS

JEREMY BENTHAM, 1748–1832, was born and died in London. He was a precocious boy, an omnivorous reader of books, a sensitive person who spent many hours quietly in his own rooms. He was graduated with a B.A. from Queen's College, Oxford, at the age of fifteen and received an M.A. three years later. He studied law, listened to lectures by Blackstone, and took chambers in Lincoln's Inn; but he had a strong distaste for the practice of law. The generosity of his father and a legacy at his father's death enabled him to devote his time to reading and writing. His early political inclinations put him on the side of the Tories, but he gradually changed his views until he became recognized as an intellectual leader of the radicals. In 1776 he published *Fragment on Government* in criticism of Blackstone. He spent some years in Russia with a brother who was in business there. In 1789 he published his greatest work, *An Introduction to the Principles of Morals and Legislation*. In 1790 he was made an honorary citizen of France. He worked for many years, though unsuccessfully, to establish an institution wherein a thousand men sentenced by the criminal courts could be trained to be useful and industrious citizens; it would be, in his own words (perhaps a bit facetious) a "mill for grinding rogues honest, and idle men industrious" (*Works,* ed. John Bowring, Vol. X, p. 226). He set himself a schedule for writing and reportedly turned out ten to fifteen folio pages a day, most of which were devoted to discussion of timely social topics. He became particularly interested in drawing up systematic codes of laws to replace the confused legislation which had grown up historically in various states. He offered his services in this connection to various heads of state (to President James Madison, among others). Other important works among his voluminous writings are *Defence of Usury* (1787), *A Table of the Springs of Action* (1815), and *Constitutional Code for the Use of All Nations and All Governments Professing Liberal Opinions* (1830).

JAMES MILL, 1773–1836, born in Forfarshire, Scotland, lived in England during his adult life and died in London. He was graduated from the University of Edinburgh in 1790, then took a divinity course for four years, was licensed to preach, but came later to consider himself an agnostic. He was befriended by Sir John Stuart, in whose train he went to London in 1802. He supported himself by journalistic writings in the fields of philosophy and economics. His great work, *History of India,* begun in 1806, was published in three volumes in 1817. He thus came to be appointed to a position in India House in 1819 and held positions of increasing responsibility in that organization for many years. In 1808 he came into close relations with Bentham and was usually recognized as the favorite in the faithful band about that master of the utilitarian school. His chief philosophical work was the two-volume *Analysis of the Phenomena of the Human Mind,* published in 1829. He wrote many articles which, because of the official nature of his position at India House, he published anonymously. Among these were a series of articles in the Supplement to the *Encyclopaedia Britannica* between 1816 and 1823.

BENTHAM AND JAMES MILL were the two philosophical leaders of the large group of Philosophical Radicals who regarded utilitarianism as a gospel to be spread abroad with loyal devotion to the common creed. Others in the group were William Allen, a Quaker agitator against slavery; Francis Place, who worked for the reform of Parliamentary elections; George Grote, the historian; John Austin, the gifted writer on principles of jurisprudence; and David Ricardo, who was persuaded by James Mill to effect an organization of his economic views in what then became his *Principles of Political Economy and Taxa-*

tion (1817). Not since the days of the Epicureans and Stoics had a number of men of genuinely independent minds come together so consciously and so zealously to defend a common philosophical thesis as a remedy for the ills of the times.

Bentham rejected with scorn many of the shibboleths current in the moral and political writings of his English and Scotch predecessors. The appeal to men's "moral sense" he deemed a covert means of maintaining uncriticized prejudices, for men can always be trained, he supposed, conscientiously to cherish any doctrines their teachers choose to fasten upon them. The resort of the Scotch school to "the principles of common sense" he regarded as a confusion of the *mores* of the time with scientifically ascertained conclusions. The Lockian ideas of social contract and natural rights and natural laws he considered to be unwarranted and *a priori* assumptions of tenets which had no empirical justification; and he referred to the American Declaration of Independence as "a hodge-podge of confusion and absurdity." [2] He derided the principles of English common law as a tangle of inconsistent notions, the main value of which was to afford large fees to avaricious lawyers. The teachings of divines about the eternal fitness of things or honor or character he condemned as a use of words with vague emotional associations but no intellectual content.

In the place of any and all these shibboleths he desired to put one clear definition of the standard of right conduct. This he first called the principle of utility and, later, the greatest happiness principle. The school of thought he founded got its name from the earlier term, and has always been known as utilitarianism. Bentham expressed the principle as follows.[3]

By the principle of utility is meant that principle which approves or disapproves of every action whatsoever, according to the tendency which it appears to have to augment or diminish the happiness of the party whose interest is in question: or, what is the same thing in other words, to promote or to oppose that happiness. I say of every action whatsoever; and therefore not only of every action of a private individual, but of every measure of government.

And happiness and unhappiness, Bentham went on to insist, mean exactly the same as pleasures and pains respectively. Happiness is a collective term for many pleasures and comparative freedom from

[2] From his letter to John Bowring, dated Jan. 30, 1827. See *Works*, ed. Bowring, Vol. X, p. 63.
[3] *Principles of Morals and Legislation*, chap. 1, sec. 2.

attendant pains; unhappiness is a collective term for many states of consciousness among which pains predominate.

Bentham offered no proof of the principle of utility. He considered the principle to be obvious, even though he had listed many opposed positions which others had misguidedly taken. He said that proof of the principle is as impossible as it is unnecessary, on the ground that what is used to prove everything else cannot itself be proved. In his earliest work he had already written that Hume had demonstrated the principle "with the strongest force of evidence," [4] but he nowhere told what that evidence is. He did not even take account of the fact that the principle of utility was for Hume a subsidiary rather than the basic moral principle and that Hume employed it only to guide his choice of means to ends which he deemed good by the more ultimate standard of our moral sentiments.[5] He merely reported that upon reading a section of Book III of Hume's *Treatise* he felt as if scales fell from his eyes.

THE HEDONISTIC CALCULUS

Pleasures, Bentham pointed out, come from many different sources. There are pleasures of sense, wealth, skill, benevolence, malevolence, and so forth. No pleasure is in itself bad; every pleasure is in itself good. But in the complex affairs of human living pleasures and pains come, not singly or alone, but in contexts of causal interrelationships. Reason, therefore, is requisite to guide us in our selection of the pleasures which add up to the greatest happiness and keep us as free as possible from accompanying pains.

Consequently, as Bentham proceeded to say, utilitarians need a calculus by which to measure the precise pleasure value and pain value of various courses of conduct. Bentham wanted government policies and social procedures to be determined with the same scientific exactitude with which the motions and speeds of bodies are measured. So he developed what has come to be called his hedonistic calculus. The value of every pleasure and every pain can properly be estimated only through considering the pleasure or pain in the light of seven distinct considerations. These considerations are the intensity of the pleasure or pain, its duration, its certainty of occurrence, its propinquity, its fecundity or its chance of being followed by sensations of the same kind, its purity or its chance of not being followed by sensations of the opposite kind, and its extent or its hedonic qual-

---

[4] *Fragment on Government*, chap. 1, sec. 36, n.
[5] See discussion of Hume's ethics, above, p. 346.

ity in the experience of every person who is affected by it. Different persons are differently affected by the same thing; one man's meat is another man's poison, or there is a bias of sensibility which makes any stimulus (for example, music or wine or a sunset) have a specific hedonic value for one person and not perhaps for others. Every pleasure or pain, therefore, ought to be measured on the basis of the first six considerations in connection with each person who can be known to be affected in any way by the action which produces the pleasure or pain. There is not time to be so meticulous in the case of all pleasure-producing and pain-producing actions, and men, in many cases, must be content with the vague but more or less reliable beliefs which experience has gradually built up among mankind. But when there is sufficient time—when, for example, some momentous policy of government is under debate—the hedonistic calculus is the only competent means for bringing debate to a sound conclusion.

Bentham was more concerned with problems of legislation, the codification of law, prison reform and penology, and public administration than he was with the private actions of individuals. So were his earlier followers like James Mill. This fact might justify to some extent the confidence he had in his hedonistic calculus. It also led to two other consequences which he betrays in his thinking.

One of these consequences is that he dismissed the motivations of action from the realm of ethical consideration. The actual outcome of our actions, he professed to believe, is the only matter with which a moralist is entitled to be concerned. Certain motives, to be sure, are commonly praised as noble, and others are condemned as base. But praise and condemnation alike are irrelevant, except to the extent that experience indicates the normal tendency of the former motives to produce pleasures and of the latter motives to eventuate in pains. "There is no such thing," wrote Bentham,[6] "as any sort of motive that is in itself a bad one." Any motive whatsoever may in some circumstances produce more pleasure than pain and, likewise, may in other circumstances produce more pain than pleasure. Motives, therefore, from the point of view of him who accepts the hedonistic calculus, are not in themselves of any particular moral significance. The hedonic result of conduct, not the motivation of conduct, is the important thing for utilitarians to consider in their scientific determinations of right and wrong.

The other consequence of Bentham's attention to public rather than private morality is that he came increasingly to consider human

[6] *Principles of Morals and Legislation,* chap. 10, sec. 10.

beings as so many units for the legislator and administrator to manipulate. Men seemed to him to be, as his critics have sometimes put
it, so many chessmen to be moved about by superior authorities in
the social system. Men always do act, Bentham was prone to say
(though occasionally departing from this position), from the idea of
future pleasures to be gained through their acts. Legislators and administrators, in that case, can so fix pleasures and pains to certain
courses of action as to promote or discourage men in those courses.
The ultimate sanction of morality is physical, to be sure; for nature
is a system of forces which operate to bring certain pleasures to men
who act in one way and pain to those who act in another way. But
the legislators and administrators who control vast masses of men,
though inevitably limited by the way in which the physical sanctions
of nature rigorously determine many of the hedonic effects of human
behavior, may yet in their wisdom create a further subsidiary sanction of considerable importance. Through civilly controlled rewards
and punishments they may make some types of conduct desirable and
other types undesirable. The political sanction, though it can never
supersede the physical, may thus be of importance in influencing the
direction in which society will develop.[7]

ASSOCIATIONIST PSYCHOLOGY

Utilitarians generally were hopeful of accomplishing the reforms
they advocated. They entertained this hope because they believed
that they, almost alone among the political groups of their day, understood how to manipulate human nature scientifically. Utilitarianism
as a moral theory went hand in hand with a certain psychological interpretation of human nature.

James Mill's *Analysis of the Phenomena of the Human Mind* is
the most ample expression of the psychology which was common to
some extent among all the early utilitarians. James Mill acknowledged dependence upon certain predecessors—Hume and Hartley in
England, Condillac and Helvétius in France. But he carried out more
extremely—one may say more ruthlessly—the theory of association-
ism which in the other writers had been expressed more moderately.

According to James Mill, psychology can become as accurate and
as fruitful a science as is physics. Physics gained its final form when

---

[7] In addition to the physical and political sanctions Bentham listed also the popular
and religious sanctions. The former is concerned with the pleasures and pains public opinion may bestow or inflict, and the latter with the pleasures and pains which ensue by
divine edict. Bentham found the former too uncontrollable to be of service to his ends.
And he came progressively, as he grew older, to deem the latter purely fanciful.

physicists realized they must begin with the ultimate elements of body, namely, the atoms, and must then show how everything ensued according to the laws which describe the manner in which the atoms are arranged in clusters (for example, Galileo's laws of motion and Newton's law of gravitation). Psychology, similarly, ought to begin with its simplest elements, the sensations or feelings, and the ideas which are copies of these original feelings; then it ought to trace the development of all other mental phenomena through the laws of association which describe the manner in which the original elements combine.

There are two types of sequence among mental phenomena, according to James Mill. (1) There is a kind of sequence which occurs in all minds alike as the result of the natural constitution of minds. For example, an idea naturally follows the sensation of which it is a copy; and certain specific actions naturally follow upon certain specific sensations and ideas. A desire is an idea of a pleasant sensation which may be enjoyed and leads naturally to the act whereby the pleasant sensation may be brought to pass. (2) There is also a kind of sequence which will vary from one mind to another, depending upon the kind of experiences the different minds have chanced to have. This kind of sequence is the result of the fundamental law of psychology, the law of association. All association, James Mill maintained, is association by contiguity in time or in place. Association by contiguity in time reflects the successive order in experience; association by contiguity in place reflects the synchronous order. The strength of a particular instance of association will vary with the frequency with which a certain order has occurred and also with the vividness of the associated sensations and feelings. Will differs from simple natural desire in that in the case of will the idea of a certain act and the idea of a certain pleasure (which ideas may not involve any natural sequence) have come through association to be indissolvably tied together.

The natural kind of sequence, James Mill recognized, is fixed in the constitution of the human mind. It cannot be changed. But the kind of sequence which depends upon association by contiguity can be broken and can in turn be created, provided that proper arrangements are established to destroy old associations or to produce new associations. Whoever best understands the technique of controlling the associations in men's minds will thus gain the power of determining the course of men's wills and, hence, of men's resolute actions.

It was in his essay on government (contributed to the Supplement of the *Encyclopaedia Britannica* a few years before his *Analysis* was finished) that James Mill made clear the political and social bearings of the associationist psychology he sponsored. The best form of government, he there said, can hardly be learned from the instruction of experience, because experience on this point is full of confusions and seeming contradictions. The best form of government, rather, can be deduced from the principles of psychology.[8] The study of human nature enables us to divide all pleasures and pains into two classes: those which a man brings to pass for himself through his own efforts and those which a man experiences as the result of the effects upon him of others' actions. Governments have no proper business to interfere with the former class of pleasures and pains. Every man supposedly is the best judge of what he wants to enjoy and what he wishes to avoid, and he ought to be left to his own guidance in all such individual matters. Governments do, however, have the right and the duty to increase to the utmost the pleasures men derive from one another and to prevent, so far as possible, the pains men so detive. The less government we have, the better off we would be, if only it were true (as unfortunately it is not) that each of us was an agent who produced all the pleasures and pains he experienced in himself. Government is needed because of our mutual involvement in one another's pursuit of pleasures and pains. And when that needed government is in the hands of men who understand the principles of associationist psychology, vast improvement will occur in human civilization.

2. COMTE

Auguste Comte, 1798–1857, was born in Montpellier and died in Paris. In 1814 he began studying at the Ecole Polytechnique and gained admiration and even reverence for the sciences. Though his parents were Catholics and royalists, he became a secularist and republican. In 1816 the Ecole was closed by the government because of its alleged radicalism. Comte continued his study of the sciences. He was for some years intimate with the socialist leader Saint-Simon, but broke with him in 1822 and thereafter refused ungenerously to acknowledge any indebtedness. In 1826 he announced a course of public lectures which were so

---

[8] It was statements like this one which led Macaulay to speak of James Mill's philosophy as "sophisms . . . disguised with the externals of demonstrations."

acclaimed that he continued for many years to give such courses, often without receiving fees for his labors. He supported himself scantily by serving as examiner at the Ecole. But at times he appealed to John Stuart Mill and other English defenders of his views for financial aid; and he was made beneficiary of income from a fund raised by French colleagues and disciples. In 1845 he was a close friend of a Madame de Vaux who died the following year. This friendship is supposed to have been the means of making him aware of the importance of the play of the emotions in human affairs. His *Course of Positive Philosophy* appeared in six volumes between 1830 and 1842, and his *System of Positive Polity* in four volumes between 1851 and 1854. In 1848 he founded the Positive Society, in connection with which he developed the cult of the Religion of Humanity.

COMTE GAINED from Saint-Simon a belief in the possibility of steady progress in human civilization, and from his study of the sciences he acquired an almost religious respect for the precision and certainty of scientific knowledge. These two strands in his thinking he combined in a point of view which he named positivism. The term *positivism* gains its meaning from Comte's work. Negatively, he repudiated prior philosophies, English as well as German, because their speculations, going beyond the limits of empirical verification, were meaningless. Constructively, he expounded a system of the sciences, showing their interconnections and adding to those already existing the new science of sociology, which claimed to extend the methods of science to moral and political and religious problems. Positivism, Comte believed, would place philosophy on the same firm intellectual foundations on which the sciences rested.

In reflecting upon the intellectual development of mankind, Comte believed that he discerned a pattern which characterized all fields of investigation alike. This pattern he described in what he called the law of the three stages. According to this law men pass through three distinguishable stages in their thinking. These stages he called the theological, the metaphysical, and the scientific or positive. In the theological stage men explain the vast and largely unknown world in terms of the one thing they know at first hand, namely, in terms of their own passions and emotions. They suppose that the forces of nature are kindly or angry or otherwise animated by personal feelings. They treat the objective as akin to the subjective. They thus fill the world with imaginary or fictitious beings for the existence of which they have no evidence. In the next or metaphysical stage men abandon the resort to personalized agencies but still appeal to entities other than the facts of experience. They suppose they give an explanation of a thing when they do no more than classify the thing by applying to it an abstract term. They talk of essences and substances and attributes and powers. But they use these terms, which, properly understood, refer abstractly to selected aspects of the concrete things, as if the terms designated transempirical forces beyond the phenomenal world and causally productive of the phenomenal world. Then in the third or scientific stage men realize the folly of trying to go beyond the phenomena of experience. They accept these phenomena as the positive data, and they investigate, not some mysterious something upon which these phenomena supposedly depend, but the order, the sequence, and the correlation of these phenomena with one another. They thus come to a formulation of laws of coexistence and succession among events. But they regard the laws, not as causal forces presiding over events, but as generalized statements about groups of similar facts. They recognize that laws are related to phenomena as a general fact is related to a considerable number of given concrete facts. They remain intellectually within the realm of experience, importing no pseudo principles of explanation, yet making experience intelligible by bringing to light the dependable connections among its myriad specific facts.

Comte did not intend to suggest that human civilization moved from stage to stage all at once. Rather, it moves forward in one field of investigation while remaining stationary in others. Thus all three stages of development may be coexistent in a given society at a given time, one stage in one aspect of that society's accepted ideas and the other stages in other aspects. Indeed, just that kind of overlapping of the three stages Comte believed to characterize European civilization of his own generation. Men had advanced to the scientific stage, he believed, in their thinking about the solar system. But they had remained in the metaphysical stage when in their psychology they speak of a substantial soul or self which possesses conscious states and performs mental acts. And they are even in the theological stage insofar as they preserve beliefs about the divine origin and government of the universe. Sophistication in one field and naïveté in another field often coexist in a society and in the attitudes of individual men.

Comte, of course, wished to promote scientific or positive attitudes in those areas of thinking where men are still most retarded. He supposed that such areas were the moral, political, and religious concerns of mankind. Problems of morality and politics and religion lie, he maintained, in the field of sociology, and sociology is, and should be expected to be, the last of the sciences to reach mature development. For the sciences fall into a natural sequence because of the manner in which they are related to one another. Their natural order is mathematics, astronomy, physics, chemistry, biology, and sociology, each of which presupposes all those which precede it in the list and is not, in turn, presumed by any of them. Sociology, Comte held, was just coming into existence as the result of his own labors in the field.

One of the chief problems of morality, Comte believed, is to find ways to make the altruistic feelings of men (which are naturally weak) supplant or control the egoistic feelings (which are naturally strong). In his early writings Comte thought that this end could be accomplished by proper instruction concerning the dependence of every human individual upon the society to which he belonged. Humanity, he pointed out, is like a vast organism. The individual owes his language, his customs, his means of livelihood, his ideals, to the group life within which he is nurtured. Therefore, to the extent that an individual understands his indebtedness to society he will gain an orientation of his activities, Comte hoped, in the direction of public service and the common welfare. But as time went on, especially after the friendship he briefly enjoyed with Madame de Vaux, Comte came to recognize that he could not so confidently trust the individual's powers of reason to direct aright the activities in which the individual expresses his feelings. Men, he decided, are not sufficiently rational to be made altruistic through instruction and the increase of understanding of the facts of social interdependence. The problem of moral training and transformation of egoistic human nature requires a discipline of the feelings or affections. And this training, he became convinced, can be affected only through a carefully planned religious life to which all men, especially in their formative years, will be subjected. He called the new religious system he created for the proper moral training of human affections by the name of the Religion of Humanity.

The Religion of Humanity, as he conceived it, is a religion which in its ideas and its practices is harmonious with the scientific or positive stage of human development. It sponsors no beliefs concerning theological doctrines or metaphysical principles. It is religion in the sense that it is a means to transform human nature into a nobler product than human nature originally is. It aims to create in its adherents new emotions of unselfish devotion to altruistic ends, to bring men's feelings into harmony with the most advanced scientific interpretation of the needs of society, and to promote the unity of all individuals in the pursuit of the common good. Comte modeled the institutions of the Religion of Humanity, at least in many respects, upon the practices of the Catholic Church.[9] He promoted a calendar in which many holy days are named for persons who seemed to him to have been noble servants of mankind, and he organized services on those special days in order to give solemn recognition of the characters of these noble servants and their contribution to human welfare. He devised a system of nine sacraments through participation in which men would be induced solemnly to consecrate their wills to altruistic ends. He selected certain documents from world literature which he considered worthy of inclusion in a positivistic library for educational purposes.

As the result of Comte's leadership Positivist societies were organized in London and other cities. These flourished for a time and have continued to have some degree of influence. Many of Comte's critics, however, regarded the ceremonies of the Religion of Humanity as bizarre. Some who had gladly followed the positivistic teaching of Comte's earlier years deplored what they considered the fantastic trend of his later years. John Stuart Mill, for example, wrote *Auguste Comte and Positivism* in 1865, in the first part of which he gave a favorable interpretation of positivism, and in the second part of which he condemned the extravagance of the organized Religion of Humanity.[10] The more permanent parts of Comte's influence have proved to be his creation of the science of sociology and the conception of a positivistic philosophy. In various forms, which are all similar to Comte's position, positivism has been one of the philosophical traditions of the last hundred years.

3. JOHN STUART MILL

JOHN STUART MILL, 1806–1873, was born in London and died in Avignon, France. He was educated by his father in a strict manner which he later described as "a course of Benthamism." [11] He began the study of Greek at the age

---

[9] T. H. Huxley called the Religion of Humanity "Catholicism without Christianity."

[10] He even spoke of the "melancholy decadence of a great intellect." See *Auguste Comte and Positivism* (London, Truebner, 1865), p. 199.

[11] *Autobiography* (London, Longmans, Green, Reader, and Dyer, 1873), p. 64. His father, James Mill, was an orthodox devotee of Bentham's ideas.

of three. He read historical works and many of the classics at an early age. When he was twenty years old, he experienced a period of depression, which he himself attributed to excessive emphasis on development of intellect and a consequent neglect of the emotions. "The cloud gradually drew off," he reported.[12] But he had become convinced that attention to outward results of conduct ought to be balanced by a "cultivation of the feelings," such as could best be gained through poetry and art. He expressed himself in ways so unlike orthodox utilitarian words that Carlyle hailed him as "a new mystic." In 1838 he called Bentham and Coleridge "the two great seminal minds of England in their age." [13] His philosophical position remained, he believed, in the utilitarian tradition; but he made many concessions to the opponents of utilitarianism in psychology, logic, and ethics. As early as 1823 he had, through his father's influence, obtained a minor position with the East India Company, and he held positions of increasing importance with that company until the company was dissolved in 1858. He had a long love affair with a Mrs. Harriet Taylor and married her after her first husband's death. He attributed to her many of the ideas he developed in his later works. She probably did make him less extremely individualistic than the orthodox utilitarians and more sympathetic with socialistic plans for the betterment of society. In 1858 he retired to Avignon, France. He returned to England to run for Parliament in 1865 and was elected a member of the House of Commons. But he was not re-elected and again retired to Avignon, where he spent the rest of his life. Among his many writings are *A System of Logic*, 1843, which received many revisions until the eighth edition appeared in 1872; *Principles of Political Economy*, 1848; *Of Liberty*, 1859; *Considerations on Representative Government*, 1861; *Utilitarianism*, 1863; *Examination of Sir William Hamilton's Philosophy*, 1865; *Auguste Comte and Positivism*, 1865; *Autobiography*, 1873; *Three Essays on Religion*, 1874. Many of his essays are gathered together in his *Dissertations and Discussions*, Vols. I and II in 1859, Vol. III in 1867, and Vol. IV in 1875.

12 *Ibid.*, p. 141.
13 "Bentham," *Dissertations and Discussions* (London, John W. Parker and Son, 1859), Vol. I, p. 331. This essay had previously been published in the *London and Westminster Review* (August, 1838).

JOHN STUART MILL's *Logic* is one of the great books of the nineteenth century. Its reputation in its own day and ever since is primarily due to its clear formulation of what Mill called the five canons of inductive proof. Mill was not the first logician to describe the methods of inductive inquiry. Francis Bacon, for example, had spoken of the tables of presence and absence and degrees, and David Hume had drawn up rules which improved upon Bacon's statement.[14] But Mill's language in his definition of his five canons is a model of meticulous clarity; it has been repeated, more or less *verbatim*, in many textbooks on logic during the hundred years and more since it first appeared.

Logic is not primarily concerned, Mill maintained against what he considered the Aristotelian tradition in logic, with formal relations among terms and propositions in deductive processes like immediate inference and the syllogism. Deductive reasoning has, to be sure, a legitimate place in logic and plays a role in scientific method. So Mill gave an analysis of this branch of logic, calling it "the logic of consistency." This branch of logic is useful in helping a thinker to organize his knowledge, once he has gained the knowledge, and to build this knowledge into the structure of a consistent system. But there is much more to logic than formal logic. Logic, Mill said, is "the science of the operations of the understanding which are subservient to the estimation of evidence."[15] Its prime concern is to promote the discovery of new truth. One can never discover a single new particular matter of fact by resort to deductive procedures. One may resort to deductive procedures to develop the formal implications of an already accepted generalization. But one ought always to regard these implications as tentative hypotheses to guide further inquiry until and unless they are verified by evidence in fresh investigations. The integral processes of human thinking begin and end in observations of particular facts, so that generalizations are virtually logical devices for helping the mind to move profitably from particulars already observed to further particulars which will have evidential value. Mill therefore devoted the bulk of his *Logic* to describing inductive methods and placed deductive reasoning in a subsidiary position within the course of experimental thinking.

As his logical system developed and led on into a general theory of knowledge, Mill became involved in some difficulties. Not only did he

---

14 For Bacon's tables, see above, pp. 271–272. For Hume's rules, see *A Treatise of Human Nature*, Bk. I, Pt. 3, sec. 15. For Mill's canons, see his *Logic*, Bk. III, chap. 8.

15 *Logic*, Introduction, sec. 7.

not surmount all these difficulties but he seems in some cases to have been unaware that the difficulties existed. The difficulties resulted from Mill's allegiance to two disparate intellectual influences. On the one hand, he sought to describe the procedures he found scientists and other thinkers about him to be using in their more successful work; and on the other hand, he remained faithful to the empirical philosophical traditions as these had been instilled in him by the firm educational training he received from his father. He made corrections in his father's theories when, in editing his father's *Analysis of the Phenomena of the Human Mind* in 1869, he deemed corrections requisite. But he retained more presuppositions than he was aware of from the psychological and epistemological theories of his father and from the traditions of empiricism in Locke and Berkeley and Hume as his father had led him to interpret these classic authors.

One illustration of such an unresolved difficulty in Mill's logical writings may be summed up here. On the one hand, Mill insisted that the function of logic is to enable us to get beyond the casual and subjective associations of our limited experiences and to ascertain the objective order of "the course of nature." [16] Our experience may be a chaos of random feelings and irrelevant events; it may obscure rather than disclose the order, or the many types of order, which prevails among the things and events of the natural world. We cannot indeed appeal to anything beyond experience. But we can appeal from limited personal experience to a broad and instructive experience. We ought not to accept psychological plausibility for logical assurance. We cannot trust a feeling, even though it be vivid, or a belief, even though it be strong. We need evidence. And an experience can be called evidence only if it has logical significance. Mill gave his definition of evidence. "Evidence," he wrote, "is not that which the mind does or must yield to, but that which it ought to yield to, namely, that, by yielding to which its belief is kept conformable to fact." [17] But he did not follow up this definition by indicating how one may concretely determine the evidential value of an experience.

On the other hand, however, Mill continued to accept his father's theory that all the facts of experience are "feelings or states of consciousness." We begin, he thought, with simple conscious elements. He would always take these simple elements as evidence. He even suggested in one passage that if we could (as he thought we cannot)

[16] This phrase, quoted here from *Logic*, Bk. III, chap. 4, sec. 1, appears also in many other places in the book.
[17] *Logic*, Bk. III, chap. 21, sec. 1.

get back to the first impressions in the consciousness of an infant, we should have elements which would be free from the contamination of later accretions and associations and so would be of prime evidential value.[18] But this psychological innocence is hard to recover. The original simple elements, he continued, come to be bound together by the laws of association into stable groups or "things," even into what are, psychologically considered, inseparable wholes. We have no facts except mental facts. Matter, Mill said in a famous phrase, is "but a permanent possibility of sensation." [19] Matter, he meant, is not an actuality beyond experience which contains the possibility of producing future sensations in us; rather, it is a name for the possible sensations we may come to have or can conceive ourselves or other persons to have in certain eventualities. There is in this case no such thing as an objective order in contrast to a subjective order of experience. There is no such thing as the course of nature in contrast to the successions of our own and other people's mental facts. There are but the poor associations of limited experience in contrast to better associations of broader experience. All the groupings of feelings by the laws of association would have the same origin; fancies and the inductive generalizations of science alike would be results of the same laws of association. For if all facts are feelings or mental facts, no one fact would have evidential value concerning any order except the order among the feelings. All sequences and all correlations would be among the feelings, though some sequences might be said to be unusual and others more normal.[20]

Mill's theory of induction reflects the difficulty discussed in the preceding paragraph. When Mill dealt with logic from the background of associational psychology, he made the worth of an induction depend on the number of instances in favor of a certain way of connecting phenomena. He even regarded the ideal induction as an exhaustive enumeration of all possible relevant sequences, though he recognized reluctantly that complete enumeration is usually impossible in practice. When, however, he dealt with logic as analysis

[18] *An Examination of Sir William Hamilton's Philosophy* (London, Longmans, Green, Longmans, Roberts and Green, 1865), p. 147.

[19] *Ibid.*, p. 200.

[20] Mill's position on this point has been compared by some critics, and justly, with a truncated Berkeleyanism. If one espoused Berkeley's theory that the only realities (other than minds) are ideas and, at the same time, denied the existence of God, one would drift into Mill's quandary. A denial of the existence of God would deprive an otherwise Berkeleyan thinker of the means Berkeley himself had for distinguishing between those ideas which constitute "the mighty frame of the world" and other ideas which occur in merely private minds of individual persons.

of the objective order of nature, he made the worth of an induction depend on the manner in which crucial instances of a phenomenon are selected for special consideration. He even acknowledged that a single instance, handled with experimental skill, may at times "be sufficient for a complete induction." [21] But he hurried on honestly to confess that neither "the wisest of the ancients" nor (by implication) he himself could account for the strange way in which a single instance may prove of more logical worth than "myriads of concurring instances." Certainly no one could account for the evidential significance of a single instance as long as he operated on the basis of associational psychology and the subjectivistic premises of classical empiricism.

What Mill was trying to do in his inductive logic was to find a way of distinguishing between *post hoc* and *propter hoc,* that is, between a subjective psychological sequence and an objective natural sequence. He turned to a discussion of the law of causality as a means of effecting this end. But the kind of account he gave of the law of causality prevented him from accomplishing his end. He was eager to insist that the idea of causality is not imported rationalistically into our analysis of experience. He therefore argued that the law of causality is a generalization from experience. And it is a generalization which, far from preceding and guiding other generalizations, is a final and very abstract generalization. The law of causality, he wrote, is the principle that "the invariable antecedent is termed the cause; the invariable consequent, the effect." [22] We get various other generalizations first, and then we make a further generalization concerning the nature of those prior generalizations. The law of causality is thus an end product of the operation of the psychological law of association, so that *propter hoc* turns out to be nothing more than *post hoc* after all. The proffered law thus fails to give a technique for getting beyond subjective associations to an analysis of "the course of nature." It is rather a faith, empirically indicated but never verified, that experience, made sufficiently ample, will prove more uniform in its sequences than actually human experiences are in their occurrence in individual persons.[23]

[21] *Logic,* Bk. III, chap. 3, sec. 3.

[22] *Logic,* Bk. III, chap. 5, sec. 2.

[23] Mill's *Logic* made his difficulty about causality so clear that many empiricists since his time have been concerned with belief in uniformity of nature as the central "problem of induction." Until empiricists came to regard experience as something other than a succession of "feelings and states of consciousness," they had no epistemology to justify them in taking experimental work to be an analysis of an objective order of nature. Cf. below, the treatment of John Dewey's philosophy, p. 499.

MILL'S ETHICS

Mill's ethical theory, like his theory of logic, is the product of a mind that was trying to harmonize ideas he had been taught to accept as the fundamental principles of his school of thought and certain critical principles he was led to formulate in the light of his own moral experiences. Mill always regarded himself as deeply loyal to Bentham's utilitarian position. But he became sensitively aware of certain values which he thought Bentham had not merely ignored but even, at times, explicitly denied. He believed that he could correct a certain narrowness in Bentham's views without repudiating Bentham's essential principles. More orthodox Benthamites accused him of abandoning utilitarianism, and the opponents of Benthamism thought his reservations were inadequate. In any case, his essay entitled *Utilitarianism* is so eloquent a writing that it has come to be regarded, by both its defenders and its opponents, as a definitive statement of the utilitarian school.

Mill's statement of the fundamental principle of his ethical system is as follows.[24]

The creed which accepts as the foundation of morals, Utility, or the Greatest Happiness Principle, holds that actions are right in proportion as they tend to promote happiness, wrong as they tend to produce the reverse of happiness. By happiness is intended pleasure, and the absence of pain; by unhappiness, pain, and the privation of pleasure.

So far the voice of Bentham. But Mill at once proceeded to specify that pleasures (and similarly pains) cannot be evaluated solely on the basis of quantity. He thus repudiated the hedonistic calculus. Pleasures (and, similarly, pains) are not homogeneous in quality and therefore cannot be handled quantitatively. Pleasures differ from one another *in kind*. Human beings have vast capacities for enjoying pleasures of many kinds. They have animal appetites, to be sure, but they also have higher faculties. And the pleasures derived from exercise of the higher faculties are so disparate from pleasures derived from gratification of animal appetites that no good judge would hesitate to pronounce in favor of the former.

It is quite compatible with the principle of utility to recognize the fact, that some *kinds* of pleasure are more desirable and more valuable than others. It would be absurd that while, in estimating all other things, quality is considered as well as quantity, the estimation of pleasures should be supposed to depend on quantity alone.[25]

[24] *Utilitarianism,* chap. 2, par. 2.
[25] *Utilitarianism,* chap. 2, par. 4.

Here is the voice of Mill in what he took to be gentle correction of Bentham.

Mill feared that the hedonistic principle would repel many persons —all those persons, in fact, who thought of pleasures in connection with gratification of the senses. By emphasizing quality of pleasures he hoped to make hedonism more acceptable to people of refinement and good breeding. Few human beings, he thought, would consent to live a sheerly animal existence, even if thereby they had intense pleasures. They would not be willing to play the role of a fool, a dunce, or a rascal, even if they thus had uninterrupted pleasures. They are beings of greater sensitivities than are other animals, and they are ashamed to give over their lives to what would satisfy those other animals. And so Mill came to the conclusion he expressed in the following famous words.[26]

It is better to be a human being dissatisfied than a pig satisfied; better to be Socrates dissatisfied than a fool satisfied. And if the fool, or the pig, are of a different opinion, it is because they only know their own side of the question. The other party to the comparison knows both sides.

When Mill turned to explain by what criterion we may determine the pleasures of higher quality, he did not work out a consistent position. He maintained in a closing section of his *Logic* that the cultivation of a noble will is as justifiable an end for men to pursue as ever could be the promotion of happiness. But he there went on at once to add that nobility of will or character is to be estimated by reference to the happiness which over a considerable time will abundantly result from the many actions of this kind of character.[27] But this earlier and somewhat equivocal solution of his difficulty did not satisfy him. In the *Utilitarianism,* where he gave his most mature and last statement of his position, he asserted only that the test of quality is the preference which "competent judges" or people with "capacity for the nobler feelings" uniformly exhibit. He does not seem to have realized that in conceding the importance of qualitative distinctions among pleasures, he was yielding an important point to the advocates of reliance upon moral sentiments. Bentham had thundered against just this position, denouncing it as a piece of unwarranted subjectivity and as an obstacle to practical reforms in social life. In rejecting the sufficiency of the hedonistic calculus, Mill virtually rejected hedonism. For pleasure ceases to be a standard of value

26 *Utilitarianism,* chap. 2, par. 6.

27 *Logic,* Bk. VI, chap. 12, sec. 7. This passage was not in the first edition of the *Logic.* It was added in the third edition in 1850.

if pleasures have to be judged in the light of some quality or qualities these pleasures have or have not. This quality, or these qualities, would become the standard by which pleasures and, hence, human conduct are to be judged. Mill never defined the quality which makes a pleasure a noble pleasure. He left the matter to the taste or the moral sensitivity of good judges, and he did not attempt to tell how we may make ourselves good judges or recognize good judges when we encounter them.

Mill included in his *Utilitarianism* a chapter entitled "Of What Sort of Proof the Principle of Utility Is Susceptible." Early in that chapter he gave two arguments which have often been quoted. They are so famous that they may be quoted again here.[28]

The only proof capable of being given that an object is visible, is that people actually see it. The only proof that a sound is audible, is that people hear it: and so of the other sources of our experience. In like manner, I apprehend, the sole evidence it is possible to produce that anything is desirable, is that people do actually desire it.

No reason can be given why the general happiness is desirable, except that each person, so far as he believes it to be attainable, desires his own happiness. This, however, being a fact, we have not only all the proof which the case admits of, but all which it is possible to require, that happiness is a good: that each person's happiness is a good to that person, and the general happiness, therefore, a good to the aggregate of all persons.

These passages have probably not been quoted so much in subsequent works on ethics as in textbooks on logic. The textbooks on logic have frequently listed them as samples of obvious logical fallacies. The first, it has often been said, is a fallacy of equivocation in language; for whereas visible means *capable* of being seen, desirable means, not *capable* of being desired, but *worthy* of being desired. The second has been quoted by the textbooks as an instance of the fallacy of composition.

MILL'S SOCIAL PHILOSOPHY

Mill's social philosophy is historically important because to a large extent it molded the thinking of liberals between 1860 and the outbreak of World War I. Here, too, as in logic and ethics, Mill meant to adhere to the Benthamite school but introduced various qualifying considerations. His essay on *Representative Government* granted much more clearly than Bentham had been willing to concede in his *Constitutional Code* that suitable political institutions cannot be

[28] *Utilitarianism*, chap. 4, par. 3.

determined abstractly from the general principles of human psychology, but also depend upon such other factors as the cultural level and the historically developed customs of a society. He also pointed out that representative government or democratic institutions did not automatically furnish safeguards against the abuse of power in the tyranny of a majority over a minority. He here virtually abandoned the contention of his *Utilitarianism* to the effect that when each man pursued his own good, all collectively would be pursuing the common good.

Most influential of Mill's social writings was his essay *On Liberty*. His central thesis is the desirability of allowing great freedom of opinion and even of action to individuals. "If a person possesses any tolerable amount of common sense and experience, his own mode of laying out his existence is the best, not because it is the best in itself, but because it is his own mode." [29] The silencing of open discussion of any topic is morally evil, partly because it fosters an assumption of infallibility in the silencers, partly because it shuts off the chance of increase in understanding moot issues. Liberty of discussion is the only social cure for "the deep slumber of a decided opinion," so that "all restraint, *qua* restraint, is an evil." [30] Mill knew by personal experience that people are not always receptive to instruction, and that they often are not even willing to listen to carefully framed ideas of their opponents. But, at least, he did believe that liberty of discussion was more likely than any form of social control or censorship to eventuate in increase of intelligence and knowledge in individuals and societies. Mill would not grant as complete liberty to men in their actions as in their opinions. But even in action he would allow a man to act freely, even if he did not act wisely, provided merely that he did not make himself "a nuisance to other people." [31] He thus followed the orthodox utilitarian supposition that the less government a society has, the better for that society. He would often even leave the exercise of restraint, where restraint is imperatively necessary, to the unorganized pressure of public opinion rather than utilize the coercion of laws and judges and police force.[32]

[29] *On Liberty* (London, John W. Parker and Son, 1859), p. 121.
[30] *Ibid.*, p. 170.
[31] *Ibid.*, p. 101.
[32] Mill did come in his later years to sympathize on many points with the socialist program of reform. But his essay *On Liberty,* his most influential work in the field of social philosophy, made no concessions of that kind.

4. SPENCER

HERBERT SPENCER, 1820–1903, was born at Derby and died in London. He was not sent to schools and had few contacts with other boys, but was educated at home by his father and an uncle. At the age of 17 he went into railway engineering and spent about ten years in that line of work. Then he supported himself for about another ten years by journalism. In 1850 he published his *Social Statics*. About 1857 he conceived the outlines of a comprehensive system of all human knowledge which he called the Synthetic Philosophy. To the execution of this grandiose project he devoted himself for forty years. He financed the project in part by subscriptions, collected mostly in England and America. He came to the United States in 1882 and gave a series of public lectures; and he was hailed by both business leaders and many intellectuals as the embodiment of enlightenment for an age of science. He worked with zeal on successive volumes of the Synthetic Philosophy, even when he was a semi-invalid and at the price of making himself almost a recluse from society. The Synthetic Philosophy, when completed in 1896, consisted of ten volumes: *First Principles,* 1862; *Principles of Biology,* 2 vols., 1864–1867; *Principles of Psychology,* 2 vols., 1870–1872; *Principles of Sociology,* 3 vols., 1876–1896; and *Principles of Ethics,* 2 vols., 1879–1893. Some of these works were revised in subsequent editions. His many other writings were amplifications of themes advanced in these ten volumes, for example, *Man versus the State,* 1894.

HERBERT SPENCER has been known for almost a hundred years as the chief exponent of what is often called the philosophy of evolution. Even Charles Darwin, referring to him in a personal letter, said of him: "I suspect that hereafter he will be looked at as by far the greatest living philosopher in England; perhaps equal to any that have lived." [33] Few critics today would concur in Darwin's tribute. But all critics are likely to agree that Spencer was the first philosopher and, perhaps, the most notable to turn the idea of evolution into the organizing principle of an all-embracing world view.

The materials which Spencer included within his embracing system came to him from many sources. Spencer was prone to insist that he

[33] *The Life and Letters of Charles Darwin* (London, 1887), Vol. III, p. 120.

was influenced only slightly by the thoughts of others and boasted that his ideas were developed from within his own mind. He did not judge altogether aright on this point; he confused independence of judgment (in which he excelled) with originality of views (in which he was not conspicuously pre-eminent). Most of his factual material was borrowed; for he was not an experimental scientist at all. His fundamental principle of evolution came to him, not from Charles Darwin in all probability, but from Lamarck.[34] He then generalized from Lamarck's position and made the principle of evolution into a general cosmic principle. He was influenced also by Sir William Hamilton's theory of the unconditioned (though he preferred to refer to the absolute as the unknowable), by Comte's positivistic attitude, and by the individualism of the social theories of the Philosophical Radicals. He quite probably could not himself have traced his indebtedness to his sources. But he was in quite a few respects a typical child of the nineteenth century and followed intellectual trends of his time. He did, to be sure, cast aside, with an indifference which approached contempt, the classics of philosophy; he explained how he refused to be bored by the works of Plato or Locke or Kant. But he absorbed current ideas easily and made them so firmly his own as to come soon to regard them as originating within his own mind. The historian ought to recognize, however, that these current ideas, when put in the context of the engulfing principle of evolution, often assume a significance they do not elsewhere have.

THE UNKNOWABLE

First Principles was the first volume of the Synthetic Philosophy to be written and published. It contains Spencer's basic conceptions. Among these, of course, is the principle of evolution which dominates the thinking of the subsequent volumes as well. Spencer's statement of this principle is well known and often quoted.[35]

Evolution is an integration of matter and concomitant dissipation of motion; during which the matter passes from an indefinite, incoherent homogeneity to a definite, coherent heterogeneity; and during which the retained motion undergoes a parallel transformation.

The principle, Spencer held, is applicable in physics, in biology, in psychology, in sociology, even in ethics. The business of philosophy,

---

[34] Not directly from Lamarck, to be sure. He was reading Lyell's *Principles of Geology*, rejected Lyell's arguments against Lamarck, and therefore concluded in favor of Lamarck. See his *Autobiography* (New York, D. Appleton and Company, 1904), Vol. I, p. 201.

[35] *First Principles*, sec. 145.

he maintained, is to arrange the materials of the many sciences systematically. Ordinary knowledge is un-unified knowledge; scientific knowledge is partially unified knowledge; philosophy is completely unified knowledge.[36] Each of the major branches of science—and Spencer named four: physics, biology, psychology, and sociology—has its own special principles and reaches its own special conclusions. But philosophy goes further. The principle of evolution is the philosophic principle which enables us to correlate the special principles of the several sciences and to reach a generalization which organizes the generalizations of those sciences. Thus philosophy brings the whole of human knowledge into a coherent whole of significantly related parts.

Human knowledge, Spencer set forth, deals with phenomena, that is, with the manner in which reality appears within our experiences. But in all of our thinking we are constantly aware of a more-than-phenomenal reality which forever eludes our explicit knowledge. Reality is represented in our thoughts rather than directly presented. We call some phenomena "outer phenomena" and explain them by reference to space and time, matter and motion and force; we call others "inner phenomena" and explain them as sensations or states of consciousness. But all these phenomena, outer and inner alike, are manifestations to us of a reality which is not exposed in our experiences and yet is constantly involved. This reality is the absolute. Or, since from the very nature of our mental processes we cannot get beyond appearances, it is the unknowable. It is an actuality in which we human beings have, and properly, an "indestructible belief," [37] but it baffles all our attempts to ascertain its intrinsic nature.

The unknowable, Spencer decided, is the concern of religion. Spencer was not a markedly religious man; his interest in religion was primarily sociological. He liked to trace the development of religion from its earliest form (which he believed to be ancestor worship) through its successive stages of animism and polytheism and monotheism to its final stage in the vague recognition of the mystery of the unknowable. Superstitions about the absolute gradually give way, he pointed out, as science and philosophy become more adequate, to a simple affirmation of an inscrutable power beyond the range of human knowledge. Religion in this sense can never be displaced by science, however developed our knowledge may become; for there will always be, as there has always been, the ultimate mystery of

[36] *First Principles,* sec. 37.
[37] *First Principles,* sec. 26.

existence. This mystery is ever approached and never solved. It cannot be solved. Science can never displace religion, because science deals with the phenomenal and relative. Nor can religion oppose science, because the concern of religion is with what lies beyond experience. Conflicts between religion and science have occurred repeatedly in history. But these conflicts have been due to failure to understand the utterly disparate realms with which religion and science are concerned. As history evolves toward its goal, the conflicts will cease. Evolution will bring eventual balance or adjustment. And science and religion will supplement each other in peaceful harmony.

THE SPECIAL SCIENCES

The various sciences, Spencer held, illustrate in their several ways the basic law of evolution. In every field there occurs during the course of evolution a constantly increasing multiformity. And concomitantly and correlatively thereto there also occurs a constantly increasing equilibrium among the diverse forms of existence. And always the goal of evolution is a state of complete adjustment or harmony.

Physics has as its basic special principle the law of the persistence of force. All the other laws of physics specify the particular manner in which force, unchanged in its total amount, manifests itself in particular and local conditions. Transformation yields to transformation in the never ceasing evolution of patterns of greater complexity. But the succession is not chaotic; it is ordered. It is ordered in such fashion that clash of force against force gives way to co-ordination of forces in balanced systems. And the vast order of the complex cosmos has as its as-yet-unreached goal the perfect equilibrium of harmonious forces.

The evolution of life, of mind, and of society, within the context of the physical cosmos, also manifests the principle of persistence of force. But life and mind and society are the subject matters of three further sciences, each of which in its turn has its basic special principle.

Biology rests upon the foundation of physics but introduces new ideas. Life, Spencer said, is a name for certain processes of interaction between organism and environment. Life obeys the law that with the greater diversification of organic forms comes greater adjustment of internal conditions to the external conditions of the environment. In the earlier stages of life struggle and destruction prevail. But as evolution continues, increased complexity of organic forms results in the elimination of certain occasions of conflict and promotes more harmonious interaction. And life will be perfect, Spencer thought he could conclude, when inner conditions are so developed that they permit entirely peaceful adjustment to the outer forces.

Psychology, as Spencer conceived it, is a branch of biology, that branch, namely, which deals specifically with the phenomena of consciousness. Consciousness is a developed form of life in which an organism has come into the possession of improved means of adjustment to outer conditions. The senses are tools of adjustment in the service of the organism. Thinking is a further and more elaborate form of adjustment, extending the area of an organism's adjustment throughout a larger area of the environment.

One of the most interesting features of Spencer's discussions in his psychology is his effort to reconcile the claims of the rationalist and the empiricist concerning the nature of human knowledge. Spencer's basic sympathies, it may be said, lie with the empiricist. All ideas, he granted, arise originally from experience. They arise from experience in the history of the race, but they do not all arise from experience in the development of the individual. In accord with the contentions of Lamarck, with whom he sided against Lyell, Spencer argued that an idea achieved by a certain organism through experience may, like other acquired characteristics, be so built into the structure of that organism that it is transmitted to the future generations. What appears from experience in the history of the race may then appear from intuition in the development of an individual. Such, Spencer said in illustration of his position, are our ideas of space and time. Thus the advocates of empiricism and of intuitionism are both, in their different ways, correct in their theories. The more complex an organism becomes in the course of evolution, the more intuitive ideas it will have. Thus the supposition of innate ideas becomes reconcilable, in Spencer's judgment, with the empirical theory of knowledge. And since the goal of evolution is always perfect adjustment and balance, the goal of psychological evolution will bring complete harmony between intuitively discerned principles and the course of experience.

In his sociology Spencer treated a society as an organism, an evolving organism. Every type of society is fitted into some place in the developing panorama of social forms. One of the leading generalizations of this sociological scheme is that society naturally evolves from military societies to industrial societies. The former is relatively homogeneous, the latter is marked by ever increasing diversities of function and, hence, by ever increasing multiformity. Societies outgrow military activities, Spencer supposed, as they become sufficiently industrial. The goal of social evolution therefore is an era of world peace, in which complete adjustment will be effected and strife will be eliminated in mutual and interdependent exchange of products.

EVOLUTION AS A MORAL CRITERION

The *Principles of Ethics* was the part of the Synthetic Philosophy in which Spencer took most interest and most pride. He here summed up the ethical implication which his use of the principle of evolution seemed to him to have throughout his review of the sciences. He expressed his conclusion in these words: "The foregoing exposition shows that the conduct to which we apply the name good, is the relatively more evolved conduct; and that bad is the name we apply to conduct which is relatively less evolved." [38]

Spencer regarded the course of evolution as furnishing us with the major criterion of moral judgment. For evolution guarantees, he thought, that life will become broader, more complete, more rich, more harmonious. But he wished to do more than to uphold his evolutionary standard. He wished also to point out that every one of the other ethical theories which philosophers have advanced will, if thought through sufficiently, turn out to coincide in practical judgments of value with his basic theory. The moral sense school, he contended, is an indirect and less articulate version of his own theory. For the moral sensitivities of cultivated men, though these sensitivities can indeed be morally trusted, are the result of ideas which men have accumulated, one by one, over the years, concerning the means whereby human development may best be promoted. In the individual person these sensitivities are intuitive, but in the race they are gained through observation of the changes which mark the rise from older levels of society to more developed levels. Similarly with the hedonism of the utilitarian school. Pleasure, Spencer insisted, ought to be thought of in its biological context. Thus viewed, it is a subjective indication of the growth of an organism in the realization of its powers and, hence, of movement in the direction of evolutionary advance. Pleasure is a useful guide in determining the relative worth of different human choices, even though the genuine norm of value is the degree to which any choice promotes evolutionary progress. [39] Similarly also with the

---

[38] Vol. I, sec. 8.

[39] Spencer objected when John Stuart Mill once referred to him as an anti-utilitarian. He esteemed Mill for his candor and generosity of judgment. But he believed he himself might be called a utilitarian, even though he made the principle of utility subsidiary to the principle of evolution.

age-old quarrel between egoism and altruism. Egoism, Spencer said, is the original or primitive nature of man. But the more evolution advances and the more complex social relations become, the more men's egoistic impulses become modified, until in the highest and most mature societies altruistic interests completely drive out all base egoism. Thus Spencer, confident of the embracing catholicity of his evolutionary views, sought to absorb the rival positions of other schools into a role of contributing to the superior wisdom of his own central principle.

In his earliest work, *Social Statics,* Spencer had taken a very much more radical position than even the Philosophical Radicals had taken. He had pushed individualism to an anarchistic extreme. He had granted to an individual the right to ignore the state, to "adopt a condition of voluntary outlawry," [40] and even to refuse to pay taxes if also he relinquished police protection. Spencer retained this attitude throughout his life; yet in his *Principles of Ethics* twenty-five years later he expressed it in a much less provocative manner. He made more clear (what, to be sure, he had indicated from the start) that his "social statics" dealt, not with the moral relations of men in the imperfect societies of our semi-evolved state, but with the "absolute ethics" of the fully evolved men in a fully evolved society. No science of ethics is possible, he reflected, insofar as one seeks to determine exactly how imperfect men ought to act in imperfect societies. Failure to realize this simple truth, he believed, had handicapped all previous framers of ethical systems, and he did not intend to add one more to their list of failures. He therefore proclaimed that he was picturing the conduct men would exhibit when the goal of evolution had been reached. The state would disappear because strife and conflict would be superseded by complete adjustment. Moral struggle between an impulse to evil and a sense of right would no longer occur because every impulse would be in accord with right. Even choice would disappear because everyone and everything would be automatically good.

When Spencer turned from his picture of the goal of evolution to a discussion of contemporary moral problems, that is, to "social dynamics," he had little to say; for contemporary moral problems, he thought, could not be treated scientifically. He could only hope that men would hasten and not retard the march of evolutionary progress. The picture of perfect men in perfect societies might at least stimulate men to conduct themselves currently in accord with the demands of the higher levels toward which evolution is tending.

40 *Social Statics,* 1st edition, chap. 19, sec. 1.

DISSOLUTION

An account of Spencer's philosophy ought to include reference to his supposition that evolution is not the whole story of either cosmic or human destinies. Spencer professed a cyclic theory. That is, he maintained that evolution continues until the greatest complexity of form and the most complete adjustment among things has been reached, that the state of evolutionary perfection will prove unstable, and that then dissolution or disintegration will occur—and all will return to its primitive homogeneous condition. Then evolution once more, then again dissolution, and so on, forever.

But in his Synthetic Philosophy the recognition of dissolution occupies an inconspicuous place, as, indeed, it probably did in Spencer's thought. The idea of dissolution may have seemed deductively requisite for the rounding out of a system of the cosmos. But Spencer was so busy urging men to help evolution to occur that he had no time to consider dissolution in detail. He acknowledged that dissolution must occur. But he remains the philosopher of evolution.

XV

The Twentieth Century in Europe

1. BERGSON

HENRI BERGSON, 1859–1941, was born and also died in Paris.
He studied at Lycée Condorcet and École Normale
Supérieure. In 1881 he began teaching, first at the Lycée
in Angers, then at the Lycée in Clermont-Ferrand, the
Collège Rollin, the Lycée Henri IV in Paris, the École
Normale Supérieure, and, finally, from 1898 on, at the
Collège de France. In 1914 he retired from teaching and
was active on a French commission to the United States
during World War I and, later, on the Commission for
Intellectual Coöperation of the League of Nations. Serious
ill health limited his activities during the last twenty years
of his life. But shortly before his death he rejected the
exemptions given him by the Pétain government at Vichy,
and he went, old and ill, to register as a Jew with the
German authorities in possession of Paris. His sympathies
in later life had come to be with the Catholic position, but
he firmly refused to change his status as a Jew during a
time when his fellow Jews were subject to persecution.
His chief writings were *Time and Free Will* (1889),
Matter and Memory (1896), *Introduction to Metaphysics*
(1903), *Creative Evolution* (1907), *The Two Sources of
Morality and Religion* (1932).

BERGSON, LIKE KANT before him, was a searching critic of the traditional forms of both rationalism and empiricism. But he opposed
the older philosophies out of a very different concern and for a very
different reason from those of Kant. Kant had wished to justify the
procedures of the physical sciences of his day and had argued that
mind has fixed and necessary ways of experiencing the world. Bergson wished to justify the longings of men for freedom from mechanism and necessity and argued that the life force (*élan vital*) is creative
of ever new personal and even cosmic lines of development. The very

title of his book *Creative Evolution* was revolutionary. Most people at the turn of the century viewed creation and evolution as alternate theories of the world. He rejected the theory of creation when creation was supposed to have been an act, or a series of acts, which occurred long ago and was finished and over. He rejected the theory of evolution when evolution was supposed to be a drive toward an inevitable and foreseeable goal. He was in his early days a semidisciple of Spencer. But his mature philosophy involved a complete abandonment of Spencer's formulas. Spencer thought of evolution as a march toward a state of adjustment of inner to outer conditions. Bergson came to think of evolution as a process by which the life force remakes outer conditions in the interest of some inner need. Evolution, as he viewed it, is a perennially creative process and moves in ever novel directions.

Bergson's first book was *The Immediate Data of Consciousness.*[1] This book is a defense of the thesis that we are aware of our conscious life in two different ways. On the one hand, we find through direct awareness that we are the pure, pulsing quality of dynamic process, moving and moving with power, now in this and now in that direction, hemmed in somewhat by the limitations of the body through which we reach out and act upon the world, but not determined in our course by the body or consisting of a mere function or consequence of the body. We are bits of vital energy. This vital energy eludes formal definition; it cannot be adequately expressed in the quantitative formulas of science. On the other hand, we come to think of ourselves in terms utilized by scientific psychology. We then view ourselves as a linear series of discrete sensations and feelings and ideas, each of which is a definite entity which can be measured in intensity and extensity; we thus seem to be dependent upon bodily states and subject to the laws which give the mechanical conditions of each momentary state of consciousness. The former way of regarding consciousness discloses the real self; the latter way substitutes for this real self a pictorial and symbolic schematism, scientifically fruitful but inadequate to "the immediate data of consciousness."

ANALYSIS AND INTUITION

In order to substantiate his position about the immediate data of consciousness Bergson was led to formulate a general theory of knowledge. This he did in his *Introduction to Metaphysics*. There are, he maintained, two different ways of knowing anything. One is the

---

[1] When this book *Essai sur les données immédiates de la conscience* was put into English, its title was given the unfortunate translation of *Time and Free Will*.

symbolic way of science. In following this way we move around a thing, observe its externalized aspects, and analyze it into parts and subparts until we have cut up the original integral thing into as small bits as we wish. This method is followed in physics (with its atoms, and so forth), in biology (with its cells, and so forth), in psychology (with its mental states, and so forth). Motion, then, is viewed as a series of points, none of which moves; and life and mind are viewed as series of static elements. The other way of knowing anything is by entering into it and identifying oneself with it, intuitively discerning the unique quality of the thing and respecting the integrity of its unified, concrete occurrence. The scientific way is often better practically because it enables us to predict, to manipulate, to classify under standard concepts. The intuitive way, however, is requisite for metaphysics because it alone enables us to grasp the unimpaired fullness of being of the individual thing.

Thus Bergson contrasted analysis with intuition, symbolic portrayal with direct understanding, practical efficiency with theoretical adequacy. No error has been so constant an obstacle to sound philosophy as the supposition that the terms into which a thing is analyzed can be regarded as giving the real nature of the thing. Analysis is always incomplete. Furthermore, analysis is often falsification, because none of the items separated out by analysis, and not even all of those items collectively, can capture the unique quality of the whole with which analysis started. Analysis, therefore, is destruction of reality and substitution of fictions for the true being of things.

Empiricists and rationalists alike, Bergson held, have commonly committed the blunder of taking the terms of analysis as substitutes for the original realities. Empiricists, particularly in psychological analysis from Locke to Hume and Spencer, began with artificial entities manufactured for various practical reasons and never recovered the genuine self with its vital energy. Rationalists, dissatisfied with the pictorial results of the empiricists' analysis, resorted to conceptual analysis and attributed real being to "the soul" or "the mind" or "the spiritual substance." But the concepts of the rationalists, as much as the analytical bits of the empiricists, lack that driving quality of process and becoming which is the genuine self. Only by intuition can the integrity of the self be recovered.

Bergson was thus led to conclude that there are no inert states, no dead things, no static entities. Everything is mobility or process. He liked the word *durée* which is commonly translated "duration." Duration is not at all like a measured extent of time such as appears in the symbol *t* of physical equations. It is the quality of the inner life of ourselves and of everything else. We sophisticated modern men become so involved in measuring things around us that ordinarily we overlook the duration in ourselves. But this duration is what philosophers ought to emphasize in order to prevent devotees of the sciences from leading themselves and others to accept the results of scientific analysis as the truth about the world. There are no things, Bergson said; there are only processes or events or becomings or durations. A "thing" is the conceptualized artifice we get when we conceive a duration as halted and try to take, as it were, a cross section of it. Philosophy, therefore, is anything but the synthesis of the sciences that Spencer took it to be. It reverses the scientific direction of analysis and deals with the qualitative wholes which analysis has not destroyed.

CREATIVE EVOLUTION

The full purport of Bergson's theories of duration and of intuition becomes clear in his striking work *Creative Evolution*. The story of the evolution of life, even the story of the development of the cosmos, can be understood as the constantly creative work of vital energy. There is no unchanging substance behind the multitude of changes in nature. The reality of everything is incessant novelty. Evolution has no predestined end. It is not bound within the limits of laws that reflect the routine of the past. There are no mere repetitions. There is unpredictability at the root of all change. This unpredictability is not merely relative to our ignorance of what things fully are. It is an absolute unpredictability due to the way in which creative energy may, at any moment, break through the forms which have already been achieved by past operations of life and may freely produce new forms which the old forms could not themselves generate. The diversity of forms of living things is a consequence of the way in which creative energy presses out irresistibly in all sorts of directions from every successive *status quo*.

In a magnificent metaphor Bergson tried to make his position clear. Suppose we have, he wrote, an enormous mass of iron filings, and suppose we also have an invisible arm which presses powerfully through the iron filings. At times the power of the invisible arm is momentarily stayed and the filings are at rest. Then the arm resumes its exercise of power and pushes again in some new direction through the filings. Men may try to explain, Bergson said, the arrangement which at some moment of rest the filings happen to exhibit. The mechanists, he pointed out, would make their explanation in terms

of laws governing the motion of the filings. The old-fashioned creationists would try to make their explanation in terms of some
over-all plan to which the filings are subservient. Both mechanists
and old-fashioned creationists make the same error: they fail to take
account of the invisible arm and its inexhaustible power. The form
of the filings at any moment of arrest symbolizes the species of life
which occur at any one time in the history of the world. The arm
symbolizes the creative impulse of vital energy. One cannot give a
sound explanation of the position of the iron filings if one omits reference to the invisible arm. Similarly, one cannot give a sound explanation of the evolution of species if one omits reference to vital
energy.

Bergson granted that Darwin's theories of struggle for existence and
survival of the fittest have some value as principles of explanation in
biology. But he deemed these theories quite insufficient because they
in no way account for the appearance of the variations among which
struggle and selection may then occur. The cause of the appearance
of the variations, he claimed, can be no other than the vital energy.
He adduced various considerations in support of this judgment, such
as the following three. (1) The fully developed eye, which gives power
of vision, did not, of course, appear all at once. It took many generations to develop. During some of these intervening generations the
rudimentary eye was a sensitive spot, so that organisms with the
variation were at some disadvantage in competing with organisms
without the variation. The rudimentary eye was a handicap rather
than an asset during this time. Yet it survived. In order to explain
why a variation like the rudimentary eye was selected for survival
while it was slowly developing into the fully formed eye, we cannot
resort to any mechanical theory. We are, rather, led to recognize the
driving force of a vital impulse making its way through the resistance
of matter, fashioning matter to satisfy its demands, and eventually
accomplishing its purpose at the end of a series of generations. (2) The
eye of the vertebrate and the eye of the pecten (a species of mollusk)
are very similar. Yet the two types of organic life have no connection
through interbreeding and evolved in quite different environmental
conditions. Again, we cannot account for the amazing facts by a
mechanistic hypothesis. We are, rather, led to accept the hypothesis
of a vital impulse with yearning to see, driving through matter and
accomplishing its purpose in more than one area of life. (3) In the
eye we are confronted with a contrast between the simple function
the eye serves (namely, the unitary act of vision) and the complex

structure of many parts, all of which in their interrelations are requisite to effect the act. Once more, the facts make the mechanistic hypothesis incredible and point to the theory of the dynamic force of a vital urge working its will upon bodily materials.

LIFE AND MATTER

Many passages in Bergson's *Creative Evolution* are composed in terms of a dualism of life and matter. Vital energy, or the life force, operates to create new organs and new species of organism. Matter is the stuff upon which this vital force operates to satisfy its cravings and to realize its will. This dualism is expressed in the metaphor of the invisible arm and the iron filings, in the contrast of function and structure in the eye, and in numerous other passages of like tone.

But Bergson did not intend to have these dualistic expressions pass for his final cosmological position. Frenchman though he was, he did not stand in the Cartesian tradition. He regarded Plotinus as much more his spiritual ancestor than anyone else. For him, as for Plotinus, matter is the limit in the externalization and deterioration of mind. Vital energy, he maintained, is ultimately the only reality. But, separated as this vital energy is in countless individual beings, it becomes arrested and, for a time at least (like the invisible arm), static or nearly so. Life degenerates into inert forms and appears as matter. Matter is the sodden and lethargic or atrophied residue from the creative impulses of former times. New life, therefore, always has the task of working upon and through the deadening legacy of its own weary past. Matter is what life becomes as life loses the dynamism of its creative vigor.

Bergson used an effective metaphor to clarify his position. The whole life of the universe is like a vessel full of steam under high pressure. Jets of this steam are constantly being thrown out. But these jets, separated out in minute drops, condense or materialize and then fall back. New jets may hold these drops up for a moment, infusing new life into them. The steam is the reservoir of vital energy, the jets are divisions of evolution, the drops are individual organisms, and each drop, in its falling back, is a material world. The metaphor, Bergson warned, must not be taken too literally, for the vessel and the jets are determined by mechanical conditions and operate necessarily, whereas life, even when life has to operate through the retarding matter of its own past, is still free and creative.

The course of change in the world, Bergson said, may be viewed as a reality making its way forward in the midst of a reality which is undoing itself. Life and matter seem like two opposed realities. Were there no matter, life would be entirely free in its creativity. Insofar as life meets the inverse movement of its own past, it has to express its creativity through matter; and matter is sheer necessity. Hence, the course of evolution seems full of retrogressions as well as of advances; it takes a sinuous path and often exhausts its energy in combating obstacles it has raised against itself. But even the matter against which life struggles is really a form of life—exhausted life, life at low ebb, but life after all.

The reservoir of vital energy Bergson called God. God, then, is the source of all life. God is creative, free, capable of endless novelty of expression. God's creation is never complete; it did not occur once and for all, it continues without cessation, and its outcomes are not in any way constrained by the past course of creation and the present state of life and matter.

TWO TYPES OF MORALITY

Bergson's last book was *The Two Sources of Morality and Religion*. Here he exhibited great skill in carrying out, in problems of morality and religion, the opposition he always maintained between analysis and intuition, science and philosophy, matter and life. That opposition here becomes one between static morality and dynamic morality, and between static religion and dynamic religion.

Static morality is the morality of obligation. It arises in "closed societies" and conserves the established values of past creativity. It involves the observance of taboos, conventions, conformity to fixed standards. It varies, of course, from one closed society to another. But in each instance of its occurrence it is concerned with restraints imposed on individuals in order that the stability of the group may be maintained. Without such static morality a society would dissolve in a welter of undirected impulses. Although any single one of the conventions of a group may be challenged, the totality of recognized obligations has the force of duty without which social decay would at once ensue.

Dynamic morality is the morality of aspiration. It is not relative to any established order of society. It is a ferment from which novelty may arise. It is not a steady pressure upon individuals, as is static morality; nor are its aims clear. It appeals to ideals which lie beyond the recognized values of life—ideals unrealized as yet and usually incompatible in some respects with convention. It is the revolutionary morality of the reformer who will hazard what has already been achieved in the hope of gaining something better. It is ejaculatory in its appearance in human affairs, intense when it comes, but coming at irregular intervals. And its ideals are normally somewhat blurred in outline, so that the prophetic souls who proclaim these ideals may not themselves know just what is involved in their pursuit. It often leads to social conflicts by the challenge it issues to conservative consciences.

Neither type of morality is found apart from the other, though the manner in which the two types are mixed varies from place to place and from time to time. The former comes from the structure of a society, and the latter comes from the vital energy which in one fashion or another creates every social structure in the panorama of human history. The former, when fulfilled, eventuates in pleasure (which always accompanies the easy and smooth performance of human functions); the latter brings joy (which is the satisfaction of bringing some new life into the world). The former is infra-intellectual, because it depends on personal habit and social conformity; the latter is supra-intellectual, because it hopes for more than it can prove to be within men's grasp. The two types of morality, however, for all the contrast between them, are not antithetical in their occurrence. They could hardly be antithetical since the former was, from the point of view of some earlier stage of evolution, the kind of thing the latter now is. The latter is not always worthy of trust, nor would it always be desirable if carried out; for there are many dead ends and failures in evolution. But the two types of morality are certain to continue to compete for men's loyalties as long as evolution continues. As it is life that produces matter, so aspiration, when successful, establishes new bonds of solemn duties.

TWO TYPES OF RELIGION

The history of religions, Bergson observed, is one long record of error and folly. But in making this strong statement, he was not wholly condemning religion. Religion, with all its deficiencies, has its essential role to play. It has, in fact, two essential roles to play. One of these roles is played by static religion, the other by dynamic religion.

Static religion has the role of protecting men's feelings against the dissolving effects of intelligence. Bergson returned here to his point that the kind of analysis which intelligence gives of life is destructive of the vigor of vital energy. Intelligence breaks down the life force into mental states in a mechanically conditioned system. It destroys hopes which it cannot prove to be warranted by the causal forces of the material environment. It generates fears through its instructions concerning the limitations of human powers and the inescapable fact of death. It tends, unless counteracted by some other influence, to make men submissive, inert in the face of challenge, timid to embark upon adventure. Religion, however, is this other counteracting force. Religion is not a product of men's fears, Bergson insisted; rather, religion is a socially approved technique of opposing men's fears and of providing cure for the disastrous effects men's fears might have upon their resolute living. The taboos of religion, the mythological fantasies about "another world," and the many untenable suppositions about spirits and gods may be, when examined critically by human intelligence, nothing but the "error and folly" by which Bergson confessed the course of religion in history to be characterized. Bergson would not defend any particular form of taboo or myth or fantasy. But he did point out that society needs the kind of thing which religion offers to men. Society needs this kind of thing lest it be submerged in the despair intelligence breeds in men. Religion is a defensive reaction of human nature against the manner in which intelligence substitutes necessity for freedom, matter for vital energy, static entities for dynamic processes, reasonable doubt for courage, and repetition of routine exercises for creativity of novel achievements. Bergson did not deny that any and every religious system is full of absurdities, but he insisted that the role of religion in society is desirable and that nothing but religion can perform this particular role.

Dynamic religion has the role of making men sensitive to their dependence upon, and their share in, the reservoir of vital energy in the world. Bergson here gave expression to the mystic urge within him. The mystic, he held, establishes contact, elusive and perhaps vague, but nonetheless real, with the creative source of all life. Dynamic religion is thus the prophetic drive which gives birth to successive systems of static religion and which, finding each such system in turn inadequate to its sensitivities, pushes forward to new expressions of its joyous visions. The human sponsors of dynamic religion are strong souls who dare much. They love the life urge which they mystically sense. They find that life urge itself to be love—love of new life. Mysticism, Bergson contended, does not properly issue in withdrawal from action (as he thought it did in Plotinus); much less does it issue in release from life (as he thought it did in the Nirvana of the Buddhists). Rather, it issues in heightened creativity in imitation of the vital energy of the world.

The two forms of religion, like the two forms of morality, are interpenetrating, Bergson pointed out, in human history. Ever at strife with each other in each successive social situation, they are harmonious in their total roles in evolution. For the static religion of each present is but the slumbering form of the dynamic religion of its own past.

2. RECENT TRENDS

THE NEARER WE come down to our own times, the more difficult it is to select, out of the large number of competing voices, the individuals whom future historians may recognize as leaders of twentieth-century philosophy. Therefore, we shall not continue here to trace the complex of ideas which constitutes the total philosophical position of any single thinker. We shall content ourselves with noting certain trends of opinion, trends which, in perhaps a variety of different ways, enter into the reflections of groups of philosophical writers. We shall be doing full justice to no one person. But we may characterize the climate of opinion during the last few decades.

All three trends which are here to be considered are matters of current controversy. They are not finished positions. They are moot points in contemporary debates. Advocates of each of the three trends often differ radically among themselves. But in all three cases, the name usually assigned to the trend is a battlecry around which zealous proponents rally.

REALISM

One characteristic emphasis of twentieth-century philosophy is realism. The realistic trend arose in an animus against idealism. It was directed against Berkeley's thesis that *esse* is *percipi* and, even more, against the Kantian principle that mind or reason is constitutive of the experienced world. It sought to undo the Copernican revolution which Kant had claimed to have effected. It was intended as a rejection of the Hegelianism which, broadly diffused in continental thought, had also flourished in England and America during the last few decades of the nineteenth century and the opening years of the twentieth. It sought to maintain, in one form or another, that a real world exists independently of our experience or knowledge of it, and even of all experience and all knowledge. The many men who called themselves realists had little in common except their aversion to idealism. When they developed their positive positions, they quickly proved to be in disagreement with one another. But they all taught that mind, far from being the source of the world or even the source of the order of experience, appears within a world antecedent to it, and that mind, if it is to know the world, must make all its ways of thinking conform to the nature of this antecedent world.

Two main types of realism have appeared which have gone under the labels of critical realism and new realism (or neo-realism).

According to the advocates of critical realism, the data of experience are subjective effects in the mind which indicate the presence of external things and, perhaps to some extent, the nature of these external things. We begin with "appearances" and seek, in our cognitive life, to make inferences from these appearances to external objects, which are "independent of us and our perceptions." [2] Critical realists were sometimes agnostic concerning the possibility of reaching accurate knowledge of external objects and, at other times, quite ready to borrow the views of physical scientists as reliable conclusions about the external world. They stood in the Lockian tradition. They claimed to avoid certain of Locke's difficulties and confusions. But if one takes the writings of the critical realists as a body of literature, one finds in it, as one finds in Locke, a hesitant alternation between practical confidence that physical sciences inform us about the real nature of objects and theoretical agnosticism concerning our ability to know anything other than our own subjective experiences.

The new realism was a more original form of realistic theory. Some of the new realists maintained that the many bits or items of experienced data are in themselves neither mental nor material. These data may be called neutral entities. When some of these neutral entities are brought into certain relationships by awareness, memory, expectation, and other such processes, they can be said to constitute a mind and so to be mental. When these same or any other neutral entities are brought together into certain other relationships, they can then be said to constitute a material thing. These other relationships are established by making a kind of logical construction. When, for example, we say that we see an inkstand (or any other particular thing), we are virtually judging that the given item of our present sensory experience can be correlated with a vast number of other more or less similar items in other perspectives (actual or possible). And it

[2] The words here in quotation marks are from Bertrand Russell's early book *The Problems of Philosophy*, Home University Library edition (New York, Holt, 1912), p. 42. Lord Russell did not long hold to this type of realistic position but became an advocate of new realism instead.

is only the system of all such items in all these perspectives that can properly be called a material thing. The system of such items has, of course, no genuine ontological status; it may even, without impropriety, be called a fiction. Mind and matter thus turn out, both of them, to be ways of ordering data which, apart from these orderings, are neither mental nor material. Thus, according to the advocates of the new realism, there cannot be a dualism between mind and matter; nor will there arise any epistemological problems of the sort with which empiricists have traditionally been beset.[3]

LOGICAL POSITIVISM

Another trend of twentieth-century philosophy has been in the direction of what is called logical positivism. This movement arose among a group of central European thinkers (especially in Vienna, Prague, and Berlin) who are known as the Vienna Circle. It spread (partly as the result of the totalitarian attacks upon the integrity of university life) to Cambridge and Oxford in England, and was then widely, if thinly, diffused in the United States. The movement is also called logical empiricism.

Logical positivism is based upon a study of differences among various types of sentences or linguistic expressions. Some sentences have cognitive meanings, others have only noncognitive meanings, and still others have no meanings at all. But a further and very important distinction must be made. Some sentences with cognitive meanings are purely formal propositions of an analytical nature, and other sentences with cognitive meanings are factual propositions of a synthetic nature.[4]

Logical positivists have made considerable use, for their special purposes, of modern theories of mathematics. Pure mathematics, they point out, is a strictly deductive enterprise which begins with arbi-

---

[3] For the further investigation of the realistic trend in recent philosophy, the student may consult such books as the following:

George E. Moore, *Philosophical Studies,* International Library of Psychology, Philosophy, and Scientific Method (New York, Harcourt, 1922).

Bertrand Russell, *Our Knowledge of the External World,* Lowell Lectures (Chicago, Open Court, 1914).

The New Realism (New York, Macmillan, 1912), six essays by six different men.

Essays in Critical Realism (London, Macmillan and Co., Ltd., 1920), seven essays by seven different men.

The last two of these books represent the American version of the realistic trend in recent philosophy.

[4] Advocates of logical positivism have often made contributions to the study of semantics and the syntax of language and so find some kinship with a current Oxford group known as advocates of "philosophical analysis." But only the major positions of the logical positivists can be reviewed here.

trarily defined postulates and proceeds, by means of the principles of logic, to develop the implications of those postulates. Therefore mathematics does not, indeed, it cannot, make possible any pronouncements upon the existential world or upon any matter of fact in that world. It is a body of propositions, each of which follows necessarily from certain prior propositions, except the preliminary postulates and definitions which set up the logical system. The *Principia Mathematica* (3 vols., 1910–1913), of Alfred North Whitehead and Bertrand Russell is often regarded as one of the most momentous exhibits of the nature of mathematical thinking.

Mathematics, according to the language of some advocates of logical positivism, is not concerned with truth but only with validity. Truth (or falsity), in this vocabulary, is a property of only those propositions which deal with matters of fact; whereas validity (or invalidity) is a property of propositions which correctly (or incorrectly) state the necessary logical relations of one formal proposition to another formal proposition. Mathematics, according to the language of other advocates of philosophical analysis, is concerned with *a priori* truth but not with factual truth. *A priori* truth, in this vocabulary, is what validity is in the former vocabulary. But the two ways of speaking, though differing linguistically, agree in the intended meaning.

The advocates of logical positivism then proceed to point out that many propositions asserted by many people on many occasions are logically akin to mathematical propositions. Consider, for example, the propositions "All bachelors are unmarried" and "All men are mortal." These propositions, like mathematical ones, are analytic. They do not, strictly interpreted, affirm the existence of bachelors and men. They are definitions, or partial definitions, of the senses in which the subject terms of the propositions are being used. They are valid in the sense that one cannot, in any respectable discourse, use a term and then refuse to abide by the logical implications of one's own definition of that term. But these propositions make no claim to truth about any existing matter of fact.

Factual sentences aim at factual truth and require, for their meaning and for their truth, something other than and more than logical validity. A factual statement is meaningful if, and only if, we can indicate the kind of situation which, at least theoretically, would make its confirmation or disproof possible. And, correlatively, a factual statement is meaningless if no situation can be indicated which, in principle at least, would furnish such confirmation or disproof. The criterion of factual meaning is verifiability by reference to existing situations. Meaningful statements are true, of course, when they receive confirmation, and false when they receive disproof.

With this much of the position of logical positivism many empiricists agree who are nonetheless unwilling to call themselves logical positivists. Their unwillingness is due to their dislike of further contentions which advocates of logical positivism are prone to make. For among factually meaningless sentences advocates of logical positivism frequently put all metaphysical and ethical sentences.

Logical positivists tend to deride metaphysics in the sense of speculations about noumena or absolutes beyond the range of possible experience. So far, so good, in the estimation of most schools of empiricists. But, having discarded metaphysics in this special (and supposedly objectionable) sense, logical positivists often seem to suppose that they have disposed of metaphysics in all other senses, too. They reject as meaningless Aristotle's early metaphysical speculations about a prime mover, but they also reject, and without careful consideration, the inquiries which Aristotle made in the later and more empirical parts of his *Metaphysics*. They reject as meaningless the efforts of Aristotle and many subsequent empirically minded metaphysicians to define the generic traits of existence. They clarify the issues with which they deal, but they confine their attention to certain selected issues and are too sweeping in their dismissal of all other problems which they summarily call meaningless.

In similar fashion, advocates of logical positivism usually regard all sentences which contain the words "good" or "right" or "ought" as merely emotive. Such sentences, they often say, have only noncognitive meaning. That is, these sentences are taken to indicate attitudes of approval or disapproval on the part of the persons who utter them but to indicate nothing whatsoever about the situations to which the sentences purport to refer. Such sentences, therefore, are neither true nor false. Ethical sentences are merely expressions of subjective emotions in the speaker.

Other empiricists, empiricists who accept the requirement that meaningful sentences must find confirmation or disproof in existing situations, attack the logical positivists as needlessly radical. Logical positivism, they say, is a type of thought which has cathartic value in its attacks upon loose thinking, verbalisms, equivocations, and intellectual fuzziness. But it has gone beyond this service to philosophy when it is turned into a too hasty assault upon all metaphysical and ethical reflections.

Space does not permit a full consideration of the contemporary debate. But one illustration may be given of the kind of thing which is being said. One logical positivist has written that "the word cause, as used in everyday life, implies *nothing but* regularity of sequence, because *nothing else* is used to verify the propositions in which it occurs." [5] But other empiricists point out that when most people inquire into the cause of a particular fire, they are not meaning by cause any kind of regularity. Rather, they are trying to identify a particular agent or agency which produced this particular fire. Cause, these other empiricists say, may mean regularity of sequence, but it may also mean an efficacious and productive factor in one particular existing situation. Logical positivists are prone to ignore, if not overtly to deny, the dynamic elements in nature because they think too narrowly of "situations" as collocations of sensory data. They ban efficacy from nature because they cannot isolate a sensory datum, or a collection of sensory data, which is this efficacy. Logical positivists thus operate, the other empiricists charge, with an attenuated empiricism. They move too much within the dialectics of an artificial theory of what they suppose empiricism requires them to maintain, rather than examine freshly the full contents of the world as they experience it.[6]

EXISTENTIALISM

Another trend in twentieth-century thinking is called existentialism. This trend is in marked contrast with all the other philosophical currents of the time. Indeed, it is a violent rejection of all the major philosophical systems of the modern world. Some of its unsympathetic critics refuse to call it a philosophy at all; they regard it as an

---

[5] Moritz Schlick, "Causality in Everyday Life and in Recent Science," reprinted in *Readings in Philosophical Analysis*, ed. Herbert Feigl and Wilfrid Sellars (New York, Appleton-Century-Crofts, 1949), p. 516.

[6] For the further investigation of logical positivism, the student may consult such books as the following:

A. J. Ayer, *Language, Truth and Logic* (London, Gollancz, 1936).

L. Wittgenstein, *Tractatus Logico-Philosophicus* (New York, Harcourt, 1922).

———, *Philosophical Investigations* (Oxford, Blackwell, 1953).

R. Carnap, *The Logical Syntax of Language*, International Library of Psychology, Philosophy, and Scientific Method (London, Kegan Paul, Trench, and Truebner, 1937).

Herbert Feigl and Wilfrid Sellars, eds., *Readings in Philosophical Analysis* (New York, Appleton-Century-Crofts, 1949). This book contains many useful recent essays, some by logical positivists and others from kindred points of view.

unreasoned and unreasoning and therefore quite arbitrary act of will. The facts are that existentialists differ among themselves a good deal in the manner in which they relate reason and will. In all cases, however, existentialism revolves around an act of will which each existentialist must make for himself. Existentialism is, in each of its sponsors, a highly personal matter. Some of its exponents are defiantly atheistic; others are devoutly religious, even Christian. It is, wherever it is found, a resolute commitment of the entire personality, entailing a compulsive assurance that a final truth has been reached about one's place in the world.

To expound existentialism, one must write as if he were tracing the biography of an existentialist. One may deal in this biography with certain ideas, but one will deal primarily with emotions and attitudes and volitions.

Let us consider one such possible biography. Let us consider how a man might respond to his experiences. He has certain sensations—certain visual sensations, certain tactual sensations, and so forth. He has also certain emotions and feelings—certain fears, certain vain hopes, certain hesitations. He has certain nebulous ideas—perhaps beliefs which other people tell him they hold but which he cannot share. And he has a vague sense of unexplained mysteries in the world around him and within his own soul. He finds these sensations and feelings and ideas a jumble of unrelated items, without rhyme or reason, and he falls into the mood of despair. Then a change occurs in his consciousness, a change which perhaps comes suddenly with a kind of apocalyptic insight. He comes to know his purpose in the world, and he finds the world amenable to his purpose. Everything which before was drab and meaningless now stands forth as existing for the sake of yielding to his purpose. Perhaps his new insight is a revelation from God, and his purpose is then given him by divine grace. Perhaps his new insight is an intuition that he stands alone in a godless universe and is master of his destiny and capable of forcing all things to conform to the pattern of his own resolute purpose. But whether divine revelation or godless resolve, his insight confers on everything the meaning it will for him hereafter and forever have. He has gained a conviction of truth which is final.

Historically considered, existentialism goes back to Kierkegaard (1813–1855), a Dane who revolted against the Hegelian influences in the academic world of his time, against the Christian teachings of the churches in his country, and against the tyranny (as he felt it) of the social conventions around him. But no existentialist is in any detail a model whom other existentialists must follow. Existentialism is a personal attitude which, in any and every age, some few men take. What makes existentialism conspicuous in the twentieth century is that certain of its advocates have made themselves vocal by enunciating a somewhat systematic outline of its principles. Perhaps one does violence to the existentialist commitment by speaking of its principles or by reducing it to a system. But since some existentialists have ventured themselves to do this kind of thing, we may take account of the manner in which they try to formulate their position.

Some existentialists begin with the principle that existence is prior to essence.[7] This strange dictum, if clear in the biographical transition from confusion to clarity in an existentialist's experience, is philosophically quite obscure. The English word *existence* is awkward here. One might better turn to the German and say that *Existenz* is prior to essence. In any case, the world cannot be deduced in Hegelian fashion from the interplay of categories. What exists cannot be determined by reason. Existentialists often seem to be affirming that existence is amorphous until and unless form is given to it by a man's personal will. They seem to be untroubled by the criticism that in this case the world is likely to have a different form for each different existentialist. Existentialists are often deeply concerned with determining their relations to one another and to other persons; yet their position is such that each person is bound to find himself living in an entirely different world from that in which those with other commitments find themselves living.

If an existentialist begins with the principle just mentioned, he is likely to proceed to a further principle that the commitment of a person is not a sheerly rational decision. The commitment is not, to be sure, deliberately anti-rational. But reason is only a phase of a person's nature. And commitment involves the entire and integral person. Commitment is an act in which feeling and reason, desire and hope, creative impulse and aspiration are all involved simultaneously and in inextricable combination. And the test of truth cannot be evidence from sense experience, such as natural scientists utilize, or rules of reason, such as logicians provide, or biological value in promoting survival. The test of truth, rather, is the triumphant sense of finality which a commitment gives to him who makes the commitment with unlimited devotion. Triumphant living is living and dying in the firm assurance that one has established beyond all doubt the full meaning of one's self and one's world.

[7] This theme is in Sartre's existentialism but not in Heidegger's, for example.

Existentialism is a point of view which has been turned to many uses by its different adherents. It has sometimes been used in Europe, and it has almost exclusively been used in the United States, by Protestant theologians who have been hard pressed for a means of asserting their creeds. Protestant theology has never had, as Catholic theology has had in such men as St. Augustine and St. Thomas, philosophical exponents whose positions have remained normative over the centuries. Protestant theologians, consequently, have essayed to use successive trends of thought as trends have appeared from time to time. At present, one of their devices has been to resort to existentialism. Karl Barth (1886–   ) in Germany and the members of the so-called neo-orthodox group in the United States have been using just this device. They disparage both natural theology, with its appeal to evidences of God in nature, and rational theology, with its classic cosmological and ontological arguments, and even theology based on the Kantian postulates of practical reason. Neither nature nor history, they are prone to say, can be organized meaningfully, unless and until, by an act of faith, a man imparts to both nature and history a transcendental meaning which nature and history themselves could never furnish us. The critic of this kind of existentialist theology cannot but wonder why it is that the transcendent meaning allegedly given to nature and history so frequently turns out to enable theologians then to affirm many of the dogmas of historic Calvinism. But such seems to be the case.

Existentialism seems to be developing both a moderate and an extreme form. In moderate form it is another empirically minded revolt against the abstractions and *a priori* theories of the Hegelian tradition. Its peculiar mark of distinction from many other empiricisms is its insistence that assent is not a result of a purely intellectual estimate of probabilities, but a response of the whole unitary man. In extreme form, however, it is a violently anti-intellectualistic and voluntaristic romanticism. As regards ethics, it is an exhibition of willfulness; and as regards ontology, it is an indulgence in caprice.[8]

[8] For the further investigation of existentialism, the student may consult such books as the following:

J. P. Sartre, *L'être et le néant* (Paris, Gallimard, 1947). Translated into English in part by Hazel E. Barnes under the title *Existential Psychoanalysis* (New York, Philosophical Library, 1953).

M. Heidegger, *Existence and Being* (Chicago, Regnery, 1949).

———, *Sein und Zeit*, (Tübingen, Niemeyer, 1953).

XVI

Philosophy in the United States

IN THE EARLY history of the United States, philosophy was, if not an echo, at least an adjunct, of philosophical reflections which had their home in Europe. Some American thinkers had notably independent minds and their writings exhibit their great ability. Jonathan Edwards (1703–1758) and Ralph Waldo Emerson (1803–1882) are important figures in American intellectual history. But independence is not originality. And for the most part, American philosophical minds before 1890 carried on European traditions. Locke's *Treatise of Civil Government,* both directly and through its French admirers, guided much of political thinking in the formative years of the American republic; and his *Essay Concerning Human Understanding* was an accepted text for more than a century in courses of instruction at both Harvard and Yale. Samuel Johnson (1696–1772), president of King's College (now Columbia University), used Berkeley's philosophy in his theological speculations. Noah Porter (1811–1892), president of Yale, and even more James McCosh (1811–1894), president of Princeton, followed teachings of Thomas Reid and later members of the Scotch school of common sense; they and their books helped in the wide dissemination of Scotch realism in American colleges in the second half of the nineteenth century. Laurens P. Hickok (1798–1888) and Charles E. Garman (1850–1907), both professors at Amherst, Felix Adler (1851–1933), founder of the Society of Ethical Culture in New York, and George H. Howison (1834–1917), professor at the University of California, were among those who presented, in one way or another, principles taken over from Kant. The St. Louis movement in philosophy furthered the study of Hegel, and its most outstanding member, William T. Harris (1835–1909), founded the *Journal of Speculative Philosophy* to promote philosophy in general and Hegelian philosophy in particular. The absolutism of Josiah Royce (1855–1916), professor at Harvard, was a later chapter in the story of Hegelianism in the United States.

The history of philosophy in the United States before 1890 [1] is akin to philosophical history in certain other periods. The Romans went to school to the Greeks, and the peoples of western Europe went to school to classical antiquity. Aristotle significantly remarked that philosophy only begins to flourish when men have leisure.[2] This last point need not be overstressed. Americans, unlike the Romans and the peoples of western Europe, were themselves transplanted from the countries from which they derived their philosophical stimulus and were as entitled to develop the great European traditions as were European followers of these traditions. But the new land, new problems, new relations of men to men and of men to nature, new political and social conditions, new aims and objectives—these were bound to have their effects on philosophy. Philosophy in the United States since 1890, with its roots in western Europe and Rome and Greece, is an important and creative chapter in the intellectual development of western culture. It may perhaps seem to historians of the future the most fertile aspect of twentieth-century thought.

The leading figures in philosophy in the United States since 1890 are not all Americans. Santayana was a Spaniard whose home was in the United States from 1872 to 1912 (less than half his almost eighty-nine years); but his books were all published in the United States, and nowhere else but in the United States has he been very influential. Whitehead was an Englishman who did not come to the United States until 1924 when he was already sixty-three years old; but he then lived at or near Harvard until his death in 1947, and he wrote most of his philosophical works during this period of his American residence. The United States has been fortunate in having such non-Americans as participants in the intellectual development of the country and has been further enriched by other thinkers who came to it as refugees from totalitarian oppressions. But most of the philosophic minds who have taught and written philosophy in the United States have been native Americans.

Some historians have been inclined to speak of recent philosophy in the United States as typically and indigenously American. No objection need be made to this way of speaking, unless the words be interpreted too narrowly. Philosophy in the United States *is* part and parcel of American life. But it is cosmopolitan, not provincial, in quality. It takes account of the broad spaces of time and eternity as fully as ever did Aristotle or Spinoza or Hume. The historian must

[1] The year 1890 is, of course, an arbitrary date. It is chosen here because it was the year in which William James's *The Principles of Psychology* appeared. That great work, more than any other single thing, marks the beginning of a new period.

[2] *Metaphysics*, 981b23.

point out that philosophy in the United States is heir to the whole of western culture and has roots deep in European thought. But the historian should also recognize that philosophy in the United States is making fresh contributions to the development of western culture. Of these contributions, certainly the western world, and probably the entire world, must take account.

1. JAMES

WILLIAM JAMES, 1842–1910, was born in New York City, and died at his summer home in Chocorua, New Hampshire. He had little formal schooling as a boy but received more education from associations with his father and his friends and from extensive travels. In 1861 he began studies at Lawrence Scientific School, Harvard, first in chemistry, later in anatomy and physiology. In 1864 he entered Harvard Medical School, from which he received an M.D. degree in 1869. In 1865 he went with Agassiz on an expedition to Brazil. He had several long sojourns in Europe where, among other things, he heard lectures on Kant at the University of Berlin and studied with Helmholtz at Heidelberg. In 1870 he had the severe spiritual crisis which he later described, without reference to it as his own.[3] He taught at Harvard most academic years between 1872, when he was appointed instructor in physiology, and 1910. He became professor of philosophy in 1885, professor of psychology in 1889, and professor of philosophy again in 1897. The subjects he taught indicate the wide range of his interests: physiology; psychology; Herbert Spencer; evolution; ethics; logic; general problems of philosophy; Renouvier; Hegel; Locke, Berkeley, and Hume; Descartes, Spinoza, and Leibnitz; Kant; metaphysics; philosophy of nature; history of philosophy. He gave many lectures and addresses to both popular and learned audiences. Among his published books are *The Principles of Psychology,* 2 vols. (1890); *The Will to Believe and Other Essays in Popular Philosophy* (1897); *The Varieties of Religious Experience* (1902); *Pragmatism* (1907); *The Meaning of Truth* (1909); *A Pluralistic Universe* (1909); *Some Problems of Philosophy* (1911); *Essays in Radical Empiricism* (1912).

[3] *The Varieties of Religious Experience* (London, Longmans, Green, 1913), pp. 160–161.

WILLIAM JAMES CAME into philosophy from the study of the medical sciences. This fact is not without significance for an understanding of his philosophical attitude. He had a basically therapeutic concern in all his reflections. He wished to help his fellow men (as well, of course, as himself) to live more vigorously, more wholesomely. He felt a moral obligation to face facts without flinching. But he wanted men, after they had been thoroughly honest in accepting all the bits of truth they could glean from scientific discoveries, to go on to lead rich and happy lives. He would never take any scientific conclusion as *the* final truth about the universe. He would acknowledge any well-evidenced conclusion, but he would insist that the world was full of odds and ends and left room for other conclusions, too. And if the first conclusion seemed to restrict human freedom severely, he was ready to expect that the next conclusion would prove to remove the restrictions. He was, so to speak, a physician of the soul. He thought of the *sciences* as enabling men to make a reliable diagnosis, at least the best diagnosis possible at the moment, of their predicament in the presence of entangling forces. And he thought of *philosophy* as enabling men to prescribe cures for the ills the diagnosis revealed. These cures, he hoped, would save those who are discouraged or afraid. They would also serve as bracing tonics for those who, though tolerably strong, might yet need some new strength in the continuing battle of life.

James's early essays manifest his therapeutic concern. In these essays he examined those current theories which, unless they were rightly interpreted, might seem to some individuals to subject them to forces beyond their power to control and thus to hamper their effective living. In 1880 he commented upon the theory of evolution as presented by Darwin and turned into a cosmic formula by Spencer. He was quite willing to accept Darwin's positive discovery that life was threatened by the play of environmental forces, but he insisted that this theory, although emphasizing the hard requirements of the struggle for existence, still left considerable room for individual initiative. He was more severe against Spencer's way of turning the scientific theory of evolution into a philosophy of an inevitable trend toward a fixed goal. He called Spencer's theory of automatic progress an "obsolete anachronism" because it made the human mind little more than a passive victim of external forces.[4] In 1882 he attacked Hegelianism because that manner of thought, with its uniform pat-

---

[4] William James, "Great Men and Their Environment," *The Will to Believe and Other Essays* (New York, Longmans, Green, 1921), pp. 223, 233, 254.

tern of thesis and antithesis and synthesis, was a "mouse-trap" in which all who enter the door "may be lost forever." [5] In 1884 he excoriated deterministic theories because they limit the future to repeating the routine uniformities of the past and deny the presence of new possibilities.[6] And in 1895 he wrote another essay with the title "Is Life Worth Living?" He here explicitly asked the question which had been implicit in the earlier essays. Life will be worth living, he answered, if we do not think of ourselves as caught within the fixed structure of that portion of the world the scientists have reduced to a fixed order. The world of our natural knowledge lies within a vaster unseen world. The former and narrow world may seem to confront us with riddles we cannot solve. But the latter world, we are entitled to hope, may permit us to find solutions to these riddles. We ought then heroically to trust the demands of the moral life and to affirm fearlessly that life is worth living.[7]

James's early essays led up to the reformulation of his position in the most famous single essay James ever wrote, namely, "The Will to Believe," published in 1896. James was concerned in this essay with the way in which our volitional nature determines, at least on many points, the beliefs by which we guide our lives. He accepted the control of volition over belief as giving the actual psychology of human opinion; he furthermore sought to show to what extent and in what contexts such control is justifiable. Men cannot know, he pointed out, the full truth about the world in advance of deciding how to act in that world. We are often forced to act without the knowledge we should like to have, and we ought not to allow our lack of knowledge to hamper our effective and dynamic activities. When we can obtain evidence by which to settle a question, we ought to respect that evidence; and when we can delay decision on a question where evidence is lacking, we ought to suspend judgment. But when we are confronted by an option, and when that option is living, momentous, and forced upon our immediate need to decide and to act with vigor, we are entitled to exercise a will to believe. Our passional nature may, because indeed it must, decide every genuine option when our intellectual nature, through lack of evidence, is unable to guide our decision.

James had no intention of encouraging premature belief on matters which scientific investigation could resolve. He did make two

5 "On Some Hegelisms," *ibid.*, p. 275.
6 "The Dilemma of Determinism," *ibid.*, p. 121.
7 "Is Life Worth Living?" *ibid.*, pp. 51, 54.

main applications of his principle of the will to believe. These applications were to moral and to religious questions. In moral questions, he pointed out, our firm and confident belief in our own powers or in the integrity of our friends may be the sufficient cause which produces those powers and that integrity. In religious questions we face the forced option of relating ourselves to the vast unknown world which engulfs the little area of our limited knowledge. We are then entitled to believe that this vast unknown world is such as to establish and preserve our values, to sympathize with us in our failures, and to turn these failures eventually into successes.

James did not so much as try, in his early essays, to work out a systematic theory of the world in support of his gospel of courage and high hopes. He was not, and he openly declared to his friends that he was not, a systematic thinker. He tried to see how much light each of various theories shed upon the world, but he trusted none of the theories as a total view or a last word. He could be tolerant of even contradictory theories, for he thought the world itself to be as full of inconsistencies, as unfinished, as inchoate in the relation of part to part, as his own ideas of the world. He could embrace simultaneously one belief in rigid causal necessities and another belief in unforeseeable chances. He could do this because, as he maintained, that which is in theory an insoluble impasse may be in practice an opportunity which courageous men may turn to glorious achievement.

THE STREAM OF CONSCIOUSNESS

The most influential philosophical idea which James presented in his *Principles of Psychology* is that of the stream of thought or the stream of consciousness.[8] James's great book is not an altogether consistent one.[9] James wanted a psychology which would further the therapeutic point of view of his earlier essays. Although he did not free himself entirely from older ideas, he advanced a genuinely new view in his idea of the stream of consciousness.

James was unalterably opposed to the traditional supposition that consciousness can be correctly described in terms of simple ideas or sensations or any other mental elements which later come to be built

---

[8] James called chapter 9 of *The Principles of Psychology* "The Stream of Thought." He was using the term *thought* to mean not simply intellectual processes but all forms of consciousness, sensations, feelings, emotions, volitions, and so forth. The term *stream of consciousness* is clearer and has come to be more frequently used.

[9] Even so ardent an admirer of James as John Dewey insisted on this point. Dewey sometimes took James's *Principles of Psychology* into his classroom and went over selected chapters in detail (for example, chapter 17, "Sensations"), pointing out how James oscillated between older and his own novel positions.

up into complexes in accord with psychological laws. The simple ideas or other mental elements may indeed be carved out of the stream of consciousness. But they are not original building blocks. They are artificial entities, discriminated by attention for the practical purpose of guiding phases of consciousness to more satisfactory outcomes. The integral stream of consciousness is prior to all such abstracted elements. It is not a chain of discrete entities but a flowing stream of interpenetrating pulses of awareness. We all make such remarks as that the same realities, realities like a chair or a star or the quality of green, come before our thought over and over again.[10] But our consciousness of these things is never twice the same. What we call the same thing is always appearing in new contexts, suffused with new emotions, transformed even by being recognized as the "same." The stream of consciousness has its psychic overtones, its fluctuating intensities, its sharp outlines and its vague fringes.

Nothing is easier, James granted, than to treat the stream of consciousness as a function of the brain and nervous system of the organic body. And James did indeed himself give considerable attention to physiological matters. But he firmly insisted that there is much more to consciousness than is represented by brain processes and other bodily functionings. He claimed that there is no evidence to show that the brain produces consciousness. Rather, indications are that the brain is an instrumentality which consciousness uses in its efforts to act efficaciously upon the world. Just as we use our hands to accomplish certain purposes, so we use our brains. Our consciousness is full of many ideas, fanciful and practicable; and our brains sift out these ideas, discarding the fanciful and directing the practicable into such bodily activities as help to realize the ideas. Thus the brain serves the useful end of localizing our purposes at appropriate points of contact with the rest of the world. Consciousness thus finds the body an indispensable tool. But consciousness is fuller and richer than the organic body in its dynamic occurrence and can never be exhaustively understood by viewing that part of it which manages to push visibly through bodily barriers.

Consciousness, James held, is not primarily a matter of cognition or intellectual activities. Older theories of the mind made it too much a merely knowing affair. Consciousness is impulsive, affective or passional, and volitional throughout its course, and is only intellectual at times. And when intellectual or reflective processes do occur, they are given their occasions, their problems, and their im-

[10] *The Principles of Psychology* (New York, Holt, 1890), Vol. I, p. 231.

portance by the way in which they have their setting in the earlier and more fundamental types of consciousness. As early as 1881 James maintained that willing dominates knowing and even perceiving, or that "perception and thinking are only there [that is, in consciousness] for behavior's sake." [11] He sympathized with Kant's contention that mind contributes to the structure of experience. But against Kant he insisted that the contribution of mind is piecemeal and without pre-established requirements, because mind is always in the service of more basic kinds of consciousness and has to proceed provisionally and experimentally in the service of these other kinds of consciousness. To say this, he explained, is not to make knowing a matter of obstinate or capricious pretense; for knowing cannot make willing more fruitful unless it gives genuine enlightenment. It is to say, rather, that knowing enlarges the range and increases the degree of success which the impulses of life may have in the world.

RADICAL EMPIRICISM

In the course of the ten or twelve years after the publication of his *Psychology* James developed his position in the direction of what he chose to call "radical empiricism." He used the adjective *radical* because his empiricism, as he viewed it, corrected the classic empiricisms in two important respects.

One of these respects concerned the nature of consciousness. He asked the question "Does 'consciousness' exist?" [12] and provocatively answered this question in the negative. He meant by this negative answer to deny that there is any entity or stuff, any subjective existence, such as Locke and his followers supposed to be the immediate facts of experience. There is indeed a function in experience which we may, if we choose, call by the abstract name *consciousness*. The cloud, the physical cloud which obscures the physical sun, may mean rain. Insofar as the cloud obscures the sun, it is a physical object; insofar as the cloud means rain, it is a mental object. Perceiving and knowing, meaning and believing, like loving and hating, are processes that frequently occur. But these processes occur in the same complex of events in which walking and gesturing and shining and raining occur. There is but one primal stuff, namely, experience. James made the comment that his position was akin to natural realism.[13] When we perceive an object, we do not have some representative effect of the object before us; we have the real physical object before us. And

[11] "Reflex Action and Theism," *The Will to Believe and Other Essays*, p. 114.

[12] This question is the title of an essay he published in 1904. This essay is reprinted in *Essays in Radical Empiricism* (New York, Longmans, Green, 1922), pp. 1–38.

[13] See "A World of Pure Experience," *Essays in Radical Empiricism*, p. 76.

two or more persons may, indeed often do, perceive the same identical physical object. The field of consciousness, if we use that term, is a collection of physical things cut out from the rest of the physical world by virtue of new functional relations which our perceiving or knowing those objects establishes among them. Consciousness is thus a function which objects not previously mental come to have when grouped in certain ways. Mind and consciousness indeed occur; but they occur in the natural world in which also all sorts of other non-mental relations occur, and they are as natural in their occurrence as those other nonmental relations. Minds, then, are not private solipsistic worlds. Minds are rather occurrences in the natural world; they sometimes meet one another and share common objects; they are open to objective examination as genuinely as any of the other types of occurrence in experience.

The second respect in which James distinguished his radical empiricism from prior empiricisms was in emphasizing the efficacious role of mental processes. He refused to put the natural world and its processes on one side and mind on the other side and then to make mind the witness of events in which it did not share. He insisted that mind participates in the course of nature. Perceiving, knowing, believing, thinking—these occurrences make a great difference in the direction of the changing world. They are such that, when they occur, the world does not go on in the manner in which it otherwise might go on. They bring about natural fruitions and exhibit unique possibilities of the natural world.

From the outset of his thinking, James had regarded the world as pluralistic. He rebelled indignantly against all monisms, against all theories which treated the world as headed inevitably in a set course. His radical empiricism intensified his conviction that the world is an unfinished lot of things, some of them closely related to one another in mutual interdependence, others of them loosely related and subject to being reshuffled in many novel ways. Mind is, among other things, exploration of possibilities tentatively considered. Hence, the world within which mind occurs is open to the introduction of novelty. And there is not, in the present state of things, any clear indication of limits beyond which, to a resolute person, new and hitherto nonexistent relationships may not come to pass. We live in a multiverse rather than in a universe. Or, if we wish to continue to use the familiar word *universe,* we are forced to speak of a *pluralistic universe.*[14]

14 James's Hibbert Lectures bear the title *A Pluralistic Universe* (New York, Longmans, Green, 1909).

PRAGMATISM

In the first decade of the twentieth century (which was also the last decade of James's life) James was in great demand as a lecturer on philosophical subjects, before both academic and civic audiences. He also wished, as he explicitly stated, to compose a full and, so far as possible, systematic statement of his mature views. From the combination of external pressures on his time and his own inner desire there came in 1909 the book *Pragmatism, a New Name for some Old Ways of Thinking*. He was not satisfied with the book; but it is the work on which, more than anything else, his fame among philosophers rests.

The word *pragmatism* had been coined, as a term for a definite doctrine, by Charles Sanders Peirce (1839–1914), to whom James acknowledged considerable indebtedness. Peirce meant by pragmatism, not a general philosophical position, but a specific logical theory, the theory, namely, that the meaning of an idea is the sum of all the practical consequences which might conceivably ensue from the truth of that idea. To think about a thing is to prepare to deal with that thing in certain specific ways and to make adjustments to the outcome of the ensuing action. An alleged idea which has no consequences is not an idea at all. And what purport to be two ideas are, if they involve no differences in expected consequences, but one and the same idea.

James adopted the pragmatic method wholeheartedly. Theories, he said, are instruments, and ideas are plans of action. Theories are not summaries of past experience in which we can then rest as if we had already an assurance of possessing the truth about the world. Theories, rather, lose meaning at once if they no longer cause us to dip again and again into the course of events. The treasured formulas to which men are prone to give eulogistic names like "first principles" and "ultimate categories" usually prove to be obstacles rather than aids to thinking. For they lead men to relax from the attitude of experimental investigation. And in a changing world the best formulas of the past require constant retesting, revamping, reconstruction. Beliefs are not pictures of the past; they are, rather, predictions of factors upon which we can rely as we move on into the precarious future—predictions which may or may not turn out to be fulfilled by events. We all rely on a fund of truth accumulated in the past. But unless we take this fund of truth and go forward with it to grasp new facts, open-mindedly revising old estimates and adding new truths as we go along—unless we proceed in this way, the old truth becomes a dead mass of verbiage. To think is to be prepared to do.

James, then, after sponsoring pragmatism, gave to the pragmatic position a twist which was characteristic of his therapeutic concern. Pragmatism, he went on to say, is not simply a theory of meaning; it is also a theory of truth. An idea is true when it works; and an idea works when it leads to satisfactory outcomes. The kind of working and the kind of satisfaction are matters in regard to which James was exceedingly generous. One kind of working is to find our expectations verified in observed facts—in facts observed through the senses and witnessed by as many observers as wish to participate in the processes of verification. Another kind of working is to find ourselves strengthened in courage to meet our daily tasks and comforted in our hopes for joys we do not now possess. We may consider any idea true, James said, if it "proves itself to be good in the way of belief." [15] But ideas can be good in many ways. They can be good in anticipating correctly the facts in the natural world, in fitting in congenially with other beliefs, and in giving cheer to all sorts and conditions of mankind. James did not care to distinguish among these objective and subjective kinds of goodness.

Peirce protested against James's version of pragmatism. He refused to accept the emotional gratifications of some beliefs as relevant to judgment upon the truth of those beliefs. He protested that emotional gratifications vary with the personalities and temperaments of those who weigh the worth of beliefs. He pointed out that to call beliefs true when the beliefs give emotional gratification is to allow that a given belief may be true to one man and false to another man. He rejected the alleged evidential value of private satisfactions. Truth, he maintained, is public, not private. Truth is what is corroborated by a number of men who, setting aside their hopes and fears, accept only the evidence they jointly ascertain. Truth is not equivalent to utility; for utility depends on the needs and interests of individuals, and truth is the same for all individuals. Peirce even proposed to abandon the term *pragmatism* because it had been corrupted by its indiscriminate use, and suggested that he might better speak of his strict logical theory as *pragmaticism*.

James, however, never yielded to Peirce's demands for making a sharp distinction between public evidence and private satisfaction.

[15] *Pragmatism* (New York, Longmans, Green, 1907), p. 76.

JAMES'S GENEROUS FAITH

The closing chapters of James's books show how he kept returning to his persistent therapeutic point of view. He did not perhaps himself entertain many beliefs for which he could not adduce objective evidence. But he wanted to leave to others a source of comfort he did not himself need or use. In the last chapter of his *Varieties of Religious Experience* he remarked that some day the impersonal view of science may appear to have been "a temporarily useful eccentricity" rather than a thoroughly sound position.[16] In the last chapter of *A Pluralistic Universe* he wrote that life always exceeds logic,[17] by which phrase he meant that privately entertained visions of realities beyond our finite experience may become true for him who cherishes the visions. And in *Pragmatism* he insisted that we are not justified in rejecting any hypothesis which brings consequences useful to life.[18] But in all these chapters, it is important to note, James was primarily concerned, not to establish any view of the world he himself advanced, but to increase men's tolerance of the faiths of others, even when those faiths seemed bizarre. Belief in God, he wrote, means pragmatically that tragedy is provisional and hope for salvation is justifiable. Belief in design in nature means pragmatically that we may have confidence in the future. Belief in free will means pragmatically that we need not restrict our hopes to repetition of what has already happened but may anticipate novelties far better than what is past. James throughout was protesting against taking any scientific or philosophical scheme as a final truth. He wanted to reconsider all questions and to seek new solutions, solutions that would make him impatient if they ever became a new orthodoxy.

2. SANTAYANA

GEORGE SANTAYANA, 1863–1952, was born in Avila, Spain, and died in Rome, Italy. He was brought to the United States in 1872 and was chiefly resident there until 1912. He attended Boston Latin School and Harvard College (1882–1886), studied at Berlin (1886–1888), took a Ph.D. degree

---

16 *The Varieties of Religious Experience*, Gifford Lectures (New York, Longmans, Green, 1902), p. 501.
17 *A Pluralistic Universe*, p. 329.
18 *Pragmatism*, p. 273.

at Harvard (1889), and studied at Oxford (1896–1897). He taught at Harvard from 1889 until he resigned his professorship in 1912. After 1912 he lived in Europe—in England between 1914 and 1918, otherwise partly in Paris and chiefly in Rome. He wrote several books of verse: *Sonnets and Other Verses* (1894), *Lucifer* (1899), *A Hermit of Carmel and Other Poems* (1901), and *The Poet's Testament* (1953). He wrote one novel, *The Last Puritan* (1935). Among his philosophical works are *The Sense of Beauty* (1896), *Interpretations of Poetry and Religion* (1900), *The Life of Reason,* 5 vols. (1905–1906), *Three Philosophical Poets* (1910), *Character and Opinion in the United States* (1920), *Soliloquies in England* (1922), *Scepticism and Animal Faith* (1923), *Dialogues in Limbo* (1925), and *Realms of Being,* 4 vols. (1927–1940), which, depending on *Scepticism and Animal Faith* as an introduction, are often referred to as a series of five volumes. He wrote three volumes of an autobiography under the general title *Persons and Places* (1944, 1945, 1953).

SANTAYANA'S ALMOST sixty years of literary productivity fall into two fairly distinct periods. In the earlier period Santayana devoted himself to appreciative criticism of the cultural achievements of mankind, especially of those branches of mankind which developed western culture and so are the sources of the traditions of the western world. His first two books are concerned with art and religion, and these were followed by the five volumes of *The Life of Reason,* a widely influential work in the United States from the day of its appearance until the present. All of these books, to be sure, reveal certain assumptions about the kind of world within which such human enterprises as art and religion arise and flourish. But their explicit aim and their major effect have been to direct attention, not so much to this world and its ontological structure, as to the way in which men through the centuries have cultivated the life of the imagination. Santayana expounded with sympathetic yet exacting skill the successes and failures, the pathos and irony, the measured and partial glory of men's efforts to transform the raw materials of nature into the finished products of civilization. He was at heart a poet, taking delight in the visions men have entertained of the world, though he appraised these visions, not so much for their degree of truth, as for their charm and for the elevation of mind they might occasion in those who (as he usually did not) believed them. And he was a moralist, judging human institutions and practices, human arts and sciences, human manners and ideals, for their relative contributions to a sane and wholesome and yet joyous life.

Santayana never abandoned the interests and the convictions of this earlier period of his philosophical writing. But he did deplore a misunderstanding which, as he thought, many readers made of his *Life of Reason*. He deplored the way in which, when he spoke of the moral considerations which prompted men to order experience, he was interpreted to be resolving the order of the cosmos into a human contrivance or convenience. He protested against this interpretation.[19]

The whole *Life of Reason* was written with an eye to describing experience, not the cosmos. . . . I was rather carried away, at that time, by a kind of humanism and liked to degrade, or exalt, all things into the human notions of them, and the part they played, as counters, in the game of thought. It was a modern attitude which I hope I have forgotten—*schlecht und modern,* as Goethe says, or Mephistopheles.

Although retaining his earlier interests and convictions, he became more and more eager to make explicit and to elaborate the hidden epistemological and metaphysical assumptions of his earlier writings. And so he turned, in his *Realms of Being,* to a full statement of his theory of knowledge and to metaphysical forays in which he tentatively disclosed such bits of ontological belief as his theory of knowledge permitted him to claim. Back of experience, supporting the occurrence of experience but not disclosing itself within experience, is the cosmos. Back of appearance is reality. And although we may not be able to penetrate the secrets of the substantial world, we can at least, Santayana thought, salute it in its inscrutable efficacy and omnificent power. And salutation of the substantial world, though it will have no bearing upon *its* unfeeling course, will keep *us* tolerably free from ontological caprice and superstitious fancy. "The appearance of things is always, in some measure, a true index to their reality." [20] And unless we frankly and boldly take account of their reality, our enjoyment of their appearance will degenerate into willful sentimentality. Thus the direction of Santayana's later reflections changed. He did not so much alter his former views as bring to explicit statement what before had been tacitly assumed and leave unsaid what before had been recorded with passionate eloquence.

19 In a letter to the author under date of Nov. 15, 1933. This letter was written at a time when he had published the first of his four *Realms of Being* and was at work on the other volumes.

20 *Some Turns of Thought in Modern Philosophy* (Cambridge, Cambridge University Press, 1933), p. 37.

"THE LIFE OF REASON"

The Life of Reason rests upon a fundamental principle which Santayana learned from the Greeks. This principle is the Platonic-Aristotelian contention that the good life for man results when natural impulses are harmoniously developed in accord with reason. Man has in his nature, Santayana maintained, two elements—impulse and ideation. Each of these elements, if allowed to function apart from the other, leads to moral disaster. Impulse, uninformed by understanding of its intent and possible outcome, leads to brutality; ideation, unconnected with the dynamic forces of the physical and social worlds, leads to wild and insane fancies. These same two elements, united effectively in living, spell out such advances as man can make toward rational happiness. Impulse, guided by ideas, becomes aware of its ideal possibilities of expression in an organized life; and ideation, leashed to the exigencies of action, becomes relevant to the course of affairs. Thus impulse becomes art, and ideation becomes wisdom.

The subtitle of *The Life of Reason* is *The Phases of Human Progress*. Santayana cherished no illusions about progress. He did not regard it as inevitable or constant. He did not suppose it to rest upon any cosmic trend. Progress, he thought, is occasional, spotty in its occurrence in human history, precarious in its continuity. But it is possible. It is possible because human nature, like other raw materials in the natural world, can be refashioned so as to bring some of its fairer potentialities into actuality. Human progress has been spasmodic in the history of mankind. Barbaric intrusion of crude impulses and fantastic assertion of untenable notions have now and again wrecked the latent promise of certain individuals and even of certain societies. But bit by bit across the centuries mankind has learned, slowly and piecemeal, how to leaven natural impulse by ideas that define their best fulfillment. Santayana professed entire agreement with the Aristotle he admired when he insisted that "everything ideal has a natural basis and everything natural has an ideal development." [21] Both parts of this often-quoted formula are requisite to Santayana's position. On the one hand, the good life for man is not a native possession or an original endowment; it ensues only from training, discipline, and the instruction of long stretches of experience. On the other hand, the good life is not gained by contemning nature and by seeking to foist upon man the alleged authority of

[21] *The Life of Reason* (New York, Scribner, 1905), Vol. I, p. 21.

some other-than-human sanction of moral value; it comes, if it come at all, by exploiting resources of the autonomous individual.

In other words, as Santayana was wont to say, the good life is an art. It is, indeed, the inclusive and final art. Any activity, he wrote, becomes an art when it is conscious of its aim and is informed by a sound theory of its adroit advance toward its ideal outcome. There are, indeed, many arts. Some of the arts are instrumental in the sense that they, like all feats of engineering, subserve efficiently ends beyond their own practice. But others of the arts are "fine" or intrinsically desirable, in the sense that their practice and their products adorn human life with moments of delight and achieve bits of ideal perfection within the texture of natural events. But all the instrumental and fine arts are subsidiary to the inclusive art of living. They contribute to the supreme art of the life of reason insofar as they enable man to turn the random and possibly disastrous play of natural impulse into a life patterned by rational pursuit of ideal ends.

Santayana, with imaginative historical justice, liked to say that in natural philosophy he was a convinced disciple of Democritus, and that in moral questions he was a loyal follower of Socrates. He was not, in the first of these phrases, espousing uncritically an ancient theory of the nature of the atoms and the void. For he was willing quite humbly to accept all the instruction which modern scientists could furnish concerning details of the structure and processes of the physical world. He was only insisting that he, like Democritus, refused to read into the course of the physical world any dialectical play of ideas or any providential scheme. His tribute to Democritus was preliminary to his more important affiliation with Socrates. His *Life of Reason* followed the teachings of Socrates that a vision of ideal beauty or any other such inclusive principle could be the technique for introducing particular beauties and values into human relationships, human institutions, human laws, human thoughts and ideas— into the whole scene of human life in which the drive of impulse inextricably involves mankind.[22] As some of the subsidiary arts give gracious patterns to material substances and material forces, so the inclusive art of the good life gives pattern to the welter of impulses and fashions human affairs to meet in some measure the requirements of moral ideals.

The successive volumes of *The Life of Reason* trace the way in which Santayana would apply his general principle to various aspects

[22] Santayana's position is constantly reminiscent of such passages in Plato as *Symposium*, 210.

of human life. The titles of the separate volumes indicate these various aspects: *Reason in Common Sense, Reason in Society, Reason in Religion, Reason in Art, Reason in Science.* The volumes are too rich in their insights into both human history and human aspirations to be summarized here. But some few points may be mentioned in order to illustrate Santayana's procedure.

"REASON IN COMMON SENSE"

Reason in Common Sense deals with the moral interests which have helped to guide the development of such ordinary and widespread human beliefs as those in natural objects, natural laws, a system of nature, the minds of oneself and one's fellow men, and so forth. These beliefs, Santayana granted, may well be true, at least in some careful form of their expression. But he was not concerned to establish their truth; he was concerned, rather, to show their genesis in the needs of human nature. Experience is initially a chaos of sensations, emotions, ideas, and impulses.[23] It was a chaos in the primitive days of man on this earth, and it is a chaos again in the early days of each human child. This chaos, or flux, receives the first imprint of a bit of rationality when some item of the flux arouses interest, satisfies desire, or appeases unrest. This item of the flux generates belief in a real object, when the item is taken, not in its isolation, but in its seeming connections with other items, so that such items may be sought more resourcefully and may be controlled in their recurrence. Man's eagerness for satisfactory experiences induces him to marshal the items of his experience into causal sequences and to treat the objects he comes to believe in as independent in status and constant in meaning. The objects believed in are disclosed, not to sense, but only to belief; that is, the objects believed in are not items in the immediate flux of experience. But the objects believed in are taken to explain experience and to account for the growing degrees of order experience assumes. And the objects of belief become eventually, when man has become sufficiently sophisticated in handling his experience, a system of natural objects, which system stretches far beyond the immediately visible and conditions all human experiences of it. Thus, from the moral needs of human nature eventuate the common-sense beliefs which all men everywhere normally entertain.

Santayana did not mean that the natural world is a product of human imagination working upon the subjective materials of experi-

---

23 Santayana here showed the influence of William James's treatment of "the stream of consciousness." Santayana had been James's pupil for some years.

ence. He never forgot that in ontology he was a disciple of Democritus. The natural world, he always firmly maintained, is ontologically and chronologically prior to experience; matter is prior to life. He was trying to drive home an understanding of quite a different point. This point is that the beliefs of men in natural objects and a system of nature may very well not plumb the depths of the objectively and independently existing world. The beliefs, even if true (as they most likely are), are concerned only with those phases of the objective world which are indicated in experience. And we have no logical and no moral right complacently to assume that the objective world has obligingly recorded all its secrets in our limited experience of it. No one probably, Santayana thought it safe to guess, has entirely ordered his own experience; no one has invented a belief which takes account of all the experiences of other men as well as of his own; and no one has the slightest ground for supposing that the entire fund of all human experiences exhausts the fertility and richness of objective existence. Our best sciences—and Santayana always had respect for the work of careful investigators of the natural world—can record no further phases of existence than those which worm their way into the course of experience and give us some bit of evidence of their presence in the world about us. Man occurs in nature, and, to a limited extent, nature occurs in human experience. But man is tiny, and nature is vast. And we ought not proudly to suppose that nature so occurs in man as there to disclose itself fully. We lift into our theories of nature only those aspects of objective nature which concern our efforts to increase the rationality of experience.

NATURAL, FREE, AND IDEAL SOCIETY

Santayana, in a number of effective metaphors, expressed the manner in which he believed ideals may supervene in human life to transform the brute forces of blind nature. One of these metaphors is his classification of human activities as natural society, free society, and ideal society. Natural society is a name for the relationships in which a man stands because of the accidents of his birth, and for the qualities and activities which ensue in his life because of those relationships. A man, if he is to exist at all, must be born in some one specific place and at some one specific time, of some specific parents, and in an environment molded by specific linguistic, political, economic, and cultural forces. He must also be a body of a certain sort, with its specific assets and liabilities, powers and limitations. He can never escape, nor ought he to wish wholly to escape, the consequences of his particularity. But he is not required to remain unchanged in his natal relationships. Natural society is a basis for his life, without wise recognition of which he would have no point of departure to better things. But he can aspire to better things. He can enter into free society, that is, into new relationships which he chooses for their affinity with his tastes, their congruity with his ideals, and the enlargement they give to the expression of his powers. Love is one of Santayana's illustrations of both natural society and free society. Love has its basis in animal lust and finds its fulfillment in many goods beyond the gratification of passion: in the joys of parentage, the sharing of interests between two persons or among the several members of a family, the protection of helpless children and the education of those children in ways for which other institutions like schools cannot afford an easy alternative. Government is another illustration. In words quite parallel to Aristotle's, Santayana pointed out that governments arose in order that men might live and are justified when they enable men to live well. Existing governments may be appraised by the degree to which they have enabled their citizens to advance from the merely natural level of society to the free level. Friendship is still another illustration. Friendship may exalt and beautify an already existing natural relationship (as between a child and a parent) , or it may be the free choice of companions selected discriminatingly out of a wide range of possibilities of social life. In either case, friendship, more indeed than any other single feature of human affairs, may be taken as the measure of the degree to which advance has been made from the natural to the free. It may have its basis in the glow of animal association, but it finds its fulfillment in the enjoyment of good fellowship, in the exhilaration of giving and receiving mutual services, and in the satisfactions of shared ideas and beauties.

Ideal society is quite another thing. It is not Utopia, for the fancying of which Santayana had little concern. It is not, in the narrow sense of the word *society,* a society at all. It is the speculative life of Aristotle,[24] that is, a life spent in the contemplation of ideas. Santayana sometimes called entrance into ideal society the spiritual life. He once claimed that he himself preferred to be a rational animal rather than a pure spirit.[25] In his many years of retirement after 1912, years devoted to reading and writing, he seemed to many critics to be choosing ideal society insofar as a person can do so and yet continue to live at all. In the dramatic mythology of his *Dialogues in Limbo*

---

[24] See above, pp. 64–65.
[25] *The Realm of Essence* (New York, Scribner, 1927), p. 65.

he is himself the Stranger from earth who chooses to visit Limbo, where Democritus, Alcibiades, and other souls have ceased to be their historical persons and have become essences which symbolize possible ideas and ideals for contemplation. But, as he acknowledged, a man may cultivate ideal society without wholly detaching himself from the life of reason.[26]

I do not forget . . . the relation of the spiritual to the rational life. Suppose that instead of mysticism I was considering taste: the poet or musician may, in moments of ecstasy, lose himself entirely in the intuition of his ideal theme. It is a limit to one movement in the Life of Reason. To revert to humanity and morality he has to consider the healthfulness of such rapture: he has to re-introduce it into the political life. Yet the moral world (being animal and spontaneous in its elements) does have those windows. I have been looking out of one lately; but, as you seem to suspect, with no intention of jumping out of it.

Santayana remained a poet when he became a philosopher. He knew enough about mathematics to realize how thrilling a geometrical system could be as an esthetic object, how enticing equations of ellipses and other curves could be whether or not such curves actually occurred in the natural world. He viewed all sciences and all religions as material for esthetic contemplation. The affirmations of scientists and theologians are always either true or false; but the ideas affirmed, apart from any affirmation of their truth value, are adventures of the imagination, adventures to be enjoyed for the charm of their esthetic qualities. And so Santayana reviewed, with kindly and detached irony, the history of men's beliefs about the heavens and the earth, about man and his destiny, about politics and education. He deemed any man impoverished, impoverished both intellectually and morally, who did not for some portions of his life take time out from his practical affairs for the enjoyment of ideas. Even the man in free society who works out his rational success finds the world indifferent to the goods he may and ought to cherish. Hence, even he needs now and then to restore his inner calm and to renew his moral poise by periodic excursions away from moral pressures into the serenity of ideal society. This contention is perhaps the way in which Santayana chose to say for our day what Plato had said in calling a philosopher a spectator of both time and eternity.

"REASON IN RELIGION"

Santayana treated religion, as he treated art and science and society, as a phase of man's effort to live the life of reason. In the religious

26 Quoted from a letter to the author under date of Jan. 28, 1929.

life, he held, man envisages his greatest joys, defines his ultimate ideals, and seeks the conversion of his soul. But though religion aims at the life of reason, it largely fails to attain it.

The aim of religion at the life of reason and the failure of religion to attain it can be correlated, Santayana maintained, with two distinguishable elements in the historic course of the religions of mankind. These elements are a deep moral consciousness and a poetic conception of things.[27] Historic religions have erred in confusing these two elements and then in supposing that the former is somehow dependent on the latter. Santayana would revise this judgment upon the role and relation of the two elements. He regarded the moral consciousness as the basic content of all religious aspiration and, also, as the permanently precious phase of religious life. The poetic conception of things, if taken as a dramatic moment in the life of the free imagination, may well add persuasive power to the lure of the ideals which aspiration has discerned; it may charm men's minds and foster their active conformity by the beauty of its imagery and the sensitivity of its symbolism. But this same poetic conception of things, if taken as a literal set of doctrines about the world and man, becomes a pseudo science, a spurious explanation of the natural in terms of the mythological. One may enjoy the imaginative constructions of religious doctrines as one would enjoy a sonnet or a symphony; but one does damage to the religious life if one thinks that the doctrinal formulas can rival scientific conclusions, or can even supplement the findings of scientific investigations, concerning the structure of the existential world.

The existence of God, Santayana wrote, is in one sense obvious and in another sense of no religious concern.[28] It is of no religious concern insofar as it is taken to be, like an astronomer's affirmation of the existence of another planet or a chemist's affirmation of the existence of another element of matter, an affirmation of an existential substance or power within or behind nature. All such existences, if they be discovered, require interpretation in the light of the bearing they have upon the efforts of men to achieve their aspirations. And it is this bearing which religious doctrines ought to set forth. Athena, for example, is not an existence which one would empirically find if one ventured to enter the cella walls of the Parthenon; rather, she is a symbol of the meanings and values which Athenian citizens might well cherish. So with the gods of other religions. The existence of God

27 *Reason in Religion*, p. 55.
28 *Ibid.*, p. 158.

is obvious, however, insofar as it is a recognition of the effective role which imaginative symbols have in the moral commitments of mankind.

Among the fine qualities which religions ought to cultivate in human life Santayana listed three: piety, charity, and spirituality. These qualities effect a man's wise adjustment, respectively, to the past, the present, and the future. Piety is a man's reverence for, and gratitude to, the natural and social factors which have made his life possible and afforded him some measure of rational happiness. It is the foe of, and remedy for, excessive self-esteem, blatant pride, and arrogance. Charity is that fine moral balance whereby a man, while holding firmly to his own aspiration, generously recognizes the differing aspirations of others.[29] And spirituality is living constantly in the light of ideals one professes to cherish. It is in antithesis to the worldliness which becomes absorbed in the instrumentalities of life (wealth, outward success, fame), and also to the fanaticism which, discerning some single good, is blind to the other possibilities of moral achievement. Equipped with these three virtues and undiverted from them by irrelevant doctrinal assertions, human life would gain religious quality and overcome the customary failure of traditional religions to exemplify adequately the life of reason.

INTUITION AND ANIMAL FAITH

Moral philosophy, Santayana acknowledged, was his "chosen subject." [30] But as years passed, Santayana, without abandoning the themes of *The Life of Reason,* became involved in contemporary controversies and so took pains to formulate an epistemology. He had always presupposed, as was said above, a contrast between nature and experience. Nature, he assumed, conditions experience but is not disclosed in its essential being within experience. Experience is the seat and sanction of all values but is a kind of madness which does little to fathom the secrets of nature. He took over the term *madness* from Plato. Madness may indeed be insanity; but *normal* madness is the prudential sanity which, saluting nature at a distance, then devotes itself to strictly human affairs. Normal madness includes such human affairs as the imagery of the senses, the delights of love, and the fancies

---

29 In one passage Santayana wrote: "Charity will always judge a soul, not by what it has succeeded in fashioning externally, not by the body or the words or the works that are the wreckage of its voyage, but by the elements of light and love that this soul infused into that inevitable tragedy." *Persons and Places* (New York, Scribner, 1944), Vol. I, p. 95.

30 *Soliloquies in England* (New York, Scribner, 1922), p. 257.

of religion.[31] To defend the assumptions of this dichotomy between experience and nature, Santayana developed explicitly the theory of knowledge of his later series, *Realms of Being*. This theory of knowledge rests upon a fundamental distinction between two types of human activity which, though often confused, are disparate in content and in issue. These human activities are intuition and animal faith.

Intuition, Santayana held, is immediate awareness. It has as its content, not the natural objects in which men may believe, but only and exclusively certain essences or "appearances." He acquired from James, he specified, "a sense for the immediate: for the unadulterated, unexplained, instant fact of experience." [32] But he platonized James's position when he affirmed that every instant fact of experience is a disembodied essence rather than a particular existential item. "Nothing given exists," he repeatedly proclaimed.[33] Insofar as a man confines himself to the content of intuition, he has no assurance of any existence, no ground for belief in any existence, no evidence for any fact. He also has no possibility of suffering from illusion. Pure intuition is a rare thing in most human lives, because men allow other activities to supervene upon intuition. Perhaps they cannot prevent other activities from so supervening. Pure intuition is an activity suitable to such people as poets, mystics, and epicureans, who delight in reveling in the luscious quality of detached moments of experience. But for most people pure intuition is an interruption to life and can be risked only rarely and for a special purpose. The special purpose is to use pure intuition as a limit in the wholesome purification of the mind from prejudice. Pure intuition is not so much an end in itself as a propaedeutic; it is the chastity of the intellect and ought to be surrendered only to legitimate and wise belief.

Animal faith is belief such as is maintained during the practical affairs of living. It is maintained to justify and make reasonable the business of meeting the forces of the world. It has as its content the natural objects which allegedly, and perhaps actually, constitute the substances of the world and the forces with which these substances play upon one another. Animal faith is expressed in beliefs in bodies, in the self, in other minds, in a system of nature. To assume such existences is requisite to the efficient performance of the vital functions. These assumptions are not an impertinence to life, though an

---

[31] *Dialogues in Limbo* (New York, Scribner, 1926), p. 46.

[32] "Brief History of My Opinions" in *Contemporary American Philosophy* (New York, Macmillan, 1930), Vol. II, p. 251.

[33] The phrase occurs, for example, as the title of chapter 7 of *Scepticism and Animal Faith*.

absurdity to intuition. They can hardly be said to be deliberately chosen. They are prior to criticism, because the animal organism is living before it begins to reflect. Animal faith is more primitive as well as chronologically earlier than intuition. It is the confident assurance men have in what yet was not first given and, indeed, can never, even in the end, be given, in experience. But it is involved in memory, in expectation, in fear, in hope, in choice of means, in selection of ends. It is unavoidable on the part of animals (including men). It always involves the risk of error; but without it life in any form, therefore, among others, the rational life, cannot occur.

As in *The Life of Reason* Santayana spoke of rationality as the happy union of ideation and impulse, so in *Realms of Being* he described knowledge as successful use of intuition of essence to guide animal faith. "Knowledge," he wrote, "is faith mediated by symbols." [34] The essences we have immediately before us in intuition may, when taken alone without reference to anything beyond themselves, give rise to poetic visions. They may, when given reference in the heat of passion or in slipshod fashion, give rise to error and illusion. But they also may, when given reference according to the fruitions of animal action and animal faith, eventuate in what we ordinarily call knowledge. This knowledge does not lay bare the mysterious nature of external realities, but it does give rise to beliefs which find justification in the practical issues of life. Knowledge is a leap of faith from the immediate of which we are aware to the hidden objects beyond the reach of intuition. This leap is not knowledge if made recklessly; but it becomes knowledge when tested by sufficient experience in the daily interaction of a living animal and the world around him. To intuition all the ideas of wild fancy and reasonable belief are alike essences on a par with one another, so that skepticism concerning their truth value is the only tenable possibility. But to animal faith the essences of intuition are symbols of dynamic forces in nature and, hence, cues to efficient action, so that knowledge arises and grows with experience.

THE UNKNOWABLE

Little further need be said concerning Santayana's metaphysics. He often repudiated metaphysics as an idle pretense to knowledge. His critic then ought perhaps to speak, not of his metaphysics, but of his assumptions about the real world. The existence of a real world beyond human experience, if not certain to the skeptic, is at least

[34] This sentence is the title of chapter 18 of *Scepticism and Animal Faith*.

"unquestioningly to be assumed." [35] This world is the fundamental presupposition of animal faith. Santayana sometimes liked to speak of it in terms of "atoms and the void." At other times he preferred to speak of it as the unknowable. "With qualifications," he wrote, " . . . I belong to Herbert Spencer's camp." [36] But whether he talked of himself as a disciple of Democritus or of Spencer, he was not committed to any particular analysis of reality, an atomic analysis or any other. He was more than willing to put the burden of venturing descriptions of the unknowable world upon the shoulders of physical scientists. He liked to shrug his own shoulders freely in such matters. He wished merely to insist that substance (or many substances) are ontologically and epistemologically prior to our existence and our speculations. He found it indispensable, in order to account for our animal contacts with substance, to believe that substance is in flux, is unequally distributed through space, and composes a cosmos of more or less interrelated things. He found certain further beliefs reasonable presumptions, such beliefs, for example, as that substance remains always constant in quantity and that the modes of substance are determined in all respects by their causal antecedents.[37] These various articles of belief do not, all together, carry one very far. And, indeed, in such points of theory Santayana did not wish to go far. He was still the moralist when he ventured to discuss substance. He was concerned, not to describe the natural world (for he deemed that world unknowable in its objective reality), but to indicate the human attitudes men might most profitably take toward that world. His doctrine of substances was really a warning to men that they need to be humble in the presence of forces greater than their petty strength. His doctrine of causal determination was a challenge to men to find wisdom by disciplining their hopes in accord with nature's possibilities. He was willing to call himself "a decided materialist—apparently the only one living." [38] But he used this language in order to dismiss ontological problems and to turn again to consideration of the roles which substances play in human experience. He remained a moralist even when he ventured outside the field which most philosophers would call the province of moral philosophy.

[35] "The Unknowable," *Obiter Scripta* (New York, Scribner, 1936), p. 188.
[36] *Ibid.*, p. 162.
[37] For the "indispensable properties" and the "presumable properties" of substance, see *The Realm of Matter* (New York, Scribner, 1930), chaps. 2 and 3.
[38] *Scepticism and Animal Faith* (New York, Scribner, 1923), p. vii.

3. WHITEHEAD

ALFRED NORTH WHITEHEAD, 1861–1947, was born in Isle of Thanet, a town near Canterbury, England, and died in Cambridge, Massachusetts. He entered Cambridge University in 1880, studying principally mathematics but continuing to read widely in the classics and poetry. He became a fellow of Trinity College, Cambridge, in 1885, and taught at Cambridge until 1910. He was elected to the Royal Society in 1903. In 1910 he resigned his Cambridge post and moved to London where he became associated with the University of London as teacher and as administrator. His teaching up to this time was in the field of mathematics, though his work always had philosophical import. In 1924 he accepted an appointment as professor of philosophy at Harvard University, taught there until 1937, and was professor emeritus until his death. His first writings were in mathematics, for example, the article on mathematics in the eleventh (1910) and subsequent editions of the *Encyclopaedia Britannica; Introduction to Mathematics* (1911) in the Home University Library; and, in collaboration with Bertrand Russell, *Principia Mathematica,* 3 vols. (1910–1913). Among his later and his philosophical writings are *Principles of Natural Knowledge* (1919), *The Concept of Nature* (1920), *Science and the Modern World* (1925), *Religion in the Making* (1926), *Symbolism* (1927), *Process and Reality* (1929), *Adventures of Ideas* (1933), *Nature and Life* (1934).

WHITEHEAD, UNLIKE OTHER prominent philosophers in the United states, came into philosophy from the field of mathematics. This biographical point is not without significance for an understanding of the nature of the philosophical position he eventually reached. For from his study of mathematics he learned both the utility and the limitations of abstract thinking; and as he extended the range of his reflections, he saw that the same kind of utility and limitations characterized the abstractions made in other bodies of knowledge. Mathematics, he maintained, is thought which seeks complete generality; and it gains this complete generality by ignoring the concrete details of all matters of fact and by formulating the purely abstract conditions which these matters of fact exemplify. Mathematics is successful just because it avoids consideration of the concreteness of *every* matter of fact and specializes in the rigorous analysis of the general conditions of *all* matters of fact. The science of mathematics thus becomes relevant to everything but fails to instruct us concerning the full nature of anything.

Philosophy, Whitehead said, stands in marked contrast with mathematics. Philosophy is the critique of abstractions. It is reflection which keeps watch of the fully concrete realities of the world and seeks to measure the degree of adequacy which any proffered abstractions have relatively to these concrete realities. The philosopher has as one of his requisite tasks a kind of oversight of the special sciences; he has the function of explaining the nature of the abstractions each special science uses and of compelling attention to the full concreteness of things. He needs to keep in mind that the full concreteness of things is never exhausted in the analyses of any one science, or even in the analyses of any set of sciences.

With this view of the relation of scientific abstractions to concrete realities, Whitehead formulated a philosophy of the natural sciences. He sought to attain a concept that would serve to unify all the natural sciences and to place them in their due relation to one another. The required concept is the concept of "nature." [39] *Nature,* in this sense of the term, is everything there is for sense awareness, for knowledge, for emotion, for thought. But it does not include awareness or emotion or knowledge or thought. It is "closed to mind." Whitehead could properly take this position even though he also pronounced firmly, from his earliest to his latest writings, against theories of "the bifurcation of nature." He was unwilling, when he came to metaphysics, to regard reality as divided into two realms, nature and mind. But for the methodological purposes of the natural sciences the exclusion of mind from nature was, he supposed, a useful procedure. Nature is a pragmatically justified abstraction from reality.

Abstractions, Whitehead went on to say, must be made with care. Not all abstractions are equally useful, and some abstractions are quite misleading. He pointed out that by what he called "the method of extensive abstraction," [40] natural scientists may reach such concepts as points, instants, time as a series of extensionless instants, all-nature-

[39] Whitehead was not setting forth, as some of his readers supposed, his theory of what the real world around us is. He was, rather, so abstracting from the real world as to find a basis for scientific work. He did not intend the concept of "nature" to be regarded as a metaphysical principle. He expressed, in more than one conversation with the author, his regret that some of his readers misconceived the intent of his analysis.

[40] He defined this method in his *Principles of Natural Knowledge* (Cambridge, Cambridge University Press, 1919), chap. 8. Students who desire to do so may find his exposition of the method there. Space does not permit discussion of the method here.

at-an-instant, event-particles, and so forth. But we ought to realize that these entities are not concrete realities. We ought to realize that from no assemblage of these entities, however numerous, can we ever recover the concrete realities by abstraction from which we reach the concepts. We ought not to suppose that such entities are the ultimate building blocks of the universe. To make that faulty supposition is to commit "the fallacy of misplaced concreteness," that is, to regard an artificial abstraction, however useful as an abstraction, as the description of a concrete natural entity.

Whitehead went on [41] to criticize the concepts which were fundamental in the Newtonian theory of nature and to revise the Newtonian theory of nature so as to bring it in line with contemporary scientific ideas. Among his criticisms of the Newtonian world two may be mentioned here.

One of these criticisms is directed against the Newtonian concept of particles of matter, each of which, existing at some specific point in space at some specific moment of time, is what it is by virtue of its own intrinsic nature. This concept, Whitehead insisted, is the outcome of unimaginative empiricism. We find no concrete entity of the type of Newton's particles. What we find is always some occurrence or event, changing in nature with its temporal advance and owing its nature to the relations in which it stands to the nexus of events in which it is involved. No event is what it is because of its separate being. Every event takes account of other events about it (though this "taking account" is not necessarily or even usually on the level of cognition). The concrete world is a vast nexus of events, each of which stands in mutual relevance with each other event and is what it is because of this relevance. Newton's particles have, and concrete events do not have, the property of "simple location." A bar of iron, for example, is a concrete reality. It may appear to casual observation to be unchanged over a period of many days. But it is still an event. For, as Whitehead once took pleasure in saying, it takes time to be iron. It takes at least enough time to permit a particle to revolve once about a nucleus. To exist is to occur. There are no instantaneous configurations of matter. Moreover, the concrete events are not isolated entities. Rather, they are constantly undergoing changes due to influences which come to them from their environment and which they prehend in their own ways. To prehend is to take account of another entity and to become modified in some specific manner by so taking account. Prehension is the way in which any event includes

[41] Notably in his *Science and the Modern World* (New York, Macmillan, 1925).

aspects of other events as part of its own essence or its own pattern of occurrence.[42] Newton's particles, each of which has simple location, have their intrinsic nature completely through themselves and then enter adventitiously into merely external relations with one another. Whitehead's events, each of which penetrates and is penetrated by all other events, are patterned in their being by the internal relations in which they occur relatively to one another.

A second of Whitehead's criticisms of the Newtonian concept of nature concerns the ontological status of sense qualities. Newton's particles could not be colored or fragrant or have any sensory qualities because the qualities, on the one hand, undergo constant fluctuations, and the particles, on the other hand, are already complete in their nature and cannot be modified except by external relations. The Newtonian theory of nature thus led on logically, as Locke's use of it in his philosophy shows, to banishing sense qualities from nature and relegating them to a subjective status in the mind of the observer. This theory, Whitehead insisted, is contrary to the facts of experience. Sense objects, he maintained, ingress into events when and if certain definable conditions are met.[43] A flannel coat, for example, becomes blue, or a concert room becomes filled with a note. The color and the sound are not "in the mind" in the sense of being elsewhere than they appear. They are in the event. They are characters which come and go in events with the development of the pattern of the events. They are exactly when and where they appear.

HIS ACCOUNT OF EXPERIENCE

Whitehead was an empiricist in the sense that he would require every idea to be tested by its adequacy for the interpretation of particular concrete facts. But he differed greatly from the classical empiricists in his conception of experience. He refused to begin by listing simple ideas or any other detached psychical elements and then to try therefrom to determine the limits of human knowledge. He proffered, in criticism of the classical procedure, a view of experience which is, in some respects, novel and which enables us to reach much more

---

42 See *Adventures of Ideas* (New York, Macmillan, 1933), p. 300.

43 Whitehead defined "objects" as "elements in nature which do not pass." See *The Concept of Nature* (Cambridge, University Press, 1920), p. 143. They are not concrete entities but are characters concrete entities may come to have. Unlike events, they may occur over and over again, that is, may be the same character in many events. And Whitehead defined "ingression" as one form of prehension. When an event prehends an entity, we have physical prehension. But when an event prehends an object, we have conceptual prehension or ingression. See *Process and Reality* (New York, Macmillan, 1929), p. 35.

knowledge of the real world than the classical empiricists supposed.

In the first place he regarded sense experience as making us aware of complexes of fact. The discerned, he wrote, is given in its context with the discernible. We do not, for example, experience separately the color of a wall or the extensiveness of a patch of color. Rather, we experience "color away on the wall for us." [44] The color is a sensory item, but it is an abstraction from the integral experience. The wall is given as colored in its relation to us as its observers; it is given as standing in spatial relation to what lies beyond it and is not immediately discerned; it is given also as coming out of something prior and leading on into something subsequent. Any moment of experience may be compared to a vector. For in addition to having its own intrinsic pattern, it points beyond itself in various ways and so involves a broad context of occurrence. The ways in which a sense experience points beyond itself are its significance. Significance is not added to facts as a more or less hazardous or even gratuitous interpretation or judgment; it is intrinsic to the directly discerned as genuinely as any quality or extensiveness of a sensory item.

In the second place, Whitehead regarded sense experience as only one of the modes of human experience. Human experience is often obscure and always fragmentary; yet, if attended to fully, it penetrates deeply into the nature of concrete reality. It is not primarily cognitive; it is surely not primarily sensory. Human experience has various modes. The mode of conceptual analysis and cognition is highly sophisticated and is made possible through the more elementary modes of perceptivity. But within pure perceptivity (that is, within perceptivity considered apart from any conceptual analysis which may actually accompany it) two different modes of experience may be distinguished. These two modes Whitehead called presentational immediacy and the perception of causal efficacy. [45] They doubtless occur conjointly in human experience. But presentational immediacy is a mode of experience of only fairly high-grade organisms and is not very fundamental, even in human experience, as a source of information about the world around us. Presentational immediacy is precise (and herein lies its value), but it is also, when taken apart from other modes of experience, quite trivial. The color or the taste of a substance, for example, gives us little information about the full nature of that substance. Perception of causal efficacy, in contrast to pre-

---

[44] *Symbolism* (New York, Macmillan, 1927), p. 13.
[45] See *Symbolism*, p. 17 especially, but throughout chaps. 1 and 2.

sentational immediacy, is vague and unmanageable, but it is also "a heavy, primitive experience" [46] which puts us in direct contact with the dynamic urgency of events. It makes us aware that we are involved in a world of looming forces which impinge on us, sustain or threaten, pull or push, promote or retard, control or modify, or otherwise forcefully affect both ourselves and one another. It gives us to understand that events do not succeed one another as do the discrete integers or as, perhaps, the series of sensory images in the classical empiricist's description of experience. It gives us to understand that events interpenetrate, move along, grow, sweep, compel.

Presentational immediacy, apart from perception of causal efficacy, is blind to the dynamic course of events. Its sensory items, then, are but a kind of decorative futility upon the realities of the world and are likely to be illusory because they enable us to deal with appearances only.

Perception of causal efficacy, apart from presentational immediacy, is confused. It is a mode of experience akin to that of living things (like plants) which exist on a noncognitive and even a nonsensory level. It would make us aware of forces we need to take account of, but it would leave us unaware of methods of dealing with these forces, of measuring the strength of various forces, of determining fruitful points of contact with the forces, of using the forces to assist us in gaining our ends instead of meeting destruction at their hands.

The effective union of the two modes of perceptivity in human experience makes experience fruitful in an understanding of the world. The data of presentational immediacy, then, are symbols of the dynamic forces of the world; they make our contact with these forces manageable. The perception of causal efficacy gives significance to the data of presentational immediacy and enables us to turn these data into evidence for scientific knowledge and humane practice.

COSMOLOGY

Whitehead's criticisms of scientific abstractions and philosophical traditions culminated in his own cosmology. He felt driven to attempt to formulate a cosmology in order that he might combat the stubbornly retained Newtonian attitude of popular thought and might provide a scheme more in accord with contemporary scientific discoveries. He aimed to construct a framework of general ideas by which everything we encounter in our experience can be interpreted, of

[46] *Symbolism,* p. 44.

which everything we encounter in our experience will be a particular instance. He called this grand enterprise an essay in speculative philosophy.

There is, Whitehead maintained, one all-embracing fact, which is the advancing and constantly expanding history of the universe. There are no independent entities. There are, to be sure, individuals within the universe. But individualization is not independence. Every actual entity pervades the entire world, finding its own specific and unique ways of being prehended in all other actual entities. And, in turn, every actual entity reflects the entire world, incorporating into the unity of its pattern prehensions from all other entities. Every entity thus has its intrinsic and its extrinsic reality, the former of which is the pattern of its prehension of all other entities, and the latter of which is the pattern of its aspects in the prehending unities of the other entities. The universe is an organism in that the character or pattern of its totality ensues from the characters or aspects of its interrelated parts; and each individual within the universe is an organism in that it brings prehensions from all other things into the unity of its own character or pattern. Whitehead's cosmology is thus, as he put it, a philosophy of organism.

The "final real things" of which the world is composed Whitehead called by several different names in his various chapters—events, actual entities, occasions of experience, even "cells." Each of these names has its respective relevance to one or another of the points he was discussing. In any case, or rather in all cases, the final real things are processes occurring in a vast cosmic context and reflecting in their nature the influences of that context. They may, in light of the fact that they reflect the context of their occurrence, be called social entities. One point which Whitehead recurrently emphasized is that these final real things are not fixed or static. A particular event may exhibit, when during a certain course of time its intrinsic pattern is not altered by any distracting prehension, an enduring continuity of character for a considerable period. But that enduring continuity of character is not undifferentiated sameness. It is rather the re-iteration of a pattern, each occurrence of which requires a certain lapse of time and a certain rhythmic variation of development. The bar of iron mentioned above seems fixed only because the pattern of its occurrence, too brief to be detected in sense awareness of it, occurs over and over again without noticeable alteration. An exploding rocket is no more genuinely an event than is the bar of iron.

Inherent in the very nature of reality, therefore, is process or passage. Passage is always from the potential to the actual. There is room for novelty in a world so constituted. And, Whitehead firmly maintained, we do actually observe the constant emergence of novelty. An actual occasion absorbs into itself prehensions from other occasions and so advances to a new phase of development. Nature manifests evolutionary expansiveness. There is, to be sure, necessity in the world, too. For all processes begin within the limits of the actual, as man, for example, needs food, warmth, and shelter as conditions of his higher activities. But the environment yields to the exercise of intelligence, so that to the extent that intelligence takes part in change, the range of necessity is narrowed and the field of creativity grows. What nature manifests on the human level, it manifests in less conspicuous manner on lower levels. In some events necessity appears to be dominant. Elsewhere, as in human events where intelligence takes charge, creativity is amply evident. And to the extent that creativity occurs novelty appears within the expanding universe.

The philosophical doctrines of creativity and novelty required some consideration of the nature and role of natural law. This consideration Whitehead gave in several places in his writings.[47] He reviewed several theories maintained in modern and contemporary times, rejected some, and finally came to a definition of his own position. He rejected, for example, the theory of natural law as imposed by divine power (the deistic notion). He rejected also the theory of natural law as generalized description of observed sequences (the positivistic notion). He rejected this last because he recognized that there are vast areas of order in the universe and wanted a theory of law which would account for the occurrence of these areas. He was not satisfied to make law a way in which we human investigators sum up what we find in nature; he wanted a theory of law which accounts for what we find. So he came to espouse—with qualifications to be noted below—the more rationalistic theory of law as immanent in events. Natural laws are nature's habits before they are our formulas about nature. Each law sets forth a common character which pervades nature (or at least large areas of nature with which we are dealing in our observations and our inquiries). This theory fits in with Whitehead's previous contention that actual entities are constituted through their interconnections and that their interconnections are an outcome of their characters; that is, the philosophy of organism has the consequence that community of development prevails through large areas of the universe.

47 Notably *Adventures of Ideas,* chaps. 7 and 8.

Whitehead accepted the theory of natural law as immanent, as was said above, with certain qualifications. The qualifications are important to his position. One qualification is that the laws, or at least some of the laws, are probably statistical in character, setting forth a norm around which nature's habits approximate. Another qualification is that the laws themselves may well evolve. Nature's habits may change. What is a genuine law at one epoch of the history of the universe may give place to another and different law at another epoch. A third qualification is that the theory of law as conventional interpretation is also in a sense acceptable. It is acceptable, however, in a sense that makes it compatible with the theory of law as immanent. We do not grasp nature throughout the inexhaustible richness of its full being, but we touch it at certain points which concern us most. Our human approach to nature determines which of the many habits of nature we chance to discover. Nature may illustrate many sciences we human beings have never formulated, as well as those we have formulated. We are nonetheless obligated, in our dealings with nature, to receive instruction and not to impose subjective fancies. Convention is not caprice. Convention may settle *which* laws we find but not *what* laws we find. Even when we realize that our conventional approach to nature is a function of our own stage of human culture, we must needs expose our minds to nature's objective ways.

DOCTRINE OF GOD

Whitehead was concerned to bring his cosmology to completion in a doctrine of God. His discussion of God is obscure at many points. He himself knew that it was obscure. The claim of exactness in ultimate philosophical speculation, he said, is "a fake." [48] He was clear enough about what he did not want to be taken to be affirming. He was a fearless critic of traditional theological conceptions of western culture. He praised Hume's critique of some of these conceptions in the *Dialogues* as a masterpiece. He dissented from the supposition that God is a first cause or a creator of the world. He denied that God is omnipotent and even that God has an already completed nature. But when he went beyond dissent to positive assertion, he was neither exact nor clear.

In the first extended discussion of God in his published writings (*Science and the Modern World*) Whitehead referred to God as the

---

[48] See the closing sentence of his Ingersoll Lecture at Harvard Divinity School in 1941 in P. A. Schilpp, ed., *The Philosophy of Alfred North Whitehead* (Chicago, Northwestern University, 1941).

"principle of concretion" in the universe. His point seems to have been as follows. Any empirical philosophy (and he regarded his own philosophy as a form of empiricism) is committed to acknowledge that existence cannot be demonstrated by abstract reason. Existence must be encountered in experience. The universe is the particular universe it is and is not lots of other things which might vainly be imagined. There is requisite, therefore, some principle of concretion, that is, some metaphysical ground which limits the vast possibilities of existence to the actual world. And if God is the principle of concretion to explain why the actual world is what it is, God cannot then be accounted for by anything more ultimate.

In saying that God is the principle of concretion, Whitehead did not wish to imply that God is the metaphysical ground of evil as well as of good. In his later treatments of God (*Religion in the Making* and *Process and Reality*), he chose to think of God as one actual entity within the world. God, then, like all other actual entities, even if far more vast than most other actual entities, is in interaction with the world. God prehends the rest of the world, and it prehends God. And when God is thus conceived, Whitehead was led to distinguish two phases of God's existence: the primordial and the consequent. God is not infinite in all respects but is limited by his own goodness. He is expressed in the love which runs through the world and which may be taken as a progressively potent force in the course of events. The primordial nature of God is his activity in limiting the vast possibilities of being to that which is good. God, in this sense, is the savior of the world, or the dynamic urgency which keeps the world from so developing as to issue in the total destruction of all values. In his perceptivity are preserved and fused all the diverse values which emerge with the evolving creativity of the universe. And the consequent nature of God is the way in which, through the interaction of God with the rest of the world, the world process points ahead to greater values than have yet been actualized. It is the way in which values impossible in the light of existing actualities may yet be made possible and brought to pass. God, in his consequent nature, is what makes the world process progress in the direction of ever greater good.

Whitehead did not maintain that he had demonstrated or could demonstrate the truth of his theological position. He proffered his conception of the nature of God as part of his speculative philosophy. And a speculative philosophy, he granted, functions, not as a body of established knowledge such as a special science may accumulate by piecemeal investigation of selected actualities, but as a point of view which, consistent with all that is known, yet seeks to guide future reflections toward a more embracing understanding of concrete reality.

4. WOODBRIDGE

FREDERICK J. E. WOODBRIDGE, 1867–1940, was born in Windsor, Ontario, and died in New York. He was graduated from Amherst College in 1889, studied at Union Theological Seminary from 1889 to 1892, and at the University of Berlin between 1892 and 1894. He received honorary degrees of LL.D. and Litt.D. from a number of institutions. He taught philosophy at the University of Minnesota from 1894 to 1902 and was professor of philosophy at Columbia University from 1902 until 1939, when he became professor emeritus. He was dean of the Faculties of Political Science, Philosophy, and Pure Science at Columbia University from 1912 to 1929. He became Theodore Roosevelt Professor at the University of Berlin (1931–1932). He was one of the founders of the *Journal of Philosophy* in 1904 and one of its editors from 1904 until his death. His philosophical writings include *The Purpose of History* (1916); *The Realm of Mind* (1926); *The Son of Apollo: Themes of Plato* (1929); *An Essay on Nature* (1940). His many philosophical articles and lectures were so important to his students and friends that a collection of them was made and presented to him in book form on the occasion of his seventieth birthday; this book is *Nature and Mind* (1937).

WOODBRIDGE IS NOTABLE for his contributions to the fields of history of philosophy and metaphysics. He dealt with the history of philosophy for several decades in his academic lectures, as well as in his witty and penetrating book on Plato's main dialogues. He was a leader, possibly *the* leader, in the movement in the United States in the twentieth century which made the history of philosophy one of the major philosophical disciplines. He also did much to revive metaphysics, rescuing it from the inferior status to which modern epistemologists had relegated it and re-establishing it as a *first science* in Aristotle's sense of that term.[49] He was aware of his debt to Aristotle and called himself both humanist and naturalist in the meaning these terms have in the traditions which stem respectively from Plato and Aristotle. But he handled Aristotelian ideas freely in developing

[49] See above, pp. 67–68.

his own position. His metaphysics may be said to be that revision of Aristotle's metaphysics which he deemed requisite in the light of modern scientific and philosophical thought.

Woodbridge emphasized the importance of metaphysics and was indeed bound to emphasize its importance, because of the undeviating realism of his habits of mind. He was a realist for some years before the various "schools" of realism began to crop up in England and the United States. But his realism was not a doctrine. It was an attitude. It was the attitude expressed in the remark he was fond of quoting from Matthew Arnold: "Things are what they are and the consequences of them will be what they will be; why then should we wish to be deceived?" This kind of attitude was bound to generate doctrines when it was firmly sustained through a course of philosophic reflections. It was bound to generate metaphysical doctrines. For it was the attitude that whatever more the world may be, the world is at least all that we do or can find it to be. Apart from the doctrines it generated, his realistic attitude was one of respect for the full integrity of the subject-matter we find before us in every form of our experiencing of phases of that subject-matter. The world is not a product of our thought. The world is prior to our thinking about it. Knowledge, Woodbridge realized, may, at times, be won by means of experimental activities in which the objects we are investigating are transformed or even destroyed in the course of our experimentations with them. But knowledge is neither transformation nor destruction of its objects. Our hands or our instruments (that is, our own bodies or other bodies we control) are what transform or destroy objects. Our minds do not transform or destroy. Our minds may, and indeed often do, capture the nature of the objects as they were before they were transformed or destroyed, even though our minds only gain that knowledge during or after the transformation or destruction. Knowledge is intellectual vision in which objects, or some aspects of some objects, are disclosed. Knowledge may be superficial or penetrating; but in either case, it is, as far as it goes, cognizance of what is there to be known. If we observe things without prejudice, turn them over, and experiment with them in various ways, we "see" what things are. This seeing is what the Greeks called θεωρία. A realist of Woodbridge's type sees the spectacle of the world as the Greeks saw a spectacle at the theater.

"What we repeatedly need," Woodbridge wrote, "is at once the most naive and profoundest realism we can express." [50] And he might well have added that only a realism which began by being naive could end by being profound. For only if the things we see and hear and touch are natural objects, can further investigation of them render us acquainted with more of nature's ways. Every item of experience, Woodbridge maintained, is an occurrence in the natural world. There are sensations if that word mean processes of sensing; but there are no sensations if that word be taken to mean mental states. We are not justified in supposing that things as they appear to us in sense experience are not things as they really are. The alleged illusions (like the straight stick, half immersed in water, so that it "appears" bent) can all be explained, not by treating them as subjective (and inaccurate) images of external things, but by understanding the physical relativities among natural things and events. Relativity there certainly is among the items experienced; but the relativity is never to the mind but only to one or another body (sometimes, but not always, to that particular body which is the percipient organism). Our interpretations of the observed items may sometimes be false, and our practical reactions to them may be awkward and in need of training. But whatever we observe is to that extent real. Whatever "appears" also is—and is as it appears. And from the basis of this kind of naive realism we can properly proceed, Woodbridge held, to further analyses of the objects we observe and to further discoveries of more objects, until our realism becomes the "profoundest" view men in our day, with our instruments and techniques, can possibly achieve of the world of nature.

METAPHYSICAL PRINCIPLES

None of the great metaphysical systems, Woodbridge granted, can be taken as absolutely true. Nonetheless, from Democritus and Aristotle in the ancient world to Hegel and Spencer in recent times, the enterprise of metaphysics is one of "the supreme attempts of intelligence at integration." [51] In metaphysical reflections a man sees the universe under those of its aspects which are most universally present throughout it. For the universe has certain general characters in addition to the specific characters it exhibits in the variety of distinctive things which the special sciences examine. Metaphysics keeps the mind of man from being divided into compartments as he listens to first one specialist (like an astronomer) and then another specialist

[50] *The Realm of Mind* (New York, Columbia University Press, 1926), p. 115.
[51] "Metaphysics," *Nature and Mind* (New York, Columbia University Press, 1937), p. 105.

(like a psychologist). Doubtless knowledge is best gained through specialization. But understanding requires integration. And metaphysics is a means—when competently done, it is the best means—to this integration and, hence, to this understanding.

Although recognizing the value of integrated understanding, Woodbridge made his chief contribution to metaphysics in the form of a series of separate analytical essays on a series of separate metaphysical points. His preference for this way of expressing his metaphysical convictions was a consequence of his inveterate realism.[52] He did not wish to lose sight of the concrete realities which alone could exercise epistemic control over his own or anybody's reflections. One may properly analyze concrete realities by using highly abstract concepts. But by such a procedure one soon gets to the limit of his powers to report on the varied panorama which nature exhibits. One is in danger of turning his metaphysical analysis into an arbitrary dialectical system and of ignoring all but some favored selection of nature's diverse traits. One needs to return often, not to some earlier idea of his own abstract system, but to concrete nature itself, and to begin another and fresh line of analysis. The various lines of analysis, if done skillfully, will supplement one another; they will, put side by side, give rise to the integrated understanding in which metaphysical wisdom culminates. But integrated understanding is not the same thing as intellectual mastery of a dialectical system. It is, rather, a vision of the concrete world by means of a succession of telling perspectives. It is, in other words, θεωρία.

Woodbridge was both disciple and critic of Aristotle in metaphysics. And his wide scholarship in intellectual history taught him the need of safeguarding his use of Aristotle against misinterpretations which had arisen in the course of the Aristotelian tradition. Where Aristotle had spoken of matter and form, Woodbridge spoke of structure and behavior. Structure and behavior are two ultimate ideas to which the analysis of nature leads. The two ideas, capable of separate treatment, are significant in juxtaposition. Structure is of many types. There are physical (mechanical) and chemical structures, biological structures, mental structures. Structure, varying enormously in types, is in some form everywhere in nature. We can speak of nature as a manifold of structures. Woodbridge chose quite carefully to say that

---

[52] Friendly critics have also pointed out that during the years when he was at the height of his intellectual powers, Woodbridge was burdened with the administrative duties of a great university and so had little time for sustained development of a system. One cannot deny that this view has some plausibility. But the main reason for Woodbridge's preference for separate analytical essays is probably that given in the text above.

nature *is* structure, rather than that nature has structure. He thereby hoped to avoid the supposition of a *materia prima* which comes to be structured or of a something-I-know-not-what which lies behind the structures we empirically discover. Structure, he noted, is not a cause or agent. It is absolutely inert. It is not itself a happening, but it is manifest in all happenings. Structure is *matter* in the metaphysical sense of that term; that is, it is the principle of particularity in things, or it is that to which we inevitably come when we point to the difference between some *kind* of thing we may be thinking about and a particular instance of that kind of thing. And everywhere behavior, as our investigation of nature eventually teaches us, is correlative with structure. Behavior cannot be reduced to structure any more than structure can be reduced to behavior.[53] Furthermore, behavior can only be defined in terms of the end served. These ends do not operate; they are not efficient forces; they ought not to be read back, like Bergson's vital impulse, into the structures as if they were resident powers which produced the behavior. Behavior, we can do no more than point out, is everywhere teleological in outcome. It cannot be empirically identified, except by pointing to the ends accomplished in nature. We discover a certain structure and may be able to ascertain how its parts are related to one another; but we do not feel content that we understand it until we also note how it behaves and what end it thereby effects. An agent with a certain structure behaves in such a fashion as to keep time; another agent with another structure behaves so as to produce fruit and seeds. We thus tend to discriminate structures and their respective behaviors by the ends they serve. Hence we are justified in saying that the teleological character of behavior constitutes the intelligibility of nature.

Consideration of structure and behavior, therefore, seemed to Woodbridge to necessitate the further consideration of teleology. Nature, he repeatedly insisted in his essays, is a domain of changes which point to certain definite, specific ends, and which, unless thwarted by untoward circumstances, effect these ends. This teleology, however, is *natural* teleology. It needs no explanation; that is, it does not have to be accounted for. It is a generic trait of nature. It is a fact to be used practically in the arts, and it is a fact to be referred

[53] Woodbridge was here taking a stand against the attempt (found in different ways in Bergson, Whitehead, and Dewey) to make events the one ultimate kind of existential entity. As he was fond of saying, he could think of the birth of a child as an event, but he had trouble in trying to think of the child as an event. There are things and events, however much these two ultimate considerations stand in one-one correspondence with each other; or, in his more technical language, there are both structures and behavior.

state of things into the past through our realization of some new state of affairs.

And what has just been said of the way we human beings operate can also be said, *mutatis mutandis,* of all agents in nature, inanimate as well as animate. Many agents lack all consciousness of their own activities and of the ends their activities effect. But inanimate agents do nonetheless act, and act efficaciously. They, too, "push" the former state of what they act upon into the past through their productive actualization of a new present.

One may represent time by a line, and the successive instants of time by points on the line. But one must then, in his spatial representation of time, compare time, not to a line already drawn (in which past, present, and future are all, so to speak, completed and over), but by "a line in the drawing." [55] The present, however, cannot be represented by one of the points on the line. It must, rather, be represented by the drawing of the line. Only the past is on the line. And as the line is drawn, each point already on the line recedes farther and farther away from the place where the continued operation of the drawing of the line is still going on. So each finished event of the past recedes farther and farther away from the present into the past. The past is thus built up, bit by bit, by continued activity of present agents. The past is a product of successive presents.

History, of course, is continuous. But its continuity is not due to the way the past pushes forward through the present into the future. Its continuity is due, rather, to the fact that the present (that is, existing actualities) must act, if they are to act at all, upon the legacy the past has left to them as materials for their reconstruction. History will exhibit periods of more or less uniform character, insofar as present actualities preserve relatively unchanged their habits of action. History will show rapid and revolutionary change, insofar as present actualities alter their line of attack or, in the case of rational agents, their purposes. But in any case, the activity of reconstruction of material is always a process of the conversion of the potential into the actual. It is much fairer to regard the passage of nature as going, not from past to future, but from potential to actual. It is not the past in the sense of a period of time which sets limits to present activities. It is, rather, the potentialities (and lack of potentialities) of the materials from the past which set those limits. "The world," Woodbridge concluded with justice, "is always fresh and always

[55] *Ibid.,* p. 38.

old." [56] The legacy from the past is ever transformed, and so novelty appears; and nothing else exists to operate upon, and so continuity with the past is maintained.

THE REALM OF MIND

Woodbridge was led, by his consideration of epistemological speculations in modern centuries, to formulate a theory of mind. The term *mind,* he pointed out, has come to be used in two senses. The senses are distinct, though significantly related. Mind is, on the one hand, a name for certain activities, such as perceiving, thinking, feeling—activities performed pre-eminently by human beings but, to some degree at least, by other living things, too. Mind is, on the other hand, a name for the realm in which thinking goes on. In the former sense we may speak of many minds; in the latter sense, of one objective mind.

When we speak of mind in the sense of the many individual minds, we are dealing, Woodbridge held, not with a certain kind of object, but with certain activities. The term *mind* here refers to what some bodies do rather than to what they are. Walking, digesting, and breathing we call physical activities; thinking, remembering, and perceiving we call mental activities. It is the same object which performs both sets of activities, namely, the organic body of a living individual. Mind is not an agent. The agent in the activities of thinking, remembering, and perceiving is the same as in the activities of walking, digesting, and breathing. Doubtless the two kinds of activities are performed in such intricate involvement with each other that each becomes what it is by virtue of the presence of the other. We walk when and where we walk because we think and plan in a certain manner; and we perceive what we perceive because we walk in a certain direction. But the mental, however closely related with the physical, cannot be reduced to the physical; and the physical, in spite of the entanglement of idealists in the dialectic of their speculations, cannot be reduced to the mental. Men's bodies come to be related to more physical objects than those with which they are in physical contact, because their mental activities bring them into relations with the past which is gone, with the remote in space, with the inferred which is not visible. And, reciprocally, men's minds come to be related to one another in society, in morals, in various phases of culture, because, willy-nilly, their bodies inhabit neighboring areas on the surface of the earth. The mind (in the sense of the term when we speak of

[56] *Ibid.,* pp. 82–83.

many minds) is so related to the body that thereby it both unites the body, and is united by the body, with many other things. We must therefore conclude that when certain organic bodies think and remember and perceive, they are led, not into another realm than the physical realm in which those bodies walk and digest and breathe, but into new relationships with other physical objects in the one and only realm for the existence of which we have the slightest evidence. When bodies perform mental activities, they are still in the natural world; but they are in the natural world in an enriched and vastly altered way. Woodbridge used a telling metaphor in summing up his position.[57] As a lens, placed among many rays of light, will focus those rays in a clearly patterned picture, so an organic body, united to other physical objects by activities of thinking and remembering and perceiving, will focus the meanings of its situation in rational discourse. A body without a mind has a narrow range of physical contacts and is confined in those contacts to physical pressures. The relation of mind to body is such that a body with a mind has the range of its contacts amplified and the course of its contacts rendered intelligible.

When we speak of mind in the sense of objective mind, we are dealing, Woodbridge insisted, with the natural world. His position is in intentional opposition to the Lockian theory that the realm of mind is a private realm apart from nature. Since the body (and not an alleged spiritual substance) is the agent which thinks, thinking occurs in the same realm in which the body moves. The world is a physical world, to be sure; but it is also a *mundus intelligibilis*. An individual mind, that is, the mental activity of a particular organic body, unites that body with the intelligibility of nature. We human beings (and possibly other living things) have ideas. But an idea is not a mental replica or a mental representative of a physical thing. Woodbridge was fond of saying that Spinoza understood, best among the moderns, the nature of an idea. "The order and connection of ideas," Spinoza said, "is the same as the order and connection of things." The two orders are one and the same order. For an idea is an object in its logical connections. In walking, a man is exploring the spatial aspect of nature; in thinking, he is exploring the intelligible aspect of nature. He is, so to speak, exploring objective mind. We may get ideas through physical stimuli and then through events in our nervous systems and brains. But the mechanism by which we get ideas is not an indication of what ideas are: it is only an indication

---

[57] *The Realm of Mind*, pp. 103–104.

of one way in which the body which thinks is tied to the rest of the world. What we call having ideas is a disclosure of nature's intelligible structures. We use physical means for the transmission of ideas —spoken words, written symbols, the gestures of mutes, the flags on a ship at sea. We can use physical means for the communication of ideas because the physicality and intelligibility of the world are not ontologically separable. Objective mind is a dimension of the natural world, a dimension which is explored by those physical bodies with organic structure and, hence, with ability to perceive, remember, and think.

NATURALISM AND HUMANISM

Woodbridge liked to call himself a naturalist. He was prone to say that the word *naturalism* was not (like idealism or materialism) a sectarian word. A naturalist in philosophy is a man who is willing to investigate the heavens above, the earth beneath, and the waters under the earth, making no commitment in advance as to what he will find, and ready to accept without hesitation whatever is discovered. In fact, however, Woodbridge was a naturalist in a more special sense. He was a naturalist in the sense of the tradition which stems from Aristotle. But the Aristotle he admired was the Aristotle whose *Ethics* re-expressed in systematic form the humanistic position set forth by Plato in the *Republic*.

Woodbridge's naturalism was such that he found it easy and, indeed, imperative to go on, almost without interruption, from metaphysical reflections about the general traits of nature to an exhibition of man's moral life as a special instance of structure, behavior, and teleology. We ought to have, Woodbridge would say, a naturalistic theory of nature and a humanistic theory of man. We ought not mythically to read moral significance into nonhuman nature; nor ought we to measure man, as we do measure cyclones and river currents, by speed and physical energy. Naturalism without humanism is likely to be brutalizing; for it emphasizes efficiency in the use of tools and machines, progress in inventions to increase the range of human control within nature, and the importance of industrial and commercial assets, but it leaves unconsidered and, hence, unregulated the ends for which efficiency is to be used. Humanism without naturalism is likely to be sentimental, as it was at times among the literary scholars of the early Renaissance; for it exults in the great achievements of the past—in ancient literature, ancient art, and ancient culture generally—and longs for repetition of just these same values. A union of naturalism and humanism yields a balanced philosophy. The finest flowering of moral values and civilized arts, Woodbridge taught, has its roots in the potentialities of nature's raw materials, so that exploration of nature in the physical and biological sciences increases man's possibilities of consequent moral development. And raw materials of nature, understood in the light of their teleological possibilities, are a stimulus to human aspiration and to rational efforts to turn aspiration into actual possession of values. Naturalism is more concerned with means, and humanism with ends. But ends give means a moral status, as means give ends a practical basis. To say that means and end are happily adjusted is to say that man has found his due place in nature, and nature one of its fulfillments in man. And to say either of these things is also to say that human life, precarious and quantitatively insignificant as it is in the face of the vast and potent forces of nonhuman nature, is qualitatively enriched so as to become rational and joyous.

5. DEWEY

JOHN DEWEY, 1859–1952, was born in Burlington, Vermont, and died in New York City. He was educated in the public schools of his native city and at the University of Vermont, from which he graduated in 1879 at the age of nineteen. He taught school for three years, two of them in South Oil City, Pennsylvania, and the other in a village near Burlington. He had read the Scotch realists and Auguste Comte when studying at Vermont, and, upon his return to teach school in the neighborhood, he read extensively in other philosophical classics under the guidance of his friend and teacher Professor A. P. Torrey. He submitted two articles to the *Journal of Speculative Philosophy;* and when the editor of that journal, Dr. W. T. Harris, accepted and published them in 1882, he decided to follow his already half-formed resolve and to devote his life to philosophy. He borrowed enough money to enable him to go to The Johns Hopkins University for graduate work, where he came under the influence of Professor George S. Morris and made a thorough study of German philosophers, particularly Hegel. Morris went to the University of Michigan in 1883, and Dewey was invited the next year to an instructorship in philosophy under Morris. Dewey taught at Michigan from 1884 to 1894 (except for one year which he spent as teacher at the University of Minnesota). From 1894 to 1904 he was head of the Department of Philosophy, Psychology, and Pedagogy at the University of Chicago. In 1904 he was offered a professorship at Columbia University, which he accepted, and began his teaching there in 1905. He taught at Columbia for twenty-five years (except during two years spent in lecturing in Japan and China and in advising Chinese officials on educational problems). He retired from teaching in 1930 and was professor emeritus until his death. His influence upon both educational theory and educational practices was more extensive than that of any other person of this century. His writings are voluminous, both in philosophy and in educational, political, and social matters. Among his more important philosophical books are *The School and Society* (1900); *Ethics,* in collaboration with James H. Tufts (1908), second edition (1932); *How We Think* (1910); *Democracy and Education* (1916); *Reconstruction in Philosophy* (1920); *Human Nature and Conduct* (1922); *Experience and Nature* (1925), second edition (1929); *The Public and Its Problems* (1927); *The Quest for Certainty* (1929); *Art as Experience* (1934); *A Common Faith* (1934); *Logic, the Theory of Inquiry* (1938).

JOHN DEWEY WAS A prolific writer in the field of philosophy during an unusually long period of time. His first philosophical articles appeared in 1882, and he continued the writing of philosophy until his death seventy years later. During the earlier part of this period he expressed some views which he later abandoned. He felt profoundly the influences of certain great thinkers of the past and of his own day. These influences, however much they contributed to his thinking, never made him a partisan of any tradition. Nor was he an eclectic, piecing together bits of borrowed wisdom. He was, rather, a person with a keen and penetrating flair for observing facts, and knew how to measure the value of all the ideas he encountered by their adequacy in reporting the facts faithfully. He was always open to new ideas and ready to revise previous ideas. He took many years to work out his own mature and independent position. This position he finally presented in the second (revised) edition of *Experience and Nature* in 1929, which may be accepted as the definitive expression of his philosophy.

Dewey described his own intellectual development in the phrase

"From Absolutism to Experimentalism." [58] He also spoke of his theory of knowledge as instrumentalism. And in the second edition of *Experience and Nature* he came to the point where he chose to speak of his philosophy as "either empirical naturalism or naturalistic empiricism" or even naturalistic humanism.[59] What these various labels mean can best be explained by considering some of the influences in use of which, and in reaction against which, he came to his mature position. No sketch will be given here of stages in his development; but an account of his mature position will be given in terms of the intellectual forces which contributed to his development.

HIS AFFILIATIONS WITH HEGEL

In his earliest writings Dewey showed profound influences from the Hegelian tradition. In his mature life he looked back upon his early days and reported that he had originally come close to being a good Hegelian.[60] He was, almost from the outset of his philosophical career, restively critical of both the absolutism and the idealism of the Hegelians. But he profited, and he acknowledged that he profited, from his early training at Hegelian hands. He always retained, in even the final form of his mature position, certain affiliations with Hegelian ideas. These affiliations are sometimes unsuspected by his readers because they occur along with rejections of other Hegelian ideas. But they can be pointed out. And only when one notices them, will one fully understand the form of Dewey's mature position.

In the first place, Dewey was led through his study of Hegel to reject the dualism between experience and nature which Locke had fastened on so much of the empirical tradition in modern philosophy. Human experience, he insisted, is not a separate, nor is it a private, realm of being. It is part and parcel of the natural course of events. Experience occurs *within* nature and is *of* nature, or, conversely, nature is directly (if incompletely) disclosed in experience. This view of the relation of experience and nature may not be orthodox Hegelianism. But it is what Hegel's discussion led Dewey to believe.

[58] He used this phrase as title of the philosophical autobiography he wrote for *Contemporary American Philosophy* (New York, Macmillan, 1930), Vol. II, pp. 13–27. This autobiography was written about the same time as the revised version of *Experience and Nature*.

[59] *Experience and Nature*, 2d ed. (New York, Norton, 1929), p. 1a.

[60] He said just this in a personal letter to the author dated Jan. 5, 1923. In the same letter he stated that a student of philosophy is more likely to end up with a sound empiricism if he approaches philosophy through Hegel than if he approaches philosophy through other types of modern philosophy.

In the second place, Dewey learned from Hegel that thought participates, and participates effectively, in the historical process and is, indeed, one of the potent factors in shaping the course of events. Thought makes a difference. Locke was wrong, Dewey again maintained, in supposing that the real essence of things is completely what it is before thinking about those things begins. And Hegel was right in holding that thought enters into the determination of what things become and, hence, truly are. Hegel spoke of history as a thesis-antithesis-synthesis development, and Dewey modified this conception considerably when he spoke of thinking as a doubt-inquiry-answer experience.[61] Dewey modified the Hegelian conception because he deemed it too rigid and schematic; he realized that thinking is not a routine repetition of a pre-established and set pattern. But he nonetheless did get from Hegel the conviction, a conviction he always retained, that thought has the function, not of laying bare some fixed reality which is prior to the occurrence of thought about it, but of sharing in the fashioning of reality. He deplored the interpretation which classical empiricists often gave of both nature and knowledge in terms of unchanging entities like "substance" or "matter" or "mind." He preferred to think with Hegel that nature and knowledge can be better characterized by such categories as history, culture (*Geist*), process, change, becoming.

In the third place, Dewey learned from Hegel that thought, at least significant thought, is a social affair. "The only possible psychology," Dewey once wrote, " . . . is a social psychology." [62] And the only possible theory of knowledge is one which, as in Hegel, treats thought as working itself out in its social context. Thought is a phase of culture. No matter how much the genius of an individual makes him stand out as intellectual leader, mind is always and everywhere a process of interaction of organism with both physical and social environment. The genius as truly as the plodding person arises in a special society at a special time in cultural history and must operate in relation to the cultural milieu. He need not be a slave to convention; he may (and, in the case of a genius, he will) participate in reconstruction of the cultural milieu. But thought goes on, not inside heads and nervous systems, but in the inclusive historical situation in which heads and nervous systems provide certain momentary centers for social relationships.

[61] See, for example, *How We Think* (Boston, Heath, 1910), chap. 8.

[62] P. A. Schilpp, ed., *The Philosophy of John Dewey* (Chicago, Northwestern University, 1939), p. 18.

HIS DEBT TO BIOLOGICAL CONCEPTIONS

Though Dewey thus retained in his mature position certain points which had come to him from his early study of Hegel, he did drift steadily away from the orthodoxy of the Hegelian tradition. Other influences supplemented, or even supplanted, the influence Hegel originally had with him. Among these other influences the most notable where Charles Darwin's theory of evolution and William James's psychology. Dewey was deeply affected by developments in the biological sciences during the second half of the nineteenth century. His other ideas were so organized by conceptions derived from these biological sciences that his mature philosophy may be said to be more biological in character than any other philosophy since that of Aristotle. Under the influence of biological conceptions all traces of both idealism and absolutism finally disappeared from his thought, and a thoroughly naturalistic framework of ideas emerged. This biological influence is conspicuous at a number of fundamental points in Dewey's mature position.

In the first place Dewey came to regard the historical process, not as the unfolding of an inclusive cosmic design, but as the interaction of multiple factors in constantly varying conditions. Life, he said, life as studied empirically in biology, *is* interaction. Life, however, is not the only instance of interaction. It is a special case of interaction. It is that kind of interaction in which one of the interacting factors (the organism) turns the forces which play upon it into means for its own conservation, renewal, and advance.[63] Its degree of success in making the forces about it contribute to its own survival and well-being varies with circumstances. Eventually all organisms die, unable to keep up indefinitely the process of their self-renewal. Even while organisms continue to live, their interactions with their environment may entail, on the one hand, untold misery, thwarting of impulse, and stunted growth, and, on the other hand, health, prosperity, and increase of power. Experience therefore—human experience, to be sure, but the experience of all living things, that is, the interaction of these living things with their environment—is a two-way affair. It is an undergoing of effects from, and it is an action upon, the environment. Men in particular, but all living things generally, need to accommodate themselves to some forces at the same time that they manipulate other forces to their own advantage.

Dewey proceeded to extend the conception of interaction to the

[63] *Democracy and Education* (New York, Macmillan, 1916), pp. 1–2.

entire world. Nature is a collective term for "things interacting in certain ways." [64] We often use the singular noun existence; but we mean, or ought to remember to mean, many existences. And these many existences are a mixture of ordered recurrences of recognizable patterns of behavior and of more or less novel "processes going on to consequences as yet indeterminate." [65] We classify the many existences in certain groups or species. But we ought not to suppose that these species are any more fixed and permanent ontologically than biologically. They are constantly shifting, subject to strange variations, generative of new and equally temporary species of things. Things play upon one another in ways so varied that no single formula can be adequate to their endless diversities. Nature abounds in vicissitudes. Nature is not uniform or homogeneous. Nature is, in one place or another, both stable and precarious, ordered and confused, finished and uncompleted, typical and unique, routine and creative.

In the second place, Dewey came to emphasize, in accord with Darwin's biology and James's psychology but in opposition to Hegelian and other modern epistemologies, that experience is not primarily a cognitive affair. Thought is part of the technique whereby an organism either adjusts itself to, or effects modification in, the environment. Thought is not coextensive with experience. Indeed, it forms no part of the experience of many living things. And even in men, it forms but a small part of their experience. Men suffer and enjoy; they possess and encounter. Then, in order to avoid suffering and to gain enjoyment, or in order to possess happily and to encounter profitably, thought supervenes in living. But it is as occasional in its occurrence as it is valuable in its fruits. So far is the real from being identical with the rational, Dewey said in rejoinder to Hegel, that the real becomes the rational only at sporadic moments. Thought may turn experience from blind blundering to intelligent foresight. But thought could not perform this function were not experience basically a matter of undergoing, that is, of suffering and enjoying. Thought originates as a biological variation in organic behavior and is "selected" for survival because it brings to pass that undergoing will less often be suffering and will more often be enjoying. Or, to put the point in technical language, whereas for Hegel thought is constitutive, for Dewey it is reconstructive.

In the third place, and again in accord with modern biology and

[64] *Experience and Nature,* 2d. ed., p. 4a.
[65] *Experience and Nature,* 2d ed., p. 48.

in frank opposition to Hegel, Dewey maintained that just as thought is not coextensive with experience, so experience is not coextensive with nature. Experience does not occur "everywhere and every-when." [66] Life, or experience (which Dewey defined as interaction of organism with environment and so made equivalent to life), occurs within a system of nature which had a long existence before life or experience began to occur, and which continues to exist, in large part, without any dependence upon life or experience. Experience is occasional in nature, not omnipresent. Experience presupposes nature as the environment within which it occurs; but nature neither presupposes nor requires experience. Nature is such that within it occur experience and hurricanes and eclipses; but just as nature is not a hurricane or an eclipse, so it is not experience.

NATURALISTIC EMPIRICISM

A further explanation is here required for a full understanding of Dewey's empiricism. *Experience,* he pointed out, is a double-barreled word. The first and primary meaning is that given above, namely, interaction of organism and environment. Then, by extension, the word *experience* gets a derivative or secondary meaning and is used to indicate the natural scene, or portion of the natural world, within which the process of interaction of organism and environment occurs.

This kind of extension of meaning of a word is not peculiar to the one word *experience*. It occurs in connection with other words in the language, words which have no connection with philosophical controversy. Take, for example, the word *walk*. We say that we know a man by his walk, and we also say that a man proceeds down the walk. Walk means a certain process and also the scene where that process occurs. The first meaning is primary, and the second derived. But it is highly important to note that the process is not an activity of the organism by and in itself. No organism could walk if it were separated from some solid basis of floor or ground. Walking is a process in which organism and environment interact. The floor or ground participates in the process of walking or assists the process of walking to occur. That is why the path along which the process of walking occurs comes in turn to be itself called a walk. The path is called a walk, even when not being used by any organism for the activity of walking. But it is not a walk except because it has been,

[66] *Experience and Nature,* 2d ed., p. 3a.

and may again be, the scene of some organism's walking. Nature contains walks because organisms and the ground beneath their feet co-operate in walking.

So with the term *experience*. Experience (the interaction of organism with environment) is not internal to, or a private possession of, an organism. Some philosophers have slipped into the error of supposing so. Perhaps they have slipped into that error because the organism is the only constant factor present in many experiences. The environment of the many experiences may be stars and rivers, judicial decisions, factory methods, church services, and the furniture of a room. But what is constant in these many experiences is no more requisite for their occurrence than what is variable. Properly considered, experience is a function of two factors jointly and of neither one exclusively; and no one can draw a sharp line through experience to divide what part results from the organism and what part results from the environment.

Thus, by extension of meaning, experience is used for the scene within which the experience process occurs, as walking is used for the path over which the walking process occurs. And so Dewey was led to speak of nature as experience. Nature is not primarily experience, any more than a stretch of ground is primarily a walk. Nature *becomes* experience; that is, nature enters into a type of interaction with organism which it did not always have. The stretch of ground existed before it became a walk, and natural things existed before they became experiences. Dewey never intended to suggest that experience is a kind of stuff or neutral material out of which organisms manufacture nature. He called things experience, not because of what they are made of, but because of the way they sometimes function.

In *Experience and Nature* the three terms *nature, existence,* and *experience* are used almost interchangeably. In the table of contents of the book, five of the ten chapters use the term *nature,* three use the term *existence,* and two use the term *experience.* The three words, as was just said, can almost be interchanged with one another. But not quite. They all refer denotatively to the same vast system of things and events which stretches far beyond us in both space and time. But in referring to this same vast system of things and events, they refer to it for different (though not in any way inconsistent) reasons. This system of things and events is called *existence* because it stands before us and has to be taken account of; it cannot be deduced from first principles, but it is inevitably encountered—and only by being encountered may it ever become known. This system is also called *nature* because it contains the forces which condition the occurrence, the duration, and the disappearance of every thing in turn. It is the seat of all the potentialities which have ever been actualized and will ever or can ever be actualized. And, finally, this system is called *experience*, because in the interaction of organism and environment, many of the characteristics and traits of nature are laid bare. "Experience thus reaches down into nature; it has depth." [67] Experience (in the primary sense of the term) enters into possession of some portion of nature, and enters into possession of this portion in such fashion as to make other portions of nature accessible—accessible to knowledge and accessible to possession and enjoyment. Dewey called the whole of nature experience because he wanted to emphasize how extremely opposed he was to such theories as that of Locke. In Locke, experience was a kind of curtain which hangs between the mind and the external world and rather hides than discloses that external world. But in Dewey, experience is an interaction with nature such that some of the things that transpire in nature are immediately discerned and others may therefrom be reliably inferred. There are many *practical* difficulties, Dewey realized, in the way of the extension of our knowledge of nature. Some things may be too minute or too rapid in occurrence for us to detect, too far off in space or in time, too intricate in structure to be analyzed with our existing instruments. Practical difficulties, however, may be overcome, as they have been overcome in the past, with improvement of apparatus or with change in the human line of attack. But there is no *theoretical* limit to knowledge—no limit imposed because of an alleged inaccessibility of nature to experience. Dewey called nature experience because natural objects enter cognitively, as they enter physically, into the interaction of organism with environment.

When we use the term *experience* in its primary sense for interaction of organism and environment, we may always properly inquire *whose* experience is being referred to. Experience is mine or yours or his or hers or its.[68] But when we use the term *experience* in its derivative sense for the scene in which interaction of organism and environment occurs, then no possessive pronouns are particularly significant. A house may always be somebody's property; but we may set forth the properties of a house without knowing whose it is. So an experience may always be involved in interaction with some or-

---

[67] *Experience and Nature*, 2d. ed., p. 4a.
[68] Experience can be *its* because interaction of organism with environment may be the interaction of a nonhuman form of life (of a vegetable, for instance).

ganism; but we may set forth the characteristics of experience without mentioning whose organism is concerned. Trees and stars, tables and chairs, institutions and customs, and endless other things are all experience (in the derivative sense of the term). We may analyze these things and discover the traits of experience, as we may analyze a house and even number the bricks it is made of. And so we are entitled to say, for example, that all the sciences, the physical and social sciences, investigate the traits and properties and relations of experience. As a house may be described accurately without reference to an owner, so experience can be described accurately without reference to a self. And when anyone so describes experience, Dewey maintained, one is at the same time describing nature.

It was this position which Dewey had in mind when he said that his mature philosophy could be called empirical naturalism or naturalistic empiricism.

DEWEY'S RELATION TO JAMES

Dewey's relations to William James have often been misunderstood. Dewey was willing to call himself a pragmatist; he sympathized with James's attacks on the classical empiricists and the rationalists. But of many of James's contentions he did not at all approve. He did feel greatly indebted to James's *Psychology,* though even here he acknowledged that James frequently lapsed, certainly in his vocabulary and probably in his thought, into the subjectivistic attitudes of the prebiological schools of psychologists. He deplored the sentimentalism which James mixed up in a confusing way with his pragmatic ideas. James, trying to rally other thinkers to a sense of party solidarity in the pragmatic cause, included Dewey among those who had seen the light. But Dewey owed little to James's *Pragmatism.* For one thing, Dewey had pretty well worked out the main features of his own theory of knowledge before *Pragmatism* appeared, and, for another thing, Dewey disliked the way in which *Pragmatism* and others of James's later books returned in their closing chapters to the loose sentimentalism of the *Will to Believe* essays.[69] Dewey was very much closer in his intellectual affiliations to Peirce's pragmaticism than to James's pragmatism.[70] And so, though he continued to employ the adjective *pragmatic* often, he was restive in being labeled a pragmatist without qualification. He invented the terms *instrumentalism* and

[69] For Dewey's own statements on these points, see his autobiographical essay "From Absolutism to Experimentalism" in *Contemporary American Philosophy,* Vol. I, pp. 23-24.

[70] For the issue between pragmaticism and pragmatism, see above, p. 461.

experimentalism in order to differentiate his brand of pragmatism from that of James and other writers of the sentimental wing of the pragmatic school. He defined his position over against James in a review which he wrote on *Pragmatism* and published as an essay entitled "What Pragmatism Means by Practical." [71]

In this historically important essay Dewey accused James of mixing up three senses in which one thing or another may be said to have *meaning,* and sought to clear himself from identification with James by distinguishing these three senses. (1) We may ask what meaning an *object* has. The object (as here understood) is something already given in experience and thus empirically vouched for. And we can properly answer the question by saying that the meaning of the object is the effects which, supposedly, the object will produce and we shall therefore have to take into account. (2) We may ask what meaning an *idea* has. And we may answer this question by saying that the meaning of the idea is the investigations which the idea leads us to make and the changes which the idea causes us to produce in objects. These two senses, (1) and (2), are quite compatible. They will both be found, interinvolved with each other, in any considerable instance of reflective procedure. Both objects and ideas have meanings which involve the future. The meaning of an object modifies our ideas, and the meaning of our ideas modifies the object. And the two kinds of modifications are the *practical* consequences which, in their inter-relationships, a pragmatic theory of knowledge ought to bring to attention. But (3) we may also ask what meaning a *belief* has. And we can here answer only that the meaning of the belief is the consequences the belief has in the emotional attitudes of him who entertains the belief. The belief, being a settled opinion which is accepted as true, is not an idea tentatively examined and experimentally used as a guide in further inquiry. It "has its logical content already fixed." [72] It is not a factor in a process of reflection. It is something to be enjoyed, to be prized. Its value is a present possession. Hence it closes the door against change and induces contentment with a settled way of regarding one's relations to the world (or to some special aspects or parts of the world).

Pragmatism, Dewey pointed out, had begun by granting that truth is a matter of agreement between idea and fact. But the distinctive point about pragmatism was that it found the agreement to consist, not

---

[71] Published in *Essays in Experimental Logic* (Chicago, University of Chicago Press, 1916), pp. 303–329.
[72] *Ibid.,* p. 313.

in a static and timeless relation, but in a temporal process which consists in the development of ideas and the search for new facts until through reflection ideas and facts are at last found to be in accord. And Dewey found James turning away from a properly pragmatic theory when he commended beliefs for the emotional satisfactions they produce in the minds of those who entertain them as finalities. He complained that James confused the genuinely pragmatic value of an idea and the quite nonpragmatic value of a belief. And because James's widespread influence had lured people into complacent satisfaction with cherished beliefs, Dewey came more and more to prefer his own distinctive labels and to call himself an instrumentalist or an experimentalist.

THEORY OF VALUATION

Dewey carried his philosophical principles into so many areas of human interest that no review can here be given of his many contributions to contemporary thought. But one further matter deserves attention here because it is a matter which deeply concerned Dewey through all periods of his philosophical activity. Dewey wanted to extend to moral and social problems the methods of investigation which had been eminently successful in the natural sciences. In order to effect this extension, he had to maintain, over against much contemporary philosophical writing, both of two theses. One of these theses is that moral judgments are about empirical matters of fact. The other is that moral judgments can be experimentally confirmed.

In order to defend the thesis that moral judgments are judgments about matters of fact, Dewey had first to maintain that values are objective occurrences in nature. And this he consistently and earnestly did. Values are as objective natural occurrences as colors or weights or sizes or shapes. Certain classical theories of nature had, of course, banned sense qualities from nature, and, even more, theories of modern centuries had similarly banned esthetic and moral traits from nature. But Dewey always refused to assent to these sentences of exile. Empirically considered, he insisted, things are found to be poignant and tragic, good and bad, beautiful and ugly, and so forth. Things "are such immediately and in their own right and behalf." [73] Esthetic and moral traits belong to nature as really as do mechanical structures and physical traits. Experience, Dewey was fond of saying, is often consummatory. And in saying this, he was, of course, using the term *experience* not for some private realm apart from nature, but for

[73] *Experience and Nature*, 2d ed., p. 96.

the natural world as it enters into interaction with living, possibly with thinking, organisms. Nature, in other words, has a qualitative character, or, rather, natural objects have many and diverse qualitative characters, which arrest attention and are enjoyed (or suffered) in their esthetic immediacy. Various natural mechanisms and instrumentalities lead up to and eventuate in natural ends. Nature is full of ends as well as of means. To make this last statement is not to suggest that nature pauses in its temporal course. A natural end is not a termination of change and passage. Natural ends, like everything else in nature, have consequences of certain sorts of which we may take account. But nature has ends in the sense of moments of certain intrinsic intensity, or experiences of marked value (good or bad). Natural objects are *had* much more widely and generally than they are *known*. And these objects as *had* objects are distinguishable, apart from consideration of their generative conditions and their eventual outcomes, in terms of their qualities as directly experienced.

The consummatory experiences or natural ends in the world around us are not all goods. Death and disease are ends as truly as birth and well-being. And of the natural ends which are intrinsic goods, the variety is enormous. Choice among ends, apart from reflection, is arbitrary and amoral. Goods are naturally prized; but they need also, if their pursuit is to be intelligent, to be appraised, to be evaluated in their relative worth, to be made into moral ends. Prizing and appraising, Dewey maintained, are two distinct human attitudes toward actual and possible goods. The primitive, immature, impulsive attitude is merely to prize. But some natural goods are alternatives, and all natural goods are precarious in their occurrence and inevitably require planning and thoughtful care in order to be abundantly won. Thus prizing passes gradually into appraisal. Prizing passes into appraisal because enjoyment often ceases to be a fact and becomes a problem. And for the solution of the problem, criticism is needed. And with the emergence of criticism, the moral life is born.

Appraisal is the process of forming a critical judgment whereby natural goods are sorted out. Some of them are perhaps discarded; new ones are sometimes discovered; and all are put into classifications of mediocre, better, and best. Dewey sought to explain the nature of appraisal by pointing out that appraisal is a species of cognitive experience or reflective process. In all reflection there is a constant play between ideas and facts; ideas are developed and tested, and facts are discovered and observed, until the ideas and facts are, at least in successful reflection, brought into agreement or accord. So in that species of reflection which is moral criticism. In moral criticism the ideas are appraisals, and the facts are prizings; and reflection must continue, if the criticism is to be sound, until prizing and appraising are brought together into a mature and unified judgment. Men's moral judgments differ from one another, Dewey recognized, as do their beliefs in other than moral matters. There are some beliefs which men do hold as a matter of fact, whether the beliefs are sound or absurd; and there are also certain beliefs which men accept at the end of ample consideration. The former may be called beliefs *de facto;* the latter, beliefs *de jure.* So in the field of morals, there are certain immediately experienced goods, whether wisely or foolishly enjoyed; and there are also certain reasonably accepted goods which have been appraised and deemed worthy. The former may be called goods desired; the latter, goods desirable.[74] There could be nothing desirable unless there were first something desired. The desirable is the desired-in-the-light-of-critical-appraisal. The merely desired may be, and often is, the shallow and specious good, which, upon full and intelligent inquiry, will be judged bad or indifferent. Natural and un-criticized goods are, so to speak, the *data* of moral judgments. In the immediate *feel* which they have in experience there may be no notice-able differences among uncriticized natural goods and critically ap-praised goods. But through appraisal, judgments of worth may be made whereby the many goods receive determinations of their relative worth.

Having thus emphasized the importance of appraisal, Dewey pro-ceeded to give an account of some of the steps whereby sound appraisal can be effected. Three such steps may here be quickly summarized. (1) Ends and means must be evaluated together. We cannot justifiably take certain prized goods as ends and thereby sanc-tion any means which would enable us to possess those goods. Ends and means are factors in the integral process of the moral life. (2) Every means has its intrinsic character as good, bad, or indifferent. Hence, from an isolated good prized by itself, we are led through reflection to consider the moral quality of a larger segment of experi-ence, namely, the moral quality of achieving the prized good by the device of the chosen means. And the mature moral judgment which then results may considerably change the original prizing of the iso-lated end. (3) Every end is, in the context of the natural world and its causal connections, an occurrence with its consequences. When a particular end is appraised, the critic raises his sights, and, instead

[74] *Experience and Nature*, 2d. ed., p. 402; also chap. 10, *passim.*

of cutting himself off from further outcomes by reiterating his preliminary desire for the particular prized end, he re-evaluates this end in its connections with a larger range of pertinent considerations. Thus a rough kind of casual appreciation of an abstracted item of experience gives place to a refined judgment of a comprehensive system of means and ends. Something will still be prized after thorough appraisal has been made. But that something will be the end which effects an organization of subsidiary activities in an integrated plan. This end Dewey called an "end-in-view." An end-in-view is as concrete as any other end, and it is prized as is any other end. But it differs from all other kinds of end in that it has received critical evaluation and has become reasonably justified. It is still desired, but it is also desirable. And provided that criticism has been comprehensive and intelligent, the end-in-view is "finally" desirable.

Dewey was criticized on the ground that the process of appraising ends by consideration of their further consequences involved an endless *regressus*. His critics seemed to take the stand that an end which was viewed in the light of its further consequences became thereby a merely instrumental good. They thus supposed that Dewey was denying that his ends-in-view really had intrinsic value.

This adverse criticism missed the point of Dewey's position.[75] Dewey was recommending a kind of moral appraisal which retained consideration of the intrinsic moral quality of every item of experience. He wished to include reference to the intrinsic value of means as well as the intrinsic value of ends. His intent was, not to turn from intrinsic to instrumental values, but to take both into account. He was urging people to enlarge the range of considerations, every one of which might well be an item with both its instrumental and its specific intrinsic worth. Of course, he could not specify, particularly when he was dealing abstractly with the general nature of moral situations, how enlarged a range of considerations would be requisite to make appraisals reasonably just. He could not specify this, he granted; but the reason he could not specify this, he insisted, was that no such specification is either theoretically or practically possible. No one can tell *a priori* how much of nature may be relevant to the proper handling of moral issues. No one can tell *a priori* how much evidence is sufficient to support any judgment about matters of fact. Moral issues are no more subject to the charge of uncertainty than all

<hr />

[75] Dewey replied to the criticism several times. One effective reply he made is "Theory of Valuation," in *International Encyclopedia of Unified Science* (Chicago, University of Chicago Press, 1929), Vol. II, No. 4, particularly pp. 45–48.

other empirical issues. But after a certain amount of evidence, we become reasonably assured about the diagnosis of a disease and about the best method for its treatment. And similarly, after a certain amount of appraisal, we become reasonably assured about the worth of certain ends and the moral desirability of using certain means to secure these ends. More than reasonable assurance no critic has a right to demand of an empiricist. And Dewey, of course, regarded the rationalistic claim to absolute certainty, whether in physical problems or moral issues, as a false security which but tempted rationalists to premature complacency. After all, he remarked, reasonable assurance is intellectually more respectable than illusory sentiments of certainty.

Conclusion

AN HISTORIAN OFTEN ends his story of the past at some point long before his own day. If he brings his narrative down to the date at which he himself is writing (as is the case with this historian), he is likely to gain a new sense of the relation of past and present. He must interrupt his work at the present, not because his story has any natural termination there, but because he, as historian, can go no further— and the ways of a prophet are not congenial to one who has learned to take account of the vicissitudes of history. The story of our philosophical traditions is interrupted, not finished. Time will go on. New intellectual currents may well ensue. These currents may so transform the material of our traditions as to change their significance from what it is today into something else that we cannot now envisage.

John Dewey once said: "Tradition looks forward as well as backward." If tradition looked backward only, it would be cruelly binding and oppressive. But it looks ahead, too. It looks ahead as a Greek temple on a promontory into the blue Aegean looks eastward toward each rising sun. It looks ahead, wondering what the new days will bring forth, curious to witness new deeds, hoping the new deeds will equal the best of the past and occasionally reach new levels of creative genius.

We all march forward with our traditions. These traditions need not be our masters. They will not be our masters if we are wise. They will be, rather, our opportunities. They give us some degree of understanding of ourselves and our world, in order that we may then reach ahead intelligently. We are fortunate in that we do not need to begin afresh, like primitive men, with almost no ideas. We have a heritage. We need not wallow sentimentally in admiration of that heritage. We may use it and use it critically. We may use it for—well, only some future historian can tell for what we will use it. But of one thing we can be sure. The manner in which a man chooses to use his heritage of tradition is the final test of the quality of his manliness.

Bibliography

THIS BRIEF bibliography is not intended to send students of the history of philosophy away from the original writings of the great philosophers. Those original writings are much more important than even an exhaustive bibliography of secondary literature. But an effort is here made to mention at least one secondary work which will supplement the discussion of each chapter of the present book. Sometimes two secondary works are suggested; and three, in the case of Plato. Books on twentieth-century philosophy are difficult to list, because criticism here has been controversial rather than historical and expository. The author has ventured to include references to some of his own historical articles in order to reinforce interpretations of moot points dealt with summarily in the present book.

BURNET, John, *Greek Philosophy: Part I, Thales to Plato* (London, Macmillan and Co., Ltd., 1924). Particularly good on the period from Thales to the Greek Sophists.

TAYLOR, A. E., *Socrates* (London, Davies, 1932). Far less skeptical than the present book on our ability to distinguish between the ideas of Socrates and the ideas of Plato.

——, *Plato: The Man and His Work* (New York, Lincoln MacVeagh, 1927). Follows the wise procedure of treating each dialogue of Plato as a separate piece of philosophical literature.

FIELD, G. C., *Plato and His Contemporaries: A Study in Fourth-century Life and Thought* (New York, Dutton, 1930). Presents Plato's philosophy as an integral part of Greek culture in his day.

WOODBRIDGE, F. J. E., *The Son of Apollo: Themes of Plato* (Boston, Houghton Mifflin, 1929). A witty and penetrating evaluation of certain ideas which appear repeatedly in Plato's major dialogues.

JAEGER, W. W., *Aristotle: Fundamentals of the History of His Development* (Oxford, Clarendon Press, 1934). An epoch-making piece of scholarship in enabling us to understand the probable line of development in Aristotle's philosophical writings.

MURRAY, Gilbert, *Five Stages of Greek Religion* (New York, Columbia University Press, 1925). Excellent treatment in chapter 3 of the Cyrenaic-Epicurean and Cynic-Stoic traditions.

KATZ, Joseph, *Plotinus' Search for the Good* (New York, King's Crown Press, 1950). A clear and systematic presentation of one of the dominant themes in Plotinus.

McGIFFERT, A. C., *A History of Christian Thought*, 2 vols. (New York, Scribner, 1932–1933). Fairly complete coverage on intellectual currents among all groups of Christians from the first century to Erasmus.

COPLESTON, Frederick, *A History of Philosophy: Mediaeval Philosophy, Augustine to Scotus* (London, Burns Oates, 1950), Vol. II. A model for intellectual history—clear, learned, well written.

GILSON, E. H., *History of Christian Philosophy in the Middle Ages* (New York, Random House, 1955). A systematic review of Christian philosophical thought by a foremost authority of our day, from the early Greek and Latin theological writers of the early Christian days to the fourteenth century.

——, *The Philosophy of St. Thomas Aquinas* (Cambridge, W. Heffer and Sons, 1924). One of the major works of one of the great medievalists of this century.

BURTT, E. A., *The Metaphysical Foundations of Modern Physical Science* (New York, Harcourt, 1925). Particularly good on the period from Copernicus to Galileo and on the bearing of scientific discoveries upon philosophical developments.

RANDALL, J. H., *The Making of the Modern Mind*, rev. ed. (Boston, Houghton Mifflin, 1940). Particularly good on the Copernican revolution, the Cartesian revolution, and the Newtonian world.

HAMPSHIRE, Stuart, *Spinoza* (Harmondsworth, Penguin Books, 1951). A brief but well-balanced interpretation of Spinoza, and worthy of a better format.

LAMPRECHT, Sterling P., "Hobbes and Hobbism," *The American Political Science Review*, Vol. XXXIV, No. 1 (February, 1940).

STRAUSS, Leo, *The Political Philosophy of Hobbes* (Oxford, Clarendon Press, 1936). Particularly good on the historical relations of Hobbes to Bacon, Aristotle, and so forth; makes Hobbes more of a Hobbist than the interpretation given of Hobbes in the present book.

LAMPRECHT, Sterling P., "The Early Draft of Locke's *Essay*," *Journal of Philosophy*, Vol. XXIX, No. 26 (December, 1932).

——, "John Locke and His Essay," A Tercentenary Lecture (New York, Columbia University Press, 1933).

GIBSON, James, *Locke's Theory of Knowledge and Its Historical Relations* (Cambridge, Cambridge University Press, 1917). Regards Locke's *Essay* as much more of a consistent whole than does the chapter on Locke in the present book.

WOODBRIDGE, F. J. E., "Berkeley's Realism," in *Studies in the History of Ideas* (New York, Columbia University Press, 1918), Vol. I. A brilliant presentation of a much neglected aspect of Berkeley's philosophy.

LAMPRECHT, Sterling P., "Empiricism and Epistemology in David Hume," in *Studies in the History of Ideas* (New York, Columbia University Press, 1925), Vol. II. In spite of an unfortunate and improper misuse of the word *epistemology*, this article represents the same line of criticism of Hume as the chapter on Hume in the present book.

LAIRD, John, *Hume's Philosophy of Human Nature* (London, Methuen, 1932). Treats Hume as consistently the phenomenologist he was in the first book of the *Treatise*, but is particularly good on Hume's treatment of the idea of necessity.

ROYCE, Josiah, *The Spirit of Modern Philosophy* (Boston, Houghton Mifflin, 1892). Chapters 4–8 give brief but helpful analyses of Kant and his German successors.

STEPHEN, Leslie, *The English Utilitarians*, 3 vols. (London, Duckworth,

1900). Discursive and much preoccupied with biographical matters, but written in the penetrating manner which made Stephen a great critic.

ELLIOT, Hugh, *Herbert Spencer* (London, Constable, 1917). Written by a man who, like Spencer, regards philosophy as a synthesis of scientific knowledge.

PERRY, R. B., *The Thought and Character of William James,* 2 vols. (Boston, Little, Brown, 1935). A delightful interpretation of James, of many of James's contemporaries, and of American life at the turn of the century.

FISCH, H. M., ed., *Classic American Philosophers* (New York, Appleton-Century-Crofts, 1951). Contains a general introduction to recent American philosophy and special introductions to each of several important figures in philosophy in the United States.

Index

(Bold-face figures indicate main references.)